THE BISHOP'S BOYS

Wilbur and Orville Wright, at the height of their fame, pose informally on the rear porch at 7 Hawthorn Street in June 1909. Typically, Orville's modish suit, wingtip shoes, and Argyll stockings contrast with his brother's austere dark suit and high button shoes.

THE BISHOP'S BOYS

*A Life
of
Wilbur and Orville Wright*

TOM D. CROUCH

*W. W. Norton & Company
New York · London*

The text of this book is composed in Century Expanded, with
display type set in Century Nova and Nuptial Script. Composition and manufacturing by the Haddon Craftsmen, Inc.
Book Design by Charlotte Staub.

Photos drawn from the collection of the Wright State University
Archives appear on pages

Photos drawn from the collection of the National Air and Space
Museum, Smithsonian Institution appear on pages

First Edition

Library of Congress Cataloging in Publication Data
Crouch, Tom D.
The Bishop's boys : a life of the Wright brothers / Tom D.
Crouch.
p.   cm.
Bibliography: p.
Includes index.
1. Wright, Orville, 1871–1948. 2. Wright, Wilbur, 1867–1912.
3. Aeronautics—United States—Biography. I. Title.
TL540.W7C76 1989
629.13'0092'2—dc19
[B]   88–19585

ISBN 0-393-02660-4

W. W. Norton & Company, Inc.
500 Fifth Avenue, New York, N. Y. 10110
W. W. Norton & Company.
37 Great Russell Street, London WC1B 3NU
1 2 3 4 5 6 7 8 9 0

CONTENTS

ACKNOWLEDGMENTS

Acknowledgments are a special problem when a book has been in the making as long as this one, but there is no doubt where my greatest debts lie. Any author assessing the Wright brothers must be forever grateful to a pair of early scholars, Marvin W. McFarland and Charles Harvard Gibbs-Smith. That is especially true in my case—both were friends, guides, and mentors.

The members of the Wright family have extended themselves on my behalf for over ten years. The best I can offer is the book itself, along with my thanks, to: Ivonette Wright Miller and Harold Miller; Susan and Horace Wright; Wilkinson and Marion Wright. Thanks also to John Jameson, who gave his time generously over the telephone. Mrs. Elizabeth Rehling, daughter of Agnes Osborn and an old friend of the family, shared her mother's memories, and her correspondence with Katharine Wright.

Rick Young, a fellow Wright scholar, has for years been willing to drop everything for a discussion of some obscure point relating to the Wrights. He invited me to assist in building a replica of the 1902 glider. The hours spent helping to fly that machine—and lugging it back up the slope for the next try—have added to my understanding of what the Wrights accomplished, and how they lived and worked on the Outer Banks. For that, and for his friendship, my thanks. Ken Kellett, who built and flies a replica of the 1903 airplane, also provided an opportunity to crew that machine.

Howard Wolko, special assistant for technology with the Aeronautics Department of the National Air and Space Museum, helped me to understand how an airplane flies, and how the Wrights designed their machines; he also allowed me to serve as his partner in a recreation of the 1901 wind-tunnel experiments. Others who have made important contributions include Eugene Husting, Peter Jakab, Richard Hallion, Dr. Douglas Robinson, and John Gillikin.

As always, I am indebted to librarians. Patrick Nolan and his colleagues at the Wright State University Archives deserve special thanks for their assistance and courtesy. The staff of the Dayton and Montgomery County Public Library also went far out of their way to help. In addition, my thanks to: the staff of the Manuscript Division, Library of Congress; the Library and Archives staff of the National Air and Space Museum; the crew at the Library of the National Museum of American History; and Bill Diess and his colleagues at the Smithsonian Archives.

It is customary to include one's wife and children in the list of acknowledgments. Those who have not lived through the process of writing a book may not realize the price family members pay for the finished product. Nancy, Bruce, Abby, and Nate—thanks.

Tom D. Crouch
Fairfax, Virginia
December 30, 1989

THE BISHOP'S BOYS

HUFFMAN PRAIRIE, OHIO

May 25, 1910

Early on the morning of May 25, 1910, three passengers stepped off the Dayton, Springfield and Urbana interurban at a simple wooden platform marked Simms Station. They had ridden the eight miles out from their home in Dayton, Ohio, in less than half an hour. The trip had become a part of the fabric of their daily lives during the past six years, but for Wilbur and Orville Wright and their father Milton, this was a special day.

They waited for the train to pull away, then crossed the road and walked through the gate into the field that everyone in this part of Greene County knew as Huffman Prairie. The hangar door was open, and a small party of workmen were already wheeling out an airplane. It was one of the new machines, a Model B. Milton thought the craft looked smaller than the 1905 Flyer he had seen the boys fly here so often; it didn't have the big elevator out front. This one had wheels, as well. The days of catapulting the machine down a long track and into the air were gone forever.

Orville, who was doing all the flying now, went to work immediately. Wilbur stayed with his father, explaining the preparations needed to get the machine safely into the air. They were at it all day. Orville made fourteen flights before dusk, most of them training hops to give the three new men, Frank Coffyn, Art Welsh, and Ralph Johnstone, an opportunity to get the feel of the controls. Johnstone would be dead within six months; Welsh had just over two years to live.

Late that afternoon, Wilbur took a seat on the exposed lower wing next to his brother. They circled the field for just over fourteen minutes. It was the only time they would ever fly together, something they had promised their father they would never do. Just this once, for the sake of history, he had relented.

Then it was Milton's turn. The old man had never flown before. The opportunity had always been there—he had simply never asked. Now he climbed up next to his youngest son for the first time. They remained aloft for 6 minutes, 55 seconds, never climbing above 350 feet. Orville had been unnecessarily worried about his father's reaction. At one point during the flight Milton leaned close to his son's ear and shouted above the combined roar of engine, propellers, and slipstream: "Higher, Orville. Higher."[1]

On that spring morning in 1910 Milton Wright was eighty-one years old, but an observer might have put him as much as a decade younger. He stood ramrod straight and had the look of an Old Testament patriarch, with his neatly trimmed white beard and clear, penetrating eyes.

No pictures were taken that day, but it is safe to assume that Milton wore a plain black suit and hat with a white shirt and tie, the clergyman's uniform. He had scarcely stepped out of his door dressed in any other way since his ordination as a minister over half a century before.

From his clothes, he could have been a simple country parson, retired after a lifetime of tending his flock. In fact, Bishop Milton Wright is remembered today as the most controversial figure in the history of the Church of the United Brethren in Christ. Small wonder. He created a permanent national schism in the church over a matter of principle; waged a decade-long courtroom struggle with old friends and colleagues for the control of church property; then threatened to create a second split in the church branch he had led away from the original group.

He was a man who refused to recognize shades of gray. Negotiation and compromise were not in his vocabulary. Once he had decided on a course of action, he could not be moved.

Milton had inherited that strength of will and dedication to principle from his father, and passed it on to his own children. He had taught them that the world was not a friendly place for honest men and women. Temptations beckoned. Unscrupulous persons lay in wait, eager to take advantage of the weak and the unwary. Friends would fall away in times of trial, accepting the easier road of accommodation with error and injustice. Ultimately, the strength of family bonds offered the only real support one could hope for in life.

Wilbur and Orville Wright, his two youngest sons, had based their lives on the principles laid down by their father. It was Milton's proudest boast that they continued to make their home "beneath the paternal roof." Neither of them would ever marry, nor find better friends or stauncher supporters than the members of their own family circle.

The world looked at these two men and saw a corporate entity: the Wright brothers. Indeed, their ability to function as a team was nothing short of extraordinary. Their father had once told a reporter they were "as inseparable as twins." Perhaps so, but they remained very different men. They understood that fact—it was one of the secrets of their success. Each of them was prepared to rely on the other's strengths and to compensate for his weaknesses.

In the spring of 1910, Orville was thirty-eight years old. He stood five feet eight inches tall and weighed one hundred forty pounds. Wilbur, aged forty-three, was an inch and a half taller and weighed, usually, a pound or two less. His bony, angular frame made him seem much taller and thinner than he was.

You had to look closely to notice the family resemblance. Orville was on the pale side, with dark hair, "getting very thin to the crown," as one reporter noted. He had sported a reddish mustache since high school. Once full, almost a handlebar, it was now clipped short, just bushy enough to cover a pair of very thin lips that turned up at one corner when he smiled. "The jaws are never clenched," a friend noticed, "as one would expect to be the case with a man of determination." George Burba, a Dayton reporter, described his hands as "small, and uncallused."[2]

He was very particular about his appearance. This family paid a good deal of attention to the proprieties of dress. During their "scientific vacations" at Kitty Hawk, where the local hostesses were pleased when summer dinner guests arrived wearing shoes, the Wrights had faced the grit and wind of each new day with a clean tie and fresh celluloid collar.

Even so, Orville had a reputation as the "swell" of the family. His niece Ivonette remembered that he always knew what clothes suited him. "I don't believe there was ever a man who could do the work he did in all kinds of dirt, oil and grime and come out of it looking immaculate."[3]

His pale complexion was a matter of choice—and some pride. During the three years (1900–03) when they returned from Kitty Hawk each fall tanned by the wind and sun of the Outer Banks, Orville would immediately go to work bleaching his face with lemon juice. Carrie Kayler, the housekeeper, remembered that Orville would have gone pale again weeks before his brother.[4]

Wilbur was much less concerned about such things. Their sister Katharine made it a practice to inspect him periodically, ensuring that his clothes matched and were neat, clean, and pressed. He had given the most important speech of his career to a group of distinguished Chicago engineers in 1901 dressed in clothes borrowed from Orville.[5]

Orville had fine, regular features, and was the more conventionally handsome of the two. Wilbur was darker, and much more striking. A high domed forehead, together with his lean face and strong features, had made him the delight of caricaturists in Europe and America. "The countenance," a French observer noted, "is remarkable, curious. The head [is that of] a bird, long and bony, and with a long nose. The face is smooth-shaven and tanned by the wind and the country sun. The eye is a superb blue-grey, with tints of gold that bespeak an ardent flame."[6] An English reporter mentioned his "fine-drawn, weather-beaten face, strongly marked features, and keen, observant, hawk-like eyes."[7] Another observer thought he had the look of "a man tempered like steel."[8]

Their personalities were quite as different as their appearance. Orville was impulsive—"excitable" was the word his father used. "His thoughts," Milton said, were "quick."[9] He was the enthusiast of the pair, ever on fire with new inventions, and the optimist as well, the one who always saw the brighter side. The airplane had been Wilbur's idea, but Orville was the one who supplied the drive that carried them through the difficult times when a solution to the problems of flight seemed to recede too far.

Milton once remarked that Orville, "unlike his brother, whom fright could not rattle," suffered from timidity. With family and intimate friends he was a charming and delightful conversationalist, with a reputation as a tease and an incorrigible practical joker. Among strangers, however, he was painfully, almost pathologically shy. He would outlive his brother by more than forty years, and attend hundreds of award ceremonies, yet he absolutely refused to speak in public. He would not so much as offer an after-dinner thank you. One friend explained that "words simply failed him."[10]

Orville, much more than Wilbur, fit the image most Americans had of a "born" inventor—a man who found his fullest expression in devising new mechanical solutions to the everyday problems of life and work. As a youth he built his own printing press, and helped to devise a new and improved bicycle wheel hub. In 1913, after Wilbur's death, he received the prestigious Collier Trophy for the development of an automatic pilot system, and invented the split flap, an innovation employed on some U.S. dive bombers during World War II.

In later years, his inventive instincts frequently took a Jeffersonian turn. He would fill Hawthorn Hill, his home in Dayton, with a variety of "labor saving" gadgets of his own design, from an "efficient" circular shower bath to an intricate plumbing system and a special set of chains and rods that allowed him to control the furnace from the upstairs rooms. He designed and patented toys; modified his favorite easy chair with a special reading stand that could be shifted from arm to arm; developed tools to remove the damask wall coverings during spring cleaning; and produced a bread slicer and toaster designed to turn his morning toast a precise golden brown.

Wilbur, much more outgoing than his brother, was a gifted public speaker who never failed to delight an audience. "He is never rattled in thought or temper," Milton noted. Cool, aloof, and controlled, he had struggled to overcome fits of severe depression in his young manhood, developing an enormous self-confidence in the process. At the same time, he had the capacity to isolate himself at will. "He could cut himself off from everyone," a family member recalled. "At times he was unaware of what was going on around him."[11]

He was a voracious reader with, as his father remarked, "an extraordinary memory." His command of history, philosophy, science, and literature astounded Europeans who came to the flying field expecting to meet a rustic and untutored mechanic. Wilbur once told his father that he hoped to become a teacher. With his gift for devising simple illustrations to explain difficult concepts, he would have been a good one. A pasteboard inner-tube box enabled him to teach the fundamentals of three-axis control to a Patent Office examiner. He explained the real function of a rudder to officers of a federal court using nothing more than a string and a piece of chalk.

Yet, if the brothers were different in so many ways, they shared an extraordinary ability to analyze their experience. They were acute observers, who moved beyond surface appearances to achieve an understanding of fundamental principles. Both of them understood the world in terms of graphic and concrete images; more important, they could apply these observations of physical and mechanical reality to new situations. It was the very core of their shared genius.

But such observations do not provide an answer to our most basic question: How were these two men, who had always seemed so ordinary to their friends and neighbors, able to achieve so much?

It was a question the Wrights themselves found difficult to answer. They had kept a meticulous record of the evolution of their technology in diaries, notebooks, letters, and photographs. They knew precisely what they had done, and when. As to why they had done it, and how they had succeeded where so many others had failed, they were far less certain. Once, when a friend suggested that sheer genius might be the only explanation, Wilbur remarked that he doubted that to be the case. "Do you not insist too strongly on the single point of mental ability?" he asked. "To me, it seems that a thousand other factors, each rather insignificant in itself, in the aggregate influence the event ten times more than mere mental ability or inventiveness. . . . If the wheels of time could be turned back . . . it is not at all probable that we would do again what we have done. . . . It was due to a peculiar combination of circumstances which might never occur again.[12]

It was typical of Wilbur to give a thoughtful, honest answer to a difficult question. Those who would understand the Wright brothers and their invention would do well to follow his advice. Turn back the clock and retrace the long chain of circumstance. The story begins with the extraordinary man who was their father.

BOOK ONE

Family

chapter 1

TAKING UP THE CROSS

1829-1853

M ilton Wright first saw Huffman Prairie from the seat of a farm
wagon on a late fall afternoon in the year 1848. It had been
a long day. Samuel and John Quincy Wright had driven their
visiting Indiana cousins, Milton and his brother William, fifty miles
since sun-up. They had gone to Dayton to hear the Freesoil speakers
on the courthouse steps. There was no fooling these boys. The Mexican War, just concluded that spring, had been the Devil's work. The
words of James Russell Lowell were ringing in their ears:

> They just want this Californy,
> So's to bring new slave states in.

Then it was on to Xenia, to visit another cousin William, who was
apprenticed to a chairmaker. They drove down the Yellow Springs
Road late that afternoon, turning onto the Dayton-Springfield Pike
just at the corner of William Huffman's cow pasture. Cousin Samuel
urged the team on through the little farm town of Fairfield, Ohio,
toward his father's homestead near the village of West Charleston on
the National Pike.

For twenty-one-year-old Milton Wright, it had been a day full of
unrecognized portents. It was the first time he had ever seen Dayton,
the city where he would spend so many years of his adult life. And
the first time he had seen Huffman Prairie, where he would one day
fly with his sons.[1]

Extended family visits were to form a central element in the pattern

Wilbur and Orville Wright inherited strength of character, firmness of purpose, and absolute confidence in their own abilities from their father, Milton Wright, seen here as a rising young churchman.

of Milton Wright's life. He was a man with a great sense of family, who sought to maintain contact with his most distant aunts, uncles, cousins, nephews, and nieces either through personal visits in the course of his church travels or by letter. After his marriage to Susan

Koerner in 1859, he added her relatives to the list of family members with whom he wished to remain in touch.

In later years all of this would find a natural expression in his hobby—genealogy. Milton Wright was conscious of his position as a single link in a long familial chain connecting the past, present, and future. He scoured the nation for books and manuscripts, church records, tombstone inscriptions, and anything else that would fill the gaps in his knowledge of the family tree.[2]

His surviving correspondence includes letters to historical societies, relatives, suspected relatives, local genealogists, and complete strangers who might be able to add to the store of minute details he had amassed on his background. Like all good historians, Milton Wright was aware that the "facts" he had gathered were a mixture of the "reliable," the "uncertain," and the "probably fictitious."[3] The experience taught him a lesson. He would document his own life with extraordinary care in half a century's worth of pocket diaries and in his bulging correspondence files. The importance of documentation was a lesson that he passed on to his children, along with his enthusiasm for genealogical research, and so much else.

By the 1890s, Milton could take justifiable pride in his ability to trace "the genealogy of my foreparents on all sides for as far back as my great-grandfather's great-grandparents, and some of them farther." When asked for information on the family background, he could respond with a lineage that sounded like an American version of the "begats" of Noah:

Dan Wright (my father) was the third son of Dan Wright, who was the third child of Benoni Wright, who was the tenth child of Samuel Wright, who was the fifth child of James Wright, who was the *second* son of Samuel Wright, our first American ancestor of the name, who was born in England about the year 1600, settled at Springfield, Massachusetts in 1637 or before, less than twenty years after the landing of the Pilgrim Fathers at Plymouth Rock.[4]

That first American Wright, Samuel, was the great-great grandson of John Wrighte, who, with his wife Olive, had purchased Kelvedon Hall, Essex, in 1538. Samuel, a Puritan, was part of the "Great Migration" to Massachusetts, arriving in Boston in the early 1630s. He was among those who established Springfield Township in 1636. In the absence of an ordained Puritan minister for the local Congregational church, he was appointed to "dispense the word of God for the present." He moved to Northampton in 1656 and died there nine years later, asleep in his chair.

Samuel's great-great grandson, Dan Wright (never Daniel, as Milton Wright was careful to point out), was born in Lebanon township, Connecticut, on April 7, 1757. A veteran of the Revolution who saw service at Bemis Heights and Saratoga, he worked as a carpenter and farmer following his discharge from the patriot army. He married Sarah Freeman in 1785 and settled in Thetford Township, Orange County, Vermont, where their third son, also Dan, was born on September 3, 1790.

Young Dan, Milton Wright's father, was well educated in the country schools of Vermont, and taught a session himself before joining his older brother Porter and sister-in-law Lois on a farm in the Genesee Valley of New York in 1813. The following year, the entire Wright clan—the elder Dan, his wife Sarah, and their four children, Asahel, Porter, Dan, and Eliza—pulled up stakes and moved west. They traveled overland to Olean, Pennsylvania, then rode a flatboat down the Allegheny and Ohio rivers to Cincinnati. After a quick survey of available land, the family settled on a farm near Centerville, eight miles south of Dayton, in Montgomery County, Ohio.[5]

Dan, the youngest son, was the first to leave. He married a local Centerville girl, Catherine Reeder, not yet eighteen, on February 12, 1818. Milton Wright took great pride in the fact that his mother was the product of two first-generation Ohio families. Her maternal grandfather, John Van Cleve, had the dubious distinction of being the only white settler to be killed by Indians within the city limits of Cincinnati. Legend had it that her mother, Margaret Van Cleve, was the first white woman to set foot in what became Dayton.[6]

In February 1821, Dan and Catherine Wright and their sons—two-year-old Samuel and Harvey, an infant of five months—followed what had become a family tradition, moving west. They set up housekeeping on an eighty-acre farm in the green woods of what was soon to be Rush County, Indiana. The first winter was difficult. Dan had purchased his land from a speculator who had promised that a finished cabin would be ready to accommodate the young family. When the Wrights reached their homestead, they found the promised shelter occupied by a family of twelve, recently arrived from Virginia. Rather than forcing this brood out into the cold, the Wrights moved into one half of a larger double cabin that housed the proprietor, his wife, and six children.[7]

Dan completed work on his own cabin that spring. It was a simple affair—the walls were "chinked" with dried grass and wood chips, but not "daubed" with mud. There was a wooden puncheon floor, however, and a good solid roof. The family girdled trees the first year and cut them the second, clearing a total of ten acres, five of which were planted with corn each season. There were no cattle or horses for plowing; the work was done by hand with a hoe. Catherine bore a third son here, George, who died in infancy.

Dan sold this tract to a Mr. Parker in 1823, and moved his family to a new farm a mile and a half to the southeast. With later additions, the Wright place would eventually grow to a full quarter section, 160 acres. Four more children were born here—Sarah (Nov. 21, 1824); Milton (Nov. 17, 1828); William (Feb. 29, 1832); and Kate, who died at birth, probably in 1834.

Dan and Catherine, setting down roots on the Indiana frontier, maintained close contact with the other members of the Wright family who had come west together in 1814. Asahel, Dan's eldest brother, wrote often. He had established himself as a farmer, postmaster, and storekeeper on a 113-acre lot in the village of West Charleston, Bethel Township, Miami County, Ohio. He proudly reported that his new place included "a two-story hewed log house, 24 feet by 20, shingled roof, Porch on each side—a hewed log cabin, a log barn with a shingle roof—60 feet by 24—60 acres cleared & well fenced, an orchard of 120 good apple trees, plenty of Peach trees, a large spring of never failing water near the house—a good smoke house & corn crib besides."[8]

Asahel's letters to Dan covered a range of topics, from politics (Dec. 26, 1828: "I suppose you know that Jackson is to be our next President. I consider the fact a poor compliment to the intelligence & candor of the American people, and well calculated to strengthen the faith of them who believe that it falls not to the lot of man to give permanency to a free government.") to local farm prices (Feb. 20, 1829: "Wheat is now one dollar a bushel in this part of the country"). He described the opening of the Miami and Erie Canal between Cincinnati and Dayton, and offered a running account of progress on the National Road, from congressional debates on funding through the actual construction of the highway past his front door.

Of course there was family news to relate—condolences on the death of relatives, wishes for the speedy recovery of a sick wife, and congratulations on the birth of a child. On February 20, 1829, Asahel wrote to welcome Dan and Catherine's "fine new son" into the family, and to express the hope that "his life may be long, and a blessing to you, himself, and his country."[9]

That boy, Milton Wright, would grow up on the raw, trailing edge of the frontier. When the family moved into the area, Rush County had not yet been organized. Wolves, wildcats, bears, wild boar, and the occasional Indian trapper still roamed the woods. Clothing was homemade linsey-woolsey and grain was still ground with hand mills and hominy mortars. It was a far cry from Asahel Wright's store in settled, stable Ohio, where customers purchased calico and "domestic plaids" by the yard and the "best green coffee" was to be had at 20 cents a pound.

"Society," as a Rush County pioneer noted, "was in a chaotic state." The population was a mix of older frontiersmen, farm families filtering north from southern Indiana and Kentucky, and new arrivals from the more settled East. Violence was a way of life. One observer said that elections were an excuse for "bloody demonstrations of strength and pluck." A resident of Tippecanoe County recalled that "black eyes, bruised noses, and bit fingers" were local badges of honor.[10]

They called themselves "Hoosiers," though no one was quite sure why. Some claimed it was derived from the words of an old backwoodsman who, upon hearing a knock at the door, would bellow out, "Who's Yere?" James Whitcomb Riley, the Indiana poet whom Milton Wright so admired, related a tale popular in the southern part of the state. A stranger entering a tavern after a savage, eye-gouging brawl noticed a strange object on the floor and inquired, "Whose ear?" In fact, the word probably stemmed from "hoozer," a term applied to backwoods mountaineers in the dialect spoken in the Cumberland mountain country that was home to so many who settled southern Indiana.

Those who sought to bring the first trappings of a settled community to east-central Indiana often had a difficult time of it. According to local tradition, the first newspaper in Rush County, the *Dog-Fennell Gazette*, was a single-sheet affair printed on only one side. Subscribers were asked to return their back issues so that the publisher could print his next number on the reverse.[11]

Like so many youngsters who grew up in this environment, Milton Wright would eventually forget the hardships while retaining his fond memories of the family cabin, his first schoolhouse, and "the old log church on top of the hill where my mother was a member."[12] We know almost nothing of the personality of the woman who worshipped in that church. Milton, who offered such clear and perceptive characterizations of his seventeenth-century ancestors, spoke of his mother in terms so pious as to be empty of meaning.[13]

By contrast, the memory of his father would always remain sharp and distinct. Milton tells us nothing of Catherine's appearance, but he describes Dan down to the film that covered one of his deepset blue eyes, the result of an accident suffered while working on his brother Porter's Genesee Valley farm in the winter of 1813.

"He was five feet nine inches in height," Milton recalled thirty years after his father's death,

> and straight as an arrow. He weighed about one hundred and fifty pounds. His features were regular. . . . His temples were slightly sunken, and his head and forehead high. His hair was dark, straight and thin, but not inclined to baldness, even at seventy. He was grave in his countenance, collected in his manners, hesitating in his speech, but very accurate. Unless much excited, there was little change in his countenance and manners. He did not push acquaintance with strangers.[14]

Milton's graphic portrayal of his father can be read as a remarkably accurate description of his own sons, Wilbur and Orville. Nor was the resemblance limited to physical features or mannerisms. Dan Wright passed his strength of character, sureness of purpose, and sense of high moral resolve along to his son and grandsons as well.

"In reform," Milton noted, "he was a generation ahead of his times." Dan Wright was a man with very firm beliefs and a willingness to stand up for them, whatever the cost. He was an ardent abolitionist, voting for the Liberty Party candidate James G. Birney in the election of 1844. That alone was enough to get a man strung up in some parts of southern Indiana.[15]

Dan Wright's fierce egalitarianism and independent spirit were reflected both in his abhorrence of Freemasonry and "all of its satellites," and in his refusal to join an established church. He had undergone conversion in 1830, and was a devoted reader of the Bible, but could not find a local congregation he regarded as being sufficiently vehement in support of the antislavery cause.

Dan Wright was a total abstainer in a country where a man's worth was often judged by the amount of "Monongahela-Durkee" he could absorb before collapsing. Nor was it enough to speak out in favor of temperance. On more than one occasion he accepted a lower price for his corn than most of his neighbors because he refused to sell to the high-paying local distillers.[16]

Dan Wright's opinions would have a profound impact on Milton, who cast *his* first vote for John P. Hale, the Liberty Party candidate in 1852. Milton relished the memory of schoolboy debates with "ignorant and incredulous" Rush County classmates who recognized the "outrage and uncertainty" of slavery but feared "saucy free negroes and the danger of them walking with and marrying white girls." His antislavery sentiment led to "a lively interest in politics." When the Civil War began in 1861, Milton, then a young preacher in Grant County, Indiana, saw the conflict as part of a divine plan to end slavery. "The president does not mean it; congress does not mean it; but I am confident the *Lord* means it, and will bring it to pass."[17] Driven by such absolute confidence in his own moral judgment, Milton would make it his business in life to show others the way to the light.

He was twelve years old when his father sold the second Rush County place and purchased a farm, complete with an unfinished frame house, in Orange Township, Fayette County, Indiana. The move seems to have been a turning point for the boy. "It was here," he recalled many years later, "that I labored with strong hands, for I had almost my full growth at fifteen, and from my twelfth year had almost perfect health, though I was in delicate health for the six years preceding that time."[18]

Milton found the Fayette County teachers more competent than those in Rush County, where the local Kentucky emigrants "cared little for education." The boy who had once argued elementary cosmology with classmates "so ignorant as to think that the earth might be set upon a great rock," now "devoured books with remarkable rapidity, considering the time I had for reading, and with a memory which at that time was a marvel to the family."[19]

He sought to improve himself in every way. He practiced public speaking while at work in the fields, "often attracting the ears of the family, and sometimes the neighbors." Sam, his oldest brother, taught him algebra, while Harvey, next in line, encouraged his "desire and efforts for careful mental improvement" and advised him to "train" his mind to think. "I did it daily, purposefully, and sometimes laboriously and as systematically as a 13 year old knows how. I did this till hard thinking was so much a habit that I had to regulate this tendency."[20]

Much of this hard thinking was directed toward the subject of religion. Milton Wright had become a "seeker of religion" at the age of eight, following a conversation with his mother. He described himself as "a praying child, although never in the hearing of anyone." He attended church, listened attentively to the preaching, and often left the services "powerfully impressed" and "fully resolved to be converted."[21] Time and again, his resolve wore off after a month or two.

The searching, questioning, and doubting came to an abrupt end in June of 1843. While laboring in his father's corn field, fifteen-year-old Milton Wright experienced conversion. "It was not by forces, visions, or signs," he recalled in later years, "but by an impression that spoke to the soul powerfully and abidingly. . . . There was no sudden revolution from great anguish to ecstatic joy, but a sweet peace and joy [which I had] never known before."[22]

The future bishop believed that he owed his "religious impressions" to his mother, who had converted just before his birth in 1828. Catherine's piety had certainly made an indelible impression on her children—each of her surviving sons chose the church as his career.

Samuel Smith Wright, the older brother whom Milton thought "endowed beyond any of the family in physical and mental powers," planned to enter the ministry, but died of typhoid in 1842 while away from home teaching school to raise money for his education. Harvey grew up to be a Primitive Baptist minister, "well known in his church, throughout his State, and in neighboring states." William, the youngest, became a United Brethren preacher, but suffered an attack of "dyspepsia" which "so impaired his health that his wit in conversation and public speech were never fully regained." As a result, Milton recalled, he was "so slow in utterance" as to weary his congregation.[23]

In spite of the credit Milton gave his mother for directing all her children down the path of righteousness, it is clear that his own religious attitudes were more closely aligned with those of his father. Catherine was a Presbyterian by choice, but usually attended the Methodist Episcopal church close to her home. Like his father, Milton rejected both those faiths. He could not accept some of the Presbyterian tenets and disliked the fact that the Methodist churches seemed "largely filled by persons, who, in his judgment, seemed to be there from motives of popularity."[24]

Certain of his own convictions, he remained outside of the established churches for five years following his conversion. Finally, late in 1846, Milton turned his attention to the Church of the United Brethren in Christ. He had known John Morgan, an itinerant preacher of the sect, for many years, and regarded him as "one of the best and grandest men [I] ever knew." After studying the "usages and doctrines" of the faith in some detail and attending a major church conference in Andersonville, Indiana, he decided that the Brethren, "respectable, but not cursed with popularity," suited him. Following a Sabbath sermon at Dan Wright's home in 1847, the Reverend Joseph A. Ball of the United Brethren White River Conference baptized both Milton and his brother William into the faith by total immersion.[25]

At the time of Milton Wright's entry, the Church of the United Brethren in Christ was just forty-seven years old. The denomination was a product of the wave of evangelical pietism that had swept over the United States late in the eighteenth century. Philip William Otterbein, spiritual father of the church, was a German Reformed minister who had immigrated to Pennsylvania in 1752. Working with Mennonite leader Martin Boehm, Otterbein had staged a series of highly successful revival meetings among German immigrants in the backcountry of Pennsylvania, Maryland, and Virginia.[26]

Otterbein's highly personal and emotionally charged approach struck directly at the heart of traditional Calvinism. He rejected predestination out of hand, emphasizing the importance of the individual conversion experience, a personal relationship with God, scripture, and the moral life as evidence of sanctification.

The Church of the United Brethren in Christ was established by a group of admiring and like-minded evangelical preachers meeting at Frederick, Maryland, in 1800. Before Otterbein's death in 1813 the church remained little more than a loose amalgamation of congregations. Gradually, however, a church structure emerged. The first General Conference was held in 1815. Two years later the group adopted a Confession of Faith and a *Book of Discipline.* By 1830 the scores of frontier converts flocking into the circuit meetings in Kentucky, Ohio, and Indiana had diluted the original ethnic German flavor to the extent that English was adopted as the official language for preaching and church publications.

In theology and church polity the Brethren had general links to the Methodist, Mennonite, and German and Dutch Reformed traditions. The original pietistic strain remained very strong. Ritual was regarded as of so little importance that individual congregations were free to adopt any form of baptism or communion they chose.

The rapid growth of the church required the adoption of the first governing Constitution at the General Conference of 1837. The original document proved so weak and unpopular, however, that it was replaced by a much stronger constitution only four years later.

The Constitution of 1841 reflected both the individualism and the democratic viewpoint common to so many of the frontier converts who now made up the bulk of the membership. It established a single clerical rank—presiding elder—to which fully ordained ministers were admitted. All basic decisions affecting the church were to be decided by vote at a quadrennial General Conference attended by clerical delegates representing the local conferences, or geographic subdivisions of the church. These local conferences met annually to set regional policy, ordain ministers, and conduct other business.

Five bishops, the sole governing authorities linking the congregations into administrative districts, were elected to a four-year term by the delegates to each General Conference. The notion of life tenure for bishops, as in the Methodist pattern, was anathema to a church dominated by frontier egalitarians.

The new Constitution also underscored a reform tradition that was already well established in the church. Good Brethren were exhorted to forswear alcohol, and unofficially encouraged to support the antislavery cause. Membership in the Masonic order, or any other secret society, was specifically forbidden. In that regard, they were in good company.

By the third decade of the nineteenth century, Freemasonry, which had been so popular with American and French revolutionary leaders, was widely regarded as an elitist cabal, its sole purpose to offer members an unfair preference in business, social, and political situations. The notion of a secret privileged brotherhood that cut across the lines of nation and religion struck the wrong chord in a country where it was believed that men and women ought to be able to rise in life solely on the basis of their own merits. Moreover, the Masonic Lodges, with their secret rituals, cabalistic symbols, and ceremonial garments, seemed almost sacrilegious to many evangelical Christians of the sort who founded the United Brethren Church.

The Brethren were not alone in their opposition to secretism. Anti-Masonic feeling functioned as an important organizing principle in American politics during the decade 1826–36. Thurlow Weed, William Henry Seward, and other rising young politicians used the issue to rally anti-Jacksonian support. Established leaders attached themselves to the movement as well. Ex-President John Quincy Adams, for

example, campaigned for the governorship of Massachusetts on the
anti-Masonic ticket. After 1835, voters lost interest in the question of
secret societies, but the issue remained very much alive among evangelical groups like the Brethren. Within the church, anti-Masonic
sentiment was strongest in the West, where the original prohibition
against secret societies in the Constitution of 1841 was repeatedly
reaffirmed.

The church stand on such political and moral issues as alcohol,
slavery, and secret societies was far more important to Milton Wright
than any theological fine point. He represented a new generation:
while committed to the essentials of pietism and a personal religion,
he rejected much of the emotional fervor that had marked the church
during the years of the great revivals. He would do his best to win
souls for God, but he reserved his heart and his energy for the fight
to lead men and women onto the path of righteousness here on earth.

Milton had chosen his course in life. Two years after joining the
church he was licensed to exhort, or offer comment on scripture during services. He preached his first sermon on November 17, 1850; was
admitted to the White River Conference, the local church governing
body, in August 1853; and was regularly ordained as a minister three
years later.

Milton would not earn a regular church salary until he was appointed a full circuit preacher. In the meantime, he continued to live
at home and work his father's fields. He began teaching in local
schools in 1849 to earn additional money, and would continue to do so
off and on for the next decade. In April 1852, the school examiners of
Rush County certified him as a "gentleman of good moral character"
qualified to teach orthography, English grammar, reading, writing,
arithmetic, and geography in the common schools.[27]

Milton once remarked that he was "fond of science, fond of youth
and children," and had been "an enthusiastic lover" of the teaching
profession "after experience had taught [me] the art of governance
by mental and moral forces."[28] He would remember his successes
with great pride—the backward children he had helped to catch up
with their class, the poor student who went on to medical school, the
wayward boys whom he had taught self-discipline.

He also put his teaching experience to use in raising his own children, each of whom was taught to read through the first McGuffey
before they entered school, "except my daughter, whom my second
son taught." Many years later he became incensed at the techniques

employed at the Dayton elementary school: "My youngest grandson was turned over to me after a teacher had taught him to *guess* at words!" he complained. "It was a hard job to break him from *guessing.*"[29]

In 1853 Milton was appointed supervisor of the preparatory department at Hartsville College, a United Brethren institution. The position would also enable him to take a number of college courses, including Greek. But he became ill and could not return the following year. Although he never graduated from college, he took great pride in the honorary degree of doctor of divinity awarded many years later by Western College, another Brethren school.

Marriage was much on Milton's mind during his year at Hartsville. The notion of family was so important to the young clergyman that he determined to exercise great care in selecting a wife, and cautioned his brother William to take a similar approach: "I would by all means advise you to marry just as soon as you find somebody you are sure you want to have for a companion. Don't wait to get fixed only wait to find the *person* but *be sure* about that first."[30]

Milton was not a man to allow his heart to govern his head. Back in Fayette County he had fallen "deeply in love" with the "uncommonly good looking" third daughter of neighbor Thomas Stephens, but had not proposed marriage because "I could never think she was the right one for me." Perhaps not, but there had been some very deep feeling involved. Three quarters of a century later, in January 1916, Milton still remembered this girl he had "always much admired." "Still do," he concluded.[31]

Following the time-honored tradition of older brothers gone off to college, Milton filled his early letters home to William with news of his romantic prospects. "I live very well here," he told his brother, "but alas! I can find my 'lovely fair one' nowhere." He must have met Susan Koerner within a few weeks of sending that letter.

chapter 2

MILTON AND SUSAN

1853-1869

Susan Catherine Koerner remains in the shadows of the Wright family. Unlike her husband, she did not keep a diary or leave extensive reminiscences behind. Only a few of her letters have survived. She died of tuberculosis on July 4, 1889, long before her sons became famous and reporters flocked to interview all the members of the family. Even Milton, the inveterate genealogist and record keeper, failed to document her background as fully as he did the myriad branches of his own family.

She was born near Hillsboro, in Loudon County, Virginia, on April 30, 1831, the fifth and last child of John and Catherine Koerner. Her father, John Gottlieb Koerner, was a native of Foerthen, near Schleitz, Saxony, who had emigrated to the United States in 1818 to avoid conscription. He worked as a carriage maker in Baltimore for a time before marrying Catherine Fry, the daughter of John Philip Fry (sometimes given as Fryer), an American-born farmer of Swiss extraction, on April 10, 1820.

The couple moved in with the bride's parents on a seventy-acre farm in the lovely, rolling countryside three miles southeast of Hillsboro. Koerner continued to follow his trade, apparently operating a small carriage shop on the farm, as well as a forge in town.

Philip Fry's will was recorded in the Loudon County Courthouse on March 27, 1824. The document was finally probated seven years later, in September 1831, a few months after Susan's birth. This length of time, combined with a suit in chancery filed by John Koerner on his wife's behalf on December 12, 1831, suggests that there may have been some family difficulties relating to the will. In any case, John and Catherine sold the land to one William Brown on September 12, 1832, and set out for Union County, Indiana, where a number of relatives had already settled.[1]

They prospered in the new country. The sale of the Virginia farm had enabled them to buy 170 acres of good Indiana bottom land. When their grandson Orville visited the Koerner farm and workshop fifty years later, it resembled a small village, with twelve to fourteen buildings, including a carriage shop furnished with a foot-driven lathe.

Koerner was just the sort of man to delight an intelligent grandson. "He did not accept all that he heard or read," Orville remembered with obvious admiration.

> It was his habit to read newspapers aloud to his family, and when, as invariably happened, he came to something that interested him because of approval, disapproval, or for any other reason, he would interpolate comment without changing his tone or rate of utterance. It was impossible for a listener to tell just how much that he seemed to be reading was actually in the paper and which ideas were his own. One by one, members of the family would study the paper afterwards to see if various surprising statements were really there. No matter how commonplace a newspaper article may have been, it was never colorless when he read it.[2]

Koerner and his family had converted from Presbyterianism to the United Brethren faith soon after arriving in Indiana. He remained a prominent member of the church for over fifty years. His daughter Susan experienced conversion and joined the Brethren at the age of fourteen, in 1845.

Susan was very close to her father, and apparently spent a good deal of time in his carriage shop as a young girl. Her children remembered her as having considerable mechanical aptitude. She designed and built simple household appliances for herself and made toys, including a much-treasured sled, for her children. When the boys wanted mechanical advice or assistance, they came to their mother. Milton was one of those men who had difficulty driving a nail straight.

Wilbur and Orville had their mother to thank for their lifelong penchant for tinkering, and, ultimately, for their extraordinary ability to visualize the operation of mechanisms that had yet to be constructed. That ability, coupled with their fascination with technological problem solving, would carry them far.

Hollinger,

12 N. Main St.,
Dayton, O.

Susan Wright (c. 1870), was a shy, quiet woman who loved to work with her hands.

Susan was a scholar as well. "Like myself," Milton Wright reported with his usual modesty, "in school she excelled." Her father sent her on to Hartsville College, a rare opportunity for a woman of that time and place. She studied literature and "came within three months of graduation." But, according to Milton, she "was not ambitious for the degree."[3]

The most striking feature of Susan's personality was her painful shyness. Milton regarded it as an asset, and spoke with pride of her modesty and quiet demeanor. Her son Orville, who inherited the quality from her, saw the pain engendered by intense shyness. Just after her marriage, he once told his friend Jess Gilbert, Susan went to a strange grocery store. On being asked where the items should be delivered, she became so flustered that she could not recall her own name.[4]

We know little of their courtship except that it was a long one. When they met at Hartsville in 1853, Milton was twenty-four and Susan twenty-two. Both wanted to be absolutely certain that the other had the character and strength of purpose required to face the difficulties of a Christian life.

Following his year at Hartsville, Milton returned to a farm he had purchased in Grant County. He taught at Neff's Corner for two years, 1854–55, and conducted a revival in Indianapolis in the fall of 1855. Ordained a minister of the faith at Abingdon, Indiana, in August 1856, he was posted to the Andersonville Circuit, near the family home in Fayette County. It was a particularly appropriate assignment—he was replacing a man who had created a minor scandal on the circuit when it was discovered that he was a Mason. Then, in the early spring of 1857, Milton accepted a call to join an Oregon mission.

"Mother was much affected yesterday about my going to Oregon, but was resigned," he wrote in his diary on May 28. "She said that she prayed that her sons might be ministers, and she ought not to complain."[5]

On June 19, as he was getting ready to leave, Milton had a "private talk" with Susan. He proposed, and asked her to accompany him to Oregon. Milton did not record her response, but it appears that she said yes to him and no to Oregon. They would be married after his return, if both of them were still willing.[6]

Susan was now twenty-six. If all went well, Milton's mission might last as long as three years. Clearly, this was a woman who wanted to be very sure of her partner in life.

Milton proved steadfast. The two and a half years from June 1857 to November 1859 were to be a forecast of their marriage. A rising churchman, he would spend most of his life on the road. There were churches to be visited, conferences to be attended, the work of the Lord to be done. The letters that passed between them now were the first of hundreds that would bind their lives over the next thirty years.

Milton left home in late June with a party of five destined for the United Brethren missionary circuits of Oregon. They traveled by train east through Dayton, Xenia, Columbus, Pittsburgh, Altoona, Harrisburg, and Philadelphia. From Amboy they journeyed up the North River to New York by steamboat, arriving in the city in time for the Fourth of July celebration. "Little balloons, shooting crackers, cake, pie, orange, [and] pineapple sellers, the firing of cannon and all sorts of parades seem to be the order of the day," Milton wrote William. "And tonight they expect to have fireworks."[7]

For a young minister fresh from a Hoosier cornfield, New Yorkers seemed daunting. "The military companies were out strutting about this forenoon," he told William. "Some of them pretty hard folks— hard looking I mean." Three of Milton's companions—Mr. Dougherty, his wife, and daughter—were caught up in a "riot of Bowery Boys," escaping into a doorway just as the rowdies approached them.[8]

They sailed aboard the *Illinois* at 2:00 P.M. on July 6, bound for Panama. Milton, fascinated by the sea, found it difficult to sleep. "I went forward at night, and for hours saw the moonlight dance on the waves." While most of the passengers suffered from seasickness, he flourished. "My berth was No. 102; my seat at table 63." The world was full of new sights and sounds—Watling Island, where Columbus had landed; flying fish and porpoise "nearly the length of a man"; the fortifications at Kingston, Jamaica; fruit sellers, beggars, and native divers calling for dimes to be thrown into the clear water; "Sixty colored girls" carrying baskets of coal aboard the ship "with snatches of song and dance."[9]

They journeyed across Panama by rail, passing "villages, huts, trees, swamps, mountains, Panama soldiers, Indians," and mosquitoes, then boarded the *Golden Age*, and sailed for San Francisco on July 18. Milton was shocked that "not a few" church members took part in a dance on board. A Spaniard present that evening remarked to the Americans that their nation was but a child. "A very large child," Milton replied.[10]

They touched at Acapulco and Manzanilla, "sorry towns." Milton had a slight chill on July 26, the first symptom of the dreaded Panama fever. By the time they reached San Francisco he was a very sick man, his fever so high he almost fainted simply walking aboard the *Commodore,* the ship that would carry them on to Portland. T. J. Connor, a fellow mission worker, nursed him through the delirium that followed, when, as Milton later recalled, "my thoughts with painful vigor flew over the universe."[11]

His recovery was very slow. Milton was still "quite weak and stupid" when they transferred to the *Hoosier* at Oregon City for the final leg of their journey to Butteville, Oregon. He preached his first sermon in Oregon on August 23, then began a slow tour of the Willamette Valley circuits as he regained his strength. Milton fell in love with the Oregon wilderness during his first weeks in the territory. "The breezes had a peculiar roar in the trees," he wrote, "and the memory of the sound was lasting."[12]

Posted to the Lane County Circuit in mid-September, he was still too ill to accept. Instead, he was asked to take over the preparatory department of Sublimity College, an embryonic United Brethren school. He opened classes on November 23 with twenty-seven "scholars." Under his leadership, Sublimity grew and prospered. He spent the next two years teaching and administering the school, and making the rounds of various Oregon circuits as a preacher.

Milton remained in close touch with his family by mail. William received constant letters describing his life in the Oregon wilderness; there was also a steady flow of letters to and from Susan, "the girl I left behind."

His first tour of missionary duty completed, he sailed from Portland on October 7, 1859. His plan was to return home, marry Susan, and come back to Oregon to spend his life in the service of the West Coast conference. As before, he enjoyed the trip, attending a lecture on Arabia by the renowned traveler Bayard Taylor in San Francisco before boarding the steamer *Sonora,* bound for Panama. Taylor and his wife; Lansing Stout, U.S. representative from Oregon; and U.S. Senator Joseph Lane were among his fellow passengers.

Arriving at Panama City, they received word that "Ossawatomie" John Brown had been captured by Virginia authorities following a raid on the U.S. arsenal at Harper's Ferry. Senator Lane, who would run as the Southern Democratic candidate for Vice President with John C. Breckinridge in 1860, remarked, "I would have him hung higher than Hammon without judge or jury!" Milton, while never a violent man, felt some admiration for Brown, and chided the senator for making a remark obviously intended to reach the ears of the press.[13]

He arrived back home in Fayette County on November 14, 1859, after an absence of two years, four months, and nineteen days. "Mother," he noted in his diary, "almost overcome with joy."[14]

Milton visited the Koerners the next day. Apparently all doubts were now resolved. One week later, on November 22, he obtained a marriage license. He and Susan were married by the Reverend John Fohl shortly after three o'clock on the afternoon of November 24—Thanksgiving Day—1859. He was four days short of his thirty-first birthday; she was twenty-eight.

The long years of waiting had been worthwhile. This was to be a very successful marriage. A quarter of a century after his wife's death in 1889, Milton continued to honor their anniversary, her birthday, and the anniversary of her death. On July 4, 1908, he wrote a poignant letter to his son Wilbur, who was preparing to give his first public demonstration flights in France: "I went to your Mother's grave this forenoon, and laid a little bunch of flowers on her grave. Nineteen years ago she departed. Of course I miss her most. Her benediction rests on you. She was so humble, cheerful, meek, and true. . . ."[15]

It is clear that he regarded Susan as the ideal wife and helpmate. The best advice he could give his daughter was that she strive to attain "some of her Mother's love of calm and solitude," so that she might "Flourish like the palm."[16]

Susan was a good and dutiful wife, even by the rigorous standards of the period. There was assuredly much more to her than that, however. She was a woman with a will, if not a constitution, to match her husband's. She accepted Milton's religious calling as her own. Her duty, as she saw it, was to create a home that would provide him with loyalty and support, and to raise the children into healthy, strong adults with the moral fiber that would enable them to take their place as good Christians and model citizens.

Her health was never good. She suffered periodic bouts with malaria, rheumatism, and a variety of other ills. Yet she bore Milton seven children—the first when she was twenty-nine, the last when she was forty-three. She packed and moved her family twelve times in thirty years of married life—without a complaint. She was a capable, independent woman, devoted to her family.

The dream of returning to Oregon faded as the young couple settled into married life. They moved into their first home, a farm near Rushville, late in 1859. Milton earned $25 a month teaching the winter term at the New Salem subscription school, six miles southeast of town. "Here my wife and I were happy," he reported. As a professional experience, it was a good deal less pleasant. "Some of the large scholars were insubordinate, and injured the discipline of the school," he recalled. In April 1860, they moved to Andersonville, where Milton accepted a teaching position at Neff's Corner. Again, it was a "less pleasant experience" than it had been when he taught here in 1855.[17]

Finally, in the fall of 1860, he received a regular church appointment to the Marion Circuit. The couple moved back to Milton's Grant County farm, four miles east of Fairmont, where they established their first real home in a hewed log building on the lot. They would spend the next four years here, while Milton rode various White River Conference circuits. In addition, as he later recalled, "I tried to farm a little."[18]

Their first child, Reuchlin—named for Johannes Reuchlin (1455–1522), a German theologian and humanist—was born here on March 17, 1861. Milton, convinced that the name Wright was too common, was determined to give his children distinctive first names.

Having married relatively late in life, Milton and Susan were the proudest of parents. "Reuchlin weighed about twenty pounds a month ago," Milton informed his brother William on November 27, 1862. "His flesh is solid—his cheeks red—and he is just as full of life and good nature as he can be."[19]

Lorin, the second son, was born in Dan Wright's home twenty months later, on November 18, 1862. Dan had died on October 6, 1861; Milton, hurrying to his father's bedside, had arrived too late. Now his widowed mother supervised Lorin's delivery. The boy was named for a town selected at random on a map; the parents thought it sounded nice.

Milton's letters to other members of the family were soon filled with news of childhood ailments and accidents, as well as a surprising amount of detail on the children's development. He was, and would remain, a very observant father. Lorin was down with a fever. Reuch, (pronounced "Roosh"), had burned his hand "smartly" on the stove, but was recovering. He was a year old when he began to walk; Lorin walked at eleven months, and was soon "running about."[20]

The Wrights were on the move again in 1864, living in a series of rented houses as Milton moved from circuit to circuit in the Marion, Dublin, and Williamsburg districts. Late that fall, he acquired additional property, a five-acre farm with a three-room house near Millville, eight miles east of New Castle, Indiana. He paid $550 in cash, with the promise of $200 more to be paid within two years, interest-free. Family tradition has it that the property was purchased with money presented by the Wright and Koerner families at the time of Milton and Susan's wedding.[21]

For the moment, the farm was only an investment, not a home. Milton's church salary at this point was approximately $200 a year; the family could also count on perhaps $35–50 a year in money from crop and timber sales from the Grant County Farm. As the owner of two farms, Milton now received not only the extra share of crop money but an additional $20 a month in rent for the Millville farm.[22]

Like all good Brethren, Milton was a pacifist. During the Civil War he did not enter the Army or preach sermons to the troops, yet there was no doubt where he stood on the issues. "May it prove to be an irrepressible conflict in the fullest sense of the term, ending oppression's rule," he remarked in a letter to a friend. "I made no party speeches," he told his children many years later, "but I, on many occasions, condemned slavery and advocated the Union cause."

Those wartime sermons were described as "temperate in word, but radical in principle." He was invited to deliver special sermons on the occasion of the recapture of Fort Sumter and the death of President Lincoln. Like the President, he argued that leniency and understanding should be extended to the defeated Confederacy.[23]

Not long after the end of the war, they finally moved onto the Millville farm. Susan gave birth to their third son, Wilbur—named for Wilbur Fiske, a clergyman whom Milton admired—here on April 16, 1867.

The boy was born with a head his father described as being "two stories high." Milton, a long-time amateur phrenologist, was concerned but found some humor in the situation. Later, he would tell reporters that while his son's appearance had improved with age, it was several years before Susan could find a hat that did not look silly on the youngster.

"Willy," as his father insisted on calling him for several years, took his first step on February 4, 1868, when he was ten and a half months old. After that there was no stopping him—"At fifteen months, when turned into a room he seemed to see all the mischief available in it at a glance, and [he] always found the greatest first."[24]

The year after Wilbur's birth, the family returned to Hartsville, where Milton had been named the first professor of theology in the history of the United Brethren Church. The post was an indication of his rising position within the loosely knit hierarchy. Milton did well both as pastor of the college chapel and in his teaching and administrative duties. His success helped to lay the foundation for the establishment of the church's first professional training school, the Union Biblical Seminary, later Bonebrake Theological Seminary.

Milton would have good reason to remember the General Conference of 1869 in years to come. For the first time in the placid history of the Church of the United Brethren in Christ, there were serious signs of dissension. The key issue related to the continued support of the anti-Masonic doctrine established in the Constitution and the church *Discipline* of 1841.

A group of young ministers—Liberals, as they would come to be called—argued that the church must be brought into step with the times. Secret societies no longer aroused the horror that they had in 1840. The Masonic order had grown from a membership of perhaps 5,000 during the 1850s to as many as 200,000 members by 1865. Membership in a lodge or fraternal order offered a sense of belonging and identity so often missing in the lives of Americans who had left farms, small towns, or villages for the big city. During the years after the Civil War, businessmen and professionals joined these organizations in unprecedented numbers. The church must reflect the change in social values, the Liberals argued, or suffer the consequences of declining membership and lost revenue.

Others, including Milton Wright, were appalled at the suggestion that the church should abandon its traditional stand on this issue. In time, this group of conservative churchmen would be most inappropriately dubbed the Radicals.

Milton Wright's obsessive rejection of Freemasonry was rooted alike in his background and personality. As a social reformer, he was never to move beyond the classic liberal causes of his youth—the abolition of slavery, temperance, and women's rights. He believed in, and would fight for, absolute equality of opportunity for all men and women. He was free of the nativist taint, and in later years would assist Asian church groups on the West Coast. Masonry—perceived as an elitist conspiracy whose only real purpose was to confer unfair advantage on its members—ran counter to his most cherished values.

An open, forthright person, Milton abhorred secrecy as a matter of general principle. The lodge swore a man to oaths that could not be divulged to wife, children, friend, or pastor. Anyone who took such an oath, he believed, set the lodge above family, church, or state.

Then there were the religious problems. Milton had little serious interest in theological hairsplitting, but he was no Bible-thumping orator. His religion was, in fact, too cerebral for many of the Brethren. Nevertheless, he was a firm Christian. The man of broad vision and courage who supported unpopular social reforms could also argue that Masonic prayers excluded the name of Jesus Christ to "satisfy and gratify" non-Christians.[25]

Ultimately, what would set Milton apart from the other Radical leaders was his extraordinary resolve. A Hartsville classmate once characterized him as "more than ordinarily cautious, conservative and methodical in all that he undertook, and when once he decided his course he was hard to turn from it."[26] None of that had changed. Milton saw life as a series of clear-cut moral choices. The real test of character was to be found in willingness to choose the path of virtue and follow it, whatever the cost.

Most men and women lacked the strength of will required for the task. It was not the path to friendship, popularity, or political success; the temptation to seek harmony and consensus was very great. Yet moral issues were beyond compromise or negotiation. There was no middle ground. Milton Wright saw himself as one of God's chosen few—a man made of sterner stuff, who was willing to stand up for the right in the face of any opposition from weaker souls.

The Radical-Liberal split in the United Brethren Church was a perfect case in point. It seemed so simple to the Liberals. The internal dispute that threatened the church did not involve any central questions of theology. They regarded the anti-Masonic stance of the church fathers as a piece of antiquated baggage that had to be jettisoned in order to bring doctrine into line with a changing social order.

That, to Milton Wright's way of thinking, was expediency. He wanted no part of a "Creed on Wheels" which could be altered at will to meet changes in public tastes and attitudes.

For the moment, the Radicals prevailed. There had never been a serious possibility of a Liberal victory in 1869. It was clear, however, that the issue was far from resolved. Two distinct factions had emerged in the church leadership. The questions at issue would expand, for the specific problem of Freemasonry masked a deeper rift over the general question of change in traditional church doctrine and polity.

Those who favored such change had suffered a temporary defeat, but time was on their side. Their cause would obviously prove popular with the general membership.

The Radicals recognized the need to buttress their position. As one important step, they sought to maintain strict control over the all-important church publication program. The United Brethren Printing Establishment, based in Dayton, Ohio, was one of the best-equipped religious printing houses in the nation.

Its most important product, *The Religious Telescope,* was a weekly newspaper that carried the official church position into Brethren homes across the nation. The editor of the *Telescope,* like the bishops, was elected at the quadrennial General Conferences. In 1869, the Radicals chose their most vocal spokesman, Milton Wright, for that honor. Quite unexpectedly, Milton had become one of the most influential men in the church. The Wright family would be moving to Dayton.

chapter 3

THE PREACHER'S KIDS

1869-1881

No. 7 Hawthorn Street is today a vacant lot. Henry Ford moved the two-story white frame house that once stood here to Greenfield Village in the fall of 1936. Transplanted to a plot of manicured grass, framed by shrubs and trees, the structure remains a central feature of Ford's vision of small-town America.

The house looked very different when the Wright family moved here in April 1871. The lovely porch that wraps around the front and down one side was missing; there were no pale green shutters on the upper-story windows. Those additions lay twenty years in the future. In the early spring of 1871 the house smelled of raw lumber and fresh paint.

Standing here today, it is difficult to believe that a house was ever wedged into the lot, only thirty-seven feet wide. This was a tight, cramped, urban neighborhood. No more than two feet separated the Wrights' house from its neighbor to the north. You had to turn sideways to pass between the two buildings.

It was a modest enough home inside, as well. What appears to be the front door, the Wrights used as the guest or visitors' entrance. Family and friends entered through a side door that opened into the sitting room. The Sunday parlor was to the left, with the narrow, closed stairwell leading to the four bedrooms on the upper story beyond that. The dining room and kitchen were to the right.

There was an attic above the bedrooms, and a partial cellar beneath the rear of the house. A cistern furnished running water to the sink,

In spite of moves to Iowa and Indiana while the children were growing up, the house at 7 Hawthorn Street in Dayton, Ohio, seen here on a fall day in 1897, was always home. The wraparound porch and shutters were Wilbur and Orville's handiwork.

supplementing the pump just outside the kitchen door. A carriage shed and outhouse stood at the rear of the lot along the fence.

The city gas lines had been extended through the neighborhood, but the house was not yet connected. Oil lamps provided light, and coal stoves heat. There was a wood-burning cook stove in the kitchen.

The Wright family came to Dayton in June 1869, immediately after Milton's election as editor of *The Religious Telescope*. They rented a house on Third Street until November of that year, when they moved into "John Kemp's large brick [sic] on Second Street, just east of the Railroad." Milton purchased the Hawthorn street house from James Manning, the builder, for $1,800 on December 21, 1870, while it was still under construction. The family moved in four months later.

The area was still popularly known as Miami City then, although the name had officially been changed to West Dayton when the city annexed the neighborhood in 1869. West Dayton lay on the far side of the Miami, in a great bend of the river just below the point where Wolf Creek empties into the larger stream.

This was a streetcar suburb, the result of a classic pattern of urban expansion that would change the face of cities across America. The West Side had begun to blossom in 1869 when W. P. Huffman and H. S. Williams established the Dayton Street Railway. Both men had extensive real estate investments in the city, Huffman in the populated eastern section of town and Williams across the river on the West Side. The two entrepreneurs scarcely expected to make a great deal of money from streetcar fares. Rather, they hoped that the availability of cheap transportation would increase the value of their landholdings, and encourage the sale of new lots and homes in outlying areas to workmen previously forced to live within walking distance of the industrial and commercial core of the city.

The venture was particularly important for Williams. On February 27, 1868, he had recorded the platting of "a new addition to Miami City" in the Montgomery County deed books. The new plat centered on a large tract of land south of West Third Street, an area left undeveloped because of its distance from downtown Dayton.

The horse-car line was extended over the bridge and down the length of Third Street by the end of 1869. As Williams and Huffman had hoped, stores and shops sprang up along the main thoroughfares, with residential areas appearing a block or two back from the business district. Real estate values soared, and, as one local historian noted, "the proprietors [of the streetcar line] were astonished when it was found that from the first the traffic paid a profit on the investment."[1]

Unlike the modern developer who packages subdivisions complete with finished houses, utilities, streets, and shopping centers, nineteenth-century speculators like Williams were content simply to chop the land up into small urban lots for sale to individual builders. Quite often, smaller-scale proprietors would buy several lots, hoping for a quick rise in land values; a suburban lot might pass through several hands before a house was actually constructed on it.

The early history of the house at 7 Hawthorn Street is typical. On May 4, 1868, John A. Francis purchased lot 111 of the Williams tract, along with several others, from the proprietor for $300. Six months later Francis sold this lot to Anna Manning for $350. Anna and her husband, Dayton carpenter James Manning, held the land for over a year before beginning construction of a house sometime in the early spring of 1869. Milton bought it before the work was finished.[2]

In time, West Dayton, like so many other suburbs of its kind, developed a character all its own. Officially part of the city of Dayton, it nevertheless remained somewhat isolated by the Miami. The residents announced that they were citizens of *West* Dayton. They organized campaigns urging their neighbors to patronize local businesses, and to join West Side clubs and civic organizations.

Hawthorn, a block south of Third and Williams, and half a block east on Fourth, was a typical West Side residential street. Most of the houses were newly constructed by small-scale speculators like the Mannings, or individual workmen who purchased lots and built their own inexpensive homes. The sudden availability of reasonable housing drew working-class citizens into the area. Milton Wright's neighbors were carpenters, day laborers, wagon makers, foundry workmen, bookkeepers, seamstresses, house painters, salesmen, clerks, laundresses, machinists, firemen, and stenographers. The census records covering Hawthorn and the surrounding streets reveal that Milton, one other clergyman, and a physician were the only professional men living in the area in 1890.[3]

While the Wrights were by no means rich, they were wealthy enough by the standards of Hawthorn Street. Milton's salary had increased from $900 a year as a presiding elder and circuit preacher to $1,200–1,500 as an editor. In addition, his travel costs and related expenses were covered by special collections taken up by the congregations he visited. The real estate investments of the previous decade were now yielding $40 to $60 a month in rents plus money from the sale of crops grown on both farms. By the turn of the century, oil had been discovered on the Indiana land, further increasing the family income.[4]

Milton Wright was forty-three years old when the family came to 7 Hawthorn. His wife Susan was forty, and four months pregnant. Their sons—Reuchlin, Lorin, and Wilbur—were ten, eight, and four at the time.

Twins, Otis and Ida, had been born in the Second Street house on March 7, 1870. Ida died at birth; Otis lived only one month and two days. The fact that both Milton and Susan had seen brothers and sisters, as well as the children of friends and neighbors, die in infancy made their own loss no less traumatic. Milton would continue to honor the twins' birthday for over a quarter of a century.

Orville, the sixth child, was born in the upstairs front bedroom at 7 Hawthorn Street on August 19, 1871. As usual, Milton had chosen a distinctive first name, in this case honoring Orville Dewey, a Unitarian minister whom he admired.

Katharine, the youngest child and only surviving daughter, was born precisely three years to the day after Orville. Variant spellings of her name were common on both sides of the family. The choice of Katharine suggests that her parents wanted to commemorate the family name while giving this child the same sense of distinction as their sons.

Milton kept precise records of the development of his younger children, just as he had of the older boys. Orville, he noted, began to walk when he was a year old, and Katharine at ten months.

The West Side was a good place for children to grow up. The neighborhood was expanding rapidly, but there were still open "commons" where Reuch, Lorin, and their friends could stage an impromptu game of "one old cat" or "town ball." "Fox," a variant of hide-and-seek played over several city blocks, was another favorite. A West Side contemporary of the older Wright boys recalled that the smaller children, including young Wilbur, had to agree to be "it" if they wanted to play.

The Wright youngsters faced the usual childhood problems. Wilbur became lost one morning when Reuch and Lorin abandoned him on the way home from Sunday School in order to go swimming. Thereafter, he developed a standard response when threatened by his brothers—"I'll squall." It remained a catch phrase in the family for years.[5]

His older brothers also introduced him to the fine art of rolling grapevine cigars. The three of them were lighting up behind the woodpile on Second Street one day in 1870 when Wilbur burned his fingers and dropped the match into a pile of shavings. The result was a "lively blaze."[6]

Orville, in turn, did his best to burn down the Hawthorn Street house. He and Ed "Jamsie" Sines, his best friend from down the block, built a fire against the back fence that threatened to burn out of control. Three-year-old Katharine saved the day by running for her mother. Orville's first biographer, John R. McMahon, reported in 1930: "He still likes to make and see fires, the larger the better." Recalling these incidents in a letter to Reuchlin many years later, Milton remarked that "Fire departments can sometimes be useful."[7]

Drawing on his own experience as a younger brother, Wilbur delighted in teasing Orville and Katharine. He taunted his brother with nonsense phrases based on the youngster's mispronunciation of words until Orville came running after him with a rock. Katharine, he discovered, could be made to cry with the crook of a finger, or a grimace.

Milton took justifiable pride in his success as a disciplinarian. "I governed them," he told a reporter who asked about the early behavior of his famous sons. "They were pretty good boys, but mischievous. I had little trouble with them."[8]

There would be a few spankings for the really serious offenses. Orville once attempted to escape a whipping by hiding in the cellar. Both boys protested that they did not deserve the punishment meted out for throwing rocks at a passing carriage. Wilbur received his last switching at the age of twelve for hitching his sled onto a passing wagon.

But if there were occasional disagreements among the children, and a need for discipline, there was also much affection in this family. Milton and Susan were warm, loving, and protective parents, who encouraged a close relationship between their children. As in any group of brothers and sisters born over a thirteen-year period, the bonds were especially strong between those children who were closest in age. Reuch and Lorin, eldest sons, were particularly close, as were Orville and Katharine, the two youngest.

Wilbur was in every sense the middle child. Four and a half years younger than Lorin, he was the tag-along little brother. In high school he tended to draw his friends from an older circle met through Reuch and Lorin. He was the youngest member of a local men's club otherwise composed entirely of his elder brothers' classmates.

Four years older than Orville, Wilbur took his own responsibilities seriously. He told Orv stories, taught him to build kites, and served as an unofficial guide and adviser to his gang of friends. At the same time, he was careful to maintain a respectable distance from childish goings-on.[9]

In later years Wilbur and Orville would point to a very strong relationship stretching far back into their childhood. In the will prepared in May 1912 shortly before his death, Wilbur stressed that the two had been "associated . . . in all hopes and labors, both of childhood and manhood."[10] And on another occasion he wrote: "From the time we were little children, my brother Orville and myself lived together, played together, worked together, and, in fact, thought together. We usually owned all of our toys in common, talked over our thoughts and aspirations so that nearly everything that was done in our lives has

been the result of conversations, suggestions, and discussions between us."[11]

Those words have been cited time and again to illustrate the lifelong bond between the two brothers. In fact, Wilbur was overstating
their relationship as children in order to underscore the importance of
the full partnership that they enjoyed as adults. As boys they were
as close, and as far apart, as any brothers separated by a four-year
difference in age. They would scarcely begin to bridge that gulf in a
serious way until 1889, the year in which Orville left high school and
Wilbur emerged from a period of extended illness and depression.

Katharine's relationship with her brothers was far more subtle, but
no less important. She was especially close to Orville. He was the one
who pulled her about the neighborhood in his wagon, protected her,
and insisted that his own friends include her in their games.

When the brothers were away from home in later years, Wilbur
tended to write to his father. Orville, far more often, directed his
letters to Katharine. They are charming letters, flecked with warmth
and humor. Within the family circle, Orville was generally regarded
as being much less articulate than his brother, yet his letters to
Katharine are among the clearest and most human documents among
the thousands of pieces of Wright family correspondence.

In childhood, both Orville and Katharine looked up to Wilbur as
their big brother. As adults, they enjoyed a close personal relationship
based on the foundation of mutual concern, support, and respect that
had been laid when they were very young. The three became allies and
confidants—closer to one another than to anyone else in the world.

The importance of early experience in forging the depth of affection
and bonding that they enjoyed as adults can be seen in something as
simple as the use, throughout their lifetimes, of private childhood
nicknames. They were Will, Orv, and Kate to their friends, even their
father. In letters to one another, however, Wilbur would always be
Ullam, short for Jullam, the German equivalent of William. Orville
was Bubbo, or Bubs, as close as Wilbur could come to saying
"brother" at the time of Orville's birth. Katharine was Swes, or Ster-
chens, both affectionate diminutives for *Schwesterchen*, German for
"little sister." A close observer of the family once commented that
"such nicknames were spoken in fondness and perhaps expressed a
jealous affection within a family circle inclusive and aloof from the
world."[12]

The early years in Dayton were happy and successful ones for

Milton. By 1873, after four years editing *The Religious Telescope*, he had cemented his position as the leading spokesman of the conservative cause within the United Brethren Church.

He was a good editor, who refused to employ the official weekly as a weapon against those who disagreed with him. As one church historian noted: "He always aimed to give those of differing opinions from his own their full share of space proportionate to the numbers they represented...."[13] At the same time, he had no intention of advancing the Liberal cause. "My idea of a church paper," he wrote, "is not one that panders to false tastes, sinful weaknesses, and by stimulating good fellowship with all things, rises into a popularity not unlike that of many secular papers. Jesus did not thus pander; the Bible does not; but the unscrupulous politician or editor does."[14]

Far from attempting to negotiate a compromise that might have made him more popular within the church, Milton Wright had become a national leader of the dwindling anti-Masonic movement. He attended the first meeting of a National Christian Association Opposed to Secret Societies in Pittsburgh in 1868, and delivered a major address to the National Anti-Secrecy Association at Cincinnati in 1872. His remarks at the 1875 meeting of that organization were reprinted in full in the Pittsburgh papers and the *Christian Cynosure*, a National Christian Association paper. His speech to the State Anti-Secrecy Society of Illinois in 1878 was also widely reprinted.[15]

Milton spoke out on other issues, too. He attended the National Temperance Convention in 1868–69, was present at the Christian Amendment Convention in Cincinnati, and argued forcibly for women's rights. By 1877 he was well on his way to becoming the most visible United Brethren clergyman since Otterbein, and the most outspoken.

The Radicals approached the General Conference of 1873 apprehensively. As they feared, the Liberals came to the meeting, which opened in Dayton on May 15, with an expanded program of reforms. In addition to relaxing the traditional attitude toward secret societies, they now suggested that representation to the General Conference be expanded to include lay delegates, as well as presiding elders. They also sought to institute a system of proportional representation to the General Conferences. This meant that the local conferences would no longer come to the quadrennial meetings as equals. Those conferences with the largest number of churches would dominate.

Milton was not confident that the conservatives would win if matters came to a vote. Rather than testing their strength, the Radicals resorted to a parliamentary gambit. The Constitution of 1841 specified that a vote of at least two thirds "of the society" was required to amend any provision of the original document. The conservatives argued that the phrase referred to the entire church membership, not simply to the delegates attending the General Conference. They were successful—action on the proposed changes would be postponed for another four years. In addition, Milton Wright was reelected to the post of editor.[16]

Over the next four years the Radicals redoubled their efforts to buttress the conservative position. Milton remained the unquestioned leader of the party. He argued the case in the editorial pages of *The Religious Telescope*, and traveled thousands of miles carrying his message to as many individual congregations and local conference meetings as possible.

The Radical campaign succeeded. Delegates to the General Conference of 1877 not only rejected the Liberal proposals out of hand, but incorporated a much stronger statement on secret societies into the church *Discipline.*[17]

Milton Wright rode the crest of this last burst of conservative enthusiasm to election as a bishop of the church in 1877. He was charged with responsibility for the West Mississippi District, composed of fifteen separate local conferences stretching from the Mississippi to the Rockies. Over the next four years he would help to organize and attend a grand total of fifty-seven local conferences, traveling six to eight thousand miles a year. In addition, he organized special religious meetings and revivals throughout the area, gave speeches, sermons, and addresses, as well as attending to the purely administrative details of his office.

The family remained in Dayton for a year after Milton's election, but the additional travel proved too burdensome for the new bishop. In June 1878 they put the house at 7 Hawthorn Street up for rent and moved to a home on Iowa Street, in Cedar Rapids, Iowa. Two years later, in 1880, Milton built a new home in Adair, Iowa.[18]

The children adapted quickly to life in Cedar Rapids. The place was very much like Dayton. The Cedar River divided the town, just as the Miami separated Dayton from the West Side. There were fewer trees, and the prairie countryside had a different look to it, but down by the rapids which gave the town its name, or out among the rolling hills, there were still plenty of places to intrigue an adventurous seven-year-old like Orville.

Milton once said of his youngest son that "enthusiasm always made him a leader among boys. Happily," he continued, "his leadership was never toward vice." Soon after arriving in Cedar Rapids, Orville was in command of an "army" of fifteen or twenty boys. Wilbur, at eleven, was drafted into service as a strategic consultant, basing plans for the forthcoming campaign on his reading of Plutarch.[19]

"Orville loved to tell his mother of his army and its progress," Milton recalled. "And as he did so, placing his hands on the seat of a chair, he would punctuate his narrative by his heels flying into the air. It is a wonder that overenthusiastic political meetings have never learned that method of punctuation and emphasis, for it is the natural language of exhilaration."[20]

Orville's exhilaration, his incessant curiosity, and his mother's apparently boundless patience are apparent in the earliest letter that has survived from any of the children.

> April 1, 1881
>
> Dear Father,—I got your letter today. My teacher said I was a good boy today. We have 45 in our room. The other day I took a machine can and filled it with water then I put it on the stove I waited a little while and the water came squirting out of the top about a foot. . . . The old cat is dead.[21]

It was the first of hundreds of letters that would tie Milton to his children over the next two decades. The Wright youngsters learned to write good, clear letters at an early age—their father insisted on it.

chapter 4

MOVING ON

1881-1885

M ilton had become a professional traveler in the service of his God. He was absent from home for months at a time, crisscrossing the West to visit the far-flung Brethren congregations in his charge. It was not a life a loving husband and father would much enjoy. Susan and the children were inundated with letters demanding news of home, and informing them of his health, progress at work, and the sights, sounds, and wonders that came his way.

Those letters were a part of the children's education, enabling them to see the larger world with greater clarity than any lesson in a geography or history book. They traveled vicariously through the Dakotas and Montana only five years after Custer's Last Stand:

> This is the region of the Flathead and of the Blackfeet Indians. These vallies are of considerable consequence, the tribes were ever friendly to the Whites and easily civilized. Missoula is a town about the size of Dublin, Indiana. The tunnel over the mountains is not in repair and we went up the steepest grades I ever saw cars climb. We had two locomotives before, and one behind, and all their strength moved us very slowly. The ascent was in the midst of the wildest mountain scenery, and the track had a horse-shoe bend and some very short curves. The descent was more gentle, but the scenery wild all the way to Missoula, and indeed to Clark's Fork of the Columbia.[1]

St. Paul was more than just a spot on a map for young Katharine. Her father had been there:

St. Paul is a very pretty city at the head of navigation on the Mississippi, and eight miles below St. Anthony's Falls at Minneapolis. It is almost three times as large as Dayton, and Minneapolis is larger than St. Paul. They, like Chicago, are cities of marvelous growth, in a wonderful wheat-producing Country.[2]

Milton's description of a fair that he attended in Los Angeles confirmed that California was an agricultural paradise.

I saw a great quantity of apples, pears, peaches, oranges, quinces, persimmons, etc. Saw a cabbage 45 inches around, a sweet potato 36 inches, a beet 56 inches, two pumpkins as big as boulders. One weighed 182 pounds, the other 203 pounds. Some fine plates-full of pomegranates as large as big apples. Among the vegetables were onions 20 inches around, squashes 4 feet long and 38 inches around—breakfast squashes understand, and a mess for a small family. One was three feet long and 56 inches round. Peanuts, grapes as big as plums etc. etc.[3]

Of course Orville and Kate would want to hear about the sea serpent rumored to frequent the waters around Santa Monica.

Eight witnesses testify. It was from 60 to 120 feet long—its head from three to six feet in diameter—It roared like a dying horse—it spouted water like a whale—it had a bright crest on its head—it stuck out its tongue above its head—it had black bright eyes—it lashed the sea into foam.[4]

It was "probably a fish story," Milton admitted, adding that he was going to Santa Monica the next day to see for himself.

In later years Orville spoke with pride of the advantages they had enjoyed growing up in the Wright household: "We were lucky enough to grow up in an environment where there was always much encouragement to children to pursue intellectual interests; to investigate whatever aroused curiosity. In a different kind of environment, our curiosity might have been nipped long before it could have borne fruit."[5]

Milton's letters to his children, designed to stimulate curiosity and portray new people and places, were a part of that environment. So were the presents he brought back from his trips. Milton recognized the importance of a gift as a means of ensuring that a child felt needed, and specially remembered. Birthdays were always an occasion in this household, and, while the bishop and Susan regarded Christmas trees and Santa Claus as unnecessary pagan survivals, there were always presents by the children's breakfast plates on Christmas morning.

Milton was a firm believer in the educational value of toys, and took genuine delight in selecting things that would stimulate the imagination of his children and inspire their curiosity. One such gift, purchased during the course of a church trip and presented to Wilbur, then eleven, and Orville, seven, soon after the family's move to Cedar Rapids, Iowa, would prove particularly significant. It was a toy helicopter designed by the French aeronautical experimenter Alphonse Pénaud.

Milton paid perhaps 50 cents for this variant of Europe's oldest mechanical toy—and the world's first powered flying machine. In its earliest form, dating to the fourteenth century, the idea was simple enough. A stick with a four-bladed rotor fixed to the top was set in a hollow spindle held by hand. When a string wrapped around the stick was pulled, the rotor rose out of the spindle and into the air.

The toy is a perfect illustration of play as the inspiration for technological innovation. From the time of Leonardo, when portrait painters used the little helicopter to quiet fidgety young sitters, to that day in 1878 when Milton Wright presented the gadget to his sons, rotary-wing toys were to intrigue and inspire generations of children, a few of whom would, as adults, attempt to realize the dream of flight for themselves.

Sir George Cayley (1773–1857), the English baronet who constructed the first man-carrying gliders, was just such a child. His early notebooks include sketches of the toy, and suggestions for its improvement. In 1784, Launoy, a French naturalist, and Bienvenu, a mechanic, flew a new, self-propelled version before the members of the French Academy of Sciences. Twin rotors were fixed to the top and bottom of a shaft that ran through the center of a small wooden bow. Holding the bow in one hand and turning the rotors with the other, the bowstring twisted around the shaft, flexing the bow. When released, the little craft bumped up against the ceiling, to the great delight of the assembled savants.

It remained for Pénaud to substitute skeins of rubber for the cumbersome bow. Octave Chanute, a civil engineer who was to play an important role in the story of Wilbur and Orville Wright, regarded Alphonse Pénaud's helicopter as "the best of its kind." "These models, when built in varying proportions, would either rise like a dart to a height of some fifty ft., and then fall down, or sail obliquely in great circles, or, after rising some 20 or 25 ft., hover in the same spot for fifteen or twenty seconds, and sometimes as many as 26 seconds, which was a much longer flight than had ever been obtained before with screws."[6]

Obviously, a single toy cannot shape the course of a life. Still, the little helicopter that Milton Wright brought home to Cedar Rapids in the fall of 1878 made a very big impression on his two youngest sons. Orville described the result in court testimony offered in 1912: "Our first interest [in flight] began when we were children. Father brought home to us a small toy actuated by a rubber spring which would lift itself into the air. We built a number of copies of this toy, which flew successfully. . . . But when we undertook to build the toy on a much larger scale it failed to work so well."[7]

Orville's first teacher remembered the incident as well. One day in 1878, Miss Ida Palmer, of the Jefferson School in Cedar Rapids, noticed the boy hunched over his desk fiddling with two pieces of wood. When she asked what he was doing, he explained that he was assembling the parts of a flying machine, a larger version of which might enable him to fly with his brother. It can only have been one of the small copies of the Pénaud model that the brothers had constructed. To her credit, Miss Palmer reprimanded Orville but did not confiscate the craft.[8]

A quarter of a century later young Milton Wright, Lorin's son, reported that his uncles were still making helicopters "out of bamboo, paper, corks, and rubber bands and allowed us to run after them when they flew them."[9] There can be no doubt that Orville regarded his father's gift as a major event in his life. In 1929, at the height of his feud with officials of the Smithsonian Institution, Orville became incensed when a Smithsonian curator confused the Pénaud helicopter with the Dandrieux butterfly, another flying toy of the period. He wanted the details of the incident to be recorded accurately, and was determined that Pénaud, one of the two or three early aeronautical experimenters the brothers most admired, should receive full credit.

The credit was all Milton's—he knew a great deal about children in general and his sons in particular. The time he took out from a hectic schedule to select a stimulating gift had been very well spent.

Both parents were great believers in formal and informal education alike. Their home was filled with books, and the children were encouraged to read at an early age. But Milton, himself an ex-teacher, had some strong ideas on education that occasionally conflicted with school policy. Miss Esther Wheeler, who taught several of the Wright children at the Seventh Street School in Dayton, had clearer memories of the father than his sons. "Bishop Wright did not believe in ten month school," she recalled in 1909,

> and would tell his boys to take half a day off now and then. The Bishop and I have clashed over that proposition many times, but he was set in his ways and could not be won over by any sort of argument. He had much faith in his children and believed that they could keep up with their classes and miss a few days also. Whether he was right in allowing them to remain away, I will not try to answer, but his boys were excellent scholars, just as he argued they would be.[10]

Like his older brothers, Orville started school late. Susan had intended otherwise, enrolling him in kindergarten back in Dayton at the age of five. She walked him to school on the first day, then saw him off, neatly dressed, each morning. Weeks later she discovered that he had stopped attending after that first day. He walked down the block to his friend Ed Sine's house each morning and returned home on time each afternoon. Home tutoring began shortly after that, and continued until the family moved to Cedar Rapids, where he finally started school in the second grade.[11]

Orville was a good student. That first year in Cedar Rapids he won first prize—a picture of Miss Palmer—for best penmanship in class; he was also moved on to the third reader before the end of the year. To do so, he had to read out a passage from the second reader for visiting school officials. They were amused when Orville literally raced through the required passage, holding the book upside down. Any child who had memorized the text, they decided, deserved promotion.[12]

Eleven-year-old Wilbur was a sixth grader at the Washington School in Cedar Rapids that year. Emma Fordyce, his teacher, who knew Orville as well, remembered Wilbur as being "less communicative" than his little brother and "too dreamy" to get into trouble. Then, as later, history and geography were his favorite subjects.[13]

If Wilbur was quiet, and tended not to volunteer information in class, he was nonetheless already very sure of himself. Back at Garfield School in Dayton he had once been severely reprimanded by a teacher for failing to arrive at the correct answer to an arithmetic problem on the blackboard. A young girl was instructed to help him with the problem; several minutes later the students returned. Wilbur had convinced the girl that he was correct, and together the two of them then convinced the teacher. (Thirty years later, the young girl,

Orville Wright was eight in 1878. . . .

now Mrs. D. L. Lorenz, greeted Wilbur when he came to New York to fly for the Hudson-Fulton Celebration.)[14]

Orville and Reuchlin were on the opposite ends of the educational scale when the family moved to Iowa. Reuch graduated from Coe's Collegiate Academy in Cedar Rapids in 1878, the year Orv began school. There is some suggestion that he intended to enter the clergy—his high school graduation speech was entitled "The Evidences of Christianity," and in the fall of 1879 he enrolled at Western College, a Brethren school only ten miles south of Cedar Rapids that turned out many ministers over the years. The next summer Reuch assisted his father in teaching a special Fourth of July Sunday School class at a local church.[15]

Reuchlin did not return to college in the fall of 1880. Instead, he took the state teaching examination on November 2, and taught one term at an elementary school a few miles south of Cedar Rapids. It seems clear that this break in the pattern of his life marked the beginning of a serious rebellion against parental authority.

Many years later, in 1907, Reuchlin's nineteen-year-old daughter Helen "declared independence" in a similar fashion and took a job in town. In describing the situation to Wilbur and Orville, Bishop Wright remarked that Reuch was having "about the same experience with her [Helen] that I had with him when he was about the same age, only I managed not to let him break away. After a year or two he became and remains most dutiful."[16]

Reuchlin's "rebellion" almost certainly involved the natural desire of a young man to achieve some measure of detachment from the family. Wilbur, Orville, and Katharine's experience would prove that Milton, on the other hand, was a possessive father reluctant to allow his children to leave home and explore life on their own. Reuch did return home, although time would show that the reconciliation was by no means as happy or complete as Milton suggested.

By the spring of 1881, Milton Wright was weighed down by the burdens of his office. Ironically, he had lost a great deal of political ground while serving as one of the five highest officers of his church. He had relinquished control of the all-important weekly church newspaper, isolated himself from the center of church activity in Ohio and Indiana, and spent four difficult and exhausting years serving the needs of small, scattered congregations in the Far West.

Milton was not adept at the skills required to win friends and influence people. As an administrator he had "personally offended" a num-

. . . his brother Wilbur was twelve . . .

and sister Katharine was four.

ber of presiding elders. His limitations as a politician were apparent. Reconciliation, negotiation, and compromise, the tools of the effective vote-getter, were foreign to him. Moreover, he would never trust men who possesed those skills. His written descriptions of various Dayton political contests over the years are studded with words like "scheming," "malicious," and "treacherous." There were no moral gray areas in his world. Right was right. Wrong was wrong. No amount of under the table negotiating would ever change that.

But if Milton refused to make back room deals, others would. "In one conference," a church historian reported, "an evil man had the ascendancy and used all his arts, not only to hold his friends, but to injure the bishop's influence, when he found it could not be made to implicitly serve his purposes."[17]

As a result, Milton Wright was in a very weak position when the eighteenth General Conference of the Church of the United Brethren in Christ met at Lisbon, Iowa, in 1881. "Of course he could not expect much support from the Liberals," a fellow churchman remarked. "Then, he had alienated some persons on the Radical side, because in certain cases he was not compliant to their wishes."[18] He was neither reelected a bishop nor reinstated to his old editorial post.

Without strong leadership at the conference, the Radicals could no longer hold off the Liberal drive for pro-rata representation. While the major issues—membership in secret societies and lay representation at the General Conference—remained in abeyance, that victory virtually guaranteed that the forces of change would ultimately triumph within the church. It was only a matter of time.

Milton returned to the Whitewater District as a presiding elder, riding the circuit as he had done at the outset of his career. The family relocated once again, this time to a farm in Henry County, near Richmond, Indiana, not far from Wilbur's birthplace.

The return to Indiana represented a political defeat for Milton, but he was not entirely unhappy with the situation. After four years of almost constant travel and the pressure of high church office, he was anxious to spend more time with his family. Susan's health was failing—by 1883 she was exhibiting the unmistakable early symptoms of tuberculosis. She welcomed the move back to Richmond, where she would be close to her widowed mother and childhood friends.

Milton had by no means given up the Radical cause, however. Free of the administrative burdens he had shouldered during his years as editor and bishop, he could concentrate on attempts to generate fresh support for the conservatives.

In addition to his normal clerical duties, Milton set himself up as a writer, editor, and publisher in defense of church Radicalism. In October 1881, he issued the first in a series of *Reform Leaflets*, small pamphlets "intended to be laid between the leaves of some oft-used book for preservation and future reference." The first issue listed fifty reasons for opposing secret societies; subsequent numbers continued to hammer away at the Liberal arguments for modernization of the church.[19]

Late in 1881, Milton founded a monthly newspaper, the Richmond *Star*, dedicated to building support for the conservative cause. In spite of the fact that "every effort was made by some officials to suppress it," the *Star* became self-supporting after its first year.

While never a moneymaking proposition, the paper served as a rally-ing point for Radical sentiment in the church, and enabled Milton to mend a few fences within his dwindling ranks.[20]

In spite of Milton's reduced salary and the expenses related to his publications, the family budget was large enough to enable the two eldest sons to continue their education. Reuchlin, having returned to the family circle, entered Hartsville College, his parents' alma mater, as a sophomore in the fall of 1881. Lorin enrolled as a freshman.

The boys spent two academic years rooming together. Perhaps significantly, it was Lorin who remained in closest touch with their mother by mail. "I and Reuchlin are clean out of money again," he wrote to Susan on October 31, 1882.

> I have spent for pens 10 cents; Hair cutting 25; Paper 20; Drilling .05 cents; Speller .05 cents; Club Treas. $2.50. I paid both mine and Reuch's assessment and $1.57 for cooking; Shaving Cup .15; Necktie 50 cents. Making in all five dollars and 37 cents since I wrote last. Reuch gave me $ five of the last money you sent. We owe Prof. Fix $2.25 for wood and we have not paid for Room rent or tuition. We get scholarships for $14.00. We will owe some more before you can send some down so please send enough down so we won't always be out of money.[21]

Lorin assured his mother that they were trying "to get along cheaper." They roomed with the college president, and boarded with a Mrs. Case, who was "nearly starving before we had her cook for us."[22]

The Brethren schools were a far cry from the best American higher education could offer. Hartsville had an enrollment of some fifty-two students during the year 1882–83. Lorin's shaky grammar, his re-quirement to purchase a speller, and the fact that he made some extra money teaching Spencerian penmanship to fellow students, does not speak highly of the entrance standards.

Still, Lorin at least seems to have thrived at Hartsville. During his freshman year he served as secretary of the Philomatheon Literary Society, and delivered an address entitled "Building for the Ages" at the anniversary exercises on June 14, 1882.[23]

A little education was apparently enough for both boys. Instead of returning to school in the fall of 1883, they moved back to Dayton and took rooms in a boardinghouse at the corner of Third and Euclid. Lorin found work as an assistant bookkeeper at the Van Arsdall & Garmen Carpet Store, while Reuchlin took a job clerking in a lumber-yard.

Wilbur began his senior year at Richmond High School in September 1883. His schedule of classes would daunt a modern honors student: Greek, Latin, geometry, natural philosophy, geology, and composition, with general scholastic averages of 94, 96, and 95 for the first three terms.[24]

He was an athlete as well, excelling at gymnastics and particularly, his father would recall, "as an expert on the turning pole." He enjoyed riding the high-wheel bicycle he had purchased with his own money, and may even have developed an interest in a young woman classmate. Milton and Susan talked of sending him on to Yale.[25]

Orville seemed destined for commerce. As a six year old back in Dayton he had gone from house to house with his wagon collecting bones for sale to the local fertilizer plant. In Richmond, he pressed Katharine into service helping him collect scrap wood and metal for delivery to a junkyard. He also built and sold kites to his playmates, and organized a local amateur circus performance.

Wilbur made his pocket money assisting his father on the Richmond *Star*. Family tradition has it that he constructed a special machine to fold the papers for mailing. He also helped his brother build a six-foot treadle-powered wood lathe. Orville would later recall that this was their first joint venture in technology.

The few idyllic years in Indiana came to an end in June 1884, when Milton decided to move the family back to Dayton. Certainly, it cannot have been an easy decision—their twelfth move in a quarter of a century of married life. Henry County was home, close to the place where Milton had been born and both of them had grown up. Their farm was at the center of the preaching circuits for which Milton was responsible, and near Richmond, Indiana, where his Radical newspaper was published. Susan, now fifty-three and already in poor health, not only had Milton home more often but was close to her aging mother, her sister, and childhood friends.

Wilbur was about to graduate from the high school in Richmond. The move was so quick and abrupt that he would not be able to attend the commencement exercises with his classmates, or officially complete the courses required for graduation. They would not even be able to return to their own home. The lease held by the family renting 7 Hawthorn Street still had sixteen months to run.

Yet the reason for the move was clear to everyone: Milton, rested and refreshed, was ready to return to the fray. The General Conference of 1885 was only a year away, and he would find it easier to marshal his forces in Dayton, the city that remained the unofficial headquarters of the church and the home of its publishing house.

On June 14, 1884, Milton and his youngest sons, Wilbur and Orville, carefully loaded their worldly goods onto the Dayton train. The boys, assisted by Lorin and Reuch, who were already living and working in Dayton, would supervise the move into a rented house at 114 N. Summit Street. Susan and Katharine would follow on June 17.

Milton remained behind in Indiana for a few more weeks on business. On June 20 he received a letter from his wife. The new house, she informed her absent husband, was "in miserable order."[26]

chapter 5

TIMES OF TRIAL

1884-1889

F ew outside the family circle knew or understood Milton Wright
better than his fellow clergyman, A. W. Drury. "By his strain
of Puritan blood, by primal instincts, and by association," Drury
pointed out,

> Milton Wright was committed to moral reform. His outlook was not
> confined to his own Church but extended to society at large. From first
> to last he was opposed to slavery, the rum traffic, and secret societies.
> His position in the earlier part of his career was strictly that of the
> Church at the corresponding time. His being made editor in 1869, and
> Bishop in 1877, was with the understood purpose on the part of the
> majority in the General Conference to make stronger the historic posi-
> tion of the Church in regard to secret societies. Under the stress of
> experience, and with changed conditions, the Church, almost uncon-
> sciously to itself, came to change . . . but Bishop Wright, with some
> others, stood by the position of the Church without change.[1]

By the time he came back to Dayton in the spring of 1884, it was
apparent that church opinion was running heavily against Milton and
the other members of the dwindling Radical party. Moreover, there
was a personal price to be paid for continuing the fight against Liberal
elements within the church. Milton had failed to win reelection as a
bishop in 1881. Now the presiding elders of the quarterly White River
Conference voted to cut his already reduced salary by one quarter
because he was no longer living in his district.

The system of proportional representation approved in 1881 would give the Liberals control of the majority of votes at the upcoming General Conference of 1885. *The Religious Telescope*, once a bastion of conservative strength, now supported a more lenient attitude toward secret societies: "We are living in another age," wrote Bishop Weaver, a one-time Wright supporter. "Our ecclesiastical machinery must be adjusted to meet these days, and not the days of our fathers."[2]

With power in their hands at last, the Liberals were quick to act for a final resolution of the controversy. On the second day of the conference, which opened in Fostoria, Ohio, on May 14, they pushed through the appointment of a thirteen-man committee to study the need for a thoroughgoing reform of the church structure. The group reported back four days later recommending that the General Conference amend the basic church documents to meet the needs of the modern Brethren.[3]

For the next day and a half, the conference debated the questions that had split the church since 1869. Over the futile objections of Milton Wright and the Radicals, the delegates created a twenty-seven member Church Commission that was empowered to rewrite the Constitution, Confession of Faith, and *Discipline* according to their view of the will of the majority. The results would then be submitted to a vote by all members of the church. The commission itself would oversee the voting, which was to be completed prior to the General Conference of 1889.

The twenty-year-old split in the United Brethren leadership was no longer simply an internal matter. The apparent Liberal victory attracted considerable attention in the press. The Dayton *Daily Journal* applauded the creation of the commission as a victory for the forces of modernity over outmoded tradition, characterizing the Liberals as young men of "advanced thought" and "education" who were devoted to "religious progression." Milton and the Radicals, on the other hand, were portrayed as "men whose ages are in keeping with their antiquated ideas," so set in their ways "that the magnificent oratory of the opposition was powerless to move them."[4]

Religious traditionalists of other faiths took a different view. The *Lutheran Standard*, for example, charged that "the United Brethrens have permitted false notions of expediency to triumph over Righteousness in their action on secretism." Under the Liberal element, the church, which once "had a noble record on the subject," was now "giving way to a craving for popularity." Milton and his colleagues were urged "to stand up for the right . . . rather . . . than yield to the encroachments of lodgery."[5]

Confident of their success, the Liberals sought to solidify their position. And their first step was to elect Milton Wright bishop of the West Coast, responsible for all church activities in California, Washington, and Oregon. As one Liberal explained to a reporter, the action "would send him clear across the Rocky Mountains, where he could not disturb them."[6]

For the next four years Milton would spend six of every twelve months on the road, looking after his West Coast congregations. The other six months would be spent in Dayton, marshaling support for the final battle to be fought out at the General Conference of 1889. If the Liberals believed that Milton Wright would recognize the hopelessness of his situation, they were mistaken. The bishop was never one to accept a vote on a matter of principle.

Milton and other conservative leaders banded together to form a Constitutional Association, which would hold independent annual conferences for the next four years. In addition, the group established its own newspaper, the *Christian Conservator,* which began publication in July 1885. From the outset, Bishop Wright was the single most important figure in shaping editorial policy. As a sign of his confidence in the *Conservator,* he immediately ceased publication of the Richmond *Star.*

Milton faced another set of problems at home. Reuchlin was having an especially difficult time of it. He had married Miss Lulu Billheimer, the daughter of United Brethren missionaries, on April 27, 1886. The arrival of a child was always a welcome event in the Wright family, but the birth of Catherine Louise thirteen months later severely complicated Reuch's already dismal financial situation.

Susan wrote to her absent husband in July 1889 complaining that Lulu's relatives were "still sponging off" Reuchlin, who had "no work, and no prospect of it," and was "clean out of money." By the end of the summer her patience was wearing thin. "I told him he could come to our house," Susan explained to Milton, "but not a cent of my money should go to feed the Billheimers." It was scarcely "worthwhile to try to help him till he shakes the Billheimers off."[7]

Reuchlin and Lulu continued to struggle along in Dayton through the winter. Finally, in February 1889, Reuch boarded a train for Cincinnati and points west, vowing to send for his wife when he found work. A month later the bishop put Lulu and baby Catherine on a train

Reuchlin, the eldest of the Wright children, was a restless young man who distanced himself from the family in later life.

for Kansas City, where his son had taken a bookkeeping job with the South Missouri Lumber Company.

They remained in Kansas City for thirteen years. Little Catherine Louise died early in 1892. The lumberyard job proved unsatisfactory and Reuch found employment with the Kansas City, Memphis, and Birmingham Railroad. Then, in 1901, convinced that outdoor work would improve Reuch's delicate health, the family moved to an eighty-acre farm near Tonganoxie, Kansas, where they would remain for the next ten years, raising Jersey cattle and seed corn.[8]

Reuch, Lulu, and their three children—Helen Margaret, Herbert, and Bertha Ellwyn—built a good life for themselves in Kansas. But the distance separating Reuchlin from the family back in Ohio was as much psychological as geographic.

Reuch's growing alienation was obvious, and puzzling, to other members of the family. "I'd like to do something for Reuch," Katharine told her father in 1902, "but a person can't do anything to please him. He is suspicious of everything."[9]

In time, Reuchlin would reveal apparent feelings of inferiority. In 1901, for example, he agreed to negotiate the sale of the 160-acre Adair County, Iowa, farm which Milton had deeded jointly to all four of his sons. Convinced that he had been cheated on the deal, Reuch informed his father that he would pay each of his brothers the difference from his own share. "I don't want them to feel that their interests have been injured by anything I did."[10]

In this case, it seems unlikely that Wilbur's half-hearted response did much to reassure his older brother. "Some matters connected with the sale seem to have . . . led you to fear that we felt disposed to blame you," he wrote. "We certainly have no such feeling. We saw . . . that if foresight had been equal to hindsight, we might have realized a little more from the sale . . . but as we felt that any of us would have made some errors, we had no disposition to blame you."[11]

Reuchlin became increasingly defensive over the years. He was grateful to receive one of the cash gifts which Wilbur and Orville distributed to members of the family in 1910; at the same time, he wanted his father to understand his financial situation: "I myself have never been a great money maker, but I have managed so far to keep most that has come to me. I am a money saver rather than a money maker."[12]

The depth of Reuchlin's isolation and estrangement from his family would become painfully obvious at the time of Wilbur's death of typhoid in the spring of 1912. Reuchlin, Katharine, and Lorin each received a bequest of $50,000. As useful as the money was, Reuch apparently did not believe he deserved an equal share and returned $1,000 to his father. "This is not intended exactly as a gift," he wrote. "It is some of Wilbur's money and I am inclined to think perhaps if he had more time for deliberation he might have made some provisions differently in his will." The money, he told Milton, "is yours to use or give away or do whatever you desire with it that may give you the most pleasure."[13]

The bishop would have none of it. The money was returned to Reuchlin with the comment that Wilbur's last will and testament was to be regarded as "sacred writ."

For a time, Milton and Susan feared that Lorin, their second son, would follow his older brother's course, drifting away from the family. Like Reuch, he found it difficult to make a decent living in Dayton.

Lorin left for Kansas City, and the hope of more profitable employment, in the spring of 1886. He returned home that fall, broke and disappointed, but was off once more early the next year, this time settling in Coldwater, Kansas, forty miles southeast of already fabled Dodge City. Lorin arrived in town before the railroad, when Coldwater still lay at the end of a sixty-mile stage ride. It was not until winter set in in late November, however, that the young Ohioan had his first real taste of isolation. Looking out the window of the Comanche County Courthouse one day, Lorin saw a wolf loping down a city street through the snow.[14]

Gradually, he took on the coloration of his new environment. He outfitted himself with a cowboy hat, practiced his marksmanship at a gun club, and spoke of joining a hunting expedition headed into the Indian Territory—Oklahoma. He would dine out for the rest of his life on his stories of the Kansas frontier in the roaring eighties. Bat Masterson was still marshal of nearby Dodge when Lorin arrived in Coldwater. The Younger boys, Jim, Bob, and Cole, were behind bars, but Lorin knew the men who had ridden with them, and after them, a decade before.

He had tasted adventure in Kansas, and was making a living of sorts, but he was homesick. Even the fascination of the prairie landscape had begun to fade by 1888. "We were over on Mule Creek where there are quite a number of small stunted trees," he told Katharine. "They look fine to a person who has not seen a tree for a year nearly."[15]

He thought that his guitar might ease the winter loneliness. Could Wilbur make a box and ship the instrument via Wells Fargo? Lorin became increasingly anxious for news of home as well. "What does Will do?" he asked Katharine in November 1888. "He ought to do something. Is he still cook and chambermaid?"[16]

Lorin's sarcasm masked a genuine concern for his brother, who at twenty-one was having great difficulty getting started in life. Wilbur had thrived during the months immediately following the family's

Lorin, the second son, sampled life in a Kansas cow town before settling into a quiet existence at home in Dayton.

Wilbur (center rear) was the youngest member of the Ten Dayton Boys, a social club founded by Lorin (right front), Reuchlin (rear second left), and seven of their high school chums.

return to Dayton. He enrolled at Central High, not to complete work for graduation but in order to better prepare himself for Yale. Two of his certificates of proficiency survive from this period, one for a course in Cicero (grade 83.5), and the other in rhetoric (grade 87). His friends, next-door-neighbor John Feight and Ed Ellis from down the block, remembered him as an outstanding athlete. Feight recalled that he played on the Central High football team, and was one of the swiftest runners in the school.[17]

He was mature for his age. Reuch, Lorin, Ed Ellis, and six other young West Side men accepted him as the youngest member of an informal social club known as the Ten Dayton Boys. Singing was a favorite pastime; Ellis reported that Wilbur had a fine bass voice.

Suddenly, all of that changed. Milton Wright describes what happened:

> In his nineteenth year when playing a game on skates at an artificial lake at the Soldier's Home near Dayton, Ohio, a bat accidentally flew out of

the hand of a young man . . . and struck Wilbur, knocking him down, but not injuring him much. A few weeks later, he began to be affected with nervous palpitations of the heart which precluded the realization of the former idea of his parents, of giving him a course in Yale College; but, tenderly caring for his invalid mother, he, for a few years, pursued a large course in reading, which a retentive memory enabled him to store for future use.[18]

Milton summarized three years of his son's life in that brief paragraph, raising more questions than he answered. The accident at the Soldier's Home was clearly a turning point for Wilbur. It brought an end to any serious talk of going to college, and marked the beginning of a period of withdrawal and depression. Friends and neighbors, even family members like Lorin, wondered at the sudden transformation of an active and athletic young man into a housebound "cook and chambermaid."

The details of the accident and its aftermath are so sparse that we cannot be certain when it occurred, or what the extent of Wilbur's injuries actually were. Most biographers have dated the incident to March 1885. If so, then the bishop's remark that Wilbur was in his nineteenth year at the time is incorrect. He did not turn eighteen until April 1885.

Moreover, Dayton school records indicate that Wilbur was enrolled in the rhetoric course in March and completed the work with high marks that June, surely a difficult task for a student with injuries to the mouth and face. With this in mind, the winter of 1885–86 seems a more likely period for the accident to have occurred.

Milton stated that the initial injury was minor, but he did not see his son for some weeks after the accident. It is clear that the accident itself was less worrisome than the heart palpitations and digestive complications that developed in its wake. It was the first step in a chain of events all too familiar to many nineteenth-century American families. A sudden accident, an apparently simple illness, followed by the appearance of far more serious complications leading to lifelong debility.

Milton Wright had seen it happen in his own family. Many years before, William, his most promising brother, had lost his "wit in conversation and public speaking" following what seemed to be nothing more than a minor attack of "dyspepsia." Milton blamed such problems on damage to the nervous system, which was particularly susceptible to shock and injury during periods of severe illness, stress, or physical trauma. The body was then open to attack and permanent damage might be done to the heart, stomach, brain, or other vital organs.

The family insisted on a period of extended rest for Wilbur when the first sign of serious complications developed. They could begin to relax by the end of the year—the immediate crisis had passed. Among the many things for which Milton offered thanks in his diary on December 31, 1886, was the fact that "Wilbur's health was restored."

But the accident, complications, and the long recuperation left an indelible mark on the young man. In his own mind, he was now a "potential invalid," convinced that his once robust constitution was so fragile that any thought of returning to his former active life was out of the question. Wilbur had always assumed that he would attend college. "Intellectual effort is a pleasure to me," he told his father.

> I have always thought that I would like to be a teacher. Although there is no hope of attaining such financial success as might be attained in some of the other professions or in commercial pursuits, yet it is an honorable pursuit, the pay is sufficient to enable me to live comfortably and happily, and teaching is less subject to uncertainties than almost any other occupation. It would be congenial to my tastes, and I think with proper training I could be reasonably successful.[19]

But that dream was now beyond his grasp. A permanent teaching post would require a college diploma which, in view of his uncertain health, "might be time and money wasted."

Unable to chart a new course that appealed to him, Wilbur fell into a depression born of frustration, indecision, and self-doubt. Friends left home, launched their careers, and established families of their own while he remained at home, prey to feelings of vulnerability and a growing sense that he might be unequal to coping with an ordinary, independent life. Always deeply introspective, he began to withdraw into himself.

In 1902, when an acquaintance, George Spratt, voiced similar doubts about his own ability and capacity, Wilbur responded with some sage advice:

> I see from your remark about the "blues" that you still retain the habit of letting the opinions and doings of others influence you too much. . . . It is well for a man to be able to see the merits of others and the weaknesses of himself, but if carried too far it is as bad, or even worse, than seeing only his *own merits* and others' *weaknesses* . . . there was no occasion for your "blueness" except in your own imagination. Such is usually the case.[20]

When Spratt refused to snap out of his depression, Wilbur renewed the attack: "I am sorry to find you back at your old habit of introspection, leading to a fit of the blues. Quit it! It does you no good, and it does do harm."[21] Wilbur understood what damage a severe case of the "blues" could do, and advised Spratt to pull himself out of his depression by sheer force of will and strength of character. That was what he had done, though it had taken some time to accomplish.

Unable to formulate new goals and unwilling to continue brooding, Wilbur simply chose to ignore his own problems and devote himself to nursing his mother. Susan Wright now required constant care. Her tuberculosis, which had first appeared in 1883, was already much worse. By 1886 she had become a helpless invalid.

For Milton, the loving husband and dedicated churchman, the illness created an impossible dilemma. In order to remain at home and care for his wife he would have to resign his duties as bishop of the West Coast and abandon the fight against the Liberals. The older boys could be no help—Reuchlin was overwhelmed with family problems of his own, while Lorin was off in Kansas seeking his fortune. The younger children, Orville and Katharine, aged fifteen and twelve, required taking care of themselves.

Wilbur, whose own plans had been forestalled by ill health, was happy to step into the breach. He did not feel that he was being particularly self-sacrificing. It was a son's duty to care for his parents. In addition, a period of rest and quiet at home would benefit his health, and give him an opportunity to pursue his own interests. Most of the world would come to regard the invention of the airplane as Wilbur's finest moment. Milton thought otherwise:

> His mother being a declining, rather than a suffering invalid, he devoted himself to taking all care of her, and watching and serving her with a faithfulness and tenderness that cannot but shed happiness on him in life, and comfort him in his last moments. Such devotion of a son has rarely been equaled, and the mother and son were fully able to appreciate each other. Her life was probably lengthened, at least two years, by his skill and assiduity.[22]

Milton's large and varied library became Wilbur's preserve during the years 1886–89. "He . . . used his spare time to read and study, and his knowledge of ancient and modern history, of current events and literature, of ethics and science was only limited by the capacity of his mind and his extraordinary memory."

The *Encyclopaedia Britannica* and *Chamber's Cyclopedia* were at his fingertips, as were those classics of history and biography which the bishop cherished—Plutarch's *Lives,* Gibbon's *Decline and Fall of the Roman Empire,* Guizot on the history of France, Greene on the history of England, and Boswell's *Life of Samuel Johnson.* There were sets of Hawthorne and Sir Walter Scott, and popular science alongside theological works. Milton, never a man of narrow religious temperament, had even purchased the works of the "demon atheist," Robert Ingersoll.

Wilbur was clearly emerging from his shell by the spring of 1888, three years after the accident. The time had been well spent. He knew that he was now as well read as any college graduate, and that he had the makings of a clear and confident writer and speaker. The long hours spent nursing his mother had made him feel needed and useful once again. Moreover, he had enlisted in the United Brethren fight as his father's strong right arm in Dayton.

That spring, Wilbur published a short tract entitled *Scenes in the Church Commission During the Last Day of Its Session.* His first piece of published writing, it was a lucid, concise, and professionally strident bit of Radical propaganda. He had gathered the material for the pamphlet three years before, in the fall of 1885, when the Church Commission established by the General Conference of 1884 met in Dayton. Milton, like all of the bishops, had been named to the commission. True to form, he refused to attend what he regarded as an illegal and unconstitutional body. He left for the West Coast as usual late that summer and was in Oregon when the first session was called to order on November 16, 1885.

The Religious Telescope announced that the commission would conduct its business in closed-door sessions. Wilbur, following the proceedings with obvious interest, was not surprised. "It seemed entirely proper, and indeed fitting," he wrote, "that a body meeting to legislate secrecy in, should also legislate in secret."[23]

In fact, visitors were to be admitted, although the commission had chosen not to advertise the fact. Wilbur did not attend until the final session on November 23, when he heard a debate that raged through the afternoon. A great many Liberals were as philosophically opposed to secret societies as Milton Wright, but feared that the absolute prohibition of these organizations was driving members out of the church. They sought to abolish penalties for membership in a lodge, but to include a statement in the new Constitution suggesting that Christians "ought not" to belong.

Others took a harder line. The president of the commission went so far as to argue that the position on secretism, like the classic abolitionist stand of the church before the Civil War, placed the Brethren in an untenable political position. "We made a great mistake on the slavery question," he maintained. "Our opposition was not judicious. Other churches, by taking a milder course, were enabled to do a great work in the South, while our church was not able to do anything."[24] Wilbur—Milton Wright's son, Dan Wright's grandson—was appalled.

Before the close of the session, the commission managed to produce a draft of a new Constitution and Confession of Faith to be put to a vote by all church members in an election which the commission would oversee. Wilbur, who had made very careful notes on the alterations to the traditional documents approved at this session, was outraged to discover that the official versions of the new Constitution and Confession published in *The Religious Telescope* in January 1887 did not match those approved by the commission. Apparently the Liberal leadership had illicitly introduced further alterations.

Most of the members of the Constitutional Association, led by Milton Wright and his friend and ally Halleck Floyd, argued for a complete boycott of the election. Such decisions were the work of the General Conference, not a special commission; the vote was illegal and divisive. Over the next year and a half the Radicals increased their already heavy travel schedules to include attendance at local conferences in order to argue against the election.

Wilbur joined the fray in the spring of 1888, transforming the rough notes taken three years before into the most effective Radical pamphlet of the entire campaign. *Scenes in the Church Commission* was first sold through the *Conservator*, then given away by the thousands at local conferences and to church congregations.

The general election was held later that year. The Liberal commissioners charged with responsibility for the voting had stacked the deck in their favor, distributing ballots with a large "X" already printed in place to indicate the Liberal position. To vote for change, a member had only to return his ballot unmarked. In order to vote the Radical position, the printed response had to be erased and the new vote written in.

The Radicals had expected something like this, and called for a boycott of the election. The rules stated that a two-thirds majority was required for the passage of any suggested change. Milton reasoned that if only one third of the church members could be persuaded not to vote, the conservatives would win by default. The Liberals, on the other hand, argued that they could win with a two-thirds majority of those voting.

Both sides assumed that they had won. The Liberals obtained their two-thirds majority on each of the four issues: the new Confession of Faith; the new Constitution; the admission of lay delegates to the General Conference; and the specific question of secret societies.

The Radical boycott had succeeded as well. A total of 54,250 church members cast the preprinted ballots; the total membership of the church in 1888 was 204,517. Three quarters of the members had not voted. Obviously the Liberals would appear at the General Conference to argue for the validity of the election, while the diehard Radicals would argue against it on the basis of their reading of the two-thirds rule.[25]

Recognizing that a final confrontation at the conference might shatter the church, most members of the old Radical faction were ready to capitulate and join hands with the victorious Liberals. Bishop Wright would have none of that. He continued to work at a frenzied pace, and Wilbur relished the opportunity to enter the fight on his father's behalf, distributing thousands of copies of *Scenes in the Church Commission* and other conservative pamphlets.

"The tract is producing a big stir," he told Milton. "The Liberals can't hold still, and every movement they make only draws out some new admission." Three thousand of the little booklets were mailed that summer, with an additional 1,100 copies ready for distribution at the General Conference. "When we begin to circulate them *free,*" he noted with some relish, "there will be fun."[26]

Wilbur continued to write articles and editorials of his own responding to attacks on his father. There were those, like the Reverend W. J. McGee, who wondered at the presumption of this young man who dared to argue important issues with elder churchmen. Wilbur was more than able to to defend himself—and get in a few licks of his own at the same time.

> Your complaint that I am only a boy sounds rather strange coming from the lips of a Liberal. They have been complaining for years that the Radicals were "old fogies," "antediluvians," etc., and rejoiced that they would soon die off. Now to suit the exigencies of the times you complain that they are too young! You seem to infer that I am too young to tell the truth. Is there any precise age at which men become able to speak the truth? I know children not five years old who tell the truth. It has not been the custom, therefore, to grade the truth of statements by the age of the person giving voice to them.[27]

The tone of feisty self-confidence indicates the extent to which Wilbur had left depression behind. At an age when most young men were breaking their family ties, he had enjoyed his first success and achieved some measure of visibility, not by striking out on his own but by writing in support of his father's cause.

All of the Wright family crises came to a head during the spring and summer of 1889. Milton had worked feverishly since the general election, traveling from congregation to congregation Milton gathering signatures on petitions he would carry to the General Conference of 1889. It was the one time in his life when work came before family.

Susan was sinking rapidly. Back in August of 1888, just after Milton had left home on his annual West Coast trip, Wilbur wrote: "Mother thinks that while it is not absolutely necessary on account of her health that you should return before your time is up, yet she would feel more comfortable if you were here."[28] Milton was still in Indiana when he received the letter, about to catch a train for Oregon. It must have been a difficult moment for him. His presence would be a great comfort to Susan, who had spent so many years of her life waiting for him to return home. Still, there was the Lord's business to be done. He compromised, continuing on his journey, but returning to Dayton several weeks earlier than usual.

The leaders of the United Brethren Church gathered for the General Conference at York, Pennsylvania, on May 9, 1889. Each man knew that the time for parliamentary maneuvering or compromise had passed. The conference opened, as usual, with a joint message from the bishops. The address called attention to the work of the Church Commission over the past four years, and noted that the vote of 1888 establishing a new Constitution and Confession had been legal and binding upon the conference. Five of the six bishops signed the message. Milton was the lone dissenter.

The final vote to accept or reject the work of the commission, and the new Constitution and Creed, came at 4:00 P.M. on Saturday, May 11. The result was overwhelming—111 for adoption, 20 against. Still hoping to avoid a catastrophic split, J. W. Hott spoke for moderate Liberals, expressing "our deep regret that any of our brethren should not be able to cheerfully acquiesce in the decision of the great majority of the votes of our people," and honoring the Radicals for "their faithfulness to their beliefs."[29]

Good wishes were not enough for the diehard remnant of the Radical party. On the morning of Monday, May 13, Bishop Kephart read a proclamation signed by all the bishops except Milton Wright, declaring that the new Constitution and Confession of Faith were now in effect. Milton and fourteen of the twenty delegates who had voted against the commission were no longer present. They had rented the Park Opera House in York, and now proceeded to conduct business as the "lawful" General Conference under the provisions of the old Constitution.

The Radicals remained in session until May 20, completing arrangements for the organization of what would be known as the Church of the United Brethren in Christ (Old Constitution). Milton, the only bishop to withdraw, was unanimously reelected by the conservative conference on May 16. Horace T. Barnaby, Halleck Floyd, and Henry J. Becker completed the roster of bishops.[30]

Bishop Wright was the undisputed head of the Old Constitution church. As one of his colleagues remarked, "if Philip William Otterbein can be truthfully called the founder of the Church of the United Brethren in Christ, Milton Wright, with equal truth, can be called the preserver of that Church." Bishop Milton Wright "stood like a hero," noted the *Christian Conservator*, now the official organ of the Old Constitution church. "When all the other bishops faltered and fell prostrate before the commission compromise with the world, he stood faithful among the faithless, and deserves great credit from every United Brethren."[31]

He returned to Dayton exhausted, on May 21, 1889, to face his most bitter crisis. Susan was near death. The end came early on the morning of July 4. "About 4:00, I found Susan sinking," he wrote in his diary, "and about five awakened the family. She revived about 7:00 somewhat, but afterwards continued to sink till 12:20 afternoon, when she expired, and thus went out the light of my home."[32]

She was buried at four o'clock on the afternoon of July 6 in a "beautiful lot" which Milton had purchased in Woodland Cemetery. Two days later he was back at work, arranging for the publication of the new *Discipline* adopted by his church. There were legal problems to be tackled. He was particularly anxious to begin proceedings to test the ownership of the United Brethren Printing Establishment. On August 12 he boarded a train for Union City, Pennsylvania, bound for his first local conference as the leading bishop of the reorganized church. The struggle would go on—Milton would see to that.

chapter 6

THE TIES THAT BIND

Summer-Winter 1889

Milton Wright faced an uncertain future in the late summer and early fall of 1889. For all his dedication to reforming society, he had never been able to tolerate fundamental change in his own life. Suddenly, church and family, the very cornerstones of his existence, seemed to be crumbling beneath him.

Susan, his wife of thirty years, was gone. The eldest boys, Reuch and Lorin, were grown and living far from home. Will and Orv, at twenty-one and eighteen, might choose to strike out on their own at any time. Even Katharine, the baby of the family, was remarkably self-assured for a fifteen year old. Within a few years, Milton might find himself entirely alone.

The prospect was yet more frightening when seen in the context of the church situation. In cutting the Gordian knot of a twenty-year-old controversy, Milton had severed his ties with the organization to which he had devoted his entire adult life. The knowledge that he was in the right did little to ease the sense of estrangement from those who had been his closest friends and colleagues for forty-two years.

Milton was a genuine conservative, who had no intention of accepting the inevitability of change. He saw no way in which the old institutions could be improved. The best that he could hope was to lead his flock down the path blazed by the church fathers, and to somehow restructure his family to fill the gap left by the death of his wife. Only by shoring up the old foundations could the stability of church and family be restored.

The first step in rebuilding the church was to complete the task of separating the Liberal and Radical branches into two distinct organizations. Initial stocktaking indicated that the minority group was not in such desperate straits as Milton had feared. They had taken 15,000 to 20,000 members with them, perhaps 10 percent of the total church population. This included a disproportionately large number of leaders. The Radicals had expected the older ministers to side with them, but the support of a great many young fire-eaters came as a pleasant surprise.

Even with so many local leaders, reorganization would be daunting. Milton Wright and his colleagues must reconstruct their church from the ground up. At the local level, seceding Radical supporters had to be gathered into new congregations. While several local conferences in Indiana and Ohio had cast their lot with the Radical minority, new districts would have to be organized in the rest of the nation. Finally, the local and regional elements must be linked through an entirely new national support structure. The bishops, in their report to the first General Conference in 1893, gave a bleak assessment: "Our missionary, church-erection, Sabbath-school, publication and educational funds and property were largely in the hands of those who had gone out from us, and these funds were turned against us. All of our great connectional interests required readjustment, and some of them reconstruction."[1]

The question of property rights was foremost in their minds. The arguments began with the very name of the church. Obviously, both groups believed they had a right to call themselves the Church of the United Brethren in Christ. Within a few months of the separation, the need to distinguish the two organizations led to the addition of the phrase "Old Constitution" or "New Constitution" in parentheses after the church name. It was one of many arguments that would continue for decades to come. As late as May 1901, the New Constitution bishops were still requesting that their Old Constitution counterparts adopt a new name. Bishop Wright and his colleagues replied that they were not only satisfied with their name, "but it is sacred to us as a symbol of the faith it represents."[2] They suggested that the New Constitution Brethren might feel free to change *their* name at any time.

The disposition of real property belonging to the old church represented more serious problems. Who was to control the church building and grounds when a congregation was split down the middle? What was one to do with a Liberal minister presiding over a Radical flock? Could the congregation evict the pastor from the parsonage? Could the minister force his decision as to which branch represented the true faith on an unwilling congregation? The search for solutions to these and other problems was complicated by the bitterness that separated the two factions.

The single most valuable church asset, the great printing establishment in Dayton, was the object of the first of the major lawsuits that would follow over the next five years. Bishop Wright, who served as Old Constitution publishing agent from 1889 to 1893, set the process in motion on July 26, 1889. Accompanied by two colleagues, he presented William J. Shuey, New Constitution publishing agent, with a written demand that the facility be turned over to them. Naturally, Shuey refused.

The New Constitution board of trustees, headed by Daniel L. Rike, immediately petitioned the Montgomery County Court of Common Pleas for a hearing. After considerable legal manuevering, including an unsuccessful Radical petition to the U.S. District Court in Cincinnati for a change of venue, the case came to trial on June 17, 1891.

In addition to determining ownership of the printing plant, the decision would indicate the probable disposition of millions of dollars worth of real estate that would eventually come before the courts. Both sides hired batteries of lawyers and imported distinguished theologians to buttress the fine points of their legal and theological arguments.

Milton and the Radicals contended that those who supported the original Constitution and Confession of Faith represented the true church and had a right to control all property. The Liberals insisted that in amending the Constitution they had operated within established procedures and produced a document with which the majority of the members agreed. After nine days of testimony, the panel of judges issued a unanimous ruling in their favor.

The Old Constitution Brethren were unwilling to allow matters to rest there. The case made its way through the appellate court system, and was finally heard by the Supreme Court of Ohio on June 13, 1895. Once again, the high court handed down a unanimous decision in favor of the Liberals.[3]

Milton was reelected bishop at the General Conference of 1893, as he would be at every conference until 1905. In addition, he was named Supervisor of Litigations, and charged with carrying forward the series of lawsuits over disputed church property. The decision to pursue a great many simultaneous suits was not an easy one; the United Brethren had long believed that good Christians should settle their differences out of court. But the bishops recognized that they had little choice if they were to "inspire faith and restore confidence in our people." "If we should not maintain the trust confided to our care, by the pious living and sainted dead," the council noted at the General Conference of 1893, "we could not expect future benefactions to our church."[4]

Between 1893 and 1900, suits involving local property disputes between the two branches of the church reached the supreme courts of seven states: Indiana, Pennsylvania, Oregon, Illinois, Michigan, Missouri, and California. Milton and the Old Constitution Brethren lost every case but one, that brought in Michigan, where legislation favored the control of property by local bodies as opposed to national organizations such as the General Conference. The control of church property in the Dominion of Canada was decided in a single case in which the Radicals won their suit in the lower courts, but lost to a reversed decision handed down by the court of appeal.

The period of litigation was costly for both groups, sapping energy and funds that might have been better used. A. W. Drury reported that the New Constitution Brethren drew out a total of $35,510.06 from the coffers of the printing firm. In addition, local funds were raised to defend individual churches and parsonages. Bishop Musgrave estimated that the Old Constitution branch had raised and spent some $10,000 "in defense of its sacred rights."[5]

The process of separating the two churches was completed by 1900. Partisan bitterness was frozen into place as officials faced one another time and again in the courtrooms. There would be no reconciliation.

It was the busiest decade of Milton Wright's life. In addition to heading the defense team, he remained the leading churchman of the Old Constitution branch, participating in virtually every phase of the rebuilding process. He traveled incessantly, visiting congregations and organizing new conferences. By 1900, he had achieved his original goal: the Church of the United Brethren in Christ (Old Constitution) was the very image of the organization into which John Morgan had baptized Milton so many years before.

Bishop Wright attacked the problem of preserving his home with the same fierce determination he had brought to the task of rebuilding his church. In his experience, a tightly knit, unified family was the best defense against the pressures of an essentially wicked world. Dan Wright's home had been just such a bastion of morality, besieged by the hard-drinking, pro-slavery Southern roughnecks who had dominated Rush and Fayette counties during his youth.

Milton's own fight against those who sought to corrupt the pure tradition of the United Brethren Church only confirmed the absolute importance of the family. But the various crises surrounding the church schism and the death of his wife had placed all of that in jeopardy at the very moment when Milton felt most need of it. He was not at all certain that he had the strength to carry on his mission alone. Consciously or unconsciously, he set to work binding his three youngest children to him for life.

He began by promoting his daughter to her mother's role even before Susan's death. "Be good. Learn all you can about housework," he wrote in October 1887, when she was thirteen. "Do not worry Mother. Be my nice pet daughter." As Susan's illness grew worse, Milton made clear exactly what he would expect of a "nice pet daughter." "Take especially good care of yourself," he instructed her in May 1889. "You have a good mind and good heart, and being my only daughter, you are my hope of love and care, if I live to be old."[6]

After Susan's death, Milton frequently reminded his fifteen-year-old daughter that she was now the emotional center of his life. "Home seems lonesome without you," he wrote on August 9, 1889, while Katharine was visiting family friends just a month after the funeral. "But for you we should feel like we had no home."[7]

Nor was it enough to elevate Katharine to the role of woman of the house. Milton did his best to reshape his daughter in his wife's image. Susan had been a very shy and quiet woman, whereas even as a child Katharine had exhibited what was then generally referred to as spunk. That was fine with Milton—up to a point. He once noted in his diary that "Katharine has been a good girl, for her chance." Whatever that may be taken to mean, there was no doubt he saw some room for improvement in his daughter.[8]

"I am especially anxious that you cultivate modest feminine manners," he counseled her. "And control your temper, for temper is a hard master." Twenty years later he would complain to Wilbur: "If she had inherited some of her mother's love of quiet and solitude, she might 'Flourish like the palm tree,' for she has a fine constitution."[9]

Milton placed many more demands on his daughter than he ever would on his sons. By the time she left for Oberlin Prep in 1893, she was her father's unofficial partner—the voice of parental authority in his absence. Milton provided Katharine with a detailed itinerary of his travels, so that she could *immediately* forward all mail. If there were financial matters to be taken care of when he was gone, Katharine was responsible.

Never a man to leave much to chance, Milton was careful to provide his daughter with detailed instructions. "I send . . . a draft for Lorin," he wrote in the fall of 1892, "out of which is to be paid the office, the orders I have sent, and the money for the watch." Katharine was to "take what is left for paint on the house, if the boys paint soon—and what is needed to live on & deposit the rest." While she was at it, she could also deposit in the church accounts a $15,000 draft that he had received from a New York bank. That was only the beginning.

> I also send the [church] statistics of Cairo, Illinois and East Des Moines for 1892. Lay these away carefully in the left-hand pigeonholes in my desk. I also send the statistics on East Des Moines for *1891*. Put these on that Statistical Chart, carefully, and then also lay in the same pigeonhole. Do not send the post office addresses of the E. Des Moines Annual Conference preachers. Put them in the same place. They are particular.[10]

Seldom satisfied, Milton usually had a complaint or two to lodge with Katharine: "I want you to raise a racket if the boys do not send me the *Conservator* as soon as it is in print—two copies—and not wait for me to get it by the mailers. I have not seen last weeks paper yet! A week after it is in print!"[11]

There was nothing extraordinary for the period in Milton's assumption that Katharine would, as she grew older, accept the responsibility of running his household. The dutiful daughter who devoted her life to caring for a widowed father was the epitome of female virtue in the life and literature of the period. Yet it is safe to assume that few widowed fathers were as demanding as Milton Wright. As in the case of his sons, whom he also encouraged to remain at home, Bishop Wright had no intention of restricting Katharine's intellectual growth. His egalitarian views included an insistence on the right of women to an education and entry into a profession. Katharine had always excelled at school. Graduating from Central High School in 1892, she took the school year 1892–93 off to read and study on her own before enrolling in the rigorous Oberlin Preparatory School in September 1893.

Her two older brothers had failed to complete their studies at

Hartsville, a church school that scarcely qualified as second rate. Katharine graduated from Oberlin (Class of '98), a great university, and as much a center of the struggle for women's rights as it had been a hotbed of abolitionist sentiment a generation before. There was never any doubt, however, that Katharine would return to her duties at home following graduation.[12]

As Milton was enlisting Katharine's help in the fall of 1889, he could take heart that at least one of his older sons had returned. Depressed, homesick, and stunned by news of his mother's death, Lorin had ended his self-imposed exile on the Kansas prairies and rejoined the family in Dayton.[13]

Lorin worked with his father and brothers for a time printing and distributing Old Constitution tracts and pamphlets, but there was little money in that. After marriage to Ivonette Stokes, his childhood sweetheart, on January 12, 1892, he found steadier work as a book-keeper.

Lorin and Netta, as she was known in the family, had four children over the next decade—Milton, Ivonette, Leontine, and Horace. Life was not easy for the young couple with a growing family. By the time Horace arrived, Lorin was struggling with a string of part-time second jobs, and barely making ends meet.[14]

Wilbur watched his two older brothers with interest and a great deal of sympathy. Reuch and Lorin were talented men with more formal education than most of their contemporaries, yet both of them gave the impression of being constantly overwhelmed by responsibility and circumstance. They suffered from chronic poor health, and seemed to be perpetually on the brink of failure. What had gone wrong for them? It was puzzling, and more than a little frightening, for Wilbur was by no means certain he could do any better under similar circumstances.

He had emerged from the depression following his hockey accident four years earlier a self-assured and confident young man, yet still unable to reach a firm decision as to his own future. Ill health had put a college education and teaching career beyond his grasp. Life in the business world held little interest for him. Wilbur, who knew himself so well, could see no reason why he should succeed where his brothers had failed. It was a frustrating time.

Assessing his situation in the late summer of 1889, Wilbur recognized that he was fortunate in one regard—he was not burdened with the family responsibilities that made life so difficult for Reuch and Lorin. For the moment, he was content to work out his destiny within the safety of his father's house. If he would not be forced to explore new challenges, neither would he risk destitution and failure.

Orville had not passed through a psychological crisis of the sort that plagued his brother, but he would face very real problems setting himself up in life. All across America young people were finding it much more difficult to strike out on their own than their parents and grandparents had. Times were hard. The long-wave depression of the 1890s led to a rise in the number of young adults who were forced to remain at home, waiting to inherit a house, farm, or business from their parents. Recent demographic studies have shown that this was especially true in Middle Western urban areas like Detroit. Presumably, Dayton was not much different. Orville was anxious to establish himself as a printer. The only way to do that, for the time being, was to continue living under his father's roof.

Nothing could have pleased Milton more. As Reuchlin's experience had demonstrated, the bishop did not relish the idea of his children leaving home under the best of circumstances. He bound Katharine to him because he needed her. He seems to have regarded the boys as his hostages to fate.

The depth of Milton's desire to insulate and protect his sons from the harsh treatment that the world meted out to honest folk was never more apparent than in the late summer and fall of 1908, when Wilbur was making his first public flights in France. "I wish you could be in the home circle," Milton wrote that September, at a time when his world-famous son was besieged by admiring throngs. "You are so *alone,* if not lonely."[15]

Milton was certain that he knew what Wilbur must be feeling. "I have had some experience in being thousands of miles away from home, away from my family," he reminded his son. "But I was in my own country and amid my own language. In 1859 I was a full month distant, and mails about six weeks en route. In 1885, 1886, 1887, and 1888, I was about 7 or 10 days away. I do not like to have you so far from us all, with your cares and experiments."[16]

Surrounded as he was by "those who have a lack of sympathy, and even inward hostility," Wilbur must be suffering from the "lack of home sympathy."[17] Milton cautioned him to mind his health and to be careful while flying, but he was far more concerned about what those "hostile strangers" might do. He warned his son to be especially alert to the danger of sabotage. "Before making a flight," he suggested, "you should inspect your machine carefully, to be sure that no one has tampered with it."[18]

If the French did not kill Wilbur, Milton feared, they would most certainly attempt to rob him. "Astute experimenters," he advised, "will catch up with you, prevent your profit, and steal your credit, as well as [your] cash, at last."[19]

Time and again he reminded Wilbur that the applause of the multitude was not to be trusted. "The ties of blood relationship," he admonished, "are more enduring and more real."[20]

But if Milton sought to protect his children from the harsh reality of the world, it is also clear that he was very much afraid of being abandoned by them. He struggled to mask those feelings. "As long looked for," he wrote to thirty-nine-year-old Wilbur in August 1908, "you [and Orville] are both far away, probably never to be much at home after this. But I . . . [will] say little about it." Still, Wilbur and Orville could scarcely avoid reading between the lines of a letter received in July 1908. "We miss you," their father remarked, "but while your business goes forward I have to accept the inevitable."[21]

Milton would grow more demanding in years to come, creating considerable tension in Katharine's life after her graduation and return home. She and her brothers accepted this side of their father's nature without complaint, however. Bishop Wright had faced problems with Reuchlin, but there was never the slightest sign of rebellion among his three youngest children. They revered him, never doubting that he wanted only what he thought best for them. More important, they believed he knew what was best for them.

Nor was there any question who was the head of the household. Wilbur spoke for all of them in a letter written to Milton while the printing establishment suit was being heard by the Ohio Supreme Court in December 1898.

> I hope that Mr. Young [the Old Constitution attorney] will insist strongly that there is no law in America requiring churches to leave the essentials of faith and practice to be legislated upon from time to time as majorities may dictate . . . it is the privilege of churches to protect the rights of their legitimate spiritual children in future times, by "extraordinary and impractical" restrictive rules . . . for the protection of those who have inherited the spirit of the founders.

"The Fathers knew what they were doing," Wilbur concluded. "They had a right to do it; the Court is bound to protect that right."[22]

Clearly, Wilbur regarded the church situation as a metaphor for life—"The Fathers knew what they were doing." Wilbur, Orville, and Katharine were deeply involved in and affected by their father's prob-

lems. They never doubted the righteousness of his cause or the way
in which he attempted to resolve the difficulties he faced. Like Milton,
they came to believe in the essential depravity of mankind. The world
beyond the front door of their home was filled with men and women
who were not to be trusted.

Gradually, they would become as isolated as their father—and as
combative. The ten-year fight in the courts for the property rights of
the Old Constitution church served to draw them closer together. An
honest person was well advised to expect the worst of others, and to
rely on the security and support of the family.

The reorientation of the Wright family following Susan's death was
a continuous process, not completed until Katharine's graduation
from Oberlin in 1898. It involved the working out of a new set of
dynamics. As father and daughter began the complex task of establishing a framework for family leadership within which both could
function, Wilbur and Orville were exploring the advantages of a partnership between brothers.

chapter 7

A BUSINESS FOR BROTHERS

1889-1891

The year 1889 was a turning point for each member of the Wright family. It brought the sadness and uncertainty of Susan's death and the dissolution of the old church. But there was a sense of new beginnings as well, particularly for Wilbur, who emerged from the four years that he had spent convalescing, reading, and nursing his mother to discover that his younger brother had caught up with him.

Orville turned eighteen that August, a little more than a month after his mother's funeral. He had come back from Indiana with the family in 1884 under something of an academic cloud. Involved in some bit of mischief, he had been sent home from the sixth grade with a warning that he would not be allowed to return to school unless accompanied by one of his parents. Busy packing, Susan simply kept the boy out of school for the last few weeks before the move to Ohio. As a result, Orville did not receive his sixth-grade certificate, and had to prove himself before being allowed to enter the seventh grade.[1]

His reputation for mischief was apparently well founded. Miss Jennings, his eighth-grade teacher at the second district intermediate school in Dayton, found it necessary to seat him in the front row where she could keep an eye on him. He retained that seat the following year, 1887, when both he and Miss Jennings were promoted to the ninth grade.

Orville was not an outstanding student, but he got by. His ninth-grade marks included a 79 in Latin, an 86 in algebra, and a 92 in botany. Orville raised all of his grades during his sophomore year, earning a 90 in Latin, geometry, and history; his tenth-grade instructors credited him with good deportment and "medium" habits of application.[2]

Nor was he a particularly memorable pupil. William Werthner, his ninth-grade instructor in botany, later described him as "a quiet, reserved boy, faithful in his work, but not strikingly different from the rest . . . whom I would have forgotten had not his sister Kate in after years also attended our school and told me she was the second of her family to recite in my classes."[3]

In truth, Orville was more interested in printing than in schoolwork. While the family was still living in Richmond he had become fascinated by the line illustrations in magazines of the period. After reading up on the subject in *Chamber's Cyclopedia*, he tried his own hand at cutting wooden printing blocks, using the spring of a broken pocket knife as a scribe. Wilbur presented him with a proper set of wood-cutting tools that Christmas.

When they arrived back in Dayton, Orville was delighted to discover that his old friend Ed Sines, who still lived in the neighborhood, boasted a small printing outfit. When that proved inadequate, Wilbur and Lorin traded an old boat for a more professional press, which they presented to the young printers. Milton pitched in with twenty-five pounds of used type.

The first major project undertaken by the firm of Sines & Wright was a small newspaper, *The Midget*, aimed at their eighth-grade classmates. Milton suspended publication when he discovered that the first issue included an entire page consisting of the name Sines & Wright printed twice diagonally across the sheet. Their readers would feel cheated, he explained. It was probably just as well. The issue contained a notice that the next number would include Miss Jenning's thoughts on "The Inherent Wickedness of School Children." Orville's already shaky academic record might not have stood the shock.[4]

Before long the printing operation had taken over the "summer kitchen" at the rear of the Wright house, and the boys were accepting commissions for the job printing of handbills and advertising circulars, as well as letterhead, business cards, envelopes, and tickets. They boasted that Sines & Wright would "do job printing cheaper than any other house in town."[5]

Orville spent two summers as an apprentice at a local printing shop to improve his skills and, with Wilbur's assistance, designed and built

Orville Wright (center rear) had already lost his enthusiasm for formal education when he posed on the steps of Dayton's Central High School with Paul Laurence Dunbar (left rear) and other members of the Class of 1890.

his first professional press out of a damaged tombstone, buggy parts, scrap metal, and odd items scrounged from local junkyards. He could now accept contracts for bigger jobs, including the publication of church pamphlets. The first of these was Wilbur's *Scenes in the Church Commission*, issued under a new imprint—Wright Bros.: Job Printers, 7 Hawthorn Street. It was the first time that phrase— the Wright brothers—had appeared in print.

At the time of his mother's death, Orville had already decided that he would not return to Central High School for his senior year, 1889– 90. He had abandoned the regular program the year before, enrolling in special advanced courses intended to prepare recent graduates for college. As a result, he lacked several credits and would not be able to graduate with his class.

It was no matter. Orville had little interest in higher education—he wanted to be a printer, and by 1889 he knew the basics from the bottom up. He had constructed a press capable of handling sheets of up to eleven by sixteen inches, and had mastered a variety of special- ized professional techniques, including stereotyping, the art of cast- ing columns of set type into sheets of wet cardboard.

Orville had a much stronger commitment to the enterprise than did Sines. When a local grocer paid his advertising bill with two dollars' worth of popcorn, Sines argued that they should split the fee and eat the profits. Orville preferred to resell the popcorn to another grocer and buy additional type. Unable to resolve the dispute, Orville bought Sines out, becoming sole proprietor of the printing firm. Sines continued to work as an employee until the Wrights sold out completely in 1899.

Orville began work on another, larger, press in the spring of 1888. Like its predecessor, the new press was built up of a collection of scrap parts. The frame was constructed of four-foot lengths of firewood, while the framework of a folding buggy top was used to ensure a uniform pressure of the type on each sheet. Orville again drew on Wilbur's services as a consultant during the process of design and construction.

By July, he reported to his father that the new press was almost complete. With a makeshift inking arrangement Orville was already printing five hundred sheets an hour; when the final system was in place, his speed would double. The press was large enough to print a double page of the *Conservator* at once.[6]

Ed Sines recalled that the new press intrigued professional printers:

> E. C. James, I think he was pressman for a Chicago [printing] house at that time, came to the [Wright] print shop almost every time he was in the city. One day he walked into the front office and asked if "that Wright press is running today." When we told him it was running at that time he said he would like to see it. Well, he went back into the press room, stood by the machine, looked at it, then sat down beside it and finally crawled underneath it. After he had been under the machine some little time he got up and said, "Well, it works, but I certainly don't see how it does the work."[7]

When the new press went into operation Orville expanded his printing services. He could now bid on lucrative church and business contracts for tracts, pamphlets, and annual reports. Milton, who served as Old Constitution publishing agent from 1889 to 1893, was able to direct considerable business to his son.

On March 1, 1889, Orville began publication of a weekly newspaper, *The West Side News*. It was intended to function as the keystone of his small printing enterprise, producing enough income to justify his decision to quit school, forego college, and devote all his time to publishing. He was betting that the residents of West Dayton had sufficient pride in their own identity to support a local newspaper, which, he promised, would represent "the interests of the people and business institutions of the West Side. Whatever tends to their advancement, moral, mental, and financial, will receive our closest attention."

The first few numbers were distributed free of charge. The original subscription rate, 50 cents per year, or a penny a week, was later raised to a quarter a month, or a dime for six weeks. Readers found hard news in short supply. The bulk of the copy was made up of clippings from other newspapers and magazines, an occasional editorial, and short snippets of broad humor. (March 1, 1889: "The city elections will be held Monday, April 1. Vote early and often.")

By the end of April, *The West Side News* had begun to show a profit. Orville moved his equipment out of the old carriage shed at the rear of 7 Hawthorn into rented quarters at 1210 West Third. Far more important, Wilbur's name now appeared on the masthead as editor. Orv was satisfied to list himself as printer and publisher.

We have no way of knowing how Orv drew his brother into the project, but it was probably not a very difficult job. Wilbur was intrigued by the possibilities of the little paper. It would give him an opportunity to do some writing and to read extensively for clippings that could be reprinted. Even the preparation of advertising copy represented the sort of challenge that he enjoyed. Still, work on the four-page, four-column weekly was not particularly demanding. The expansion of the paper into a daily was almost certainly his idea.

The last issue of *The West Side News* appeared on April 5, 1890. Old subscribers found the first issue of its successor, *The Evening Item*, on their doorsteps on the afternoon of April 30. If *The West Side News* was an advertising sheet with pretensions, the Wrights promised their readers that the *Item* would contain "all the news of the world that most people care to read, and in such shape that people will have time to read it." Subscribers would receive "the clearest and most accurate possible understanding of what is happening in the world from day-to-day," and were reminded that "it is not always the largest papers that do this most carefully and successfully."

Advertisers could expect the paper to "boom up the business interests of the West Side and increase the value of West Side property. If there is anyone on the West Side who does not think it worth a cent a day to have a daily paper here, it must be that he has no property interests in the West Side and does not know how to read."[8]

The novice editors did their best to deliver on their promises. In addition to scouring the West Side for local news, they subscribed to a wire service, which enabled them to include "about the amount of telegraph news furnished by Dailies outside Cincinnati." A typical issue (May 2, 1890), featured a headline story on international affairs ("Czar Scared—He Runs Away to Escape Assassination"), followed by the welcome news that the "boys" down at the Columbia Chain Bridge Works had finally received their back pay. There was an account of the traffic jam created when a Consolidated Tank Line wagon broke down in front of the *Item* office on Third Street, and a challenge offered by Dr. Brown and George Sharkey, checker champions of neighboring Browntown, to meet any and all comers from Miami City.

James Gordon Bennett, William Randolph Hearst, and Joseph Pulitzer were building empires on sensational stories and banner headlines. The Wrights were not averse to trying their hands at some small-scale yellow journalism in the hope of attracting a few additional subscribers. An account of a fire at a Montreal insane asylum was headlined: "Roasted in Red, Roaring and Terrible Flames." "Death Locked in the Juice of a Poisonous Root" told the story of a French Canadian family that fell victim to a mess of bad parsnips. "Died for Love—Tragic Suicide in an Ohio Hotel" and "Leprosy— Dread Disease Among Chicago's Millions" were self-explanatory— and, the Wrights hoped, irresistible.

But if the brothers had a weakness for lurid headlines, they also provided their readers with first-rate coverage of local events that the larger city dailies overlooked. When Terrence Powderly, head of the Knights of Labor, a pioneer industrial union, wrote to a West Dayton friend with a description of labor unrest in Detroit and Chicago, the Wrights knew about it, and so did their subscribers.

The *Item* gave West Side citizens a detailed record of the daily events—large and small—that made up the life of their community. The badly decomposed body of John Danner, a sixty-eight-year-old man who had been missing for a week, was found floating face down in the Miami Canal that May. The remains of an unidentified black child were discovered in the hydraulic channel near the Ohio Rake Works several days later. City detectives were at work on both cases.

West Dayton had been a racially mixed neighborhood since the end of the war, and, as stories in the *Item* suggested, race relations were not always the best. In the spring of 1890 one Will Adkins was set upon by a gang of "colored youths" near the Flying Dutchman, a local tavern. Wilbur reported that "one of the Negroes got Adkins finger in his mouth and bit entirely through it. It will be months before the finger will be in condition to use again."

Not all of the news was bad. The economy was looking up. One day in late April a local factory shipped thirty-three carloads of threshing machines out on the noon train. Local merchants, anxious to take advantage of the better times, filled the back pages of the *Item* with advertisements for spring sales.

The *Item* offered comment and opinion as well as local, national, and international news. The Wrights spoke to city hall on behalf of the West Side, calling attention to the poor condition of the streets and sidewalks, leaky sewers, and the deficiencies of the streetcar companies. Wilbur addressed the major issues of the day—labor unrest, the farm problem, and the monetary crisis—from a traditional Republican perspective in an editorial column on the second page. While he sympathized with the workingman and expressed moderate admiration for labor leaders like Terrence Powderly, he was certain that no one would really benefit from a strike.

But the Wrights, with their stubborn independence, would never be rigid adherents of any party. They argued that the time had come to forget the old war-related issues on which the Republicans had first come to power, to "bury the bloody shirt," cease "eulogizing the war," and face the future. Wilbur wrote some of his strongest editorials in support of issues that would eventually be espoused by the Democrats. He argued the cause of woman suffrage, and opposed the jingoists who favored the expansion of American power and influence overseas. The Mexican War remained a great stain on the American escutcheon—"Another such blot shall not soil her fair name."

In gauging the fitness of a politician for office, the Wrights believed that honesty and personal morality were far more important than a man's party, or his stand on any particular issue. By that measure, James G. Blaine, the "plumed knight" who had been the Republican standardbearer in 1884, was not "a Presidential possibility." Blaine, as one contemporary noted, "had wallowed in spoils like a rhinoceros in an African pool."

The brothers had an opportunity to examine two leading Republican candidates in the fall of 1891, when Joseph Benson ("Fire Alarm Joe") Foraker (two-term governor of Ohio and future U.S. senator) and William McKinley (Ohio governor and future President) visited Dayton. They disagreed with almost every aspect of McKinley's program. Still, as twenty-year-old Orville remarked to his father, he "looks like an honest man." It was the highest compliment they could pay a politician, and overrode any compunction they might have about his platform.

Foraker's speech was humorous, "and enjoyed more by the crowd than McKinley's," but the brothers were not impressed. "A few minutes look at Foraker and I left," Orville wrote to his father. "If he is an honest man he ought to sue his face."[9]

By any standard, *The Evening Item* was a good local paper. Unfortunately, the Wrights were financially ill-prepared to battle for a niche in the highly competitive city newspaper market. In the spring of 1890, Dayton boasted twelve newspapers, the largest of which, the *Herald* and the *Journal,* had invested in the new high-speed presses that enabled them to produce thick, illustrated editions complete with advertising supplements, special features for Mom and the kids, and a sports section for Dad.

Wilbur and Orville did not expect to make their fortunes in journalism, but neither could they afford to lose their shirts. They had launched the *Item* with very little capital, and had no savings to invest. Their father, living on a reduced salary until the new church was functioning properly, could not offer much help. Any loss would mean going into debt, a prospect that was anathema to the Wrights. They had lost their gamble. The last issue of *The Evening Item* appeared in August 1890, less than four months after start of publication.

The brothers returned to the far less risky business of operating a job printing plant. The firm of Wright & Wright prospered to a modest extent, catering to the printing needs of West Side merchants. They gave up their office at 1210 West Third, transferring operations to a second-floor room in the Hoover Block, a building on the corner of Third and Williams only a block and a half from Hawthorn Street.

Wright & Wright published a wide variety of materials, ranging from church, club, and association directories to the annual reports that state agencies required of local savings and loans, programs for school and YMCA functions, posters, and the usual line of business cards and letterhead. Several times a year they put together special holiday shoppers for local merchants. "Thanksgiving Tid-Bits," issued in October 1891, was typical, containing announcements of various sales and specials "enlivened" with a string of feeble jokes and riddles.

"What animal falls from the clouds? Rain Deer."

"What is worse than raining pitchforks? Hailing Omnibuses."[10]

The brothers were involved in one other failed newspaper venture. Late in 1890, Paul Laurence Dunbar, an old classmate of Orville's at Central High, launched a paper aimed at Dayton's black community, *The Tattler*. Born in Dayton on June 27, 1872, the son of freed slaves, Dunbar was the only black member of the class. He became class poet, editor of the *High School Times*, and president of the Philomatheon Society, the school debating club. Like Orville, Dunbar dropped out of school during 1889–90, but returned the following year to graduate. He had always been far more a leader than Orville.

Dunbar, who had grown up on the West Side, had known Orville since childhood. Many years later Orville said that they had been "close friends in our school days and in the years immediately following." Dunbar had contributed poetry to the *West Side News* as early as March 1889, and continued to publish in that paper and its successor until the summer of 1890. Legend has it that he was working in the back room of the print shop with Orville one day and scratched four lines of doggerel on the wall:

> Orville Wright is out of sight
> In the printing business.
> No other mind is half as bright
> As his'n is.[11]

Dunbar's idea of a paper for the black community was almost certainly inspired by the fact that he had a friend in the printing business. Wilbur and Orville published the early issues on credit, obviously hoping that the black community would prove more receptive to Dunbar than West Dayton had to them. "We published it as long as our financial resources permitted," Orville later recalled. "Which was not very long." Only three issues of *The Tattler* are known to have been printed. The most interesting thing about the short-lived paper was an article in the first issue. Headlined "Airship Soon to Fly," it dealt with the efforts of a Chicagoan, E. J. Pennington, to fly a dirigible airship.

Two young bachelors still living at home did not require a great deal of money. As they scrambled to establish themselves as printers and publishers, they were also working out the boundaries of their own relationship. It was not always an easy task. Orville, who had drawn his brother into the printing business, occasionally sensed that he was being treated more as a younger brother than as full partner. There were times, as in the summer of 1892, when he felt the need to assert himself.

That July, Wilbur and Orville had agreed to design and build a new Wright press for another printing firm, Matthews & Light. Then Lorin presented the brothers with a rush contract for a United Brethren printing job. They decided that Wilbur should continue work on the press while Orville returned to the shop to fulfill the church contract. All proceeds were to be evenly divided.

A few weeks later, Orville felt that his half of the bargain involved more work, and insisted that Wilbur set construction of the press aside and join him in printing and binding the church pamphlets. Anxious to appease his brother, Wilbur agreed. Still dissatisfied, Orville then insisted on a complete renegotiation of their agreement. Exasperated, Wilbur drew up a mock "brief" for presentation to the "Circuit Court of 7 Hawthorn St."

The complaint was couched as a broad, humorous parody of a legal document, but the depth of ill-feeling on both sides was apparent. The plaintiff, Wilbur, alleged that his brother had "exhausted his vocabulary . . . in order to insult the plaintiff." To please him, Wilbur had stopped working on the press and performed "girls work" at the shop, "although said defendant [Orville] well knew that the pay for such work was but small and that said plaintiff, being unfamiliar with such work, would be able to accomplish little." Orville was aware that time away from the press would mean a financial loss to the firm, and had intended the arrangement solely "as an insult." Wilbur had humored his brother only "for the sake of peace in said firm." The demand for a new split of the profits was the last straw.

> Plaintiff further states that while, as a member of said firm, he is willing to stand his share of the expense entailed upon said firm for the gratification of the pleasure of said defendant alone, nevertheless, he is not willing that the defendant should have all the fun and said plaintiff all the expense.
> Plaintiff further says that he was first insulted, then cheated, and then accused of having a dishonest and tricky business character. . . .

Wilbur petitioned the "court" for a decision as to an equitable distribution of the money earned on both jobs, as well as an order directing Orville to "apologize for his insulting conduct, and requesting him to keep his mouth shut in future, lest he should again be guilty of befouling the spotless and innocent character of others."[12]

No record of the results has survived, but the episode offers fascinating insight into the relationship between the two brothers.

The use of humor to defuse a potentially difficult situation was a family characteristic. Wilbur, Orville, and Katharine each possessed an extraordinary sense of humor. Laughter, particularly if it was the result of an "inside joke," would offer a release from a great many personal disagreements over the years.

There is no escaping the fact that the Wrights were a litigious family. The children had grown up in the midst of an extended debate over the central meaning of the frame of church government. Their father was a superb parliamentarian who enjoyed nothing more than a good argument. From 1889 to 1900 the conduct of a series of intricate church-related lawsuits became a part of their daily lives. Wilbur, in particular, was heavily involved in the preparation of real legal briefs supporting the Old Constitution position. After 1902, Milton—and through him his children—was to become embroiled in yet another church legal controversy that would ultimately lead to the bishop's retirement.

The Wrights were firm believers in the rule of law. The courts existed to protect the rights of the innocent. Small wonder that Wilbur later received high marks as an effective witness during the airplane patent suits of 1910–12; he was drawing on a lifelong familiarity with the law.

Finally, Wilbur and Orville were men who took great delight in arguing with one another. "I love to scrap with Orv," Wilbur once remarked. "Orv is such a good scrapper."[13] In time, they would learn to argue in a more effective way, tossing ideas back and forth in a kind of verbal shorthand until a kernel of truth began to emerge. Their ability to argue through to the solution of a problem would prove very useful to them. It was but one of the important elements of an enormously successful partnership that was fully launched by the late summer of 1892.

chapter 8

BICYCLES BUILT BY TWO

1892–1896

Wilbur and Orville had the house to themselves for most of September and October 1892. The bishop was on the road, and Katharine, who had graduated from Central High School in June, was enjoying an extended visit with Reuch, Lulu, and the children in Kansas City.

"We have been living fine since you left," Wilbur assured his sister on September 18.

> Orville cooks one week and I cook the next. Orville's week we have bread and butter and meat and gravy and coffee three times a day. My week I give him more variety. You see that by the end of his week there is a big lot of cold meat stored up, so the first half of my week we have bread and butter and "hash" and coffee, and the last half we have bread and butter and eggs and sweet potatoes and coffee. We don't fuss a bit about whose week it is to cook. Perhaps the reason is evident. If Mrs. Jack Spratt had undertaken to cook all fat, I guess Jack wouldn't have kicked on cooking every other week either.[1]

The time alone gave the brothers an opportunity to resolve their recent squabble and to discuss business in general. Wilbur had little interest in the print shop. With the collapse of his editorial responsibility for *The West Side News* and *The Evening Item*, there was not much work for him to do. That was the root cause of their disagreement that summer.

Orville, too, was discovering that a printer's life was not all he had hoped. With the job printing facility up and running, Ed Sines handled most of the day-to-day work. Like his brother, Orville was bored and looking for a new challenge. They began to cast about for a business enterprise that could be run in addition to the print shop—something that would provide a supplementary income, hold their interest, and allow them to exercise their joint talents.

The talk between them flowed most easily when they were peddling along one of the back roads leading out of Dayton. Orville had splurged and bought a new Columbia "safety" bicycle for $160 early that spring. A few weeks later, Wilbur, ever the more cautious of the two, invested $80 in a used Columbia. By fall, cycling had become a shared passion.

"We had a good rain Tuesday," Wilbur told Katharine in his same letter of September 18, "and the roads were good for bicycling." That Thursday, unable to resist temptation any longer, they locked up the print shop at four-fifteen in the afternoon and rode south out of town on the Cincinnati Pike, bound for the great Indian mound at Miamisburg, 25 miles away. In no particular hurry, they indulged in several quick laps around the dirt track at the Montgomery County Fairgrounds.[2]

By five o'clock they were back on the Pike, struggling up a hill that seemed to go on forever. "We climbed and then we 'clumb' and then we climbed again," as Wilbur put it. He asked a farmer mowing hay in a neighboring field if they were not "getting nearly to the top of the world." The man responded by pointing to the summit of a "mountain" three quarters of a mile farther on. "Centerville," he told them, "is the highest point in the county."

Riding into Centerville, the Wrights confronted a bit of their own heritage—the lovely two-story brick dwelling where their great-uncle Asahel had run a store from 1816 until 1826. By the time they reached the mound and started for home, "it was so dark we could hardly see the road." Undeterred, they raced along through the night, "more by feeling than seeing," following the two light streaks on the road where wagon wheels had rolled the gravel smooth. Disaster was narrowly averted when a loaded farm cart suddenly appeared in their path. "This experience set Orville's imagination (always active, as you know) to work," commented Wilbur. "Pretty soon he clapped on brakes and nearly threw himself from his 'bike' to keep himself from running down a hill into a wagon just crossing a little bridge. When he came to the place he found no hill, no bridge, and no wagon, only a little damp place in the road which showed up black in the night."[3]

By 1892, the "merry wheel" had become a national craze. Journalists touted the bicycle as a "boon to all mankind," a "national necessity," and a "force that has within it almost the power of a social revolution." The Smithsonian scientist WJ McGee, assessing "Fifty Years of American Science" for the readers of *The Atlantic Monthly* in 1896, termed the bicycle "one of the world's great inventions." The Detroit *Tribune* went a step further, predicting history would prove that "the invention of the bicycle was the greatest event of the nineteenth century."[4] And the authorities who prepared the Census of 1890 insisted: "Few articles created by man have created so great a revolution in social conditions."[5]

The invention that was to exercise such influence on American society and technology was launched as a business in 1878, when Colonel Albert Pope began producing high-wheel "ordinaries" in the corner of a Hartford, Connecticut, sewing-machine factory. Sales were encouraging, but the appeal of such cycles was limited to athletic young men willing to risk life and limb in erratic flight through crowded city streets and down rutted country lanes. Wilbur had owned such a machine when he was in high school back in Richmond.

The introduction of the "safety" bicycle to the American market in 1887 marked the beginning of the genuine cycle era. With its two wheels of equal size, sturdy triangular frame, and trustworthy chain-drive system, the safety enabled an entire nation to taste the freedom of the road.

The industry enjoyed phenomenal growth. The number of manufacturers in the field climbed from 27 to 312 in only seven years; total production, estimated at 40,000 machines a year in 1890, reached a peak of 1.2 million by 1895. As the historian David Hounshell has noted, these figures add new meaning to the term "mass production."[6]

The bicycle bridged the gap between the age of the horse and that of the automobile. It marked the first convergence of technologies crucial to automobile production, ranging from electrical welding and work on ball-bearings to experience with chain and shaft transmission systems, metal-stamping technology, and the manufacture of rubber tires.

The millions of bicycles pouring out of American factories created an insatiable appetite for personal transportation. A young fellow could ride his bicycle back and forth to work six days a week quicker than the horse cars could carry him, then peddle out into the countryside for a Sunday outing with his best girl. He went where and when he pleased, under his own power and at his own speed.

The sheer exhilaration of cycling captivated a generation of Americans accustomed to the restraint of high, tight collars, ankle-length skirts, and corsets. Nothing in their experience could compare with the thrill of racing down a steep hill into the wind, and the newfound sense of personal independence was irresistible.

The bicycle craze swept through West Dayton in the fall of 1892. Ed Sines and some other neighborhood men bought the stock of a bicycle manufacturer who was going out of business. They organized a local cycle club, held races, and sponsored group excursions. Most of them also joined the YMCA Wheelmen, one of the great national cycling associations that sanctioned local races.

Wilbur preferred long country rides to track racing, but Orville fancied himself something of a "scorcher." He won at least three races during this period; in later years, however, he would admit that his racing career had been less than spectacular. "You'll never know how I used to envy you and some of the other fellows in those days," he once said to his old friend and rival Peter Klinger. Why, Klinger asked, should the inventor of the airplane envy anyone? "If you'd eaten as much dust as I did," Orville responded, "you'd know!"[7]

Wilbur and Orville were much better known as bicycle mechanics than as racers. The two young men who had constructed printing presses from scratch were already legendary mechanics on the West Side. Now they found themselves besieged by friends in need of bicycle repairs. The second business for which they had been searching was literally thrust upon them.

Milton always believed that the cycle business was Wilbur's idea. Perhaps so. Wilbur was certainly the one who broached the subject soon after his father's return to Dayton on October 25, 1892. They would begin on a small scale, he explained, with a rented storefront that would serve as both showroom and repair shop. With the continued assistance of Ed Sines, they could cover both the new bike store and the print shop without any additional help. The bishop approved of the plan—there was obviously money to be made in the bicycle trade.

The brothers' bright dreams of business expansion were almost dashed on November 6. Milton left home late that afternoon to meet the train bringing Katharine back from Kansas City. When the two of them arrived at the house, they found Wilbur doubled up in pain.

The bishop immediately summoned Dr. Spitler, the physician who had nursed Susan through her final illness.

Wilbur, suffering from appendicitis, was in far greater danger than he had been at the time of the hockey accident. Dr. Spitler was a fine diagnostician who kept up on the latest advances. Appendicitis had been identified, described, and named by Reginald Heber Fitz, a Boston pathologist, only six years before.

An appendectomy was the indicated treatment in acute cases—as one surgeon noted, the idea was to "get in quick and get out quicker." But it was still a very new and dangerous operation, and Dayton was far from the mainstream of surgical advance. St. Elizabeth's, the first real hospital in the city, was only twelve years old. Anesthesia was primitive and, while the need for antisepsis in the operating room was well known, death as a result of postoperative infection was still common. Dr. Spitler chose not to risk sending his patient under the knife. He prescribed rest, a bland diet, and the avoidance of cold. It worked, though Wilbur was still suffering from recurring pain in mid-December.

As his health improved, the brothers took the first steps toward establishing the bicycle shop. In December 1892 they rented a storefront at 1005 West Third Street, and began laying in a stock of parts for the opening of the Wright Cycle Exchange the following spring. The repair business would be their bread and butter, but they would also sell new bicycles and offer a complete line of parts and accessories. Anxious to build a reputation as scrupulous businessmen, they refused to push the cycling geegaws that flooded the market. They regarded cycle dealers who urged local city councils to require the use of bells and lights as little more than thieves.[8]

The Wrights took a similar approach to the sale of bicycles. A cycle, they realized, was a major investment. Between 1890 and 1900, the mean annual wage of the American worker (total wages paid divided by the average total number of wage earners) hovered around $440. A good boy's bicycle cost from $40 to $50; adult bikes began at $50, with the finest machines priced at $100 and up. At those prices, the brothers were careful to emphasize the quality of the products they sold.

Over the years, they would carry at least eight brands of cycle: Coventry, Cross, Duchess, Envoy, Fleetwing, Halladay-Temple, Smalley, and Warwick. These were the best machines on the market. Like other dealers, they developed time-payment plans, and accepted trade-ins as a means of enabling their customers to afford a higher-quality cycle for their hard-earned dollars.

Some trade-ins represented a pure loss; they refused to resell the cheap safety bicycles accepted in trade. Orville gave one such machine, a Viking, to his friend Paul Dunbar. A pair of high-wheel models turned in for new safety bikes did provide some amusement: they produced a gigantic bicycle-built-for-two using a pair of the large four-foot front wheels. No one who watched Wilbur and Orville peddling their monster along the streets of the West Side would ever forget the sight.

Trade boomed during spring and summer of that first year. By the fall of 1893 the bicycle shop was their primary business. When the volume of work became heavy at the print shop, they hired Lorin to give Ed Sines a hand.

The Wrights moved to larger quarters at 1034 West Third that year, and renamed their enterprise the Wright Cycle Company. But competition was growing stiffer. In 1891, there had been only four bicycle shops and one repair facility in the city; by 1892–93, the number had grown to fourteen, including the Wrights.[9]

Small-scale operators had a difficult time of it. Business flourished in the spring and summer, when bike and accessory sales and the repair trade were all at a peak. In the fall and winter, however, there were so few customers that it scarcely seemed worthwhile to remain open. Wilbur discussed these difficulties in a business report to his father in the fall of 1894:

> The bicycle business is fair. Selling new wheels is about done for this year, but the repairing business is good and we are getting about $20 a month from the rent of three wheels. We get $8.00 a month for one, $6.50 for another and the third we rent by the hour or day. We have done so well renting them that we have held on to them instead of disposing of them at once, although we really need the money invested in them.[10]

He went on to request a $150 loan, to which Milton agreed, but the brothers continued to face financial difficulties. Two weeks later Wilbur wrote again to tell his father they had decided to close the store at 1034 West Third and consolidate their two firms at the print shop. "There is hardly enough business to justify us in keeping so expensive a room any longer."[11]

Beset with business problems, Wilbur was reassessing the decisions that had brought him to this point in life. He admitted his basic discontent and remarked that he was once again thinking of taking a college course.

> I have thought about it more or less for a number of years but my health has been such that I was afraid that it might be time and money wasted to do so, but I have felt so much better for a year or so that I have thought more seriously of it and have decided to see what you think of it and would advise.
>
> I do not think I am specially fitted for success in any commercial pursuit even if I had the proper personal and business references to assist me. . . . I have always thought I would like to be a teacher. Although there is no hope of attaining such financial success as might be attained in some of the other professions or in commercial pursuits, yet it is an honorable pursuit, the pay is sufficient to live comfortably and happily, and is less subject to uncertainties than almost any other occupation. It would be congenial to my tastes and I think with proper training I could be reasonably successful.[12]

The problem, Wilbur noted, was money. He would need $600 to $800 to get through college. He could earn most of that, "or at least enough to help along quite a bit," by continuing to work in the bike shop. Still, he would have a difficult time without a loan from his father. Milton agreed that "a commercial life" would not suit him well, and offered to help with "what I can in a collegiate course."

There the matter rested. Wilbur did not pursue his father's offer, nor, so far as we know, did he ever raise the issue of college again. He may have felt that he was too old. He would certainly have been reluctant to ask Orville to accept full responsibility for their joint enterprises. Whatever the reason, he decided to redouble his efforts to make the bicycle shop a success.

In the spring of 1895 the Wrights attempted to expand beyond an exclusively West Side market. They opened not one but two bike shops that season, centralizing the printing and bicycle repair business in a rented building at 22 South Williams Street, just around the block from 7 Hawthorn, and opening a downtown bicycle showroom at 23 West Second Street.

They were also experimenting with imaginative advertising, and tried particularly to attract the high school crowd. When rumors circulated that a copy of an upcoming test had been stolen from a teacher, the Wrights immediately printed up advertising flyers resembling a standardized Central High test sheet, then hired a student to distribute them between classes. Each question and answer extolled the virtues of the Wright Cycle Company.

They explored other ways in which their printing facility could enhance the cycle business. The first issue of *Snap-Shots of Current Events*, a weekly publication aimed at Dayton cyclists, appeared on October 20, 1894. *Snap-Shots* contained enough topical articles, humorous sketches, and jokes to justify charging a subscription fee, but it was primarily intended to promote the Wright Cycle Company and the other West Side merchants who advertised in its pages. The little journal enjoyed a modest success, running until April 17, 1896.[13]

In the fall of 1895 the Wrights reassessed their operation. The downtown store, opened with such high hopes the previous spring, had sapped their time and energy without attracting many additional customers. Competition remained the major problem. There were three other bike shops within two blocks of their showroom. They chose not to renew the lease, and retreated back across the river to the main shop on South Williams.

They had already decided to expand their operation in a different direction. The brothers had given a great deal of thought to how they could apply their peculiar strengths to improving their business position. They reasoned that the best way to increase sales was to market a better product, as Orville explained to their father in October 1895: "Our bicycle business is beginning to be a little slack, though we sell a wheel now and then. Repairing is pretty good. We expect to build our own wheels for next year. I think it will pay us, and give us employment during the winter."[14]

The Wrights had been riding, selling, and repairing bicycles for almost three years when they decided to produce their own brands. They knew the strengths and weaknesses of the various models on the market, and were certain that they could design and build a superior product. It was precisely the sort of challenge that most appealed to them. Orville, in particular, took enormous delight in devising highly personal solutions to mechanical problems.

Ed Sines recalled how eagerly Orville rose to meet any new technical challenge:

Why there was that 10-key adding machine. After I left the Wrights [in 1896] I learned book-keeping. One day I told Orville about a new adding machine that the office had bought. I told him there were nine rows of keys on it, nine keys to the row. "Too many keys," he said. He told me he could make one with just ten keys, and I laughed at him. Sure enough, some time later he showed me a model of it, made with sticks tied together instead of metal rods. And it worked too.[15]

Orville (shirtsleeves) and Ed Sines working in the bicycle shop, 1897. Ivonette Wright Miller never forgot her Uncle Orv's blue tick apron, nor that he always emerged from the shop looking as though he had stepped "right out of a band box."

The brothers transformed the back room and upstairs of the South Williams Street store into a light machine shop. The tools were simple: a turret lathe, a drill press, and tube-cutting equipment. They installed a line shaft on the ceiling to drive the machinery. The design and construction of the single-cylinder internal combustion engine that would power the shafting was a pure pleasure. Fueled by the city gas piped in to light the shop, the engine was a joint project. "The boys have tried their gas engine," Milton told Reuch on March 17, 1896. "Orville's plan to raise the valves and regulate the explosions works all right. It simplifies much and gives increased regulation of the explosions. Wilbur's governor works well and his plan to obviate the necessity of the water jacket promises success. The trade opens well, and lack of capital seems their greatest hindrance."[16]

And there were other opportunities for ingenuity. They devised an electrical welding apparatus to be used in building bicycle frames, and designed their own oil-retaining wheel hub and coaster brake. They had no intention of mass-producing bicycles after the fashion of the large manufacturers. Each of their machines was a hand-built original, made to order.

The official announcement of the Wrights' new line came in the final issue of *Snap-Shots* on April 17, 1896:

> For a number of months, the Wright Cycle Co. has been making prepara-tions to manufacture bicycles. After more delay than we expected, we are at last ready to announce that we will have several samples out in a week or ten days and will be ready to fill orders before the middle of the month. The Wright Special will contain nothing but high grade mate-rials throughout, although we shall put it on the market at the exceed-ingly low price of $60. It will have large tubing, high frame, tool steel bearings, needle wire spokes, narrow tread and every feature of an up-to-date bicycle. Its weight will be about 22 pounds. We are very certain that no wheel on the market will run easier or wear longer than this one, and we will guarantee it in the most unqualified manner.[17]

They named their original model the Van Cleve, in honor of those pioneer Van Cleve ancestors of whom Milton was so proud. Always the top of the Wright line, the Van Cleve initially sold for $60 to $65. By 1900, with sales down and enthusiasm for cycling on the wane, the price dropped to $50.

They also unveiled the St. Clair, a lower-priced line, in 1896. Named in honor of Arthur St. Clair, first governor of the Northwest Terri-tory, these machines sold for $42.50 during the peak years of 1896 and 1897; the price had fallen to $30 when production of the line ceased in 1899. The Wrights may have built and sold at least one sample for a third brand, the Wright Special, priced at $27.50 in 1897.

Both men's and women's models were available. Customers could choose to have their bicycles finished with a variety of brand-name seats, tires, and handlebars. Every model was brush-painted with five coats of rubber baking enamel, either black or carmine. The Wrights built their own wheels with both wooden or metal rims, according to customer preference. The key mechanical elements, the cranks and hubs, were also built in the shop.

The production of their own line of machines marked a turning point in their financial fortunes. By the spring of 1898, Orville reported with some pride that they were "getting in better shape" and "keeping very busy. The wheels," he continued, "are selling very well." During the years of peak production, 1896–1900, Wilbur and Orville constructed perhaps three hundred bicycles. They were by no means rich, but they had established themselves as reasonably successful small businessmen. In a typical seven-month period (February–August 1897) the print shop showed a profit of $127.29. The rest of their income, perhaps $2,000–3,000 a year, came from the bicycle shop.

Most of their friends and neighbors on the West Side must have assumed that the Wright boys would be pleased to spend the rest of their lives splitting their time between the print shop and the bicycle business. In fact, their attention had already begun to wander.

As early as the summer of 1896 Orville was fascinated by a new kind of vehicle chugging along the streets of the West Side. Cordy Ruse, a close friend and a part-time employee at the bike shop, had designed and built the first automobile in Dayton. Orville and Cordy fiddled with the machine for hours, discussing the intricacies of ignition, carburetion, and differential gearing systems.

Wilbur was less interested. He recommended that Cordy fasten a bed sheet beneath the machine to catch the parts that fell off as it lurched down the street. When Orville suggested they build a car of their own, Wilbur expressed doubt that there would ever be a market for such a noisy contraption.

For once, he was wrong. One wonders what he would have thought of a prediction from the editor of the Binghamton, New York, *Republican* who on June 4, 1896, remarked that the invention of a successful heavier-than-air flying machine would likely be the work of bicycle makers. "The flying machine will not be the same shape, or at all in the style of the numerous kinds of cycles," he maintained, "but the study to produce a light, swift machine is likely to lead to an evolution in which wings will play a conspicuous part."[18]

It was not such an outrageous prediction. Bicycles and flying machines were both in the news that summer, and there were many who saw at least a metaphorical connection between the two. It seemed difficult to describe the sense of freedom, control, escape, and speed experienced in cycling without making a comparison to flying.

One minister informed his congregation that the bicycle was "a scientific angel, which seems to bear you away on its unwearied pinions," and a second praised the machine that "enables us to fly in this life before we get the traditional angelic wings."[19]

Budding poets filled newspapers and cycle magazines with similar praise:

> Hurrah, hurrah, for the merry wheel,
> With tires of rubber and spokes of steel;
> We seem to fly on airy steeds,
> With Eagle's flight in silent speed.[20]

James Howard Means, a wealthy Bostonian, had retired as manager of the family shoe factory to promote the cause of flight. In an article published in the 1896 number of his influential journal *The Aeronautical Annual,* Means noted the tendency to equate cycling and flying: "It is not uncommon for the cyclist, in the first flash of enthusiasm which quickly follows the unpleasantness of taming the steel steed, to remark: 'Wheeling is just like flying!' "[21] He urged those who sought to fly to pay serious attention to the bicycle. Once in the air, the operator of a flying machine would have to balance his craft and control its motion through the air. Balance, control, and equilibrium were all problems thoroughly familiar to the cyclist.

Human beings would learn to fly just as they had learned to ride a bicycle, with practice. "To learn to wheel one must learn to balance," Means pointed out. "To learn to fly one must learn to balance."[22]

The manned glider was the aeronautical equivalent of the bicycle. Only when he had mastered his craft during repeated short glides would a prospective aviator be ready to move on to experiments with a powered machine.

Within seven years, Wilbur Wright, the man who had turned his back on Cordy Ruse's horseless carriage, would prove the truth of those words. In so doing, he would also fulfill the outrageous prophecy of the Binghamton editor: the airplane would indeed be the work of bicycle men.

chapter 9

HOME FIRES

1898-1905

T he years 1896–99 were quiet ones in the Wright household. Business at the bicycle shop was steady, with enough growth each year to be encouraging. In 1897 the brothers transferred the company to a new shop, at 1127 West Third, a house that had been remodeled into a duplex storefront. The owner, Charles Webbert, rented the other half of the building to Fetters & Shank, undertakers.

The Wrights were kept busy honing their carpentry skills. They remodeled the back room at 1127 West Third into a well-equipped light machine shop, complete with line shafting driven by the old gas engine. They fixed up the house as well, adding the porch, installing shutters on all the windows, and doing some remodeling upstairs.

With Katharine away at college and the bishop still on the road, the two men had a great deal of time by themselves. Orville, at least, developed a serious pride in mastering the culinary arts. When they tired of their own cooking, they boarded with a widow down the block.

There was plenty of relaxation, as Ed Ellis, Wilbur's best friend, recalled in 1909:

> Years ago when they were in the bicycle business, the country runs with "all the trimmings" were a regular thing with them. I have camped for weeks at a time in a party with Wilbur Wright, when the canoe (of his own make), the gun, fishing tackle and other paraphernalia were as dear to him as to any of us. . . . I remember that during that camping stint of ours, Wilbur and I tramped some four miles trying to buy some chickens. We "got" the chickens.[1]

Wilbur had been a member of the Ten Dayton Boys, the social club formed a decade before when he was still in high school. Beyond two formal annual dinner meetings, however, the group was now inactive. Cycling offered a social outlet for both brothers. They sponsored local races as a means of promoting the shop, and participated in the long weekend "runs" into the surrounding countryside. They were singers as well, members of an informal local chorus.

Music was something that all the family enjoyed—usually. "Orv began lessons on the mandolin," Katharine reported to her father in 1900. "We are getting even with the neighborhood at last for the noise they have made on pianos. He sits around and picks that thing until I can hardly stay in the house."[2]

We know that Orville took the mandolin with him to Kitty Hawk in 1900. The harmonica was Wilbur's instrument, as Lorin's daughter Ivonette recalled:

> At Christmas time it was customary to get together Christmas morning, in the early years. . . . I remember one year when the box from our Kansas cousins was opened. One of the gifts was a small mouth organ with horns protruding from it to increase the sound. After the excitement of opening all the presents had subsided a bit, Uncle Will, who was sitting on the stairway landing, with his long legs stretched out in front of him, started to play the instrument with all the flourishes he could command. He played the melody and accompaniment as if he had done it for years. None of us was aware that he knew how and were all convulsed with the way he carried it off.[3]

In one significant respect, the three youngest Wright children set themselves apart from their contemporaries. Wilbur was twenty-nine in 1896, Orville twenty-five, and Katharine twenty-two. They were ripe for marriage, yet none of them showed any serious interest in the opposite sex. They seemed bound by an unspoken agreement to remain together and to let no one come between them.

Many years later, older residents of Richmond recalled that Wilbur had courted a young lady in high school. There is nothing to indicate that he ever looked twice at a woman again in his life. Those who knew him after 1900 suggested that potentially eligible women actually frightened him. Charles Taylor, for many years employed as a mechanic at the bicycle shop, remembered that Wilbur

> would get awfully nervous when young women were around. When we began operating at Simms Station on the outskirts of Dayton in 1904, we always went out on the traction cars. If an older woman sat down beside

him, before you knew it they would be talking and if she got off at our
stop he'd carry her packages and you'd think he had known her all his
life. But if a young woman sat next to him he would begin to fidget and
pretty soon he would get up and go stand on the platform until it was
time to leave the car.[4]

Sex was a subject on which the entire family maintained silence.
That was to be expected in any late Victorian American household.
Still, the fact that the brothers and their sister were unmarried fascinated the public after 1908. When queried about his marital status,
Wilbur simply replied that he did not have time for a wife and an
airplane. Charles Taylor was probably closer to the truth. "Will kept
saying he didn't have time for a wife," he remarked, "but I think he
was just woman-shy—young women at least."

Perhaps. But Wilbur, with his extraordinary sense of his own
strengths and limitations, may simply have felt that freedom from
family responsibilities was an essential element in his ability to concentrate his attention and energies.

Certainly, he was always scrupulously careful with women. He
regarded any suggestion of an illicit involvement as the worst slur on
his character. This was most apparent in June 1909, when French
newspapers reported that a Lieutenant Goujarde, an officer stationed
at Champagny, had named Wilbur as a co-respondent in a divorce suit.
He claimed that Mme Goujarde, an aeronautical enthusiast, had se-
duced Wilbur in order to win a bet with a friend. The two were
reported to have lived together for two weeks in a Le Mans hotel.

The story quickly found its way into the American press. It appeared in the Dayton *Daily Herald* on June 8, beneath a banner
headline. Friends and family rushed to Wilbur's defense. "In the first
place, he is too clean a man, he is too moral a man to do a thing like
that," Ed Ellis told reporters.[5] Lorin retorted that his brother was
"not that kind."[6] Wilbur spoke out in an open letter to the editor of
the *Daily Herald*. "The French people seem amused that I do not
smoke or drink wine," he noted, suggesting that the whole thing had
been a bad joke akin to the European cartoons that showed him with
a pipe in his mouth blowing billows of smoke.[7]

Rumors of romance would continue to plague Wilbur to the end of
his life. None was ever confirmed. It seems unlikely that he would
ever have trusted himself so far with anyone outside the family.

Wilbur's tendency to distance himself from women seems to have
been the result of a fear that romance would interfere with the more

important things in his life. Orville was simply very shy. Jess Gilbert, a high school friend, remembered a particularly telling episode:

> By someone's super-salesmanship, Orville had been inveigled into one of those gatherings we called "a party," all free from restraint except that we must be home in bed not later than ten o'clock, just about the time the boys and girls start out nowadays. The picture of that party has lingered in mind all of these years, though the howling noise has died down. Orville sat in a straight-backed chair just inside the parlor door all evening, genially aloof from our games of Kiss the Pillow, Post Office, Forfeits and other stimulating enterprises. He was not disdainful; not haughty, not offensive. He simply preferred to have a passive part in our exuberance. He chose to be himself.[8]

Gilbert's story is reinforced by a photograph taken at another Dayton party during the 1890s. The happy faces of young men and women, gathered around a couch, are the central image. Off to one side, seated by himself and staring away from the camera, is Orville.

Ironically, it was Orville, the shyest and least socially adept of the young Wrights, who came closest to marriage during this period. Agnes Osborn had been Katharine's closest friend since grade school. During the months immediately after her graduation, Orville's friendship for Agnes developed into something more. There were evenings of chess and romantic boat rides on the old canal. Agnes's younger brother Glenn, the proud owner of a Wright bicycle, remembered that Orville came calling dressed in his best suit, and loved to play practical jokes on his sister.

Tradition in the Osborn family has it that Orville actually proposed marriage. Whatever credence is attached to such family stories, the romance came to nothing. Perhaps Agnes, a very religious girl, was put off by Orville's cynical remarks on the United Brethren controversies. His practical jokes were certainly a bit rough for her taste. Another intriguing family story suggests that she really had her cap set at Wilbur, much more the courtly gentleman than his younger brother, but entirely unattainable. The most likely explanation is that Orville was simply never very serious about the whole thing.[9]

Katharine's attitude toward men and marriage was much more complex. In a world where marriage was assumed to be every young woman's goal, she went off to Oberlin as determined as her brothers to resist romantic impulses.

She had any number of close female friends. Surviving snapshots show them in their full skirts, shirtwaists, and hats, smiling Gibson

Katharine, second from the right in this group of Oberlin co-eds, was the only college graduate in the family.

Girls sitting on the steps of a college building or preparing to climb onto their bicycles for a picnic in the country. She brought them home during the holidays, and visited in their homes. Several of these young women remained her lifelong friends, but there is nothing to indicate that Katharine was ever serious about a man.

More important, she lost few opportunities to reassure her father and brothers that she had no intention of even enjoying a simple evening with a man. She poked fun at the efforts of her friends who sought to impress potential beaux.

Katharine's need to satirize romance was never more evident than when she attended her first Oberlin class reunion in June 1900. "I know you'll want to hear about Mag [Margaret Goodwin]," she wrote to her two "bubbos." "Caesar [a male classmate] was with her on the train. If possible, he looked even worse than he used to look. Of course, Mag was snippy to him as usual. She told him the true state of her feelings. Anyway, she's going to get paid up all right for he simply insists on taking her to the ball game Saturday. G. Harrison asked me, so I'll save a quarter there."[10]

The message was unmistakable. You are not to worry, this fellow Harrison is nothing more than a free ticket to the ball game.

"Mr. Sheffield," another old friend, also visited: "called on us last evening—in a *dress suit*. . . . You never saw anything so affected in all your days," she assured her menfolk from home. "He had a goatee which adds to his ridiculous appearance. He was just as friendly as ever but he is such a dude and so affected *I* couldn't be natural and cordial."[11]

All too often, men were a source of anger and frustration in Katharine's life, particularly when they refused to recognize her authority or accord her the respect that she deserved. Such a reaction is not at all difficult to understand on the part of a young woman trying to assert herself in a man's world. Charles Taylor, whom Wilbur and Orville left in charge of the bike shop when they went to Kitty Hawk in 1902, was one of her favorite targets: "The business is about to go up the spout, to hear Charles Taylor talk. Say—he makes me too weary for words. He is your judge, it seems. . . . Today I got wrathy and told him that I was tired of hearing him discuss your business. . . . Mr. Taylor knows too much to suit me. I ought to learn more about the store business. I *despise* to be at the mercy of the hired man."[12]

"I simply can't stand Charles Taylor," she remarked the next month, "so I steer clear of the store. I have been in twice to telephone but we never said a word to each other! Imagine."[13]

She was justifiably outraged when the women teachers at Steele High School, where she taught after 1899, were unfairly put upon by the male establishment on the occasion of a teachers' meeting in Cleveland in the fall of 1903.

Mr. Miller, of the Big Four [railroad company] office, has offered to let fifteen [teachers] go on the Wednesday afternoon train, the Twentieth Century Limited. He suggested that the men of the high school let the women go on the afternoon train and he would let them [the male teachers] go at midnight. But the motto at High School is "Men first—if anything is left, women served." So the men are making a great row and it will probably end in no one going on that fast train.[14]

Katharine insisted on her right to exercise power within her legitimate spheres—the home and the school—as little Carrie Kayler could testify. Milton hired fourteen-year-old Carrie in 1900 to assist Katharine with the housekeeping. She left for a short time after marrying Charles Grumbach, then was lured back with the promise that her husband would be taken on as a handyman. The Grumbach's were still working for Orville at the time of his death in 1948.

During the years immediately after Carrie's arrival, Katharine

proved to be a demanding taskmaster. Ivonette recalls the first visit
of Octave Chanute, the great Chicago engineer, to the Wright home
in June 1901:

> Katharine, the hostess, had decided on melons for dessert and gave
> instructions that if one melon, on cutting, proved to be better than the
> other, Carrie was to make sure that Mr. Chanute got a piece of the bet-
> ter one. When the time came, Carrie saw that one of the melons was
> hardly ripe enough to serve and took the liberty of cutting up the remain-
> ing one in small pieces so that everyone could have at least a taste.
> Carrie's impartiality evoked Katharine's displeasure and for a while,
> it seems, there was some doubt in Carrie's mind that she would ever be
> forgiven.[15]

During the early years of their relationship, Katharine lost few
opportunities to ensure that Carrie towed the mark. She was also
careful to let her father and brothers know that the responsibility for
managing their household sometimes weighed heavily on her, as in
October 1902, when she remarked that she was "getting grey with
troubles over washer women."[16]

Immediately after graduating from Oberlin, Katharine went to
work as a teacher of English and Latin at Steele High School, which
had replaced old Central High as Dayton's principal secondary school.
She remained at Steele until 1908, leaving behind a generation of
students who adored her. But in her classroom, as in her home, Katharine insisted on her right to dominate the scene.

"The children who sit in my class are not so nice as they were last
year," she wrote to Orville in the fall of 1901. "I have five or six
notoriously bad boys assigned to my room. I was ready for them, and
nipped their smartness in the bud."[17] When school opened in 1902, Orv
asked his sister for a list of "the first week's victims," adding: "I like
to see someone else catch it beside us."[18]

If Katharine struggled under the special handicaps imposed on a
single working woman, she also took great pride in her job, and in the
responsibility that went with it. "School began Monday," she informed her "Pop" on September 12, 1900.

> I have a room on the third floor—the northeast one, overlooking the
> river. It is the prettiest room in the whole building. I have thirty-eight
> pupils sitting in my room. Then I have five Latin classes—three begin-
> ning, one second year and my January classes of last year consolidated
> into one. The work is very pleasant and will not be particularly hard. I
> like the first year pupils better than Juniors and Seniors.[19]

She fought for additional duties, hoping for the opportunity to teach a class in Greek, and relished the chance to address the one hundred and fifty attendees at a parents' night celebration.[20]

In addition to affording Katharine an opportunity to make her mark in the world, the job also offered some relief from the loneliness that gripped her after 1900, when her father and brothers were absent on their fall and winter trips. "School begins next Monday," she remarked to Milton in September 1900. "I am not sorry, for it has been lonesome for me this summer." It was the same thing the following year. "School begins on the 16th. I wish it would begin right away. I am tired of doing nothing."[21]

In time, Katharine took on some of her father's psychological coloration. She shared Milton's subconscious fear of abandonment and was always careful to let her father and brothers know how difficult things were for her when they were not around. One day seemed very much like another. "The house is so lonesome that I hate to stay in it, but I can't rest as well anywhere else," she noted in the fall of 1903.[22]

She suffered from a string of colds, had trouble with her digestion, and voiced frequent complaints of "utter exhaustion." But the men were not to worry. "I'll be all right when you all get home again," she assured them. A little guilt might bring everyone back together more quickly.[23]

Nor did Katharine want to be forgotten during her own absences from home. Before leaving for a stay with friends in the summer of 1905, she arranged for a relative, Emma Dennis, to come in each day to take care of the house. A graduate of the Milton Wright School of Management at a Distance, Katharine then proceeded to bombard everyone with precise instructions as to their daily activities.

July 10, 1905: I wish you would telephone to Joe Boyd to cut the grass about the middle of the week. It gets so coarse when allowed to grow too long. And please put up one string for that honey suckle vine. . . . And see that the flowers get some water. . . . Get up early Sunday morning and see that the children [Lorin's] get washed and off to Sunday School![24]

July 13, 1905: You could tell our Emma to get some chickens and make sandwiches and deviled eggs et cetera if you wanted to have them out in the country for dinner. . . . Milton [Lorin's son] could go out later and take the basket if you went before Emma was ready. And maybe Netta [Lorin's wife] could go along to entertain Emma. Or Emma could get dinner at home and you could make ice-cream, or buy some for dessert. . . . And tell Emma to have my room cleaned. . . .[25]

July 17, 1905: I hope things are going all right. Tell Emma to give you a change in the lunch, if you get tired of the fare. Be sure to water the flowers.[26]

July 19, 1905: I'll bet dollars to donuts that the grass wasn't trimmed a speck. *I* can cut the grass, it's the trimming *I* can't stand.[27]

July 27, 1905: I hope Emma won't break the family purse with her grocery bills. I'll be home soon.[28]

August 1, 1905: I hope Emma will have something decent to eat. She won't boss that ranch after I strike the place, I can promise her that. I hope things haven't been too uncomfortable. If you lay it on too thick about missing me, the neighbors won't believe you. I'd be moderate about it, if I were you.[29]

The letters are laced with Katharine's dry and infectious humor, but it is a safe bet that Emma left thankfully.

In assuming the role of female head of the family, Katharine had done precisely what her father expected of her. Yet there were times, particularly as he grew older and more dependent on her, when the bishop felt the need to remind Katharine that she was, after all, his daughter, and not really a full partner at all.

His attitude toward Katharine in this regard was very different from that toward his sons. In the thousands of pages of letters and diaries that he left behind, there is not a single angry word directed at either Wilbur or Orville. He could reason with them. He expected his daughter to do as she was told—and quickly.

In the fall of 1908, when Katharine was supervising Orville's hospital care following a flying accident at Fort Myer, Virginia, Milton became convinced that she was neglecting her duty to keep him informed. "The natural inference," he remarked in the most curt terms, "is that you are down with typhoid fever. We are so ashamed to tell the many inquirers after Orville's condition that for four days we have no word from you, so we have to say that we suppose it is because you are sick. But if you are down sick, news might disturb you. So I will close."[30]

On one isolated occasion Milton went much further, addressing Katharine in a fashion that can only have caused her some measure of genuine anguish. Upon learning that Wilbur, Orville, and Katharine had taken a balloon ride in France in 1909, he wrote to tell his daughter that "It does not make much difference about you, but Wilbur ought to keep out of all balloon rides. Success seems to hang on him." He also let her know that he would "do as I please when you

. . . come home. The idea of my making thirty-thousand dollars, and being bossed by you, who can save nothing, is ridiculous."[31]

It is important to realize that Milton did not attack Katharine with malicious intent. Allowance must be made for the fact that he was an eighty-year-old man, lonesome for his children and concerned for their welfare so far from home. At the same time, the letter underscores the extent to which Katharine served as a target when her father was displeased, and the lengths to which he would go to remind his daughter of her subordinate role in the great scheme of things.

Katharine found real satisfaction in her father's house, but there can be no doubt that the Wright men were the primary beneficiaries of the arrangement. Milton could continue his church work, crisscrossing the country and fighting his battles, confident that the haven to which he had always returned was in the best of hands.

Wilbur and Orville enjoyed the benefits of life within a warm and stable family, while escaping the responsibilities that consumed the time and energy of married men. Katharine, far more than the others, paid a considerable physical and psychological price. It was her most important and least recognized contribution to the work of the Wright brothers.

Theirs was not a house without children. Some of the most vivid impressions of life at 7 Hawthorn during the decade after 1896 come from the four youngsters who spent almost as much of their early lives with their grandfather, aunt, and uncles as they did with their parents. Lorin and Netta lived on Horace Street, only a block or so away from both the house and the cycle shop. Their children—Milton, Ivonette, Leontine, and Horace—were the family favorites.

"Grandpa Wright's house was a favorite place. He and my Aunt Katharine and my Uncles Wilbur and Orville spent many days entertaining us there," Leontine recounted. "Sometimes there was picture taking, fascinating candy making, good reading sessions, and good games indoors and out."[32]

Ivonette had similar happy memories. "When my mother had an errand taking her downtown, and had one child she couldn't take with her, we were dropped off at the bicycle shop, and either Orville or Wilbur, or both, baby-sat us. They were never too busy to entertain us."

Orville was Ivonette's particular favorite. "If he ran out of games he would make candy. If he happened to be busy with something else, he would make caramel, which was easier to make and the kind children couldn't eat fast. If he had time, he made fudge with a long

Wilbur, Orville, and Katharine did not have children of their own, but Lorin's children (clockwise), Ivonette, Leontine, and Milton (Horace not shown), were very much a part of their lives.

thermometer to test how long it should be boiled. It was beaten to the right consistency and it was delicious."[33]

The children, at least, appreciated Orville's brand of humor. He was, Ivonette recalled, "a terrible tease," who would stop at nothing to carry off the perfect joke. As the youngest, "Bus" was usually the butt of his uncle's elaborate schemes.

During many of our Sunday dinners they used to tease me as to whether they had enough potatoes, since I always liked mashed potatoes. One Sunday Uncle Orv remarked, "It seems funny how Bus's plate always makes for the mashed potatoes," and with that my plate started to move towards the mashed potatoes he was serving. It turned out he had pasted a thread to the bottom of my plate which he pulled toward him.[34]

Orville was the more patient of the brothers. "Wilbur would amuse us in an equally wholehearted way," Ivonette noted, "but not so long."[35]

Both brothers took the business of entertaining the children very seriously. Milton, Lorin's oldest boy, remembered the magic lantern shows and other theatrical spectaculars. "There were two characters that took part in the shadowgraph shows, Sam Bonebrake, who was tall and thin, and Jim Higgenbotham, who was short and fat and had a high squeaky voice. There was always a big build-up before each show. Uncle Orv and Uncle Will spent hours in the shop making these jointed sheet metal figures."[36]

Holidays were always a special time. Christmas trees had been absent from the Wright house when Wilbur, Orville, and Katharine were small, but Milton had mellowed by the time his grandchildren arrived. All of them recalled the tree, the presents, and songs sung by the entire family. Horace remembered that Valentine's Day was also

something of an occasion in our house. After dark we would put our valentines at the door, stamp our feet, and run. One year Uncle Orv put on a yellow raincoat, a top hat and when he heard the kids coming down the street, slipped out the back door and around the corner so he would be following us as we approached his house. I had slipped in the gate and was going up on the porch when Uncle Orv turned in the gate, caught me under his arm, and carried me into the house. As they all sat around laughing, I slipped out and down the street to a light. In my collection of comic valentines I found one of a pig in a top hat and coat very similar to the one Uncle Orv had used. It had a verse on it about his piggish ways, and I left it while they were still laughing on the inside.[37]

"In the afternoon," Ivonette recalled, "Orville, Wilbur, or Katharine read to us." *The Goop Tales, Alphabetically Told,* by Gelett Burgess, was a particular favorite. The book described, in humorous verse, the various faults that were to be avoided by good children:

> Roderticus was meek and mild
> He softly spoke, he sweetly smiled
> He never called his playmates names
> He was polite when playing games
> But he was often in disgrace
> Because he had a dirty face.[38]

When Wilbur was flying in France in 1908, he received a letter from Gelett Burgess requesting an interview. He replied that he would be very pleased to meet the author of the book he had read more times than any other. Burgess was delighted, assuming that Wilbur was referring to one of his volumes of essays. Wilbur was too much the gentleman to admit that he meant *The Goop Tales.*[39]

Milton's grandchildren were the second generation to benefit from his taste in educational toys. Nor had Wilbur and Orville lost their enthusiasm for mechanical playthings. "When we were old enough to get toys," Ivonette remembered, "Uncle Orv and Uncle Will had a habit of playing with them until they were broken, then repair[ing] them so that they were better than when they were bought."[40]

Of course not all presents were store-bought. Milton had returned from his church trips laden with brightly colored stones, dried flowers, and other souvenirs for his children. Wilbur and Orville continued that tradition. "When they took their glider to Kitty Hawk," said young Milton, "I thought it must be a fine place to take a vacation, particularly after they sent me such fine souvenirs as a dried horseshoe crab and bottles containing genuine sea water and sea sand."[41]

Milton Wright applied the disciplinary skills he had honed on his own children to his grandchildren as well. Young Milton and Ivonette retained vivid memories of a closet set beneath the stairs of the house on Hawthorn Street. It was a large walk-in affair, with a small window high up on the wall; the closet was kept furnished with picture magazines and reading material. A disobedient child was simply ordered into solitary for a period of enforced reading and serious thinking.[42]

"My grandfather had other methods of punishment," Ivonette recalled. "He would put us on the floor, turn a chair over us, and sit on it so we couldn't get up. When he thought our dignity had a jolt, he would let us out." A rambunctious child was often sentenced to a term sitting on top of the icebox, where he or she would at least no longer be underfoot.[43]

Lorin's youngsters were not the only children in the family. Every effort was made to remain in close touch with the Kansas Wrights. Reuch and Lulu had lost little Catherine in 1892, but their three remaining children—Helen Margaret, Herbert, and Bertha Ellwyn—were family favorites and, from time to time, the object of some concern.

Reuch, Lulu, and the children visited Dayton in the spring of 1901. It was not a pleasant occasion. Lulu was out of sorts, complaining about her husband's lack of ambition and inability to get ahead. But it was her treatment of young Herbert that most concerned the Dayton Wrights.

"A bright manly little fellow," Herbert seemed to be unfairly put upon. The boy refused to stand up for his rights in disputes with his sisters. Parental decisions usually went against him. At one point Lulu had remarked that the boy ought to be taken out of school and put to work in business as soon as possible.

As the psychologist Adrian Kinnane has suggested in his outstanding study of Wright family dynamics, the episode had special psychological meaning for Wilbur. The bicycle business was no longer booming. The cycle craze had peaked in 1896–97; within two years sales had begun to drop precipitously. The slump was inevitable. The huge sales boom of the 1890s had saturated the market.

But the poor business climate was not the real reason for Wilbur's malaise. In spite of his interest in cycling and the mechanical aspects of bicycle repair and construction, he felt "trapped" in a "commercial pursuit" for which he was ill-suited, and which had not enabled him to develop his latent talents and abilities.

Wilbur feared that Herbert was in danger of being caught in the very same trap from which he himself was struggling to escape. The situation was serious enough to warrant a long letter to Lulu. "Please understand that I am not presuming to blame either of you, or even to assert as a fact that there is any blame or cause for it," he stressed.[44]

> But . . . I could not help wondering whether he [Herbert] would ever have a chance to develop his best qualities and choose a life work in which these qualities would be an assistance instead of a hindrance. When I learned that you intended to put him into business early I could not help

feeling that in teaching him to prefer others to himself you were giving him a very poor training for the life work you had chosen for him, for in business it is the aggressive man who continually has his eye on his own interest who succeeds. . . . If Herbert were less retiring and more self-assertive than he is I would entirely agree to putting him into business early for that is the best training in the world for a business life and is the path which practically all the leaders in the business world have followed. I agree that a college training is wasted on a man who expects to follow commercial pursuits. Neither will putting a boy who has not the aggressive business instinct, to work early, make a successful business man of him.[45]

Wilbur concluded that Herbert, like his father and uncles, had "talent sufficient to make him really great." He was not self-assertive, however, and would require the thoughtful guidance of his parents.

If left to himself, he will not find out what he would like to be until his chance to attain his wish is past. You may say that he ought to be more aggressive or that if he was really determined to be a great scientist or a great doctor or a great business man that he would find means to accomplish his end without assistance from his parents. But this is really saying that he must exercise talents that he has not got, in order to get a chance to develop talents he already has.[46]

Wilbur cited his own experience, and that of his brothers, as proof. "I entirely agree that the boys of the Wright family are all lacking in determination and push," he admitted to Lulu. "None of us has as yet made particular use of the talent in which he excels other men, that is why our success has been very moderate. We ought not to have been business men." Herbert could suffer a similar fate if Lulu and Reuch did not provide careful guidance.

There is always danger that a person of his [our] disposition will, if left to depend on himself, retire into the first corner he falls into and remain there all his life struggling for a bare existence (unless some earthquake throws him out into a more favorable location) when if put on the right path with special equipment he would advance far. Many men are better fit for improving the chances offered to them than in turning up the chances for themselves.[47]

It must have been an extraordinarily difficult letter for Wilbur to write. The Dayton Wrights had never found it easy to get along with Lulu under the best of circumstances. The decision to send her a letter filled with criticism of the way in which she was raising her children can only have been inspired by a conviction that the matter was of overriding importance.

For fourteen years, from 1885 to 1899, Wilbur had allowed life and opportunity to pass him by. He had drifted passively along, nursing his mother and fighting his father's battles rather than striking out on his own to acquire the education needed for what he regarded as the most suitable career—teaching. Rather than stepping boldly toward his own goals, he had taken the easy path, joining forces with his younger brother to run two small businesses, an occupation for which he believed he had little talent. He had talked of breaking free, dreamed of going to college and seeking to explore his own potential, but he had lacked the courage, or the energy, to do anything about it.

Wilbur had by no means given up on himself. He had always known that the great opportunity of his life might still lie in the future. If so, he meant to seize it without hesitation—and follow wherever it might lead.

Only now, in the spring of 1901, had he begun to realize that an "earthquake" had already occurred. He had a new hobby so fascinating and challenging as to be all-consuming, giving him a new sense of purpose and direction in life. In the upstairs room at the bike shop, Wilbur and Orville were hard at work on their second glider.

BOOK TWO

Wings

chapter 10

THE YEAR OF THE FLYING MACHINES

May-September 1896

I t was the summer of the Front Porch Campaign and the Cross of Gold. William Jennings Bryan, at thirty-six the youngest man ever nominated for the office of President, traveled ten thousand miles between July and November 1896, giving six hundred speeches to an estimated five million of his fellow citizens. To his friends, he was the "Boy Orator of the Platte," "the Great Commoner," and the "Silver King." Republican newspapers dismissed him as "an irresponsible, unregulated, ignorant, prejudiced, pathologically honest and enthusiastic crank."

William McKinley preferred to let the electorate come to him. Thousands of them did just that. Delegations from every corner of the nation were headed for Canton, Ohio, that summer. They were met at the station by a brass band and marched to the lawn of the McKinley home for an audience with the great man. Portly, and balding, he spoke of a full dinner pail and a sound dollar, and was as rock-solid as he looked.[1]

Americans followed the progress of the campaign in the pages of their daily papers. Those newspapers, and the men who ran them, had become a power in the land. The average newspaper reader of the 1890s remembered his daily paper of the decade before as a thin, spiritless thing. For centuries, the scope of such publications had been limited by the necessity of setting type by hand and printing one sheet of paper at a time.

Technology had changed all that. The combination of the linotype machine, the curved stereotype plate, and the high-speed rotary press, all introduced in the 1880s, enabled a publisher to set a vast amount of type in a short period of time, and to print up to 18,000 standard-sized papers an hour on both sides of a continuous roll of newsprint.

Technology had provided the means of mass-producing newspapers. The effort to take economic advantage of that potential transformed the practice of journalism in America. It was no longer enough to inform the reader; the goal was to stimulate, provoke, and titillate.

New features designed to catch the attention of the great mass of readers filled the mushrooming pages. In 1896, "Dorothy Dix" (Mrs. Elizabeth M. Gilmer) began to write the first "advice to the lovelorn" column for the New Orleans *Picayune.* Cartoonist Richard F. Outcalt developed the first modern comic strip character, "The Yellow Kid," for the *New York World.*

The "sports page" grew to become one of the thickest and most popular sections of the paper. The big story in the spring of 1896 was the incredible success of the U.S. team at the first modern Olympic Games, held in Athens that April. Beset by transportation problems, the exhausted young American competitors arrived on opening day, and went on to win nine out of twelve events.

As usual, a mixture of good news and bad dominated the front pages that summer. A tornado swept through St. Louis, taking four hundred lives. Gold had been discovered on Rabbit Creek, three miles from Dawson in the Yukon Territory of Canada. The U.S. Supreme Court, ruling in the case of *Plessy* v. *Fergusson,* approved the doctrine of "separate but equal," legalizing de facto segregation. Utah was admitted as the forty-fifth state.

Shorter articles called attention to technical curiosities of some interest. The Duryea brothers, Frank and Charles, continued to win road races with their "horseless carriage," just as they had in 1895. The giants of the new industry, they would produce thirteen automobiles before the end of the year. Up in Detroit a mechanic working for the Edison Company was the object of some humor. It seemed the fellow had built an automobile of his own in a local shed, only to discover that the thing was too wide to get through the door when complete. Henry Ford was forced to rip out the front of the building to get his machine to the street.[2]

For all of the pride that Americans took in their native ingenuity, nothing delighted newspaper readers so much as short comic pieces on eccentric inventors off in pursuit of an impossible dream. Flying-machine inventors were a particularly inviting target.

John Trowbridge had fixed the image of the aeronautical experimenter in the public mind with his story poem, "Darius Green and His Flying Machine." The hero, "like many another country dunce," believed that "the air was also man's domain," and was determined to conquer the skies. Young Darius set to work

> With thimble and thread,
> and wax and hammer,
> and buckles and screws,
> and all such things as genius use.
> Two bats for a pattern,
> curious fellows!
> A charcoal pot and a pair of bellows.
> Some wire and several old umbrellas;
> a carriage cover for tail and wings;
> a piece of harness,
> and straps and strings,
> these and a hundred other things.[3]

Encased in this contraption, the inventor leaped from the barn loft, only to thump into the yard below, surrounded by "a wonderful whirl of tangled strings, broken braces and broken wings, shooting stars and various things." The poem was reprinted in newspapers, anthologies, and school textbooks. For the thousands of Americans who chuckled over Darius' plight, the message was clear: If God had intended man to fly, He would have given him wings.

A wealth of educated opinion buttressed such popular skepticism. Had not Simon Newcomb, a leading American astronomer, argued that "the first successful flyer will be the handiwork of a watchmaker, and carry nothing heavier than an insect"? Another authority, Rear Admiral George Melville, the Navy's chief engineer, was even more forceful. "A calm survey of certain natural phenomena," he argued, "leads the engineer to pronounce all confident prophecies for future success as wholly unwarranted, if not absurd." John Le Conte, a well-known naturalist, had assured the public that "a flying machine is impossible, in spite of the testimony of the birds."[4]

As evidence of a bleak future for flying-machine inventors, the skeptics had only to open their daily papers on virtually any day in the first half of 1896. Captain John W. Veiru, "an old steamboatman and mechanic," had unveiled plans for a fish-shaped, paddlewheel flying machine. Victor Oches, a convict serving three to five in the Kings County, New York, jail, asserted that his craft would travel at speeds of up to 300 mph, and "do away with battleships." Oches offered his invention to the public at the cut-rate price of $25,000—provided a full pardon was thrown into the bargain. Chicagoan Arthur de Bausset planned to construct an enormous airship; Captain Charles E. Smith, of San Francisco, was the sole incorporator of the Atlantic & Pacific Aerial Navigation Co.

An unidentified Harlem merchant was reported to have been "inoculated with the bacilli of aeronautica." "A good, hard-headed, common sense, cent-per-cent commercial man" during the work day, he returned home each evening to labor over a flying machine. Yet another New Yorker had to be restrained by police when he sought to fly his ornithopter from a lumber pile near the 155th Street bridge. Cleveland inventor Ralph Koesch was developing a "spiral winged aircraft," while the Reverend Mr. B. Cannon, of Pittsburgh, Texas, based his Ezekiel Flying Machine on biblical descriptions.

Charles Avery, of Rutherford, New Jersey, suffered two fractured ribs and was bleeding from the nose and mouth when rescued from the shattered remains of the flying machine in which he had hurled himself from a cliff. Avery attributed the catastrophe to "a poor start."[5]

Gradually, beginning in June and July 1896, the skepticism receded. Wild-eyed, cliff-jumping birdmen continued to appear in the papers, but they were overshadowed by a spate of stories dealing with successful aeronautical experiments being conducted by some of the world's most reputable engineers and scientists. Large steam-powered models with wingspans of up to fourteen feet were cruising through the air near the nation's capital. In Germany, and on the windswept dunes south of Lake Michigan, human beings had actually glided on the wings of the wind. If Alexander Graham Bell, the revered inventor of the telephone, believed that powered flight lay just around the corner, perhaps the whole business was worth more than a good belly laugh.

QUANTICO, VIRGINIA
MAY 5-6, 1896

Late on the afternoon of May 5, 1896, two distinguished-looking gentlemen stepped from a Washington train onto the platform of the tiny station at Quantico, Virginia. It was an unlikely setting for great events. One observer described the place as a "drab hamlet," a cluster of shabby buildings nestled in a remote cove on the Potomac shore, forty-one rail miles south of Washington, D.C.

The two visitors proceeded through the center of town, past a shanty with a pine board nailed over the door announcing "Meels Served At All Ours." Moving across an open field to the riverbank, they rang a large dinner bell hung from a post to catch the attention of the boatman who would row them across the narrow channel to Scott's Island.

The island looked idyllic in the quiet of that spring afternoon. Only a few acres in extent, it was covered with a thick growth of oak and pine; the land sloped gently away from steep bluffs marking the southern shore toward a marsh that blended almost imperceptibly into the Potomac on the north.

The island was the private preserve of the Mount Vernon Ducking Club, an exclusive organization of Washington sportsmen. Within the year it would become a favorite retreat for newly elected William McKinley. It was an elegant establishment, with a clubhouse, dining hall, and several well-maintained cottages set on the bluffs. But this sportsman's paradise held few attractions for the two visitors. Samuel Pierpoint Langley and Alexander Graham Bell had come on more serious business.

They made their way toward the marsh, where a flat-bottomed scow was moored in a small cove. Dubbed the *Ark*, the strange craft featured a wooden structure almost as wide and long as the boat itself built on deck. Three large windows on either side of the deckhouse were sealed with heavy wooden shutters. A spidery wooden superstructure on the roof supported a single twenty-foot rail extending over the rear of the boat.[6]

Four workmen rose deferentially and escorted Langley and Bell into the deckhouse. Inside on a table lay two large winged models, broken down into subassemblies. The models—numbered, respectively, 5 and 6—represented the culmination of ten years' effort to develop a practical flying machine.

They were works of the machinist's art, glistening with copper pipes, brass fittings, and thin-walled steel-tube fuselages. When completely assembled they would look virtually identical to the unpracticed eye. Both machines sported two sets of tandem wings, spanning fourteen feet; from the tip of the thin forward bowsprit to the end of the cruciform tail, each measured over ten feet in length. Both were powered by delicate, lightweight steam engines driving twin propellers. The overall effect was of a pair of wispy dragonflies.

Bell had little to offer in discussion, but Langley fired one question after another at the men, determined to ensure that all preparations for the coming test flights were complete. Then, satisfied, he led the entire party back to the clubhouse for a fine meal and a good night's sleep.

At sixty-two, Samuel Pierpont Langley, secretary of the Smithsonian Institution for the past decade, had earned a reputation as the unofficial chief scientist of the United States. His interest in the problems of flight dated from 1886, when he attended a lecture on aeronautics at a meeting of the American Association for the Advancement of Science.

He was inspired to undertake a series of experiments to determine whether it was possible to construct a machine that would fly. Through precise measurements made with specially contrived instruments, he probed the laws of aerodynamics, being careful to emphasize that his interest was purely scientific. The program would not result in the construction of an airplane, but would "find the principles on which one should be built."

Langley presented the results of his research in *Experiments in Aerodynamics*, published by the Smithsonian in 1891. His most significant observation was a simple affirmative statement: "The most important general inference from these experiments . . . is that . . . *mechanical flight is possible with engines we now possess.*"[7]

The scientific community was skeptical. Some colleagues questioned the care with which the secretary had conducted his experiments; others argued that his conclusions were not supported by his experimental results. Langley, fearing for his reputation, set out to provide a practical demonstration of the validity of his work.

Between 1887 and 1891, he and his staff constructed more than one hundred flying models sporting various wing, tail, and propeller combinations, each powered by strands of twisted rubber. None met his expectations. He then turned to the design of even larger craft, with wingspans in excess of ten feet, to be propelled by small steam engines. With Smithsonian funds, he mounted a five-year effort to launch these machines into free flight. One model followed another— the first was too heavy, the second too light, the third too weak. The little engines were refined and perfected during this period. Experiments were conducted with catapult launching systems. For all of this preparation, there had not been a single successful flight. Trial after trial had ended with the craft falling into the water off the end of the launch rail. By the spring of 1896 Langley's critics were feeling rather smug.

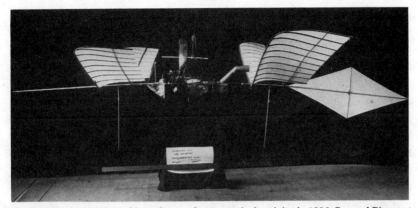

The Wrights were inspired by a flurry of aeronautical activity in 1896. Samuel Pierpont Langley had flown two of his Aerodromes, including Number 6, over the Potomac that year.

Aerodrome No. 6 was ready to go by 1:10 on the afternoon of May 6. Luther Reed, superintendent of the Smithsonian carpentry shops, stood behind the machine, ready to pull the lever that would release a powerful streetcar spring and send the craft rushing down the rail once again. One of the guy wires holding the frail wings in place snapped at the moment of launch, allowing the left forward wing to bend sharply up. The sight of their precious Aerodrome arcing violently into the river was a familiar one to the launch crew, but no less disappointing. Fishing the remains out of the water, they found the wing and both propellers smashed and the engine severely damaged. There would be no more tests with No. 6 that day.

The second model, No. 5, was hoisted into position and prepared for a trial by three o'clock. Each member of the party was at his appointed place. As before, Reed would operate the catapult from a scaffold. Bell stood on the narrow deck beside a nervous Smithsonian photographer. Number 6 had entered the water too quickly for the fellow to snap a picture. Langley was angry, and let him know that it was not to happen a second time.

With one hundred fifty pounds of steam in the boiler and the propellers spinning at top speed, Reed pulled the release. No. 5 left the rail twenty feet above the water, dropped three or four feet, then moved into the wind, angling up some 10 degrees from the horizontal. The men who had grown so accustomed to failure were struck dumb.

The machine began a slow climbing turn, circling the houseboat twice as it gained altitude. It was 100 feet in the air when the steam was exhausted 90 seconds after launch. The propellers ground to a halt and the little machine settled gently onto the river. It had traveled 3,000 feet through the air, over half a mile, at a speed of 20–25 miles per hour.

Stunned silence gave way to a ragged cheer. The crew retrieved the craft, dried and reguyed it with great care. They launched it again at five o'clock that afternoon. The second flight was another triumph. Langley was ecstatic. His belief in the possibility of heavier-than-air flight had long threatened to blot one of the most distinguished careers in American science. Even his colleagues at the Smithsonian were concerned lest the secretary's aeronautical obsession damage the reputation of the Institution.

The flights of May 6, 1896, were his vindication. As he noted in his diary that evening: "These experiments were beyond comparison the most satisfactory which have yet been made, and they have probably no parallel in the history of the subject."[8]

RHINOW HILLS, GERMANY
AUGUST 2–10, 1896

Early Sunday morning, August 2, 1896, Robert Wood, a correspondent for the Boston *Transcript*, met Otto Lilienthal on the platform of Berlin's Lehrter Station. Lilienthal, dressed in a flannel work shirt, twill knickerbocker trousers with thickly padded knees, heavy brogans, and a close-fitting knit skullcap, arrived just before dawn, accompanied by his fourteen-year old son and a mechanic from his machine shop. He looked the image of an athlete—compactly built, broad-shouldered, barrel-chested, with a head of curly red hair, a full beard and mustache, and a ready smile that had etched deep lines around his eyes.[9]

Together, the four men boarded a train headed for the Rhinow Mountains, a range of lush hills forty miles to the north. This excursion was a weekly ritual for Lilienthal, who retreated to the seclusion of Rhinow each Sunday to continue a series of manned glider flights that had brought him world fame since 1891. Fascinated by bird flight since boyhood, Lilienthal had begun his serious study of aeronautics in 1879.

He published the results of his laboratory research in a book, *Der Vogelflug als Grundlage der Fliegekunst (Birdflight as the Basis for Aviation)*, which appeared in 1889. *Vogelflug*, and his other articles, provided a foundation of solid research for other men who sought to fly.[10]

The laboratory tests and publications were the necessary preliminaries to the real business of designing a flying machine. Unlike Langley and most other experimenters, Lilienthal did not believe in the value of models. He was convinced that the conquest of the air would begin with manned gliders. Only by testing a series of unpowered craft for himself could an engineer achieve the process of refinement that would lead to a successful powered machine capable of sustained flight with a pilot on board.

Between 1891 and 1896 he completed nearly two thousand glides in sixteen separate glider types. Most of these were simple monoplanes with stabilizing surfaces at the rear, but Lilienthal also experimented with biplane designs and variations of his standard bat-like monoplane. Ribs and other covered portions of the craft were constructed of split willow and bamboo. The wings, which resembled "the outspread pinions of a soaring bird," averaged between 10 and 20 square meters in area and were covered with cotton twill sheeting doped with a special colloidal solution that created an airtight surface.

The normal glide ratio of these machines averaged eight feet of forward flight for every foot of fall. In all Lilienthal machines, the pilot hung upright between the wings, controlling the craft by shifting his own weight to alter the center of gravity. Hence the term "hang glider."

Nowhere had Lilienthal's work found a more receptive audience than in the United States. This name was familiar to many readers of American newspapers and magazines; accounts of his exploits provided a rich source of material that captured the imagination of the public. Wood was the latest in a string of reporters dispatched to satisfy the American appetite for news of the "flying man."

At the site, Lilienthal supervised the unloading and assembly of the glider, a biplane with a twenty-foot wingspan and a six-foot gap between the upper and lower wings. Wood was enthralled by the sight of the machine taking shape on the grass.

So perfectly was the machine fitted together that it was impossible to find a single loose cord or brace, and the cloth everywhere was under such tension that the whole machine rang like a drum when rapped with the knuckles. . . . Here was a flying machine, not constructed by a crank, to be seen at a county fair at ten cents a head, or to furnish material for

encyclopedia articles on aerial navigation, but by an engineer of ability
. . . a machine not made to look at, but to fly with.[11]

While Wood positioned his camera, the other three men carried the glider up to the crest of a hill. Lilienthal crawled underneath, worked his arms into a set of cuffs that would give him leverage on the machine, grasped a bar near the forward edge of the wings, and stood "like an athlete waiting for the starting pistol." As the wind freshened, he took three steps downhill and was immediately lifted into the air. Flying straight out from the summit, he passed over Wood's head at an altitude of fifty feet, "the wind playing wild tunes on the tense cordage of the machine."

A sudden gust caught the left wingtip, lifting it and sending the craft into a broad, sweeping turn from which Lilienthal recovered with a powerful throw of his legs. He swooped low over the fields at the base of the hill, "kicking at the tops of the haystacks as he passed over them." Approaching the ground, he kicked forward to raise the leading edge of the wing, brought his craft to a dead stop in the air, and dropped easily to earth.

The young reporter found it difficult to contain himself. "I have seen high dives and parachute jumps from balloons," he exulted, ". . . but I have never witnessed anything that strung the nerves to such a pitch of excitement, or awakened such a feeling of enthusiasm and admiration as the wild and fearless rush of Otto Lilienthal through the air."[12]

Toward the end of the afternoon, having witnessed ten flights, Wood wanted to try his hand at gliding. Lilienthal agreed and ordered the machine taken only a dozen yards up the slope. Wood quickly discovered that simply standing in one place balancing the glider was so difficult as to give him a feeling of "utter helplessness." "As you stand in the frame, your elbows at your side, the forearms are horizontal, and your hands grasp one of the horizontal cross-braces. The weight of the machine rests in the angle of the elbow joints. In the air, when you are supported by the wings, your weight is carried on the vertical upper arms and by pads which come under the shoulders, with the legs and lower part of the body swinging free below."[13]

The weight of the machine was reduced with each step as he ran downhill into the wind until, suddenly, he was airborne. "I was sliding down the aerial incline a foot or two from the ground. The apparatus dipped from side to side a great deal. . . . The feeling is most delightful and wholly indescribable. The body being supported from above, with no weight or strain on the legs, the feeling is as if gravitation had been annihilated. . . ."[14]

Wood left the Rhinow Hills that evening prepared to write the finest account of Lilienthal's personality and experiments available in English. But there would be no opportunity for follow-up interviews. The following Sunday, August 9, Otto Lilienthal stalled and fell from an altitude of fifty feet while flying a standard monoplane glider. He died the next day in a Berlin hospital.

News of Lilienthal's death, coming in the wake of the extended coverage of Langley's successful flights over the Potomac, drew wide attention in the American press. The German experimenter was portrayed not as a fool who had tossed his life away to no purpose but as a martyr to science. The newspaper reading public was treated to its second aeronautical hero of the summer of 1896. A third was still to come.

chapter 11

OCTAVE CHANUTE

June-September 1896

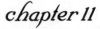

When Octave Chanute arrived in Miller, Indiana, aboard the eight o'clock train from Chicago on June 22, 1896, Samuel Langley's triumph over the Potomac was still very much in the news. Otto Lilienthal had less than two months to live.

Chanute supervised four young assistants as they loaded an assortment of boxes and crates filled with camping gear and the parts of two disassembled gliders into a wagon bound for the wild dune country bordering the southern shore of Lake Michigan.

He was sixty-four years old. With his short, stocky figure, decided paunch, fringe of gray hair, and neatly trimmed Van Dyke beard, he bore a remarkable resemblance to William Shakespeare—or so Wilbur always thought.

A native of Paris, born on February 18, 1832, Octave was the eldest of Joseph and Elise Sophie Debonnaire Chanut's three sons. In 1838, Joseph accepted a position as vice-president of newly established Jefferson College in New Orleans. Six-year-old Octave went with him. He would not see his native France again for forty years. Sophie, now separated from her husband, remained behind with her two youngest sons.

Joseph was extraordinarily protective, refusing to allow his son to mix with American playmates. Tutored at home, the boy did not learn English until he was eleven. This sheltered upbringing deprived Octave of much of the normal cultural baggage picked up by most boys of his generation. He was an undeniably prudish adult, who did not

Octave Chanute, a leading American civil engineer, led a group of young glider enthusiasts into the Indiana Dunes in 1896.

drink, smoke, dance, or swear. In later years, his two daughters enjoyed poking fun at their father's ignorance of such common slang expressions as "fourflusher" and "ace in the hole." Card games and colloquial English were lifelong mysteries to him.

Joseph and Octave remained in New Orleans until 1844, when the father resigned his college position, packed up, and caught a train for New York. There Octave finally entered school. It must have been a difficult time for a sheltered boy with a thick French accent. There is evidence of that even in his name—when schoolmates insisted on dubbing him the "naked cat" *(chat nu)*, he changed the spelling to Chanute, suggesting the correct pronunciation.[1]

In 1849, having decided on a career in engineering, the ambitious seventeen year old traveled to Sing Sing, New York, and presented himself to Henry Gardner, the chief engineer of the Hudson River Railroad. Told that there were no jobs available, Chanute offered to work for nothing. Impressed, Gardner put the young volunteer to work as a chainman, the lowest-ranking member of a surveying team.

Chanute rose rapidly in the profession. Before and after the Civil War he moved through positions of increasing responsibility with one Western railroad after another. Like most of his colleagues, he was not a company man, but was employed to perform a specific job, usually the extension of a rail line farther west. When the task was complete, there was always another railroad ready to bid for his services.

In 1867—the year in which Wilbur Wright was born—Chanute moved his growing family west to Kansas City, where, in addition to continuing work on his current railroad contract, he supervised the construction of the first bridge across the Missouri River. Its completion in 1869 firmly established the thirty-seven-year-old Chanute as an engineer with a national reputation.

Other major railroad and construction contracts were to follow. Chanute served as chief engineer and superintendent of the Leavenworth, Lawrence & Galveston Railroad Company during the early 1870s. In addition, he designed and supervised construction of the Union Stockyards in Kansas City in 1871, and offered essential advice on water, sewer, gas, and transit problems to growing Midwestern cities. His contributions to the urbanization of the West were substantial. It seemed only fitting that one of those towns—Chanute, Kansas—was named in his honor.

Chanute reached the pinnacle of his career in 1873, when he was named chief engineer of the reorganized Erie Railroad. At the time, Western newspapers were filled with tributes to his character and achievements. The Leavenworth *Daily Tribune* praised him as "a gentleman in every respect," while the *Parsons* [Kansas] *Sun* protested "against New York taking from us one of the ablest and best brain men in the state." One Illinois journal termed him the "ablest as well as one of the most popular men in the West."[2]

He spent ten difficult years working for the Erie. The railroad had suffered during the previous decade under the management of the most outrageous band of stock manipulators in American history—"Uncle Dan'l" Drew, "Jubilee Jim" Fiske, and Jay Gould. By the time Chanute arrived, the road was bankrupt and in receivership. Nevertheless, as chief engineer Chanute was able to complete several important modernization programs, including a double tracking of the entire line.

He was also heavily involved in the work of professional societies during this period, serving as president of both the revitalized American Society of Civil Engineers and the engineering section of the American Association for the Advancement of Science, as well as chairing important ASCE technical committees.

In 1875, close to collapse, Chanute treated his family to a four-month vacation in France. He returned to America refreshed and relaxed—and interested in aeronautics. During the course of his European trip he apparently read a few articles on the subject in European journals. He found the work of the English engineer Francis Herbert Wenham particularly interesting. In 1871, Wenham and a colleague, John Browning, had conducted the first experiments with a "wind tunnel"—a device that enabled them to study the reaction of a series of small test surfaces placed in an artificially induced flow of air inside the wooden tunnel.

Chanute recognized that this was solid engineering research at its best. Quite apart from any bearing on the flying-machine problem, these studies could be of extraordinary value to a working engineer. Chanute himself had long been puzzled by the way in which certain roof designs were susceptible to destruction in high winds. A better understanding of the impact of gusting winds on suspension bridges might prevent tragedies such as the catastrophic loss of Charles Ellet's Wheeling, West Virginia, bridge in 1854. The study of air resistance might also lead to more efficient locomotive design.

But there was little time in his life for anything as frivolous as aeronautics. Always the practical man of business, he would keep his growing interest in the flying machine a careful secret for another decade. At a Kansas City dinner party in the 1880s, a friend asked Chanute how he spent his leisure time. "Wait until your children are not present," he replied, "for they would laugh at me."[3]

He finally retired from the Erie in 1885. Rejecting lucrative contracts for work in Latin America and Asia, he established himself as a consulting engineer in Kansas City. From 1880 to 1885 he had chaired an ASCE committee on the problems of wood preservation, a major concern in view of the nation's increasing dependence on railroad ties and telegraph and telephone poles. By 1890 Chanute's reputation in the new field was so well established that he settled permanently in Chicago and founded a firm specializing in wood preservation. Within five years, with his business running smoothly, he could relax and spend some time on the problem that had intrigued him for twenty years.

Chanute began to gather information on aeronautics in about 1884. He scoured bookshops and libraries, subscribed to newspaper clipping services, and launched into correspondence with virtually every major flying-machine experimenter in the world. Twice, at Buffalo in 1886 and at Toronto in 1889, Chanute sponsored major aeronautics sessions at meetings of the American Association for the Advancement of Science. While controversial, the Buffalo meeting was responsible for drawing Samuel Langley to the subject. On both occasions Chanute was careful to maintain the discussion on a high professional level, and to avoid any appearance of "enthusiasm."

In 1893, encouraged by the professional response to the Toronto session, Chanute agreed to organize an International Conference on Aerial Navigation, to be held at the World's Columbian Exposition in Chicago. For the first time he would be going beyond a professional society and speaking to a larger public.

Beginning with London's Crystal Palace in 1851, the history of the nineteenth century had been punctuated by a series of great international fairs. Vienna, New York, Philadelphia, and Paris—each in turn had mounted a stunning display of the scientific, mechanical, and artistic wonders of the age. In honor of the four hundredth anniversary of the discovery of America, Chicago planned a fete that would dwarf all predecessors.

A great "White City"—a collection of neoclassical buildings, broad avenues, and canals—rose from 686 acres of reclaimed marshland fronting Lake Michigan. From the top of the enormous wheel that would immortalize the name of its designer, George Ferris, to the midway dive where Little Egypt captured the hearts of a generation of American males with her "hootchy-kootchy dance," the World's Columbian Exposition was a marvel.

Milton Wright was passing through Chicago on October 20, 1892, and witnessed the great Columbian Exposition Parade that marked the opening of the fair. Wilbur and Orville made the trip to Chicago to "do" the fair in the spring of 1893. Neither of them left an account other than to remark to friends that they had enjoyed the bicycle exhibits. It was the first time either brother had ever been away from home, and they probably saw as much of the fair as Milton did when he returned on October 24 for a complete three-day tour.

The bishop visited twenty-seven of the state exhibit buildings, sixteen of the foreign pavilions, the Art Gallery, the government fisheries display, and the Electrical Department. He rode the Intramural Railway for an hour; admired a giant Redwood plank and the exhibition of polished woods in the Forestry Building; saw a live gorilla; and visited the "aboriginal villages." In all likelihood, he passed up Little Egypt.

The opportunity to attend a session of the Congress of Religions was the high point of Milton's visit. This was only one of a number of congresses designed to add a touch of intellectual class to the great fair. Leaders in a variety of fields—scientists, writers, artists, philosophers, engineers, and theologians—were invited to hold international meetings on the Exposition grounds. The object was to explore the state of the art in their disciplines, and lay a foundation for future work.[4]

The most newsworthy of these congresses was officially known as the International Conference on Aerial Navigation. Held on August 1–4, 1893, the meeting was the work of Octave Chanute and a colleague, Albert Francis Zahm, a young Johns Hopkins Ph.D. in physics who was teaching at Notre Dame. Zahm had conceived the notion of a congress devoted to aeronautics and worked to overcome Chanute's initial reluctance to take part. Ever conscious of his reputation, the older engineer agreed to cooperate only if fair officials promised to assist him in avoiding "publicity and cranks . . . by all possible means."[5]

It was an overwhelming success. Chanute was able to convince some of the nation's leading engineers, men whom he knew to be interested but hesitant to write on the subject, to offer papers. Moreover, it provided an opportunity for him to introduce a number of the young engineers who had conducted experiments to a wider professional audience.

To Chanute's surprise, the public was equally enthusiastic. The Pittsburgh *Dispatch*'s response was typical: "The Chicago Conference undoubtedly marks a new era in aeronautics. It brought together many scientists and engineers who have been engaged seriously on the problem of flight. The subject, it was shown, is one for the study of men of broad knowledge, and accurate training, and is no longer to be considered the hobby of mere cranks."[6]

Coming in the wake of the Chicago conference, the publication of *Progress in Flying Machines* in 1894 marked Octave Chanute as the international authority on the history, theory, and current status of aeronautical studies. The book was an updated version of a series of articles he had published in the *American Engineer and Railroad Journal* since 1891. Covering virtually everything that had been accomplished in the field since the time of Leonardo da Vinci, it quickly became the basic text for all would-be aviators.[7]

At this point Chanute was anxious to move beyond the lectern and the printed page and conduct flying-machine tests of his own. As an engineer, he was accustomed to investigating a project on paper, then transforming theory into practice. It would have been out of character for him to have devoted twenty years of spare-time research to aeronautics without applying the results to an actual flying machine.

An admirer of Lilienthal, Chanute agreed that the manned glider offered the most direct approach to solving the problems of successful powered flight. The actual business of constructing a glider was quite beyond him, however; he was not at all handy and had no skill in carpentry or metalworking. As a railroad chief engineer and a bridge builder, he was accustomed to developing a general plan, then supervising the work of the assistants who would carry it through.

Chanute had always recognized the importance of encouraging younger men. In the 1880s and early 90s he had offered help to several men, including Edward Huffaker, who later served as Langley's aeronautical assistant at the Smithsonian, and John Montgomery, a Californian who had made the first glider flight in the United States in 1885. Chanute had provided a forum for these experimenters to present their work at AAAS meetings, and at the conference in Chicago.

Even this limited experience had taught him a lesson. Young fellows like Huffaker and Montgomery who insisted on becoming involved with flying machines were apt to be difficult, opinionated, and far more eager to pursue their own ideas than to take instructions or advice from Chanute. Still, he recognized that by hiring talented young newcomers to build and test gliders for him, he was not only adding to the store of aeronautical knowledge but supporting engineers who might someday play a major role in solving the problem of flight.

Chanute began his own glider design program in 1895, with the construction of some small flying models. He chose Augustus Moore Herring as his assistant. Herring was no newcomer to flight studies. Born into a wealthy Georgia family in 1865, he had studied engineering at the Stevens Institute of Technology in Hoboken, but did not graduate. He worked at a variety of jobs following the collapse of his consulting firm in the panic of 1893, but his real love was aeronautics.[8]

During the early 1890s Herring had constructed several unsuccessful gliders, as well as one very interesting biplane flying model powered by rubber strands. In the spring of 1894 he began work on the first of three successful gliders based on original Lilienthal plans obtained from Germany. Short flights made with these machines came to Chanute's attention as a result of an article on the subject in the New York press. The initial involvement of the two men was short-lived. Herring left Chanute's employ in May 1895 for Langley's more lucrative Aerodrome program at the Smithsonian.

A talented egotist, Herring found it impossible to remain with Langley. The secretary insisted on being informed of every detail, and refused to allow the young engineer the free hand he believed was essential if they were to make progress with the Aerodromes. Langley, for his part, came to regard Herring as an ingrate who made few substantial contributions to the program. In fact, a comparison of the Langley models before and after Herring's short tenure in Washington suggests that he was most responsible for the major changes that led to the successful flights of May 1896.

Herring and Langley reached a parting of the ways in December 1895. Chanute cabled his old assistant as soon as he heard the news, inviting him to join a crew of workmen in Chicago who were constructing a series of gliders that would be tested in the Indiana Dunes that summer. Herring accepted, and agreed to bring the remains of his last Lilienthal glider with him.

Chanute had developed a multiwing design. The workmen dubbed the craft the "Katydid." Even Chanute had to admit that the profusion of wings, struts, and wires gave it a distinctly insectlike appearance. The machine featured twelve wings—each six feet long by three feet wide—set on either side of the fuselage. The original plan called for positioning eight wings in front, and four wings at the rear.

William Avery, a carpenter in Chanute's neighborhood, had constructed the Katydid and decided to stay on to fly the craft. William Paul Butusov, an emigrant Russian seaman who had come to Chanute

in the summer of 1895 claiming to have made fabulously successful
secret glider flights in the wooded hills near Mammoth Cave, Kentucky, was the third member of the team.

They were comfortably ensconced in a camp pitched deep in the
dunes by late afternoon on June 22, 1896. Herring assembled, rigged,
and made a first short tentative flight with his Lilienthal before dusk.
Chanute's hopes of keeping their activity a secret were dashed when
an observant stationmaster at Miller wired news of their arrival to the
Chicago *Tribune*. A reporter showed up in camp the next morning.
Before the week was out, Chanute had joined Langley on the front
pages of American newspapers.

Chanute, at sixty-four, did not glide at all. Herring made most of
the early flights, with Avery and Butusov taking over the piloting on
occasion. The performance of the two gliders was disappointing. The
Lilienthal proved to be awkward, dangerous, and difficult to control.
The Katydid was no better: the best flights obtained during the first
period on the dunes were under one hundred feet in length.

The party returned to Chicago on the Fourth of July, disappointed
by bad weather, the poor performance of the gliders, and the plague
of reporters that had descended on the camp. They remained in the
city for a month and a half. Avery repaired the multiplane, while
Butusov constructed a glider of his own—the Albatross. Herring
spent his time building what would prove to be the most important
and influential hang glider of all time.

During his spare time on the dunes, Herring had flown a small
monoplane kite with a flexible cruciform tail that had much impressed
Chanute. As the older man later recalled, he had discussed with Herring the possibility of building another glider loosely based on the
kite. They had agreed that the craft would also feature another idea
that Herring had been toying with—a cruciform tail, free to move in
any direction so as to maintain stability. Chanute provided some simple sketches and asked Herring to work out the details.

That was not the way Herring remembered it. He pointed to the
striking resemblance between the 1896 "two-surface" glider and
some models that he had flown in New York in 1892, and three years
later at the Smithsonian. Albert Zahm, who was teaching physics at
Catholic University in 1895, had seen those models, and agreed with
Herring. In 1908 he went so far as to comment: "It is sometimes said
that the best French airplanes are copied from the Americans . . .

Chanute and his young assistants tested a variety of machines on the Dunes. Augustus Moore Herring is shown here with the famous "two-surface" design. The dogs were Chanute family pets, Rags and Tatters.

Farman's airplane resembles the Wright brothers; theirs resembles Chanute's glider of 1896, and this in turn resembles Herring's rubber driven model. . . ."[9]

It is clear that Herring played a more important role than was generally recognized at the time. He was responsible for the cruciform tail unit, and may well have suggested the general configuration. Chanute financed construction; contributed to the general design; and provided the all-important Pratt truss system, a combination of solid struts and flexible wires that transformed the structure into a single beam that would resist bending or torsion.

It was a simple, elegant design, quite unlike the studied complexity of the Katydid, or Butusov's enormous Albatross, which resembled a cross between a gigantic bird and a sailing schooner. All three craft were shipped back to the lakeshore by boat in mid-August. This time the camp was established five miles farther down the beach in the hope of avoiding reporters.

Flight testing, which began on August 29, convinced the group that the triplane wings of the new glider provided too much lift at the front of the structure. In the wake of Lilienthal's death in Germany only three weeks before, this was cause for serious concern. Avery suggested removing the bottom wing to produce the final "two-surface" configuration.

With that accomplished, longer flights of over 150 feet became commonplace within a day or two. Eventually, the distance through the air grew to 359 feet, with the machine remaining aloft for up to 14 seconds. While the Katydid and the Albatross, which was to be launched into the air from a huge ski-jump ramp, proved less than successful, the little group was overjoyed with the performance of the small biplane. Their craft was much superior to the famed gliders constructed by Lilienthal. They had taken a major step forward.[9]

Flights continued until the rough weather set in that September. The Chicago newsmen located the second camp as easily as they had the first, and were soon spreading word of the new glider. Octave Chanute, long famous among the small circle of international aeronautical enthusiasts, now became a public celebrity. The invention of the airplane, no longer a subject of jest, seemed to be just around the corner.[10]

chapter 12

WINDMILLS OF THE MIND

August 1896-July 1899

T he typhoid struck suddenly late in August 1896. Katharine, preparing to leave for her junior year at Oberlin, was convinced that Orville had contracted the illness from a tainted well just inside the rear door of the bicycle shop. His condition deteriorated rapidly. By the end of the month Orville hovered near death. His temperature reached a peak of 105.5 degrees, then fell, finally stabilizing at 103. Dr. Spitler offered little encouragement. The infection would have to run its course.

Bishop Wright was, as usual, absent from home on a church trip. He had actually packed his bags and left for the station when he received Katharine's wire, then thought better of it. There was very little he could do. He instructed Katharine and Wilbur to seal the suspect pump, and to first boil, then chill any water consumed at home. They were to move Orville to the best room in the house and sponge him "gently and quickly with least exposure, followed by rapid friction."[1]

Orville spent September deep in delirium. Katharine and Wilbur took turns sitting by his bed, feeding him a steady diet of milk and beef broth. Milton, who returned home on September 4, divided his time between assisting with Orville's care and catching up on church and family business.

Whenever possible, he spent his evenings "with Lorin's." Young Milton, Lorin's eldest and his grandfather's favorite, excited by the festivities being staged to mark Dayton's centennial anniversary, marched back and forth for the bishop, demonstrating "how the drum major keeps time and how the soldiers drill."

Daytonians were feeling very proud of themselves. Folks in the East could no longer look down their noses at the citizens of a state that had dominated the national political scene for the past quarter of a century, contributing five of the seven Presidents elected between 1868 and 1900.

Still, honest Daytonians had to admit that their own Gem City was the very definition of an average American place. The precise center of U.S. population in 1870, Dayton remained at the statistical center of the top one hundred American municipalities surveyed in the Census of 1900: the fifth largest city in the state, the forty-fifth largest in the nation.

After one hundred years, this most typical of American cities seemed poised on the brink of unprecedented expansion and prosperity. The population had doubled between 1870 and 1880, then increased by another 60 percent to reach 80,000 in 1896. Most Daytonians were employed in the one thousand factories, machine shops, and foundries that dotted the city. Dayton was a national center for the production of farm implements, bicycles, metal castings, and railroad cars.

By the 1890s, however, the National Cash Register Company—"the Cash"—dwarfed all other Dayton employers. The cash register was born in the Empire Restaurant at 10 South Main in 1878. Discouraged by slow sales, inventor James Ritty sold his patents to local businessman John H. Patterson in 1883. A marketing genius, Patterson created a sales team, armed them with a spiel that no merchant could resist, and turned them loose on an unsuspecting world. The firm was selling 13,500 registers a year by 1890. Patterson was well on his way to becoming a legend, and Dayton had acquired a new economic backbone.

Change was sweeping over the city. Dayton boasted twelve miles of paved streets; municipal water, gas, and sewer lines extending into every corner of the city; and a skyscraper, the eleven-story Riebold Building. A complex web of telephone and electric power lines had been spun above the streets. You could board a streetcar on the West Side, transfer to an interurban train, and travel to every corner of the state—and beyond—in record time.

Dayton's pride in all these achievements was wrapped up in the great Centennial Celebration, which opened at Van Cleve Park on September 14, 1896. As one observer noted, the three days of speeches, pageantry, and parades "outdid anything that Dayton, or even some larger and older cities, had ever witnessed."

Orville missed the entire event. Milton kept his room supplied with fresh flowers, while Wilbur and Katharine read to him. He was unconscious most of the time, and the reading was, as much as anything, a means of helping them to pass the time while they nursed their brother.

Wilbur welcomed the opportunity for some quiet thinking. Late in August he had run across a short item in the paper that startled and intrigued him: Otto Lilienthal was dead.

Wilbur had thought a great deal about Lilienthal over the past several years. It had begun with the helicopter toy. Neither he nor his brother had ever forgotten the sense of awe and wonder inspired by the sight of the little thing bobbing up and down against the ceiling. Thereafter, they paid particular attention to bits of aeronautical news in the papers.

They had first run across Lilienthal's name when they were producing *The Evening Item*. In July 1890, the news service to which they subscribed had included an item on him. Will recast it in humorous terms and carried the article in the issue of July 26:

"Needs More Wings"
A German named Lilienthal, after experimenting for 23 years with artificial wings, has succeeded in raising himself, weighing 160 pounds, with the aid of a counter weight, lifting 80 pounds. How to raise the other 80 pounds is still beyond him.

They did not forget Lilienthal. One account of his exploits, an article entitled "The Flying Man" that appeared in the September 1894 issue of *McClure's Magazine*, was especially intriguing. Now he was gone.

For Wilbur, it was a turning point. "My own active interest in aeronautical problems dates back to the death of Lilienthal in 1896," he reported a few years later. "The brief notice of his death which appeared in the telegraphic news at that time aroused a passive interest which had existed from my childhood, and led me to take down from the shelves of our home library a book on *Animal Mechanism* by Prof. Marey, which I had already read several times."[2]

Wilbur must have leafed through that book as he sat by Orville's bed. It was a disappointment. Etienne Jules Marey, a French physician and photographer, had included a few photographs of birds in the air, but provided no clues as to the basic mechanism of flight.

Orville's fever broke early the next month. On October 8 he sat up in bed for the first time in six weeks. Tapioca and other soft foods replaced the milk and beef broth. Everyone in the house could begin to relax. Katharine, already late for the fall term, left for Oberlin the next morning. Milton caught a train for Marion, Ohio, where he met with the local Brethren and attended an enthusiastic Bryan meeting at the fairground. The bishop noted laconically that "a man jumped onto my head off the Fairground fence, but did not kill me."[3]

Orville was still too weak to return to the bicycle shop. As he lay in bed, Wilbur brought him up to date on what had happened during his illness. They spent some time discussing Lilienthal's death. Wilbur may also have mentioned the other bits of aeronautical news. Langley, back at work at the Smithsonian after a summer vacation, had flown another of his Aerodromes. Augustus Herring had returned alone to the Indiana Dunes in the early fall and flown his own copy of the Chanute-Herring two-surface glider that had proven so successful earlier in the summer.

The questions were obvious. What sort of catastrophe could have taken the life of Lilienthal, a man with two thousand glides to his credit? Who would replace him? What of Langley and Chanute? Would their successes lead to continued efforts to develop a full-scale powered machine? What did the future hold for those who sought to fly?

The spark of curiosity flickered over the next two years, but it did not die. "In the early spring of 1899," Orville recalled two decades later, "our interest in the subject was again aroused through the reading of a book on ornithology." The book was probably James Bell Pettigrew's *Animal Locomotion, or Walking, Swimming and Flying, With a Dissertation on Aeronautics.* Wilbur once told Octave Chanute that he had read Pettigrew's work. It is the only other book either of them mentioned as having been among their earliest research.

In any event, the study of flight in nature was important to them at the outset. "We could not understand that there was anything about a bird that could not be built on a larger scale and used by man," Orville explained. "If the bird's wings would sustain it in the air without the use of any muscular effort, we did not see why man could not be sustained by the same means."[4]

Much later, Wilbur would corroborate Orville's belief:

My brother and I became seriously interested in the problem of human flight in 1899. . . . We knew that men had by common consent adopted human flight as the standard of impossibility. When a man said, "It can't be done; a man might as well try to fly," he was understood as expressing the final limit of impossibility. Our own growing belief that man might nevertheless learn to fly was based on the idea that while thousands of the most dissimilar body structures, such as insects, fish, reptiles, birds and mammals, were flying every day at pleasure, it was reasonable to suppose that man might also fly. . . . We accordingly decided to write to the Smithsonian Institution and inquire for the best books relating to the subject.[5]

Richard Rathbun, assistant to Samuel Pierpont Langley, received that letter on the morning of June 2, 1899. The letterhead indicated that the correspondent, Wilbur Wright, was, with his brother Orville, the proprietor of the Wright Cycle Company at 1127 West Third Street in Dayton, Ohio. The fellow came straight to the point: "I have been interested in the problem of mechanical and human flight ever since as a boy I constructed a number of bats of various sizes after the style of Cayley's and Pénaud's machines. My observations since have only convinced me more firmly that human flight is possible and practicable." It was "only a question of knowledge and skill." The final success, when it came, would not be the work of any single individual. Rather, he believed, "the experiments and investigations of a large number of independent workers will result in the accumulation of information and knowledge and skill which will finally lead to accomplished flight."

Wilbur assured the officials of the Smithsonian that he was serious. "I am an enthusiast," he admitted, "but not a crank in the sense that I have some pet theories as to the proper construction of a flying machine." He wished only to avail himself "of all that is already known and then if possible to add my mite to help on the future worker who will attain final success." To achieve that goal, he requested copies of "such papers as the Smithsonian Institution has published on this subject, and if possible a list of other works in print in the English language."[6]

Rathbun scarcely gave Wilbur's letter a second thought. Since Langley's success with the small Aerodromes in 1896, the Institution had been flooded with a steady stream of letters from would-be aviators. The announcement in 1898 that the secretary had received a grant of $50,000 from the U.S. Army Board of Ordnance and Fortification for the construction of a full-scale, man-carrying version of the

Aerodrome flown at Quantico did little to improve the situation. Every aeronautical crank in the nation was now aware that the Smithsonian Institution had money to spend on flying-machine experiments. At least this latest enthusiast had not included the usual plea for government funding.

Rathbun prepared a quick answer to the letter, and passed it on to a clerk who gathered together the handful of pamphlets to be enclosed. They were reprints of articles originally published in the *Smithsonian Annual Report:* Louis-Pierre Mouillard's "Empire of the Air"; Otto Lilienthal's "The Problem of Flying and Practical Experiments in Soaring"; Samuel P. Langley's "The Story of Experiments in Mechanical Flight"; and E.C. Huffaker's "On Soaring Flight."

In addition, Rathbun included a few suggestions for further reading: Octave Chanute, *Progress in Flying Machines;* Samuel Pierpont Langley, *Experiments in Aerodynamics;* and James Howard Means, *The Aeronautical Annual.* The Langley, he noted, could be purchased from the Smithsonian for one dollar, postage included. The entire package was in the mail to Dayton the next morning. Wilbur wrote back the following week, offering his thanks for the prompt service and placing an order for *Experiments in Aerodynamics.*

It was the most important exchange of correspondence in the history of the Smithsonian. The receipt of those pamphlets set in motion a chain of events that would culminate in the invention of the airplane.

Wilbur's letter deserves close attention, for it contains a number of important clues suggesting how the brothers were drawn into the flying-machine problem. Consider, for example, the fact that the letter is written in the first person singular. There is no indication that Orville was also interested in flight.

In later years the brothers would claim that Wilbur had simply written "I" when he meant "we," but Wilbur was well aware of Orville's touchiness on the subject of an equal division of labor, profits, and credit. Had aeronautics been a joint interest in 1899, Wilbur would have spoken in the plural.

When Wilbur wrote to his father on September 3, 1900, admitting for the first time that he was actually going to fly a glider at a place called Kitty Hawk, he did not mention Orville's involvement. In her own letter to Milton, Katharine said that, "If they can arrange it, Orv will go down as soon as Will gets the machine [the glider] ready." That statement alone indicates how secondary Orville was at the outset. He was never one to remain behind tending the store when there was work to be done on a project that really interested him.[7]

Small wonder that Milton would always believe Wilbur had "drawn" Orville into "the flying machine problem."[8] It is true that the bishop's assessments must be accepted with caution. As a father, he made every effort to avoid favoring one son over the other, always insisting that "they are equal in their inventions, neither claiming any superiority over the other." At the same time, he found it impossible to disguise his belief that Wilbur was the more talented of the two, and the senior partner in their joint enterprises. A decade later he wrote to Wilbur, then flying in France,

> I think that, aside from the value of your life to yourself and to our-
> selves, you owe it to the world, that you should avoid all unnecessary
> personal risks. Your death, or even becoming an invalid, would seriously
> affect the progress of aeronautical science. . . . Outside of your contacts
> and your aviations, you have much that no one else can do so well. And,
> alone, Orville would be crippled and burdened.[9]

Orville, who was seriously injured while flying at Fort Myer, Virginia, during this period, did not receive a similar letter. The following year Milton told Katharine, who was traveling with her brothers in Europe, "It does not make much difference about you, but Wilbur ought to keep out of all balloon rides. Success seems to hang on him. . . ."[10] And at the time of Wilbur's death in 1912, Milton noted: "In memory and intellect there was none like him."[11] The best he could say of Orville was that his "mind grew steadily, and in invention, he was fully the equal of his brother."[12]

Any impression of Wilbur's dominance vanished abruptly after the fall of 1900. From that time forward, the brothers made a concerted effort to present a corporate personality to the world. Regardless of which one generated a piece of "official" correspondence, it was invariably written in the first person plural. They held all funds in a joint account. Checks were signed "The Wright Brothers," with a small "OW" or "WW" to indicate which of the two had written the check.

In order to understand why the Wrights attempted to disguise Wilbur's initial leadership, one must recall how all the members of this family defined their relationships through formal and informal covenants and agreements. It was a lesson learned from their father. From Milton's point of view, the Liberal attempt to breach an existing agreement, the Church Constitution of 1841, had necessitated the

United Brethren schism. The mock trial over the division of labor at the print shop indicates the extent to which adherence to agreed conditions was essential for good relations within the family. The strength of the lifelong bond between Milton, Wilbur, Orville, and Katharine suggests an unspoken but no less binding agreement to remain together as a mutually supporting family unit.

The strongest of all the ties within the family, those binding Wilbur and Orville, can only be understood within this context. Once Orville had fully committed himself to the flying-machine experiments, there was a firm understanding between them that Wilbur's initial leadership would be ignored. Otherwise, no matter how significant Orville's later contribution, he would always appear to have been in some sense the lesser member of the team.

The sequence of events seems clear. Memories of a childhood toy, coupled with a few books and some newspaper articles, set in motion a process that would end with the development of the first practical airplane. The reality was far more complex. Thousands of Pénaud helicopter toys had been sold in America, and millions of people around the globe were sufficiently fascinated by flight in nature to read an occasional book on the subject. Very few of them attempted to build their own wings.

Wilbur's peculiarly receptive frame of mind had set the Wrights apart. As he explained to his sister-in-law Lulu, he was much troubled by the fact that he had not been able to take advantage of those talents in which he "excelled other men." He had made a detached assessment of his own personality and knew his strengths and weaknesses. But he had never tried to put that knowledge to work for himself.

Wilbur was thirty-two years old in the spring of 1899. He realized that now was the time. He needed a challenge, a measure of himself— a problem that matched his skills and abilities.

The recognition that flight was such a problem did not come in a blinding flash of insight, but grew slowly during the years 1896–99. By the time he wrote to the Smithsonian, however, he had already made his decision. He would conduct a series of aeronautical experiments, picking up where Lilienthal, Chanute, and Pilcher had left off, and adding his own "mite" to the accumulation of engineering knowledge on which the final solution would be based. Wilbur had absolutely no idea how close that final solution was, but he assumed it was so distant he would not be involved in attaining it.

He began with a thorough course of readings based on the Smithsonian materials and Rathbun's suggestions. He obtained a copy of Chanute's *Progress in Flying Machines,* located copies of the *Aeronautical Annual* for 1895, 1896, and 1897, and read through back issues of popular magazines in search of flying-machine articles.

His initial foray into the morass of conflicting opinion, speculation, and guesswork that passed for the literature of aeronautics was an education. "Contrary to our previous impression," Wilbur observed,

> we found that men of the very highest standing in the profession of science and invention had attempted to solve the problem. . . . But one by one, they had been compelled to confess themselves beaten, and had discontinued their efforts. In studying their failures we found many points of interest to us.
>
> At that time there was no flying art in the proper sense of the word, but only a flying problem. Thousands of men had thought about flying machines and a few had even built machines which they called flying machines, but these were guilty of almost everything except flying. Thousands of pages had been written on the so-called science of flying, but for the most part the ideas set forth, like the designs for machines, were mere speculations and probably ninety per cent was false. Consequently those who tried to study the science of aerodynamics knew not what to believe and what not to believe. Things which seemed reasonable were often found to be untrue, and things which seemed unreasonable were sometimes true. Under this condition of affairs students were accustomed to pay little attention to things that they had not personally tested.[13]

Wilbur spent three months, from June to August 1899, sifting through the chaff of aeronautical history and theory to arrive at a far more accurate understanding of the state of the art than men like Langley and Chanute who had spent decades in the field and written books on the subject. How did he do it?

Wilbur was a man who established a goal with care, then never lost sight of it. He was the perfect engineer—isolating a basic problem, defining it in the most precise terms, and identifying the missing bits of information that would enable him to solve it. Other students of the subject lost themselves in a welter of confusing detail; they were lured into extraneous, if fascinating, blind alleys that led away from the basic problem. Not Wilbur. He had the capacity to recognize and the dogged determination required to cut straight to the heart of any matter.

Some experimenters—Langley, for example—had come to the field with their own preconceptions and cared little for the lessons to be learned from previous theorists. Chanute, on the other hand, had attempted to gather all the available information on the subject as an end in itself.

Instead, Wilbur went to the books in search of answers to the most fundamental issues. What did one *have* to know to fly? What portions of the flying-machine problem were well in hand? What problems remained to be solved? He emerged from his reading with the answers to those questions. Incredible as it may seem, no other major experimenter had taken such a reasonable approach to the work of his predecessors.

Wilbur summarized his conclusions in a lecture to a group of Chicago engineers in the fall of 1901. "The difficulties which obstruct the pathway to success in flying machine construction are of three general classes," he noted. Such a machine would require wings that would lift it into the air; a power plant to move it forward with sufficient speed so that the air flowing over the wings would generate that lift; and a means of controlling the machine in the air.[14]

It seemed obvious that the basic solutions to the first two problems had already been achieved. Lilienthal, Langley, Chanute, and others had actually constructed wings that would lift them into the air. More important, Wilbur knew how they had done it. During the course of his reading, he had found the simple equations and the precise engineering data that would enable him to design his own wings when the time came. As his work progressed, he would undoubtedly encounter unknown aerodynamic problems, but he was confident that the groundwork was in place.

The same was true of power plant research. Langley's steam-powered Aerodromes of 1896 had made unquestioned free flights of impressive length powered by onboard engines. Obviously the little Langley steam engines could not be used to power a full-scale machine, but the success of 1896 had demonstrated that it was possible to build an engine and propeller combination that would propel a set of wings into the air.

Over the next few years automobile experimenters would be concentrating all their energies to develop lighter and more powerful internal combustion engines. When Wilbur needed a power plant, the technology would be there for the taking.

Not all his contemporaries agreed with that. Samuel Pierpont Langley would spend the greater part of his time and resources between

1898 and 1903 developing the perfect aeronautical engine. He believed that surplus power would be required to overcome unforeseen aerodynamic inefficiencies.

Wilbur would have none of that. Long before he built a powered machine, he would have calculated precisely how much horsepower would be required to fly it. He would provide just that much, plus a bit of a margin, and trust to his calculations. The key difference between the attitude of these two men can be seen in their approach to the power plant question. Time would prove Wilbur Wright correct, and Langley disastrously wrong.

Wilbur's brilliant analysis of the flying-machine problem had led him to the area of balance and control. So far as he was concerned, in the summer of 1899 "the problem of equilibrium constituted the problem of flight itself." This area he would make his own.

There were good reasons why the fundamentals of aerodynamic control remained a mystery. To conduct research on active control systems, one had first to be able to fly. Model wings could be tested in flight, or in the safety of the laboratory; the power of an engine and the thrust of a propeller could be measured on the ground. But to test a control system one needed a flying machine large enough to carry a human being who could operate those controls.

The complexity of the joint issues of aircraft stability and control, and the inability to break out traditional modes of thinking, also worked to retard serious advances. The airplane was the first vehicle that would require control in three axes of motion. These axes can best be understood as three imaginary lines around which a machine in the air is free to rotate: Pitch (a horizontal line running from wingtip to wingtip); roll (a horizontal line running through the center of the craft from nose to tail); and yaw (a vertical line running directly through the center of the craft).

It was relatively easy to visualize the need to control an aircraft in yaw and pitch, and to imagine how that might be accomplished. The lessons of surface transportation could be applied directly: it seemed obvious, for example, that a rudder placed on the tail of a flying machine would function in the same way that it did on a ship. Going one step further, a horizontal rudder, or elevator, should enable an aviator to turn the nose of his craft up or down to climb or descend. Elevators already served precisely that function on primitive submarines.

In fact, the control of pitch and yaw would prove much more difficult in actual practice. As the Wrights were to discover, an aircraft rudder and a ship's rudder function in different ways. And while the elevator worked roughly as predicted, determining its optimum size and placement would prove the most difficult of the many control issues that the Wright brothers faced, and the last to be resolved.

Roll control was uniquely difficult—the fact that it might be necessary or desirable to control this axis did not even occur to many experimenters. Everyone realized there would have to be a means of balancing the wingtips, but men and women accustomed to the engineering of surface transportation rarely considered that a pilot might actually want to induce a roll.

The conceptual problems and the impossibility of testing any control system without first learning to fly were serious enough. But lurking behind them was the notion that it might not be wise to trust the operator with full control of his machine. Things would happen so quickly in the air. There would be no opportunity to pull over to the side of the road to think a while. Could a human being remain alert and capable of reacting instantly to sudden potentially catastrophic changes in the attitude of the craft? Would it not be better to design an inherently stable aircraft, one that would fly a straight and steady course, automatically maintaining equilibrium in all three axes? The pilot would intervene only when a change in direction or altitude was required.

Between 1875 and 1900, the search for stability dominated the development of active control systems. Octave Chanute, for example, had sought inherent stability in pitch and roll by means of the confusing array of multiplane wings rocking back and forth on the Katydid, and the spring-mounted cruciform tail of the 1896 two-surface machine.

Samuel Langley had actually achieved automatic stability in his 1896 Aerodromes. As an experimenter working with flying models, he had little choice but to do so; any model airplane flying free of control from the ground must be inherently stable. It must resist any force acting to move it from straight and level flight, and have some capacity to restore its balance if upset by wind gusts, for there is no pilot on board to operate controls.

Such inherent stability was not as difficult to achieve as one might suppose. Alphonse Pénaud had demonstrated automatic stability as early as 1871 with a series of small models powered by twisted skeins of rubber. A simple four-bladed tail was an essential element of the design. The two vertical vanes on the top and bottom of the tail provided yaw stability, tending to keep the model pointed into the wind. Pitch stability was achieved by mounting the tail at a slight negative angle to the horizontal. This forced the nose up, which, Pénaud reasoned, was considerably better than having it pointed down.

But Pénaud's most interesting contribution was his means of achieving roll stability. He gave the wings a slight dihedral, angling the tips up from the center of the machine. When the airplane was flying in balance, the airflow over the right and left wings was equal. If the craft tipped to one side, however, the low wing would move into a position parallel to the airstream, thus increasing the lift on that side and raising the wing back into equilibrium.

Langley incorporated all of the Pénaud features into his steam-powered Aerodromes of 1896, and planned to follow the same pattern in the large manned machine he was constructing for the Army. The Great Aerodrome, as it was already known, would have no provision for roll control. The pilot would be able to move the tail up and down for takeoff and landing; he would also have some control over a large rudder centered beneath the craft. Under normal circumstances, however, he would keep his hands completely away from the controls. In point of fact, Langley was building the world's largest model airplane.

Wilbur's philosophy of control was diametrically opposed to Langley's. He believed that the operator of any vehicle ought to have a means of controlling the motion of his craft in every available axis— an idea firmly rooted in his experience as a cyclist.

The bicycle differs from all other surface vehicles in that it is inherently unstable in both yaw and roll. The cyclist must steer with the handlebars while at the same time maintaining lateral balance through subtle shifts in body position that will keep the machine upright. It was just as James Means had suggested: "To learn to wheel one must learn to balance. To learn to fly one must learn to balance."[15]

Wilbur's intuitive grasp enabled him to move beyond Means's simple notion of balance to a recognition of the positive virtue of absolute control. He realized that one could take advantage of the subtle links between control in roll and yaw to produce a more maneuverable, and therefore safer, aircraft. The operator of the Langley Aerodrome would have to negotiate wide flat turns with the rudder alone; the wingtips might dip slightly into the turn, but would automatically balance themselves once again as a result of dihedral. How much better and safer, Wilbur thought, to have the ability to intentionally lean, or roll, into a much tighter and fully controlled turn—as with a bicycle.

This essential truth had escaped Wilbur's predecessors in the field. His grasp of the control issue is a perfect illustration of his approach to technical problem solving. He had an extraordinary ability—perhaps genius is the word—to mix essential principles involved in a given mechanical situation, and to apply that understanding to the solution of problems which, on the surface, seemed quite unrelated.

It was an intuitive process, based on visual and tactile perceptions. What Wilbur could see and feel, he could understand. Consider, for example, the way he reduced the complex business of turning a bicycle to the left into a series of concrete, graphic images:

> I have asked dozens of bicycle riders how they turn to the left. I have never found a single person who stated all the facts correctly when first asked. They almost invariably said that to turn to the left, they turned the handlebar to the left and as a result made a turn to the left. But on further questioning them, some would agree that they first turned the handlebar a little to the right, and then as the machine inclined to the left, they turned the handlebar to the left and as a result made the circle, inclining inwardly.[16]

The development of a system to control an airplane in flight rested on this foundation—Wilbur's understanding of how a bicycle is turned to the left.

chapter 13

"A FRACTIOUS HORSE"

June–September 1899

C ontrol was everything. But what sort of experimental approach
would enable Wilbur to balance a machine in the air?

"After reading the pamphlets sent to us by the Smithsonian,"
Orville recalled, "we became highly enthusiastic with the idea of
gliding as a sport." While the notion of rushing through the air at
breakneck speed must have appealed to these two cyclists, there were
better reasons to follow Lilienthal and Pilcher, the two most experienced gliding pioneers. Gliding was perfectly suited to Wilbur's intuitive grasp of the links between flying and cycling. Continued practice
was the only way to devise, test, and refine an effective control system, while at the same time exploring the remaining aerodynamic and
structural problems.[1]

"Now there are two ways of learning how to ride a fractious horse,"
he explained to the Chicago engineers in 1901.

One is to get on him and learn by actual practice how each motion and
trick may be best met; the other is to sit on a fence and watch the beast
a while, and then retire to the house and at leisure figure out the best
way of overcoming his jumps and kicks. The latter system is the safest; but the former, on the whole, turns out the larger proportion of
good riders. It is very much the same in learning to ride a flying machine; if you are looking for perfect safety, you will do well to sit on
the fence and watch the birds; but if you really wish to learn, you
must mount a machine and become acquainted with its tricks by actual trial.[2]

171

It was easy enough to speak of bucking horses, or bicycles, but Lilienthal and Pilcher had both died in accidents. The problem lay in the means of control. The pioneers had flown hang gliders, with weight shifting as their only means of control. It was an imprecise, uncertain, and dangerous technique. The pilot who threw his legs in the wrong direction in a moment of panic or confusion might send his machine skittering into an irreversible attitude. That had happened to Lilienthal.

Moreover, weight shifting placed an absolute limit on the span and area of the wings. With a craft any larger than Lilienthal's, a shift in the position of the pilot's legs would not alter the center of gravity sufficiently to change the attitude of the glider.

Unwilling to risk his life aboard an unsafe machine of limited size, Wilbur was determined to build his glider around an effective mechanical control system. Roll control would be the major problem. There were no mechanical analogies on which he could draw.

His first clues came from observations of bird flight. "I . . . conceive Lilienthal's apparatus to be inadequate," he told Chanute, "not only from the fact that he failed, but my observations . . . convince me that birds use more positive and energetic methods of regaining equilibrium than that of shifting the center of gravity."[3]

Wilbur believed that birds balanced themselves in roll by altering the aerodynamic characteristics of their wings. But how? Could the shape or position of a wing be altered so as to mimic the attitude of a bird in flight? It did not take him long to come up with the answer.

> The thought came to me that possibly it adjusted the tips of its wings . . . so as to present one tip at a positive angle and the other at a negative angle, thus . . . turning itself into an animated windmill, and that when its body had revolved . . . as far as it wished, it reversed the process and started turning the other way. The balance was controlled by utilizing dynamic reactions of the air instead of shifting weight.[4]

A bird balanced by turning the forward edge of one wingtip up and the other down. The image of "an animated windmill" stuck in Wilbur's mind. "Here," he noted, "was the silent birth of all that underlies human flight."[5]

Now there was a new problem. How could the same thing be achieved with man-made wings? It came to Wilbur while working alone in the bicycle shop one day in July 1899. He picked up a rectangular inner-tube box from which the end tabs had been ripped, and began idly twisting it in his hand. Twisting . . . that was the answer.

Rather than treating each wingtip as an independent unit, he would throw a complete helical twist across the entire wing structure in either direction.

A simple cardboard box suggested a mechanical analogue to the twist of a bird's wing. Wilbur's graphic imagination, the extraordinary path that led from his hand and eye to his mind, was at work once again.

Orville was taking Katharine and Harriet Silliman, a visiting Oberlin classmate, around town that day. Wilbur explained the principle when they returned that evening. "We began construction of a model embodying the principle demonstrated with the paper box within a day or two," Orville recalled.[6]

The small model of split bamboo, paper, and strings convinced Wilbur that he could achieve the required torsion with the sort of structure he had in mind. After playing with it for a few days, he set to work on a biplane kite with a span of five feet and a chord (straight-line distance from the leading edge to the trailing edge) of thirteen inches. The two wings were trussed together with six struts, jointed at the top and bottom, and wires crisscrossing between the wings along the leading and trailing edges. There was no fore and aft trussing. A fixed elevator was attached to the midpoint of the central trailing edge strut.

He would control the kite with a stick held upright in each hand. Fixed lengths of line ran from the top and bottom of each forward outboard strut to the bottom and top of the control sticks. When the operator tipped the upper end of both sticks toward the machine in the air, the top surface would move to the rear, causing the average center of pressure on the wings to shift behind the center of gravity. The kite would nose up. An opposite motion of the sticks would result in a dive. Pointing the top of one stick toward the kite while pointing the other away from it would cause the little craft to roll off to one side. Reverse the sticks and it would roll off to the other side.

Work on the kite was under way at the end of the first week in July, when Bishop Wright brought his young grandson Milton up the backstairs of the bike shop for an inspection. On July 24, Orville, Katharine, Harriet Silliman, Agnes Osborn, and a few of their friends set out on a chaperoned camping trip. When the tent housing the male campers blew down in a storm, everyone crowded into the remaining shelter for the rest of the night. From that point on, Camp Rain-in-the-Face was enshrined in West Side legend.[7]

Wilbur visited the camp on Sunday, August 6. He drew Orville aside, the others recalled, engaging him in animated conversation. The kite worked. Wilbur had flown it the week before. It dived, climbed, and rolled to the right and left on command. John and Walt Reinieger and some of the other neighborhood boys had tagged along. At one point Wilbur put the kite into too steep a dive, causing the lines to go slack. The boys threw themselves to the ground as the little craft swooped down at them.

"We felt that the model had demonstrated the efficiency of our system of control," Orville noted. "After a little time we decided to experiment with a man-carrying machine embodying the principles of lateral control used in the kite model already flown."[8]

It was a major decision, not lightly made. It was one thing to send a small kite darting about the sky, and quite another to risk one's life aboard such a craft. Still, if they moved slowly, the danger might be contained.

Wilbur outlined his plan confidently to Chanute:

> I shall in a suitable locality erect a light tower of about one hundred and fifty feet high. A rope passing over a pulley at the top will serve as a sort of kite string. It will be so counterbalanced that when the rope is drawn out one hundred & fifty feet it will sustain a pull equal to the weight of the operator and apparatus, or nearly so. The wind will blow the machine out from the base of the tower and the weight will be sustained partly by the upward pull of the rope and partly by the lift of the wind. . . .[9]

"In this way," Orville noted, "we thought we would be able to stay in the air for hours at a time, getting . . . a maximum of practice with a minimum of effort."[10] Lilienthal had spent a total of several hours in the air—ten seconds at a time over a period of six years. He had made two thousand sweeps down a hundred hills, each flight over in the blink of an eye.

Wilbur hoped to soar at the end of a kite line until he became adept at the controls. While kiting offered "no guarantees," he thought it would enable him to "escape accident long enough to acquire skill sufficient to prevent accident."

That was the plan. Accomplishing it was another matter. Wilbur at least knew where to begin. During his research he had uncovered two equations and some precise data that would allow him to engineer his flying machine.

Engineering was the key. The Wright brothers functioned as engineers, not as scientists. Science, the drive to understand the ultimate principles at work in the universe, had little to do with the invention of the airplane. A scientist would have asked the most basic questions. How does the wing of a bird generate lift? What are the physical laws that explain the phenomena of flight?

The answers to those questions were not available to Wilbur and Orville Wright, or to anyone else at the turn of the century. Airplanes would be flying for a full quarter century before physicists and mathematicians could explain why wings worked.

How was it possible to build a flying machine without first understanding the principles involved? In the late twentieth century, we regard the flow of technological marvels from basic scientific research as the natural order of things. But this relationship between what one scholar, Edwin Layton, has described as the "mirror image twins" of science and technology is a relatively new phenomenon. Historically, technological advance has more often preceded and even inspired scientific understanding.

The roots of the flying machine lie not in scientific theory, but in the experimental work of a group of eighteenth-century engineers who were interested in windmills. The Englishman John Smeaton—a founder of modern engineering—was the most important. A native of Whitlock, near Leeds, his list of achievements includes the rebuilding of the Eddystone Light; navigational improvements to rivers and the draining of the Fens; strengthening the piers of the old London Bridge; the design of a pumping engine to provide water for London; the construction of the bridges at Perth, Coldstream, Banff, and Hexham; water-supply systems for Edinburgh, Deptford, and Greenwich; preliminary work on the Forth and Clyde Canal; and the design of lighthouses and harbor improvements for St. Ives in Cornwall, and Ramsgate.

Smeaton also made important contributions to engineering research. His experimental studies of optimum piston size and stroke, cylinder volume, and engine operating temperatures led to basic improvements in steam engine design. He was not concerned with underlying physical principles—the why of the thing. Instead, he produced tables of precise engineering data to assist his colleagues in designing more efficient engines. In so doing, he provided a starting point for the theoreticians who would found the science of thermodynamics.

Smeaton took precisely the same approach to increasing the efficiency of windmill blades. His most important contributions were embodied in a 1759 paper for which he received the Royal Society's Gold Medal. Smeaton had no interest in flying machines, yet his work was crucial to the early history of aeronautics.

For Smeaton, precision measurement was the key to understanding. Like Wilbur, he asked specific questions. How much pressure was exerted on a plate immersed in a fluid stream? How much lift was generated? How much resistance was encountered? Did a change in the size or shape of a plate affect its efficiency? Did the magnitude of the forces alter with a change in the velocity of the stream?

He conceived instruments that would measure minute shifts in speed and pressure, devised whirling arms that would rotate their various test surfaces rapidly through the air, and observed the changing patterns of the water flowing past objects placed in test tanks. Clever fingers and a quick eye could coax a surprising amount of information out of such primitive apparatus.

Smeaton did not gather random information. His goal was to help engineers design blades that would extract a maximum amount of work from the energy of wind and water. Such a man would want to know the total amount of fluid pressure on his blade. Smeaton could help him there. As an appendix to his paper, he included a table showing the coefficient of air pressure (.005). This number was a standard multiplying factor used to calculate the total air pressure on a surface set at an angle of 90 degrees to a fluid stream.

Smeaton also uncovered the basic relationship between the variables of speed, surface area, and angle of attack. And he studied the efficiency of various blade shapes. The fact that the wings of a bird are cambered, or arched, had been known for centuries, but Smeaton was the first researcher to measure the difference. He had no idea why a cambered surface provided more lift, or upward force, than a flat plate, nor did he really care. It was enough to demonstrate that it was so, and to make the information available to other engineers who could put it to good use.

Sir George Cayley of Brompton Hall, in Kent, was the first man to use the data collected by Smeaton in designing a flying machine. Cayley not only built and flew the first gliders, he also conducted research that confirmed and expanded the findings of his predecessors. From his time to that of the Wright brothers, flying-machine experimenters would continue to depend on the original work of the English engineers.

The most important line of research during the nineteenth century involved the study of the lift and drag (resistance) encountered by specific airfoil (wing cross-sectional) shapes through a range of angles of attack. Unlike the coefficient of air pressure, these figures (soon to be known as the coefficients of lift and drift, or drag) were not constant multiplying factors, but experimentally determined numbers that varied for each wing shape at each angle of attack.

Virtually every major experimenter undertook to determine these figures for himself. It was this drive to test a variety of surfaces under different conditions that had led Wenham and his colleague John Browning to the invention of the wind tunnel. The early tunnels were nothing more than long empty boxes with both ends removed. A fan blew a stream of air over a test surface, while the operator did his best to measure the forces at work.

By the time the Wrights entered the field, so many studies had been conducted that it was no longer easy to differentiate between accurate data and the faulty product of flawed experiments. Whatever information an experimenter chose to trust, at least the equations for using this data to predict the behavior of a wing were well established.[11]

Wilbur and Orville discovered two formulas in the published work of Lilienthal and Chanute—one for calculating the lift that would be produced by a particular wing under certain conditions, and the other for predicting the amount of drag. The basic lift equation looks daunting to the lay eye:

$$L = k \times S \times V^2 \times C_L$$

Broken down into its components, the equation becomes easier to understand:

$$
\begin{aligned}
L &= \text{Lift in pounds} \\
k &= \text{Coefficient of air pressure} \\
S &= \text{Total area of lifting surface} \\
V^2 &= \text{Velocity (headwind plus air speed) squared} \\
C_L &= \text{Coefficient of lift}
\end{aligned}
$$

Wilbur began solving the equation by inserting two pieces of information he believed to be valid. He knew that John Smeaton had established a figure of .005 as the coefficient of air pressure. Other experimenters had disputed that value, but the Smeaton coefficient remained in common use. Lilienthal and Chanute had both employed this figure in their calculations and they had flown. That was good enough for the Wrights.

Values for the coefficient of lift were much less certain. The lift coefficient (C_L in the equation) varied with every airfoil shape (wing cross-section), at every angle of attack. Once again, the Wrights decided to put their faith in Lilienthal's results.

The German experimenter had conducted his own airfoil research before building his first glider, and had included a table of coefficients for lift and drag through a range of angles of attack in an article entitled "Sailing Flight," published in the *Aeronautical Annual* for 1896. Referring to that table, Wilbur found the lift coefficient for the range of relatively low angles of attack at which he would be operating—7 to 10 degrees. He began his calculation with the coefficient (0.825) given for an angle of 10 degrees.

The coefficient might only be accurate for an airfoil precisely like Lilienthal's—a circular arc with a camber of 1 in 12. Which is to say, the chordline, an imaginary straight line running from the leading to the trailing edge of the wing, was twelve times as long as the distance from the chord to the top of the arch at the center of the wing. The Wrights did not intend to copy the Lilienthal airfoil so closely, but they assumed that the performance of the wing shape they did construct would be approximately the same.

Using the equation was now a matter of give and take. Wilbur's first step was to estimate the total amount of weight his craft would have to lift—his own weight, one hundred forty pounds, plus the weight of the machine itself. A quick check of the tables of weights of materials available in a standard engineering handbook indicated that his kite/glider would weigh perhaps fifty pounds. One hundred and ninety pounds would be the goal—the total amount he planned to lift into the sky.

Next, he had to choose a reasonable velocity—the speed of the wind in which he would fly. A few trial calculations indicated that he would have to operate in a headwind of 10 to 20 miles per hour. A wind velocity as low as 10 miles per hour would require an enormous wing; a 20-mile per hour wind sounded positively dangerous. He used a compromise figure of 15 miles per hour in his calculations.

With these decisions made, Wilbur solved the equation for an estimate of the amount of wing surface area that would be required to operate under his conditions:

$$L = k \times S \times V^2 \times C_L$$
$$190 \text{ (total weight)} = .005 \times S \times 225 \text{ (15 mph 2)} \times .825$$

(from Lilienthal table)

$$190 = .928 \times S$$
$$S = 190/.928$$
Surface area $= 204.74$ square feet

The use of the equation was a first step in the design process. Wilbur now knew that a craft weighing one hundred ninety pounds, with a surface area of 200 square feet, would fly in a 15-mile per hour wind. How was he to arrange that surface area?

He had decided that the Chanute biplane glider of 1896 was a distinct improvement over the classic Lilienthal monoplane. Moreover, that design seemed made to order for his wing-twisting control system. Cables linking the front and rear edges of the upper and lower wingtips would connect to a foot control. It was a closed system. By shifting his feet to one side the pilot would pull the trailing edge of the wingtip on one side down, while allowing the leading edge of the tip on the opposite side to rise. The entire wing structure could be twisted to the right, recentered, and twisted to the left at will—just like the cardboard box and the kite.

A great deal of thought went into the design of the airfoil for those wings. Lilienthal, Chanute, and most other experimenters had used the simplest curvature—the arc of a circle. Their wings were evenly curved from front to rear, with the peak of the arch falling at the midpoint. The Wrights chose a different pattern, moving the peak forward to a point only three or four inches back from the leading edge. In addition, they would build a much shallower wing, with a camber of only $\frac{1}{23}$, as opposed to the $\frac{1}{12}$ selected by Lilienthal and others.

These changes, they realized, might invalidate the Lilienthal lift coefficients on which they had calculated their wing design. They took that chance because of a fear that the wind striking the broad forward slope of the deep Lilienthal wing would significantly increase its resistance. A shallower camber, with a sharp initial rise to a peak much closer to the front, ought to reduce the problem, producing a more stable wing.

They placed an elevator in front of the wings rather than at the rear of the craft, as they had with the small fixed surface of the 1899 kite. French experimenters would refer to such a machine as a canard, because of its resemblance to a duck in flight, with its small head carried far forward at the end of a long neck. The Wrights did not invent that design, but it was not the obvious choice.

Why did they choose the canard pattern? Imagine a board standing on one edge with its flat face to the wind. The center of the wind pressure (CP) is on a line running the length of the board at the very center. As the top, or leading edge, of the board is brought forward, angling the surface toward the horizontal, the center of pressure moves forward as well. Less surface area is being exposed. As the angle of attack decreases, the CP continues to move toward the front until, when the board is horizontal, the CP rests on the narrow leading edge, the only surface now exposed to the wind.

Earlier theorists had assumed that CP would travel to the leading edge of a cambered wing at a zero angle of attack, just as it did on a flat board. If so, the Wrights reasoned that a forward elevator would be more effective than one on the tail of the craft. If the CP moved forward onto the elevator itself, pitch control would become much more precise than if the surface was located at the rear. A surface set forward of the wings with a slightly negative angle of attack when at rest might also provide some pitch stability.

The rough lineaments of the first Wright glider were in place by the end of September 1899, three months after Wilbur had sent his first letter to the Smithsonian. Having determined to fly, he was not wasting any time. He would tackle the construction problems one by one as the work progressed. The conception—the design—was the important thing. And in that area Wilbur now felt a real confidence.

chapter 14

"KITTY HAWK, O KITTY"

October 1899-October 1900

T he construction of the machine would have to wait a while. The brothers spent the fall and winter of 1899–1900 assembling their next year's stock of Wright bicycles. Business at the shop would keep them busy through the following spring and summer.

Wilbur was able to devote a few idle hours to the selection of a testing ground. The kite/glider could not be flown in Dayton—the machine would not lift in a wind of much less than 12 to 15 miles per hour. If Wilbur was to remain in the air for any length of time, he had to find a spot where there were strong, steady winds day in and day out. The ideal site would also offer seclusion, hills for gliding, and soft sand to ease the shock of landing.

Casting about for advice, Wilbur wrote to Octave Chanute for the first time on May 13, 1900. He was familiar with Chanute's work, having read *Progress in Flying Machines* and a handful of his magazine articles. Wilbur introduced himself with characteristic humor as a fellow "afflicted with the belief that flight is possible to man. My disease has increased in severity," he added, "and I feel that it will soon cost me an increased amount of money, if not my life."[1]

He explained that the bicycle business required his full attention for nine months each year. Any "experimental work" had to be confined to the slack months from September to January. Wilbur asked for comment on his plan to kite a man-carrying machine from a tower, adding that he would be "particularly thankful for advice as to a suitable locality where I could depend on winds of about fifteen miles per hour without rain or too inclement weather."

Chanute, always happy to welcome a new enthusiast, sent a prompt reply. He was encouraging, but did not fully approve of Wilbur's plan for tethering his machine to a tower. Restraining ropes were both an unnecessary complication and a safety hazard.

As for a test site, Chanute "preferred preliminary learning on a sand hill and trying ambitious feats over water." San Diego, California, and St. James City, Florida, both offered constant offshore winds, but neither had the advantage of sand. Some other spot "on the Atlantic coast of South Carolina or Georgia" might be preferable.[2]

Wilbur refused to indulge in guesswork when he could lay his hands on solid fact. He wrote to the U.S. Weather Bureau in Washington requesting information on prevailing wind conditions in various parts of the United States. Bureau chief Willis Moore responded by sending the August and September 1899 numbers of the official *Monthly Weather Review*. The September issue, which included articles on several experimental instrument kite programs and a table of the average hourly wind velocities recorded at 120 Weather Bureau stations, was especially interesting.[3]

The table confirmed that Chicago was the windiest city, with an average daily velocity of 16.9 miles per hour for the month of September. But Wilbur had already rejected Chicago, and all other urban areas. Chanute's experience in 1896 had shown that any flying-machine experiments conducted near a city would immediately attract the attention of the press, something Wilbur hoped to avoid at all cost. Nor could any of the other four stations recording average winds of over 13.5 miles per hour meet the requirements of isolation, suitable hills, and sand.

Moving down the list, Wilbur discovered that the sixth-highest average wind in the United States (13.4 mph) had been recorded at Kitty Hawk, North Carolina. He had never heard of the place. Few people had. Still, while the average wind was on the low side for the calculated performance of the planned kite/glider, additional tables in the journal indicated that Kitty Hawk offered a reasonable number of clear, rain-free days each fall, with occasional winds much above the average. It would bear looking into.[4]

On August 3, 1900, Wilbur wrote to the Weather Bureau office at Kitty Hawk. Joseph J. Dosher, the sole bureau employee there, sent a short reply indicating that the beach near his station was a mile wide and clear of trees and other obstructions. The winds in September and October blew from the north and northeast. Wilbur could board in the village, but housing would be a problem—he would have to bring a tent and camp out.[5]

As an afterthought, Dosher passed Wilbur's letter on to William J. Tate, a local postmaster, notary, and Currituck County commissioner. Bill Tate responded on his own, mentioning the "relative fitness of Kitty Hawk as a place to practice or experiment with a flying machine, etc."

> In answering, I would say that you would find here nearly any type of ground you could wish; you could, for instance, get a stretch of sandy land one mile by five with a bare hill in the center 80 feet high, not a tree or bush anywhere to break the evenness of the wind current. This in my opinion would be a fine place; our winds are always steady, generally from 10 to 20 miles velocity per hour.

Tate was obviously a man of some warmth. He closed his letter with an invitation that was difficult to resist: "If you decide to try your machine here & come, I will take pleasure in doing all I can for your convenience & success & pleasure, & I assure you you will find a hospitable people when you come among us."[6] Kitty Hawk it would be.

On August 10, Wilbur told Chanute that "It is my intention to begin shortly the construction of a full-size glider." The work of building this machine was split between Dayton and Kitty Hawk. Before his departure, Wilbur cut, steamed, and bent the ash ribs that would give shape to his wings, and carefully fashioned the fifty or so additional wooden pieces. Components that could not be obtained at Kitty Hawk, including metal fittings and fasteners and spools of the 15-gauge spring steel wire for trussing the wings, were purchased at home and packaged for shipment. Yards of glistening sateen fabric were cut and sewn into the panels that would cover the finished wings.

Unable to find long pieces of spruce for the main wing spars and elevator support at a local lumberyard, Wilbur asked Chanute for advice. He recommended a Chicago lumberyard, but suggested that the material could surely be obtained in Cincinnati.[7] Rather than continuing the search at home, Wilbur decided to take a chance on being able to purchase the spars cut to size in Norfolk, Virginia, the largest city on his route to the Outer Banks.

Wilbur could no longer avoid breaking the news to Milton. The bishop was aware of his son's interest in flight, but he had no idea that Wilbur planned to take to the air himself. "I am intending to start in a few days for a trip to the coast of North Carolina in the vicinity of Roanoke Island, for the purpose of making some experiments with a flying machine," Wilbur admitted on September 3.

> It is my belief that flight is possible, and, while I am taking up the investigation for pleasure rather than profit, I think there is a slight possibility of achieving fame and fortune from it. It is almost the only great problem which has not been pursued by a multitude of investigators, and therefore carried to a point where further progress is very difficult. I am certain I can reach a point much in advance of any previous workers in the field even if complete success is not attained just at present. At any rate, I shall have an outing of several weeks and see a part of the world I have never before visited.[8]

We have no way of knowing how Milton, always so concerned about the physical welfare of his children, reacted to the news. Katharine tried to soften the blow, following Will's letter with one of her own two days later. "We are in an uproar getting Will off," she noted. "The trip will do him good. I don't think he will be reckless. If they can arrange it, Orv will go down as soon as Will gets the machine ready."[9]

Wilbur boarded a Big Four train at Union Station at six-thirty on the evening of Thursday, September 6. He was setting off on the great adventure of his life. Other than the trip to the World's Columbian Exposition in 1893, he had ventured no farther than a bicycle ride from Dayton in the past decade. Now he was traveling southeast through the night toward the most remote and isolated spot on the East Coast of the United States.

Arriving at Old Point Comfort at six o'clock the following evening, he loaded his gear onto the steamer *Pennsylvania* for the short trip across historic Hampton Roads, where the James and York rivers flow across the mouth of the Chesapeake Bay into the Atlantic. Saturday morning was spent in a futile search for the spruce wing spars. He had no more luck in Norfolk than in Dayton. Close to collapse in the humid, 100-degree heat of Indian summer on the Virginia peninsula, Wilbur finally settled for white pine spars. Even so, he could only find the substitute material in sixteen-foot lengths, two feet shorter than required for a wing designed to fly in a 12-mile per hour wind. He would simply have to wait for a wind above 15 miles per hour.

Wilbur had studied his maps, and knew that here in Norfolk he was within sixty miles of his destination. Kitty Hawk lay midway down the

first leg of a long ribbon of sand that began at the southern edge of
the city and ran south in a great arc paralleling the coast of North
Carolina. These were the fabled Outer Banks, a thin chain of barrier
sand islands ranging from a few hundred feet at the narrowest point
to perhaps three or four miles at the widest, broken by a series of
channels or inlets that connected the wild Atlantic to the shallow
inland sounds separating the back of the Banks from the swampy
wilderness of mainland Carolina.

But there was no way for a traveler to make his way down the
length of the Banks; there were no roads, and no bridges across the
inlets or the sounds. Wilbur boarded another train that carried him
south to Elizabeth City, North Carolina, a few miles above the spot
where the Pasquotank River entered Albermarle Sound.

Arriving at four-thirty on the afternoon of September 8, he checked
into the Arlington Hotel and visited the city docks to find out the price
of transport to Kitty Hawk. Wilbur was startled to discover that "no
one seemed to know anything about the place, or how to get there."
Not until Tuesday, the 11th, was he able to find a boatman, Israel
Perry, willing to ferry him down the Sound and across the head of
Roanoke Island to the Outer Banks. Perry explained that his boat, a
flat-bottomed fishing schooner, was anchored three miles down the
Pasquotank, in the relatively deep water mid-channel just inside the
entrance to the Sound.

"We started in his skiff," Wilbur recalled,

> which was loaded to the gunwale with three men, my heavy trunk and
> lumber. The boat leaked very badly and frequently dipped water, but by
> constant bailing we managed to reach the schooner in safety. The
> weather was very fine with a light west wind blowing. When I mounted
> the deck of the larger boat I discovered at a glance that it was in worse
> condition if possible than the skiff. The sails were rotten, the ropes badly
> worn and the rudder post half rotted off, and the cabin so dirty and
> vermin-infested that I kept out of it from first to last.[10]

They started down the Pasquotank immediately after dinner in a
wind so light that it was nearly dark by the time they entered the
Sound and turned east toward the Banks. "The water was much
rougher than the light wind would have led us to expect," Wilbur
noted. "Israel spoke of it several times and seemed a little uneasy."
The reason for the skipper's unease became apparent when the wind
shifted to the south and east and began to grow stronger. Even a
landlubber like Wilbur could see that Perry's flat-bottomed scow, with

its large deck cabin and light load, was ill-equipped to make its way against the growing headwind. "The waves which were now running quite high struck the boat from below with a heavy shock and threw it back about as fast as it went forward. The leeway was greater than the headway. The strain of rolling and pitching sprang a leak and this, together with what water came over the bow at times, made it necessary to bail frequently."[11]

By eleven o'clock that night high winds were driving the boat dangerously close to the north shore. Perry was struggling to make his way past the North Point light so that he could swing up into the channel of the North River and take shelter behind the point. Just as they drew abreast of the river, a gust blew the foresail loose from the boom with a "terrible roar." "The boy and I finally succeeded in taking it in," Wilbur reported in his journal,

> ... though it was rather dangerous work in the dark with the boat rolling so badly. By the time we had reached a point even with the end of the point it became doubtful whether we would be able to round the light, which lay at the end of a bar extending out a quarter of a mile from the shore. The suspense was ended by another roaring of the canvass as the mainsail also tore loose from the boom, and shook fiercely in the gale. The only chance was to make a straight run over the bar under nothing but a jib, so we took in the mainsail and let the boat swing round stern to the wind. This was a very dangerous maneuver in such a sea but was in some way accomplished without capsizing. The waves were very high on the bar and broke over the stern very badly.[12]

The condition of Perry's schooner belied his seamanship. Stern to the wind, he worked the craft around and back up into the safety of the river channel. The three men—skipper, deck hand, and passenger—collapsed on the deck, drenched by the waves, exhausted but relieved. Through it all, Wilbur maintained his sense of humor. "Israel," he noted, "had been so long a stranger to the touch of water upon his skin that it affects him very much."

They remained at anchor in the North River making repairs until mid-afternoon of the following day. Wilbur, unwilling to touch any of the food aboard the schooner, subsisted on a single jar of jam that Katharine had tucked into his bag.

Looking across the choppy waters in the fading afternoon light of September 12, Wilbur could just make out the dark line of trees that marked the Outer Banks. It was nine o'clock when they tied up at the dock in Kitty Hawk Bay. Venturing ashore for the first time in two

Wilbur and Orville chose the fastness of the North Carolina Dunes for their glider trials. Their hosts, the William Tates, posed for Orville on the front porch of their home in the fall of 1900. Mrs. Tate would manufacture new dresses for her youngest daughters from the wing fabric of the discarded 1900 glider.

days early the next morning, he met a young man who guided him up a sandy lane to the Tates' home, a two-story frame house, sided with unplaned lumber weathered by the elements to a splotchy slate gray.

Wilbur received a warm welcome. He arranged to lodge and board with the Tates, at least temporarily. There was only one request. Having inspected the shallow open well in the yard, Wilbur asked for a pitcher of boiled water each morning, the danger of typhoid never far from his mind.

He set to work immediately, assembling the glider beneath a canvas shelter erected in the Tates' front yard. The woodwork and rigging went quickly enough. Mrs. Tate donated her sewing machine so that Wilbur could cut down the larger panels of wing fabric presewn in Dayton. "I have my machine nearly finished," he reported to Milton on September 23, taking care to assure his father that there was nothing to fear.

> In my experiments I do not to expect to rise many feet from the ground, and in case I am upset there is nothing but soft sand to strike on. I do not intend to take dangerous chances, both because I have no wish to get hurt and because a fall would stop my experimenting, which I would not like at all. The man who wishes to keep at the problem long enough to really learn something positively must not take dangerous risks. Carelessness and overconfidence are usually more dangerous than deliberately accepted risks.

The letter indicates how little Milton knew of his son's plan. Wilbur had to explain that his machine was a glider—"It is not to have a motor, and is not expected to fly in any true sense of the word."[13]

Orv appeared at the Tates' door on Friday, September 28, equipped with a tent and cots, as well as coffee, tea, sugar, and a few other items unavailable in Kitty Hawk. He had talked a young man named Dillon into watching the shop. Cord Ruse would come in periodically to take care of the repair work; Katharine reported with some pride that she and Lorin were "managers."

Orville shared his brother's room at the Tates for a few days, while they were putting the finishing touches on the machine. When complete, the craft had a span of 17 feet 5 inches, with a 5-foot chord and a total surface area of roughly 177 feet, including 12 square feet of forward rudder. The total weight, without a pilot, was just under fifty pounds. The pilot would lay prone in a cutout section of the lower wing, with his feet resting on the T-bar controlling the wing warping. The elevator was fixed at the leading edge. The rear could be flexed up or down with a hand control to govern pitch.

The Wrights moved out of the Tate house on October 4, pitching their tent half a mile away. The weeks and months of dreaming were over. The time had come to test their theories in the laboratory of the sky.

Flight was still a hobby, scarcely more than an excuse for the brothers to take a vacation in a remote place. Perhaps that is why their records of the 1900 experiments are so scanty. Neither of them ever mentioned the day they first left the ground.

It was probably Wednesday, October 3—the day before they set up their camp at the edge of the dunes. On October 14, Orville informed Katharine that they were "having a fine time" and had tried the glider on three different days. He described a crash on the third day, October

With work on the 1900 glider complete, the Wrights pitched a tent on the dunes.

10, that had prevented any further flying since that time. He also mentioned that on Tuesday, October 9, the wind was blowing at 36 miles per hour, surely too high for an attempted flight. October 7 was a Sunday, a day of rest when the brothers always refused to fly in deference to their father.

Joe Dosher's daily weather log indicates that the winds were "light" from Thursday (October 4) through Monday (October 8). Wilbur went aloft on the kite during the first day of testing, and experience would show that a wind of at least 25 miles per hour was required to get the machine into the air with so much weight aboard. Dosher would not regard a 25-mile per hour wind as "light." On Wednesday, October 3, he reported that a "fresh" wind was blowing from the northeast. It was the only possible day in the first two weeks of October when Wilbur could have flown aboard the kite.[14]

They began the morning with a series of unmanned flights. Within a few minutes, Wilbur found it impossible to resist trying his hand. Orville and Bill Tate stood at the right and left sides of the machine, each grasping a wingtip and holding fifteen or twenty feet of coiled line attached to either side of the craft.

Wilbur stood inside the cutout in the lower wing, grasping the two inside lower ribs. At his signal, all three men trotted forward into the wind until the craft began to lift, at which point Wilbur pulled himself aboard, stretching his feet out to the T-bar at the rear and placing his hands on the elevator control.

Orville and Bill Tate began to play out the line as slowly and carefully as possible given the excitement of the moment. Many years later Orville told John McMahon that Wilbur reached an altitude of perhaps fifteen feet on that first foray into the air when the glider began to bob rapidly up and down. Wilbur, experiencing trouble, began to yell: "Let me down!" A sustained tug on both tether ropes settled the craft gently back onto the sand. Orville had difficulty containing himself. Why come down again just when things were getting interesting? Wilbur could only comment: "I promised Pop I'd take care of myself."[15]

Those first few seconds aloft convinced Wilbur of the need to continue testing the glider as an unmanned kite. Typically, he had devised a simple but effective system of instrumentation that enabled him to record all the forces acting on the machine in flight. Joe Dosher had loaned the brothers a hand-held anemometer with which to gauge the wind speed. The pull of the glider on a standard spring fish scale provided a measure of the drag, or total air resistance.

Readings were taken with the craft flying empty in a variety of wind speeds, and loaded with various weights of chain. At times it was flown as a pure kite, with all the controls tied off; more often, additional lines enabled them to control it from the ground.

The test sessions lasted for three to four hours on each of the first two days, after which bad weather and high winds brought a temporary end to the experiments. By the morning of Wednesday, October 10, the wind had fallen to 30 miles per hour. Orville reported that "the Kitty Hawkers were out early peering around the edge of the woods and out of their upstairs windows to see whether our camp was still in existence."[16]

They resumed the kite experiments later that morning, carefully recording the parameters of each flight: the weight of the chain loaded on board; the wind velocity; and the amount of drag encountered. That afternoon they moved the tower to the top of Look-Out Hill, a small rise just south of the village at the edge of the dune field. Orville described their testing procedure to Katharine:

> Well, after erecting a derrick from which to swing our rope with which we fly the machine, we sent it up about 20 feet, at which height we attempt to keep it by the manipulation of the strings to the rudder [elevator]. The greatest difficulty is in keeping it down. It naturally wants to go higher & higher. When it begins to get too high we give it

a pretty strong pull on the ducking string, to which it responds by making a terrific dart for the ground. If nothing is broken we start it up again. This is all practice in the control of the machine.[17]

They had the machine on the ground and were adjusting the control lines when, as Orville recalled, "without a sixteenth of a second's notice, the wind caught under one corner, and quicker than thought, it landed twenty feet away."[18]

It was over in a flash—the right side of the machine was completely smashed. The front and rear struts were broken in several places; the ribs were crushed and the wires snapped. The brothers dragged the pieces back to camp and spoke of going home.

Things looked brighter the next morning. The damage was extensive, but not irreparable. Wilbur and Orville had the woodworking skills, and it would be a shame to abandon the tests so soon. They had been out only three days, and had made only one abortive attempt at a manned ascent.

As Orville reported: "The next three days [October 11, 12, and 13] were spent in repairing, holding the tent down, and hunting; mostly the last. . . ."[19] It was a respite from the excitement of experimentation, and their first opportunity to look around. They were fascinated by what they found.

Wilbur admitted to his father that he looked upon his stay in Kitty Hawk as "a pleasure trip, pure and simple." Both brothers relished the elemental nature of the place. Kitty Hawk was a series of houses and a store or two scattered through the marshy woods along Albermarle Sound; there were no harbors or wharfs in the wild Atlantic surf. The fishing boats put out from villages facing the Albermarle— Kitty Hawk, or Manteo and Wanchese on nearby Roanoke Island— and entered the ocean through Oregon inlet, a few miles to the south.

A few minutes walk along the path leading south out of Kitty Hawk and they were in another world, far from the trees and marsh grass. The three great Kill Devil Hills, enormous mountains of sand, were the first in a series of dunes stretching forty miles down the Banks to Cape Hatteras. There was little vegetation beyond a few stunted trees and shrubs that took root in the wind-blown hollows behind a dune. Many years later, when asked by an artist to describe the place where the world's first airplane had flown, Orville remarked that it was "like the Sahara, or what I imagine the Sahara to be."

They were captivated by the undeniable romance of the region.

Even the place names—Currituck, Albermarle, Pamlico, Nags Head, Wanchese, Manteo, Ocracoke—had an exotic ring to two city boys from Ohio.

The earliest chapters of American history had been written on the shifting sands and shallow waters of Dare and Currituck counties. Giovanni da Verrazano and the crew of *La Dauphine* had cruised this coast in 1524. Verrazano came ashore at the Nags Head Woods, very near the spot where Wilbur and Orville would camp during the years 1901–03. He remarked upon the "sweet savours" of the trees, and kidnapped an Indian lad for presentation at the French court.

The English followed in Verrazano's wake. Gazing across Kitty Hawk Bay, Wilbur could see the lonely pines of Roanoke Island, the site of the first English colony in the New World—the Lost Colony, which vanished without a trace.

Later, this had been Blackbeard's country. The pirate died in a sea battle fought off Ocracoke in 1718. His decapitated body had swum three times around the *Adventure Galley* before sinking beneath the waves, or so the Bankers told the Wrights.

Not all the local pirates had operated at sea. Many of the place names reflected a sinister past. Nags Head and Jockey's Ridge, for example, recalled the exploits of the legendary eighteenth-century wreckers who ventured onto the crests of the dunes leading a horse with a lantern tied around its neck. The bobbing light, resembling the stern post lantern of an inshore vessel, lured mariners onto the treacherous shoals where their cargo could be salvaged.

The origin of other place names remained a puzzle. By Blackbeard's time the spot Verrazano had dubbed Arcadia was already appearing on coastal maps as Chickahauk. Whether this was a corruption of "chicken hawk" or a version of some long-forgotten Indian word is uncertain. Another century would transform it into Kitty Hawk.

It had always been a harsh and unforgiving country. "But the sand! The sand is the greatest thing in Kitty Hawk, and soon will be the only thing," Orville exclaimed. He noted that the dune on which they were camping rested on what had once been a small house—fierce winter storms sweeping across the Banks had buried the homestead beneath a mound of sand. The rotting upper branches of a shade tree protruding above the dune were all that remained to mark the spot. Bill Tate was in the process of tearing down a house near the Wright camp site "to save it from the sand."[20]

The Wrights had never encountered anything like a storm on the Banks. "The wind shaking the roof and sides of the tent sounds exactly like thunder," Orville wrote to Katharine a few days after arriving in Kitty Hawk.About two or three nights a week we have to crawl up at ten or eleven o'clock to hold the tent down. When one of these 45-mile nor'easters strikes us, you can depend on it, there is little sleep in our camp for the night. . . . When we crawl out of the tent to fix things outside the sand fairly blinds us. It blows across the ground in clouds. We certainly can't complain of the place. We came down here for wind and sand, and we have got them.[21]

The winter cold of the Outer Banks cut straight to the bone, as Wilbur told his father later, in November 1903: "In addition to . . . 1, 2, 3 and 4 blanket nights, we now have 5 blanket nights, & 5 blankets & 2 quilts." They ended up at last in "shoes & hats, and finally overcoats."[22]

A plague of black flies and mosquitoes descended on the isolated dune country in the late summer and early fall. "They chewed us through our underwear and socks," Orville would report to Katharine in 1901. "Lumps began swelling up all over our bodies. . . . Misery! Misery!"[23]

But there was another side to the Outer Banks:

> The sunsets here are the prettiest I have ever seen. The clouds light up in all colors in the background, with deep blue clouds of various shapes fringed with gold before. The moon rises in much the same style, and lights up this pile of sand almost like day. I read my watch . . . on moonless nights without the aid of any light other than that of the stars shining on the canvas of the tent.[24]

Ultimately, it was the Bankers themselves who most appealed to the Wrights. They were a wild, undisciplined, and self-reliant lot, eking out a marginal existence by moving from one job to another with the changing seasons—fishing in the spring and summer, hunting in the fall, and a winter's work at one of the U.S. Lifesaving Service Stations located every ten miles or so down the Banks.

There was "little wealth and no luxurious living" in Kitty Hawk. The houses were small and austere. The Tate home, for example, was unpainted inside and out; the floors and ceilings were of unvarnished pine. While clean and comfortable, the furnishings were in stark contrast to the overstuffed Victorian splendor of the Wright parlor. "He has no carpets, very little furniture, no books or pictures," Wilbur reported.

There may be one or two better houses here but his is much above average. . . . A few men have saved up a thousand dollars but this is the savings of a long life. Their yearly income is small. I suppose few of them see two hundred dollars a year. They are friendly and neighborly and I think there is rarely any real suffering among them. The ground here is a very fine sand with no admixture of loam that the eye can detect, yet they attempt to raise beans, corn, turnips, &c. on it. Their success is not great but it is a wonder they can raise anything at all.[25]

Subsistence farming was impossible in the thin, sandy soil, although virtually everyone kept a little vegetable patch. "Our pantry in its most depleted state would be a mammoth affair compared with our Kitty Hawk stores," noted Orville.

Our camp alone exhausts the output of all the henneries within a mile. What little canned goods, such as corn, etc., [there is] is of such a nature that only a Kitty Hawker could down it. Mr. Calhoun, the groceryman, is striving to raise the tastes of the community to better goods, but all in vain. They never had anything good in their lives, and consequently are satisfied with what they have. In all other things they are the same way, satisfied in keeping soul and body together.[26]

"Trying to camp down here reminds me constantly of those poor Arctic explorers," he told Katharine. They appointed Mr. Calhoun their agent, and authorized him "to buy anything he can get hold of, in any quantities he can get, in the line of fish, eggs, wild geese, or ducks."[27]

The brothers, unaccustomed to being thought of as rich men, were startled to discover that their arrangement threatened to destroy the local economy.

The economics of this place were so nicely balanced before our arrival that everybody here could live and yet nothing be wasted. Our presence brought disaster to the whole arrangement. We, having more money than the natives, have been able to buy up the whole egg product of the town and about all the canned goods in the store. I fear some of them will suffer as a result.[28]

Hunting and fishing were the major commercial enterprises. Each season tons of fish were shipped north to Baltimore and other East Coast cities. The late nineteenth century taste for exotic millinery led to the decimation of the local egret and heron colonies.

The Banks were a hunter's paradise. "The people about Kitty Hawk are all Game Hogs," wrote Wilbur. Game laws were universally ignored. Each fall thousands of migratory wild fowl were destroyed by professional hunters armed with small artillery pieces known as punt guns.

In the fall of 1894, six years before Wilbur Wright stepped onto the Kitty Hawk dock for the first time, a young Massachusetts man accompanied one of these boisterous hunting parties to the Outer Banks. The experience made an indelible impression on nineteen-year-old Robert Frost.

Disappointed in love, Frost had left home to see something of the world outside New England. He arrived in Norfolk aboard a coastal steamer, and walked south out of town into the Dismal Swamp. He stumbled across a boat carrying a party of hunters down the Dismal Swamp Canal, which connected Norfolk with Elizabeth City via the Pasquotank River. They invited the young man to join them on the voyage across Albermarle Sound for some duck hunting on the Outer Banks.

"And it was a rough crowd of—of *gentlemen,*" he recalled many years later. "I went with them, without a gun. And I was afraid for my life all the time. They were drinking all the time, you know, and shooting in all directions. Really, really a wild expedition. I didn't think I'd ever see my mother again."[29]

Frost made his way back home, returned to school, and eventually married the girl he thought he had lost. But he would never forget Kitty Hawk. Returning in 1953, the year of the fiftieth anniversary of powered flight, one of his most frankly autobiographical poems recalled his memories of that first trip to "Kitty Hawk, O Kitty," "dark Hatteras," and "sad Roanoke."

When the Wrights came to Kitty Hawk in the first year of the new century, they found an area in the throes of change. Local fishermen still paid tribute to "Mad Mabe," the witch of Nags Head Woods, to ensure fair weather and a good catch. Orville's gasoline cooking stove was a curiosity in the neighborhood "more feared than those 'bars' up on North River, where Israel Perry wouldn't land 'for a thousand dollars.'"[30]

Bill Tate, whom Orville described as "postmaster, farmer, fisherman, and political boss of Kitty Hawk," was particularly intrigued by the Wright camp:

> He gets interested in anything we have. . . . [He] wants to put acetylene gas in his house because he saw my bicycle gas lamp, has decided to buy our gasoline stove when we leave. . . . Mr. Tate would also like to spend

his remaining days—which might be few—in experimenting with flying machines. . . . Tate can't afford to shirk his work to fool around with us, so he attempts to do a day's work in two or three hours so that he can spend the balance with us and the machine.[31]

Dr. Cogswell, Tate's brother-in-law, warned Orville that Captain Bill would "be dead before Christmas from excitement if we don't get out."

The locals were never completely certain what to make of the brothers. They created an enormous splash in the little community. "We need no introduction in Kitty Hawk," Orville remarked. "Every place we go we are called Mr. Wright. Our fame has spread far and wide up and down the beach."[32]

They were likable enough, friendly, invariably well dressed—and polite to a fault. Yet the down-to-earth fishermen of the Outer Banks remained dubious of these two Yankees who arrived at the very onset of the winter storm season and spent their time skimming down the dunes on enormous white-winged contraptions. After all, the Bankers were a "practical, hard-headed lot who believed in a good God . . . a hot hell . . . and, more than anything else, that the same good God did not intend that man should ever fly!"[33]

The Wrights were back in the air with the repaired glider/kite just three days after their accident. They had learned some important lessons. Never again would they attempt to fly the craft from a tower; Chanute had been correct in that regard. Nor would they ever again rig the lower wing at a dihedral angle, as they had, experimentally, during the early trials. Side gusts catching the upturned tips were too much of a problem. From now on the wings would be rigged level, or, as in 1903, with a cathedral, or slight down arch.

They spent the afternoon of October 17 testing the performance of the craft over a wide range of wind and load conditions. Dan Tate, Bill's half brother, pitched in to assist with the trials. They flew the machine empty (fifty pounds), and loaded with twenty-five and fifty pounds of chain.

There was no question of repeating Wilbur's kite ascent of the first day. The machine would not leave the ground under these conditions in anything less than a 25-mile per hour wind. Fortunately, young Tom Tate, Dan's son, was more than willing to take an occasional ride on the kite. The ascents were not made for Tom's amusement: while he weighed forty pounds less than either of the brothers, he pre-

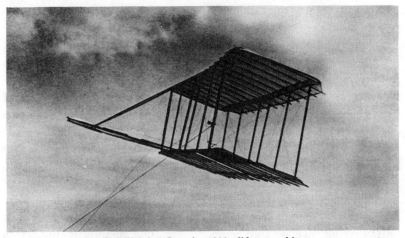

The Wrights flew the 1900 glider as a kite.

sented almost the same surface area to the resistance of the air as did an adult—one more bit of information to be recorded in the notebooks.

The Wrights finished the day with a clear idea of what their machine could and could not do. The result was a puzzling mix of satisfaction and confusion. The overwhelming disappointment was that the machine simply did not generate the amount of lift predicted by Wilbur's calculations. When flown as a kite, the empty craft would not fly in a wind of less than 22 miles per hour. This was 4.5 miles per hour (20 percent) higher than the predicted lift of even the reduced wing. As Wilbur noted, "either the curvature or the area should have been greater."[34]

The problem might indeed be found in the fact that the Wrights were flying with an airfoil camber of only 1 in 23, as opposed to the 1 in 12 favored by Lilienthal and Chanute. Moreover, the camber had grown even flatter as the Wrights' steam-bent ribs gradually straightened out with time. It was a point to be considered in the design of their next machine. For the moment, airfoil design would remain a matter of guesswork. The only sure means of making longer flights in lighter winds was to substantially increase the wing area.

The unmanned tests also gave them an opportunity to explore the control responses of a full-scale machine. Here again, there were problems. Forced to operate the controls from the ground, they discovered that it was very difficult to manipulate the wing-warping and rudder mechanisms simultaneously.

The wing-warping system for lateral control seemed satisfactory, but there were problems with the elevator. "We tried it with the tail [elevator] in front, behind, and every other way," Orville told Katharine. "When we got through, Will was so mixed up that he couldn't even theorize. It has been with considerable effort that I have succeeded in keeping him in the flying business at all. He likes to chase buzzards, thinking they are eagles, and chicken hawks, much better."[35]

Convinced that the mysteries of pitch control would remain unsolved so long as they were restricted to kiting, the brothers were forced to try making free glides. The additional lift generated by a craft moving forward into the wind would be enough to support an adult in flight.

The following day, October 18, they set out for the sand hills a mile or so south of camp, only to find that the wind had died before they arrived. Undaunted, they began tossing their unmanned machine off the brow of a dune to see what would happen. "We were greatly pleased with the results," Orv told Katharine, "excepting a few little accidents to the machine."

> It would glide out over the side [of the dune] at a height of 15 or twenty feet for about 30 feet, gaining, we think, in altitude all the while. After going about 30 feet out, it would sometimes turn up a little too much in front, when it would start back, increasing in speed as it came, and whack the side of the hill with terrific force. The result generally was a broken limb somewhere, but we hastily splint the breaks and go ahead.[36]

The experience of simply tossing the machine loose into the air, watching it fly after a fashion and return to earth without catastrophic damage gave them confidence in its strength, resilience, and basic airworthiness. The next day was perfect for gliding. The technique was the same one used to get Will aloft on the kite the first time. The wing-warping control remained tied off throughout the tests. The two men at the wingtips continued running with the machine as long as possible, depressing a wingtip by hand when necessary. When the machine outran the men at the tips, Wilbur—who made most, if not all, of the flights—landed.

They had originally planned for the pilot to pull himself back into a sitting position for landing. In practice, it proved unnecessary. The prone position looked dangerous but was perfectly safe, except for the occasional mouthful of sand.

The problems with the elevator seemed to vanish completely. Wilbur could bring the craft back to earth with such precision that two thin lines, the tracks of the skids, extended back twenty or thirty feet from the point where the machine finally came to rest.

By the end of the day, glides of three to four hundred feet, lasting as long as fifteen seconds, were commonplace. Wilbur finished the day with a grand total of perhaps two minutes flying time.

But the facts and figures on paper mask the excitement of the moment. The exhilaration was incredible. Racing down the slope, holding his machine within five feet of the surface, Wilbur was traveling twice as fast at the end of a flight as at the beginning. He was flying—experiencing sensations known to only a handful of human beings.

Light winds returned the following day. There would be no more manned glides before they broke camp for the return to Dayton on October 23. The 1900 Wright glider, the machine on which they had first taken to the air, was no longer of any use to them. But the $15 that went into its construction had been money well spent. Repaired many times, the machine was held together by a collection of splints and splices, its once-glistening French sateen fabric patched and grimy.

Just before they boarded Perry's boat for the trip across the Sound, the brothers carried the machine back down the trail going south out of town and gave it one last toss from the top of a dune. It came to rest in a sand hollow. Some weeks later Bill Tate's wife trudged out to the spot with a pair of shears and removed the sateen. She gave it a good wash and fashioned it into two new dresses for the Tate girls.

When the Wrights returned in the fall of 1901, the skeletal remains of one wing could still be seen protruding from the sand. That last piece of the original Wright glider disappeared forever in a 93-mile per hour gale that swept over the Banks on July 25, 1901.

chapter 15

"NOT WITHIN
A THOUSAND YEARS. . ."

October 1900-August 1901

T he news that Wilbur had actually flown at Kitty Hawk surprised Octave Chanute. He had received the first letter from Dayton only six months before. The new correspondent seemed promising enough, a practical man who tempered his enthusiasm with the kind of down-to-earth common sense that appealed to a working engineer. He was particularly impressed by the reduction in drag achieved through the use of the prone pilot position. "This is a magnificent showing," he wrote to Wilbur, "providing you do not plow the ground with your noses."[1]

Chanute hoped that the Wrights would pay attention to his gentle warning. These young men were entirely too daring, stretching themselves out on the lower wing of their machine and flying with a control system that was positively dangerous. Anything other than automatic stability was, he thought, an invitation to disaster.

Then there was this wing-twisting business. Chanute coined the term "wing warping" to describe the Wright technique, but he did not grasp the basic principle. He never would. Whereas Wilbur's experience with cycling had stretched his imagination and focused his attention on the need for active control in all three axes of motion, Chanute's career had limited his thinking.

Safety, strength, and stability were the watchwords on which Chanute had built his distinguished reputation. He had devoted his life to laying thousands of miles of steel rails and had constructed enormous stationary structures—bridges and stockyards. It was not the sort of work that prepared a man to solve the problems of controlling a machine balanced on the head of a pin in the sky.

Some men might have overcome the limitations of personal experience and tradition. Chanute was not one of them. He could conceive the problem of flight control in only two dimensions. The idea of a roll axis did not even occur to him when Wilbur described his notion of twisting the wings to raise or lower the tips. Chanute was convinced that wing warping was nothing more than a means of turning (yawing) a machine in the air by increasing the drag on one side. There was nothing new in that. Louis-Pierre Mouillard, the French experimenter, had employed precisely the same principle in a glider constructed in Egypt in 1896–97. Chanute himself had paid for its construction.[2]

Chanute had no intention of alienating the Wrights. They were so certain that their approach to control was correct, he decided to refrain from comment, avoid potential areas of disagreement, and do what he could to assist them. In time, they would come round to his way of thinking.

The Wrights were puzzled by Chanute's attitude. Had they been in his place, there would have been a thousand questions. How did the pilot actually operate the controls? How were the cables arranged to accomplish the twisting action? How much pressure was required to twist the wings or flex the elevator? What was the reasoning behind that forward elevator?

Chanute had not asked about any of those things, nor had he made any special reference to the problems of balance and control. Apparently he was content to remain in the dark about the most important aspects of the Wright machine.

The brothers took Chanute's measure very early on. Technically, they had already gone beyond him. Sure of their position, they were ready to move on to the next step—the construction of a new, improved glider. The last thing Milton Wright's sons needed was a pat on the back from established authority.

Why then, did the Chanute correspondence remain so important to the Wrights? That it was important—to both parties—can scarcely be doubted. From the time of Wilbur's first note of May 13, 1900, to Chanute's last on May 14, 1910, a total of 435 letters would pass between them. The sheer bulk of the exchange was extraordinary, averaging one letter every eight or nine days over an entire decade.

Consciously or unconsciously, the Wrights used Chanute as a means of sharpening their own thinking. What had really occurred?

Why? In what direction would they move in the future? Why? The need to get it all down on paper, to explain their ideas in terms that were clear enough for another person to understand, became so important that the hours spent at Katharine's desk in the parlor preparing another letter to Chicago were an integral part of the process of invention.

But there were problems. Chanute believed above all in the importance of sharing information. He was quite certain that when the airplane did come, it would be the result of a cooperative effort. While he had encouraged the young engineers with whom he was directly associated to protect their ideas with patents, he also insisted that they make the results of their joint experiments available to the widest possible audience. There was no telling what bit of data might prove crucial to the work of another experimenter.

Chanute hoped that the Wrights would allow him to present the details of their work to the world in the same way. He broached the subject with great care. "I have lately been asked to prepare an article for *Cassier's Magazine,*" he wrote on November 23, 1900, "and I should like your permission to allude to your experiments in such brief and guarded way as you may indicate."[3]

Wilbur hedged, noting that "it is not our intention to make a close secret of our machine, but at the same time, inasmuch as we have not yet had opportunity to test the full possibilities of our methods, we wish to be the first to give them such a test." The Wrights offered to give Chanute any information he wanted for his own use, but asked that there be "no publication in detail of the methods of operation or construction of our machine."[4]

Disappointed but eager to assure them that he could be trusted, Chanute wrote back on November 29, enclosing two pages from the manuscript of his article "covering *all* that I have said about my own experiments, and what I have just added about yours." It described the Wrights' work in a single paragraph focusing on the importance of the prone pilot position in reducing air resistance to one half of that encountered by previous experimenters. Published in the June 1901 issue of *Cassier's* under the title "Aerial Navigation," the article was the first public notice of the Wright aeronautical experiments.

Wilbur published two technical articles of his own that summer. The first, "Angle of Incidence," appeared in the July 1901 issue of *The Aeronautical Journal,* the official organ of the Aeronautical Society of Great Britain. The second article, "Die Wagerechte Lage Während des Gleitfluges" ("The Horizontal Position During Gliding

Flight"), was published that same month in the *Illustrierte Aeronautische Mitteilungen.*

Both articles were short and straightforward. In preparing "Angle of Incidence," Wilbur did not even mention that he had actually conducted flying-machine experiments. The German article was a plain statement of the fact that the author had made landings in the prone position at speeds of up to 20 miles per hour without injury or danger. Wilbur illustrated the piece with a single photograph of the 1900 glider being flown as a kite. That photograph, and a scattering of others over the next two years, would spark a renaissance in European aeronautics. The words of Wilbur and Orville Wright could be ignored or misread, but the message of their photographs was unmistakable. The Wrights were flying.

Wilbur's desire to return to Kitty Hawk with a new machine embodying the lessons of 1900 was apparent in his letters to Chanute. This year they planned to stay longer—for six to eight weeks in September and October—establishing a permanent camp at the Kill Devil Hills, complete with a hangar to house the new glider.[5]

The design of the 1901 machine was complete by mid-May. This time, the brothers refused to cut any corners. In 1900, the calculations had called for a glider with a surface area of over 225 square feet in order to operate in a 15-mile an hour wind. Aware that Kitty Hawk would offer winds averaging only 13–14 mph, the Wrights had nevertheless settled for just 165 square feet of wing. It was a mistake they would not make again. This year they would not only stick to the calculations, they would build in a margin of safety.

With a twenty-two-foot span and a chord of seven feet, the 1901 Wright machine was the largest glider ever flown. The total surface area of 315 square feet, including the elevator, was two and a half times that of the 1900 craft. The area, weight, and other features of the glider matched the calculated requirements for an aircraft flying at a 5-degree angle of attack.

The Wrights removed one more uncertainty, abandoning the shallow wing camber of 1 in 23 employed in 1900. The Lilienthal lift and drag tables were based on an arch of 1 in 12. That was what the Wrights would use.[6]

With the design complete, Wilbur and Orville felt it impossible to postpone getting back into the air. On June 19 they informed Chanute that "changes in our business arrangements" would enable them to leave for Kitty Hawk much earlier than originally planned.[7] That change had come in the person of Charles Taylor.

Charlie was an old friend. Born on May 24, 1868, near Cerro Gordo, Illinois, he had quit school after the seventh grade and worked at a variety of mechanical trades before meeting Henrietta Webbert at the Jolly Young Men and Girls Club in Kearney, Nebraska, in 1892. Four years later, married and finding it difficult to establish themselves in Nebraska, the couple moved to Dayton, where Henrietta's brother said there were jobs to be had. Charlie worked at Stoddard Manufacturing for a time, then established his own machine shop.

The Wrights met Charlie through his brother-in-law, who owned the building where the Wright Cycle Company was located. They liked him at once, and directed business his way. Charlie helped to plan the production of the oil-retaining wheel hub of which the Wrights were so proud, and machined the original coaster brakes for the Van Cleve bicycles.

Eventually Taylor tired of struggling as an independent and took a job with the Dayton Electric Company. Strolling home after work on a hot Saturday night in June 1901, he stopped off to say hello to the Wrights, who were open late that evening. "One of the brothers, I forget which, asked me how I would like to go to work for them," he remembered many years later.

> There were just two of them in the shop and they said they needed another hand. They offered me $18 a week. That was pretty good money; it figured to 30 cents an hour. I was making 25 cents at the Dayton Electric Company, which was about the same as all skilled machinists were getting. The Wright shop was only six blocks from where I lived— at Calm and Grant streets—and I could bicycle to lunch. Besides, I liked the Wrights. So I said all right and I reported in on June 15. That was in 1901.[8]

Katharine always had trouble with Charlie. She found him altogether too sure of himself for a "hired man." Then there were the cigars—Charlie smoked them one after another, consuming up to twenty a day. But Wilbur and Orville knew that Charlie could be counted on to get the job done. They must have been convinced that he was honest as well, for they were about to trust him with their livelihood.

Just a year before, Wilbur had explained to Chanute that they could not afford to allow a hobby to interfere with their business. Now they were hiring Taylor to watch the shop at the height of the season because they could not wait an extra month to resume their experiments. It was out of character—and a clear indication of shifting priorities.

Four days after Charlie started work, Wilbur told Chanute they would leave for Kitty Hawk by July 10. Chanute immediately wired Dayton to ask if he could pay a personal visit on the afternoon of June 26. There was a dinner that evening, but it seems likely that the three men, lost in conversation, scarcely noticed what they were eating. The discussions continued into the next day, right up until Chanute caught the afternoon train for Tennessee, where he planned to visit Edward Chalmers Huffaker, an assistant who was at work on a new glider designed by Chanute.

One of the most experienced and best educated aeronautical experimenters in the United States, Huffaker was a graduate of Emory and Henry College, and held an M.S. in physics from the University of Virginia. His interest in flight was inspired by Langley's work, and that of the American expatriate Hiram Maxim. He had written to Chanute in 1892, describing his own experiments with a series of glider models. Chanute invited the young engineer to offer a paper at the great aeronautical meeting in Chicago.[9]

The Wrights listened politely as Chanute described his contract with Huffaker, unaware that a plan linking them to the Tennessee engineer was already forming in the mind of their guest. While Chanute did not broach the subject, he was a firm believer in the team approach to aeronautics, and regarded his own experience at the Indiana Dunes as a model. By gathering a small group of talented young enthusiasts at an isolated site for a period of intense testing, he had been able both to compare the performance of various glider types and to encourage a cross-fertilization of ideas.

Wilbur and Orville's new round of glider tests offered a golden opportunity to do it all again. Huffaker should be sent to join the brothers at Kitty Hawk with the glider that he was completing. Chanute also had George Spratt, a young physician from Coatesville, Pennsylvania, in mind as a possible team member.[10] Spratt had never constructed a machine or seen a glider fly, but his thoughts on the subject intrigued Chanute.

George Alexander Spratt had first written to Chanute in April 1899. He had been fascinated by flying creatures since boyhood—"Flying has been the dream of my life," he confided. "I never scared a bird up or saw it cross a valley, but what I longed to go with it and envied it." The young man devised an apparatus to measure the lift of curved surfaces, and conducted test flights with a large model glider that proved rather disappointing.

He refused Chanute's offer to pay for the materials to be used in building a full-scale version of his glider, remarking that he would "bungle" the job and waste the money. What better experience than two weeks with the confident Wright brothers?

Chanute recognized that the situation was not precisely what it had been in 1896. The Wright brothers were not his employees, and had no desire to be members of any team. Still, Chanute intended to take full advantage of the fact that they were polite and would be unwilling to offend him.

Two days after leaving Dayton, he wrote to Wilbur, expressing his disappointment in the Huffaker glider. "The mechanical details and connections of the gliding machine . . . are so weak, that I fear they will not stand long enough to test the efficiency of the ideas in its design. . . ."[11]

Indeed, as Chanute described it, the machine sounded like a disaster waiting to happen. Huffaker had constructed the wing struts of cardboard tubing, designed the wings to fold for easy storage, and attached the fabric so as to automatically vary the curvature of the wing with changes in pressure. The Wrights found it difficult not to laugh when they first saw the thing.

Having disarmed the Wrights, Chanute offered a proposal. "If you were not about to experiment, I should abandon the machine without testing, but perhaps it will stand long enough to try it as a kite, and to make a few glides from a height of 15 or 20 feet." If the Wrights thought they could "extract instruction from its failure," he would ask Huffaker to join them at Kitty Hawk at his expense. They could call on Huffaker for assistance with their tests in exchange for their help with his own trials. "The latter," Chanute hastened to add, "I expect to be brief." In addition, Chanute offered to send George Spratt along, "if you think you want more assistance."[12]

Was the letter an offer of help or a call for assistance? The Wrights had no need of help, and would find the presence of two strangers in their camp a trial and an inconvenience. Still, if Chanute was honestly asking for their assistance in testing his craft and training his people, they could not easily refuse.

"As to Mr. Huffaker's trip to Kitty Hawk," Wilbur replied on July 1, "I do not feel competent to advise you, as you alone can judge whether the probable advantage would justify the expense involved." They could not accept Chanute's offer to send Spratt as their helper. "If, however, you wish to get a line on his capacity and aptitude and give him a little experience with a view to utilizing him in your own work later, we will be very glad to have him with us."[13]

Sensing their reluctance, Chanute wrote back on July 3, assuring Wilbur that Spratt was "discreet concerning other people's ideas," and that Huffaker was "quite reliable." "I mention this," he concluded, "as you told me that you have no patents."[14]

Wilbur responded briskly:

We have felt no uneasiness on this point, as we do not think the class of people who are interested in aeronautics would naturally be of a character to act unfairly. The labors of others have been of great benefit to us in obtaining an understanding of the subject and have been suggestive and stimulating. We would be pleased if our labors should be of similar benefit to others. We of course would not wish our ideas and methods appropriated bodily, but if our work suggests ideas to others which they can work out on a different line and reach better results than we do, we will try hard not to feel jealous or that we have been robbed in any way.[15]

The Wrights left for Kitty Hawk on Sunday, July 7. A storm much worse than any they had experienced the previous fall held them in Elizabeth City for several extra days. "Anemometer cups gave way at 93 miles per hour," Wilbur reported to Chanute, " . . . the highest speed [ever] recorded."[16] Just before crossing the Sound they wired traveling instructions to Huffaker and Spratt, and to Chanute, who was also planning to join them.

They reached Kitty Hawk dock on Thursday evening and spent the night at the Tates. The following morning they loaded all their camping equipment and lumber onto a beach cart and drove to the campsite at the Kill Devil Hills, where Will had flown the fall before. They were off to a bad start:

After fooling around all day inside the tent, excepting on a few occasions when we rushed out to drive a few more tent pegs, our thirst became unbearable, and we decided upon driving the Webbert pump, no well where we could get water being within a mile's distance. Well (pun), we got no well; the point came loose down in the sand and, we lost it! Oh misery! Most dead for water and none within a mile! excepting what was coming from the skies. However, we decided to catch a little of this, and placed the dish pan where the water dripped down from the tent roof; and though it tasted somewhat of the soap we had rubbed on the canvas to keep it from mildewing, it pretty well filled a long-felt want.[17]

Work on the hangar for the new glider began on Monday, July 15, and continued for three days. Orv thought it "a grand institution, with awnings at both ends; that is, with big doors hinged at the top, which we swing open and prop up, making an awning the full length of the building at each end. . . ."[18]

Huffaker arrived in camp the following Thursday, "and with him a swarm of mosquitoes which came in a mighty cloud, almost darkening the sun." That, Orville added,

> was the beginning of the most miserable existence I have ever passed through. The agonies of typhoid fever with its attending starvation are as nothing in comparison. But there was no escape. The sand and grass and trees and hills and everything were crawling with them. They chewed us clean through our underwear and socks. Lumps began swelling up all over my body like hen's eggs. We attempted to escape by going to bed, which we did at a little after five o'clock. We put our cots out under the awnings and wrapped up in our blankets with only our noses protruding from the folds. . . . The wind, which until now had been blowing over twenty miles an hour, dropped off entirely. Our blankets then became unbearable. The perspiration would roll off us in torrents. We would partly uncover and the mosquitoes would swoop down upon us in vast multitudes.[19]

The following night, the three campers set up their beds in the open air beneath wooden frames supporting mosquito netting. At first all went well. "But what was our astonishment when in a few minutes we heard a terrific slap and a cry from Mr. Huffaker announcing that the enemy had gained the outer works and he was engaged in a hand-to-hand conflict with them. All our forces were put to complete rout."[20]

The campers finally stumbled upon the expedient of burning old tree stumps, collected from a sand hollow a quarter of a mile from camp, to drive off the mosquitoes. Spratt, who arrived in camp on the evening of July 25, dragged his bedding out into the open, but returned a few minutes later, agreeing that the smoke was preferable to the mosquitoes. Wilbur wrote to Chanute on July 26, hoping to catch him before he left for Kitty Hawk—"You should by all means bring with you from the North eight yards of the finest meshed mosquito bar you can find. Except for the mosquitoes, our camp life has been pleasant but exciting at times."[21]

They finished the glider on July 26. Between the mosquitoes and the midday heat, it had not been an easy task.

They made seventeen glides on Saturday, July 27. As in 1900, Wilbur was the sole pilot. Problems were apparent from the outset. The first flight ended with a quick nose down into the sand. With each trial,

They returned to Kitty Hawk with a new machine in 1901. As in 1900, Wilbur did all the flying. Bill (left) and Dan Tate (right) helped to launch him into the air.

Wilbur moved a few inches more to the rear, attempting to shift the center of gravity farther back and bring the nose up.

The craft remained in the air, but Wilbur, forced to stretch his arm far forward to the control, found that full up or down elevator was still required to maintain command of the machine. "In the 1900 machine," he would later explain, "one fourth as much rudder [elevator] action had been sufficient to give much better control."[22]

Time after time the glider flew an undulating pattern, as Wilbur struggled to maintain an even keel. Twice it climbed rapidly out of control, then stalled, or stopped dead in the air. Screams from the ground sent the pilot scooting rapidly forward toward the leading edge. To everyone's relief, the glider pancaked straight down from an altitude of twenty feet, landing without injury to pilot or machine.

The forward elevator, they realized, had saved the day. That expanse of surface out in front of the main wing had prevented the glider from nosing over or falling off on one wing. It happened again a few minutes later. This time the machine had even begun to fall backward before Will brought the nose down sufficiently to flutter safely back to earth.

This early indication that the forward elevator would help to keep the nose up in a stall was encouraging, but the basic problem remained. As Orv explained to Katharine, "this is precisely the fix

Lilienthal got into when he was killed." For the first time since they had begun their experiments, the brothers were genuinely frightened.

Huffaker, whose aeronautical experience had been limited to some work on the Langley models in 1896, failed to recognize the danger, and regarded their work as an overwhelming success. He was particularly impressed by a long glide of 315 feet in 19 seconds, which he thought was probably the best anyone had ever made. "We think," Orv noted, "that at least three or four better have been made before."[23]

Pitch control was the problem. Wilbur found it impossible not to overcontrol. They reduced the size of the elevator to 10 square feet, reducing the lift at the forward end of the machine and making the elevator a bit less sensitive. It did not help. As in 1900, they decided to pause and gather a full range of data while flying the glider as an unmanned kite before risking any further damage to craft or pilot.

The results were not encouraging. Total lift remained only one third of that predicted by the Lilienthal tables, and the angle of attack was still much higher than expected. Empty, the machine would not kite at an angle as low as 3 or 4 degrees in a wind of less than 23 to 25 miles per hour. Wilbur recorded their disappointment: "As we had expected to devote a major portion of our time to experimenting in an 18-mile wind without much motion of the machine, we find that our hopes of obtaining actual practice in the air reduced to about one-fifth of what we hoped, as now it is necessary to glide in order to get sustaining speed. Five minutes practice in free flight is a good day's record. We have not yet reached so good an average as this even."[24]

Although they had not fully tested the controls, it was apparent that the 1901 machine was less responsive than its predecessor. The brothers attributed this to the deeper camber of the 1901 wing, over which the center of pressure might move more slowly. They were also afraid that the center of pressure was reversing directions at small angles of attack.

That was the heart of the control problem: How to govern the movement of the center of pressure around the center of gravity. The two points coincided when the airplane was flying straight forward in a balanced condition. The elevator and wing-warping controls enabled the pilot to alter the position of the center of pressure to restore balance or to maneuver.

The Wrights had concluded that the airstream striking the upper surface of the deeply curved wings of 1901 not only increased resistance but caused an unexpected reversal of travel of the center of pressure. To confirm their suspicions, they removed the upper wing and kited it separately. At relatively low wind velocities the surface soared high overhead at a steep angle of attack. As the wind velocity increased, the angle of attack decreased and the pull of the kite line approached the horizontal. Finally, in very high winds of over 25 miles per hour, the wing nosed down at a negative angle, forcing the brothers to pull it up off the sand with the tether ropes.

Their fears were confirmed. The deep camber of 1 in 12 was leading to a reversal of the center of pressure at low angles of attack, a condition that created the unexpected pitch problems. In addition, a comparison with the drift measurements made in 1900 showed that the new craft had much greater head resistance. Late in July the Wrights ceased testing and remodeled the machine to correct the defects. They reshaped the leading edge spar and added a new spar near the midpoint of each wing supporting a series of short uprights that were used to truss the ribs into a much shallower camber.

Huffaker had scarcely given a thought to his own machine. His attempts to fly were so pathetic that he had given up early on, abandoning the tattered remnants of the Chanute-Huffaker glider to deteriorate slowly in the sand.

By the time Chanute finally arrived in camp on August 5, Huffaker was brimming over with enthusiasm for the Wrights and their glider. "He is astonished at our mechanical facility," Wilbur noted, "and, as he attributes his own failures to the lack of this, he thinks the problem solved when these difficulties are overcome, while we expect to find further difficulties of a theoretical nature which must be met by new mechanical designs."[25]

Very soon after putting the rebuilt machine back into service on August 8, the Wrights tried a new means of launching the glider, kiting it up to an altitude of twenty or thirty feet in a wind of 17 to 20 miles per hour, then cutting loose to glide back to earth. In this way they hoped to make repeated flights from the sand flats, and avoid the time-consuming drudgery of carrying the craft back uphill after every flight. In practice, however, the machine kited at far too steep an angle for launching a glide.

Reduced to gliding, they were pleasantly surprised to find that Wilbur was able to stretch his distance through the air to 389 feet after only a few trials. More important, the reduction in camber had solved the pitch problem. "The machine with its new curvature never failed to respond promptly to even the smallest movements of the rudder [elevator]. The operator could cause it to almost skim the ground, following the undulations of its surface, or he could cause it to sail out almost on a level with the starting point, and passing high above the foot of the hill, gradually settle down to the ground."[26]

With the pitch control problem solved, the brothers loosened the warping cables for the first time. The foot control of 1900 was replaced by a cradle to which the warping wires were attached. When one wingtip dropped, the pilot would shift his hips, which rested in the cradle, to the high side, restoring balance. The Wrights expected the system to work perfectly, giving them an opportunity to make their first long glides under complete control. Instead, they found themselves, in Wilbur's words, "completely nonplused." They had stumbled across the edge of the most intractable of all their theoretical difficulties. If warping was applied for only a short time, they could maintain balance and make their way downhill. When prolonged warping was induced in an effort to turn, things began to fall rapidly apart.

It was a very difficult thing to put your finger on, as Wilbur later explained. "To the person who has never attempted to control an uncontrollable flying machine in the air, this may seem somewhat strange, but the operator on the machine is so busy manipulating his rudder [elevator] and looking for a soft place to alight, that his ideas of what actually happens are very hazy."[27] He described it as "a peculiar feeling of instability."

Wilbur sensed that the machine was turning, skidding really, toward the wing that presented the most surface to the air. Whatever was happening, it was dangerous. Skimming close to the ground on August 9, the left tip dropped and Wilbur shifted to his right. The craft immediately darted into the sand, throwing him forward through the elevator. The forward surface was badly damaged, and Will suffered facial cuts and bruises.[28]

Chanute left for home on August 11, as the Wrights continued to struggle with the new problem. They returned to unmanned kite tests, loading the machine with sandbags and trying to operate the wing-warping mechanism from the ground. The tests confirmed the existence of the problem, but offered no solutions.

There were a few more free glides on August 15 and 16, but the uncertainty was taking its toll. All of the flights were less than 200 feet in length. Rain had set in, and there seemed little point in continuing. The company was not improving, either. Spratt left camp soon after Chanute. To their surprise, the Wrights liked him. He had a sense of humor, and knew every plant and animal on the Outer Banks. Moreover, Wilbur felt a personal kinship with this man who was struggling with some of the problems he himself had overcome not so many years before.

Huffaker, on the other hand, was priggish, lazy, and given to borrowing personal articles without so much as a by your leave. Will thought Huffaker looked a bit sheepish when he finally left camp. He attributed it to the fact that the Tennessee man was still wearing a shirt he had put on soon after his arrival. "Well," he remarked to Spratt, "some things are rather more amusing to think about than to endure at the time."[29]

The Wrights left Kitty Hawk early on August 22. The atmosphere was very different from their departure the year before. In 1900, while the experiments had not gone exactly as expected, there had been some cause for enthusiasm and much reason for hope. Now they could see only problems. The steps taken to increase the lift of their first machine had failed dismally. They could not understand what was wrong, but they had begun to suspect that there was a fundamental problem with the information they had inherited from Lilienthal and others.

The new difficulty with lateral control was even more disturbing. The Wrights had expected to encounter a great many additional problems, but not with their wing-warping system. They had been absolutely certain of their success in that area. The realization that there was some mysterious problem with the warping mechanism was the worst blow.

"When we left Kitty Hawk at the end of 1901," Wilbur recalled a decade later,

> . . . we doubted that we would ever resume our experiments. Although we had broken the record for distance in gliding, and although Mr. Chanute, who was present at that time, assured us that our results were better than had ever before been attained, yet when we looked at the time and money which we had expended, and considered the progress made and the distance yet to go, we considered our experiments a failure. At this time I made the prediction that men would sometime fly, but that it would not be within our lifetime.[30]

A more colorful phrase stuck in Orville's mind. On the train going home, he recalled, his brother had remarked that "Not within a thousand years would man ever fly!"[31]

chapter 16

TUNNEL VISION

September–December 1901

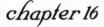

W ilbur and Orville walked through the door of 7 Hawthorn Street unexpectedly on the afternoon of Thursday, August 22. "[They] haven't had much to say about flying," Katharine wrote her father. "They can only talk about how disagreeable Mr. Huffaker was."[1]

Wilbur wrote to Chanute just a week after they were back, admitting his confusion. Would it be possible to locate one of the old 1896–97 Chanute-Herring two-surface machines? "I cannot think of any experiment that would be of greater value in the present muddled state of affairs than an actual measurement, both as a kite and in glides under specially chosen conditions, of some other machine than our 1901 model."[2]

Wilbur, always nervous in the face of uncertainty, suddenly found what he had assumed to be solid ground turning shaky. A substantial error had crept into the lift data accumulated since Smeaton's time. The Wrights had trusted that information, assuming that the success of Lilienthal, Chanute, Langley, Pilcher, was proof of its accuracy. Now it appeared that the machines flown by those men had generated far less lift than had been assumed. The Wright brothers, the first to measure the lift of their machines, were also the first to discover the problem. The performance of their two gliders indicated that the error was in excess of 20 percent. Had they known at the outset that such discrepancies lurked in the data, they would never have begun.

The wing-warping problem had popped up out of nowhere, and was even more disturbing. Wilbur had been certain that the control issue was solved. Suddenly, there was that little "hint of instability," and a profound sense of danger. Wilbur was exasperated. For the first and only time, he doubted—why should he succeed when so many others, better prepared, had failed?

> In view of our own experience and the experience of men like Langley, Lilienthal, Maxim, Chanute and Ader, men almost ideally fitted in mental equipment and training for such work, and having at their command hundreds of thousands of dollars, all of whom, like ourselves, had found the results obtained too small for the effort and money expended, and who had, one by one, abandoned the task before we had taken it up, we felt that similar conditions would probably prevail for a long time, as the problem of stability which had caused all these men to drop the problem, was yet seemingly untouched, so far as a practical solution was concerned.[3]

His self-confidence draining away, Wilbur wondered whether two years of time, money, and effort had been wasted. More to the point, if they decided to continue the work, what should they do next? They were willing to accept an error in the lift tables, but how were they to correct it? And how overcome the difficulty with the lateral control system?

It was time to get their feet back on the ground. Orville would catch up at the bicycle shop, installing some new machine tools and laying in parts and materials for next year's line of bicycles. Wilbur set out to do battle on his father's behalf once again.

For the second time in his career, seventy-two-year-old Milton Wright was moving toward a direct confrontation with most of the other members of his church. The Old Constitution Brethren could scarcely believe it—for them, one schism in a lifetime was enough. But Milton refused to consider the issue in those terms.

The problem was rooted in the years just after the founding of the Old Constitution branch. Milton served as publishing agent from 1889 to 1893, when the press of business relating to the growing number of lawsuits forced him to relinquish that office to concentrate on legal matters. He tried to keep the publishing enterprise within the family, however, proposing his son Wilbur as his successor in the post.

Wilbur lost the election to Millard F. Keiter, a preacher and rising church politician. Perhaps the Brethren, with Milton as their leading bishop and chief legal officer, were reluctant to offer the most important nonclerical position in the church to another Wright. In later

years, Keiter remarked that Bishop Wright's "unrelenting persecu-
tion" of him was a result of that defeat.

Keiter served two terms in office, 1893–1901, and was confident of
being reelected at the General Conference of 1901. Just a month
before the meeting, in April 1901, George D. Crane, a Fort Wayne
accountant, appeared at Keiter's door with an order for a complete
audit of the printing establishment books.

Milton was behind the move. For some months he had been nervous
about Keiter's handling of the publication funds, one of the most
important sources of church revenue. Rumors had circulated that the
publishing agent was dipping into the till to meet his personal needs.

Crane's report confirmed the bishop's worst fears, indicating a
shortage of some $6,800 in the accounts. The publishing board imme-
diately filed a summons with the clerk of the Huntington County,
Indiana, court on April 27, asking that a receiver be appointed to take
charge of all monies and account books until the matter could be
sorted out. The court refused to act, noting that it was up to the
General Conference to arbitrate the matter.

The publishing board controversy threw the conference into turmoil. Keiter was removed from office and the board was instructed to
obtain an official written report from Crane, after which a hearing
would be arranged for Keiter. At the hearing, held in February 1902,
Keiter convinced four board members that the accountant had been
in error, and that any remaining discrepancies were the result of
simple carelessness rather than deliberate fraud. Three other members, led by Milton Wright, refused to accept the explanation.

Milton asked Wilbur to take a look at the books. While not a trained
accountant, Will had a meticulous eye and considerable bookkeeping
experience. He went beyond a strict accounting, comparing Keiter's
published accounts in the annual reports of the printing firm with the
actual books. There were failures to report receipts, deliberate fal-
sifications, and repeated overcharges against church accounts. He
discovered that Keiter had used church funds to pay his own insur-
ance premiums, to purchase personal clothing, and to pay for stone
that went into the construction of his home.

True to form, Milton launched a pamphlet war against Keiter and
his defenders. In 1902 he issued three tracts aimed at winning a
majority of church members to his point of view. Wilbur was closely
involved in the preparation of all three—the first included his long and
detailed signed report on the publishing firm's books.

Acting without the approval of church officials, Milton also petitioned local authorities to take criminal action against Keiter, who was brought to trial for the forgery of a bequest note in the circuit court of Huntington County on April 30, 1902. The case was dismissed a week later. Not only had the Statute of Limitations expired, but there was no reference to the forgery of bequest notes in the Indiana statutes. The decision in a second case also went in Keiter's favor.

Sentiment within the church ran heavily against Bishop Wright. Keiter was not an especially appealing or believable character and few of the Brethren doubted that he was guilty. They were not, however, anxious to admit that one of their chief financial officers had defrauded the church. They had dismissed Keiter from office; any additional steps would only call undue attention to the problem and discourage future gifts. Milton forged ahead, confident that his own judgment was superior to that of the majority.

This time he had gone too far. He admitted to Katharine that old friends spoke of him behind his back as "the egotist," and the "Wise Bishop." In May 1902, Keiter, sensing a backlash against his "persecutor," leveled formal disciplinary charges, accusing Bishop Wright of libel, insubordination, and a breach of the *Discipline*, which urged good Brethren to settle their differences out of court.[4]

The presiding elders of Milton's own Fairmont Circuit appointed a special commission to investigate his conduct. A hearing was scheduled for the annual conference meeting on August 28. Milton, as bishop of the conference, issued a notice postponing the meeting until October, pleading the press of other business. The notice was ignored. Bishops Barnaby and Floyd presided over the hearing in his absence, and approved a verdict of guilty on all three charges. He was ordered to confess his error and apologize to the members of the conference and to the "offended parties" within sixty days—or face indefinite suspension.

Bishop Wright ignored the order, remarking that the session was "so startlingly [sic] out of conformity to all legality and justice that it was not to be regarded as an attempt to carry out law in the church and do justice, but to close the mouth and silence the tongue of a bishop in this church."

There was no effective mechanism for dealing with the problem until the General Conference met once again in 1905. Milton simply continued as though nothing had happened. With two exceptions, he presided over the quarterly and annual meetings of each of the local conferences under his jurisdiction in 1902, 1903, and 1904. His own White River Conference, which officially expelled him from membership in 1903, was one of those exceptions.

As always, Wilbur accepted his father's fight as his own. Through the spring and summer of 1902 he devoted considerable time and energy to the project, conducting the audit of Keiter's books, preparing a long and detailed report, and writing pamphlets. In addition, he made several trips to the administrative center of the White River Conference at Huntington on his father's behalf.

Had the timing of the church crisis been slightly different, the affair might have had a major historical impact. If Wilbur had been drawn away to conduct the audit in the fall of 1901, just after his return from Kitty Hawk, when his energies and enthusiasm were at an ebb, he could have given up on aeronautics. By the spring of 1902, his commitment to the flying-machine puzzle was stronger than ever. He found the time both to assist his father and to move his own work forward.

Octave Chanute deserves the credit for keeping the brothers going after the discouraging season of 1901. His most important contribution was a simple invitation on August 29 for Wilbur to address one of the most distinguished engineering groups in the nation, the Western Society of Engineers.

Wilbur's spirits were low when the invitation arrived. He was inclined to refuse the offer until Katharine "nagged him into going." Chanute sensed Will's waning enthusiasm, and saw the lecture as an opportunity to provide some recognition for his younger friend. Katharine agreed that the opportunity to speak to such a distinguished group would be a tonic for him—"He will get acquainted with some scientific men, and it may do him a lot of good."[5]

Indeed it did. In preparing the speech Wilbur was forced to think through everything that had occurred, going back over the basics and addressing the problems that had seemed so overwhelming after the return from Kitty Hawk. It was an excuse to cover old ground, considering the successes and failures of the past two years. If nothing else, he was determined to leave an accurate record of their efforts. If they did not return to the field, their work might have some value for those who followed.

Chanute added a new wrinkle on September 5—would Wilbur mind if the meeting was designated "ladies night"? "As to the presence of ladies," the speaker responded, "it is not my province to dictate, moreover, I will already be as badly scared as it is possible for a man to be, so that the presence of ladies will make little difference to me, provided I am not expected to appear in full dress, &c."[6]

When Katharine asked Will if his speech was to be "witty or scientific," he replied that "he thought it would be pathetic before he got through with it!" She had a "picnic" getting him off to Chicago on the evening of September 17, dressed in finery borrowed from Orv. "Clothes do make the man," she decided. In his brother's top coat, shirt, collar, cuffs, and cufflinks, "you never saw Will look so swell."[7]

The speech was all that Chanute had hoped. Wilbur spoke to an appreciative crowd of some seventy members and their wives, first outlining the problem, then calling for the lights to be lowered and launching into a description of his experiments illustrated by lantern slides of the 1900 and 1901 machines in the air, and charts showing the process of design. A stenographer was present—Wilbur's corrected version of the text would appear in the *Journal of the Western Society of Engineers*.

Did Wilbur and Chanute pay attention to each other that evening? Their remarks indicate that they were far apart. In introducing Wilbur, Chanute noted that lack of a suitable aeronautical power plant was "the great obstacle in the way. . . ." Wilbur bluntly contradicted him, arguing that when compared to the problems of stability and control, "all other difficulties are of minor importance."[8]

Chanute did take careful note of Wilbur's suggestion that the Lilienthal lift and drag tables were wrong. They had been skirting around this issue for some time. Wilbur finally brought it out into the open for the first time after returning to Chanute's home that evening. Writing to Spratt two days later, he remarked that Chanute's "faith in the Lilienthal tables is beginning to waver though it dies hard."[9]

Working with Wilbur's 1900 and 1901 data, Chanute struggled to explain the discrepancy between actual experience and the performance calculations. After analyzing the results of a single glide of August 8, 1901, he admitted: "I have tried to figure out this glide with the Lilienthal coefficients, but they do not fit at all."[10]

Still, Chanute found it difficult to accept the possibility of a fundamental error in data that had always been thought trustworthy. Perhaps he simply did not understand the mathematical procedures involved. He sent the Wrights a copy of the chapter on Lilienthal's air-pressure tables reprinted in Major Hermann W. L. Moedebeck's *Taschenbuch zum praktischen Gebrauch für Flugtechniker und Luftshiffer*, the standard engineering handbook to which all serious aeronautical experimenters referred, and asked that the brothers double-check his calculations.

Wilbur knew perfectly well that Chanute understood the "mode of calculation." The problem was not with the equation, but with the numbers that were plugged into it. To grasp the difficulty, we must return, as Wilbur and Orville did, to the basic formula devised to calculate lift:

$$L = k \times S \times V^2 \times C_L$$

Recall that in this equation:

L = lift measured in pounds
k = a constant coefficient for air pressure
S = total surface area of the machine in square feet
V = total velocity of the machine (headwind + forward speed)
C_L = a coefficient for lift that varies with the shape of the airfoil surface and the angle of attack

The surface area and velocity were known quantities. The coefficients for air pressure and lift had been inherited from their predecessors.

The Wrights, like Chanute, had followed Lilienthal's practice, using John Smeaton's figure of .005 as the coefficient for air pressure under standard atmospheric conditions. But that figure had been experimentally derived, and not everyone agreed that it was accurate. During the course of his extensive research, Chanute had identified up to fifty separate coefficients ranging from .0027 to Smeaton's very high .005. As Wilbur pointed out in 1908, the variation was not difficult to understand in view of the problems faced in trying to measure minute differences in pressure with primitive instruments.[11]

It occurred to him that both the low lift and the reduced drag of the 1900–01 machines could be explained by assuming that Smeaton's coefficient for air pressure was too high. On September 26, only a week after his speech, Wilbur called Chanute's attention to the fact that "Prof. Langley and also the Weather Bureau officials found that the correct coefficient of pressure was only about .0032 instead of Smeaton's .005."[12]

The longer Wilbur thought about it, the more certain he became. "While I have not personally tested the point," he told Chanute a week later, "I am firmly convinced that it [.005] is too high."[13]

In fact, Wilbur had already done some testing. Referring to his meticulous notes on the performance of the 1901 glider, he calculated a lower, and much more accurate, value for the coefficient of air pressure. Both he and Chanute had developed tables of reduced data for six particularly well-documented flights made between July 3 and August 17, 1901. Will used the data on wind speed and aircraft weight to calculate a coefficient of lift for each of those flights, then proceeded to work back to a calculation of the coefficient of air pressure. For the six glides in question, those coefficients ranged from .0030 to .0034. The average was .0032. He could see "no good reason for using a coefficient greater than .0033 instead of .005."[14]

Wilbur had identified and corrected one source of error in the Lilienthal calculations, but there might be others. Next, he turned his attention to the problem of lift and drag coefficients. Unlike the pressure figure, the lift and drag coefficients varied with each airfoil shape at every angle of attack.

A great many nineteenth-century engineers and physicists had struggled to chart the tiny fluctuations in lift and drag dancing back and forth over a wing set at various angles to the wind. In planning their first machines, the Wrights had referred to Lilienthal's coefficient tables for his airfoil (arc of a circle, camber of $1/12$). That information was now in question.

Wilbur and Orville had a low tolerance for guesswork. If they were to continue, there was no choice but to devise a means of checking the Lilienthal coefficients and, if necessary, correcting them. The temptation to replace uncertainty with hard facts and figures was irresistible.

It was a problem made to order: their genius for visualizing mechanical solutions to theoretical problems would be fully exercised in conceptualizing the experiment and designing the necessary apparatus. Their personal qualities—an insistence on absolute precision and an unflagging confidence in the results of their own research—were equally essential. Nothing less than absolute confidence would do, for the Wrights would be staking their lives on the numbers they produced.

The first task was to prove that a problem really existed. To accomplish that, they designed a mechanical analogue of the Lilienthal tables. According to Lilienthal, a cambered wing with a surface area of 1 square foot set at a 5-degree angle of attack should produce just enough lift to equal the pressure on a flat plate measuring .66 of a square foot set at a 90-degree angle to the air flow.

The brothers recreated that situation, mounting a bicycle wheel,

free to turn, on its side with a cambered Lilienthal airfoil of the
correct dimension fixed to the front of the rim at a 5-degree angle and
a flat plate positioned vertically one quarter of the way around the
wheel from the airfoil. If Lilienthal was correct, the wheel would
remain stationary when placed in a strong wind. If he was wrong,
either the lift of the airfoil would overpower the pressure on the flat
plate and turn the wheel in one direction, or the pressure on the plate
would be higher than the lift of the airfoil, turning it in the other.

When the Wrights discovered that they could not get satisfactory
results from their testing apparatus in a natural wind, they mounted
the wheel horizontally over the handlebars of a bicycle and rode madly
up and down the street. The pressure on the plate was much higher
than the lift of the airfoil.

The experiment proved the existence of an error somewhere in
Lilienthal's work. Was it the result of his use of Smeaton's coefficient,
as the Wrights suspected, or did additional errors lurk in Lilienthal's
measurement of the lift and drag coefficients for his airfoil? The
whole business gave them pause. Could the great German gliding
pioneer, a man for whom they had an extraordinary respect, have
made such a mistake? Why had no one noticed it before them?

The Wrights constructed their first wind tunnel to double-check the
results of the bicycle-wheel experiment. It was a simple device, a
square trough with a fan at one end driven by the overhead line shaft.
Confirmation of the error was quick in coming.

Nothing was left but to recheck all of the figures in the Lilienthal
table. They would fashion a small model of his wing, test it at every
angle of attack, and calculate the coefficients for themselves. And
they would go a giant step further. Lilienthal and most other experimenters had tested only single airfoil designs; Wilbur and Orville
would study a wide range of shapes and sizes, searching for the most
efficient lifting surface.

The original small "channel" was inadequate for the task. They
constructed a new wind tunnel, a wooden box six feet long and sixteen
inches square on the inside. To the uninitiated eye, it looked like
nothing more than a long packing crate resting on two sawhorses. In
fact, it was a delicate instrument that would permit the Wrights to
unlock the secrets of a wing.

The purpose of the tunnel was to move a smooth, steady stream of
air through the box at a constant speed of 27 miles per hour. A sheet
metal hood at one end partially shielded a two-bladed fan that was

Disappointed and puzzled by the poor performance of their machine, the Wrights returned to Dayton in the fall of 1901 and set to work on a testing device. Initially, it consisted of an airfoil test rig mounted on the handlebars of a bicycle.

The 1901 wind tunnel offered a far more precise method of gauging the performance of airfoils.

driven through the gearbox of an abandoned grinder at a speed of 4,000 rpm. It would not do for the wind to careen off the walls of the tunnel, creating eddies, swirls, and cross-currents, so the Wrights placed a "straighter"—a cross-hatch of thin wooden strips covered with wire mesh—just in front of the fan.[15]

A section of the wooden top of the tunnel was replaced by a pane of glass. This window into the heart of the tunnel looked down onto a spindly metal balance bolted to the tunnel floor: carefully crafted out of bicycle spokes and hacksaw blades, it was designed to balance lift against drag, just as in the case of the far more primitive bicycle-wheel experiment. This time the Wrights would be able to make precise measurements of what was occurring as the wind flowed around a small airfoil mounted on the balance.

The balances were not much to look at—they were delicate things, small enough to fit in a shoe box. The slightest jar would dislodge the many pins on which the various parts rested, reducing the device to an assortment of bits and pieces on the tunnel floor. Reassembly was exasperating, something akin to building a house of cards; one slip and the entire edifice collapsed.[16]

Perhaps because they were so small, fragile, and totally devoid of the aura that surrounded the gliders, it is easy to underestimate the importance of the balances. In fact, they were as critical to the ultimate success of the Wright brothers as were the gliders.

George Spratt had first suggested the notion of a testing machine that would balance lift against drag. He had played with the idea back in Pennsylvania, devising a testing instrument that operated in the open air. Spratt had not been successful, but he had described the episode to the Wrights at Kitty Hawk.

Small wonder that Spratt had failed. The difficulty of designing such a device required Wilbur and Orville Wright to draw on the full measure of their ability to visualize a complex physical problem in mechanical terms. How could they suspend a small test surface in their tunnel so that it would be free to move in response to changing conditions? How could they measure that movement? How would they translate those measurements into coefficients for lift and drag?

In all, the Wrights built three balances for their wind tunnel. The first, inspired by Spratt's notion of obtaining all the required information with one simple test, was designed to measure both the lift of a test surface and the ratio of lift to drag. It was a failure.

The Wrights then split those functions and developed two subsequent balances, one to measure lift and the other to measure the lift to drag ratio. In simpler terms, the first balance provided the raw materials for calculating the lift coefficient (C_L); the second enabled them to calculate an accurate drag coefficient (C_D).

The tunnel and balances were complete and in use by November 22. The next month was a time of hectic activity, as the brothers moved rapidly through a series of tests with perhaps 150 small model airfoils. Milton once remarked that Wilbur "systematized everything." Nowhere was that more apparent than in the wind-tunnel experiments.

Procedure was everything. No one but the operator was allowed to stand near the tunnel during a run, nor could any change be made to the upstairs room at the bike shop where the experiments were conducted. They discovered that the tunnel actually set up a circulation of air around the entire room, so that even moving a piece of furniture had an impact on the readings.

The test procedure was quite simple. The Wrights had manufactured all of their test surfaces out of 20-gauge sheet steel, cut to size with tin shears and hammered into shape. Each was about six inches square and $\frac{1}{32}$ of an inch thick. Two metal prongs were soldered to each surface so that it could be clipped in place on the balances.

The little airfoils ran the gamut of possibilities, from flat plates of various size and shape through the surfaces used by Lilienthal, Langley, and others. Most were plain sheet steel of constant thickness. In a few cases the brothers added long beads of solder to thicken the leading edges, and covered the entire airfoil with coats of wax that could be shaped. A variety of wingtip shapes and aspect ratios were also tested.

Each airfoil was run on the lift balance through fourteen angles of attack, from 0 through 45 degrees. This was meticulous, repetitive work, but therein lay the beauty of the thing. The Wrights had developed a means of taking one reading after another in rapid succession. Once a series of runs with the lift balance was complete, that instrument was removed from the tunnel and the drag balance bolted in place.

The folks at Fetters & Shank (undertakers) next door must have wondered what was going on over at the bike shop. By late November a constant staccato roar issued from the back room. "It is perfectly marvelous to me how quickly you get results with your testing machine," Chanute wrote on November 18. "You are evidently better equipped to test the endless variety of curved surfaces than anybody has ever been."[17]

When the Wrights first discovered the problem with the coefficient of air pressure, they had to assume that Lilienthal's lift and drag coefficients might also be in error. The tunnel proved that Lilienthal's figures were accurate for the ranges of angles in which they would be flying, though inaccurate at larger angles. The error in Smeaton's coefficient was entirely responsible for the poor performance in 1900 and 1901.

But the Wrights had also discovered that Lilienthal had flown with a very inefficient wing. They identified a much better surface—a "parabolic curve," with a camber of 1 in 20 and an aspect ratio of 6:1 (six inches of span for one inch of chord). As they had always suspected, the peak of the arch was only one quarter of the way back down the chord line from the leading edge. This surface, number 12 in their series of airfoils, was the one with which they would fly.

With the basic tests completed and the tables of lift and drag coef-

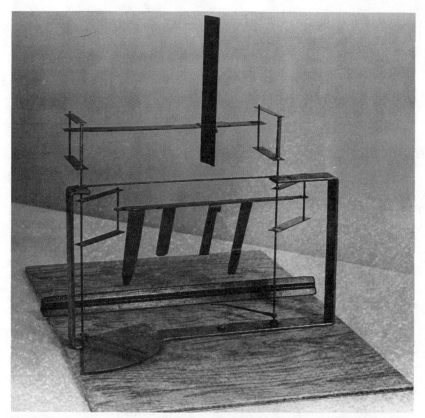

The balances were constructed of hacksaw blades and bits of wire. In the case of the lift balance, shown here, the model airfoil to be tested is clipped to the top tier. The metal "drag fingers" on the bottom tier are used to remove the force of drag, or air resistance, from the reading. The operator reads the test result on the quadrant at the base. The entire balance would fit into a box roughly 1 foot square.

ficients in place, the Wrights began a new phase of wind-tunnel research. Now they were posing other design questions. What was the ideal gap, or distance between the two wings of a biplane? How did biplane and triplane wing combinations compare in general efficiency? Should the upper and lower wings of a biplane have the same camber? What was the most appropriate aspect ratio? Did the shape of the wingtips affect the efficiency of the surface? The answers to these and other questions were tumbling out of the research process by mid-December.

Both brothers would look back on these few weeks in November and December 1901 as the psychological peak of their joint career in aeronautics—perhaps of their lives. Great moments of danger, high drama, personal triumph, and public acclaim lay ahead, but they would never again enjoy such a period of sheer intellectual excitement. Each day was filled with a sense of discoveries waiting to be made. "Wilbur and I could hardly wait for morning to come," Orville would recall, "to get at something that interested us. *That's* happiness!"[18]

They were treading absolutely new ground—and they knew it. Every run, every surface tested, every bit of data jotted down in the notebooks carried them one step farther into unexplored territory. They had the answers to questions that had been asked for centuries. The doubts and uncertainties vanished. The need to rely on the work of others was replaced by facts and figures they had verified themselves, hard numbers that they could trust.

They were certain now that success would be theirs and theirs alone. The prize was within their grasp.

chapter 17

ALL DOUBTS RESOLVED

December 1901–October 1902

C hanute constantly amazed them. "If . . . some rich man should give you $10,000 a year . . . to connect his name with progress," he wrote on December 19, 1901, "would you do so? I happen to know Carnegie. Would you like for me to write to him?"[1]

"As to your suggestion in regard to Mr. Carnegie," Wilbur responded, " . . . I think it possible that Andrew is too hardheaded a Scotchman to become interested in such a visionary pursuit as flying." And he went on: "I do not think it would be wise for me to accept help in carrying our present investigations further, unless it was with the intention of cutting loose from business entirely and taking up a different line of lifework."[2]

In fact, the brothers did not need additional money. The shop provided a steady income, and they had $3,000 in the bank—their share of the proceeds from the sale of the Illinois farm. The total out-of-pocket expenses for the flying-machine work so far, including materials for the gliders and the two trips to Kitty Hawk, had amounted to less than $300.

More important, outside funding would certainly come with strings attached. What the Wrights had achieved was entirely their own. They had no debts—financial or intellectual—and wanted to remain unencumbered.

Chanute understood their position and offered an alternative. The city of St. Louis was planning an aeronautical exhibition as part of a great fair to honor the centennial of the Louisiana Purchase in 1903.

The prize money might total as much as $200,000. Would the Wrights be interested in entering?

Wilbur was cool toward that idea as well. Two years might not afford enough time to design and build a powered machine, "which is, I suppose, the only kind that could hope to be awarded a prize of any size." The talk of the competition in St. Louis worried the Wrights. For some weeks, Chanute had been urging them to prepare an article describing the details of their gliding experiments and wind-tunnel tests. Now Wilbur commented that "it would be just as well for me to postpone the paper on our late experiments . . . as it would hardly be advisable to make public information which might assist others to carry off the prize from us."[3]

Chanute abided by their decision. On the matter of general publicity, however, there was no stopping him. During the spring of 1902, he would spread the names of Wilbur and Orville Wright far and wide.

The text of Wilbur's Chicago address had been published in the December 1901 issue of the *Journal of the Western Society of Engineers*. Chanute rushed copies off to his legion of friends. The response was immediate. Lawrence Hargrave, the Australian pioneer who had invented the box kite, wrote to thank him, commenting that Wilbur seemed to be "one of the right sort." Chanute told Wilbur that he had received similar letters from correspondents in England, France, and Germany.[4]

The Wrights could scarcely object to Chanute's wide distribution of a published paper, but they realized that unwanted publicity might endanger their work. When Chanute provided them with a list of all those who had received copies of the paper, Wilbur replied, a bit pointedly, that he had "confined" his copies to a few "personal friends."[5]

Batches of letters, many bearing foreign postmarks, began to arrive at 7 Hawthorn Street. "I am receiving from various sources letters of thanks for copies of my address," Wilbur wrote to Chanute on February 7, 1902. "As these are undoubtedly due to you I herewith forward these thanks accompanied by my own."[6]

By spring, Wilbur's patience had worn thin. "I enclose a letter from France which I take to be from Capt. Krebs, though my acquaintance with foreign customs of signing names leaves me in some doubt as to who it is from. Can you enlighten me?" Chanute returned the letter with a notation that, indeed, it was from Captain Arthur Krebs of the French aeronautical facility at Chalais Meudon. With fellow officer

Charles Renard, Krebs had built and flown the world's first navigable airship in 1884.[7]

This burgeoning correspondence was of real concern to the Wrights. It brought them face to face with a major decision: What steps should they take to protect their work? Chanute's position was clear. He advised them to "take out a patent or caveat on those principles of your machines as are important, not that money is to be made by it, but to save unpleasant disputes as to priority." Having done that, he believed they should make all their information available to fellow experimenters. With no hope of inventing the airplane himself, he could afford to be high-minded and generous. The brothers, however, believed that their experiments would lead to mechanical flight. Why should they jeopardize their own success by assisting potential rivals?

Still, they had to admit that the quality of the competition was very low. "The newspapers are full of accounts of flying machines which have been building in cellars, garrets, stables and other secret places," Wilbur commented to Chanute on February 7. "Each one . . . will undoubtedly carry off one hundred thousand dollars at St. Louis. They all have the problem 'considerably solved,' but usually there is some insignificant detail yet to be decided, such as whether to use steam, electricity, or a water motor to drive it. Mule power might give greater *ascensional force if properly applied,* but I fear it would be dangerous unless the mule wore pneumatic shoes."[8] He concluded that "some of these reports would disgust one if they were not so irresistibly ludicrous."

If the St. Louis entries were ludicrous, aeronautical research in other nations was moribund. Lilienthal and Pilcher were dead. No one had stepped forward to take their place. Arthur Krebs, Lawrence Hargrave, and the other pioneers who wrote to congratulate the Wrights had not been active in the field for many years. Others, including Samuel Langley, paid so little attention to control that the Wrights believed they stood scant chance of success.

Their quick survey of the field confirmed that there were no serious rivals in sight. Moderate publicity might even prove useful in setting them apart from the general run of fools and montebanks who were giving aeronautics a bad name.

Wilbur began to relax. He promised Chanute that he would prepare an article describing the wind-tunnel tests, with the all-important pressure tables as an appendix. The brothers approved a long description of their work to be included in Chanute's chapter for a new edition of Moedebeck's *Taschenbuch* (soon to be translated into English as *The Pocket-Book of Aeronautics*). Wilbur even promised to prepare a set of drawings of the 1901 glider as illustrations for the article.

Ferdinand Ferber was typical of the experimenters who posed little threat to the Wrights. Chanute had first mentioned his name in February 1902, noting that a certain "Capt. Ferber of Nice is in a state of admiration of your performances and wishes me to convey his felicitations."[9]

Ferber, a thirty-nine-year-old native of Lyons, was an artillery officer commanding the 17th Alpine Battery. At best a lackluster soldier, he was overweight, walked with a slouch, and looked faintly ridiculous on horseback. Although chronically near-sighted, he refused to wear spectacles. Legend has it that he once missed offering a salute to the French Minister of War, thus ensuring that he would never rise above the rank of captain.

Ferber had become interested in aeronautics in 1898 while serving as an instructor at the Ecole d'Application. He launched an extended correspondence with Lilienthal's brother Gustav, and with Clément Ader, a leading French aeronautical pioneer. By 1901 he had built and flown a series of four aircraft, beginning with a kite and culminating in a crude version of the standard Lilienthal monoplane.

In the summer of 1901, he ran across an article by G. H. Bryan, a leading member of the Aeronautical Society of Great Britain. Ferber found Bryan's discussion of Chanute's work particularly intriguing. He wrote to Chicago, enlisting in Chanute's legion of international correspondents. Four letters had already passed between them when Chanute forwarded him a copy of Wilbur's article.

"Some Aeronautical Experiments" came as a revelation, inspiring Ferber to begin work on a new glider based on the photos and descriptions of the 1901 Wright craft. Flown at Beuil in June 1902, the glider was so crudely constructed that the fabric literally flapped in the wind. The wings were flimsy, the elevator control ineffective, and Ferber did not even attempt to install the wing-warping system. "As to warping," he commented six years later, "I did not wish to employ it in 1902, as I judged it useless to begin with; so my successors, having set off along my track, did not use it either."[10]

The 1902 Ferber glider bore only a loose physical resemblance to the 1901 Wright original, and incorporated none of the Wright technology. Ultimately, that would not matter. Ferber had taken the first step, calling the attention of his colleagues to the work of Wilbur and Orville Wright. Other Frenchmen—far better engineers and mechanics than he—would follow his lead. Chanute's seed had taken root.

Chanute offered Wilbur yet another proposal in March. During a recent trip to California he had met Charles H. Lamson, a veteran flying-machine experimenter. In 1895, Lamson had built and flown the first Lilienthal glider in America. The next year he made national headlines with a gigantic man-lifting kite. Convinced that there was little money in aeronautics, Lamson then moved to Pasadena and opened a jewelry store.

Attempting to rekindle his interest, Chanute offered Lamson a contract for the construction of a new folding-wing glider. Lamson accepted. With one glider under construction, Chanute asked if the Wrights would accept a similar contract to build new versions of the two-surface machine and the Katydid of 1896.[11]

Wilbur agreed that he and his brother would oversee the production of the glider, but he let Chanute know that it was an imposition. They could not begin until after the close of the busy summer season at the bicycle shop, and would insist that he provide them with a complete set of drawings. The Wrights wanted to be sure that there was no confusion—this was to be Chanute's machine, not their own. They were not willing even to construct the craft themselves, but would hire a carpenter to work under their supervision.

Chanute accepted their terms, then changed his mind. In mid-May, he received an unexpected letter from Augustus Herring, the young engineer who had played an important role in the design and testing of the 1896 gliders. Herring was out of work and asking for help.

Chanute and Herring had parted company on less than pleasant terms before the end of the Dune trials in 1896. Herring had been eager to rush ahead to the construction of a powered version of the biplane glider; Chanute held back, insisting on additional tests. He told his friend James Howard Means that Herring "tries very sulkily those experiments that do not originate with him, and is . . . very obstinate."[12]

Still, Chanute felt sorry for the fellow. Things had not gone well for Herring. After leaving Chanute, he found a new patron in Matthias Arnot, an Elmira, New York, banker who funded the construction of another biplane glider in 1897. With Arnot's continued support, Herring constructed a powered machine the following year, a variant of the Chanute-Herring biplane glider fitted with a small compressed-air engine. Herring completed two very short hops with the little craft during the fall and winter of 1898. On the first occasion he skimmed forward over the sand of a Lake Michigan beach some fifty feet. A few weeks later he made a longer hop of seventy-three feet.

Herring's two short forays into the air proved nothing. His machine was no more than a standard hang glider with a lightweight engine capable of running for only a few seconds. Having made his brief powered hops, Herring found himself at a technological dead end. The primitive and ineffective body-shifting control system placed such limitations on the surface area that the wings could barely support the weight of the pilot and the tiny engine. Woefully underpowered, the little biplane was not remotely capable of sustained flight. If anything, Herring's 1898 powered hang glider was proof positive of the need for a revolutionary breakthrough such as the Wrights had achieved in the areas of aerodynamics and control.

Herring's dreams of moving on to a larger machine were dashed by a fire that destroyed his workshop, aircraft, and experimental engines in 1899. Arnot's death of peritonitis in 1901 cut off any hope of additional financial support. Desperate to remain involved in aeronautics, Herring swallowed his pride and came back to Chanute.

Herring knew of Chanute's interest in the two newcomers from Dayton. He had read Wilbur's paper, and been much impressed. But he realized too that Chanute believed in the value of friendly competition. So he wrote to Chicago suggesting that, given the funds for a new glider, he could "beat Mr. Wright."[13]

Intrigued, Chanute asked the Wrights to release him from their agreement so that he could offer the contract to Herring. Wilbur assured him that they would be happy to see the work go to Herring. "To tell the truth," he added, "the building of machines for other men to risk their necks on is not a task that we particularly relish."[14]

Chanute wrote back at once, explaining that Wilbur had misunderstood. He intended to offer Herring nothing more than a construction contract. Both the Herring and Lamson machines were meant as a gift to the Wrights—they could fly them to their hearts' content at Kitty Hawk during the coming season. Wilbur's rejection of the offer was polite but very firm. The Wrights were eager to build a new glider embodying both the lessons learned in their two previous seasons and the new wind-tunnel data. The last thing they wanted was to waste time testing one of Chanute's old designs.[15]

Chanute pressed the issue when he visited Dayton on July 3. If the brothers refused to test his gliders, would they allow Bill Avery or Herring, both of whom had flown the craft in 1896, to join them at Kitty Hawk? Again the Wrights were hesitant, responding by letter soon after Chanute's departure.

"It was our experience last year," Wilbur explained, "that my brother and myself, while alone, or nearly so, could do more work in one week, than in two weeks after Mr. Huffaker's arrival." If Chanute would give them enough time on their own to establish camp and conduct some preliminary tests with their glider, however, they would welcome him and his "expert" as their guests. "Provided it is equally satisfactory to you," Wilbur concluded, "reasons not necessary to mention would lead to a preference for Mr. Avery in the choice of an expert."[16]

All their attention now focused on the new glider. The calculations called for a machine slightly larger than the 1901 craft, with a wing surface area of 305 square feet. The whole point of the wind-tunnel tests had been to choose the most efficient wing surface. Number 12 on their tables of lift and drift, it was a small steel blade with an aspect ratio of 1:6 (as opposed to 1:3 of 1900 and 1901), a camber of $\frac{1}{20}$, and the peak set one quarter of the way back the chord from the leading edge.

Full scale, the new wing gave the finished machine a radically different appearance from its two predecessors. The span was over ten feet longer than in 1901 and the chord two feet shorter. To a modern eye, the 1900 and 1901 gliders seem bulky and cumbersome, with their stubby rectangular wings. The 1902 craft, lighter and more graceful, looks like an airplane.

The addition of a two-surface fixed vertical rudder at the rear of the machine also changed its look. Just as the new wing was designed to overcome the aerodynamic problems of its predecessors, the rudder was intended to deal with the control problems Wilbur had encountered at the close of the 1901 season.

The brothers reasoned that the problem stemmed from differential drag induced when the wing was warped. Take a typical example from 1901: On August 9, Wilbur was skimming along in straight and level flight when the left wingtip dropped. He shifted the hip cradle to the right to bring it back up. As the wing rose, the entire machine skidded sideways to the left. Sensing danger, the pilot dropped the craft abruptly onto the sand.

When the wing was warped, the angle of incidence of the left tip increased, to increase the lift, while that of the right tip decreased. Such action did raise the left tip, but it also increased the drag on that wing, causing it to move more slowly than the right wing and pulling the entire aircraft into the strange skid. The addition of the fixed rudder was designed to counteract that motion. When the machine began to nose toward the slow wing, the rudder would also present an angled surface to the wind, increasing the total drag on the oppo- site side and correcting the differential.

There was frantic activity in the Wright household during July and August. Wilbur dashed off a letter to Spratt, inviting him back to Kitty Hawk. If they had to put up with an "expert" who promised to rival Huffaker as a companion, they might as well have a friend along too. Another letter went to Bill Tate, asking for permission to reoc- cupy the old Kill Devil Hills site rent-free. Will, worried about the White River Conference proceedings, was torn between making a trip to Huntington on his father's behalf and remaining in Dayton to assist Orv with work on the new machine.

Katharine thought her brother looked "thin and nervous," and urged him to get on with preparations for the trip to Kitty Hawk. "They will be all right once they get down in the sand where the salt breezes blow," she wrote Milton on August 20. "They insist that, if you aren't well enough to stay out on your trip, you must come down with them. They think that life at Kitty Hawk cures all ills, you know." In truth, Katharine looked forward to their departure with mixed emotions. "Will spins the [sewing] machine around by the hour while Orv squats around marking the places to sew. There is no place in the house to live, but I'll be lonesome enough by this time next week and wish that I could have some of the racket around."[17]

They left Dayton at 9:00 A.M. on August 25, bound once again for Elizabeth City by way of Norfolk. Chanute wrote that both Lamson and Herring were ready to ship their respective machines at any time. Avery was not available. Would the Wrights accept Herring in- stead?[18]

Wilbur was blunt. They had been told that Herring was a man of "somewhat jealous disposition," and were afraid that he might use what he saw at Kitty Hawk, or claim that the Wrights had made use of something they had learned from him. Wilbur shifted the burden back to Chanute, adding: "[I]f you are also in camp during the term that he is here I do not see how any misunderstanding could arise."[19]

The first few days at Kill Devil Hills were spent putting the 1901 shed back into shape. The wind had scoured the sand from beneath both ends of the building, giving the roof, as Will said, "a shape like that of a dromedary's back." They raised the ends back into place and added corner pilings, then extended the rear to create a kitchen and living room. The sleeping quarters would be up in the "attic" this year. The brothers installed two beds running lengthwise over the rafters.[20]

They spent the morning of Monday, September 8, cleaning out the shed; killing two mice ("one with a stick, the other with gun"); and chasing several hungry razorback hogs away from the campsite. Work on the new glider began just after two o'clock that afternoon. The rest of the week passed quickly. Each wing was tested as an individual unit. The Wrights were pleased with the results: lift and drag were close to the predicted values, and the reversal of the center of pressure occurred at a much lower angle than they had hoped for.

By September 15 the struts salvaged from the old 1901 machine were in place and the complete wing set was taken out for a trial. It was, Will told Spratt, "an immense improvement over last year's machine." Four days later they made the first kite and gliding tests with the finished craft, complete with the elevator and new fixed rudder. When Wilbur wrote to Chanute on September 21, they already had fifty glides under their belts.[21]

Will was doing so well with the new machine that he could bring it to a virtual standstill in the air. And Orville was finally learning to fly. He began with short glides, accustoming himself to the use of the elevator. Teaching oneself to fly is never easy, particularly with an older brother shouting up instructions from below. The situation led to a near disaster on September 23.

It was perfect flying weather after two days of torrential rain. The Wrights were out all day, completing seventy-five glides of varying length. On the final glide Orv shifted the hip cradle to raise a dropping wing, and lost track of the elevator. The craft nosed up into a steep stall and fell backward onto the sand. The result, was "a heap of flying machine, cloth, and sticks in a heap, with me in the center without a scratch or bruise."[22]

They were back in the air a week later, rapidly gaining experience with the rebuilt machine. By October 2 they were averaging twenty-five flights on good weather days and achieving distances of over 500 feet on occasion. Those glides were the first fruits of the long winter days spent peering into the glass on top of the wind tunnel. The 1902

The 1902 glider was the result of lessons learned with two previous machines and the wind-tunnel experiments. This is Wilbur in the air on October 2, 1902. The original double-surfaced rudder was fixed and could not turn.

glider exceeded its calculated performance. The brothers could not have been more pleased.

At the same time, it was clear that the fixed rudder did not solve the dilemma of aerial skids caused by differential drag during wing warping. The problem was growing worse, and may even have been involved in Orville's spectacular crash on September 23.

Lying awake up in the rafters after his brother had fallen asleep on the night of October 3, it occurred to Orv that the fixed rudder might be at fault. In a crosswind, the additional drag of the tail could further retard the slow wing. Why not hinge the rudder, adding a new control, so that the pilot could actively turn the surface to counteract the increased drag on the low wing?

He would raise the issue carefully. All too often, he suspected, his older brother reacted against his suggestions on principle. This time Wilbur listened as Orv explained the notion at breakfast the next morning. He understood immediately, but was reluctant to add yet another control to befuddle the pilot. The movable rudder was a fine idea, but why not link it directly to the wing-warping cradle, so that the rudder would automatically move to counter the warp-induced drag? To simplify matters, a single vane could be substituted for the double surface of the fixed rudder. They began work on the new rudder later that day.[23]

The camp was crowded now. Lorin appeared unexpectedly on September 30, having come down to see for himself what his brothers were up to. He struck up an immediate friendship with Spratt, who arrived the next day. Chanute and Herring appeared four days later, in the midst of yet another rainstorm. Six bunks were squeezed into the narrow quarters up in the rafters, and the sound of Orv's mandolin accompanying a chorus of voices could be heard far into the night.

Herring set to work assembling both the "multi-wing" glider and the Lamson "oscillating wing machine." He abandoned the Lamson craft after only two days of testing. Working together, the entire team was unable to pull it into the air with a pilot on board. When tested separately as kites, the wings flew at an angle of almost 20 degrees in a 30-mile per hour wind.

Wilbur attributed the problem to structural weakness. "I noted that when there was not even enough wind for support, the surfaces were badly distorted, twisting so that, while the wind at one end was on the underside, often at the other extreme it was on top. Mr. Chanute," he concluded, "seems much disappointed in the way it works."[24]

Herring's own machine was no more successful. An altered version of the original Chanute-Herring triplane of 1896, the wings were free to rock back and forth in response to changes in the center of pressure. Herring made several faltering glides with the craft on October 13, the only day on which it was flown. His best distance was just under fifty feet.

For Herring, the whole experience was humiliating. A proud, self-confident man, he considered himself the leading American flying-machine experimenter. He had struggled for years, unfairly put upon—as he saw it—by fate and the whim of men like Chanute and Langley who gave him money, but not the freedom to develop his own ideas. He saw the 1902 Wright glider in the air on only two or three days while he was in camp. It was enough. Clearly, these newcomers had swept past him and were threatening to wrest the prize from his grasp.

The camp began to break up with Lorin's departure on October 14. Chanute and Herring left for Washington the following afternoon. Both men hoped to see Samuel Langley. Chanute did spend a few minutes with him on October 16; he described the extraordinary progress of the Wrights, and urged Langley to go to the Outer Banks to

On October 10, Wilbur was up again with a new rudder that turned to counteract the retarding effect of wing warping.

see for himself. "After seeing you," Langley wrote the next day, "I almost decided to go, or send someone, to see the remarkable experiments that you told me of by the Wright brothers." In fact Langley wired Kitty Hawk requesting permission to visit the camp, but Wilbur and Orville replied that there would scarcely be time before the close of the season.[25]

Herring, unable to see Langley, left a note, desperate either for a job or a small grant that would enable him to set off in pursuit of the Wrights. But Langley, far less forgiving than Chanute, had no intention of becoming involved with Herring ever again.

Conditions at the Kill Devil Hills were "so much easier" after Herring and Chanute's departure. The Wrights were in the air from dawn to dusk. "In two days," Orv boasted to Katharine,

> we made over 250 glides, or more than we had made all together up to the time Lorin left. We have gained considerable proficiency in the handling of the machine now, so that we are able to take it out in any kind of weather. Day before yesterday [October 21] we had a wind of 16 meters per second or about 30 miles per hour, and glided in it without any trouble. That was the highest wind a gliding machine was ever in, so that we now hold all the records! The largest machine that we handled in any kind [of weather], made the longest distance glide (American), the longest time in the air, the smallest angle of descent, and the highest wind!!! Well, I'll leave the rest of the "blow" till we get home.[26]

Glides in excess of 550 feet were commonplace. The best flights of the season came on October 23, their next-to-last day in the air. Will set the record for both time and distance with a single glide covering

622.5 feet in 26 seconds. Orv was not far behind with a flight of 615.5 feet in just over 21 seconds.

They spent their days in the air, and their nights in serious discussion. After three seasons at Kitty Hawk, they had achieved their original goals. The 1902 glider was proof that they had solved the basic problems of flight. They were ready for the next step—the construction of a powered airplane.

The basic calculations for its design were run while still in camp. They solved the lift equation as usual, but the drag formula was now especially important. Gravity had powered their earlier machines, supplying the force necessary to overcome drag and achieve flying speed. This time they would not have that advantage. Their powered machine would take off from a dead stop on level ground. Whatever combination of engine and propellers they chose would have to provide sufficient thrust to achieve flying speed and sustain them in the air.

The answers were clear. They would need some 520 square feet of wing to lift a machine with a total weight of no more than 625 pounds, including the engine and pilot. A suitable airframe of that size would weigh perhaps 290 pounds. The addition of a 140-pound pilot left 200 pounds as the upper limit for the weight of the engine, propellers, and transmission. An engine generating 8–9 horsepower would produce the thrust required to get such a machine off the ground in a reasonable headwind.

With everything going so well, the Wrights would have liked to continue flying until the end of the month, but that was not possible. Bill Tate needed to prepare his fishing boat and crew for the coming season—without his assistance, the brothers could not launch their machine. They left camp for the last time at dawn on October 28 and walked the four miles to Kitty Hawk in a cold drizzle to catch the boat for Elizabeth City—and home. They left their own glider and the two Chanute machines behind, packed away in the rafters of the shed where they would remain until the camp reopened in 1903.

chapter 18

EUROPE DISCOVERS
THE WRIGHTS

November 1902-August 1903

The Wrights scarcely paused after returning from Kitty Hawk. Orville went to work on a new wind tunnel and a final check of the lift and drag figures. Wilbur wrote to ten manufacturers of gasoline engines, asking about prices and delivery times for an engine that would weigh no more than 180 pounds and deliver 8–9 horsepower.[1]

In December, they turned their attention to the other half of the propulsion problem—the propeller. Langley, Maxim, Ader, and others had given little thought to propeller efficiency, relying on angled blades to pull their machines through the air like a screw drilling into wood. That would not do for the Wrights. They set out to engineer their propellers, just as they had their wings, achieving a specific thrust calculated in advance. Anything less would be a surrender to guesswork.

"We had thought of getting the theory of the screw propeller from the marine engineers," Orv wrote in 1908, "and then, by applying our tables of air pressures to their formulas, of designing air propellers suitable for our purpose."[2] They discovered that there was no theoretical base for the design of ship propellers. A century after the introduction of the marine screw, engineers continued to follow empirical practice of no value to the Wrights.

Reasoning their way along, the Wrights made another fundamental breakthrough. "It was apparent," Orville recalled in 1913, "that a propeller was simply an aeroplane [wing] traveling in a spiral course."

A propeller was not a screw, it was a rotary wing. Instead of being driven against the air to provide lift, it was spun, generating thrust. The formulas and coefficients used in wing design could also be applied to propellers. At first glance, as Orville pointed out in a later article, this did not seem to be a problem,

> but on further consideration it is hard to find even a point from which to make a start; for nothing about a propeller, or the medium in which it acts, stands still for a moment. The thrust depends upon the speed and the angle at which the blade strikes the air; the angle at which the blade strikes the air depends upon the speed at which the propeller is turning, the speed at which the machine is traveling forward, and the speed at which the air is slipping backward; the slip of the air backward depends upon the thrust exerted by the propeller, and the amount of air acted upon. When any of these changes, it changes all the rest, as they are all interdependent upon one another. But these are only a few of the many factors that must be considered and determined in calculating and designing propellers.[3]

The longer they studied it, the more complex the problem became.

> With the machine moving forward, the air flying backward, the propellers turning sidewise, and nothing standing still, it seemed impossible to find a starting point from which to trace the various simultaneous reactions. Contemplation of it was confusing. After long arguments we often found ourselves in the ludicrous position of each having been converted to the other's side, with no more agreement than when the discussion began.[4]

Charlie Taylor witnessed those discussions. "Both boys had tempers," he recalled. "They would shout at one another something terrible. I don't think they really got mad, but they sure got awfully hot."[5] The arguments that shocked Charlie in fact allowed them to explore every facet of a problem. Their ability to defend a point of view with real passion, while at the same time listening to the other fellow's opinion, was an essential part of the process.

The elements of a propeller theory were falling into place by early March 1903. The answers did not come in a brilliant flash of insight but were reasoned through step by step.

The design of the transmission system arose directly out of their cycling experience. Rather than bolting a single propeller directly to the crankshaft, they linked twin pusher propellers to the engine with a set of chains, achieving maximum performance with the propellers revolving at a relatively slow speed. To avoid the excessive torque resulting from two propellers spinning in the same direction, the blades were contrarotating—they simply crossed one of the hollow guide tubes protecting the propeller drive chains.

The power plant remained a problem. None of the established engine manufacturers had the slightest interest in constructing an aircraft power plant. Fortunately, the Wrights had Charlie Taylor. Charlie had never built an engine, but he had worked on them, and he was a first-class machinist. Will and Orv also had some direct experience with internal-combustion engines, having designed and built the motor that drove the line shaft in the bicycle shop.

The world's first aircraft engine would have to meet three basic requirements: it must produce 8–9 horsepower, weigh no more than two hundred pounds, and run smoothly. The least vibration or roughness would place an impossible strain on the transmission chains.

To save weight, they would cast the crankcase from aluminum. It was a chancy decision. Casting such material into the size of an engine block was work for professional foundrymen.

Construction was *en bloc*, as the French said, with the crankcase and four cylinders cast as a single unit. It was water-cooled, with a separate radiator and a waterjacket cast into the block. An air-cooled engine would be lighter, but could only be run for short periods without potentially catastrophic overheating. The savings in weight would be of little use if the finished engine refused to run.

Fuel was gravity-fed from a can mounted several feet above the engine on an inboard wing strut. There was no carburetor. Gasoline was vaporized in a beaded steel can through which air passed on its way into the engine. The resulting mixture was circulated across the hot crankcase to vaporize any remaining liquid gasoline, then run directly past the intake valves in the manifold. Ignition was make or break, with the contacts operated by cams. A battery was required for starting. A low-tension magneto driven by the flywheel provided the spark once the engine was running.[6]

Orv and Charlie began work on the engine in late December. "We didn't make any drawings," Taylor commented. "One of us would sketch out the part we were talking about on a piece of scratch paper and I'd tack the sketch over my bench."[7]

Taylor machined the crank from a single block of machine steel, using only a lathe and drill press. He drew the outline of the finished piece on the block, then drilled one hole after another until he could knock the surplus material off with a hammer. Once the part was roughed out, he turned it down to the required size on the lathe. The

Satisfied that they were ready to fly a powered machine, the Wrights, assisted by machinist Charles Taylor, designed and built their own engine. It weighed 200 pounds fully fueled and ready for flight, and produced just over 12 horsepower.

finished crank weighed nineteen pounds. "She balanced up perfectly, too," Taylor said with pride in later years.[8]

Taylor made do with what he had. He bored the cylinders out of the aluminum block with the lathe, and turned down the cast-iron pistons himself. He purchased prefabricated parts whenever possible, including the magneto and valves. A rubber speaking-tube hose served as a fuel line.

The little engine ran for the first time on February 12, 1903, just six weeks after work had begun. It was undeniably crude. The cooling system was ineffective, so that the valve box grew red hot after only a few minutes in operation. On the second day of testing, dripping gasoline froze the bearings, shattering the crankcase. They had no choice but to pull out the patterns and return to the foundry for a new casting. Charlie had the rebuilt engine back in operation by May.

The Wrights kept their plans from Chanute, who was frankly curious. "I think you had better patent your improvements," he wrote on December 9. "How far do you plan to carry your aeronautical work?" Just three days earlier he had sent them a copy of the French patent he had helped Louis-Pierre Mouillard to obtain in 1896.[9]

He did not press the point, but Chanute hoped the Wrights would

note a resemblance between Mouillard's differential drag brakes and
their wing-warping system. The Wrights did not see any connection,
nor did they dream that Chanute believed their work was in any way
related to Mouillard's primitive steering apparatus.

Puzzled, Wilbur thanked Chanute for the patent and assured him
they were applying for their own. As to their future plans, he simply
said that they were building a machine "much larger and about twice
as heavy" as the 1902 glider. "With it we will work out problems
relating to starting and handling heavy weight machines, and if we
find it under satisfactory control in flight, we will proceed to add a
motor."[10]

The brothers filed their first patent application on March 23, 1903,
with no mention of a power plant. They were patenting a flying machine, not a gasoline engine. The 1902 glider incorporated all of their
basic principles—the wing-warping system, complete with rudder.
That was what they sought to protect.

The response from the U.S. Patent Office was swift and disappointing. The Wrights were told that their drawings were inadequate and
the written description of their machine "vague and indefinite." The
examiner noted that their claims had been anticipated by at least six
other patents, and could not be allowed in any case because the device
described was clearly "inoperative" and "incapable of performing its
intended function."[11]

They had run headlong into the first of many problems with the
federal bureaucracy. For more than fifty years the Patent Office had
received a stream of applications for flying machines. In the early
1890s, officials decided that such "nuisance" applications would be
summarily dismissed unless the applicant could demonstrate that his
machine had actually flown. The Wrights knew that they could fly; it
did not occur to them that a harried bureaucrat might have difficulty
recognizing that fact on the basis of a simple patent application.

Wilbur replied that they would be glad to correct any inadequacies
in their application. He even sent a cardboard inner-tube box back to
the Patent Office in an effort to "clarify" the section describing the
wing-warping technique.

The claim was rejected a second time, the cardboard box dismissed
as "of no assistance." The examiner did offer the Wrights one useful
bit of advice, suggesting that they "employ an attorney skilled in
patent proceedings" if they wished to press their case. Puzzled and
a bit worried, they decided to set the matter aside until they had flown
the powered aircraft.[12]

Chanute spent the spring of 1903 digging out from under the correspondence that had accumulated during his absence in Europe. One letter awaiting an answer was from an old acquaintance—Major Baden Fletcher Smyth Baden-Powell.

A career officer and brother of the founder of the Boy Scouts, Baden-Powell thought of himself as an inventor. In fact, his technical gifts were limited; his enthusiasm, however, was unbounded. He had joined the Aeronautical Society of Great Britain in 1880. Founded sixteen years before by a group of gentlemen amateurs and professional engineers interested in flight, it was initially an active group, publishing the only English-language periodical devoted to aeronautics, and sponsoring key experiments, including the pioneer wind-tunnel studies of Francis Wenham and John Browning.[13]

By the time Baden-Powell joined, the Aeronautical Society had fallen on hard times. The founders had passed from the scene and interest in flight was on the wane. Elected secretary in 1897, Baden-Powell poured all of his energy into reinvigorating the group. The grateful members elected him president during his absence on duty in South Africa. Now, in September 1902, he wrote to his old acquaintance, Octave Chanute, for help in preparing a belated presidential address.

Baden-Powell apologized for having been out of touch for so long, but stressed he was "keen as ever about aeronautics." He asked to be brought up to date on events in America. In particular, he was curious about "a Mr. Wright" who, he had heard, was doing some "good work."[14]

Chanute responded immediately, enclosing a copy of Wilbur's paper and a letter describing the 1902 season. "Wright is now doing . . . well," Chanute concluded, "and I am changing my views as to the advisibility of adding a motor."[15]

Baden-Powell incorporated the contents into his address on December 4. He spoke of the "wonderful progress" that the Wrights had made, and suggested there was no reason why "such experts, having attained proficiency in the delicate art of balancing themselves . . . should not be able to soar away on the wings of the wind and remain indefinitely in mid air."[16]

The speech had a profound impact. The Wrights were not unknown in England, but Baden-Powell was the first to call attention to the triumph achieved at Kitty Hawk in 1902 and to identify them as leaders in the field. Listening closely that evening was Patrick Y. Alexander.

Alexander, the son of the manager of the Cammels steelworks in Sheffield, was brought up, according to a friend, "in an atmosphere of armaments, Naval programmes, and scientific developments generally." A shadowy figure, he had been so heavily involved in Russian railway construction projects that the newspapers occasionally identified him as a Russian. Aeronautics was his passion. Alexander owned eight balloons before 1894, had made parachute jumps, and believed that balloons, airships, and airplanes would one day be abandoned in favor of pure levitation.[17]

He was also impulsive. Three weeks and a day after attending Baden-Powell's speech in London, he knocked on the door at 7 Hawthorn Street and introduced himself. He had first called on Chanute, a complete stranger, requesting a letter of introduction to the Wright brothers. Chanute, startled by this fellow who traveled across the Atlantic at the drop of a hat, provided the letter and sent him on to Dayton. "We both liked him very much," Wilbur told Chanute after the visit, but that impression would not last. By 1907, Wilbur had become convinced that Alexander was a British spy.[18]

There is nothing to indicate that Pat Alexander was ever a "spy" in any official sense. He was an aeronautical gadfly and enthusiast, determined to learn everything he could about the Wrights, and quite willing to pass what he knew along to acquaintances at Whitehall and friends in France. Over the next five years he would become a major source of information on the brothers.

On January 3, 1903, Chanute and his two daughters (his wife Annie had died the year before) boarded the steamer *Commonwealth* in Boston bound for Alexandria, Egypt, the first stop on a combined business and pleasure trip through Europe.

Officially, Chanute was acting on behalf of the St. Louis group planning the Louisiana Purchase Exposition. Like the great fair in Chicago ten years before, the St. Louis Exposition would include a series of engineering congresses. His task was to promote the event, and to spread word of the Fair's aeronautical program.

Chanute welcomed the trip as an opportunity to meet many of his correspondents for the first time. He told Wilbur eagerly that Ferdinand Ferber "has been trying experiments with a machine similar to yours." The craft was a rough copy of the 1901 Wright glider. As Chanute noted, it was "rudely made by a common carpenter," and had no lateral control system at all. Nevertheless, Ferber had made eight to ten glides, the best of which had covered a distance of 150 feet. "He says that he is much inclined to go to America," Chanute added, "to take lessons from you." Ferber also expressed an interest in purchasing both the 1902 Wright glider and the Lamson oscillating-wing machine.[19]

Chanute was in Vienna on March 13, where he met Wilhelm Kress, an Austrian experimenter who had been heavily influenced by Alphonse Pénaud. Kress's large tandem-wing flying boat had capsized and sunk in the Tullernach Reservoir in October 1901. Chanute went to see the rebuilt machine, and reported to the Wrights that "it might fly if a lighter motor than the present one [a 30-hp Daimler] can be obtained."[20]

He was in Paris on April 4, and planned to "give several talks . . . and to promise to write something for publication."[21] In fact, Chanute had given the most important address of his long and distinguished career just two days before, at a dinner-conference of the Aéro-Club de France. The talk would have untold consequences for Wilbur and Orville Wright.

The Aéro-Club de France, founded in 1898, was the meeting place for one of the wealthiest and most fashionable social sets in fin-de-siècle Paris—the balloonists. Ballooning, for over a century the province of the scientist, soldier, and showman, had become the passion of the wealthy dilettante. A voyage aloft, dangling beneath a gaily decorated bag of hydrogen, was just the thing for a jaded young man with time on his hands and money in the bank. Members of the old balloon-making families—Paul Lechambre, Gabriel Yon, the Godards—found their services in great demand. Stories of idyllic excursions over the French countryside aboard balloons laden with picnic baskets and bottles of champagne filled the society pages of the newspapers.

By 1900, some leading members of the Aéro-Club had begun to transform the organization into something more than a sportsman's group. Henri Deutsch de la Meurthe was the leader of a faction encouraging new aeronautical technologies. For Deutsch de la Meurthe, the airplane was to be little more than a distant dream—the airship was the thing.

He had made his fortune in petroleum, and recognized that the industry's future depended on the development of a lightweight gasoline engine. He wrote books on the subject, sponsored experiments with new types of power plants, and presented President Carnot with one of the first gasoline-powered automobiles constructed in France.

His interest in aeronautics arose naturally from his enthusiasm for the internal-combustion engine. In the fall of 1900, Deutsch de la Meurthe established a 100,000 franc prize for the first airship flight from the Aéro-Club's Parc d'Aérostation at Saint-Cloud to the Eiffel Tower and back in half an hour or less.

Alberto Santos-Dumont, a wealthy Brazilian living in Paris, was everyone's favorite candidate to win the Deutsch Prize. Twenty-three years old when he arrived in Paris to study engineering in the fall of 1897, he was the son of Henriques Dumont, a Brazilian planter who had made a fortune satisfying the American craving for good coffee.

Le Petite Santos weighed only fifty kilograms and stood five feet five inches tall in his shiny patent leather button boots fitted with lifts. Dark hair, parted sharply in the center and held in place with a thick coat of pomade, capped a cadaverous face. Those who knew him assure us that his faintly comic appearance was more than offset by a cold, patrician manner.[22]

Santos acquired his first balloon, *Brazil*, in 1898. Dissatisfied with the limitations of operating at the mercy of the winds, he built a small one-man airship later that fall. Six more airships followed over the next three years. The sight of the little Brazilian chugging along just above the rooftops epitomized the spirit of la Belle Epoque.

After several abortive attempts, Santos won the Deutsch Prize on October 19, 1901. In typically grand style, he donated 75,000 francs to the Paris poor and divided the remaining 25,000 francs among the members of his crew. Popular as he was, knowledgeable members of the Aéro-Club recognized that Santos-Dumont had contributed little to aeronautical technology. While popular attention in France focused on the Deutsch Prize, a man of much larger vision, Count Ferdinand Von Zeppelin, captured the real leadership in lighter-than-air technology for Germany.

In July 1900, the count had made an 18-minute, three-and-a-half-mile flight with the 420-foot-long LZ-1. Initially, even German enthusiasts had difficulty recognizing the potential of the Zeppelin. As the *Frankfurter Zeitung* reported, the experiment "proved conclusively that a dirigible balloon is of no practical value." Zeppelin persevered. In 1909, the aging count established a sightseeing passenger air service linking major German cities.

Inspired by Zeppelin, Paul and Pierre Lebaudy, sugar refiners from Nantes, launched the first in a series of large semirigid airships in 1902. But the Zeppelin and Lebaudy programs were expensive, government-supported ventures in which the members of the Aéro-Club de France took little interest. In the wake of his Deutsch Prize victory, even Santos lost his enthusiasm for the airship. "To propel a dirigible balloon through the air," he announced, "is like pushing a candle through a brick wall."[23]

Ferdinand Ferber sensed that Aéro-Club enthusiasm for lighter-than-air flight was waning by 1902, and saw an opportunity to draw the organization into the mainstream of heavier-than-air developments. He began with an article published in February 1903.

"Expériences d'Aviation" warned Frenchmen that leadership in aeronautics had been forfeited to the United States. Ferber called for other enthusiasts to join him in gliding experiments that would enable France to recapture the lead from Langley, Chanute, and those mysterious figures, "Messrs. Orville and Wilbur Wright of Dayton, Ohio USA."[24]

Chanute's speech at the Aéro-Club on the evening of April 2 fanned the spark kindled by Ferber's article. He described his own work as well as that of Huffaker and Herring, closing with a lengthy description of the Wright experiments of 1900–02. It was a great success but not one of Chanute's finer moments.[25]

An aging widower returned in triumph to the city of his youth, Chanute exaggerated his own role and misrepresented his relationship with the Wrights. He spoke of them as his "devoted collaborators," as "young, intelligent and daring, pupils" who worked under his guidance. A newsman noted that the brothers had written to Chicago for technical information, on the basis of which they built "machines similar to those of Mr. Chanute" and were actively carrying "his" work forward to completion.[26]

Chanute's description of the Wright technology was so sketchy as to be useless to any experimenter. His reply to a question about the Wrights' lateral-control system was vague: "To regulate lateral equilibrium, he [Wilbur] operates two cords which act on the right and left side of the wing by warping [*gauchisement*], and simultaneously by moving the rear vertical rudder."[27]

Was Chanute muddying the waters to protect the Wright "secrets," or was he simply unable to provide a more accurate description? Either way, the talk did little to illuminate the basic principles of the 1902 glider. He had misled the French about a great many things. What they did understand was that *les frères Wright* were well on their way to solving the problems of mechanical flight. The comte de La Vaulx, a confirmed nationalist, described the reaction:

For most of the listeners, except Ferber and his friends, it was a disagreeable revelation; when we spoke in France rather vaguely about the
flights of the Wright brothers, we did not doubt their remarkable progress; but Chanute was now perfectly explicit about them and showed us
their real importance. The French aviators felt at last that . . . they had
been resting on the laurels of their predecessors too long, and that it was
time to get seriously to work if they did not wish to be left behind.[28]

Ernest Archdeacon was even more disturbed.

Will the homeland of the Montgolfier suffer the shame of allowing this
ultimate discovery of aerial science—which is certainly imminent, and
which will constitute the greatest scientific revolution since the beginning of the world—to be realized abroad? Gentlemen scholars, to your
compasses! You, the Maecenases; and you, too, of the Government, put
your hands deep into your pockets—else we are beaten![29]

A wealthy lawyer and a balloonist with a reputation for fearless-
ness, Archdeacon found a new mission in life. "Anxious to retain for
his nation the glory of giving birth to the first man-carrying aeroplane," the comte de La Vaulx recalled, "Archdeacon set out to shake
our aviators out of their torpor, and put a stop to French indifference
concerning flying machines."[30]

Ferber did not attend Chanute's lecture, but he was aware of the
sudden stir in Paris. He wrote to Archdeacon, suggesting that a glider
competition sponsored by the Aéro-Club would revive French
aeronautics. "Our experience has taught us that racing leads to improved machines; and the airplane must not be allowed to reach successful achievement in America."[31]

The notion appealed to Archdeacon, who offered to contribute 3,000
francs to a prize fund. In addition, he raised the issue of a glider
competition at the next meeting of the club's Technical Committee on
Aerial Locomotion on May 6, 1903. The members created a special
Subcommittee on Aviation Experiments, with dirigible builder
Charles Renard as president and Archdeacon as secretary. Over the
next five years this subcommittee would completely overwhelm both
the parent committee and the Aéro-Club itself.

Ferber's competition was never held, but he was no longer alone.
Within a matter of months the club became the headquarters for a
band of experimenters so determined to fly that they took to calling
themselves "les aviateurs militantes." They had set off in pursuit of
the Wrights too late to catch them, but not too late to write their
names large in the history of flight.

chapter 19

SUCCESS

June-December 1903

W ilbur addressed the Western Society of Engineers for a second time on the evening of June 18, 1903. There was a new confidence in his voice. The major problems were behind him now. Back in Dayton, Charlie and Orv had the engine up and running. Instead of the 8 horsepower they had expected, it developed 16 horsepower when first started and dropped off to 12 after a few seconds running time. They had overcome the propeller problem as well. Orville summed it up in a letter to George Spratt: "Isn't it wonderful that all these secrets have been preserved for so many years just so that we could discover them."[1]

Wilbur had every reason to feel confident, and every reason not to talk about it. The rejection of their patent application was a serious blow. They had no legal protection for their ideas—ideas that suddenly seemed very interesting to the French. Chanute, just back from France, had been invited to contribute an article to the *Revue des Sciences,* and was pressing for the release of additional information. "Should the warping of the wings be mentioned," he asked on June 30. "Somebody may be hurt if it is not."[2]

Wilbur was firm. "It is not our wish that any description of this feature of our machine be given at present." When Chanute sent them a copy of his article for approval, they found it riddled with errors. The author gave the camber of the 1902 machine as $\frac{1}{20}$ rather than $\frac{1}{25}$, and stated that the rudder was controlled by "twines leading to the hands of the aviator." "Really," Wilbur noted, "this is news to me!"[3]

Chanute was taken aback. How was he to describe the function of
the rudder when they had asked him not to discuss the wing-warping
system? Wilbur ignored the comment, noting that he and Orv had
called only the most substantial errors to Chanute's attention. There
were others. The article claimed that they had tested only forty-one
surfaces in the wind tunnel and that all of them had been "straight,
from tip to tip." Chanute had also claimed that the Wright machine
was guyed with "piano wire." They had allowed those minor errors
to pass, but the twines running to the hands were too much.[4]

"But," Chanute retorted, "it does not answer the question: How is
the vertical tail operated?"[5] The Wrights realized that Chanute was
not looking for a means of describing the action of the rudder without
revealing any secrets. He honestly did not know how it worked.

"The vertical tail is operated by wires leading to the wires that
connect with the wing tips," Wilbur informed him. "Thus the movement of the wing tips operates the rudder." He added quickly that this
was "not for publication, but merely to correct the misapprehension
in your mind." There was to be no further release of technical information.

> As the laws of France & Germany provide that patents will be held
> invalid if the matter claimed has been publicly printed we prefer to
> exercise reasonable caution about the details of our machine until the
> question of patents is settled. I only see three methods of dealing with
> this matter: (1) Tell the truth. (2) Tell nothing specific. (3) Tell something
> that is not true. I really cannot advise either the first or the third course.[6]

"I was puzzled by the way you put things in your former letters,"
Chanute responded on July 27. "You were sarcastic, and I did not
catch the idea that you feared that the description might forestall a
patent." Now that he understood, he would take "pleasure in sup-
pressing the passage altogether." At the same time, he believed that
a full account of the wing-warping and rudder combination "would
have proved harmless as the construction is ancient and well known."[7]

The Wrights let that pass. Many years later, in 1910, they expressed
surprise when Chanute admitted to newsmen that he had never regarded the Wright wing-warping system as anything new. In fact,
Chanute had sent them a great many signals over the years, including
both the copy of the Mouillard patent and the remark suggesting that
wing warping was well known. The Wrights chose to ignore those
signals. Wilbur, especially, enjoyed Chanute's friendship, and was not
willing to endanger it by forcing an argument.

The brothers were determined to concentrate on getting into the air with their powered machine. They refused to deal with potential distractions, including a request forwarded by Chanute from the editor of *L'Aérophile* for portraits and information to be used in putting together a biographical sketch. "Really," Wilbur responded, "we would rather not."[8]

Chanute also raised the issue of visitors to the 1903 camp. Pat Alexander was planning another trip to the United States. Would the Wrights mind if he spent some time at Kitty Hawk? Will explained that they had "made a firm resolve" that Spratt and Chanute would be the only persons allowed in camp this year. "We have so much to do, and so little time to do it." An exception might be made in Alexander's case—"We will consider the matter further when we see how things progress in camp."[9]

The machine was almost complete. It was never fully assembled in Dayton, but they had weighed the individual parts and estimated the weight of the finished craft at 675 pounds. It was more than they had planned, but the engine was producing more than the calculated 8 horsepower as well. There should be no difficulty.

The new machine was larger and sturdier than its predecessors. The ribs were built up of two pieces of wood, tacked and glued in place over supporting blocks. The end bows were pieces of bent wood manufactured by a local firm, the S. N. Brown Co., for use in folding carriages. They covered the wings, top and bottom, with a tightly woven muslin known as "Pride of the West." It was used straight off the bolt, with no additional doping to make it more airtight.

Each wing was built in three sections. The two outer bays were warped, as in the earlier gliders, but the central bay supporting the pilot, engine, and drive mechanism was rigidly trussed. There was a hip cradle for combined wing-warping and rudder operation and a hand control for the elevator. There was no throttle, but the pilot did have an engine cut-off switch.

The elevator was a double-surfaced affair designed to carry a significant proportion of the flight load, especially during the first moments in the air, when it would be operating at a much higher angle of attack than the wings. The brothers also devised a new launch system. The 1903 machine was much too large and heavy to manhandle to the top of a dune. At any rate, a gravity-assisted takeoff would hinder proof of the machine's ability for sustained flight.

The Wrights constructed a sixty-foot takeoff rail down which the airplane would ride on two bicycle-wheel hubs. One hub would be permanently attached to the forward end of the craft, the other would be carried on a small truck that supported the rear of the machine, and dropped off once it was airborne. The entire launch system—"the junction railroad," as they took to calling it—had cost very little, a marked contrast to the $50,000 that Samuel Langley had invested in the catapult system for the Great Aerodrome, also approaching completion.[10]

The 1903 season would be unlike any other. Always before the emphasis had been on testing new approaches, verifying the results of research conducted during the off-season, gaining experience in the air, and accustoming themselves to a new machine by making as many glides as possible. This year they had only one goal: to get the powered machine off the ground in sustained and controlled flight. The engine, transmission system, and airframe would require a great deal of fine tuning, so they planned to continue practicing with the 1902 glider while preparing the powered machine for its first trial.

They left Dayton at 8:55 on the morning of Wednesday, September 23, determined not to return home until they had achieved at least one powered flight. They made the trip in record time, arriving in Kitty Hawk at noon on September 26. Early the following week they were back in the air with the 1902 glider. They completed seventy-five glides on the first day, the best of which, 30 ⅖ seconds in length, broke all of their old records. It was an auspicious beginning.

Next, they must repair the damage that winter storms had done to the old building. And they set Dan Tate to work on a new building to house the glider and the powered machine. The Wrights would transform the old shelter into a real home.

They were not the only ones determined to fly a powered machine that fall. On October 14 the Wrights received a letter from George Feight, a Hawthorn Street neighbor, enclosing a newspaper report of Samuel Langley's first trial of the Great Aerodrome.

After completing the successful steam Aerodrome trials of 1896, Langley had announced that he was withdrawing from aeronautics. Having demonstrated the possibility of heavier-than-air flight, he would step aside to allow some younger experimenter to take the final steps toward a manned machine.

But as early as June 1897, Langley was remarking to Chanute that "If anyone were to put at my disposal the considerable amount—fifty thousand dollars or more—for an aerodrome carrying a man or men with a capacity for some hours of flight, I feel that I could build it and should enjoy the work."[11]

His opportunity came in 1898. On the eve of the war with Spain, Langley's friend Charles D. Walcott, director of the U.S. Geological Survey, convinced War Department officials that an experimental flying machine would be a wise investment.

The work began with a $50,000 allocation from the U.S. Army's Board of Ordnance and Fortification. Langley's approach to the problems of building a full-scale machine was relatively simple: so far as possible, he recreated the conditions that had led to success in 1896. The Great Aerodrome was a scaled-up version of the small Aerodromes. Like them, it would be launched from the roof of a houseboat anchored in the Potomac.

Langley spent much of his time and money developing a gasoline engine to power the new craft. In December 1898 he contracted with Stephen M. Balzer, a New York engine and automobile builder, for a 12-horsepower engine, together with the support structures for two propellers, transmission gears, drive shafts, and associated equipment. From the outset, Balzer's performance was disappointing. In August 1900, Charles Matthews Manly, a young Cornell engineer who worked as Langley's chief aerodromic assistant, canceled the original contract and transferred the incomplete engine to the Smithsonian, where he could personally oversee work on the power plant.

By 1903, Manly had completely rebuilt the engine, transforming it from a 6-horsepower rotary to a fixed-radial engine developing an incredible 52 horsepower. Langley was overjoyed. At last he was ready to send a human being aloft. Manly, the pilot, was less certain.

A number of questions must have occurred to Manly as he contemplated his future as the world's first airplane pilot. There was the matter of the basic structural integrity of his new machine. A simple tug on any one of the main bracing wires deformed the entire airframe. What would happen when the structure was accelerated from a dead stop to 60 mph as it sped down the launch rail?

Assuming a successful launch, would he be able to control the machine in the air? There was no mechanism for lateral control. A giant, wedge-shaped rudder was located directly at the center where it would be least effective. The all-moving cruciform tail elevator was untried.

Should the launch and flight proceed smoothly, Manly would still face his most important problem—how to land the thing. Like its quarter-scale predecessors, the Great Aerodrome was designed to land on water. The pilot, housed in a frail, fabric-sided cockpit underneath, would be the first thing to strike the surface—at a speed of perhaps 50 miles per hour. If he survived the landing he could probably count on the small floats on the main airframe to keep the machine from sinking. Unfortunately, with the Aerodrome floating on the surface, the pilot would be completely submerged. The thought of actually attempting to fly the Great Aerodrome under ideal conditions was a daunting prospect. Should it stray over dry land . . . well, best not to think about that.

The first trial flight of the Great Aerodrome was conducted on October 7, 1903, near Widewater, Virginia, just south of the old Quantico anchorage where the steam aerodromes had been flown. As the Wrights learned from the newspaper clipping, it was all over in a few seconds. Langley was not present. Manly climbed into the cockpit through the confusion of bracing wires, ran up the engine, and ordered the release. The craft moved rapidly down the rail and dived straight into the water. Drenched but undaunted, Manly agreed with Langley's assessment—it was all the fault of the launch mechanism. They immediately set to work preparing for a second trial before winter set in.

"I see that Langley has had his fling," Wilbur commented to Chanute. "It seems to be our turn to throw now, and I wonder what our luck will be."[12] At present Orville wrote to Katharine that even the elements seemed to be conspiring against them. Storm after storm swept across the Banks, forcing the brothers to venture out into the wind and rain to replace those portions of one building or another that seemed in immediate danger of being blown away.[13]

Then there were the "labor problems." Dan Tate, who signed on as a general handy man at the exorbitant rate of $7 per week, was so awkward around the machine that the brothers assigned him to outdoor duties. "Of course," Orv noted, "he was soon spoiled, and even went so far as to complain when any work was wanted on the hill."[14] That work was very hard. There were only three of them, and climbing the steep sand slope with the dead weight of the glider on their shoulders was not easy. Even with enough wind to kite the machine, the climb back uphill was marked by slips and slides as they struggled to move through ankle-deep sand.

The last straw came on October 28, when Dan refused to cut firewood. It was ridiculous, he argued, when the Wrights could buy it already cut for only $3 a cord from Jesse Baum in the village. He walked out on them at three o'clock that afternoon.

Finally, they had to contend with bitter cold. The temperature dropped lower every night. On October 25, Orv and George Spratt, who had walked into camp two days before, turned a used carbide can into a makeshift stove. The thing belched a thick cloud of smoke the first time they fired it up. "Everything about the building was sooted up so thoroughly that for several days we couldn't sit to eat without a whole lot of black soot dropping down on our plates," Orville wrote.[15]

But they persevered—the "whopper flying machine" was "coming on fine," finished and ready for ground testing by November 5. The trial did not go well. The sprockets resisted all efforts at tightening; the magneto failed to provide a sufficient spark; and vibrations from the rough-running engine damaged the propeller shafts. With no suitable shop facility available for miles around, they sent the shafts back to Dayton where Charlie could repair them.

Spratt left for home that afternoon, convinced that the Wrights were rushing toward disaster. He said as much to Chanute when they met accidentally at Manteo on November 6. Chanute, on his way to spend a few days with the Wrights, calmed Spratt down. He knew that his friends were not gamblers. It remained to be seen whether or not they would fly, but they would most certainly not risk their lives unnecessarily.[16]

Chanute had planned to come to camp with Patrick Alexander—the Wrights having finally given their approval—but the two men missed their connections in Washington. Rather than traveling hundreds of miles alone, Alexander joined Baden-Powell, who was in the United States as a delegate to the preliminary meetings on the St. Louis aeronautical program.

Chanute spent only six days in camp, November 6–12. The weather was bad. He saw little flying, but there was plenty of time for talk. For the Wrights, the conversation was discouraging. Chanute pointed out that the actual size, weight, and power of their machine almost exactly matched the calculated requirements for flight. There was no margin for error.

Orv commented to his father and sister that Chanute had "more hope of our machine going than any of the others," yet he obviously thought they had little real chance of success. Chanute described his own recent attempts to purchase the remains of *Avion III*, a large, steam-powered, bat-wing machine that the French experimenter Clément Ader had attempted to fly on two occasions in 1897. Chanute hoped to rebuild the craft, and planned to hire the Wrights to test it, but the negotiations fell through. The old machine was destined for a French museum. As if this were not enough, Chanute asked the Wrights to demonstrate the old Chanute-Herring two-surface glider at the St. Louis Exposition in 1904.

The Wrights were dumbfounded. "He doesn't seem to think our machines are so much superior as the manner in which we handle them," Orv remarked. "We are of just the reverse opinion."[17]

Having failed to interest the Wrights in his plans, Chanute arranged for W. S. Dough, of the Kill Devil Hills Lifesaving Station, to sail him back to Manteo. It was a decision he would soon regret. The man who had worked harder than any other to launch the air age simply walked away from the chance to witness the world's first airplane flight.

Work on the powered machine stood still until Charlie shipped the repaired propeller shafts back to Kitty Hawk. Nor could the 1902 glider be flown—the carbide can stove that kept the hangar comfortable had so dried the wood and fabric of the machine that it was no longer safe to use.

There was plenty of time to sit, to go over the calculations once again—and to worry. As Chanute had suggested, it would be a near thing. Everything depended on the amount of thrust delivered by the propellers. The problem was simple: the propellers were designed to produce 90 pounds of thrust at 330 revolutions per minute. That thrust would propel a 630-pound machine (the original estimated weight) at an airspeed of 24 miles per hour.

But when the finished machine was first weighed at Kitty Hawk, it exceeded their estimate by more than seventy pounds. To achieve flying speed with so much additional weight, the propellers would have to deliver an extra ten pounds of thrust. It scarcely seemed possible. Chanute estimated that they could expect a 25 to 30 percent loss of power in transmission. If he was correct, not even the addition of 4 extra horsepower over the performance originally calculated for the engine would be enough to get them aloft.

There were no loopholes. They could not reduce the weight of the aircraft, increase the horsepower of the engine, or change the fixed-gear ratio of the transmission. They could only hope that either Chanute's estimate of the loss of power in transmission was wrong, or the propellers would produce greater thrust than calculated. There was nothing to do but wait for the return of the shafts—and the ground tests that would tell them whether or not they would fly that year.

Orv noted in his diary that the value of the "flying machine stock" rose and fell in response to the mood of the moment. The long idle hours proved so frustrating and demoralizing that he took up the study of German and French, just to keep his mind off the airplane.[18]

The shafts finally arrived on November 20, and the Wrights ran their first serious tests the following day. The engine was still running rough, "jerking the chains and shaking the machine terribly." The sprockets on the propeller shafts refused to stay tight. A liberal dollop of Arnstein's Hard Cement, used to hold bicycle tires onto their rims, solved that problem. As Orv said, the stuff would fix anything from a stopwatch to a threshing machine.

The first test was a severe disappointment—only 306 revolutions per minute. The figure rose to 333 rpm after some tinkering with the engine and continued to climb during subsequent tests. In order to gauge the thrust, they placed the machine on a section of rail and attached it to a rope running over a pulley to a fifty-pound box of sand. With the engine running, they allowed the craft to inch forward. It lifted the sand and exerted an additional pull of sixteen to eighteen pounds. A few seconds of calculation revealed that the propellers were producing 132 to 136 pounds of thrust at 350 rpm. Chanute had been wrong—the machine should fly.

Wilbur and Orville spent the next week tinkering with the engine and transmission system, making run after run until they were achieving propeller speeds of up to 359 revolutions per minute. Then, following a series of six to seven runs of two to three minutes each on November 28, they detected a problem. A close inspection revealed a crack in one propeller shaft. Once again, all work stopped. This time, Orv would return to Dayton to prepare a special set of spring steel shafts.

Predictably, the weather turned mild and clear—perfect for flying—after Orville's departure. Will knew it would not last. Rather than sit and fret, he spent the long days pulling stumps and laying in a fresh supply of wood for the stove. Orv finished work on the new shafts on December 8 and boarded a train for the return trip to Kitty Hawk the next day.

Five hundred miles to the east, Samuel Pierpont Langley had completed preparations for what he hoped would be the first airplane

flight. At two-thirty in the afternoon on Tuesday, December 8, the
steam tugs *Bartholdi* and *Joe Blackburn* pulled away from a wharf
at the foot of Eighth Street in southwest Washington, D.C., with a
large houseboat in tow. The two vessels moved downstream through
blocks of floating ice to an anchorage at Arsenal Point, near the
confluence of the Potomac and Anacostia rivers. A midday calm had
given way to winds gusting up to 20 miles per hour—hardly ideal
conditions for the workmen struggling to bolt a cruciform tail and
four large wings to a steel-tube fuselage mounted on a catapult on the
roof of the houseboat.

Charles Manly was in charge. He took particular care with these
final preparations, for he was about to risk his life a second time
aboard the ungainly craft taking shape on the launcher.

At about four-thirty, Manly went into conference with Langley,
who had come out to the houseboat with a small party of friends and
Smithsonian employees. The winter sky was darkening rapidly, and
the gusts were so severe that it was impossible to keep the houseboat
pointed into the wind. Both men were aware that the test could not
be postponed—funds were gone, and the entire team had become
something of a laughingstock. Conditions were far from perfect, but
they were ready to go.

Manly stripped off his outer clothes. He would make the flight clad
in a cork-lined jacket, union suit, stockings, and light shoes. Whether
he succeeded or failed he faced a dunking in the icy waters of the
Potomac and had no intention of being weighed down by heavy garments.

The would-be aviator carefully picked his way through the jumble
of bracing wires and took a seat in the flimsy cockpit. As Manly ran
up the engine, Langley escorted his friends and guests back to the
small boats so that they could either applaud a turning point in history
or assist in Manly's rescue.

Satisfied with the sound of the engine and the operation of the
controls, Manly gave the signal for release at about 4:45 P.M. He sped
down the sixty-foot track, felt a sharp jerk, and immediately found
himself staring straight up at the sky as the machine flipped over onto
its back and dropped into the water.

Manly hung from the cockpit sides and entered the water feet first.
In spite of his precautions, he was trapped beneath the surface with
his jacket caught on a metal fitting. Ripping the garment off, he
struggled through the maze of broken wood and wire only to reach

The Langley Aerodrome was also ready to fly in the winter of 1903—or so its designer believed. Twice, on October 7 and December 8, the machine crashed into the Potomac. One reporter said it had the flying characteristics of "a handful of mortar."

the surface beneath an ice cake. Diving, he finally emerged in the open water some distance from the floating wreckage, just in time to see a concerned workman plunge under the remains of the craft to rescue him. Both men were quickly fished out of the water and carried to safety aboard the houseboat. Manly was uninjured, but so cold that Dr. F. S. Nash had to cut the clothes from his body.

Moments later, wrapped in a blanket and fortified with whiskey, this genteel son of a university professor startled the group by delivering a "most voluble series of blasphemies." Samuel Pierpont Langley's twenty-year quest for the flying machine was over.[19]

Orv arrived back in camp at one o'clock on the afternoon of December 11, having made the trip from Dayton in only two days. The machine was fully reassembled the next day. There was not enough wind to attempt a flight, but they ran it up and down the track to check the speed, damaging the tailframe in the process. The wind was still too light to attempt a flight on December 13. They spent most of the day reading. Adam Etheridge, a lifesaver from the Kill Devil Hills station, appeared in camp that afternoon to show his wife and children the flying machine that was the talk up and down the beach.

They spent the morning of December 14 finishing repairs on the tail and starting truck. Then, at one-thirty, they tacked a large red flag up on the side of the hanger, signaling the lifesavers down on the beach that they were about to attempt a flight and could use a hand. Bob Westcott, John T. Daniels, Tom Beacham, Will Dough, and "Uncle Benny" O'Neal strolled into camp a few minutes later with several young boys who had been hanging around the station that morning.

The Wrights had decided that rather than fly from the flats near camp, they would take advantage of gravity, laying their rail down the lower slopes of the big hill. That would mean moving their fragile 700-pound machine about a quarter of a mile. It was hard work, and took some forty minutes. By 2:40 that afternoon the machine sat tied on the end of the rail, some 150 feet up the 9-degree slope. They started up the engine—the sudden clatter sending the boys skittering out of sight.

While the engine warmed up, the brothers stepped off by themselves for a moment. One of them fished a coin out of his pocket. Wilbur won the toss and climbed into the pilot's position. Orv walked to the right wingtip. Will looked to both sides and reached forward to flip open the clip that held the restraining rope. Nothing happened. The weight of the machine headed downhill was putting too much pressure on the release clip. Orv called three lifesavers over and gently pushed the machine a few inches back up the slope to get some slack in the line.

Will started down the track before the crew was really prepared. Orv grabbed the upright as best he could and ran alongside to steady the craft as it rode down the rail. Before they had gone forty feet it was moving too fast for him to keep up. The machine rose into the air, and nosed sharply up to an altitude of perhaps fifteen feet. Flying at much too high an angle of attack, it slowed, stopped, and fell back to earth some sixty feet from the end of the rail.

The left wingtip struck first, swinging the craft around until the front skids hit the soft sand hard enough to splinter one of the elevator supports. Wilbur, stunned but uninjured, remained in place for a few seconds with the engine still running and the propellers ticking over. He finally reached forward and cut the engine. The first trial was over.

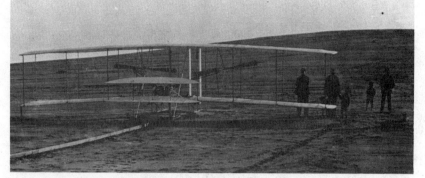

Just before the battle—December 14, 1903. The airplane is mounted on "the Grand Junction Railroad," a 60-foot monorail laid down the slope of the Big Kill Devil Hill. Wilbur stalled the machine just after takeoff, aborting the Wrights' first attempt at powered flight.

December 15 was spent making repairs to the machine. The work went quickly, but the slack wind ruled out any attempt at a second start. Orv hiked up the dunes to the village to send a wire home to Dayton: "Misjudgment at start reduced flight one hundred twelve power and control ample rudder only injured success assured keep quiet."[20]

The repairs were completed by noon on December 16. They spent the afternoon with the machine set up on the rail, waiting for the wind to pick up. The downhill launch had been a mistake. Not only would it compromise their claim to an unassisted sustained flight, but the excessive launch speed compounded the difficulties of takeoff. This time they set up the rail less than a hundred feet from the corner of the old shed.

Much of the tension was gone. Will had assured Milton and Katharine that "There is now no question [but] of final success."[21] But that final success did not come on December 16. After waiting several hours for the proper conditions, they gave up for the day.

They were up and about early on the morning of December 17. The day dawned cold and clear. A frigid 24-mile per hour wind swept out of the north, freezing the pools of standing water that had collected in the sand hollows. The Wrights were accustomed to the cold. Over a month before, Will had described how they managed at night to Milton: "In addition to . . . 1, 2, 3, and 4 blanket nights, we now have 5 blanket nights, & 5 blankets & 2 quilts. Next come 5 blankets, 2

The crew of the U.S. Lifesaving Service Station, Kill Devil Hills, N.C., made up the world's first aircraft ground crew. Proud men—and hard—they are shown here in 1900.

quilts & a fire; then 5, 2, fire, & hot water jug. . . . Next comes the addition of sleeping without undressing, then shoes & hats, and finally overcoats."[22]

The morning began with a familiar round of chores. While one man washed and shaved, the other fed chunks of driftwood into the make-shift stove that doubled for heating and cooking. Within half an hour both were dressed in white shirts, celluloid collars, and ties. Hoping that the bitter wind might abate, they remained indoors until about ten o'clock, when they decided to make a second try at flying.

As before, they tacked up the signal banner to summon the lifesav-ers, then set to work hauling out the sections of launch rail and pinning them down on the sand. Before they were quite ready, Adam Etheridge, John Daniels, and Will Dough walked into camp. They were accompanied by W. C. Brinkley, a lumber buyer from Manteo who had hiked over to the station to survey the timbers of a wrecked vessel, and Johnny Moore, a young man who lived with his widowed mother in a shack in the Nags Head woods.

Surfman Bob Westcott had the duty at Kill Devil Hills Lifesaving Station that morning; he would split his time between preparations for lunch and watching the activity in the dunes through his spyglass. Four miles down the beach at the Kitty Hawk station, Captain S. J. Payne also had a glass trained on the little party gathered around the sheds. The area was flat, and he could see that there was some activity, but could not tell precisely what was going on. Payne supposed they must be planning to try the flying machine again.

Two others, Bill Tate and Alpheus Drinkwater, had also been invited. Tate, who had not been in camp for some days, intended to stop by that afternoon once his chores were out of the way. Drinkwater was out of sight down the beach, watching the remains of one of the first U.S. Navy submarines, the *Moccasin* (A-4), which had broken loose and washed ashore while under tow. A federal employee, Drinkwater had been instructed to keep an eye on the sub until the Navy arrived. Convinced there was a promotion in it, he declined the Wrights' invitation to come up to camp that morning.

By ten-thirty the machine was set up at the head of the launch rail. A few drops of gasoline were pumped into each cylinder; the battery box was hoisted onto the wing and attached to the engine. After a final check all round, Wilbur and Orville walked to the rear and pulled the propellers through in unison. The engine coughed to life.

While the engine was warming up, the brothers withdrew. One of the lifesavers recalled that "we couldn't help notice how they held on to each other's hand, sort o' like two folks parting who weren't sure they'd ever see one another again."[23]

They shook hands and Orv climbed into place beside the engine, prone on the lower wing with his feet braced against a board tacked to the rear spar. He shifted his hips from side to side, checking the wing warping and rudder, then moved the elevator up and down. His right hand rested on a horizontal lever that had only three positions— right, center, and left. When pointing to the pilot's right, the cock connecting the fuel line to the engine was closed. To start the engine, the lever was moved to the center. When the pilot was ready to begin flight, he moved the lever one notch farther to the left, slipping the line that held the machine in place so it could move down the rail. At the same time, a stopwatch, anemometer, and propeller revolution counter were set in motion.

With Orv in place, Will turned and walked to the small group of spectators. He dispatched Daniels to man the camera pointed at the end of the rail. Orv had arranged his large box camera on its tripod before starting, and outlined the procedure; if the craft left the rail, Daniels had only to snap the shutter. Standing there shivering in the cold, he could not possibly have guessed that he was about to take one of the most famous photographs in history.

Wilbur walked back to the men with a final request—"not to look

Kill Devil Hills, N.C., 10:35 A.M., December 17, 1903. Surfman John T. Daniels, pressed into service as a photographer, caught the machine just as it left the rail, with Wilbur in mid-stride. The result is perhaps the most reproduced photograph of all time.

too sad, but to . . . laugh and holler and clap . . . and try to cheer Orville up when he started." The elder brother then strode to the right wing-tip, removing the small wooden bench that had been supporting that side of the aircraft.

At about 10:35, Orv shifted the lever to the left. Slowly, much more slowly than on December 14, the machine began to move down the rail into the teeth of a wind that was now gusting up to 27 miles per hour. Wilbur had no trouble keeping up with the craft, which rose from the track after only a forty-foot run. Daniels snapped the photo catching Will in mid-stride, apparently a bit startled by what was happening. He is the center of attention, the object to which the eye is drawn. That is as it should be.

The lifesavers broke into a ragged cheer. Bob Westcott, still watching through his telescope, let out a whoop of his own. The griddle cakes he was preparing for lunch that day were burned.

It was over very quickly. The airplane floundered forward, rising and falling for 12 seconds until it struck the sand only 120 feet from the point at which it had left the rail. You could have thrown a ball farther but, for the Wrights, it was enough. For the first time in history, an airplane had taken off, moved forward under its own power, and landed at a point at least as high as that from which it had started—all under the complete control of the pilot. On this isolated, windswept beach, a man had flown.

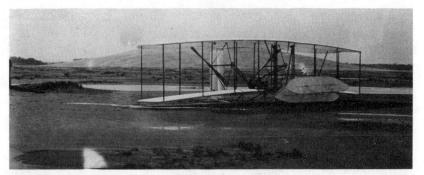

The 1903 airplane, its elevator support broken in a hard landing following the fourth
and final flight of December 17, 1903—852 feet in 59 seconds.

The small group ran forward to congratulate Orv. Then it was back
to work, carrying the machine to the starting point for another trial.
But first the Wrights invited everyone inside for a bit of warmth.
When they reemerged at 11:20, Will took his place for a flight of 195
feet. Twenty minutes later, Orv was back in the cradle, covering 200
feet in 15 seconds. At about noon, Will tried again, with spectacular
success: he flew 852 feet in 59 seconds, demonstrating beyond any
doubt that the machine was capable of sustained flight.

The distance for the men carrying the machine back to the starting
point was longer this time. When it was done, they paused for a
moment to catch their breath. The brothers, confident now, discussed
the possibility of a really long flight—perhaps all the way down the
beach to the telegraph at the Kitty Hawk weather station.

Suddenly, a gust of wind raised one wingtip high into the air. Daniels, who was standing closest, jumped to catch a strut and was carried along. The engine broke loose as the disintegrating machine
rolled over backward to the accompaniment of Daniels's screams and
the sound of snapping wires and splintering wood. When the dust
settled, the world's first airplane lay transformed into a twisted mass
of wreckage. Daniels, at least, was uninjured. For the rest of his life,
he would remind anyone willing to listen that he had survived the first
airplane crash.

The Wrights and their volunteer crew dragged what was left back
into the hangar. The earlier aircraft, the gliders of 1900–02, had simply been abandoned at the site. This time they would ship the remains
home to Dayton.

Having done all they could, the lifesavers walked back to their
station. Johnny Moore, determined to be the first to break the news,

sprinted down the beach toward Kitty Hawk. Encountering Bill Tate, he called out: "They done it! They done it! Damn'd if they ain't flew!"[24]

The Wrights ate a quiet, unhurried lunch, then strolled to Kitty Hawk themselves. They called on friends to confirm the reports of their success, but not before sending a telegram to the bishop. There was only one telegraph in Kitty Hawk, the Weather Bureau instrument that Joe Dosher used to communicate with the main office in Norfolk each day. Dosher, who had been the Wrights' first friend and contact on the Outer Banks, was on duty that afternoon. He agreed to send the message on to Bureau headquarters in Norfolk, where it would be passed to the Western Union operator for transmission to Dayton.

Just as the Wrights were leaving the Weather Bureau shack to walk on into the village, Dosher called them back. The Norfolk operator, Jim Gray, had sent a return message, asking if he could share the news with a reporter at the Norfolk *Virginian-Pilot.* The answer was an emphatic no.[25]

The Wrights had already arranged for the release of their story. Orv had given instructions to the family back in November—"If we should succeed in making a flight, and telegraph, we will expect Lorin as our press agent (!) to notify the papers and the Associated Press." By early December, Milton was busy "getting typewriter copies of the description of the Wright flyer, and copies of a sketch of the inventors" ready for distribution to newsmen.[26]

Carrie was working in the kitchen at 7 Hawthorn when the telegram arrived at half past five on the evening of December 17. She immediately took it upstairs to Milton. At some point during the roundabout transmission process Orville's name had been misspelled, but the basic message was clear. They had done it.

Success four flights thursday morning # all against twenty one mile wind started from Level with engine power alone # average speed through air thirty one miles longest 57 [sic] seconds inform Press home ####Christmas.

                                        Orevelle Wright[27]

Milton was all smiles when Katharine arrived home from school a few minutes later. Carrie agreed to hold supper while she walked the telegram and a copy of the bishop's press release over to Lorin's house. Along the way she stopped to telegraph the news to Chanute.

The message was delivered to his home just after eight o'clock that evening.[28] His response was immediate—and typical:

I am deeply grateful to you for your telegram of this date advising me of the successful flights of your brothers. It fills me with pleasure. I am sorely tempted to make the achievement public, but will defer doing so in order that they may be the first to announce their success. I earnestly hope they will do still better.[29]

Lorin went downtown to the offices of the Dayton *Journal* after supper and was directed to the desk of Frank Tunison, local representative of the Associated Press. Tunison was uninterested. His comment to Lorin became legend in newspaper circles: "Fifty-seven seconds, hey? If it had been fifty-seven minutes then it might have been a news item." Seven decades later, Lorin's daughter Ivonette could "still remember the depressed expression on my father's face when he returned."[30]

Had it been up to Tunison, the story might never have gotten out. Back in Norfolk, however, Ed Dean proved more enterprising. Dean was a friend of Jim Gray, the Norfolk operator Joe Dosher had asked to relay the Wrights' message on to Western Union. Gray told Dean about the telegram despite his instructions. Dean in turn approached his city editor, Keville Glennan, who agreed that the story was too good to pass up. The two men spent the next few hours fleshing out the sparse and enigmatic details of the telegram. Harry Moore, who worked in the *Virginian-Pilot* circulation department, also took a hand in composing the news account.

The finished story shows how heavily the three men drew on their imagination to fill in the gaps. The problems began with the headline that flashed across the front page of the paper on the morning of December 18:

FLYING MACHINE SOARS 3 MILES IN TEETH OF HIGH WIND OVER SAND HILLS AND WAVES AT KITTY HAWK ON CAROLINA COAST

They added a six-bladed "underwheel" that pushed the machine up into the air; a second propeller moved it forward through the sky. The engine was suspended beneath the "navigator's car," which also featured a "huge fan-shaped rudder of canvas" that could be moved up or down and from side to side for control. Then there was the distance flown—three miles at an altitude of 60 feet. Fortunately, one of the onlookers had preserved a record of Wilbur's first words after the conclusion of the flight." 'Eureka,' he cried, as did the alchemist of old."

When the Associated Press declined Glennan's offer to put the story on the wire, the editor sent queries to twenty-one newspapers asking if they would be interested in copying the piece. Five newspapers responded. Two of them, the *New York American* and the Cincinnati *Enquirer,* carried it in their morning editions. Perhaps inspired by the account in the morning *Enquirer,* the afternoon papers in Dayton took note of the flights for the first time. The Dayton *Herald* simply abbreviated the Norfolk piece. The *Daily News* was a bit more imaginative, if no more accurate. The story, carried in a section generally reserved for neighborhood news, was headlined: "DAYTON BOYS EMULATE GREAT SANTOS-DUMONT."[31]

It was an early indication of how friends and neighbors would react to the fact that two "local boys" had accomplished something beyond the wildest dreams of the world-famous Alberto Santos-Dumont.

The Associated Press, having rejected Glennan's story the evening before, now offered a 400-word abbreviated version to subscribers. Fantastic yarns began to appear on the back pages of newspapers across the nation. Wilbur and Orville, returning home from Kitty Hawk, found it difficult to understand how their careful plans for a low-key announcement to the press could have gone so wrong. Passing through the Chesapeake and Ohio depot in Huntington, West Virginia, early on the morning of December 23, they sent one last wire to Katharine: "Have survived perilous trip reported in papers. Home tonight."[32]

chapter 20

THE PRAIRIE PATCH

January–December 1904

The family greeted its two heroes with quiet pride and little fanfare. Carrie, aware that Mr. Will and Mr. Orv had not had a
decent meal in weeks, served porterhouse steaks and a fancy
dessert on their first evening home, assuring them "there was more
of everything in the kitchen." She was not prepared for Orville's
unquenchable thirst for milk, however. He drank glass after glass,
until Carrie began watering it down in the kitchen, certain that he
would not notice. He did, and told Carrie he was "grieved" she would
try to cheat him by dairying the milk. The story of the "dairied milk"
remained a joke between them for the rest of their lives.[1]

Christmas was especially festive that year. There was a dinner at
Lorin's, with presents for everyone. Wilbur and Orville presented a
set of silver forks and pearl-handled steak knives to Katharine, and
a two-inch micrometer to Charlie Taylor.

They expected Charlie to put his gift to immediate use. The 1903
engine had been destroyed in the accident on December 17. "They
wanted a new one built right away," Charlie recalled. "They were
always thinking of the next thing to do; they didn't waste much time
worrying about the past."[2]

Indeed, it was a time for decisions. "After several seasons," Wilbur
explained to an acquaintance,

> we found ourselves standing at a fork in the road. On the one hand we
> could continue playing with the problem of flying so long as youth and

leisure would permit but carefully avoiding those features which would require continuous effort and the expenditure of considerable sums of money. On the other hand, we believed that if we would take the risk of devoting our entire time and financial resources we could conquer the difficulties in the path to success before increasing years impaired our physical ability. We finally decided to make the attempt but as our financial future was at stake [we] were compelled to regard it as a strict business proposition until such time as we had recouped ourselves.[3]

Flight was no longer an obsessive hobby. They would turn the day-to-day operation of the bicycle shop over to Charlie and concentrate on the flying-machine business. The flights of December 17 were not the end of the quest, they lay somewhere in the middle. Frank Tunison's comment was close to the mark: fifty-nine seconds in the air would not impress a skeptical world. If they were to enjoy a financial reward for all their work, they would have to produce a genuinely practical airplane.

Work was under way on a new flying machine and engine by January 1, 1904. At the same time, the Wrights took steps to correct the ridiculous press reports arising from the *Virginian-Pilot* story. On January 5 they offered another release to the Associated Press, outlining precisely what had occurred on December 17. Newspapers across the nation and in Europe picked up the story. In addition, the account was sent to flying-machine enthusiasts in France and England, and the brothers asked Chanute to broadcast the news through his network of friends and correspondents.

Reactions varied. Predictably, the level of interest was highest in France. Ferber wrote to Chanute on January 27, thanking him "heartily" for the news. The letter reflects Ferber's extraordinary overconfidence, and indicates how little even the best-informed French enthusiasts knew about the problems that the Wrights had faced and overcome:

I was at first quite annoyed at not having been able to take this first step myself. But now, just think that this success of Wright is doing me lots of good, and is much to my advantage. I believe that people are now saying: "Why, that Captain was not such a fool after all, as the other chap has met with success." I would like to know whether Wright had already begun work on his motor last June, or whether it was the news that I was on the point of experimenting with one, which determined him to apply a motor himself?[4]

Ferber did not want the members of the Aéro-Club to be discouraged by the Wrights' success. "It is not as wonderful as they say," he commented to Ernest Archdeacon. "The experiment is not as grand as we supposed, but it does represent a new situation. . . . I think we ought to unite our efforts."[5] Archdeacon unveiled a glider of his own in January, "exactly copied from that of the Wright brothers." Constructed at the French military balloon and airship facility at Meudon, it was tested at the Aéro-Club's Parc d'Aérostation at Saint-Cloud later that spring.

Victor Tatin, a respected aeronautical pioneer, speaking at an Aéro-Club dinner-conference on February 4, reminded listeners that the reports from America were "very incomplete and often contradictory. In any case," he insisted, "the problem cannot be considered as completely solved by the mere fact of someone having flown for less than a minute . . . under conditions with which we are not very well acquainted."[6]

Tatin chided Ferber, Archdeacon, and other Frenchmen who were "slavishly copying the American gliders," and concluded with a call to arms:

Must we one day read in history that aviation, born in France, only became successful thanks to the Americans; and that the French only obtained results by carefully copying them? For us, that would indeed be glorious! Have we not seen enough French inventions carried to completion by foreigners, such as the steam-engine, gas light, steamships, and many others? Alas, are we to add aviation to them? . . . The first flying machine journey must be made in France. We need only the determination. So let us go to work!

Archdeacon rose to second Tatin:

Despite various contradictions, and a fair number of exaggerated reports published in the newspapers, it seems unquestionably true that the Wrights have succeeded in making a flight of 266 meters. . . . It is certain, gentlemen, that the results obtained are considerable, and—I do not cease to repeat—we must hurry if we wish to catch up with the enormous advance made over us by the Americans.

Just nine days after the flight at Kitty Hawk, Augustus Herring wrote to the brothers suggesting that they form a three-way partnership, with himself as third shareholder. As the "true originator" of the Chanute-Herring two-surface glider of 1896, he maintained, he had already been offered a "substantial sum" for his rights in any future patent interference suit with the Wrights.[7]

They ignored Herring's "rascality." It was an empty threat—Chanute and Herring had tried and failed to obtain an American patent for the 1896 glider. In any case, the only similarity between the glider and the Wright aircraft was the fact that all of them employed a modified Pratt truss to transform multiple wings into a beam structure.

But the incident underscored the need to obtain patent protection. While Orville set to work on the construction of two new engines— one of them experimental, the other to power the 1904 airplane—Will turned to the patent problem. The examiner who had rejected their application in 1903 advised them to hire an experienced patent attorney. Two Dayton friends, John Kirby and Will Ohmer, directed Wilbur to just such a man, Henry A. Toulmin, a lawyer with offices in nearby Springfield, Ohio.

The Wrights liked and trusted Toulmin immediately. Taking the original application as a starting point, he told them he could craft a broad, airtight patent that would stand the most severe test in the courts. He warned them at the outset that the process would take time, and advised saying as little as possible about their invention.

That meant dealing with Chanute, who was already uneasy about the Wrights' attitude toward publicity. Immediately after their return from Kitty Hawk, he suggested that they attend a meeting of the American Association for the Advancement of Science to "give the . . . first scientific account of your performances." Wilbur rejected the idea, adding that they were "giving no pictures nor descriptions of machine or methods at present." "They have grown very secretive," Chanute complained to Patrick Alexander several days later.[8]

"I was somewhat puzzled by your telegram," he wrote to Wilbur on January 20. "You talked while I was in camp of giving your *performance*, if successful, all publicity possible, and you knew I would not divulge the *construction* of your machine as I have never disclosed more than you yourself have published. Your telegram indicated a change of policy which you can more fully explain when I see you."[9]

The Wrights were wary of Chanute on several counts. In spite of his best intentions, he might release information of value to a rival. They were also concerned about the growing impression that he had played a major technical or financial role in their work. That concern was reflected in a single sentence in their Associated Press release: "All the experiments have been conducted at our own expense, without assistance from any individual or institution."

Chanute asked Wilbur to "please write me just what you had in mind concerning myself when you framed that sentence in that way." Wilbur phrased a delicate response.

> The object of the statement . . . was to make clear that we stood on completely different ground from Prof. Langley, and were entirely justified in refusing to make our discoveries public property at this time. We had paid the freight and had a right to do as we pleased. The use of the word "any," which you underscored, grew out of the fact that we found from articles in both foreign and American papers, and even in correspondence, that there was a somewhat general impression that our Kitty Hawk experiments had not been carried out at our own expense, &c. We thought it might save embarrassment to correct that promptly.[10]

Wilbur was sending a subtle message of his own to Chanute. While they had not yet seen reports of his speech to the Aéro-Club, the Wrights suspected that Chanute had told the French that the Wrights were his pupils. That had to stop.

Though neither party would admit it as yet, their relationship was already strained beyond hope of repair. Each saw the events of the past three years in a very different light. The Wrights knew that they alone had achieved a solution to the basic problems of mechanical flight. Their success was based on a series of fundamental breakthroughs. Simply put, they saw things that others missed, made correct decisions where others erred, and persevered when others lost faith.

Chanute did not agree. He saw the Wrights as extraordinarily gifted mechanics who had put old ideas into new bottles. Their genius, he thought, was to be found in an ability to make other men's ideas work. When he urged them to patent their mechanism, he was referring only to that combination of wires and pulleys that enabled them to flex a wing. The *idea* of flexing the wing, he believed, was not patentable.

The Wrights sought a patent so broad that every other flying machine would infringe on it. The value of such a monopoly would be enormous. With no serious rivals in sight, there was no reason for undue haste. The wisest course of action was to follow Toulmin's advice. They would continue working toward the production of a practical flying machine while guarding the secrets of their technology until the entire package, protected by an airtight patent, could be offered to a potential buyer—presumably a national government.

Chanute predicted that the brothers would fail to obtain more than a very narrow patent, one easily circumvented. He urged them to unveil their invention immediately. There was a fortune to be made by entering prize competitions and staging demonstrations. He raised the issue during a visit to Dayton on January 22, arguing that the upcoming St. Louis Exposition would be the perfect place to begin.

The Wrights toyed with the notion, traveling to St. Louis to inspect the flying field. It was never a serious possibility, however. Their new machine, as yet untested, would have to fly much farther than the 852 feet of 1903 to win any sort of prize. Moreover, it would be foolish to stage a public demonstration before they had a patent.

Convinced that they were wrong, Chanute nevertheless accepted their decision. The question of business strategy was now added to the growing list of issues dividing them. Just before his death in 1910—at a time when the Wrights had achieved world fame and were involved in bitter patent fights—Chanute repeated his unyielding view: "Therefore it was that I told you . . . that you were making a mistake in abstaining from prize-winning contests while the public curiosity is so keen, and by bringing patent suits to prevent others from doing so. This is still my opinion and I am afraid, my friend, that your usually sound judgment has been warped by the desire for great wealth."[11]

The Wrights faced the spring of 1904 confidently. There would be no more trips to the isolated Outer Banks. They had always known that operations would have to be transferred closer to home at some point, so they could continue to work without the expense entailed by extended stays at Kitty Hawk.

They chose Huffman Prairie as their flying field. The brothers came to this 100-acre cow pasture eight miles east of town early in the spring that year. Stepping off the DS & U trolley at a simple wooden platform labeled Simms Station, they climbed over the fence and walked out into the grass. They inspected the ground and studied the location of the trees and the newly installed telephone poles. A few months later, Wilbur offered a candid description of the place to Chanute:

> We are in a large meadow of about 100 acres. It is skirted on the west and north by trees. This not only shuts off the wind somewhat, but gives a slight downward trend. However, this is a matter we do not consider anything serious. The greater troubles are the facts that in addition to the cattle there have been a dozen or more horses in the pasture and as it is surrounded by barbwire fencing we have been at much trouble to get them safely away before making any trials. Also, the ground is an

old swamp and is filled with grassy hummocks some six inches high, so that it resembles a prairie dog town.[12]

Walking back to the platform to wait for the Dayton trolley, they decided that the field was far from perfect but it would do.

Precisely why the Wrights chose Huffman Prairie is not clear. In the mid-1830s John Leonard Riddell, foremost collector of botanical specimens in the West, had discovered three new species at the Prairie. William Werthner, the science teacher at Dayton's Central High School, led two generations of young people, including Orville and Katharine Wright, on field trips there. Orv loved that class, preserving a small notebook filled with plant descriptions and meticulous drawings of wildflowers as one of his few high school keepsakes.[13]

Perhaps it was the memory of those trips that brought the Wrights back to Huffman Prairie. Any one of a dozen fields would have done as well, but Orville knew that the Prairie had two great advantages: it lay directly on the interurban rail line and was, at the same time, relatively isolated.

Torrence Huffman, a West Side banker, was the owner. He knew the Wrights, and had seen the wild stories published in the Dayton papers over the last month or so describing goings-on with a flying machine somewhere down on the Carolina coast.

A cautious man, he had little faith or confidence in the brothers. "They're fools," he told Dave Beard, the grizzled, sixty-one-year-old farmer who worked the land adjacent to Huffman Prairie for him on shares. Still, the field was empty most of the time, and when the Wrights asked for permission to use it, he consented, asking only that they drive the cows and horses pastured there outside the fence before doing any flying.[14]

Soon the Wrights were at the Beards' door, explaining that Mr. Huffman had given his permission to use the field across the Pike. They cut the tall grass with scythes, then set to work building a wooden shed in the far corner. By mid-April they were spending most of their time inside the shed, assembling the strange, winged contraption that was the 1904 airplane.

When interviewed by reporters in later years, the Beards, like most of their old neighbors, had great difficulty describing the Wright machine. Amos I. Root, who roomed at the Beards when he drove his automobile down from Medina, Ohio, to watch the Wrights fly in 1904, thought that it resembled "a locomotive made of aluminum . . . with

wings that spread twenty feet each way." T. N. Waddell, an official
of the U.S. Census Bureau, reported that it looked something like "a
street car with the sides knocked out." The engine, he noted, was
"about the size of a waste paper basket."[15]

The 1904 machine looks just as confusing to the modern eye. Without the pilot on board to provide a point of reference, it is difficult to
tell the front from the back.

The craft was a virtual replica of the 1903 machine. Having
amassed a grand total of ninety-eight seconds' flying time in that
earlier machine, the Wrights could only guess at how its performance
or flight characteristics could be improved. There were a few differences hidden away beneath the skin of creamy muslin, however. The
wing camber had been altered from $1/20$ to $1/25$, and white pine wing
spars had been substituted for spruce. Both alterations proved to be
mistakes. The brothers would return to the 1903 pattern once again
in their 1905 Flyer.

At least the engine was an improvement. A four-cylinder in-line
model with a $4\frac{1}{8}$-inch bore, it weighed 240 pounds fully fueled and
ready for flight. The power plant developed 15–16 horsepower that
first year, and improved with age and wear. Reinstalled in the 1905
airplane, it produced 20 horsepower by the end of its second and final
flying season.

The Wrights first attempted to fly the new craft on May 23. They
had given considerable thought to this moment. By Dayton standards,
Huffman Prairie was isolated; compared to the fastness of the Kill
Devil Hills, however, it was a tourist mecca. The fifth-largest city in
the state lay only eight miles to the west, and two prosperous country
towns less than two miles to the east. Several farmhouses and all of
the surrounding fields had a clear view of the Prairie; a major traction
line carried hundreds of people directly past each day. If curiosity
seekers and newsmen came looking, there would be no place to hide.

Wilbur and Orville were astounded at the ease with which journalists had twisted the story of the first flight out of all recognition. Wild
tales about the events at Kitty Hawk were still circulating. The national magazines were as bad as the newspapers. On January 17, the
New York Herald Magazine identified the Wright machine as a balloon. The new issue of *Collier's* appeared on the newstands a week
later with a piece on "The Machine That Really Flies," including a
drawing of the 1896 Chanute glider identified as the 1903 Wright
airplane.

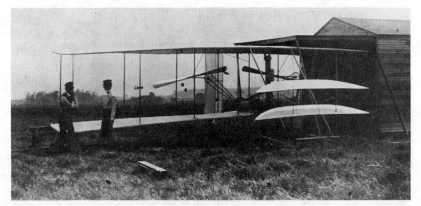

Wilbur (right) and Orville transferred operations to Huffman Prairie in the spring of 1904. Here they built and flew two more machines, the first of which rolled out of the hangar in May 1904.

"The Experiments of a Flying Man," which appeared in *The Independent* on February 4, was cobbled together from Will's two lectures to the Western Society of Engineers—lectures that had been copyrighted by the Society. The editor had even "forged" Wilbur's name to the piece. Chanute, they learned, had provided copies of the lectures and a photo of the 1902 glider. The brothers considered suing, but settled for a printed apology.

Determined to improve their handling of the press in 1904, the Wrights sent letters to the leading papers in Dayton and Cincinnati announcing that they would attempt to fly their new machine during the last week in May. No photographers would be allowed, but reporters were welcome.

A crowd of perhaps forty spectators, including a dozen newsmen, was present at Huffman Prairie on the morning of May 23. Unusually high winds gave way to a dead calm that kept them on the ground, even with the new 100-foot-long rail designed to be used on low-wind days. Finally, late in the afternoon, Will announced that they would make a demonstration run down the track. Nothing was going right. The engine proved difficult to start, and was obviously misfiring. The machine ran right off the end of the rail without rising an inch into the air.[16]

The fiasco of May 23 was followed by two days of hard rain that kept everyone indoors. Finally, on the 26th, with several hardy reporters still on hand, Orville just managed to get off the ground. Not even

Bishop Wright could become too excited about a flight of twenty-five feet.

The newsmen tried hard to find a story in what they had seen. One account described the machine as rising seventy-five feet into the air—three times as high as the actual length of the "flight." Another reporter, struggling to say something positive, commented that the Wright airplane was "more substantially constructed than any other machines of its kind."

Did the Wrights actually intend to fly for the reporters? If so, they were luckier than they knew. They had shown the press enough to be disappointing but not enough to make them look complete fools. Over the next two years the rumors of flights being made out at Huffman Prairie that circulated through the region would not surprise reporters or editors who had seen Orville actually lift off the ground for twenty-five feet. It was nothing to get excited about.

A few remained mildly curious. Luther Beard, a member of the Dayton *Journal* staff and a part-time school teacher in Fairfield, occasionally sat with the Wrights as they rode the trolley back and forth between Huffman Prairie and West Dayton. "I used to chat with them in a friendly way and was always polite to them," he recalled. "I sort of felt sorry for them. They seemed like well-meaning decent young men. Yet there they were, neglecting their business to waste their time day after day on that ridiculous flying machine. I had an idea they must worry their father."[17]

In the fall of 1904, one of Beard's students enquired if he knew what was going on over at the Prairie. The next time Beard saw Orv on the train, he asked if anything "unusual" had occurred. Orv said no, but Beard stayed in touch with them, chatting on the train and phoning once in a while. One evening Orv mentioned that his brother had flown for five minutes that afternoon, circling round and round the field. That sounded impressive enough for a couple of Dayton boys, but Beard knew that over in France the great Santos-Dumont had stayed up much longer than that, flying his dirigible airship all the way from the outskirts of Paris to the Eiffel Tower and back.

For the next five months there was little good news to report at Huffman Prairie. Flying was limited to a series of very short hops of 100 to 200 feet, most of them ending in a crash. Not until August 13 did they beat the 852-foot Kitty Hawk record. Their notebooks for the period are a litany of broken wings (the pine spars "shattered like taffy"), smashed propellers, damaged rudders, and broken supporting members.[18]

The field itself was the most difficult problem. At the Kill Devil Hills they had strong, steady winds. Here, there was usually no wind at all. When there was a breeze, it was gusty and uncertain. The Wrights were forced to use up to 240 feet of track to get up flying speed in the gentle spring and summer winds.

Laying that much track was backbreaking work. Each twenty-foot length of rail had to be carefully butted to its neighbor, checked for precise alignment, and staked into place. All too often the wind would shift just as the job was finished. When that happened, there were only two choices: to begin all over again, or risk the dangers of a crosswind takeoff.

It was a trying situation, as Wilbur explained to Chanute:

> We have found great difficulty in getting sufficient initial velocity to get real starts. While the new machine lifts at a speed of about 23 miles, it is only after the speed reaches 27 or 28 miles that the resistance falls below the thrust. We have found it practically impossible to reach a higher speed than about 24 miles on a track of available length, and as the winds are mostly very light, and full of lulls in which the speed falls to almost nothing, we often find the relative velocity below the limit and are unable to proceed.[19]

They would lay the track in the early morning calm, prepare the machine, then sit and wait for the wind to rise. At times they could see it coming in the distance, riffling the grass as it approached the launch site. There was a sudden flurry of activity as they rushed to get the machine moving down the track in time to meet the oncoming gust. If they did succeed in lifting off, the slightest drop in wind velocity deposited them back on the ground.

The dangers were appalling. Mrs. Beard kept a close watch on the Prairie through her kitchen window. When she saw the craft lift off, then fall abruptly out of sight, she would send one of her youngsters scurrying across the road with a bottle of linament. Charlie Taylor told her that every time he watched one of the brothers start down the rail, he had the feeling he might be seeing him alive for the last time.[20]

Orville made just such a hurried takeoff on August 24: the craft rose off the rail, then smashed back to earth as the supporting wind died. It was a miraculous escape. The upper wing spar came crashing down on him, broken, fortunately, just where it would have hit his back. He escaped with only bumps and bruises, but it was obvious that something would have to be done to reduce the chancy takeoffs.

Their answer was a catapult launch system. First put into operation on September 7, it consisted of a twenty-foot tower constructed at the foot of the rail. A 1,600-pound weight was drawn up to the top of the tower. A rope attached to the weight ran over a geared pulley down to the base of the tower; over a second pulley and down the length of the rail; then over a third pulley and back down the rail again to be fastened to the front of the airplane. The machine was anchored in place by means of a second rope attached to a stake in the ground.

When the pilot was ready for flight, he reached over the leading edge of the wing and released a clip holding the anchor line. With the loop open, the weight dropped, pulling the machine down the rail. They found that they could make safe takeoffs from a sixty-foot rail even in extremely light winds.

Before September 7 they had completed less than forty starts, most of which had resulted in very short flights because of insufficient air speed. Suddenly there was an unmistakable jump in performance. Now the brothers could fly the length of the field without difficulty. By September 15, they were making flights of up to half a mile in length complete with their first full turns in the air. The great break-through came five days later, when Orville flew a complete circuit of the Prairie, covering 4,080 feet in just over 1 minute, 35 seconds.

Amos Root, the eccentric operator of a beekeeping supply house in Medina, Ohio, was there that day. He had heard rumors about two young men who were actually flying from a cow pasture down in Dayton, and passed the news along to his Sunday School class. In mid-September he packed a suitcase and drove 175 miles to Fairfield to investigate the miracle for himself.

Root lodged with the Beards, who were far more impressed by the distance he had driven an automobile than by what was going on in the field across the Pike. His timing was perfect. He walked over to the Prairie on the morning of September 20 and introduced himself to the Wrights, who were quite taken with him. That afternoon he witnessed the first circular flight of an airplane in the history of the world. It was a moment he would not forget.

> When it turned that circle, and came near the starting-point, I was right in front of it; and I said then, and I believe still, it was . . . the grandest sight of my life. Imagine a locomotive that has left its track, and is climbing up in the air right toward you—a locomotive without any wheels . . . but with white wings instead . . . a locomotive made of aluminum. Well now, imagine that locomotive with wings that spread 20 feet each way, coming right toward you with the tremendous flap of its propellers, and you have something like what I saw . . . I tell you friends,

the sensation that one feels in such a crisis is something hard to describe.[21]

Root described what he had seen to the readers of *Gleanings in Bee Culture*, the journal he published for customers of his supply house. Over the next two years he continued to provide progress reports. He also offered to allow the editor of *Scientific American* to reprint his articles, but that gentleman refused. For the two years, 1904–05, when Wilbur and Orville Wright were perfecting their invention, the only accurate coverage appeared in a journal aimed at an audience of beekeepers.

By now, neighboring farmers also had begun to pay more attention to the Wrights. The Beards, the Harshmans, the Millers, and old Amos Stauffer, who farmed the land right next to the Prairie, visited the field on occasion and got to know the boys. Huffman Prairie became a topic of conversation among the DS & U crews as well. At first the Wrights had timed their experiments to avoid the passing trains. That became more difficult as the flights grew longer. On November 9, Mr. Brown and Mr. Reed, two supervisors on the Dayton-Springfield line, ordered the crew of their inspection train to hold up at the station for an extra five minutes while they watched Wilbur fly four complete circles of the field.[22]

Accidents remained commonplace. Some, like the one on November 1, were the result of simple carelessness. Orv started the engine and was conducting a pre-flight inspection when the machine suddenly edged forward—the anchor peg had pulled loose from the soft ground. He leaped onto the skid, reached forward, and depressed the elevator lever as the craft went careening down the rail. The result was a sprained shoulder and some minor damage to the machine.

Other problems required more ingenuity. The brothers had trouble orienting themselves in turns, frequently miscalculating, banking too steeply, or allowing the nose to rise so high that the aircraft stalled. The answer was a long string tied to the crossbar of the elevator. When the craft was flying straight and level, the string blew directly back toward the pilot. When banking, or flying with the nose up or down, the position of the string enabled him to gauge the attitude of his machine. It was the first flight instrument.

The last flight of the season came on December 9, almost a year after the first short hops at the Kill Devil Hills. The first year back in Ohio had been a mixture of success and disappointment. The catapult launch system had enabled them to extend their time in the air,

By November 16, 1904, when this photograph was taken, the brothers had begun to get a feel for the new machine—and the problems still to be solved.

and to make their first turns. Twice they remained aloft for more than five minutes, circling the field four or five times. That was a clear step forward.

But their performance was not consistent. The exceptional long flights were widely separated by a great many shorter hops of thirty seconds to a minute. They were really flying for the first time, and their experience in the air was growing, but accidents remained a daily occurrence and voluntary safe landings rare. The airplane was frequently operating out of control. Even during simple straight-line flights down the length of the field it would begin to undulate until it was impossible to keep it in the air.

The Wrights tried altering the center of gravity by moving the pilot position and engine slightly to the rear. Far from correcting the problem, the shift increased the undulations, making the machine impossible to control in pitch.

Puzzled, they took steps in the opposite direction, loading twenty pounds of ballast beneath the forward elevator. This increased the period of the oscillations, and helped to counter the sensitivity of the elevator. The machine was controllable, but only marginally so. The basic resolution of the pitch and elevator problems would have to wait until 1905.

BOOK THREE

The World

chapter 21

"A MACHINE OF PRACTICAL UTILITY"

January 1904-December 1905

Brevet Lieutenant Colonel John Edward Capper, Royal Engineers, a senior officer of the British military balloon establishment, arrived in Dayton to meet with the Wrights on October 24, 1904. An official representative of His Majesty's Government, he was their first potential customer.

The serious history of British military aeronautics begins with the Boer War. The handful of men who successfully pioneered reconnaissance ballooning with the Royal Engineers returned from the South African campaign with War Office approval for an expanded program of aeronautical research. The prestigious Committee on Military Ballooning authorized work on free balloons, development of a powered airship, and experiments with man-lifting kites.[1]

Strategic thinkers in England were also examining the possibility of a future war in the air. Late in January 1904, only a month after the Wrights flew at Kitty Hawk, Halford Mackinder, director of the London School of Economics and Political Science, gave a lecture on "The Geographic Pivot of History" at the Royal Geographical Society in which he argued that the next great threat to Britain's security would come not by sea, as in the past, but from the Eurasian heartland.[2] The Royal Navy would be of little value when the nations controlling the vast spaces between the Elbe and Vladivostok developed an industrial capacity and a network of railway links.

In the comment session afterwards, L. S. Amery, a rising young politician and journalist, suggested that control of the air might be the only way to counter the prospect of Eurasian hordes pouring toward

the Channel. "Both the sea and the railway are going in the future
... to be supplanted by the air as a means of locomotion, and when
we come to that ... the successful powers will be those that have the
greatest industrial basis ... those people who have the industrial
power and the power of invention and of science will be able to defeat
all others."[3]

Aware that they were starting from behind, the leaders of the
embryonic aeronautical program were eager to keep up to date on the
latest foreign developments. Thus, in June 1904, the War Office ordered Lieutenant Colonel Capper to attend the aeronautical display
and airship competition at the Lewis and Clark Exposition in St. Louis.

Thanks in part to the work of Octave Chanute, the aeronautical
program planned for the St. Louis Fair was shaping up nicely. There
would be exhibits of balloons, airships, engines, and other aeronautical paraphernalia, as well as a schedule of lectures—topped off by the
excitement of aerial competition.

The American exhibition balloonist Carl Myers, superintendent of
the races, offered a total of $150,000 in prizes to the aeronauts who
piloted their balloons and airships higher, faster, and farther than
their competitors. A grand prize would go to the pilot achieving the
best average speed during three runs over a fifteen-mile course. The
rules were stiff, including a requirement for a winning speed of at
least 20 miles per hour, but some of the world's best-known
aeronauts, including Santos-Dumont himself, were there to try their
luck.

Santos's plans to sweep the field were scotched when his airship
was destroyed by vandals. Tom Baldwin had better luck. Baldwin, a
daredevil American balloonist and parachute jumper, came to the fair
with the *California Arrow,* a one-man airship that refused to leave
the ground with its 210-pound designer on board. Fortunately, a substitute pilot was at hand. Young A. Roy Knabenshue operated a pair
of tattered captive balloons used to give visitors a bird's-eye view of
the Fair. He had already captured press attention with a spectacular
200-foot hand slide down the balloon tether cable.

Knabenshue created yet another sensation when he flew the *California Arrow* for the first time on October 25, negotiating a figure-S
over the fairgrounds. He earned substantial prize money but, like
everyone else, failed to win the grand prize.

Of course Chanute was there. He hired Bill Avery, who had flown
with him on the Indiana Dunes ten years before, to demonstrate a new

version of the two-surface glider. As there were no suitable hills, Avery devised a motorized winch to tow him into the air. Everything went fine until a twisted ankle forced his withdrawal as the only entry in the heavier-than-air competition.

Colonel Capper was disappointed with the Americans and their fair. "It is of no use whatever," he wrote, "pointing anything out to an ordinary American; they are all so damned certain they know everything and so absolutely ignorant of the theory of aeronautics that they only resent it."[4]

He did admire the "beautifully made" Chanute glider, and traveled to Chicago for a long meeting with its designer. Then it was on to Dayton to make the acquaintance of Wilbur and Orville Wright. Before his departure, Capper had asked Patrick Alexander, Baden-Powell, and others for advice on whom he should meet in America. Everyone insisted that he include the Wright brothers. Their names were well known in England now. Alexander had met them; Baden-Powell and a handful of others had corresponded with them. No one, however, had the slightest idea what they had been up to since the flights at Kitty Hawk in 1903. Capper hoped to take their measure for himself.

Sure enough, Dayton proved to be the most interesting stop on Capper's American tour. The Wrights liked him, though not well enough to show him the airplane. They let him see some photographs of the machine in flight, something they would not do for subsequent visitors, and explained the basics of their technology. Capper was impressed, and said so in his official report: "Both these gentlemen impressed me favorably; they have worked up step by step, they are in themselves well-educated men and capable mechanics, and I do not think them likely to claim more than they can perform."[5]

Capper was not authorized to negotiate with the Wrights, but encouraged them to tender a proposal for the sale of an airplane to the War Office. "We told him," Orv later recalled, "that we were not yet ready to talk business."[6]

Capper's visit, closely followed by the long flights at the close of the 1904 season, convinced the Wrights that they were in fact, ready to talk business by January 1905. But as Wilbur admitted to Chanute, "we would be ashamed of ourselves if we offered our machine to a foreign government without giving our own country a chance at it. . . ."[7]

Uncertain how to proceed, Wilbur called on his local congressman,

Robert M. Nevin, at his Dayton home on the evening of January 3. Nevin advised him to describe his machine's performance and the terms for its sale in a letter that he would present to Secretary of War William Howard Taft. Their consciences soothed, the brothers decided to forge ahead on two fronts simultaneously.

Wilbur wrote to Colonel Capper on January 10. He outlined their successes during the final weeks of the 1904 season, adding that although "no spectacular performances were attempted, the . . . results were so satisfactory that we now regard the practicability of flying as fully established." Which brought him to his main point: "There is no question, but that the government in possession of such a machine as we can furnish, and the scientific and practical knowledge and instruction that we are in a position to impart, could secure a lead of several years over governments which waited to buy perfected machines before making a start in this line."[8]

If the British government was interested in the purchase of a machine to carry two men through the air at a speed of 30 miles per hour, the Wrights could supply one. Eight days later, the brothers wrote to Congressman Nevin, describing their craft as a machine that "not only flies through the air at high speed, but lands without being wrecked."

They offered either to sell an aircraft capable of meeting government performance requirements, or to furnish "all the scientific and practical information we have accumulated in these years of experimenting, together with a license to use our patents; thus putting the government in a position to operate on its own account."[9]

Nevin was ill when the letter arrived. Unaware of his promise to take the matter up personally, a clerk forwarded the letter directly to the U.S. Army Board of Ordnance and Fortification for comment. Major General G. L. Gillispie, president of the Board, replied through Nevin's office on January 26:

> I have the honor to inform you that, as many requests have been made for financial assistance in the development of designs for flying machines, the Board has found it necessary to decline to make allotments for experimental development of devices for mechanical flight, and has determined that, before suggestions with that object in view will be considered, the device must have been brought to the stage of practical operation without expense to the United States. It appears from the letter of Messrs. Wilbur and Orville Wright that their machine has not yet been brought to the stage of practical operation, but as soon as it shall have been perfected, this Board will be pleased to receive further representations from them in regard to it.[10]

Wilbur and Orville took Gillispie's letter as a personal affront. They had told him that their machine was "fitted for practical use" and described its performance. The sons of Milton Wright did not intend to deal with those unwilling to accept their word as honest men. "It is no pleasant thought to us that any foreign country should take from America any share of the glory of having conquered the flying problem," Will told Chanute on June 1,

> but we feel that we have done our full share toward making this an American invention, and if it is sent abroad for further development the responsibility does not rest upon us. . . . If the American government has decided to spend no more money on flying machines till their practical use has been demonstrated in actual service abroad, we are sorry. . . .[11]

War Department officials have often been portrayed as short-sighted and conservative in their early dealings with the Wright brothers. That was not the case. If anything, the Army had rushed too quickly into the airplane business. The members of the Board were still experiencing serious difficulties arising out of their support for the Langley Aerodrome project. The action of the Board in granting $50,000 for the Aerodrome had been a courageous and far-sighted decision. In 1898, Langley's program seemed enormously promising, but the spectacular demise of the craft in December 1903 set the Board up as a target for congressional inquiry and censure.

Representative Hitchcock led the attack, castigating the Board for "permitting an expenditure for scientific purposes of thousands in a vain attempt to breathe life into an air-ship project which never had a substantial basis. You can tell Langley for me," Robinson added, "that the only thing he ever made fly was Government money."[12]

The Aerodrome episode became the focal point for a general congressional attack on government-funded research. The Board survived the onslaught, but it was badly burned. The career officers involved would handle the question of mechanical flight very gingerly in the future.

To make matters worse, the Langley publicity generated a flood of crank proposals from would-be aviators with surefire schemes for mechanical flight. Yet another letter, this one from two "inventors" who claimed to have solved the problem of the ages in the back room of a bicycle shop, was not calculated to impress.

The Wrights had not included any photos of their gliders or powered machines in the air, nor provided letters from eyewitnesses. In fact, they offered no proof at all, only the bald assertion that their machine worked. To expect a positive response from the War Department on that basis indicates Wilbur and Orville's inability to understand and deal effectively with a government bureaucracy.

Whitehall's reaction was strikingly different. The War Office listened to Colonel Capper, and Capper knew the Wrights. He forwarded Wilbur's letter to his immediate superiors in the Aldershot engineering command with a covering note calling "very special attention" to the proposal. "I have every confidence in their uprightness," he added, "and in the correctness of their statements. Taking their letter for granted, it is a fact that they have flown and operated a flying machine for a distance of over three miles at a speed of thirty miles an hour."[13]

Capper restated the details, pointing out that the machine was entirely heavier-than-air, and closing with a strong personal appeal:

> I wish to urge most strongly that I be permitted to answer this letter stating that I think it probable that their offer would receive consideration from His Majesty's Government. I would point out that such an answer would in no way tie His Majesty's Government to anything beyond giving full and due consideration to any offer made by these gentlemen. I cannot but feel that if these gentlemen are prepared to make any reasonable offer, their statement is a true one, and they should meet with every encouragement from us in the interest of progress in our war appliances.[14]

Capper's personal assurances worked. Although the matter of the Wright airplane was withdrawn from his hands and passed to higher authority, enthusiasm for the project took root. On February 11, Capper's immediate superior, Richard Ruck, wrote to the Wrights, inviting them to provide a description of their machine's performance and a statement of terms.[15]

They replied with a long letter on March 1, offering to provide a machine carrying two men for a distance of from ten to fifty miles through the air at a speed of not less than 30 miles per hour. Their price would be computed at a rate of £500 for each mile covered during the best of the trial flights. Alternatively, they could negotiate the sale of their patents (not yet granted) and engineering data that would permit the English to construct their own flying machines.[16]

Ruck was unwilling to purchase a machine on the basis of a trial flight of less than fifty miles. And the price for such a craft, according to the Wright formula, was £25,000, a sum far beyond his allocated resources. The matter moved up a rung in the chain of command to the Royal Engineer Committee, the War Office body charged with making scientific and technical decisions. The committee responded on April 22, suggesting that the military attaché in Washington be sent to Dayton to see the machine in the air.

On May 13, Reginald H. Brade, Assistant to the Secretary of the War Office, advised the Wrights to expect a communication from Colonel Hubert Foster, military attaché to the British Embassy. Foster, in turn, was instructed to arrange a visit to Dayton.[17]

Had Foster made contact in the spring, summer, or fall of 1905, the course of history might have been altered. Possibly the Wrights would have been willing to allow an official English visitor the privilege of witnessing a flight. But it was not to be. Foster, accredited both to Washington and Mexico City, spent the months of March through October 1905 in Mexico. He made no attempt to contact the Wrights until November 18. So far as Wilbur and Orville were concerned, it was just as well. Back in the air, they wanted no interruptions from the British or anyone else while they worked through their final difficulties.

Work began on the third Wright Flyer on May 23. They rolled the machine out for its first flight just a month later, on June 23. The new craft reflected what they had learned during the previous season. The span and chord of the wings were unchanged, but the camber was $\frac{1}{20}$ again, as it had been in 1903. The Flyer was longer than any of its predecessors and stood a bit taller as well, giving it additional ground clearance.

A pair of "blinkers"—semicircular vanes—were set between the twin elevator surfaces to prevent the sideslips so common in 1904. The propellers featured "little jokers," tabs on the trailing edge designed to halt the deformation that had been observed the year before. Both the rudder and elevator were larger than in 1904.

The most important change was in the control system. Since 1902 they had flown with the rudder directly linked to the wing-warping system. With the experience of three seasons, they decided to give the pilot full control at last. His hips would remain in the warping cradle, with his hands on two control levers, one for the elevator and one for the rudder.

Flight testing began on June 23, and continued with eight hops over the next twelve weeks. There was no improvement over the performance of the 1904 machine. The longest flight was only 19.5 seconds. Without exception, every day ended with an accident and damage to the aircraft.

The most serious mishap in two years of experimenting with powered machines occurred on July 14. Orville had been in the air for only twelve seconds when, as Wilbur reported, "the machine began to wobble somewhat and suddenly turned downward and struck at a considerable angle."[18]

The accident was a result of those undulations—Orv had lost control of the elevator. The machine smashed to earth, head first, at a speed of 30 miles per hour. The elevator and outrigger supports crumpled instantly. What was left of the machine bounced three times down the field, upending on the front edges as it slid to a stop. Orville was catapulted out of the cradle and through a broken section of the top wing. They found him, dazed and bruised, lying in the remains of the elevator.

This was the catastrophic accident they had dreaded ever since they first began gliding. Safety was much on their minds that summer. Not long after Orv's accident they received word that Daniel Maloney had been killed flying a glider designed by Californian John Joseph Montgomery.

Twenty years before, in 1883 or 1884, Montgomery had made one short, nearly disastrous glide. The first American to take to the air aboard a heavier-than-air craft found the experience so sobering that he immediately ceased flying and devoted his time to laboratory work.

Chanute met him at the Chicago meeting in 1894, and included an account of Montgomery's early work in *Progress in Flying Machines.* Disagreements over the value of the Californian's "theoretical" contributions led to a falling out, however. Chanute had not heard from him in over a decade.[19]

Suddenly, in the spring of 1905, Montgomery's name was in the headlines. This time he had built a tandem-wing glider vaguely reminiscent of the Langley Aerodrome. Rather than testing the craft himself, he hired two daredevil "pilots," Daniel Maloney and Charles K. Hamilton, who allowed themselves to be carried aloft with the glider dangling beneath a hot-air balloon. The idea was to cut loose at an altitude of several thousand feet and glide back to earth. It was an incredibly dangerous stunt to try with a craft that could scarcely be controlled except by weight shifting. Small wonder that the newspapers paid attention.

The inevitable catastrophe occurred at Santa Clara University on July 18. Maloney dropped free and maneuvered a little, then the spectators noticed that something was seriously wrong. The aircraft smashed to earth. Maloney died shortly afterwards.

All that spring, Chanute's letters were filled with the latest news of Montgomery's "bold performance." The Wrights remained silent. With Maloney's death, however, Wilbur felt compelled to comment.

The tragic death of poor Maloney seemed the more terrible to me because I knew it was coming and had tried in vain to think of some way to save him. I knew a direct warning would tend to precipitate rather than prevent a catastrophe. The Montgomery pamphlet showed an entire misapprehension of the real facts regarding the distribution of pressures and the travel of the center of pressure with increasing speed, and it seemed to me something awful that poor Maloney should cut loose high in the air and lightly cause the machine to dart and describe circles without knowing that there were critical points beyond which it would be absolutely impossible for him to right the machine.[20]

The Wrights knew infinitely more than Montgomery about the forces playing across the wings of a flying machine, and they would never have been so foolish as to release themselves in the air under such conditions. Control was the key to safety. Clearly, their own machine was often out of control in pitch. Orv's crash forced them to come to terms with the final problem.

The solution lay in some modification to the elevator. In rebuilding the forward section of the machine, they enlarged the elevator surface area from 52.74 square feet to 83 square feet; they also moved the elevator from 7.32 to 11.7 feet in front of the leading edge of the wing. The longer "moment arm" served the same function as the addition of weight beneath the elevator in 1904.[21]

The aircraft that emerged differed significantly from that of a few weeks before. It embodied all they knew about flying—and some educated guesses. Back in the air on August 24, an enormous improvement in performance was immediately apparent. After less than a week of practice Orville was flying four circuits of the field, remaining aloft for 4 minutes and 54 seconds. The accidents vanished abruptly. By September, two-, three-, four-, and five-minute flights became common—without a single serious accident.

The impact of the design breakthrough was apparent by the end of the month. On September 26 Wilbur remained in the air for 18 minutes, 11 2/5 seconds. For the first time, they ran the gasoline tank dry. The record continued to climb: 26 minutes on October 3; 33 minutes and 17 seconds on October 4.

By October 5, it was clear to a number of people that something extraordinary was happening out along the Dayton-Springfield Pike.

Wilbur flew two complete circles of the field on September 7, 1905. The Wrights were now certain that they had achieved the goal of a practical flying machine.

As their confidence grew, the Wrights began to invite selected friends and neighbors out to watch them fly. Word spread across West Dayton, and up and down the country lanes surrounding Huffman Prairie, attracting additional uninvited spectators.

Amos Stauffer was out in his field on the afternoon of October 5, cutting corn with one of his hired men. He later recalled that it was about half past three in the afternoon when the distinctive popping, clattering, flapping sound of engine and propellers drifted over from the Huffman pasture. The Wright boys were at it again. Glancing up, he saw the airplane climb into view, fly a few hundred feet straight forward, then sink back out of sight in a gentle arc. The first flight of the day had lasted less than forty seconds.[22]

There was a small crowd again that afternoon—twenty, perhaps thirty, people gathered along the fence separating the Stauffer place from Huffman Prairie. Reuben Schindler, who clerked in a Dayton drugstore, was there, arguing with tinsmith Henry Webbert about the appearance of the airplane on landing. "Like a duck," Schindler insisted, "she squatted on the ground." No, Webbert countered, it looked more like a "turkey descending from a tree."[23]

C. S. Billman, a West Dayton neighbor of the Wrights, had driven his new automobile out to the Prairie that afternoon with his wife, their daughter Nellie, and young son Charley. After the first flight of the day he was content to move from one knot of spectators to another exclaiming, "Well, she flies!"

For weeks thereafter, Charley, a wide-eyed three year old, would race through the house, arms outstretched, mimicking the sound of the airplane. The boy's performance impressed one skeptic who called on the family shortly afterwards to check on the Wright brothers' claims to have flown. "I'm about convinced," the fellow remarked. "That boy could not be a paid witness."[24]

Torrence Huffman and Dave Beard were watching from a grassy slope on the far side of the Yellow Springs Pike. They saw the workmen set the airplane into place at the head of the eighty-foot launch rail. Next, someone carried a coil box out to the lower wing and attached the leads to the engine. Two other men stepped up to the rear of the wings, counted to three, and pulled the propellers through. The engine coughed to life.

Wilbur, whose turn it was to fly, stretched himself out on the lower wing next to the engine and tested the controls. Beard and Huffman could see a helical twist run across both wings, first in one direction, then in the other. They watched the elevator rock up and down and the rudder move from side to side.

The pilot nodded to his brother, reached forward, and released the clip. The weight fell, catapulting the machine down the track and into the air. It undulated up and down as it flew the length of the field toward the two men on the slope, then swept up on one wing into the first graceful turn.

It kept right on going. Even the handful of neighboring farmers who had seen the craft off the ground before were stunned. Amos Stauffer spoke for all of them. "The durned thing just kept going round," he remarked. "I thought that it would never stop."[25]

Wilbur Wright flew thirty circles over the field on that October afternoon, landing only when his fuel was exhausted. He kept the machine in the air for 39 minutes, 23⅘ seconds, covering a total distance of 24⅕ miles in the process. This was not only the longest flight made to date, it was longer than the total of all 109 flights the Wrights had made in 1903 and 1904 put together.

They had done it. The 1905 Wright airplane was one of the most extraordinary machines in the history of technology. Capable of rising into the air, flying for an extended period under the complete control of the operator, and landing safely, it was the world's first practical airplane. Nine years of trial and error, discouragement and hope, risk to life and limb, and brilliant engineering effort had culminated in the air over this Ohio cow pasture.

With so many witnesses to an accomplishment this spectacular, newsmen at last took notice. The first press inquiries came on the evening of October 5. The next day Luther Beard of the Dayton *Journal* was on hand at the Prairie. The *Daily News* carried the story on the morning of October 6. The Cincinnati *Post* picked it up the following day. Henry Webbert told the boys that John Tomlinson at the Dayton *Journal* had offered him $50 for advance notice of the next flight.[26]

Wilbur and Orville were not eager to end the season. Chanute had not seen any of the great flights of 1904 or 1905—a witness with his credibility might be very useful to them in the weeks and months to come. They urged him to make the trip to Dayton. He arrived on November 1, but a rainstorm set in and no flights were possible.

Chanute had missed his chance to see the world's first airplane fly. He would not have another for a very long time. The brothers had reached a firm decision. They had invested an enormous amount of time and energy in solving a problem that had baffled the world's great minds for centuries. The airplane was not their gift to the world, but a product for sale.

The value of their product was not in the wood, wire, and fabric of the machine, but in the knowledge that lay behind it. Under the best of circumstances, that knowledge would be hard to protect—and circumstances were not ideal. Toulmin had finally applied for their patent, but it would not be granted until 1906. Premature disclosure of the details would seriously complicate, perhaps destroy, their legal position. Chanute might already have accomplished that in nations like Germany, which had very strict rules regarding prior disclosure.

Even the patent would not guarantee protection. The Wrights knew that patents had proved of little value in defending other inventors against infringement. A far wiser course was to reveal as little about the airplane as possible until they had a signed contract for its sale in hand. Until that day arrived, there would be no more flying.

chapter 22

"FLIERS OR LIARS"

October 1905-October 1906

T he years 1900–05 were the happiest Wilbur and Orville would
ever know. No longer drifting, they found direction and purpose
in the process of invention. Both men pushed themselves to the
limit, courting danger, tasting disappointment, and savoring triumph.
Orv distilled the sheer joy of it into that one line of a letter to George
Spratt: "Isn't it astonishing that all of these secrets have been preserved for so many years just so that we could discover them!"[1]

And now it was over. The new challenge, one they did not relish,
was to sell their invention. Wilbur had doubted whether they were
"especially fitted for success in any commercial pursuit." All of the
Wright boys, he thought, lacked the "determination and push" required in business. He was wrong. They had those things in abun-
dance, and other personal qualities—self-assurance, perseverance,
and determination—that suited them for their new role as salesmen.

But the Wrights proved to be almost as bad at business as they
were good at invention. Their ultimate success owed far more to the
quality of their product than to their marketing skills.

There have been many explanations for their difficulties during
1905–08. Most biographers place the blame on government officials in
Europe and America. It is easier to portray turn-of-the-century
bureaucrats as unimaginative dolts than to suggest a flaw in the
Wright legend.

A handful of writers have been more critical of the Wrights. Octave
Chanute thought that their "usually sound judgment" was "warped

by the desire for great wealth."[2] As Wilbur noted in disgust: "You are the only person acquainted with us who has ever made such an accusation."

The historian/engineer Percy Walker, who chronicled the Wright negotiations in England, found his explanation for their business problems in the depths of the elder brother's subconscious. Wilbur, he concluded, suffered from "a deep-rooted psychological resistance to anyone possessing his precious aeroplane, [or] even having a look at it." Struggling with delusions "of paranoiac proportions," he worked on the one hand to sell the airplane and on the other to keep it a secret from the world.[3]

The talk of mental aberration is absurd, but Walker's search for the psychological roots of the Wrights' business difficulties is worth pursuing. Any attempt to explain the career of Wilbur and Orville Wright during the difficult years after 1905 must begin with an understanding of their basic assumptions about the world. Just as their approach to the problems of flight had been conditioned by their experience with cycle technology, so they took up the challenge of selling the airplane with the memory of their father's church struggles fresh in their minds.

Milton's long battle over the Keiter issue ended in the spring of 1905. The delegates to the General Conference held at Grand Rapids, Michigan, upheld the bishop by a two-thirds majority. But the church had paid an enormous price to satisfy his righteousness. Milton, at seventy-seven, was first vindicated, then retired from all duties. An era in the history of the church, and the family, came to an end.

Wilbur and Orville were shaped in the crucible of their father's experience. They fully expected their moral fiber to be tested, as had their father's, by unscrupulous men and women. And so far they had not been disappointed. Herring had attempted to steal a share of the glory and financial reward due the inventors of the airplane. They had not heard the last of him, nor of others like him. Even Chanute and Spratt, whom they regarded as friends, failed to appreciate the scope of their achievement. Like Milton, the brothers faced a hostile world.

Chanute urged them to fly their machine at once, before the largest crowd they could find. The impact of such a spectacle would bring instant fame, he argued, and force the governments of the world to come calling on them.

Perhaps he was right. The Wrights had rejected his suggestions in 1903 and 1904 because they were unable to provide an impressive performance. In the wake of the long flights of 1905, however, they could stage a demonstration that would stun the entire world. They might have grown rich, as Chanute predicted, and avoided many of the problems that plagued them over the next five years.

But Wilbur and Orville had too little faith in the ways of the world or the motives of their fellow human beings to take the chance. Why should they demonstrate their machine in public, trusting that the world's governments, inspired by a sense of fair play, would rush forward to repay them for their efforts? Far more likely that an unscrupulous rival would copy their technology and undersell them, stealing both the money and the credit.

It was a matter of principle. The Wrights saw no good reason to swallow their pride and put themselves and their machine on public display, "making Roman holidays for accident loving crowds." They might make money that way, but it would reduce them to the level of aerial showmen such as Santos-Dumont, Tom Baldwin, and Roy Knabenshue.

"You apparently concede to us no right to compensation for the solution of a problem ages old, except such as is granted to persons who had no part in producing the invention," Wilbur explained to Chanute. "That is to say, we may compete with montebanks for the chance to make money in the montebank business, but are entitled to nothing whatever for past work as inventors. We honestly think that our work of 1900–1906 has been and will be of value to the world, and that the world owes us something as inventors."[4]

They would chart their own course, doing business directly, and on their own terms. The Wrights offered to provide a machine capable of meeting a set of performance criteria, including a minimum speed, range, and carrying capacity. Within narrow limits, the price was negotiable; other important conditions were not.

They would not allow anyone, even a potential buyer, to witness a flight or even *see* the machine, until a contract was signed. Nor would they provide interested parties with photographs, drawings, or technical descriptions of any kind before closing the deal. There were no financial risks for the buyer. No payments would be required until the Wrights had demonstrated their machine to the customer's satisfaction.

Wilbur and Orville thought it a fair arrangement that protected the interest of the buyer while preventing unscrupulous "window shoppers" from glimpsing technological details. They failed to recognize that a government functionary might take a different view. Above all, the average bureaucrat seeks to avoid looking foolish. The Wrights, intent on protecting their technology, made such men very nervous. If these fellows from Dayton could fly, why did they not do so? If they had photographs of their machines in the air, why did they not show them? Suppose they could not really fly at all—how would the contracting officer look then?

The Wrights did not regard those as valid concerns. They expected to be taken at their word. They had always done business with a handshake. What was good enough for the corner grocer was good enough for Whitehall, the Quai d'Orsay, and the U.S. War Department.

They set out in the fall of 1905 determined to sell the airplane in the same way they had invented it—on their own. The first step was to reopen contacts in Washington and London. Unable to believe that their own government could be so shortsighted as to completely reject them, they wrote directly to Secretary of War William Howard Taft on October 9, explaining that their initial proposal had received "scant attention" from the Board of Ordnance and Fortification but that they did not want to seek a buyer abroad "unless we find it necessary to do so." Their initial offer stood. They would provide a series of demonstration flights totaling one hundred miles, the price to be established on a sliding scale governed by performance.[5]

Ten days later, Orville wrote to the War Office in London to say that they were still waiting to hear from Colonel Foster, the military attaché in Washington. In addition, they were now prepared to offer immediate trial flights of up to fifty miles.

The response from the U.S. War Department was swift and predictable. Major General J. C. Bates, the new president of the Board of Ordnance and Fortification, said the Board would not consider the matter until the Wrights provided detailed drawings and descriptions of their machine, "to enable its construction to be understood."[6]

That was precisely what they would not do. Wilbur asked what sort of performance the Board would expect of a flying machine. Bates wrote back on October 24, explaining that the Board would not formulate any such requirements or take any further action on the subject "until a machine is produced which, by actual operation, is shown to be able to produce horizontal flight and to carry an operator."[7]

It would not have taken much to erase the doubts. A personal visit to Washington with a handful of the astonishing photos of the long

flights of 1904–05, accompanied by affidavits from the Huffman Prairie witnesses, would surely have convinced the Board. Secret flight
trials could have been arranged at a secluded Army base. The course
of world history would hardly have been significantly altered had the
first airplane been sold in 1906 rather than 1908, but the Wrights
would have been spared a great deal of frustration.

Yet they refused to make the effort. If their word was not good
enough, they would take their business elsewhere. For the moment,
the matter was closed.

The British response was more promising. The War Office had not
forgotten them. By mid-October 1905, even before the arrival of Orville's reminder, a clerk noticed that Colonel Foster's report on his
visit to Dayton was long overdue. A bit of checking revealed that the
attaché was in Mexico City and had not yet contacted the Wrights.
Foster wrote on November 18, immediately upon his return, asking
when and where he could witness the promised flight. Wilbur replied
that a demonstration was now out of the question, but if Foster would
come to Dayton, they would be happy to introduce him to prominent
local citizens who had seen them fly. They could then negotiate a
contract. With that out of the way, the Wrights would reassemble and
fly the 1905 machine.[8]

Bewildered, Foster explained that he was not empowered to interrogate witnesses or negotiate a contract. His instructions limited him to
observing a flight and reporting back to London. He understood that
the demonstration was a prerequisite for opening discussions, not
something that would occur after the deal was closed.

The Wrights continued to correspond with Foster, and with his
superiors in England, but they had reached an impasse. Foster
summed the situation up on December 8: "The fact seems to me that
the War Office cannot commit itself to negotiations with a view to
purchasing unless sure that your invention gives the flight it claims,
while you do not wish to show its flight until the War Office has made
some arrangement with you. Thus there is a deadlock."[9]

Even so, British officials were reluctant to drop the issue. Realizing
that the Wrights were firm in their refusal to fly without a contract,
the issue was passed back up the chain of command to the Royal
Engineer Committee for a final review. Official enthusiasm for flight
was now working against the Wrights. Capper, for example, while
reemphasizing his belief in their claims, argued against pursuing a
contract based on the mileage flown during official trials. It would be

much cheaper, he suggested, to waive the demonstration flight and insist on a fixed purchase price.

His superiors agreed that the Wrights were probably telling the truth, and that "the manufacture of a flying machine for scouting purposes has actually been effected."[10] In view of their rigidity, however, the committee recommended dropping the negotiations completely and establishing a government-sponsored flying-machine research effort. What the Wrights had done, English engineers could do. Brigadier-General James Wolfe Murray, Master-General of the Ordnance, and Colonel Charles B. Raddon, Director of Artillery, made the final decision. There would be no more dealings with the Wrights until they flew for Colonel Foster.

Perhaps the Wrights could never have closed a deal with the British. The desire of military officials to develop a home-grown flying machine was inevitable, particularly among officers like Capper, who knew the thing was possible.

Unable to make headway in either England or America, the Wrights turned their attention to France. Wilbur wrote to Ferber on October 9, giving him the first accurate account of the 1905 season and announcing that they were prepared to discuss the sale of a flying machine to the French government.

Ferber presented the letter to Colonel Bertrand, in charge of balloon and airship research for the French Army, who replied that while no money was available for such a purchase, he would consider recommending the appointment of a commission to investigate the Wright claims.

Ferber's note to the Wrights was true to form. He asked for their selling price, but warned that, "considering the progress I have made since June the Government is no longer interested in paying as great a sum as it was . . . at the time of my last two letters."[11]

"No one in the world can better appreciate your accomplishment as much as we can," Wilbur responded. "But even though France already has reached a high degree of success, it may wish to avail itself of our discoveries, partly to supplement its own work, and partly to accurately inform itself of the state of the art as it will exist in other countries which buy the secrets of our motor machine."[12] The price was 1 million francs, about $200,000.

While awaiting Ferber's reply, the Wrights sent out three more accounts of the 1905 flights. The first went to Pat Alexander; the second to Georges Besançon, editor of *L'Aérophile;* and the third to Carl Dienstbach, the American correspondent of the *Illustrierte*

Aeronautische Mitteilungen. They were hoping to hurry the French along, reawaken interest in England, and perhaps catch the attention of the Germans as well.

Alexander read his letter aloud at a meeting of the Royal Aeronautical Society. The news from America was well received and generally believed, but it had no impact on the stalled negotiations with the British government. In France and Germany, however, it created a small furor.

Besançon published the Wrights' letter along with a poor translation of their correspondence with Ferber. Seeking to underscore the military advantages of their invention to the French, the brothers had commented that the Kaiser was in a "truculent mood." Somehow, it sounded worse in the *L'Aérophile* translation. When their letter to Dienstbach appeared in the *Illustrierte Aeronautische Mitteilungen* in February 1906, it was accompanied by an editorial that questioned the validity of their claims and took the brothers to task for "attacking" Kaiser Wilhelm.[13]

American editors picked up the story from the European papers. Most of them had heard nothing about the Wrights since Kitty Hawk; skeptical then, nothing had happened since to change their minds. An editorial on "The Wright Aeroplane and Its Fabled Performances," in *Scientific American* on January 13, 1906, summed up the general reaction:

> Unfortunately, the Wright brothers are hardly disposed to publish any substantiation or to make public experiments, for reasons best known to themselves. If such sensational and tremendously important experiments are being conducted in a not very remote part of the country, on a subject in which almost everybody feels the most profound interest, is it possible to believe that the enterprising American reporter, who, it is well known, comes down the chimney when the door is locked in his face—even if he has to scale a fifteen-story sky-scraper to do so—would not have ascertained all about them and published them long ago? Why particularly . . . should the Wrights desire to sell their invention to the French government for a "million" francs? Surely their own is the first to which they would be likely to apply. We certainly want more light on the subject.[14]

The French agreed. The Wrights had been useful to enthusiasts like Ferber, Archdeacon, and Deutsch de la Meurthe, who could hold them up as a warning of the progress being made in America. If they had really flown up to twenty-five miles, however, the game was over.

Frank Lahm was one of the first to react. A native of Canton, Ohio, born in 1847, he had come to Paris in 1880 to sell Remington typewriters and stayed to establish a company of his own. By 1905, he was a very wealthy man.

Fascinated by balloons, Lahm made his first flight in 1902. Within two years he was a qualified balloon pilot and a leading member of the Aéro-Club de France. Patrick Alexander told him about the Wrights in mid-October 1905. Excited by the possibility that two fellow Ohioans had succeeded in flying, he asked Nelson Bierce, a Dayton friend, to look into the matter. Bierce reported that the brothers were men of good character who were conducting mysterious experiments with a flying machine.

Next, Lahm contacted his brother-in-law, Henry M. Weaver, Sr., a Mansfield, Ohio, manufacturer. After some confusion, Weaver arranged for a personal meeting with the Wrights at the Algonquin Hotel in Dayton on December 3. They introduced him to the Beards, Amos Stauffer, the Billmans, Huffman, and others who had seen them fly. Weaver wired Frank Lahm that evening: "Claims fully verified, results by mail."[15]

Weaver was not the only visitor to Dayton that month. Robert Coquelle, a reporter for *L'Auto*, arrived on December 12. He interviewed Wilbur and Orville, and met their witnesses. Coquelle cabled his editor: "It is impossible to doubt the success of their experiments."[16]

The first installment of Coquelle's four-part story, "Conquête de l'Air par Deux Marchands de Cycles," appeared in *L'Auto* on December 23. When the members of the Aviation Committee of the Aéro-Club met that evening, they were divided into a majority that regarded Coquelle's story as a complete fabrication and a handful who believed there might be some truth in the Wright claims.

They met again on the evening of December 29 to hear Henry Weaver's full report to Frank Lahm. Chairman Archdeacon had difficulty raising his falsetto above the hubbub, and resorted to slapping a metal ruler on the podium to call the meeting to order. Questions were shouted from the floor. If the Wrights had flown twenty-five miles, why had the American newspapers not splashed the story across their front pages? Why did they not come to France to try for the 50,000-franc prize established by Deutsch and Archdeacon for the first heavier-than-air machine to complete a circular flight of one kilometer? Who had financed their effort, and why was the American government paying no attention?

The meeting closed with the consensus that Weaver and Coquelle had been hoodwinked. Lahm thought that of all those present, only he, Besançon, and Ferber believed the Wrights had actually accomplished all they claimed.

Ferber said little that evening. He was the only person there who knew that, as they spoke, a French emissary was in Dayton concluding a contract for the purchase of a flying machine from Wilbur and Orville Wright.

Fearing that Colonel Bertrand would drag his feet, Ferber had taken the Wrights' $200,000 proposition to M. Henri Letellier, publisher of the newspaper *Le Journal.* Letellier, who knew a good story when he heard one, jumped at the opportunity to help, and placed his secretary, Arnold Fordyce, at Ferber's disposal. Fordyce left for Dayton immediately, arriving just after Christmas 1905.

Ferber sent a short note to the Wrights, alerting them that Fordyce was on his way and leading them to believe that he represented the French government. Fordyce was quick to correct the misunderstanding; he represented a private syndicate, whose members included both Ferber and Letellier. These gentlemen planned to purchase a Wright machine as a gift to the nation, in return for which they expected nothing more than the gratitude of their countrymen—and perhaps the Legion of Honor.

Puzzled, the Wrights agreed to deal with Fordyce, but insisted that the airplane would have to be turned over to the French military. In addition, the sale of a machine to France could not prohibit the brothers from continuing their negotiations with the U.S. government.

Fordyce accepted the conditions and signed an optional agreement with the Wrights on December 30. The members of the syndicate agreed to deposit $5,000 in escrow with the Paris branch of J. P. Morgan & Company by February 5, 1906; they would then have two months in which to raise the rest of the $200,000 purchase price. If the full amount was on deposit by April 5, the Wrights would journey to France and make the required demonstration flights. Otherwise, they would keep the $5,000 and the option would lapse.

Letellier had no intention of putting up the money himself. Once he received word from Fordyce that the deal was closed, he rushed to the War Ministry. While ministry officials were not certain what credence to give the Wright claims, they were willing to risk an initial $5,000. In return for serving as broker, Letellier received exclusive rights to the story for *Le Journal.*

Why did the French government move so quickly? For the same reason that the American War Department had taken a chance on Langley in 1898: a nation standing on the brink of war is more likely to invest in new weapons than one at peace. In the winter of 1905, France was locked in a struggle with Germany for control of Morocco. A scouting airplane might be just the thing to search the vast Sahara Desert for an approaching Boche army.

Having invested 25,000 francs in the option, the French government immediately dispatched a commission to meet with the Wrights. Two members of the group, Fordyce and Commandant Henri Bonel, Chief of Engineers for the French General Staff, arrived in New York on March 18, 1906. Bonel, the head of the commission, had served as an official observer at the trials of Clément Ader's *Avion* in 1897. Ader, who constructed his machine with official support from the French government, failed to fly. The experience had soured Bonel on the prospects for an early success with the airplane—he would be a difficult man for the Wrights to convince.

Captain Jules Fournier and Henri Régnier, both of the French Embassy staff in Washington, and Walter V. Berry, an American attorney retained by Ambassador J. J. Jusserand, completed the official party. In view of the $5,000 option payment and the quality of the commission members, the Wrights realized that the French government was taking them seriously indeed.

The commissioners arrived in Dayton on March 30. The Wrights refused to show them the machine, but they did arrange one more round of meetings with local people who had seen them fly. In addition, they displayed photos of the 1905 airplane cruising effortlessly over Huffman Prairie. The evidence was overwhelming. Even the skeptical Bonel was convinced.

Meanwhile, officials in Paris were having second thoughts. The crisis in Morocco had passed, the issue resolved by an international conference in favor of the French. Ministry officials telegraphed a barrage of questions to the commissioners. Could the airplane operate at altitudes above 1,000 feet? Could both the speed and weight-carrying capacity be increased?

Bonel wired the answers back—along with repeated recommendations that the government take up the option before it was too late—to no avail. The ministry sent a final telegram on the afternoon of April 5, requesting a one-year extension of the exclusive option and a guarantee that a 600-foot minimum altitude would be achieved during the demonstration trials. The Wrights refused and the commission was recalled.

Shortly thereafter, the brothers reconsidered and cabled Bonel, accepting all conditions provided that the exclusivity clause did not apply to the U.S. War Department. The War Ministry refused to reopen negotiations. The Wrights were $5,000 richer, but they had not sold their airplane. Like the British, the French were unwilling to risk public ridicule and censure over the expenditure of $200,000 for a flying machine they had never seen fly.

The Wrights were back at the starting point. Pat Alexander arrived for another visit in late April. "As near as we can make out," Wilbur told Chanute, "his trip was for the purpose of learning whether or not there was any truth in the reports that we had made a contract with the French."[17] They were now firmly convinced that Alexander was a British spy. How else could he have known about the commission, whose presence in Dayton was so secret that the members had registered at their hotels under false names?

The Wrights took it as a good sign. Perhaps His Majesty's Government was reconsidering. A letter to the War Office on May 8 led to a new round of discussions on a fixed price contract. On July 31, Wilbur wrote to Lieutenant Colonel A. E. W. Count Gleichen, who had replaced Foster as military attaché, offering to sell a machine and patent rights for $100,000. An additional $100,000 would buy exclusive use of "our knowledge and discoveries together with formulae and tables which make the designing of flyers of other sizes and speeds a science as exact as that of marine engineering."[18]

Gleichen visited Dayton on August 8. Like Capper, he was impressed. The brothers could deliver on their promises, but they would not budge on price. Gleichen pointed out that the machine alone would be worth little without the "knowledge and discoveries." The bill would be $200,000.

Even Capper agreed that the price was excessive, particularly as the value of the engineering data could not be gauged before purchase. Moreover, he now had a heavier-than-air program of his own under way at Farnborough, and was sure that his team could turn out a flying machine "within a reasonable time on much the same lines as the Wright brothers, but . . . superior to it in several respects."[19] Capper, recently promoted to superintendent of the British Balloon Factory at Farnborough, in Surrey, naturally preferred to concentrate on his own projects. In 1907 he would barely escape death when he flew a tailless glider designed by J. W. Dunne into a stone wall. A powered version of the Dunne craft developed the following year was interesting, but could never rival the Wright machine.[20]

Two years after Wright negotiations collapsed, on October 16, 1908, S. F. Cody, an expatriate American showman employed at the Balloon Factory, made the first sustained heavier-than-air flight in Great Britain. His machine, a biplane with a canard elevator and a rear rudder, was powered by twin propellers driven through chains. While not superior to the Wright craft, it was certainly built on much the same lines. The flight came only two months after Wilbur first flew in public at Le Mans, France.

To counteract the frustrations of the spring and summer of 1906, the Wrights' patents were in place. Belgium, France, and Great Britain had approved their application in 1904. The United States finally granted patent No. 821,393 (Orville Wright and Wilbur Wright, of Dayton, Ohio. Flying Machine) on May 23, 1906. Austria, Germany, and Italy followed suit that fall. At last they had achieved a measure of official recognition that could be protected in a court of law.

They were also making headway against the skeptics. A new organization, the Aero Club of America, had been formed in the summer of 1905 after a speech by Charles Manly to the Automobile Club of America. Inspired by Manly's vision of mankind's future in the air, the wealthy automobile enthusiasts organized a club patterned after the Aéro-Club de France, with the vague objective of promoting the "development of aerial navigation." Manly gave a second talk that fall, this time to the charter members of the new Aero Club. He expressed full confidence in the truth of the Wright claims.

In January 1906, the club organized the first large American exhibition illustrating the history, present status, and future prospects of the flying machine. The show, staged as part of the Annual Automobile Club exhibition at the 69th Regiment Armory in New York, was a great success. Langley, Herring, Chanute, and others contributed engines, models, and full-scale gliders. The walls were crowded with photos of balloons, airships, and flying machines. The Wrights provided the crankshaft and flywheel of the 1903 engine, along with some photographs of the 1900–02 gliders and the 1903 machine—all of which disappeared at the conclusion of the exhibition.

Critics who attended paid little attention to the Wright contribution. In describing the show for *Scientific American*, balloonist Carl Myers remarked that the efforts of Augustus Herring were "superior to the enlarged and successful machines of the Wright brothers." A few weeks later, the magazine published a critical editorial questioning the flights of 1903–05.

Something had to be done. On March 2, following a visit to Dayton by William J. Hammer, a leading member of the new club, the Wrights sent off an official account of the experiments of 1904 and 1905. It was the first public announcement in America that the Wrights had flown for distances of up to twenty-five miles.

Eight days after receiving the report, the club members adopted a resolution congratulating Wilbur and Orville for "devising, constructing and operating a successful, man-carrying dynamic flying machine." The secretary, Augustus Post, included the report and the resolution in a press release issued on March 17. Journalists descended on the Wrights, who were happy to confirm the facts contained in the release.

Even *Scientific American* now took a second look. The magazine dispatched questionnaires to seventeen Daytonians who had witnessed the flights at Huffman Prairie. The results, published in a second article entitled "The Wright Aeroplane and Its Performances" on April 7, reversed the earlier position: "There is no doubt whatever that these able experimenters deserve the highest credit for having perfected the first flying machine of the heavier-than-air type which has ever flown successfully and at the same time carried a man." The editor hoped that "they will soon see their way clear to give to the world . . . some of the immense amount of valuable data which they have undoubtedly obtained while delving into the rapidly developing science of aerial navigation."[21]

With notoriety came new acquaintances. On May 16, five weeks after the appearance of the *Scientific American* article, the Wrights received a letter from a young engine builder named Glenn Hammond Curtiss.[22] He described his factory, noted that Captain Tom Baldwin was operating his famous airship with a Curtiss power plant, and asked if the brothers would be interested in discussing their engine needs.

The Wrights and Curtiss had a great deal in common. He was about Orville's age, born on May 21, 1878, at Hammondsport, New York. An exuberant lad, he dropped out of school at fifteen, worked as a Western Union delivery boy, and earned a reputation as a bicycle and motorcycle racer. He began building motorcycles in 1900. Four years later, the G. H. Curtiss Manufacturing Company was a going concern with a stock issue of $40,000. By 1907 he was producing five hundred motorcycles annually and operating a chain of cycle shops.

Tom Baldwin drew Curtiss into aeronautics. Attracted by the reliability of the lightweight Curtiss motorcycle engines, Baldwin wrote to the young man outlining his requirements for an airship power plant. He found Curtiss a no-nonsense fellow, not eager to become involved with the flying-machine crowd.

Baldwin persevered, and became a steady customer. Following the destruction of his airship shed in the San Francisco earthquake of 1906, he shifted his entire operation to Hammondsport, convincing Curtiss that the small market for aeronautical engines might be worth cultivating after all. Wilbur and Orville were high on his list of potential customers.

Four days after receiving his first letter, the Wrights were startled to get a telephone call from Curtiss. He was in Columbus, Ohio, on business, and wanted to set up an appointment. Hard at work on a new engine design of their own, the brothers were not interested.

They met five months later, when Baldwin summoned Curtiss to Dayton to repair the engine of an airship he was operating at the Montgomery County Fairgrounds. The Wrights went out to take a look at the gasbag on September 5. Introduced to Baldwin and Curtiss, they invited them back to the bike shop for a chat.

The meeting was pleasant. Baldwin later recalled that the Wrights were friendly, exhibiting "the frankness of schoolboys in it all, and had a rare confidence in us." They even pulled out the photographs of the 1903, 1904, and 1905 machines in the air. Fascinated, Curtiss plied the brothers with questions. After they left, Baldwin chided him for being so inquisitive.[23]

The year 1906 had brought mixed blessings. The Wrights had received patent protection, succeeded in reducing skepticism in the United States, and won the recognition of the Aero Club of America. Yet they were at an impasse. A year had passed since their last flight. Negotiations with the British, French, and American governments had collapsed, and there were no new avenues left to explore.

As long as the Wrights were flying, even in secret, stories had leaked to the press—there were results to announce when it was useful. Determined neither to fly nor to release additional photographs, they had run out of ammunition with which to counter the skeptics.

The problem was especially acute in Europe. When Frank Lahm

published the full text of the letter from Henry Weaver in the Paris edition of the *New York Herald* on February 10, 1906, the paper responded with an editorial of its own. Headlined "Fliers or Liars," it summed up the doubts that were growing among the members of the Aéro-Club de France. "The Wrights have flown or they have not flown. They possess a machine or they do not possess one. They are in fact either fliers or liars. It is difficult to fly. It is easy to say, 'We have flown.' "[24]

The Wrights were frustrated but not particularly concerned. They were patient men, convinced that they would find a buyer willing to accept their terms. It was only a matter of time.

chapter 23

RIVAL WINGS

October 1906-October 1907

B y the fall of 1906, Octave Chanute was convinced that the
Wrights should unveil their machine at once. "The important
fact," he cautioned Wilbur, "is that light motors have been
developed. The danger is that others may achieve success." Would it
not be wise to reduce their asking price and fly in public before a
potential rival joined them in the air?[1]

"Our friends," Wilbur responded, "do not seem to exactly understand our position in the matter of supposed delay. If it were true that
others would be flying within a year or two, there would be reason in
selling at any price, but we are convinced that no one will be able to
develop a practical flyer within five years."[2]

Wilbur's estimate of a five-year lead over all other experimenters
was based on "cold calculation." "It takes into consideration practical
and scientific difficulties whose existence is unknown to all but ourselves. Even you, Mr. Chanute, have little idea how difficult the flying
problem really is. When we see men laboring year after year on points
we overcame in a few weeks, without ever going far enough along to
meet the worse points beyond, we know that their rivalry and competition are not to be feared for many years."[3]

Chanute agreed that he did not really understand the problem, but
wondered whether the Wrights were not too "cocksure" that theirs
was "the only secret worth knowing." Others might hit upon the
solution in less than "many times five years." "As there are many
shapes of birds, each flying after a system of its own, so there may
be several forms of apparatus by which man may compass flight."[4]

On November 1, Chanute received the latest issue of the *Aeronautical Journal,* which announced that Santos-Dumont had made a short hop in Paris on September 13 in an aircraft known as *14-bis.* On October 23, he flew the same craft a distance of one kilometer, winning both the Archdeacon Cup and an Aéro-Club de France prize. "I fancy," Chanute noted with some satisfaction, "that he is now very nearly where you were in 1904."[5]

Wilbur and Orville were not concerned. "From our knowledge of the degree of progress that Santos has attained we predict that his flight covered less than $\frac{1}{10}$ of [a] kilometer," Wilbur replied. "If he has gone more than 300 feet, he has really done something; less than this is nothing."[6]

In fact, Santos had covered a distance of 726 feet in $21\frac{3}{5}$ seconds. The French were ecstatic, hailing this as the world's first public flight of an airplane. Strictly defined, that was precisely what it was.

Between the time of Santos's short hop in the fall of 1906 and the first public flights of a Wright airplane in the high summer of 1908, a handful of European and American pioneers struggled into the air. Their aircraft were far more primitive than the Wright machine and the distances covered much shorter than those the Wrights could fly. Their activity was inspired by stories of the Wright success, and their machines were based on a sketchy understanding of Wright technology. None of that mattered. They had flown, and the whole world knew it.

The brothers took a strangely detached view—the European machines were much inferior to their aircraft; few of them incorporated any means of lateral control. None, by their definition, was a practical flying machine.

They were correct. Yet they lost something intangible by not making the first public flights. However superior their machine, Europeans saw their own colleagues fly at a time when the Wrights were still regarded as *bluffeurs.*

The Wrights had not envisaged that someone sufficiently daring might fly a considerable distance in a machine that could scarcely be controlled. That, in fact, was what occurred.

The ideas planted by Ferber, Archdeacon, and Deutsch de la Meurthe had begun to sprout in the spring of 1904. In March, the editor of *L'Aérophile* commented on the number of aeronautical projects under way in France. Stefan Drzewiecki was at work on a glider "of the Wright type," only "a little different from that of M. Archdeacon." M. Solirène was towed aloft clinging to a frail, birdlike machine; while

M. Lavezarri, a talented young painter, conducted tests with a delta-wing hang-glider kite. Léon Levavaseur, an engineer who would emerge as one of the most talented of these first-generation designer-builders, had constructed his first unsuccessful monoplane in 1903. With so many diverse projects emerging, the skies of France would soon be dotted with flying machines.[7]

This aeronautical renaissance was rooted in Octave Chanute's account of the work of Wilbur and Orville Wright. Since his address to the Aéro-Club in 1903, Chanute had either written or provided the material for a dozen major articles published in France, England, and Germany, illustrated with the photographs taken during his visits to Kitty Hawk. He even helped the staff of *L'Aérophile* to prepare a set of detailed general-arrangement drawings of the 1902 Wright glider.

Paradoxically, the articles that inspired the first generation of European flying-machine builders also misled them. Chanute made it clear that the Wrights had achieved very impressive results, and showed the world what their machines looked like. But he could not explain the underlying principles: he did not fully understand the basics of the Wright technology himself, and what he did understand he had promised not to reveal.

The general-arrangement drawings of the 1902 glider were a case in point. Chanute gave the wing camber as $1/20$, for example, rather than the correct $1/25$. Problems were even more apparent in the area of control. Wilbur provided a general description of wing warping in his 1901 paper, which was readily available in France. Chanute had slipped once or twice, revealing that the operation of the rudder was linked to the wing-warping mechanism. He had been scrupulously careful not to reveal anything in the *L'Aérophile* drawings, however. All of the trussing wires were shown, but none of the all-important control cables.

As a result, the Wright control system remained a puzzle to the French. Those who read the articles carefully noticed the references to wing warping, but the precise meaning of the phrase and the way in which it was accomplished were a mystery. The experience of one newcomer, Robert Esnault-Pelterie, was typical.

A nineteen-year-old graduate of the Sorbonne, Esnault-Pelterie made his first flights in "an exact copy" of the 1902 Wright glider near Paris in May 1904. "A great stride seemed to have been taken [by the Wright brothers] in this difficult and delicate question of the conquest of the air," he explained in *L'Aérophile*. "We confess that the magnificent results reported on the other side of the Atlantic have left us a little skeptical. But skepticism has no place in science. When an experiment seems surprising, there is a very simple means of resolving the doubts, and that is to repeat the experiment."[8]

The young engineer "scrupulously follow[ed] the instructions, directions and diagrams of the Wrights which were published in *L'Aérophile.*" The glider was "exactly like that of the American experimenters, in general dimensions, wing curvature, and the arrangement of the controls." In fact, Esnault-Pelterie used the wrong camber and could only guess at the control system. He installed wing warping, then abandoned it, fearing that the technique "magnified tensions on the wires."[9]

The machine's performance was disappointing. Certain that the Wright claims were exaggerated, Esnault-Pelterie rebuilt his craft, substituting weight shifting as the primary means of control. In so doing, he was forced to substantially reduce the total surface area. In addition, he reduced the camber to $\frac{1}{50}$ and did away with the classic Wright canard.

In addition to weight shifting, he added twin experimental *élevons* (ailerons) mounted at the midpoint of the forward struts. These surfaces, operated by hand wheels, were intended to control the glider in both pitch (when used in unison) and roll (when used in opposition).

During a long series of tests that October, Esnault-Pelterie mounted the glider on a small dolly and was towed into the air by an automobile. While the flights were generally more successful than those conducted in May, the experience convinced him that the automatic stability provided by wing dihedral, in which the wingtips were angled up from the fuselage, was superior to any attempt at active roll control.

His colleagues agreed. Automatic or inherent stability was the goal of virtually all the early European experimenters before 1908. Their most successful machine, the classic Voisin of 1907–08, retained all the external features of the Wright airplane (biplane, pusher, canard). In terms of control, however, it was a much more primitive and dangerous craft.

Gabriel Voisin, the young man who built and flew that machine, made his first flight in March 1904 aboard a glider belonging to Ernest Archdeacon. Archdeacon, with his wealth and influence, had replaced Ferdinand Ferber as the dominant figure on the French aeronautical scene. Inspired by Ferber's *type de Wright* gliders of 1902 and 1903, and by the news of the Wrights' success with their powered machine in 1903, he commissioned a glider of his own in January 1904. *L'Aéro-phile* described it as "an *aéroplane de type Wright* 1902," and noted that "apart from subsequent modifications," it was "exactly copied from that of the Wright brothers."[10]

Those modifications were considerable. The original wingspan was reduced from 32 feet to 24 feet 7¼ inches, and the wing area, roughly 301–305 square feet in the original, to only 237 square feet. The empty weight of 112–117 pounds fell to 75 pounds. While the precise camber employed by Archdeacon is not known, it was clearly much deeper than that of the Wright machine. Most important, the 1904 Archdeacon glider did not incorporate wing warping, and featured a modified elevator.

The craft was certainly far sturdier and closer to the Wright original than anything Ferber had built to date. That was to be expected, for the 1904 Archdeacon glider was constructed at the government balloon and airship facility at Chalais Meudon with the advice and assistance of the commandant, Colonel Charles Renard, one of the great French airship pioneers.

Renard's personal involvement in the Archdeacon project might have marked the beginning of a serious, government-sponsored heavier-than-air flight research program. Unfortunately, at the moment when interest in military aeronautics was blossoming in other European nations, antimilitarist sentiment and budget cuts eroded the French program. Discouraged by reduced allocations, humiliated by his own failure to win election to the Academy of Sciences, Renard took his own life on April 13, 1905.

Archdeacon shipped his glider to a test site at Merlimont, near Berck-sur-Mer, in the spring of 1904. His test pilot was a twenty-five-year-old student of architecture—Gabriel Voisin. A native of Belleville, near Beaujeau, he was a dashing fellow, and something of a ladies' man.

In later years Voisin took delight in describing the conquests of his youth, which included Marie, a "glorious blonde" seventeen-year-old schoolgirl whose "every gesture" he found "infinitely graceful," as well as an interchangeable series of housekeepers, seamstresses, dental assistants, postmistresses, landladies, prostitutes, and errant wives. Somehow, Voisin found time to experiment with boats, kites, automobiles, and engines. "My life," he recalled, "was full, and I never knew boredom."[11]

Early in 1900, while employed as a draftsman by the firm constructing the buildings to house the Universal Exposition due to open in Paris that spring, he came across a group of workmen assembling Clément Ader's *Avion* in one of the exhibition galleries. Fascinated, he clambered into the cockpit. From that moment, his life would never be the same.

In my hands were the mysterious controls which could give life to this incomparable creation. To my right and to my left I saw the mechanism which would drive the airscrew blades. The steam generator need only to be lit to animate this marvel. . . . Suspended on a tackle, the huge bird was gently lifted and swung from side to side. Why was it in this place? Why was it not up in the sky flying over us and our petty activities?[12]

Three years later, in the fall of 1903, Voisin was introduced to Colonel Renard. Impressed by the young man's enthusiasm, Renard passed his name on to Archdeacon as a potential test pilot.

Voisin first flew the Archdeacon glider from the dunes at Berck-sur-Mer on Easter Sunday, 1904. He made flights of up to twenty-five seconds in length, but ended the day so battered that Archdeacon cabled Ferber in Nice inviting him to give the *nouveau aviateur* some flight instruction.

Ferber arrived several days later. Voisin was pleased to report that his instructor "did not succeed in his trials and bent everything badly." The two continued to fly through the first two weeks of April, improving with practice. Archdeacon brought a professional photographer out to the dunes, and sent photo postcards showing his machine in the air to the members of the Aéro-Club.

At the end of the two-week gliding session, Archdeacon was "full of enthusiasm." He announced that Voisin had mastered the craft, completing flights of over sixty-five feet. The information obtained would be used to design an improved glider that would allow him "to do as well as the Wright brothers."[13]

Most of the members of the Aéro-Club shared his confidence. Now that Frenchmen had taken to the air, the world would see some real progress. And what better way to encourage development than to offer financial rewards to the most successful experimenters? By the fall of 1904, a series of rich prizes stood as benchmarks on the road toward the final victory.

The Coupe d'Aviation Ernest Archdeacon, a silver trophy valued at 2,000 francs, would go to the first man to pilot a powered airplane 25

meters (80 feet) through the air. Each of the first ten men to fly at
least 60 meters would receive 100 francs and a silver medal from the
Aéro-Club de France. Archdeacon would present 1,500 francs to the
first pilot to complete a flight of 100 meters (330 feet). That lucky
fellow would earn an additional 1,500 francs for capturing the Aéro-
Club's Prix pour Record de Distance. Together, Henri Deutsch de la
Meurthe and Archdeacon established an aptly named Grand Prix
d'Aviation of 50,000 francs for the first flight of one kilometer over
a circular course. The man who won that prize would have flown—by
anyone's standards.

Gabriel Voisin was determined to be that man. In the spring of 1905,
he was at work on a second glider for Archdeacon. Encouraged by the
trials at Berck, Archdeacon had formed a new company, Syndicat
d'Aviation, and hired Voisin as the chief engineer and sole employee.

They set out to build yet another "exact replica" of the 1902 Wright
glider, the most successful machine known to them. Unaware that
they were basing their craft on incorrect information, they assumed
that its failure to match the reputed performance of the original was
proof that the Wright claims were overblown.

In designing a second craft, they retained some external features
of the Wright glider (biplane wings and forward elevator), but rejected three-axis control in favor of inherent stability achieved
through the use of a three-cell box kite as the main lifting surface and
a two-cell kite as a tail. The glider would be towed down a wooden rail
and into the air by an automobile.

Voisin began testing the new craft in April 1905. Archdeacon, "who
knew how to open the most difficult doors," obtained War Department
permission to use Issy-les-Moulineaux, an abandoned military parade
ground north of Paris, as a flying field. The first test was scheduled
for March 25. Voisin was eager to go up, but Archdeacon insisted that
an unmanned test be conducted first with sand ballast in lieu of a pilot.
It was a wise decision. The craft rose to an altitude of thirty feet and
broke apart in the air. "Without this preliminary trial," Voisin remarked, "Issy would only have seen me on this one occasion." He
spent the next two months rebuilding the craft with a set of floats.
For safety's sake Archdeacon decided to conduct all future tests over
water.[14]

A small crowd of spectators lined the banks of the Seine between
the Billancourt and Sèvres bridges on the afternoon of June 8 to
watch Voisin fly the new glider. By three o'clock the machine had been
towed into midstream and attached to the speedboat *La Rapière*.

Voisin, secure in his saddle, ordered the boat into motion. "I had the controls ready," he recalled fifty years later. "I waited for a time and then I applied elevator." The glider rose from the water, reaching an altitude of perhaps sixty feet. The boat slowed as it approached the bridge, allowing the craft to settle gently back onto the surface after a flight of some 2,000 feet.[15]

Early the following morning one of those who had witnessed the spectacle called on Voisin. Louis Blériot was in the market for a flying machine. A thirty-three-year-old manufacturer of automobile head-lamps, Blériot was a striking man, sturdily built, with a dark face and heavy features. His sweeping mustache, clear, deepset eyes, and high cheekbones led more than one observer to remark on his resemblance to an ancient Gallic chieftain. Frédérick Collin, his mechanic, thought that Blériot's prominent nose, giving him a birdlike profile, might be evidence of predestination.

Blériot had caught the flying-machine bug while still a student, but kept his enthusiasm in check "for fear of being taken for a fool." Having seen Voisin in the air, he could no longer resist the urge to fly. Voisin accepted Blériot's money and built a glider to his new client's order, in spite of the fact that he regarded the design as dangerously unstable.[16]

Voisin tested both the rebuilt Archdeacon machine and the new Blériot glider on July 19. On the first trial an inexperienced towboat operator took off down the river "like a mad thing," damaging the Archdeacon craft. Lifting off the surface aboard the Blériot craft a few minutes later, Voisin immediately realized that the glider was just as unstable as he had feared. It rocked violently from side to side a few times, then dropped off on one wing and entered the water less than 100 feet from the spot where it had taken off. The machine was destroyed and Voisin barely escaped with his life. Far from dis-couraged, Blériot and Voisin, who was anxious to leave the ranks of hired mechanics, entered the flying-machine business as full partners three days after the trials.

While Esnault-Pelterie, Voisin, and Blériot were just beginning their work, Ferdinand Ferber was approaching the end of his. That spring he made the world's first glider flight with a passenger, his mechanic. While the newspapers made much of this, it was scarcely calculated to advance aeronautical technology.

The machine was his now standard *type de Wright* glider, this one featuring triangular wingtip "rudders" and a fixed horizontal stabil-izer resembling the spread feathers of a bird's tail. Ferber altered the glider in May 1905, adding a 6-hp Peugeot engine and a small propeller mounted on the forward elevator support. The craft was totally incapable of sustained flight. After three years of effort, Ferber was farther from the Wrights, and success, than when he started.

The year 1906 was as promising for the French as it was disappointing for the Wrights. The list of enthusiasts continued to grow. Rumanian-born Trajan Vuia unveiled a tractor monoplane powered by a 23-hp Serpollet carbonic-acid gas engine at Montesson, near Paris, on March 3. You had to look closely to see the Wright influence, but it was there. Unlike his colleagues, Vuia used both wing warping and the canard elevator.

He made three short hops on March 3, August 12, and August 19, rebuilt the craft, then made eight more hops from Issy and Bagatelle with his new *I-bis* configuration between October 6, 1906, and March 30, 1907. The best of these covered only ten meters. The Vuia II, which followed in 1907, was little more successful than its predecessor.

The Danish experimenter J. C. R. Ellehammer coaxed his monoplane through a 42-meter tethered flight over the circular track at Lindholm on September 12, 1906. Ellehammer and Vuia did not achieve sustained flight, but they did popularize the monoplane configuration, inspiring others, notably Blériot and Levavaseur, who were just entering the field.

The monoplanes were interesting, but it was Alberto Santos-Dumont who dominated the headlines of 1906 with his biplane *14-bis* (Project No. 14, second version).

The aircraft rolled out the doors of Santos's workshop-hangar at Neuilly-Saint-James in July 1906. It was one of the most awkward-looking machines ever to take to the sky. In fact, *14-bis* (most newsmen preferred to call it the *Bird of Prey*) was nothing more than another free interpretation of the basic Wright configuration—a pusher biplane with a canard elevator. The influence of Hargrave's box kite was apparent as well.

Initially, there was no lateral control, although the wing dihedral provided a measure of automatic stability. At some point in the early fall of 1906, Santos mounted two simple ailerons in the center of the outer wing bays. A forward canard cell mounted on a universal joint doubled as elevator and rudder. The pilot stood in a wicker basket cockpit set at the rear of the machine, operating the rudder and elevator with two small control wheels; the ailerons were controlled by a body harness.

Late in June, Santos announced that he was entering the competition for both the Coupe d'Aviation Archdeacon and the Aéro-Club de France 100-meter prize. Initial tests of *14-bis* were conducted with the machine running back and forth beneath an overhead wire strung between two poles. On July 14 he made an ascent with the craft slung beneath an airship.

Serious flight trials began on the Bois de Boulogne in late August. After several unsuccessful attempts to leave the ground on the 21st and 22nd, Santos replaced the original 24-hp Antoinette power plant with a new 50-hp model.

The machine flew under its own power on September 13, hopping 4–7 meters through the air. Santos lifted off a second time at four-forty-five on the afternoon of October 23, covering a distance of 50 meters at an altitude of 3–4 meters, to win the Coupe d'Aviation Ernest Archdeacon for the first public flight of over 25 meters. Everyone's favorite Brazilian was back in the headlines. Ignoring the Wright claims to flights of over 25 *miles* the previous year, the members of the Aéro-Club hailed Santos as "The Triumphant One."

Early on the morning of November 12, Santos ordered his workmen to wheel *14-bis* out of the stripped hangar pitched next to his workshop at Neuilly. The little procession moved a few hundred yards down the Rue de Longchamp, through the Bagatelle gate, and out onto an open corner of the Bois de Boulogne that served as a polo field and an exercise yard for horses. Hundreds of spectators gathered as the day wore on. Three times that morning and afternoon Santos attempted to take off. Each time he failed.

He climbed into the wicker basket for the fourth time at about four o'clock. "The vast crowd formed into two long lines down the center of the field," a *New York Herald* reporter noted. "There was a general hush as the motor began to turn, and then a shout of satisfaction as the *Bird of Prey* bounded off like a flash and was tearing through the air at nearly forty kilometers an hour."[17]

From Santos's vantage point, everything seemed to happen at once. He could hear the roar of the crowd above the engine. Looking forward, he watched the excited mass draw together in front of him. He pulled back on the wheel, nosed up over the crowd, and set the machine down in an open spot beyond. Spectators swarmed over the craft, pulled him from the cockpit, and carried him off the field in triumph.

Santos had flown 222 meters (722 feet) in 21 1/5 seconds. It was only

100 feet and 38 seconds short of the Wrights' best flight at Kitty Hawk. Santos would leave the ground in *14-bis* just one more time for a short hop of 50 meters at Saint-Cyr on April 7, 1907.

All of France erupted in a frenzy. The hero was fêted at banquets and lionized in the press. Archdeacon declared that Santos had "assuredly gained the greatest glory to which a man can aspire. He has achieved, not in secret or before hypothetical and cooperative witnesses, a superb flight . . . a decisive step in the history of aviation." "It will be partly thanks to me," Archdeacon concluded, "that my country will have been the first officially to have given birth to aviation, perhaps the greatest discovery made by Man since the beginning of the world."[18]

Across the Atlantic, Augustus Post, secretary of the Aero Club of America, announced that Santos's flight of November 12 "marks the most positive advance yet made in the science of aeronautics." American newspapers offered fulsome praise, referring to the event as "The First Important Demonstration . . . of an Aeroplane in Public" and predicting "the beginning of a new era." Wire service stories spoke of "The Aerial Revolution," and predicted "Changes in Government to Meet New Condition."

Santos dominated the headlines for the moment, but the Wrights were not forgotten. American journalists coupled their coverage of the events at Bagatelle with articles on the Wright story. Alexander Graham Bell's "Tribute to the Wright Brothers" appeared in newspapers from coast to coast. "Santos borrowed their ideas," he pointed out. "To them belongs the credit of solving the great problems of aeronautics."[19]

Bell's comment drew a strong reaction from Santos. Questioned by the Paris correspondent of the *New York Herald*, the Brazilian insisted that the inventor's remark had been "dictated by jealousy."[20]

Professor Bell is reported to have said that he believes the Wright brothers have made a machine which has flown, and that naturally they kept it perfectly secret. Almost in the same breath he is reported as accusing me of copying the designs of the Wright brothers. How could I do such a thing if the machine had been kept hidden away from every observer? The thing is altogether too absurd![21]

"There is absolutely no evidence to support the alleged statements of the Wright brothers," Santos told the newsmen. "They may have flown, but there is nothing in any report of their proceedings that inspires confidence."

chapter 24

WEALTH AND FAME

November 1906-November 1907

M ilton Wright was too preoccupied with his own problems to pay much attention to Wilbur and Orville's aeronautical experiments during the crucial years 1900–05. He seldom worried about the risks—they had promised to be careful, and his sons would keep their word.

By the fall of 1906, Will and Orv had temporarily put physical risk behind them. Yet Milton was concerned about the more subtle dangers his sons would encounter in the immediate future. He had no doubt that success would put their strength of character and sense of values to severe test. "There is much in the papers about the Wright brothers," he noted in his diary on November 30. "They have fame, but not wealth, yet. Both these, though aspired after by so many, are vain."[1]

The stream of visitors passing through Milton's house had already altered the comfortable pattern of family life. Weaver, Coquelle, Fordyce, Hammer, the members of the French commission, Pat Alexander, Baldwin, and Curtiss—all had come and gone in the past year. Will and Orv had not yet flown in public, but they were already minor international celebrities and objects of curiosity.

Thanksgiving week, 1906, was a particularly busy time. It began on November 20 with a visit from an editor of *Scientific American*. Henry Weaver, whose testimony had thrown the French into such an uproar, arrived two days later with a visitor from Paris—Frank Lahm. They stayed for two days, locked in extended discussions with Will and Orv in the upstairs room at the bike shop.

Their most important guest, Ulysses D. Eddy, arrived in Dayton on Thanksgiving Day, and called at 7 Hawthorn the following morning. Unlike the others, Eddy had little direct interest in aeronautics. He was a professional dealmaker who had learned his trade from a master, Charles Ranlett Flint.

Little remembered today, Flint was well known to readers of turn-of-the-century newspapers as "the Rubber King" and "the Father of Trusts." He had organized such giant combines as United States Rubber, the American Woolen Company, U.S. Bobbin and Shuttle, and American Chicle. The investment banking firm of Charles R. Flint & Company also profited from the sale of American arms and technology abroad—the company sold an entire fleet to Brazil, and purchased ships for Japan, Russia, and Chile. From time to time, Flint served as an overseas agent for American inventors. He had sold American electric automobiles in France and introduced Simon Lake's submarine boat to the tradition-bound czarist navy.[2]

Until recently, Ulysses Eddy had worked as a Flint agent. Not long after he struck out on his own, Eddy noticed a news article on the Wrights that appeared at the time of Santos Dumont's flight. Intrigued, and recognizing a golden opportunity for his old friends at Flint & Company, he caught the next train for Dayton.

Like everyone else, Eddy was impressed by the Wrights. The brothers planned to accompany Pat Alexander back to New York in early December to attend the second Aero Club of America exhibition, where their new four-cylinder upright engines would be on display. Eddy arranged for them to meet with Frank R. Cordley, a Flint executive, at that time.[3]

Alexander arrived in Dayton late on the morning of December 5. He ate lunch and supper with the Wrights, and discussed the lack of response from the various foreign governments. The three of them boarded the overnight train for New York at ten o'clock that evening. They attended the exhibition the following day, and dined that evening at the Century Club as the guests of John Brisbane Walker, editor of *Cosmopolitan*.

These days the Wrights' comings and goings were reported in some detail by the *New York Enquirer*, the *News*, and the *Herald*. *Scientific American*, so critical at the time of the original exhibition, now coupled its coverage of the new show with an editorial on "The Genesis of the First Successful Aeroplane." "In all the history of invention," commented the editor, "there is probably no parallel to the unostentatious manner in which the Wright brothers, of Dayton, Ohio, ushered into the world their epoch-making invention of the first successful aeroplane flying machine.[4]

The meeting with Flint & Company officials went very well. Cordley seconded Eddy's judgment: if they could strike a deal, there was money in this for everyone. Charles Flint himself was out of town, however. Cordley reassured the Wrights, and asked them to return to New York for a final conference when Flint returned.[5]

The brothers traveled from New York to Washington by way of Coatesville, Pennsylvania, where they stopped for a pleasant evening with their old friend George Spratt. Arriving in Washington on the morning of December 10, they met with Bell, Zahm, and interested parties from the Weather Bureau and the Smithsonian. Milton picked them up at the Dayton station at nine o'clock on the morning of December 12.

The telegram recalling them for the promised meeting with Charles Flint arrived five days later. Orville would make the trip alone—they did not want to appear anxious, and the absence of one brother would guarantee that no final arrangement could be made immediately.

Orv did return with a tentative offer: Flint would pay $500,000 for all foreign rights, following a demonstration flight of fifty kilometers. The Wrights were to have the American market to themselves. They would also have the right to compete for any prizes, and, after a reasonable length of time, would be free to publish anything they wished.

Will wrote to Chanute on December 20 asking his advice. Chanute replied that the deal "seems much better than I thought possible," but asked if they had considered the moral implications of turning such a potential weapon over to a European nation.[6]

A Flint agent, Mr. George Nolte, arrived in Dayton on December 26. His task was to push the Wrights into an immediate agreement. They would have none of that, and returned to New York to resume face-to-face negotiations in late January 1907. The original proposition for an outright sale of all foreign rights was no longer acceptable to either side. Flint countered with an offer to serve as an agent for foreign sales, the brothers to keep all monies earned up to $50,000; beyond that, the proceeds would be split fifty-fifty. Flint also offered an additional $50,000 for a private demonstration flight to be staged for the czar.

The Wrights rejected both proposals. They were not willing to give

Flint & Company a free hand in the sale of their invention, nor would they fly for the czar, or anyone else, until they had signed a contract for the sale of an airplane.

Flint then proposed another arrangement. The company would serve as agent for the sale of the Wright airplane in Europe, at a price and under conditions to be approved by the inventors. For their efforts, Flint & Company would receive 20 percent of all profits up to $500,000 and 40 percent thereafter. As before, the Wrights would have the American market entirely to themselves. This was very close to what the Wrights had in mind, but they still refused to act. On January 26 they left for Dayton, promising to send a proposal of their own that would embody major portions of the Flint suggestion.[7]

Wilbur returned to New York on February 5 to discuss a special sale to Germany. The specifics were not to his liking, but he did give tentative approval to the final agreement for a split up to $500,000. Company executives forged ahead. Flint himself made contact with officials in Russia. Isidore Loewe, a Flint agent who also served as director of the Mauser Gun Works, was instructed to explore matters in Germany. Coded cables were sent to Lady Jane Taylor, a well-placed Scotswoman who would see to things in England. Hart O. Berg, who was generally in charge of Flint European operations, would see what could be done in France.

The Wrights concentrated on making headway with the American government. Just this once, they gave serious thought to shock treatment. Later that spring, elements of the Atlantic Fleet would steam through Hampton Roads and up the James River as part of a great celebration marking the three hundredth anniversary of the first permanent English settlement in the New World. Thousands of spectators would attend the festival at Jamestown, which would include a small aeronautical exhibition and meeting. Suppose an airplane appeared out of nowhere, circled the fleet at anchor, and disappeared to the south—surely that would catch the attention of American officials, and most of the rest of the world as well.[8]

On March 20, Will and Orv appeared near the foot of the main bridge over the Miami with a strange contraption—an engine and propellers mounted on pontoons. The idea was to see whether they could take off safely from the shallow waters of Currituck Sound. The experiment was a fiasco—operations from the water were out of the question. The Jamestown scheme, which would require flying for a relatively long distance over the Sound, foundered.[9]

Less than a week later new hope appeared. During their visits to New York the brothers had become friendly with Courtlandt Field Bishop, the current president of the Aero Club of America. Bishop called the attention of his brother-in-law, Republican Congressman Herbert Parsons, to the Wrights' problems with the U.S. government. Parsons wrote to the brothers in early April asking to see copies of their 1905 correspondence with the Board of Ordnance and Fortification.

Having read the letters, Parsons resolved to do what he could to help. He sent a short note and copies of several recent favorable articles on the Wrights to President Theodore Roosevelt. Intrigued, Roosevelt forwarded the package to Secretary of War Taft with a recommendation that action be taken to investigate the Wright claims. Taft referred the matter back to the Board of Ordnance and Fortification, complete with his own recommendation for a favorable response and the attached notes from Parsons and Roosevelt.

The secretary of the Board wrote to the Wrights on May 11, requesting additional information on their invention and its capabilities. Orville would have to deal with this on his own—the day before the letter arrived they had received a cable from Flint. Hart Berg, superintending the marketing operation in Europe, did not share the home office enthusiasm for a supposed flying machine designed and built by two Midwestern bicycle makers. To build his confidence for the difficult months of negotiation ahead, Flint requested that the brothers travel to Europe for meetings with Berg and potential buyers.

With work under way on a new airplane and engine, it was impossible for both brothers to make the trip. Wilbur insisted that Orv should go. As he explained in confidence to his father several months later, it was a calculated move.

> When the telegram came from Flint's asking that one of us go to Europe at once, I saw instantly what was involved, and asked Orville to go. I did this for two reasons: (1) Because I wished the job of putting the final touches to the engines, and preparing the machine for shipment. I am more careful than he is, at least I think so. (2) Because it was evident that the man who went to Europe would have to act largely on his own judgment without much consultation by letter or cable. I felt that I was more willing to accept the consequences of any error in judgment on his part than to have him blaming me if I went.[10]

Orville disagreed, insisting that Wilbur would make the best impression. Setting his compunctions aside, Wilbur left Dayton on May

16, stopped for a day in New York, and boarded the *R.M.S. Campania* for Liverpool on May 18. Orville would follow once the work on the new airplane and engine was complete.

The Board's letter of inquiry arrived as Will was preparing to leave. Orv responded on May 17, noting that he and his brother had "some flying machines in the course of construction, and would be pleased to sell one or more of them to the War Department, if an agreement as to terms can be reached." Each machine was capable of carrying an operator and an observer, together with enough gasoline for a flight of 200 kilometers. The Wrights were willing "to make it a condition of a contract that the machine must make a trial trip before Government representatives of not less than fifty kilometers at a speed of not less than fifty kilometers an hour, before its acceptance by the Department, and before any part of the purchase price is paid to us."[11]

The secretary replied on May 22, requesting that the Wrights submit a definite proposal for the sale of a flying machine to the U.S. government. Orv offered to provide the aircraft described in his previous letter, together with flight instruction for an officer to be named by the Board, for $100,000. He pointed out that, "since many of the features of our flyer are secrets . . . it would not be prudent to show the machine in advance of a contract," but stressed that no payment would be required until after the promised demonstration flight.[12]

On June 8, another letter asked whether the quoted price would include sale of exclusive rights to the invention. Orv replied that an exclusive sale was no longer possible. The exchange was followed by a long silence—there would be no more letters from the Board until early October. The members, disappointed by the high price tag and the refusal to offer an exclusive sale, had decided to sit back and wait.

Things were moving more rapidly in Europe. Wilbur had arrived in London on the afternoon of May 25. Hart Berg had little difficulty picking out his new client on the crowded platform of the train station—"To begin with, it is always easy to spot an American among Englishmen." Even if other Americans had been there, Berg was certain he would have known Wilbur Wright. "Either I am Sherlock Holmes," he wrote to the home office the next day, "or Wright has that peculiar glint of genius in his eye which left no doubt in my mind who he was."[13]

As was so often the case, Berg's initial skepticism vanished after a few minutes of conversation with Wilbur. Convinced that the man meant what he said, Berg became a believer who would devote all his energies to the Wright cause.

Berg lost little time in bringing Wilbur up to date on the situation in various nations. Isidore Loewe had sent word that in Germany things were not promising. "The officials are afraid of the possible consequences of a blunder," Will wrote home. "From all accounts, every official near the Emperor is in constant terror of losing his standing." Russia, it seemed, would follow the German lead. The prospects were bleak in England as well. Only a few days before Wilbur's arrival, Lady Jane Taylor had received word from R. B. Haldane, Secretary of State for War, that "the War Office is not disposed to enter into relations at present with any manufacturer of Aeroplanes."[14]

Berg thought that Wilbur could be most useful in France. The Wrights had dominated French aeronautics from a distance for five years. The French had read about the brothers, argued the merits of their claims, and used the Wright gliders and powered machines as a jumping-off point for their own designs. Through it all, Wilbur and Orville had remained mysterious figures. The sudden appearance of one of them in Paris might help to resolve French doubts and lead to a reopening of negotiations.

Both Wilbur and Berg recognized that any talks with the French would have to be handled with care, but they disagreed on strategy. Wilbur was convinced that the best course was to deal directly with the government. Berg offered a counterproposal. Preliminary discussions had revealed that Henri Deutsch de la Meurthe was interested in creating a syndicate to produce Wright machines for sale to the French Ministry of War. That was the direction in which they should move. If they began with the government and were unable to strike a bargain, all other avenues would be closed to them. But if the notion of a syndicate failed to materialize, they could still approach the government directly. At any rate, the support of the powerful Deutsch de la Meurthe would be an important selling point when dealing with the government.

Together with Frank Cordley, who arrived from New York that weekend, Wilbur and Berg left for France on Monday, May 27. They met with Deutsch the following day. Both parties were very serious about doing business. Before finalizing any arrangements, however, Deutsch approached the new Minister of War, General Georges Picquart, about government interest in the purchase of flying machines.

Picquart spoke to Commandant Bonel, who had visited Dayton the year before, and glanced through the reports and the correspondence covering the earlier negotiations. Confident that the Wrights were all they claimed, he told Deutsch that the government would be interested in doing business, providing the machines could operate at an altitude of 1,000 feet and fulfill the other conditions discussed in 1906.

With the promise of a major French contract in hand, Deutsch returned to negotiate an arrangement with Wilbur and the Flint representatives. Together, they worked out a plan for the creation of a syndicate that would manufacture Wright aircraft for sale to European buyers. The firm would be capitalized at $700,000. The Wrights would receive $350,000 for their efforts—$250,000 in cash and $100,-000 that would remain in the company treasury as their contribution to working capital. In return, they would control roughly 47 percent of the stock. Flint & Company would deposit its entire commission in the treasury of the new firm in exchange for one-fifth ownership. Deutsch would purchase one-fifth ownership, and would handle the negotiations with the government. A consortium of other small stockholders rounded out the venture.[15]

There were serious political problems on the horizon, however. Bonel learned of the new initiative through General Picquart, and told Arnold Fordyce that Wilbur was in Paris negotiating with a completely new group of associates. Fordyce passed the news on to his employer, Henri Letellier.

Letellier was outraged. Only a year before he had sponsored an initiative that might have succeeded but for the last-minute recalcitrance of the government. Now he learned that Deutsch de la Meurthe, of all people, might succeed where he had failed. The two men were bitter rivals. Letellier's father owned the Paris daily *Le Journal*, while Deutsch had an interest in *Le Matin*.

Letellier called on General Picquart, reminding him that the previous minister had granted him the exclusive right to organize an aeronautical syndicate involving the Wright machine, and insisting that the prior commitment remained valid. General Picquart was no stranger to political intrigue. Caught up in the Dreyfus Affair less than a decade before, he had been falsely accused of forgery and served part of a prison sentence. He was promoted for his trouble, but had no intention of risking involvement in a new controversy. Legally, the 1906 agreement had expired, but it seemed to Piquart that Letellier was more likely to cause trouble. Deutsch was informed that the old arrangement stood. Flint & Company and the Wrights would have to deal with the government through Letellier and the *Le Journal* faction. Deutsch stormed off in disgust.

It did not take long for Wilbur, Berg, and Cordley to realize how much they would miss Deutsch de la Meurthe. The support of the "Standard Oil King of France" would be far more valuable than any assistance from Letellier, who, as Wilbur noted, was "too much interested in the personal and political game to suit us."[16]

Berg advised approaching the French government through Letellier's connections with the same proposition that they had worked out with Deutsch de la Meurthe. They would sell one airplane capable of flying for 50 kilometers and attaining an altitude of 300 meters with the pilot alone (10 kilometers with a pilot and passenger), for 1 million francs. The price included six months exclusive use of the invention, after which the syndicate would be free to sell additional airplanes to other nations.

On June 24, Arnold Fordyce presented the deal to Senator Charles Humbert, an associate of Letellier's who served as secretary of the Chamber of Deputies budget committee. Humbert asked that they raise their price by 250,000 francs. The additional money would be used to grease the appropriate palms along the way. Appalled, Berg and Wilbur insisted that if the original proposal was not immediately forwarded to the Ministry of War, they would pack their bags and leave for Berlin.

Humbert backed down, assuring the Americans that he would press the matter with all dispatch. It was the beginning of a period of confusion, false promises, and discouragement. They had no direct access to the government and no faith in Humbert. One conflicting message followed another, until they had not the slightest idea where they stood.

In spite of the uncertainty, Wilbur made at least a halfhearted attempt to play the tourist. He was disappointed. The problem, he explained to Katharine after visiting Notre Dame, was that "my imagination pictures things more vividly than my eyes." The reality of the great cathedral could not compare with the image planted by Victor Hugo in the mind of a young reader rummaging through the books in his father's library. "The nave is seemingly not much wider than a storeroom," he complained, "and the windows of the clerestory are so awfully high up that the building is very dark."[17] It was the same with the paintings in the Louvre. The *Mona Lisa,* he noted, was "no better than the prints in black and white."[18]

The aeronautical events did interest him. After attending several

balloon races as a spectator, he was invited to make an ascent with
a visiting American aeronaut, Allan Hawley, and two friends. The
four men launched from the Aéro-Club grounds at Saint-Cloud at
four-thirty on the afternoon of July 17. They reached a maximum
altitude of 3,000 feet, and remained in the air for three and a half
hours, finally landing some twenty miles west of Orléans. The trip
convinced Wilbur of the futility of ballooning, in which "a few glorious hours in the air are usually followed by a tiresome walk to some
village, an uncomfortable night at a poor hotel, and a return home by
slow local trains."[19]

From the roof of his hotel, Wilbur had already seen the 200-foot-
long Lebaudy airship *La Patrie* fly over the Arc de Triomphe, down
the Rue St. Honoré, and directly over the Hôtel Meurice. He estimated
that the actual speed of the craft was not more than 15 miles per hour.
Even in the relatively light 8-mile an hour wind, the craft had difficulty
making headway. He was not impressed.[20]

"As I have been very busy," he told Chanute, "I have aimed to avoid
social engagements, but have met most of the leading men interested
in aeronautics." Generally, the French were much more impressed
with Wilbur than he was with them. Ferber could scarcely restrain his
enthusiasm. "As to my impression," he told Georges Besançon,

> it was profound, and I grasped his hand and looked upon him with great
> emotion. Just think that without this man I would be nothing, for I
> should not have dared, in 1902, to trust myself on a flimsy fabric if I had
> not known from his accounts and his photographs that "it would carry"!
> Think that, without him, my experiments would not have taken place and
> I should not have had Voisin as a pupil. Capitalists like Deutsch de la
> Meurthe would not, in 1904, have established the prize you know of. The
> press would not have spread the good idea on all sides.[21]

Wilbur for his part regarded Ferber with open contempt. He was
"infected with ambition," and, for all of his admiration of the Wrights,
had apparently worked hard to scuttle the 1906 negotiations. "Since
then," Will commented, "he has done all he could to prevent us from
doing business here." In the privacy of his diary he noted that "Ferber
evidently is double-faced, but at bottom bitterly hostile."[22]

Most of the other experimenters whom he met—Tatin, Besançon,
de la Vaulx, Esnault-Pelterie, Archdeacon, and Voisin—doubted his
claims. Frank Lahm and his son, Frank Jr., a West Pointer (Class of
'01) and the winner of the first James Gordon Bennett balloon trophy
in 1906, were his only close friends.

On July 3, Fordyce told Wilbur and Berg that he would soon introduce them to a representative of the Ministry of War. Several days later, word came from the ministry that a one-year period of exclusivity would be required rather than the six months that had been offered. Wilbur would not give way. When they finally met with Major A. L. Targe of the ministry on July 9, however, he led them to believe that the original six-month period would be quite satisfactory.

Returning to the ministry for a second meeting on July 19, they met with a General Roques, who insisted on a *three-year* period of exclusivity for his government. The two Americans made it perfectly clear that their proposal was a take it or leave it one. The general then asked them to rewrite their proposal as a formal contract, complete with the six-month exclusivity clause.

Berg and Wilbur passed the document on to Fordyce, who offered to translate and forward it to the ministry. They assumed that the government would give a clearcut answer. Instead, when Berg called on Fordyce at the *Le Journal* offices on July 25, he discovered that substantial changes had been made to the text of the contract during translation. Wilbur spoke to Fordyce that afternoon, calling a halt to the entire process until his brother arrived in Paris.

As Wilbur feared, the long separation and the complexity of the negotiations placed an enormous strain on his relationship with Orville. He did his best to keep his brother informed through letters and frequent cables, but confusion was inevitable. Wilbur would cable a new bit of information and ask for comment. Orville would attempt to respond, his answer invariably arriving too late to have any impact. By the end of June the combination of slow mail and unavoidably cryptic cablegrams led to misunderstanding between them.

"I have had only one letter a week from you (these very short) in the last month or more," Orv wrote on July 11. "I have practically no information of what is going on. When you cable, you never explain anything so that I can answer with any certainty that we are talking about the same thing." Nor was he happy with Flint & Company. "They surely have had advices of what was going on," he complained, "but they have not sent me one word."[23]

Orville feared that his brother was discussing an exclusive sale of their invention to the French, something to which he was absolutely opposed. Moreover, he was concerned about a story in the *New York Times* suggesting that Wilbur had offered to sell flying machines to the French for only $500 apiece. By July 1, no longer able to stand the uncertainty, he cabled his brother:

Not approve offer to French war dept. Have not yet received any information from Flint & Co. Do nothing without I consent. Keep me informed.[24]

Wilbur received a second letter from his father subtly echoing Orville's concern. "The complaint that I have not written fully and promptly is incomprehensible to me," he replied sharply, "as I have written every few days and kept back nothing, even when giving news in a half-finished state was dangerous and liable to lead to misconceptions."[25]

Wilbur reminded them that he asked Orville to make the trip in the first place, adding: "I never for a minute was so foolish as to suppose that the final decision should be made by the man at home, who, from the nature of the case, would necessarily be less competent to form a sound judgment than the man at the seat of action."[26]

Orville had promised to join his brother in France with a finished airplane as soon as possible—"So far as his letters indicate, he spent his time on things of no use in the present situation, and left the necessary things undone." Wilbur assured his father that he had done his best. "If a serious mistake has been made it lies in the assumption that the machine would be available quicker than now seems possible. I am not to blame for this."[27]

In fact, Orville had worked hard at completing the first of a series of five airplanes, the machines the Wrights would fly in Europe and America in 1908 and 1909. They were virtual replicas of the 1905 airplane except for the seating arrangement, the controls, and a more powerful engine. The first Flyer, intended for immediate shipment to France, had already been partially assembled in Dayton before crating.

The long flights of 1905 proved that there was a limit to the amount of time a man could spend extended on the lower wing with his head elevated. That, and the requirement to carry a passenger on the coming demonstration flights, convinced the Wrights to switch to upright seating and a new warping control to replace the old hip cradle. In addition, the new system must incorporate controls allowing the pilot to teach a passenger how to fly.

The 1907 aircraft featured three control sticks. One elevator control was placed at the left hand of the pilot and another at the right hand of the passenger, or student pilot. The wing-warping and rudder controls were mounted between the two seats, on the pilot's right and the passenger's left.

With one airplane packed and ready to ship, Orville left for New York and Paris on July 18. Charlie would follow in early August, in case they chose to assemble and fly the machine. Orville arrived ten days later and was immediately drawn into the negotiations. For the first time, he had some notion of what Will was up against. Targe was out of town, and there was little to do but wait. Will left for Berlin with Berg on August 4 to check out the situation in Germany; Orv and Frank Cordley remained in Paris to superintend the work while they were gone.

Targe returned on August 6. At a luncheon that day, Senator Humbert, the man who was supposed to be presenting the Wright case to the Ministry of War, told Fordyce and Targe he believed the brothers to be frauds. They in turn assured Orv and Cordley that they did not share his view, and would see that the matter received prompt attention at the highest levels of government—a story Wilbur and Berg had heard several times over the past nine weeks. Then a new obstacle was thrown up in their path: a technical commission established to study the details of the contract proposed by the Wrights.

Will and Berg faced a different set of problems in Berlin. The situation was straightforward but little more promising. Isidore Loewe explained that the Germans were still smarting at the "derogatory" references to Kaiser Wilhelm. Anti-Wright feeling was so strong that "the military department would not be disposed to do anything even if we should be able to do all we had claimed," Wilbur noted.[28]

But Will and Berg discovered that they could cut through the initial antagonism with relative ease. Over the next several days, they met with the leaders of the new German aeronautical program, including Major Hans Gross, head of the German airship detachment; Captain Richard von Kehler, director of the Motor Airship Study Company, a society established under the personal patronage of the Kaiser in 1906; and General von Lyncker, of the German General Staff. They were also introduced to industrial leaders, including Walther Rathenau, head of the great combine controlling the German electrical industry. It was even rumored that Helmut von Moltke, legendary chief of the General Staff, was mildly interested in the Wright brothers.

Wilbur accepted General von Lyncker's invitation to develop a proposal for presentation to the German government. They hammered out the basic elements in a meeting with Loewe on the afternoon of August 7. The Wrights offered a machine capable of flying fifty kilo-

meters with a single pilot, and of making shorter flights with a pilot
and observer. The price would be 100,000 marks for the first machine,
plus an additional 50,000 marks to train a pilot. Wilbur had learned
one great lesson from the French negotiations—never again would he
offer a potential buyer exclusive ownership of his technology for any
length of time.

Before presenting the new proposal to Von Lyncker, Wilbur returned to France. Having offered an exclusive sale to the French, he
could not in good conscience open talks with the Germans until the
situation in Paris was fully resolved. He was almost pleased to find
Orv caught up in the same web in which he had been ensnared for so
many weeks. The old arguments over an appropriate translation of
the proposal continued with Fordyce, and they seemed no closer to
obtaining a firm answer.

Wilbur and Orville made one final attempt to crack the multiple
levels of corrupt bureaucracy. They translated the new German proposal into French and asked Fordyce to present it directly to the
Ministry of War. Wilbur recalled that Fordyce "made all sorts of
ridiculous objections to the form of it, saying it was not good French,
&c., &c." So far as the Wrights were concerned, that was the end of
it. On August 24, Wilbur informed the Minister of War, through
Fordyce, that all offers were withdrawn.[29]

Wilbur wrote to Chanute on September 2, explaining the situation:

> I spent two weeks in Berlin early last month and found a much readier
> spirit to negotiate than expected. Capt. von Kehler who is manager of
> the Emperor's motor airship society had shown himself exceptionally
> friendly and interested in advancing negotiations with his government.
> It was thought best however to withdraw our offers to France before
> starting there. We had a pledge from the Minister of War, Gen. von
> Einem, that if we would come to Germany we would receive fair treat-
> ment. As we found a very different spirit cropping out in the French
> negotiations, we finally decided to withdraw here and try countries we
> could trust further.[30]

In mid-September Wilbur went back to Berlin while Orville stayed
on in Paris to tie off loose ends. The Germans seemed to be the most
reasonable of men. By the end of the month, however, it was apparent
that they would not sign a contract until they had seen the Wright
machine fly. Yet Wilbur continued to regard the Kaiser as a prime
customer. "They are not engaged in experiments of their own along

that line," he told Chanute, "and would be very glad if we could put
a practical machine in their hands."[31]

Had it been earlier in the season, Wilbur might have violated his
principles and provided a demonstration flight, free of charge. He felt
that he could trust the Germans, and that such a flight might persuade
them to purchase Wright aircraft one by one rather than buying the
right to produce them. "We, however, thought it best to wait till the
opening of a new season before entering upon such a plan of doing
business," he told Chanute. "We did not like to disclose our machine
at the tail end of the year, giving our imitators all winter to manufacture copies of it. We do not wish to get into law suits before we get
the business properly organized and started."[32]

Back in Paris, Orville handled two additional requests. One, from
a Mr. Stewart of the Barnum & Bailey shows, was not the sort of
thing in which they wished to become involved. Nevertheless, he made
a quick trip to London to discuss the matter.

The second item was much more interesting. Lieutenant Frank
Lahm, the elder Frank Lahm's son, had recently asked if there was
not still a possibility of dealing with the U.S. government. While the
Wrights were not yet aware of it, Lahm's query had special significance. Lahm had been living with his father in Paris while attending
the French cavalry school at Saumur and had now been ordered back
to the United States to take command of a portion of the aeronautical
section of the U.S. Army Signal Corps. Before leaving, he prepared
a letter to the Chief Signal Officer, Brigadier General James Allen, the
highest member of the Army Board: "I have to inform you that I have
just had an interview with Mr. Orville Wright of Dayton, Ohio, in
regard to the purchase of the aeroplane invented and successfully
operated by himself and his brother, Mr. Wilbur Wright. It seems
unfortunate that this American invention, which unquestionably has
considerable military value, should not be first acquired by the United
States Army."[33]

In October, Orville received one more letter from the Board of
Ordnance and Fortification, requesting that they meet with officials of
the U.S. Army. He assured the Board that he and his brother would
welcome such a conference and that nothing would give them greater
pleasure "than to furnish the *first* machine" to their own government.[34]

Wilbur and Charlie Taylor left Paris on November 11—Charlie for
Le Havre to pick up two boxes of equipment that would be required

back in Dayton, Will directly for London, via Bologne and Folkestone. They met in London two days later and went up to Liverpool, where they sailed for New York aboard *R.M.S. Baltic* on November 16. Will would spend a day or two in the Flint offices in New York, then move on to Washington to try to arrange the meeting with officials of the Board.

Orv was still in Paris performing one final task. The brothers had every intention of flying in Europe in the spring. If they could not strike a deal with a national government, then they would make their demonstration flights and sell machines one at a time to anyone with cash in hand. For that, they would need a stock of aircraft. The parts of five airframes were awaiting completion back in Dayton. Orville, the engine expert, would explain their needs to a number of French companies interested in bidding on the construction of a series of Wright engines to be on hand by the spring.

On November 19, Hart Berg drove Orv out to Santos's old flying field at Issy-les-Moulineaux. Issy was very busy that spring and summer, thanks largely to the activities of Gabriel Voisin, whom Orville was about to meet for the first time.

The partnership forged by Voisin and Blériot in the wake of the Archdeacon glider tests of 1905 had collapsed. Convinced that he was wasting his genius attempting to build and fly machines designed by his much less talented employers, Voisin launched a new partnership with his brother Charles late in 1906.

Voisin had a vision of a new powered machine capable of winning the Grand Prix established by Deutsch and Archdeacon. The craft, a pusher biplane with a canard elevator and a box-kite tail, was a mix of the basic Wright structural elements with bits and pieces of Hargrave, Pénaud, and a dash of Santos-Dumont for good measure. Voisin was not a rich man, however. Before he could build his craft, he needed a buyer.

Henry Kapferer, a well-known engineer and automobile builder, had assisted Edouard Surcouf in the design of the *Ville de Paris*, an airship commissioned by Henry Deutsch de la Meurthe. Surcouf, recognizing in Kapferer a rich enthusiast ready to invest in aeronautics, introduced him to his friend Voisin, who sold Kapferer on his plans for a dream machine that would capture the Deutsch-Archdeacon prize.

Kapferer, attempting to cut corners, declined to purchase the 50-hp Antoinette engine recommended by the Voisins, insisting on a less expensive 10-hp Bouchet. The underpowered machine refused to leave the ground during its initial tests at Sartouville. Nevertheless, the experience was valuable for the Voisins, who set out to find another patron to fund a second, more advanced model of their new basic design.

Late in 1906, Kapferer brought Léon Delagrange to one of his meetings with Voisin. The designer listened politely to plans for a fantastic aerial contrivance, then showed his visitor a model of a slightly larger version of the Kapferer machine. Delagrange took the bait. Eight days later he placed an order for the airplane.

The first flight test of the Voisin-Delagrange I took place on February 20, 1907. It ended in near disaster when the machine literally broke in half during the takeoff run. Repairs were complete within a week, but the craft was damaged in precisely the same way on February 28.

They had worked most of the bugs out by the end of March when Charles Voisin finally nursed it into the air, covering 60 meters in 6 short seconds. Other hops followed during the summer and fall, including a flight of 500 meters in 40 seconds on November 5 with Delagrange at the controls; but the Voisin brothers were convinced that they had accomplished all that they could with their second machine.

That summer, Gabriel and Charles stumbled onto their third customer, Henry Edgar Mumford Farman, a son of Thomas Farman, the long-time Paris correspondent for the London *Evening Standard.* An Englishman by birth, Farman, who preferred to spell his first name Henri, was raised and educated in France, and spoke only halting English. He eventually regularized his position by accepting French citizenship.

Like Voisin, Farman first tried his hand at gliding, flying a homebuilt version of the Chanute-Herring glider. His next step was to approach Gabriel Voisin who, in spite of his limited experience, seemed to know more about the construction of flying machines than anyone else in France.

The Voisin-Farman I was built in a workshop in the Paris suburb of Billancourt during the fall of 1907. It was apparent that the Voisin frères had learned a great deal from their first two projects—and that Henri Farman was a natural aviator. His first attempt to fly the machine at Issy on September 30 resulted in a hop of 30 meters. Back in the air on October 15, he stretched the distance to 285 meters.

Finally, on October 26, he made four flights, the last of which—2,350 feet in 52⅗ seconds—won the Archdeacon Cup.

In less than two months, while Wilbur and Orville were struggling to make some headway with ministry officials, Henri Farman had electrified France. And the greatest moment was yet to come. All of fashionable Paris was headed toward Issy on the afternoon of November 18, the day on which Farman would try for the Deutsch-Archdeacon Grand Prix for the first circular flight of one kilometer.[35]

Wilbur and Hart Berg had scarcely stepped from their automobile that afternoon when Archdeacon came rushing up, gesticulating wildly and shouting: "Now, where are the Wrights?" Within moments, Orville was surrounded by newsmen. "There were several hundred cameras on the scene," Orv recalled, "and not one that failed to take a snap at us. . . ."[36]

Attention quickly shifted to the action on the field. Farman ran up the engine, took off, and flew 1,500 meters in an almost complete circle. It was not easy. The pilot sat behind a wheel that could be moved fore and aft to operate the elevator, and turned to the right or left for rudder control. Farman had to turn with the rudder alone, relying on the dihedral to keep the tips balanced. Should a bank become too steep, the pilot had no recourse but to use additional rudder. It was not a system designed to provide safe turns.

Farman did not capture the Deutsch-Archdeacon prize that day; he achieved that goal two months later, on January 13, 1908. The Aéro-Club judges who served as official witnesses for the flight on November 18 ruled that he had not quite closed his circle, and that the wheels of his machine had touched the earth during the course of the flight.

Orville Wright was the only man present in a position to criticize Farman's wide and wobbly turn. None of that mattered to the spectators who swarmed around Farman when he landed. For men and women who had never seen the Wrights fly, Farman had performed a miracle.

When pressed by reporters for comment on the rapid progress being made by French experimenters, Orville explained that he and his brother "never liked to pass criticisms on the work of others." Time would show "whether the methods of control used in the Farman machine are adequate to meet the conditions encountered in windy weather." Nor had Wilbur's opinion changed. "The French aeroplanists are busy," he explained to Chanute, "but up to present we see no indication of a practical machine in the near future."[37]

The Wrights claimed to have flown, but to the French the excuses that they offered for not exhibiting their machine or trying for the rich prizes that were available sounded hollow. Santos, Delagrange, and Farman had flown in full view of the public. There was little doubt as to where Archdeacon stood on the matter:

The famous Wright brothers may today claim all they wish. If it is true—and I doubt it more and more—that they were the first to fly through the air, they will not have the glory before History. They would only have had to eschew these incomprehensible affectations of mystery, and to carry out their experiments in broad daylight, like Santos-Dumont and Farman, and before official judges, surrounded by thousands of spectators. The first *authentic* experiments in powered aviation have taken place in France; they will progress in France; and the famous fifty kilometers announced by the Wrights will, I am sure, be beaten by us as well before they will have decided to show their phantom machine.[38]

chapter 25

THE RETURN TO KITTY HAWK

December 1907 - May 1908

D uring his voyage home from Europe in November 1907, Wilbur
concluded that the past two years had not been a total waste.
They had made important contacts, and a number of high-
ranking officials in Britain, France, and Germany now believed their
claims. But they had not sold the airplane, and at present, prospects
were bleak. "We will spend the winter getting some more machines
ready for the spring trade," he wrote to Milton from aboard the
Baltic. "Then we will probably put out a sign, 'Opening day, all goods
below cost.' "[1]

There was one more route left. The conversations with Frank
Lahm, Jr., and the receipt of yet another letter from the Board of
Ordnance and Fortification suggested that they might still strike a
bargain in America.

Landing in New York on November 22, Wilbur went straight to the
Flint offices for a conference with Frank Cordley. The following day
he caught the train for Washington, where he spent a rainy weekend
waiting for government offices to open on Monday. General William
Crozier, senior officer of the Board; General James Allen, Chief Signal
Officer; and Major Lawson M. Fuller met with him on the morning of
November 25.[2]

For the first time, Wilbur recognized that the Army was seriously
interested in his invention. And the Wrights were ready. They had, in
fact, decided that their rock bottom price to the U.S. government
would be $25,000, a figure Will mentioned at this first meeting. The
officers demurred. They could draw up to $10,000 from an existing

experimental fund, but a $25,000 price tag would require a congres-
sional appropriation. Will left the meeting convinced that the Army
would not take effective action before he and Orv flew in Europe in
the spring. A second meeting in Washington did not alter that assessment.[3]

But Wilbur underestimated his own impact. The Board, impressed
by his presentation, reached into a small fund left over from the
Spanish-American War to obtain the required $25,000. On December
23, General James Allen issued a solicitation for bids for the construction of an airplane.

The "Advertisement and Specification for a Heavier-Than-Air Flying Machine" required that the machine carry a pilot and passenger
a distance of 125 miles at a speed of 40 miles per hour. It must remain
aloft for at least one hour, land without damage, "and also be capable
of dismounting and loading on an Army wagon to be transported."
Moreover, it should be designed to permit "an intelligent man to
become proficient in its use within a reasonable length of time."[4]

The release of Signal Corps Specification No. 486 drew much negative comment from the press and the aeronautical community. A
writer for the *New York Globe* remarked that

> A machine such as described in the Signal Corps specifications would
> record the solution of all the difficulties in the way of the heavier-than-air
> airship, and finally give mankind almost as complete control of the air
> as it now has of the land and water. It . . . would, in short, be probably
> the most epoch-making invention in the history of civilization. Nothing
> in any way approaching such a machine has ever been constructed—the
> Wright brothers claim still awaits public confirmation—and the man who
> has achieved such a success would have, or at least should have, no need
> of competing in a contest where the successful bidder might be given his
> trial because his offer was a few hundred or thousand dollars lower than
> that of someone else.[5]

The American Magazine of Aeronautics, unofficial mouthpiece of
the Aero Club of America crowd, argued that "there is not a known
flying machine in the world which could fulfill these requirements."
James Means, editor of the *Aeronautical Annuals* which had so
influenced the Wrights, remarked to Chanute that while Minerva
sprang "fully fledged from the head of Jupiter . . . I hardly think that
the perfect flying machine will appear in such sudden fashion."[6]

Wilbur recognized the truth. Major George Squier had taken the
Wrights at their word, drafting a specification that described the
performance of their machine. "When I first learned that the Board

was advertising for bids I doubted its good faith," Wilbur told Chanute, "but am now inclined to think that I did them an injustice in
suspecting such a thing."[7]

Orville arrived home from Paris on December 13. The brothers
spent the next few weeks corresponding with the Board to ensure that
they understood all of the requirements. On January 27, 1908, they
submitted their formal proposal to sell a flying machine as described
in the circular for $25,000. It was the only bid that the Board expected
to receive. In fact, there were forty-one proposals when the competition closed on February 1.

They ranged in price from a bargain-basement $850 to $1 million.
One fellow, a federal prison inmate, valued his machine at $45 to $65
a pound, depending on the model selected; another bidder promised
speeds of up to 500 miles per hour. Nineteen of the bids were dismissed out of hand. All but three of the remaining competitors were
disqualified by their inability to post the required 10 percent of the bid
price as a bond.

The successful low bidder, J. F. Scott of Chicago, priced his nonexis-
tent machine at $1,000 because he had only $100 to offer as a bond.
Embarrassed by his unexpected success, and recognizing his complete inability to meet the specifications, he withdrew. The field was
now reduced to two bidders, the Wrights and Augustus Herring.
Technically, Herring had won the competition with a low bid of $20,-
000. The officials of the Board were in a quandary. They did not believe
that Herring could fulfill the contract. Still, he was a well-known
figure with a long-standing reputation in aeronautics; they could not
simply discount his offer. The only way to save the situation was to
find an additional $20,000 that would permit them to accept both
surviving bids.[8]

Why had Herring entered the competition? He had long since
ceased active work in aeronautics—the Wrights knew that, the Army
knew it, and Herring knew it. Yet he was convinced that he had
accomplished something significant prior to 1900 and that he ought to
be rewarded for his efforts. As the low bidder, Herring would at least
remain in the public eye. There might yet be a way to turn the situation to his advantage.

For their part, the Wrights were fully satisfied. They saw Herring
as a harmless comic figure who could do them no ill. More important,
after more than two years of effort, they had a contract. Two contracts, in fact.

Hart Berg had closed a deal with the French. Wilbur traveled to New York on March 15 to check out the particulars. The new contract would be signed not with the government but with a syndicate headed by the financier Lazare Weiller, Henri Deutsch de la Meurthe, and other French capitalists. La Compagnie Générale de Navigation Aérienne, as it was to be called, would purchase the Wrights' French patents and the right to manufacture, sell, and license Wright air-planes in France. After providing a series of demonstration flights, the Wrights would receive 500,000 francs upon delivery of the first machine, 50 percent of the founders' shares in the company, and 20,000 francs apiece for each of four additional aircraft to be delivered to the company. Although the deal was not quite as sweet as they had hoped, the Wrights agreed to the terms. Will would return to France to fulfill the new contract with the syndicate, while Orv remained in America to fly for the Army.[9]

It would be a busy spring. The machine to be flown in France still sat in a crate at Le Havre. Bariquand et Marre had won the contract to produce an engine for that craft. Now the Wrights must rush a second machine and engine to completion for the Army trials. More-over, they had not flown since the fall of 1905. Before attempting to do any flying in public, they would retire to Kitty Hawk with the refurbished 1905 machine, complete with upright seats and an impro-vised control system.

The Wrights knew that they would not be the only ones in the air in 1908. Farman continued to stretch his time and distance aloft, finally capturing the Deutsch-Archdeacon prize with a circular flight of 1,500 meters in 1 minute, 28 seconds on January 13. It was obvious that Farman, Delagrange, Blériot, Esnault-Pelterie, and others had matured; by midsummer, these Europeans were flying more than fifteen minutes at a time, and covering many kilometers. Farman flew at Ghent, Belgium, that spring, then visited the United States where he made a number of disappointingly short hops at Brighton Beach, New York, in July.

But the real excitement was generated by a group of newcomers who called themselves the Aerial Experiment Association. The AEA was born on September 30, 1907, when six people filed into the office of the American consul in Halifax, Nova Scotia, to sign articles of agreement. They were a diverse group, drawn together by Alexander Graham Bell and his wife Mabel.[10]

Thomas Watson, his assistant and friend, later recalled that Bell had spoken of the possibility of heavier-than-air flight during the course of their early telephone experiments. On one occasion Watson had stood well upwind and watched as Bell examined the wing structure of a very dead gull washed ashore on the beach.

As early as 1891, Bell, now a world-famous inventor, had conducted flying-machine experiments at his estate, Beinn Breagh,* near Baddeck, Nova Scotia. But it was his friendship with Langley, and his minor involvement in the Smithsonian Aerodrome program, that fired Bell's aeronautical interests. Encouraged by Langley, he began his own program of aeronautical research in 1896. Fascinated by kites since his childhood, Bell developed a series of new designs that would enable him to study the problems of aircraft stability.

Like the residents of the Outer Banks who had long puzzled over the antics of Wilbur and Orville Wright, the sturdy Cape Breton fishermen looked askance at Bell's kites. One local citizen reported:

> He goes up there on the side of the hill on sunny afternoons and with a lot of thing-a-ma-jigs fools away the whole blessed day, flying kites, mind you!
> He sets up a blackboard and puts down figures about these kites and the queer machines he keeps bobbing around in the sky. Dozens of them he has, all kinds of queer shapes, and the kites are but poor things, God knows! I could make better myself. And the men that visit him—old men—that should have something better to do. They go up there with him and spend the whole livelong day flying kites. It's the greatest foolishness I ever did see.[11]

By 1902, that foolishness had produced the first of Bell's famous tetrahedral kites. Loosely based on the Hargrave box kite, these large craft were built up of individual cells, constructed with triangular faces, arranged in great tetrahedral banks. Beginning with relatively simple single-cell assemblies, the kites grew to enormous multicellular aggregations, some twenty-six feet wide. The giant *Frost King* of 1905 contained 1,300 cells arranged in twelve layers. It once carried a man thirty feet into the air.

Bell was less interested in how much weight his kites would carry, or in how high they would fly, than in stability. For *Frost King* he sought absolute stability in a machine which, if powered, would be capable of flight with a man on board. Like Langley, he hoped to launch the craft from water, and immediately forged ahead with a series of hydrofoil tests.

*Pronounced Ben Vreeah—Gallic for Beautiful Mountain.

Bell's wife Mabel, a partner in the fullest sense, followed his experimental program from the outset, offering suggestions that shaped his work. It was Mrs. Bell who volunteered to put up $20,000 to create an experimental association comprised of the young men her husband had drawn into the aeronautical project.

John Alexander Douglas McCurdy and Frederick Walker ("Casey") Baldwin were the first two employees. McCurdy, the son of Bell's secretary and photographer, came home for a visit from the University of Toronto in the spring of 1906 with his friend, Casey Baldwin. Bell liked the two young men, recognizing the talents needed for his burgeoning airship program. Baldwin, a gifted young engineer, was persuaded to enter Bell's employ after his graduation in the fall of 1906; McCurdy joined the team after his own graduation the following spring.

Thomas Etholen Selfridge was the next recruit. A native of San Francisco, Selfridge graduated from West Point in 1903. After distinguished service as a troop commander during the San Francisco earthquake, his decision to pursue aeronautics seemed odd to his superiors. Bell recognized it for a carefully calculated career move:

[In the spring of 1907] a young man called upon me in Washington, an officer of the U.S. Army, who turned out to be Lieut. Thomas E. Selfridge. He showed a great deal of interest in the whole subject of aerial locomotion, and expressed a desire to witness our experiments with tetrahedral structures in Nova Scotia. I found that he had devoted a great deal of attention to the subject of Aeronautics, and what was being done in relation to heavier-than-air machines in all parts of the world with the idea that sometime or other the U.S. government would require flying machines in the army and that, when that time came, the services of an officer who had made an expert study of the subject would be in demand, and he would be sure of promotion into a field of great usefulness.[12]

Bell wrote to President Theodore Roosevelt, seconding Selfridge's official request for temporary duty at Beinn Breagh. By December 6, Selfridge was a full-fledged member of the team, having ascended to an altitude of 168 feet during a 7-minute flight aboard a new kite, the *Cygnet*.

The final, critical, member of the AEA arrived at Baddeck in July 1907. Glenn Hammond Curtiss had sold Bell an engine at the New York Aero Club show the winter before. Curtiss promised to deliver the engine in person and to instruct Bell's engineers in its operation.

Bell easily persuaded the quiet, competent Yankee mechanic to stay on as chief engineer of the new organization.

Loyalty to Bell ensured that the first AEA effort would be the completion and testing of the tetrahedral aerodrome *Cygnet*. Then "Bell's Boys," as they became known, were eager to move into the mainstream of world aeronautics. Operations shifted to Hammondsport during the winter of 1907–08, where Curtiss workmen were already putting the finishing touches on a variant of the old Chanute-Herring glider.

Test-flown from mid-January through March 1908, the little glider gave the younger members of the AEA their first real opportunity to skim through the air. It also convinced them that kites were not the future. Outvoted by his associates, Bell withdrew to Beinn Breagh to continue the kite work on his own.

The members of the AEA knew where to turn for advice. Curtiss wrote to the Wright brothers late in December, describing the creation of the AEA, and offering to furnish, "gratis," a 50-hp Curtiss engine for their own experiments. Selfridge followed with a letter of his own on January 15, 1908. He put a series of straightforward questions to the brothers. What was their experience with the travel of the center of pressure on a wing? What was "a good efficient method" of constructing light, strong ribs that would maintain their camber? How should fabric be applied? Could the Wrights offer any general advice on aircraft construction to a group of first-time builders?[13]

The Wrights answered the questions, directing the newcomers to their patents and published papers for additional details. They assumed that the AEA could not pose a threat. Bell's involvement with the group spoke well for the program—he had always defended their claims in the press and seemed to be an honest man. So long as Bell was in command, the AEA would prefer pure research to commercial enterprise. At any rate, all the information they offered was protected by their patents.

Work on the *Red Wing*, the first powered AEA machine, began at Hammondsport late in January. Selfridge, who had been among those pushing hardest to switch from kites to conventional aircraft, was the designer. Named for the red fabric (left over from the *Cygnet*) that covered its wings, the first AEA venture into powered flight displayed all the external Wright characteristics so familiar on French aircraft. It was a pusher biplane with a canard elevator and a rudder at the rear. There was no attempt at wing warping. The upper and lower wingtips were trussed so close together that they almost touched. Selfridge hoped this pattern would improve lateral stability.

Selfridge was recalled to active duty before the *Red Wing* was complete. That did not deter Curtiss, McCurdy, and Baldwin. After some preliminary runs across the frozen surface of Lake Keuka, they transported the little machine to a smooth patch of ice five miles from Hammondsport on March 12. The first test, with Baldwin at the controls, was to be a high-speed run down the ice. To the surprise of the small crowd of observers, the machine rose into the air some 200 feet from the start and flew a short distance forward until the tail buckled, sending the craft into a sharp descending turn to the right. It struck the ice with some force, breaking a runner and damaging a strut on the right wingtip. The distance from takeoff to touch down was 318 feet, 11 inches.

Far from being discouraged, the members of the AEA immediately set to work on their next project—*White Wing*. Casey Baldwin designed this craft, which was complete and ready for testing by May 9. Except that it featured wheels rather than sled runners, *White Wing* appeared to be a virtual replica of its predecessor. There was one significant difference: Baldwin had mounted two small ailerons at the upper wingtips.

The ailerons functioned like the warping wings of the Wright machine. The Wrights had, in fact, recognized that lateral control could be obtained with such surfaces—a description of them was in their patent. Bell suggested the need for a lateral-control mechanism after the crash of the *Red Wing*. Whether he first encountered the idea of the aileron in the Wright patent, or in the work of Santos-Dumont, Esnault-Pelterie, or Samuel Cody, all of whom had used them earlier, matters little. The important thing was that the ailerons transformed the AEA machine into a flyable airplane.

Casey Baldwin made the first successful flight with *White Wing* at the Stony Brook race track near Hammondsport on May 17, covering 285 feet. Selfridge tried his hand the next day: he flew 100 feet on one flight and 240 feet on another. It was Curtiss's turn on May 21. From the outset it was apparent that the skills honed in bicycle and motorcycle racing were transferable to aeronautics. On his first attempt he covered an incredible 1,017 feet. McCurdy flew 720 feet later that day, but wrecked the machine in landing. The men of the AEA abandoned *White Wing* and moved confidently toward better things.[14]

The Wrights paid scant attention. On March 23, Lazare Weiller had agreed to terms for the French rights to their invention. Two weeks later, on the morning of April 6, Wilbur caught the train for Norfolk. Memories must have come rushing back. As before, he bought lumber in Norfolk, then proceeded to Elizabeth City where he laid in a stock of supplies and registered at the Southern Hotel to await the arrival of "Little" Spencer Midgett, now skipper of the *Lou Willis*, which would transport the lumber over to the Banks.[15]

This time Will himself crossed the Sound in relative comfort and safety aboard Captain Franklin Midgett's gasoline launch, the *B. M. Van Dusen*. It was a wise decision. A few days later the *Lou Willis* once again lost her sails in a gale off the mouth of the Pasquotank, and was forced back to port for repairs. At the time, she was ferrying another load of the Wrights' lumber.

Will walked into the old camp at the Kill Devil Hills early on the morning of April 11.[16] There was not much left. The side walls and south end of the original hangar were still standing, but the roof and north side had collapsed. The floor lay beneath a foot of sand and debris. The "new" building had vanished completely, victim of a recent storm. The lifesavers had pulled the pump out of the sand and reinstalled it near the Kill Devil Hills station.

The skeleton of the 1902 wing protruded from a small dune just east of the original hangar. A crate stored in the rafters of the old structure had crashed to earth when the roof collapsed, spewing the sad remains of the two Chanute gliders onto the sand. An odd assortment of bits and pieces—ribs, spar sections, the cradle of the 1903 machine—littered the surface. Spencer Midgett, who had driven Will down to the camp in a pony cart, explained that a group of boys vacationing at Nags Head had walked down to the site and carried away everything that looked interesting.

Will hired Oliver O'Neal, a relative of Uncle Benny, and one of the Baum boys to help him put up a new building. Bad weather and ill health slowed their progress. Will came down with intestinal flu, and transporting the building materials from the landing at Kitty Hawk to the old fishing dock near the camp proved a problem. Charlie Furnas, a Dayton mechanic who had expressed a repeated desire to fly, suddenly showed up in camp on April 15. Will was pleased to have him and immediately placed Furnas in temporary command of the local building contractors.

Will and Charlie lodged with the Kill Devil Hills lifesavers. The station did not provide the most comfortable accommodations or the best food, but the company was entertaining. Will reported that Bob Westcott, the surfman who had watched the flights of December 17, 1903, through a spyglass, was discussing his plans for a perpetual-motion machine with anyone who would listen. "He did not explain its nature except that it had to do with the boiler or generator of the gas or medium rather than the engine," Will noted in his diary. "He thinks it will practically eliminate the necessity of fuel or at least reduce the quantity to insignificant proportions."

By the time Orv arrived with the flying machine on April 25, the new building was fit for occupation. The airplane went together much more quickly than its hangar. It was ready to test by May 1, the day on which the Norfolk *Virginian-Pilot* announced that the Wrights were back at Kitty Hawk and had completed a ten-mile flight out over the Atlantic.

The report was not unexpected. Newspapers had been covering the story of the Army flying-machine contract for several months and had reported the creation of the French syndicate as well. It was apparent that the mysterious Wright brothers meant to return to the air. The gentlemen of the press were determined to be there.

The *New York Herald* was first on the scene. The night editor of the *Herald* had picked up the *Viriginian-Pilot* story on the telegraph, and prepared a toned-down version for his own paper. He instructed D. Bruce Salley, a Norfolk man who worked as a local stringer for the *Herald*, to investigate the situation at Kitty Hawk.[17]

Salley registered at the Tranquil House, a Manteo hotel, on May 4. Early the following morning he hired a gasoline launch to carry him across the Sound to the old boat landing at the Kill Devil Hills. The brothers were polite to the reporter, who strolled into camp at about noon, but they did not offer much information. Convinced that the original *Virginian-Pilot* story was a hoax and that the Wrights would not be ready to fly for a few days, Salley remained in Manteo on May 6, the day on which Orv flew for the first time since the fall of 1905.

Salley *was* able to telegraph an account of that 1,008-foot hop to the *Herald.* Apparently he based his report on a telephone conversation with the men at the Kill Devil Hills station. It appeared on the front page of the paper the next morning, and was carried by the *New York Times* as well. Rain kept the Wrights, and Bruce Salley, indoors on May 7, but the reporter was back to watch from a safe distance the following day. He arrived too late to see any of the nine short flights made that morning, but he did witness the first hop of the afternoon, a 945-foot effort by Orville. Unable to contain himself, Salley once again rushed straight into camp. As Will put it, he "interrupted the experiments." Wilbur made the longest flight of the day after his departure, 2,230 feet in 59.5 seconds.

Salley's account of the events of May 7 was distributed by the *Herald* to papers across the nation, including, as Milton noted, both of the Dayton dailies and all three Cincinnati papers. As usual, the stories contained only a germ of truth. One of the Cincinnati papers repeated the earlier *Virginian-Pilot* claims that the Wrights had flown ten miles out to sea at an altitude of 3,000 feet.

Salley no longer had the Kill Devil Hills beat to himself. The editors of the *Herald,* recognizing that the story was now too hot for a mere stringer, dispatched crack reporter Byron Newton to the scene. Bill Hoster, of the *New York American,* also checked into the Tranquil House on the afternoon of May 10. Salley's experience had convinced him that the Wrights would not fly if newsmen were present. The three men set out across the Sound at 4:00 A.M. on May 11, "determined to ambush the wily inventors and observe their performance from a hiding place."[18]

Salley led them through "the noisome swamps and jungle, the thousands of moccasins, rattlers and blacksnakes, the blinding swarms of mosquitoes" to a spot where they could keep a surreptitious eye on the Wright camp. There they waited until dawn, "devoured by ticks and mosquitoes, startled occasionally by the beady eyes of a snake and at times drenched by a heavy rain."[19]

The reporters watched as the Wrights and their helpers moved the airplane out of the hangar that morning and prepared it for flight. Newton was startled by the loud, staccato popping of the engine ("like a reaping machine") and by the sight of two propellers as they "began to revolve and flash in the sun." Then came what he could only describe as the moment of miracle:

The machine rose obliquely into the air. At first it came directly toward us, so that we could not tell how fast it was going, except that it appeared to increase in size as it approached. In the excitement of this first flight, men trained to observe details under all sorts of distractions, forgot their cameras, forgot their watches, forgot everything but this aerial monster chattering over our heads. As it neared us we could plainly see the operator in his seat working the upright levers close by his side. When it was almost squarely over us there was a movement of the forward and rear guiding planes, a slight curving of the larger planes at one end and the machine wheeled at an angle every bit as gracefully as an eagle flying close to the ground could have done.[20]

The aircraft maneuvered overhead at an altitude of twenty-five to thirty feet. Judging by the speed at which its shadow moved across the sand, the reporters guessed that it must be traveling at perhaps 40 miles per hour. "Certainly," Newton commented, "it was making the average speed of a railroad train." The pilot kept the machine close to the ground, skimming up and over the crest of the big dune, then flashing back into view.[21]

They made three flights before eleven o'clock, then called it a day. On the best of them, Orv covered 2,750 yards in 2 minutes, 11 seconds. The Wrights knew that they were attracting attention. Milton had been sending clippings from the Dayton papers. Alpheus Drinkwater, the Manteo telegrapher, stopped by that afternoon with a Mr. Grant, whom he introduced as the Weather Bureau man from Norfolk. They said they were out to find a break in the telegraph line, but the Wrights noticed that they left when it became apparent that the flying was over for the day. Drinkwater made sure the Wrights knew that Salley and some other reporters had been watching them from the woods that morning.

The crowd at the Tranquil House continued to grow. The bedraggled reporters returning to Manteo that afternoon discovered that P. H. McGowan, chief American correspondent of the London *Daily Mail*, was now on hand, as were Arthur Ruhl, a freelance writer, and Jimmy Hare, a pioneer news photographer. Both had been sent down to cover the story for *Collier's* magazine.

High winds prevented any flying on May 12, but the growing crowd of reporters was back in place the next day. The Wrights had yet another visitor in camp that morning. The young man, J. C. Burkhart, claimed to be a student at Cornell, but the Wrights pegged him for a newsman. He hung around the camp and watched the first flight of the day, a 96-yard effort by Wilbur, then simply disappeared.

Jimmy Hare caught a picture of the machine in the air on the first flight of the day. It would appear with Ruhl's story in the next issue of *Collier's* on May 30, the first photograph ever published of a Wright airplane in the air. Ruhl could not restrain himself. He had met the Wrights on their return from Europe in the fall of 1907; now he boldly walked out of the woods and into camp to renew the acquaintance. Will and Orv remembered him. They had liked Ruhl in New York, and asked him to stay for lunch. Apparently nervous and guilty about the presence of the other newsmen still hidden in the trees, he declined.

The camp came alive early on the morning of May 14. At eight o'clock Will made a short hop of 656 feet with Charlie Furnas aboard. He had some difficulty with the controls and set the machine down as it approached the side of the West Hill. It was the first time two men had ever flown together aboard a Wright machine.

Orville took Charlie up a few minutes later. They remained aloft for 4 minutes, 2⅖ seconds, covering 4,506 yards over the ground. An overheated bearing compelled them to set down about halfway through their second lap of the camp area. Now it was Will's turn again, but the wind had shifted and he had trouble getting off the track. After three false starts, they retired to the hangar for lunch.

Having repositioned the track that afternoon, Will set off on a long solo aerial circuit of the Kill Devil Hills. About seven minutes into the flight, the reporters noted that the sound of the engine ceased rather abruptly when the airplane was out of sight on the far side of the Little Hill. They assumed that the pilot had simply brought the machine back to earth at some distance from the camp, as Orv had that morning, and that there would be no more flying that day.

They did not learn that there had been a serious accident until they returned to Manteo that afternoon. Drinkwater had gotten the story over the telegraph from the Kill Devil Hills lifesavers. After covering 8,909 feet, Will had become confused while operating the elevator control, and dived the machine straight into the sand at 41 miles an hour. He had suffered nothing more than severe bumps and bruises, but the airplane was a wreck. Angered at missing the big story of the day, the reporters made the best of what they had. The crash was front-page news across the nation the next morning. There was talk of the Wright brothers having destroyed their only machine, coupled with dire predictions about their ability to fulfill the Army contract or their obligations in France.[22]

It was not that serious. Will, Orv, and Charlie hauled most of the heavy bits of wreckage, including the engine and transmission, a mile and a quarter back to camp that evening. "The heat had become almost unbearable," Will recalled, "and we barely escaped collapse before reaching camp." They went back out to retrieve the rest of the equipment early the next morning. Struggling into camp, they discovered P. H. McGowan and a second unidentified reporter setting the remains of the 1902 wing against the side of the hangar for photos. The newsmen asked if they could snap a picture of the brothers as well. Orv, wearing his "Merry Widow" bonnet as protection from the sun, and Will, encased in a dog-collar arrangement used to manhaul the sand sledge, declined. "It would have been an amusing picture for private use," Will thought, "but not such as we cared to have spread broadcast."[23]

Throughout the last two weeks at Kitty Hawk they had received one communication after another from Flint & Company officials. The French syndicate was showing signs of collapse even as it was being organized. It was clear that the brothers would have to provide the promised demonstration flights as soon as possible.

With two contracts to worry about, the Wrights had little choice but to divide the workload and the responsibility. Will would leave for France immediately; there would not even be time to return to Dayton for a visit—Katharine sent his bags directly on to New York. Orv would have to complete the preparations for the U.S. Army trials on his own.

Will was uncomfortable with the situation. Leaving camp for New York on the morning of May 17, he urged his brother to complete the work on the Army machine as quickly as possible and join him in France. He very much hoped that the two of them could participate jointly in both the European and American demonstration flights. Ever the elder brother, he was leery of Orv's impetuosity. "If at any time Orville is not well, or [is] dissatisfied with the situation at Washington, especially the grounds," he told Katharine, "I wish you would tell me. He may not tell me such things always."[24]

chapter 26

THE UNVEILING

June 1908-September 1908

W ill reached New York on May 19. He wrote to Katharine at
once, thanking her for forwarding his clothing, though next
time he hoped she would "raise the lid of my hatbox . . . and
put some of my hats in before sending it on."[1]

He had scarcely a minute to himself during his two days in New
York. Reporters were everywhere, plying him with questions about
the Kitty Hawk trials and the upcoming trip to France. Flint kept him
busy, too. He scheduled Wilbur and Wu Ting Fang, the Chinese ambassador to the United States, for a visit to Thomas Edison's laboratory at East Orange, New Jersey. Fortunately, the trip was rained
out, enabling Will to conduct one important piece of personal business.

Wilbur knew the time had come to violate his longstanding policy
of avoiding publicity. On his first day in New York he noticed a
newspaper article describing the use of ailerons on the AEA *White
Wing*. "Selfridge," he informed his brother, "is infringing our patent
on wing twisting. . . . It is important to get the main features originated by us identified in the public mind with our machines before
they are described in connection with some other machine. A statement of our original features ought to be published and not left
covered up in the patent office." A magazine article explaining what
they had accomplished in simple, straightforward terms should do the
trick.[2]

The rainy day gave him a chance to propose such an article to the
editor of the *Century* magazine, who was interested. But rather than

undertaking the work himself, Will "strongly advised" his brother to "get a stenographer and dictate an article." Katharine would help in "getting it in shape if you are too busy."[3]

It was not like Wilbur to slide an unexpected project off onto his brother—particularly as he had always been the author and speaker in the family. Orville hated to commit himself to paper. The episode indicates the pressure Wilbur was feeling as he faced public demonstration flights on which the outcome of all their work would depend.

It seems not to have occurred to him that Orville, who remained behind at Kitty Hawk to close down the camp and finish the packing, would be just as busy. A complete airplane was waiting for Will in the customs shed at Le Havre, and the workmen at Bariquand et Marre should have finished at least one experimental power plant over the winter. Orv, on the other hand, would have to construct an entirely new airplane and engine and undertake all the preparations for the Army trials.

Orville traveled from Kitty Hawk to Washington in early May to inspect the proposed airplane test ground at Fort Myer, Virginia. The area, a drill field just inside the main gate, was much smaller than Huffman Prairie, but it would do.

Fortunately, the Wrights already had a friend on the scene. Lieutenant Frank P. Lahm, Jr., back from Paris, had been detailed to take part in the trials; he could promise Orv a crew of eight or ten experienced soldiers. The Wright tests would cap a busy season. Captain Tom Baldwin and Glenn Curtiss would be on the site sometime late that summer. The Army would also be purchasing the SC-1, a Baldwin-built dirigible balloon powered by a Curtiss engine, providing that it passed the operational tests. Presumably, Herring would be there with something to test-fly, although Lahm did not seem to be taking him very seriously.

Orville finally returned home to Dayton on May 23, and immediately set to work on the Army machine. "I have had all the lumber sawed up into front framing & spars," he told Wilbur. "We will be in pretty good shape as far as engines are concerned. We have the two extra bodies, with cylinders, pistons, valves, camshafts, etc. complete. About the only things lacking are the cranks."[4]

Orv also kept busy writing. It was a task he hated, but the Wrights were about to fly in public for the first time, and it was important to build up enthusiasm while at the same time underscoring what they had already achieved.

He first sent copies of a detailed letter describing the recent activity at Kitty Hawk to *Scientific American, Aeronautics,* the Aero Club of America, *L'Aérophile,* and *Mitteilungen.* But the piece for *Century,* "The Wright Brothers' Aeroplane," was his triumph. Wilbur wrote on June 28 offering a string of suggestions—Orville must be certain to mention that the "Flying Man" story published in *The Independent* had been a hoax. He should also stress that serious European interest in aeronautics dated from Chanute's lecture of 1903, and that the machines flown by Voisin, Farman, Delagrange, and others "trace their ancestry" to the drawings of the 1902 glider subsequently published in *L'Aérophile.*[5]

The advice came too late—Orville had sent his finished article to the *Century* six days before. It was not cluttered with the sort of details Wilbur requested, nor burdened with partisan claims. Step by step, Orville walked the reader through the process of invention from that day in 1878 when their father had given them the little toy helicopter to the present.

He was uncertain about its quality and offered to return part of the $500 fee paid by the *Century.* He need not have worried. The article was so well written that it remains one of the best short descriptions of the birth of powered flight.

They would need that sort of publicity. The situation in France, Wilbur remarked to Orv, was similar to how an old-time circuit rider had found religion in his district, "in other words, flat on its back." Weiller, the taxicab entrepreneur who was to head up the Wright syndicate in France, was "about scared out," and the other potential members of the group, including Deutsch de la Meurthe, were less than enthusiastic "on account of the excitement over recent flights of Farman & Delagrange."[6]

Delagrange made forty takeoffs from Paris, Rome, Milan, and Turin between January 20 and July 10. By the end of June he had remained in the air for as long as 18 minutes, 30 seconds on a single flight. Farman had won the Deutsch-Archdeacon prize; flown in France, Belgium, and America; carried passengers; and captured the European record for time aloft—20 minutes, 20 seconds.

In America, the members of the Aerial Experiment Association, determined not to be left behind, were now at work on their third powered machine, dubbed the *June Bug* by Alexander Graham Bell to commemorate a plague of small insects infesting Hammondsport that spring.

Curtiss made the first three successful flights with the new craft on June 21. By June 25 he was covering distances of up to 725 yards; two days later he raised his own record to 1,040 yards. The members of the AEA told Aero Club of America officials that they would try for the Scientific American Trophy on July 4.

The trophy was the American answer to the series of rich prizes available to French airmen. Donated to the Aero Club of America in September 1907, it was a silver sculpture, valued at $2,500, to be awarded annually in recognition of a significant achievement in mechanical flight. The first person to win the trophy three times would gain permanent possession; until then, it would stay with the Aero Club of America, which would establish the criteria for the prize and supervise each year's competition.

When the trophy was unveiled in the fall of 1907, Aero Club officials announced that the initial award would be made to the first individual to complete a straight-line flight of one kilometer in the presence of designated witnesses. The requirements for subsequent years would be devised to keep pace with the advance of aeronautics.

The AEA request for official witnesses to be present at Hammondsport on July 4 caught Augustus Post, secretary of the Aero Club, by surprise. Like everyone else, he had assumed that the Wrights would be the first to apply.

Post discussed the situation with Charles Munn, publisher of *Scientific American* and donor of the trophy. Munn immediately contacted Orville, offering to postpone the AEA attempt if the brothers would agree to take part in the competition. Orv refused, citing a competition rule requiring all entries to make an unassisted takeoff. There would not be time to add wheels to their machine.

Obviously, the Wrights could easily have won the trophy, just as they could have won all the prizes being offered in Europe. It would have been a simple matter to put wheels on their machine and choose a flying field large enough so that they could dispense with the weight and derrick launch system. The truth was that the Wrights were simply not interested in competing with latecomers who were infringing on their patents.

The Fourth of July, 1908, was a triumph for the AEA. Twenty-two members of the Aero Club, including president Allan Hawley, who had given Will his balloon ride in Paris the year before, were present. Charles Manly and Herring were there, along with a small army of newsmen and photographers. Whatever the outcome of the trial, it would be officially witnessed and well recorded.

High winds and rain prevented a takeoff until seven o'clock in the evening. Manly, who would function as the Aero Club starter, measured off the course, while Curtiss and his crew rolled the *June Bug* out of its tent-hangar, attached the tail assembly, and ran up the engine. Curtiss took off, rose to an altitude of forty feet, and immediately set the machine back down again. The tail was at a slightly negative angle, making it impossible for the pilot to hold the nose up.

With the problem corrected, Curtiss took off once again. Trailing a thick plume of exhaust smoke, he flew 5,360 feet in 1 minute, 40 seconds, winning the prize with ease. Glenn Hammond Curtiss had joined Santos-Dumont, Gabriel Voisin, and Henri Farman in the headlines.

Wilbur and Orville did not share the general enthusiasm. Orv wrote to Curtiss on July 20, citing the assistance he and his brother had given the AEA and noting that all of the key elements of the *June Bug* were covered in the Wright patent. So long as AEA members confined their activities to research and experimentation, the Wrights were pleased to allow them free use of any features of their patent. "We did not intend," Orv warned, "to give permission to use the patented features of our machines for exhibitions or in a commercial way."[7]

Wilbur meanwhile had arrived in Paris on May 29. He first checked on the progress at Bariquand et Marre; far from completing any new engines, the workmen had not even assembled the sample engine that Orv had shipped out. Company officials promised to have two complete engines ready for inspection within two weeks. Ten days later Will found that the workmen had damaged the original motor in their efforts to get it started. "They are such Idiots! and fool with things that should be left alone," he complained in his diary on June 9. "I get very angry every time I go down there."[8]

The disheartening visits to Bariquand et Marre were punctuated by a series of drives into the French countryside in search of a suitable flying field. Anxious to escape the newsmen dogging his every step, Wilbur decided against using Issy or any of the other local areas favored by the French airmen.

He settled on the Hunaudières race course, near Le Mans, a hundred miles from Paris, where he would find a measure of isolation. In addition, Léon Bollée, a Le Mans automobile manufacturer, offered him factory workspace and a team of mechanics. There were, in fact, few things Bollée would not have done for Wilbur. A sport balloonist and president of the Aéro-Club de la Sarthe, he would become the Wrights' closest friend in France.

Wilbur was in need of friends. Alone and operating under a great deal of pressure, his temper and patience grew short. Forgetting how he had felt in 1907 when his brother bombarded him with criticism from a distance, Wilbur made the same mistake.

"I am a little surprised that I have no letter from you yet," he wrote on June 3. "The fact that the newspapers say nothing of a visit to Washington leads me to fear you did not stop there in returning home. It is a great mistake to leave a personal inspection of the grounds go till the last minute."[9] Orv understood, and sent off a detailed description of the field at Fort Myer, along with a map, in his next letter.

Wilbur then launched into a new complaint. The crates containing the airplane arrived at the Bollée factory on June 16—"I opened the boxes yesterday, and have been puzzled ever since to know how you could have wasted two whole days packing them."[10]

The crates were filled with an indiscriminate mass of wood, wire, and fabric. "The cloth is torn in numerous places, and the aluminum [paint] has rubbed off of the skid sticks and dirtied the cloth very badly." That was only the beginning. The list of damage included smashed oil caps, torn magneto coils, crushed propeller supports, "badly mashed" radiators, broken seats, bent axles, and broken ribs. "I am sure that with a scoop shovel I could have put things in within two or three minutes and made fully as good a job of it. I never saw such evidence of idiocy in my life."[11]

Orville realized what must have happened—overzealous customs inspectors had opened the crates and done a catastrophically poor job of repacking. Aware that Will was wound as tight as a watch spring, he did not press the issue.

Six weeks of effort were required to assemble the airframe from the broken bits and pieces Wilbur pulled from the crates—twice the length of time he had allowed for the task. Bollée's mechanics did their best but the language barrier was a constant problem. As Will's French was rudimentary, he had to perform the most difficult tasks, like wing assembly, himself. "I was the only one strong enough in the fingers to pull the wires together tight, so I had all the sewing to do myself . . . my hands were about raw when I was not half done."[12]

The engine remained a problem. With the new French-built power plant still incomplete, Bariquand et Marre shipped the original American engine to the Bollée factory late in June. Will, his fingers still raw, spent two additional days fiddling with it on the test block, working out the problems introduced by the French crew. He was hard at work on July 4 when a radiator hose tore loose, spraying his left side with boiling water.

Bollée, who was standing behind watching, eased him to the floor and ran to fetch a vial of picric acid for the burns. Wilbur suffered an injured arm, a fist-sized blister on his side, and an even larger blister on his left forearm. The pain did nothing to improve his disposition. "I would really save time by getting into bed and staying there till entirely well," he wrote to Orville on July 9, "as nothing is done down at the shop except irritate my arm and nerves. If you had permitted me to have any anticipation of the state in which you had shipped things over here, it would have saved three weeks' time probably. I would have made preparations to build a machine instead of trying to get along with no assistance and no tools. If you have any conscience it ought to be pretty sore."[13]

At last, on the evening of August 4, they carted the airplane from the Bollée factory to Les Hunaudières. As at Kitty Hawk, Wilbur intended to set up housekeeping in the simple wooden shed that housed the machine. The hangar was provided with "a little outfit of cooking," and a larder stocked with "the finest sardines, anchovies, asparagus &c, &c," compliments of M. Pellier, "the richest man in Le Mans . . . and . . . one of the largest manufacturers of canned goods in France." There was a small restaurant near the race course, and a farmhouse within a hundred yards of the shed where he could obtain fresh milk and water.[14]

Having waited almost three years for this moment, Wilbur was anxious to fly as soon as possible, but a hard rain set in on the morning of August 5 and kept him inside for two more days. Saturday, August 8, dawned clear and windless. It was, he told his brother, "the finest for a first trial we have had for several weeks. I thought it would be a good thing to do a little something."[15]

He took off at about six o'clock that evening and flew two rounds of the field. The whole thing was over in less than two minutes. There was a sparse crowd in the grandstand. The general feeling that the Wrights were a pair of *bluffeurs* had been growing for the past year as more and more Frenchmen left the ground. A number of French airmen had come each day, however, rain or shine. Blériot was there that evening, and Archdeacon. They knew precisely what they had seen—and they were stunned. Wilbur swept through four great

Wilbur captured the imagination of the world with his first public flights in France in late summer 1908.

curves, each time banking deeply into the turn. Here was a man who could control his machine to a degree that they had only dreamed of. Truly, as the publicist François Peyrey wrote, Wilbur and Orville were *"Les Premiers Hommes-oiseaux."*

Wilbur flew eight more times at Les Hunaudières between Monday and Thursday of the following week. He turned in his best performance—seven circles of the track in 8 minutes, 13²⁄₅ seconds—on Thursday, August 13.

Men and women who had held their collective breath as Farman struggled through his wide, flat turns saw Wilbur fly a tight figure-8 with a slight motion of the hand and a flick of the wrist. It was quite beyond their experience, and proof at last that the Wrights had accomplished all they claimed.

Word of Hunaudières swept through France that week. The crowds grew larger each day as more people were drawn to see this miracle for themselves. The London *Daily Mirror* hailed "THE MOST WONDERFUL FLYING-MACHINE THAT HAS EVER BEEN MADE."[16] *The Times* agreed that the demonstrations at Les Hunaudières "proved over and over again that Wilbur and Orville Wright have long mastered the art of artificial flight. They are a public justification of the performances which the American aviators announced in 1904 and 1905, and they give them, conclusively, the first place in the history of flying machines. . . ."[17]

French newspapers like *Le Figaro* were even more enthusiastic. "I've seen him; I've seen them! Yes! I have today seen Wilbur Wright and his great white bird, the beautiful mechanical bird . . . there is no doubt! Wilbur and Orville Wright have well and truly flown."[18]

Georges Besançon spoke for the French aviators in *L'Aérophile*—"the facility with which the machine flies, and the dexterity with which the aviator gave proof from the first, in his maneuvering, have completely dissipated all doubts. Not one of the former detractors of the Wrights dare question, today, the previous experiments of the men who were truly the first to fly. . . ."[19]

Apologies flowed in from experimenters and enthusiasts across France. Archdeacon, who had tried harder than most not to believe, was one of the first: "For a long time, for too long a time, the Wright brothers have been accused in Europe of bluff—even perhaps in the land of their birth. They are today hallowed in France, and I feel an intense pleasure in counting myself among the first to make amends for that flagrant injustice."[20]

"Who can doubt that the Wrights have done all that they claim," asked the newcomer René Gasnier. "My enthusiasm is unbounded." Paul Zens commented that "Mr. Wright has us all in his hands. What he does not know is not worth knowing." Surcouf referred to Wilbur as a "titanic genius," while Léon Delagrange noted simply: *"Nous sommes battu."*[21]

Once the intial shock had washed over them, the French aviators retracted a little. Farman, in a *Le Matin* interview published on August 26, objected that "our machines are as good as his." Blériot, initially enthusiastic, later reassured his colleagues that the Wrights had only a "momentary superiority." Charles and Gabriel Voisin refused to credit the Wrights with even that much. "Where was aviation born?" they asked in a joint letter to *Le Matin.* "IN FRANCE." "Without wishing to diminish at all the merit of the aviators of Dayton, we permit ourselves to make the observation that French aviation was not born uniquely by their experiments; and that if we have derived some information—moreover very little—from their tests, they have also profited from French genius in large measure."[22]

Voisin had entered the field, built machines, and taught himself to fly, all the while convinced that the Wrights were perpetrating a hoax. A proud man with an enormous ego, he could not admit that his work, the very appearance of his machine, had been shaped by what he knew of the Wright technology. To the end of his life—he died at the age of ninety-three in 1973—he would refuse to accept that Wilbur and Orville had laid the foundation of French aeronautics.

But such criticism was scarcely noticed outside limited aeronautical circles. After years of relative obscurity, the Wrights were swept along on a wave of popular acclaim that drowned out any dissent.

Life would never be the same for the brothers after the week at Les Hunaudières. Orville had not flown publicly yet, but already they had achieved a level of international celebrity so incredible that there has not been anything quite like it since. Wilbur and Orville seemed to have accomplished nothing less than a miracle.

Even in an age that has come to regard journeys to the moon and robot exploration of the planets as commonplace, flight continues to inspire the same sense of awe and power that it did when the airplane was new. Aviation, that most hard-edged of technologies, has somehow retained a component of the magic that was so apparent to the first witnesses who saw Will fly at Les Hunaudières.

The psychological impact was stunning. If man could fly, was any goal beyond his reach? That was the one great lesson of Hunaudières—and of the flights that would follow in the summer and fall of 1908.

Having captured the attention of the world during a single week in August, Wilbur paused and shifted his operations to a larger, more suitable field known as Camp d'Auvours, eleven kilometers east of Le Mans. An artillery testing ground, it had been his first choice. Les Hunaudières, surrounded by trees, a grandstand, and other obstacles, was resorted to only when French military authorities rejected his request. Now, in the glare of publicity, the Army relented.

He made his first flight there on August 21. The atmosphere was incredible, and the crowds so large that Hart Berg and the local military commander were forced to introduce a ticket system. Wilbur was in the air day after day, breaking the few records that had been set by the French and proving his mastery to one and all.

The members of the new French syndicate were now anxious that he continue to fly in France, generating publicity to spur the sale of the Wright Flyer to governments and wealthy private individuals. Orville would have to undertake the Army trials on his own. Wilbur warned his brother to prepare for some difficulty in mastering the upright controls—"I have not yet learned to operate the handles without blunders," he admitted on August 15, "but I can easily make turns of three hundred feet in diameter." He advised Orv to "be awfully careful in beginning practice and go slowly."[23]

chapter 27

FORT MYER

August–September 1908

O rville arrived at Fort Myer on August 20, 1908. The two Char-
lies, Furnas and Taylor, were already there, supervising the
transfer of the crated flying machine from the railroad station
in Arlington to the large balloon hangar on the post where it would
be assembled. Orville initially registered at the St. James Hotel in
Washington, but was quickly moved by Albert Zahm into more prestigious quarters at the Cosmos Club.

Zahm, an old friend of Chanute's, had played a key role in organizing the great aeronautical conference at the World's Columbian Exposition fifteen years before. Now he taught physics at Catholic
University, where he was conducting studies of airship-hull resistance
with a large wind tunnel. A man who regarded himself as a mover and
shaker in official scientific circles, Zahm assumed that Orville would
enjoy the limelight.

Orville found life at the Cosmos Club "more pleasant . . . than I
expected." He met "stacks of prominent people," eager to shake his
hand and offer assistance. The newspapers, ever alert to a whiff of
romance, called attention to the society belles who flocked around
him. He handled the situation with a light touch, admitting to Katharine that he was "meeting some very handsome young ladies," yet he
would "have an awful time to think of their names if I meet them
again."[1]

But Orville was never comfortable as the center of attention. Wilbur knew how difficult life could be for a celebrity, and worried that

all the attention might distract his brother. "I fear he will have trouble with over-attention from reporters, visitors . . . &c," he told Milton. "It is an awful nuisance to be disturbed when there is experimenting and practicing to be done. I am treated with wonderful kindness . . . but too much time is wasted and nervous energy expended."[2]

Indeed, Orville complained to Katharine on August 27: "The trouble here is that you can't find a minute to be alone. I haven't done a lick of work since I have been here. I have to give my time to answering the ten thousand fool questions people ask about the machine. There are a number of people standing about the whole day long." The strain was beginning to tell, as it had on Wilbur the month before. The closing line of that letter was of particular concern to a worried sister and father. "I have trouble in getting enough sleep."[3]

The process of unpacking and assembling the machine proceeded much more smoothly than it had for Wilbur. "The goods came through in perfect shape," Orv told him with obvious satisfaction. "They were packed exactly as were the goods sent to Europe. Our trouble there is with the customhouse tearing everything loose and not fastening them again."[4]

While the mechanics uncrated the airplane and laid out the parts, Orville plotted the course for the required cross-country demonstration flights. Taking off from the parade ground, he would fly five miles to Alexandria, make a turn, and retrace his course to Fort Myer. There would be "quite a number of good landing places, though there is one large forest . . . over a mile wide in which there are no breaks whatever." He would also have to cross three deep ravines, but most of the route was over open land where he could set down in an emergency.[5]

The next task was to meet with the five officers who composed "the committee which will pass upon the trials." He already knew two of the men, Lieutenant Lahm and Major George Squier, the executive officer to the Chief of the Signal Corps. Squier had prepared the advertisement for bids and would now serve as president of the board. Captain Charles S. Wallace was an unknown quantity.

The same could not be said for Lieutenant Thomas E. Selfridge, whose presence as a member of the AEA made both of the Wrights very nervous. Predictably, the lowest-ranking member of the board, Lieutenant Benjamin Delahauf Foulois, became a particular favorite of Orville's. His avid interest in aeronautics, as evidenced by a Signal School thesis entitled "The Tactical and Strategical Value of Dirigible

Balloons and Aerodynamical Flying Machines," and his light weight (130 pounds, soaking wet) marked him as a prime candidate for pilot training.[6]

The Wright trials would cap a full summer for the members of the board, who had already served as the official acceptance panel for the Baldwin airship SC-1. Baldwin and Curtiss arrived on the post with their machine on July 20 and were flying by August 4.

Baldwin's contract required his airship to average 20 miles per hour over a measured course, with a system of bonuses and penalties for exceeding or failing to achieve that speed. Baldwin stood at the rear of the machine manipulating the rudder; Curtiss rode up front, manning the elevator control and monitoring the engine. The speed trial came on August 14, when the two men set out for Cherrydale, a little over four miles away. They covered the course at an average speed of 19.61 miles per hour. That .039 difference resulted in a 15 percent penalty deducted from the bid price of $6,750.[7]

Baldwin and Curtiss were also required to train three Army officers—Lahm, Selfridge, and Foulois—to fly the airship. Foulois was the first. The young lieutenant thought the flight "thrilling beyond words." It lasted only about ten minutes, and Foulois was kept too busy reacting to Baldwin's commands to worry about being aloft

with only a bag of air holding me up and four Oregon spruce bars held together by wire holding me in. But being airborne, with the controls in my hands and the hot engine blasting me in the face sent a surge of joy through my whole body that defied description. As we chugged around the Fort Myer parade ground, I looked eastward to the Capitol, the Washington Monument and the Lincoln Memorial glistening in the bright morning sun. It was one of those sights a person never forgets.[8]

Between flights, Foulois had ample opportunity to observe Orville Wright. It seemed to Foulois that he and his mechanics lived in a world of their own. "They paid no attention to anyone else," he recalled, "and shrugged off all questions from onlookers. They talked only to each other, as though they were on a desert island miles from civilization."[9]

Concentration was needed—the engine refused to run up to speed. The Wright contract with the Army had established a basic purchase price of $25,000 providing the machine was able to maintain an average speed of 40 miles per hour during the tests. There would be a bonus of $2,500 for each additional mile per hour, and a similar penalty for each mile per hour less. The engine had to perform without a miss. Some higher octane gasoline, a set of new oil cups, and a bit of tinkering with the magneto solved the problems.

The airplane passed the portability test on September 1, when it was loaded onto an Army wagon and moved from the balloon shed to a large tent pitched at the edge of the parade ground, where the derrick and track were already in place. There was a minor accident the next day. Orv made a test run up the track and was returning the machine to the starting point when the crossbar slipped off the rail, dropping the airplane onto the ground. The rope snapped while Marine Lieutenant Richard Creecy was straightening out the resulting tangle. The 400-pound weight grazed his jaw in passing. The damage, both to the airplane and to Creecy, was minor.[10]

Orv left the ground for the first time on September 3. As Will suggested, he took it slow and easy, flying a circle and a half of the field in 1 minute, 11 seconds. The President's twenty-one-year-old son, Theodore Roosevelt, Jr., was there for the event.

Strangely, the flight attracted little of the attention that greeted Wilbur in France. It was third-page news in the Washington *Evening Star*. The whole thing would take a bit of time to sink in. The Europeans were flying-machine connoisseurs—they knew what to expect, and Wilbur gave them more. He showed a knowledgeable crowd what it meant to really fly. That was the source of the excitement.

Washingtonians had seen Baldwin, Curtiss, and their officer-pupils chugging up and down the Potomac all day, every day. After that, Orv's circle and a half of the parade ground did not seem like much. It took a few days to realize that this was something different indeed.

Orville flew three miles the next day, and was in the air at every opportunity over the next week and a half.[11] As the flights grew more spectacular, the crowds swelled. September 9 was a red-letter day. With three cabinet secretaries looking on, Orville set three world records. On the first flight he remained in the air for 57 minutes and 13 seconds—a new world endurance record. A few minutes later he went up again, breaking his own record by remaining airborne for 62 minutes, 15 seconds. Next he made his first passenger flight in public, taking Lieutenant Lahm for a 6-minute, 24-second spin. It was a new endurance record for flight with a passenger.

On September 10, Orville remained in the air for 65 minutes, 52 seconds, shattering his record for the third time. He did it again on

September 11, with a flight of 70 minutes, 24 seconds. On September 12, with Chanute in the audience, Orville took Major Squier up and set a new record of 9 minutes, 6⅓ seconds for flight with a passenger. He went back up by himself that afternoon and shattered the basic endurance record yet again.

High winds and an engine overhaul kept him on the ground until September 17, when he was scheduled to fly with Selfridge. Orville was not looking forward to it. "I will be glad to have Selfridge out of the way," he told Wilbur. "I don't trust him an inch. He is intensely interested in the subject, and plans to meet me often at dinners, etc. where he can try to pump me. He has a good education, and a clear mind. I understand that he does a good deal of knocking behind my back."[12]

Still, Selfridge, as a member of the official board, was entitled to a ride. They took off at five o'clock in the afternoon. It was the first time Orville had flown in five days. He was dressed in his usual flying costume, a neat suit with a billed cap. Selfridge wore his uniform pants and blouse. Reporters noted that he handed his jacket and hat to a friend as he climbed aboard the machine.[13]

They made three circles of the parade ground, keeping relatively low and well inside the circle of surrounding buildings. As they began the third circle, Orville eased the nose up, climbing above 100 feet. This time he intended to make a broader turn. They were moving directly toward the wall of Arlington Cemetery when Orville heard, or felt, a slight tapping at the rear of the machine.

He looked over his shoulder and could see nothing wrong, but decided to cut the power and land as soon as he had completed a turn back toward the crowd. Two or three seconds after the first taps had alerted him, there were two audible thumps, followed by a violent shaking. The airplane slewed to the right. Orville reached to cut the power, assuming that the problem was in the transmission system. He struggled with the controls as the left wing continued to drop, pulling the nose down until the craft was headed straight for the ground. Selfridge, who had been silent up to this point, looked at Orville and murmured, "Oh! Oh!" The machine hit the ground moving at top speed and nosed over, burying Orville and Selfridge in a tangle of debris.[14]

The crowd surged across the parade ground toward the cemetery gate, three mounted troopers leading the way. Orville was pulled from the wreckage first, bleeding and unconscious. A physician in the

Orville demonstrated the performance of their machine for the U.S. Army at Fort Myer, Virginia. Tragedy, and the first fatality suffered in a powered airplane crash, came on September 17, 1908.

crowd tended him while Charlie Taylor and several officers worked their way through the wreckage toward Selfridge. Like Orville, he was unconscious and bleeding from the head. A field ambulance arrived within a few minutes, but Army physicians on the scene decided it would be safer to transport both men to the post hospital by stretcher.

As the troopers dispersed the crowd, newsmen and friends gathered in front of the post hospital to wait for the medical reports. Orville suffered a broken left thigh, several broken ribs, scalp wounds, and an injured back. He was in shock, but would survive. Selfridge was in more serious condition, with a severely fractured skull. He had been taken into surgery.

The reporters interviewed the more knowledgeable spectators while waiting for further news. Flint was there, and remarked that he hoped the crash would not blind the public to the great things Orville had accomplished earlier in the week. Chanute was the first to suggest that the accident was the result of a broken propeller blade. The final bulletin was issued at about eight-thirty that evening: Thomas Selfridge had died without regaining consciousness a few minutes after being wheeled out of the operating room.[15]

Milton was conducting family business near Richmond, Indiana, when the news arrived. If his laconic diary entry is any indication, he took it better than might be expected—"Orville injured. Orville's disaster at 5; Selfridge's death."[16]

Katharine had just come home from school when she received her telegram. She immediately contacted her superiors at Central High, requesting indefinite leave. There was packing to be done, and arrangements to be made for a trip to Washington that evening. She would nurse Orv herself, or supervise those charged with his care. Katharine had spent her last day as a full-time teacher.[17]

Wilbur was in the hangar with his airplane preparing to try for the Michelin prize when word of the disaster reached him at eight o'clock the following morning. He closeted himself in the shed for a time. Then, as François Peyrey reported, he emerged, canceled all flights for a week, and set off on his bicycle for Le Mans, where he would wait for further news.[18]

Wilbur's reaction fit a pattern that had been emerging at least since the time of the first trip to France in the spring of 1907. He was convinced that things went wrong when he was not there to prevent it. Orville was simply not as careful as he was. He wrote to Katharine on September 20:

> I cannot help thinking over and over again "If I had been there, it would not have happened." The worry over leaving Orville alone to undertake those trials was one of the chief things in almost breaking me down a few weeks ago and as soon as I heard reassuring news from America I was well again. . . . It was not right to leave Orville to undertake such a task alone. I do not mean that Orville was incompetent to do the work itself, but I realized that he would be surrounded by thousands of people who with the most friendly intentions in the world would consume his time, exhaust his strength, and keep him from getting the proper rest. A man cannot take sufficient care when he is subject to continual interruptions and his time is consumed in talking to visitors.[19]

Wilbur clearly believed the accident was the result of his brother's carelessness. "I suspect that Orville told Charlie to put the . . . screws [propellers] on instead of doing it himself, and that if he had done it himself he would have noticed the thing that made the trouble, whatever it may have been"—a mistake Wilbur did not think he would ever make. "People think I am foolish because I do not like the men to do the least important thing on the machine."[20] Perhaps now everyone would understand the necessity for such care.

There was never much question about the cause of the accident. On September 9, a split had been noted in one of the original propellers shipped from Dayton. Orville and Charlie Taylor had repaired the blade, then wired Lorin in Dayton requesting that he ship two new replacements. The "big screws" bolted in place on September 16 had the same chord as the original blades, but were six inches longer.

Following the accident, the left blade was found to be in perfect condition. The right blade was splintered and broken—a split similar to that discovered the week before in one of the old blades had opened up while the machine was in the air on September 17, flattening the blade slightly. The unequal thrust between the two blades had created the light tapping sound that Orville had heard; the differential pressure caused the right propeller support to give a little. The blade swung just far enough out of line to clip one of the guy lines holding the rudder in place. The rudder had then twisted out of position, forcing the machine into the ground.

The Army accepted the explanation without question and made it clear that the accident would not be held against the Wrights. "Of course we deplore the accident," George Squier commented,

> but no one who saw the flights of the last four days at Fort Myer could doubt for an instant that the problem of aerial navigation was solved. If Mr. Wright should never again enter an airplane, his work last week at Fort Myer will have secured him a lasting place in history as the man who showed the world that mechanical flight was an assured success. No one seems to realize at this close range what a revolution the flights portend. The problem is solved, and it only remains to work out the details.[21]

Before his release from the hospital, the Army assured Orville that the Wrights would be given a contract extension permitting them to return to Fort Myer to complete the demonstration flights in the summer of 1909. No penalties would be imposed. "I'll be back next year with a new machine," Orville told Squier firmly. "We will make good on our contract."[22]

chapter 28

POMP AND CIRCUMSTANCE

November 1908-June 1909

O rville was in the hospital at Fort Myer for seven weeks, with Katharine beside him the entire time. "The nurses are nice," she told Agnes Osborn, "but Orville likes to see me." He was incoherent for a considerable time after her arrival. "I kept him quiet all afternoon by reading to him," she noted on September 22. "He does not hear what I read, but the monotonous sound of my voice puts him to sleep often."[1]

Katharine herself was well cared for. "You never saw such kindness and consideration in all your life," she assured Agnes. "Everybody from the Secretary of War on down has offered me the town. Maj. Squier, the head of the Signal Corps [sic], the department for which the flying machine was being [built] is just about the handsomest man I've ever seen." No, she had forgotten about Captain Bailey, the surgeon in charge of Orv's case. "I never saw a more winning face than he has and I am told that he is a good surgeon."[2] Katharine's judgments of the opposite sex had mellowed.

With Chanute's help and advice, she did her best to protect her brother's interests. She was particularly concerned about the members of the AEA, all of whom were in Washington to serve as pall bearers at the Selfridge funeral. Three of them—Bell, McCurdy, and Casey Baldwin—called on Orville at the hospital on September 23, but were refused admission by the doctors. They left their cards, then walked to Arlington Cemetery to pay their respects. Passing the balloon shed where the crated Flyer was awaiting shipment back to

Dayton, they prevailed upon the Army guard to let them in. The crate was not sealed, and the sergeant on duty later recalled that Bell took at least one measurement from the wings.

Outraged, Katharine asked Chanute to investigate. After interviewing the sergeant, Chanute assured her there was nothing to worry about—Bell was only checking the wing chord.[3] Katharine was not so sure. Where her brother's interests were concerned, she could not be too careful.

Others waited, eager to take whatever unfair advantage they could. Herring arrived at Fort Myer on October 12 with an assistant, two suitcases, and a small "innovation trunk." The cases, he informed the Army and the press, contained the parts of the engine and airplane he had constructed to fulfill his contract.[4]

The newspapers had a field day. "The Herring machine is packed in a suitcase," one reporter remarked. "That is the safest way to use it." Herring could afford to shrug it off. The Wright accident placed the Army in a difficult position. The brothers had been granted an extension of their contract; Herring would gain more time too, time to milk the situation for its publicity value. Few men were more adept at that game.[5]

None of this was lost on the Wrights, who felt they had been through such things before. "I presume that poor old Daddy is terribly worried over our troubles," Wilbur remarked to Katharine after the accident. "He may be sure that, like his Keiter trouble, things will turn out all right at last."[6] They would find few real friends or supporters in the world, but they did have one another.

Orville and Katharine came back home on November 1. It would be two more weeks before he was strong enough to write to his brother. "I am just beginning to get about the house on crutches," he explained. "I sit up several hours at a time, though I suffer some from the pressure of the blood in my feet and legs, after so long a period of disuse." He walked with a cane for months and would never fully recover. For the rest of his life, the slightest vibration set off excruciating pain from an irritated sciatic nerve, occasionally sending him to bed for extended periods. He avoided travel whenever possible, and drove an automobile with a specially reinforced suspension system.[7] Air travel, he later complained, was especially painful.

Will was flying for both of them now—and flying brilliantly. Like his brother during that one short week at Fort Myer, he was setting new records at an astonishing pace. On September 21 he shattered the existing marks for both distance and duration, winning a $1,000 Aéro-

Club de France prize while ten thousand spectators looked on. He flew with the distinguished French physicist Paul Painlevé on October 10, breaking the distance and duration records for flight with a passenger.

Wilbur went after the altitude prizes as well. On November 18 the Aéro-Club de la Sarthe awarded him the 1,000 franc Prix de la Hauteur for the first flight to an altitude of ninety meters. The Aéro-Club de France altitude competition required an unassisted takeoff, a rule that seemed specifically designed to exclude Wilbur from entering. He won that 2,500 franc prize on November 23, employing an extra long rail that enabled him to dispense with the catapult. As a demonstration of his contempt for the "standing start" rule, he cruised directly above the balloons swaying at the end of ninety-meter cables, refusing to top his own recent record. Finally, on December 18, he set new world marks for distance, duration, and altitude.

Some of Wilbur's most newsworthy flights did not involve prizes. On October 7, for example, he granted Mrs. Hart Berg the distinction of being the first woman to fly. Before the month was out he also took up the first English, Russian, Spanish, German, and Italian passengers, and, on October 3, the first reporter—George P. Dicken, of the *New York Herald.*[8]

All told, Wilbur carried more than forty passengers during his stay at Le Mans. Some, like Hart Berg, Arnold Fordyce, Weiller, Deutsch de la Meurthe, Frank Lahm, and Léon Bollée, were old friends or business associates. Others, including Giovanni de Pirelli, the Italian tire manufacturer, and the Marquis de Viana, Grand Equerry to the King of Spain, were people who might someday be useful contacts. Still others, notably Léon Bollée's eleven-year-old nephew, were invited along purely for their company.

All were exhilarated. One of them, Baden-Powell, provided a detailed account of his adventure:

Having clambered in among various rods and wires one struggles into the little seat arranged on the front edge of the lower plane, and places one's feet on a small bar in front. A string is found crossing just in front of one's chest, and Mr. Wright gives directions that this must not be touched. It is a simple contrivance for cutting off the ignition and stopping the engine. In event of any accident the body will probably be thrown forward, and pressing against the string, immediately stops the engine. . . . All being ready, coats are buttoned, and caps pulled down to prevent being blown off. . . .

Then the driver bends down and releases the catch which holds the anchoring wire. The machine is off! It bounds forward and travels rapidly

Wilbur took Captain Paul Girardville aloft at Pau in 1909.

along the rail. The foreplanes are meanwhile pressed down to prevent
the machine lifting prematurely, but when about half the length of the
rail has been traversed, the lever is pulled back, the planes come into
operation, and the whole machine rises almost imperceptibly off the
track. The ascent must be very gradual. When the machine leaves the
track it glides so close to the ground that one often doubts if it is really
started in the air, but then it gradually mounts. . . .

So steady and regular is the motion that it appears exactly as if it were
progressing along an invisible elevated track. Only just now and again,
as a swirl of wind catches it, does it make a slight undulation like a boat
rising to a big wave. Mr. Wright, with both hands grasping the levers,
watches every move, but his movements are so slight as to be almost
imperceptible. Having soon reached the end of the ground, the machine
is guided round in a large semi-circle, gracefully leaning over as it turns.
. . . All the time the engine is buzzing so loudly and the propellers
humming so that after a trip one is almost deaf.[9]

Tributes flowed in: Crown Prince Frederick Wilhelm of Germany
cabled congratulations, while the Dowager Queen Margherita of Italy
traveled to Camp d'Auvours to watch him fly. There were days, Wilbur remarked to Orv, when "Princes and millionaires" seemed to be

"as thick as thieves" at the flying ground. Wilbur's social calendar was crowded with testimonial dinners offered by the Aéro-Club de France, the Société Autour du Monde, the Ligue Nationale Aérienne, and the Cercle des Arts et Sports. The French Senate suspended debate to offer him a standing ovation.[10]

Other groups offered more substantial rewards. Wilbur was awarded the 5,000 franc Commission d'Aviation prize established by the Aéro-Club de France. In addition, the club gave the Wrights a special gold medal for their combined flights in September. The Académie des Sports, the Aeronautical Society of Great Britain, the Aero Club of America, the Society for the Encouragement of Peace, and the Aero Club of Great Britain all awarded gold medals to the Wrights that fall.

Lazare Weiller's doubts had vanished. Investors clamored to join his syndicate. Wilbur completed the last of the required demonstration flights on October 10. Eight days later, in accordance with the terms of his agreement, he began to train the first Wright pilot, Count Charles de Lambert. Flight training for a second pilot, Captain Paul N. Lucas-Girardville, began on November 10.

The members of Weiller's syndicate, the Compagnie Générale de Navigation Aérienne (CGNA), did not intend to build aircraft. They would function as sales agents, contracting with Société Astra, an airship-building firm, and Chantiers de France of Dunkirk, for airframes. Bariquand et Marre would supply the engines. The firm eventually claimed that it had received fifty orders for flying machines; in fact, probably half that number were constructed. Neither the Wrights nor the investors grew rich through the venture.

Wilbur dominated the skies that fall. Most of his records for distance and duration stood until the following year. But the Europeans were quick to learn their final lessons in the art and science of flight. The most observant and adaptable of the French airmen recognized that they had rejected three-axis control all too quickly.

Louis Blériot had struggled with the control issue, moving from early attempts to achieve inherent lateral stability through dihedral to the use of ineffective wingtip ailerons. He was present for Wilbur's first public flight at Les Hunaudières on August 8—and everything fell into place. "Blériot was all excited," Ross Browne, a young American who was there, recalled. "He looked over the machine . . . he tested the wings, and Mr. Wright showed how the warping was done . . . how it worked." He was "just like a young boy." As they walked away from the flying field, Blériot announced: "I'm going to use a warped wing. To hell with the aileron."[11] His next project, the Blériot XI, did use wing warping. Eleven months later, he flew the English Channel.

Henri Farman had enjoyed far more success than Blériot. Flying his standard Voisin-built machine at Issy on July 20 that year, he remained aloft for 20 minutes, 20 seconds. For him, as for Blériot, the flights at Les Hunaudières were a revelation. For the first time the absolute importance of lateral control became clear. Farman did not directly copy the wing-warping technique; rather, he added the four large down-only flaps to the trailing edges of his wings. Esnault-Pelterie, Curtiss, and Blériot had experimented with ailerons. Farman made them work. Inspired by the sight of Wilbur Wright wheeling in narrow circles over the racetrack at Les Hunaudières, he constructed the first machine to rival the performance of the Wright aircraft.[12]

Wilbur had few illusions about the future. The French had seen him in the air; they had studied his technology in detail. Within a matter of months, the best of them would be flying as well as he. Now, while he held an unquestionable lead, Wilbur planned a spectacular performance that would cap the year 1908 and mark it as his forever.

Clearly, one impressive flight lay within the reach of contemporary technology. On October 5, Arthur Harmsworth, Lord Northcliffe, publisher of the London *Daily Mail*, announced a $5,000 prize to the first man to fly an airplane across the English Channel. Like so much else that was happening that fall, the new prize was inspired by Wilbur and Orville's performances. Northcliffe had visited Orville in the hospital at Fort Myer, and fully expected Wilbur to snatch the *Daily Mail* prize. He had already flown further and remained in the air longer than would be required to cross the Channel.

Characteristically, Wilbur weighed the risks with great care. Failure carried a high price—forced landing in the water would destroy the only Wright Flyer in Europe. The accident at Fort Myer made it all the more important for Wilbur to maintain a record of unalloyed success.

The Coupe Michelin offered an acceptable, and much safer, option. Established by the industrialist André Michelin, the prize consisted of an enormous trophy and a check for 20,000 francs to be awarded for the longest flight of 1908. As the year drew to a close, Wilbur already held the world's duration record of 1 hour, 31 minutes, and 25⅘ seconds. His closest competitor, Henri Farman, had remained aloft for 44 minutes, 31 seconds on October 2. Wilbur was determined to extend his lead even further. His own goal for winning the Michelin prize—two full hours aloft.

It would not be easy. Winter had set in at Camp d'Auvours. By December 28, when he submitted his 50-franc entry fee and announced that he would try for the prize on the last day of the year, snow covered the ground and the temperature was well below freezing. Bundled in coat, cap, and gloves, he flew for 1 hour and 53 minutes on December 30. A broken fuel line brought the first flight of December 31 to an end after 43 minutes. He took off again that afternoon in a freezing mist and flew round and round the prescribed triangular course for as long as he could stand it—2 hours, 18 minutes, 33⅗ seconds.[13]

While not as spectacular as a Channel flight, the Coupe Michelin accomplished Wilbur's goal. Not given to grand, crowd-pleasing gestures, this flight was in character—a straightforward, no-frills demonstration of his absolute superiority in the air.

Wilbur made five more flights at Camp d'Auvours. Each was a short hop of less than three minutes, giving him an opportunity to offer a few additional rides to friends and workmen from the Bollée factory. Between August 8, 1908, and January 2, 1909, he completed 129 flights—nine from Les Hunaudières, the rest from Camp d'Auvours. During those five months he established nine world records.

Wilbur's newest student, the balloonist Paul Tissandier, persuaded him to establish winter quarters at Pau, in the south of France. Nestled at the foot of the Pyrenees, Pau had begun to lose some of its appeal as a winter resort in recent years when Edward VII moved his holiday headquarters to Biarritz. Recognizing the publicity value of Wilbur's presence, the city fathers of Pau provided him with a luxurious hangar, complete with living quarters and a fully equipped shop. His meals were prepared by a chef selected by the mayor. The flying field, the Pont-Long, was a flat, open plain some six miles from Pau; 165 acres in extent, it was completely open and unobstructed.[14]

Wilbur would no longer be alone. Early on the morning of January 12, he met Orville and Katharine at a Paris train station. Back on his feet now, though still walking with two canes, Orv deserved to share the European triumph. It would have been unthinkable to leave Katharine behind.

She had prepared for the trip with some care, ordering two evening gowns in Dayton, one rose and one black. She also bought a neatly tailored traveling suit and a new hat. Her only piece of jewelry was a small diamond ring that had special significance—Orville had presented it to her on the day she graduated from Oberlin. While in Paris the year before, Wilbur had joked with his sister about spinsterish

Katharine and Orville, still recovering from the crash at Fort Myer, joined their brother in France.

schoolteachers touring the Louvre. She spent her time in Paris shopping, getting two more suits and some stylish hats.[15]

Wilbur moved south to Pau on January 14, allowing Orville and Katharine two extra days in Paris before joining him. He made sixty-four flights at Pau between February 3 and March 20. His first task was to complete flight training for Count de Lambert, Lucas-Girard-ville, and Tissandier. Ultimately, however, the sense of spectacle overwhelmed everything else. For a time Pau once again became a winter mecca attracting the cream of European society.

The newsmen and members of the aeronautical crowd who had filled the spectator seats at Les Hunaudières and Camp d'Auvours were replaced by kings and queens, captains of industry and heads of state, who trekked to Pau to witness the miracle for themselves. Alfonso XIII of Spain came with a camera slung over his shoulder, as though hoping to be mistaken for a tourist. Edward VII watched two flights, on one of which Katharine flew as a passenger.

Lord Arthur Balfour, once prime minister of England, requested the honor of "taking part in the miracle" by helping to hoist the catapult weight. Lord Northcliffe, noting that a young British lord was also assisting, remarked to Orville: "I'm so glad that young man is helping with the rope, for I'm sure it is the only useful thing he has ever done in his life."[16]

The great and near-great of Europe were fascinated and impressed by the Wrights. There was a straightforward honesty about them, coupled with rare poise, common sense, and wit. Men of wealth and power would never turn the heads of these three American heroes. "Kings," Katharine remarked to a reporter, "are just like other nice, well-bred people." She praised King Alfonso as a "good husband" for keeping a promise to his wife that he would not fly, and found J. P. Morgan and his sister to be "very pleasant people."[17]

Privately, their reactions were a bit more acerbic. Wilbur described "His Gracious Majesty &c.," King Victor Emmanuel, as so short that "his feet failed to reach the floor by at least a foot when he sat down."[18]

The Wrights were the first great celebrities of the new century. No newspaper or magazine seemed complete without a story on the three Americans. The popular appetite for images—photographs, sketches, caricatures, and motion pictures—was insatiable. Milton saw Wilbur for the first time in over a year on April 19, 1909: a local vaudeville house was headlining films of the flying at Camp d'Auvours.[19]

The smallest details of their lives seemed endlessly fascinating. It was reported that the frying pan on which Will had done his cooking in the hangar at Camp d'Auvours would be displayed at the Louvre. Wilbur did most of his flying in a soft cloth cap that Orv had bought in France the year before. Now "Veelbur Reet" caps appeared on heads all over France.

Stories about Katharine abounded. She was said to have financed the work on the airplane, solved abstruse mathematical problems for her brothers, and to be familiar with every inch of the machine. It mattered little that none of it was true. They admired Katharine for her wit and honesty, not for her supposed contributions to the invention of the airplane. King Alfonso pronounced her "the ideal American." Most of Europe agreed.

Wilbur made his last flight at Pau on March 23. Giovanni Pirelli, who had flown as a passenger at Le Mans, offered a $10,000 contract for a series of demonstration flights in Rome and flight training for two Italian pilots. Wilbur turned the airplane flown at Le Mans and Pau over to Lazare Weiller and the members of the syndicate. A new machine, its parts shipped from Dayton and partially assembled in Pau, was sent on to Rome.

Wilbur and Hart Berg arrived in the Eternal City on April 1. He would fly at Centocelle, an open plain near a military fort some twelve miles from the city. "There is a beautiful big shop here," Wilbur told his brother. "It makes a splendid place to set up the machine." The grounds were splendid as well, with a marvelous view across an ancient aqueduct toward the *campagna* and the city of Rome and the Alban Mountains in the distance.[20]

Lieutenant Mario Calderara of the Italian Navy was his first student. Neither Wilbur nor Orville was particularly fond of him. He smoked cigarettes, a vice they could not abide. Still, Calderara was an apt pupil. Wilbur did not begin training the second student, Army Lieutenant Umberto Savoia, until April 26, his next-to-last day at Centocelle. He trusted Calderara to finish the job after his departure.

The level of excitement was as high in Italy as it had been in France. Wilbur missed only three days of flying between April 15 and 27. Newsworthy onlookers, from the king and the dowager queen to cabinet ministers, ambassadors, and the great J. P. Morgan, were on hand to cheer each takeoff. Wilbur did not attempt any record flights, but he did accomplish one important first. On April 24 he took up a Universal newsreel cameraman who returned with the first motion-picture footage ever taken from an airplane in flight.

That film remains as breathtaking today as it did in the spring of 1909. It offers a real sense of what it was like to sit there beside Wilbur, exposed on the lower wing of the machine. A string—a simple instrument to enable the pilot to judge the attitude of the airplane—blows back toward your face. The horizon rises and falls at the command of the elevator. You catch a glimpse of the aqueduct looming in the distance, then flash over it and brace yourself as the pilot banks into a turn. It is an extraordinary piece of film.

By the end of April, the U.S. Army commitment was looming once again. The Wrights had been granted only a year's extension. It was time to go home. They traveled to London by way of Paris and Le Mans, fêted at every stop. Arriving in London on May 2, they were anxious to conduct a few bits of business and be on their way. The itinerary included a visit to the War Office where they met their correspondents of so many months before. A side trip to inspect the Short Brothers balloon facility at Battersea was far more important.

Wilbur moved on to Centocelle, near Rome, where he flew in April 1909. This photograph was taken by Hart O. Berg from the basket of a tethered balloon.

Two of the Short brothers, Oswald and Eustace, operated one of the most successful balloon factories in England. When the English automobile magnate Charles Stewart Rolls, who had seen Wilbur fly in France, became determined to own a Wright machine of his own, he approached the Shorts with a construction contract. The notion appealed to the brothers, who enlisted a third member of the family, Horace, and left for France to discuss the possibility with Wilbur.

Will concluded an arrangement with the Shorts, who prepared the first full set of drawings of a Wright Flyer based on measurements of the craft in France. Over the next few months, the Wrights received other inquiries from potential English buyers. Rather than create a new syndicate or turn the business over to the CGNA, they contracted with the Shorts to produce a total of six Wright machines for delivery to English customers. Wilbur and Orville were reassured by their quick visit to the factory—the Shorts could do the job.

They were in England for only two days, and attended gala banquets both nights. "If the Wright brothers and their sister had the faintest desire for social fame," one society editor noted, "they could have been fêted from Buckingham Palace downwards." They were old hands at this sort of thing, though only Katharine seems to have enjoyed it. Wilbur had summed it up back in September. Invited to offer a few after-dinner remarks to his old friends of the Aéro-Club de la Sarthe, he commented: "I know of only one bird, the parrot, that talks, and he can't fly very high."[21]

Loaded down with gold medals, honorary diplomas, and the good wishes of an entire continent, they boarded the North German Lloyd liner *Kronprinzessin Cecile* on May 4. An armada of small boats awaited them as they passed through the Narrows and into New York Harbor on the morning of May 11. This was no ordinary arrival. Other ships in the area, their decks covered with cheering, waving passengers, dipped their flags in salute. The band playing on the afterdeck was all but drowned out by the whistles and bells of the small craft moving toward the liner.

An enormous crowd was watching as they walked down the gangplank in Hoboken. Off-duty officials, anxious to shake hands with the returning heroes, packed the customs shed. There was a cursory search of their luggage. "The inspector obliged Wilbur to exhibit his medals," one reporter noted, "but it was more to satisfy his curiosity than to fulfill a duty." Then they climbed into a waiting cab provided by the reception committee and were whisked away to the Waldorf for lunch.[22]

New York officials had originally planned to stage a major homecoming celebration for the Wrights. The Congress of the United States, the Smithsonian Institution, and the Aero Club of America had each voted to award them gold medals. Congressman Herbert Parsons invited President Taft to present all three awards in a ceremony in New York soon after the Wrights' return to America. But Governor James M. Cox of Ohio lodged a stern protest, arguing that the Wright Brothers' Home Day Celebration being planned in Dayton for June 17–18 would be a more appropriate occasion for such a presentation. President Taft humorously invited Parsons and Cox to debate the issue at the White House.

The Wrights settled the dispute. They cabled New York while at sea, explaining that they wished to return to Dayton as soon as possible. There was work to be done—preparations for the Army trials at Fort Myer.[23]

The Wrights were no more pleased by Dayton's homecoming plans. "The Dayton presentation has been made the excuse for an elaborate carnival and advertisement of the city under the guise of being an honor to us," Wilbur complained to Chanute on June 6. "As it was done against our known wishes, we are not as appreciative as we might be."[24]

Approaching Dayton on the morning of May 13, they hoped for nothing more than a quiet reunion with family and friends, but were prepared for the inevitable crowd of newsmen on the platform. At Xenia, ten miles from home, Ed Ellis and several other friends boarded the train with a bouquet of American Beauty roses for Katharine, and news that ten thousand people were waiting to greet them in Dayton.

The boisterous welcome, which included an all-day party, was only the beginning. Mayor Burkhardt and a delegation from City Hall called at 7 Hawthorn Street the next day, outlining plans for the "real celebration" being planned for mid-June. Wilbur and Orville spent every spare minute over the next few weeks back at the old bike shop and in a new work area set up in the barn behind Lorin's home. They were putting together the parts for the airplane that would be flown at Fort Myer, testing propellers, and generally working to ensure a successful demonstration.

They also did some traveling, visiting Russell Alger at the Packard plant in Detroit in late May. Alger was one of a group of industrialists considering the establishment of a company to produce Wright aircraft. Two weeks later they returned to Washington for a full day of business and ceremony. Unable to attend the celebration in Dayton later that month, President Taft had invited the Wrights to the White House to accept the Aero Club of America medal.

Their train arrived at Union Station, the splendid new gateway to the nation's capital, at 8:40 that morning. The waiting reporters, many of whom had covered the Army trials at Fort Myer, recognized Orville and Katharine at once. Katharine, who had a good memory for faces, startled several of the newsmen by remembering their names.

The reception committee arrived on the heels of the reporters. A. Holland Forbes, president of the Aero Club of America, led the conquering heroes to a taxi that whisked them off to the Willard Hotel, where another crowd waited. Katharine was escorted up to the suite of rooms reserved on the fifth floor, while her brothers remained in the lobby, shaking hands and accepting the congratulations of well-wishers. As at the station, everyone seemed to recognize Orville immediately. Wilbur's face was less familiar to Washingtonians. To his great delight, Holland Forbes was mistaken for the elder Wright brother several times that morning.

Rested and refreshed, Katharine left for a small reception at the home of Mrs. C. J. Bell, wife of the treasurer of the Aero Club of Washington. Squier and Lahm walked the brothers one block west along Fourteenth Street for an appointment with their superior, Brigadier General James Allen, Chief Signal Officer of the U.S. Army.

They left the War Department at noon, accompanied by Squier, Lahm, and Allen, and walked a long block past the White House, turning up Madison Place to the Cosmos Club, where a gala luncheon was scheduled in their honor. A bastion of masculine conservatism, the club suspended a cardinal rule on June 10, 1909. In Katharine's honor, ladies were admitted to the luncheon. Wilbur and Orville found their sister, herself a career woman with moderately feminist views, already on the scene and very pleased. The 159 guests included some of the best known and most powerful figures in the city, from the aging Alexander Graham Bell to the leaders of the House and Senate.

Promptly at 2:15 P.M., the entire party walked across Lafayette Square to the White House, where they joined other dignitaries assembled in the East Room. The great double doors to the central hallway were thrown open at 2:40. Wilbur, Orville, and Katharine Wright were escorted in, accompanied by Holland Forbes and Representative Herbert Parsons of New York.

After a round of applause, Forbes offered some remarks on behalf of the Aero Club of America. President Taft's speech was brief and laced with humor. He assured the audience that, while his own girth would keep him on the ground, he shared the universal interest in flight. The work of the Wright brothers was something in which all Americans could take pride. "You made this discovery by a course that we of America feel is distinctly America, by keeping your nose right at the job until you had accomplished what you had determined to do."[25]

Back in Dayton, every member of the family was caught up in the final preparations for the Wright Brothers' Home Days Celebration on June 17–18. "You must be pretty well satiated with glory," Chanute remarked on June 16. "The harvesting of prizes, the receiving of unstinting praise, the reception of numerous medals" would now be capped by acclaim at the carnival.[26]

The Wrights were universally admired as the first real heroes of the new century. The great Homecoming Celebration staged by the citizens of Dayton on June 18, 1909, included a "living flag" composed of local grade schoolchildren.

Aware that the Wrights regarded all this as a waste of precious time, Chanute advised them to accept the inevitable. "I know that the reception of such honors becomes oppressive to modest men . . . but in this case you have brought the trouble upon yourselves by your completing the solution of a world-old problem, accomplished with great ingenuity and patience at much risk of personal injury to yourselves."[27]

The great carnival included receptions, spectacular parades, band concerts, and fireworks featuring pyrotechnic portraits of Wilbur and Orville, intertwined with the flag, eight feet tall. Bishop Wright delivered the invocation at the ceremony on June 18. His sons, clad in morning coats and top hats, received a gold Congressional Medal from General Allen, a state gold medal from Governor Judson Harmon, and a City of Dayton medal from Mayor Burkhardt. A gigantic "living flag," composed of schoolchildren dressed in red, white, and blue, topped off the festivities with a serenade. That evening the entire family gathered at the grandstand on the corner of Monument and 1st as guests of honor at a spectacular automobile parade and the closing ceremony.

Wilbur and Orville left the reviewing stand as early as possible that evening. A telegram from Washington had informed them that the crates containing the airplane had reached Fort Myer. They would be up early the next morning, off to catch the familiar ten o'clock train for the nation's capital.

chapter 29

THE WRIGHT COMPANY

June 1909-November 1909

Despite the celebrations, Wilbur and Orville had accomplished a great deal in Dayton. Wilbur knew now that the accident last September had not been his brother's fault. During the past month they had spent as much time as possible in Lorin's barn, testing a replica of the failed 1908 propeller. They cracked the first test blade after less than two minutes' running time. Obviously, the new propeller design had a weak spot on the concave side that allowed the blade to flatten and split. The problem was easily solved by strengthening the blade at that point.

"I am glad it was no carelessness of Orville that brought about the catastrophe," Wilbur told Chanute. "It is so easy to overlook some trifling detail when setting up a machine under the conditions which existed at Fort Myer, that I feared he might have failed to properly secure a nut somewhere."[1]

They were determined that nothing would go wrong this time. Nor would there be any distractions. Newsmen and everyone else were kept at arm's length. By June 24 the airplane appeared to be ready for testing. The newspapers expected that the Wrights would fly immediately, but they remained indoors for two more days, tuning the engine. The entire Senate trooped across the river on June 26 to witness the first flight of the season, but the Wrights still refused to fly. It was too windy. The newspapers charged that they were "No Diplomats" and had "Snubbed Congressmen."[2]

Critics took advantage of the situation. Carl Dienstbach, an antago-

nist of long standing, was a music critic turned aeronautical enthusiast who had attacked the Wrights in the German press as early as
1905. Since then he had published a series of articles in American
magazines extolling Augustus Herring. The delay in flying at Fort
Myer provided material for a vicious attack in *American Aeronaut:*

> we had the tragi-comic spectacle of the "kings of the air," their brows
> fresh with the laurels of Dayton's great celebration, wearing the halo of
> surpassing records on two continents and strong in their renewed coop-
> eration, doing—nothing, or, what was worse in the popular estimation,
> tinkering at a machine as if it had been the crudest experimental make-
> shift, and frightened by the lightest breath of air. . . .[3]

Their friends were as impatient as their enemies. "They tinkered
and fussed and muttered to themselves from dawn to dusk," Benny
Foulois remarked. "It seemed as if they would never say they were
ready to go." Foulois found Orville the more talkative of the two.

> When you spoke to the two of them, it would be Orville who would
> answer, and Wilbur would either nod assent or add an incomplete sen-
> tence as his way of corroborating what his younger brother had said. At
> no time did I ever hear either of them render a hasty or ill-considered
> answer to any question I asked, and sometimes they took so long to reply
> that I wondered if they had heard me.[4]

As a matter of principle, Orville would do all of the flying at Fort
Myer. He finally took to the air on June 29, beginning with four
cautious flights, the longest lasting only forty seconds. It would take
a while for him to feel easy at the controls again. The wing-warping
handle now featured a "bent wrist" control for the rudder. The pilot
simply turned his wrist to activate the rudder, while moving the entire
lever to the front or rear to warp right or left. There was also a
spark-retarding pedal on the footbar for throttling the engine.

The trials got off to a rocky start: Orv smashed a skid in landing on
the second day. Then, on July 2, the engine stopped cold while he was
in the air, forcing him to glide in for a landing—straight into a small
thorn tree.

He was badly shaken but uninjured. The airplane, however, had
suffered two broken skids, a large section of torn fabric, and several
cracked ribs. Spectators broke through the cordon of troops and ran
toward the crash. When Will reached the scene he found them stripping the tree of souvenir branches; worse, a photographer stood taking pictures of the damaged craft. Without thinking, Wilbur grabbed

The brothers returned to Fort Myer to complete the Army acceptance trials in 1909. Orville did all the flying, while Wilbur (in the derby) supervised preparations on the ground.

a piece of wood from the ground and threw it at the fellow, then demanded the exposed photographic plate.[5]

He had done the same thing once in France. On the second day of flying at Les Hunaudières, Wilbur noticed a French officer in the grandstand taking photos of the Flyer as it was being wheeled out for takeoff. He leaped over a low fence and confronted the photographer, refusing to move until he had obtained the plate. The situation at Fort Myer proved to be a bit more embarrassing. The photographer, an official representative of the War Department, finally received an apology.[6]

The damage could be repaired in a few hours; the torn fabric was more serious. Orville had to return to Dayton to prepare a new wing covering. Back in Washington on July 7, he flew again on July 12. The serious problems were behind them now. He set a new duration record of 1 hour, 20 minutes on July 20, and a new record of 1 hour, 12 minutes for flight with a passenger, Lieutenant Lahm, on July 27. That flight also satisfied the Army requirement for a one-hour minimum time aloft with an observer.

One final demonstration remained. The all-important speed trial on which the purchase price of the Flyer would be based was scheduled for July 30. The Wrights chose Benny Foulois as the passenger for this flight. They would take off from the parade ground and fly to Shooter's Hill in Alexandria and back for a ten-mile round trip. Foulois had arranged for a balloon to be tethered as a navigational aid at the turning point.

There were perhaps seven thousand people at Fort Myer that day, a smaller crowd than usual. It had rained earlier, and everyone knew that the Wrights refused to fly when the weather was less than ideal. By four o'clock the sky was clearing and the wind had fallen off. Orville announced that he would take off in an hour and a half. Major Charles Saltzman and Lieutenant George Sweet, the U.S. Navy observer, left for Shooter's Hill with a field telephone.

Foulois climbed aboard the machine fully equipped for his adventure—two stopwatches dangled from his neck, a box compass was strapped to his left thigh, an aneroid barometer to his right, and a map of northern Virginia stuck in his belt. Orville ran up the engine, then leaned over and shouted in his ear: "If I have any trouble, I'll land in a field or the thickest clump of trees I can find."[7]

As usual, Orville kept the machine close to earth after leaving the rail, pulling into a slow climbing turn as he picked up speed. They flew two rounds of the parade ground to gain altitude, then swung toward the starting line. Foulois clicked the first stopwatch and they were on their way.

"All twenty-five horses in the engine were functioning perfectly as we skimmed over the treetops toward the balloon," Foulois recalled. "The air was bumpy, and I had the feeling that there were moments when Orville didn't have full control of the machine as we dipped groundward. It was as if someone on the ground had a string attached to us and would pull it occasionally as they would a kite. But each time Orville would raise the elevators slightly, and we would gain back the lost altitude."[8]

Foulois started his second stopwatch as they banked around the balloon at Shooter's Hill. Looking down, he saw that the small crowd of spectators gathered near the cornerstone of the great Masonic Temple being constructed on the crest were waving hats, handkerchiefs, and umbrellas in salute. Orville began a steady climb as they headed back toward the Fort. Within a few minutes he achieved a record altitude of 400 feet. With the parade ground in sight, he nosed down to pick up speed and raced toward the finish line. Foulois gave both of his stopwatches a final click as they flashed past the starting derrick. Orville pulled up, circled Arlington Cemetery once, and came in for a landing.

Wilbur was the first to reach the machine—Foulois later remarked that it was the only time he ever saw him smile. The crowd had grown much larger. President Taft missed the takeoff, but drove over from

Washington when he heard that the speed trial was in progress. Now he sent a message of congratulation through the crowd.

Comparing stopwatches, the members of the official board determined that Orville had achieved an average speed of 42.583 miles per hour—2.583 over the contract requirement. The contract entitled the Wrights to make three attempts, but they elected to stand on the results of this single flight. The purchase price would be $30,000—the contract price of $25,000 plus $2,500 each for the two full miles per hour above the required speed.

The Wright brothers hit the headlines for completing demonstration flights for the Army contract, but their achievement was overshadowed by Louis Blériot, who had crossed the English Channel in his wing-warping Blériot XI five days before Orville flew with Benny Foulois. It was one of those rare moments when the entire world sensed that something extraordinary had occurred. Wilbur and Orville had flown much farther than the 23.5 miles that Blériot covered that morning, but they had not flown the Channel. Blériot not only crossed an international border; in less than half an hour he conquered a geographic barrier that had shaped the course of European history. For the English, and for all of Europe, the message of Blériot's flight was clear. As H. G. Wells noted, "this is no longer, from a military point of view, an inaccessible island."[9]

There was other news even more disturbing than the report of Blériot's triumph: Glenn Hammond Curtiss had sold his first airplane on June 26, the day the brothers had been unwilling to fly for the adjourned senators. The Aeronautic Society of New York had paid $5,000 for a machine called the *Golden Flier*.

The Aerial Experiment Association was a thing of the past. The group had met at Bell's home in Washington on September 26, 1908, the day after the Selfridge funeral, with Edward R. Selfridge representing his son's interests. Bell offered a rambling history of the AEA, assuring his associates that they had not only avoided infringing on the Wright patents but had developed a few patentable notions of their own. Coming from Alexander Graham Bell, the successful plaintiff in the most publicized patent suit in American history, that was comforting.[10]

Mabel Bell contributed another $10,000 and the group agreed to continue operations for at least six more months. Bell hoped that his young colleagues would at last be willing to assist him in developing *Cygnet II*, the latest of his powered tetrahedral kites. Instead, they returned to Hammondsport to work on the *Loon,* an abortive version of the *June Bug* designed to take off from water. In addition, they designed and built a final machine, the *Silver Dart,* named, as usual, for the color of the wing covering. It would be their most successful aircraft, the only AEA machine that met the criteria established by the Wrights for a practical airplane. Shipped from Hammondsport to Baddeck, Nova Scotia, on January 6, 1909, it was the first machine flown in Canada.

The members of the AEA, assembled at Beinn Bhreagh on January 29 for the *Silver Dart* trials, spent a great deal of time discussing patents and money. Curtiss argued that they should put a new emphasis on entering prize competitions and consider giving exhibition flights; the sale of flying machines might also be a possibility. Bell offered to transform the AEA into a business corporation—the American Aerodrome Company—which could legally undertake these and other nonresearch business ventures. Curtiss agreed to think the matter over.

While in Canada, Curtiss received a telegram suggesting a very different partnership. Augustus Herring had suggested an arrangement similar to Bell's to the Wrights in 1903, claiming that his own patent materials might serve as the basis for suits against them if they did not agree. But the Wrights could afford to ignore such threats.

Herring had been forced into the mockery of entering the Army competition to maintain the illusion that he was still an aeronautical contender. Now he had abandoned even that pretense. The Wrights had flown their machines and met the contract requirements; he could not do the same. In the spring of 1909 Herring leaked reports that he had actually flown his proposed entry in the Army competition in secret, but had decided to withdraw his bid and accept a more lucrative offer tendered by mysterious "foreign syndicates."

Aware that Curtiss wanted to enter the flying-machine business, he offered a partnership. At best, Curtiss could hope for no more than a share in any patents granted to the AEA. Orville's letter made it perfectly clear that the Wrights intended to prosecute for patent infringement. Now here was this fellow Herring, who had been around for years and who seemed to know everyone, offering the use of patent materials predating those of the Wrights.

Curtiss jumped at the chance. It was apparent that Bell was committed to research, and had suggested the formation of a company only in order to continue his association with talented young colleagues. At any rate, Curtiss, the hard-nosed business man, thought that the AEA had an amateurish feel to it that was quite inappropriate when there was money to be made. He had not seen Herring's supposed patents, but assumed they had to be better than nothing. Moreover, Herring had already put together funding for the venture, convincing Courtlandt Field Bishop, the wealthy New York banker and charter member of the Aero Club of America, to invest over $20,000. Given Herring's track record, other wealthy enthusiasts might be expected to sign up.

The Herring-Curtiss Company was officially chartered by the State of New York on February 19, 1909.[11] Shocked to read the news in the papers, Bell wired Curtiss, requesting that he clarify his position. Curtiss sent an evasive reply, suggesting that the members of the AEA might prefer to associate themselves with the new firm. Bell and the others declined.[12]

The surviving members of the AEA met for the last time at Beinn Bhreagh on the evening of March 31. Curtiss, in spite of Bell's entreaties, was not present. Without his talent, his energy, and his factory, there was little point in continuing. The group officially disbanded that evening.

In addition to his own considerable resources, Curtiss brought another useful asset to the new company. In January 1909, without discussing the matter with his AEA colleagues, he agreed to construct a flying machine for the Aeronautic Society, a group of wealthy enthusiasts spun off from the Aero Club of America. The new club rejected the restrained promotional efforts of the Aero Club in favor of active flying. Its first step was to transform an abandoned racetrack at Morris Park, in the Bronx, into a flying field. Now all it lacked was an airplane to fly. Curtiss proposed to fill that need for the rock bottom price of $5,000, including flight instruction for two student aviators.[13]

Curtiss unveiled the Aeronautic Society machine, the *Golden Flier*, with a series of short straight-line flights at Morris Park on June 16. This machine, the first that Curtiss had built on his own, featured straight biplane wings rather than the bowed surfaces drawn together at the tips that marked the AEA aircraft. In an attempt to circumvent the Wright patent, which included a description of ailerons located on the trailing edge of the wing, Curtiss mounted his lateral-control surfaces between the wings, at the midpoint of the outer bay struts. If the Wrights did go to court, he would pray for a literal reading of the patent.

Ten days after his first outing with the *Golden Flier*, Curtiss flew his first circle in the presence of five thousand paying spectators. Then he shifted operations to a larger open field at a Mineola, Long Island, fairground. There, on July 17, he flew twenty circles over Hempstead Plains, covering 25.002 miles to win the Scientific American Trophy for the second time. As in 1908, the Wrights had refused to compete with a man they regarded as an infringer.

Curtiss spent the next few weeks teaching Charles Willard and Alexander Williams, the two Aeronautic Society students, to fly. Williams's career was short-lived. The *Golden Flier* was a single-seat machine. All instruction was given on the ground, after which a novice was turned loose on a series of lengthening solo hops. Williams froze at the controls on his first attempt. The airplane stalled, fell off on one wing, struck the ground, and nosed over. The pilot survived with a fractured arm and broken thumb, but decided not to risk a second takeoff. Willard, however, proved to be a natural, and went on to a successful career as one of the best-known exhibition pilots of the time.

The Wrights had had enough. Curtiss had ignored their warnings. Rather than negotiating for the use of their patents, he had forged ahead—winning prize money, charging admission fees for flying exhibitions, and selling airplanes. They were determined to put a stop to it.

The brothers had spent their earlier years watching their father settle his church-related problems in one courtroom after another. Wilbur had helped Milton prepare legal briefs and had called for a mock family court to resolve his disputes with Orville. Neither doubted that the courts existed to defend the virtuous.

Katharine and Orville left Dayton for Washington on August 1. A week later, they boarded the *Kronprinzessin Cecile* in New York, bound for a flying exhibition in Berlin. Wilbur returned home on August 2. Two weeks later he was in upstate New York, filing a bill of complaint enjoining Glenn Hammond Curtiss and the Herring-Curtiss Company from the manufacture, sale, or exhibition of airplanes. He arrived in New York on August 19, where he filed suit to prohibit the Aeronautic Society of New York from operating the *Golden Flier* on the grounds that the machine represented an illegal infringement of the Wright patents. The case would not come to trial for many weeks. Lawyers must be selected, depositions taken, and arguments prepared. But the process was set in motion—the patent wars had begun.

On the day Wilbur filed suit, Curtiss was no longer in America. With his first airplane sold and his first student trained, he had left for France, the only American registered to participate in the great flying meet to be staged on the Plain of Bethany, near the ancient cathedral city of Reims, on August 22–29. *La Grande Semaine d'Aviation de Champagne*, as it was officially known, was conceived and funded by the leading champagne producers of the region. Seven rich prizes totaling 187,000 francs were offered to the winners of the distance, speed, and altitude competitions to be held that week.[14]

The prospect of the meet at Reims generated extraordinary excitement. All that spring and summer, the newspapers buzzed with stories of flying machines, yet scarcely anyone had actually seen one of the things in the air. The Reims meet would provide an opportunity to see not one but many airplanes in the sky at once.

The meet was billed as an international event. In fact, the French dominated the competition. But the Aero Club of America was determined to prove that the United States, the home of the airplane, could still hold its own.[15]

Wilbur and Orville Wright, the natural representatives, would not participate. True to form, they had not changed their minds. "I do not compete for trophies," Wilbur informed journalist Heinrich Adams, "unless I can win them occasionally through those flights I am obliged to make by my contracts."[16] As the inventors of the airplane, the Wrights saw no reason to compete with newcomers to the field— particularly when they regarded most of the newcomers as patent infringers. As Wilbur had once told Chanute, they refused to play the montebank game with montebanks.

The Wrights would not have admitted it, but there was an even better reason not to fly at Reims. For the first time, they could not be certain of winning. Other aviators had learned their lessons well and caught up with the masters. It would have been foolish to risk their prestige by facing their rivals in an open competition.

Aero Club of America officials had only one other choice—Glenn Curtiss. No other American had yet flown. The fact that Courtlandt Field Bishop was serving as club president sealed the bargain.

The meet at Reims was everything that the sponsors had promised—proof positive that the age of flight had arrived. Before December 31, 1908, only ten men in the world had remained aloft for as long as one minute. Eight months later, during the single week of flying at Reims, twenty-two airmen made one hundred twenty takeoffs with twenty-three airplanes of ten different types. Eighty-seven of those flights were at least three miles in length; seven of them exceeded sixty miles. One pilot covered a distance of 111⅞ miles. The maximum altitude achieved was 508.5 feet; the top speed almost 48 miles per hour. All of the records set by the Wrights in the past year were shattered.[17]

Glenn Curtiss emerged as the great hero of Reims, the first recipient of the James Gordon Bennett Trophy for the fastest average speed achieved during a twenty-kilometer run over a closed course. He brought a new airplane to France, the Reims Racer, a short-span version of the *Golden Flier* powered by a 50-horsepower V-8 engine. He took off on the morning of Saturday, August 28, and flew two blistering laps of the course, turning in an average speed of 47.10 miles per hour. It was a new world record, and the best time of the meet. The fastest man alive as a result of a 137-mile per hour run across the sand flats of Ormond Beach, Florida, with his motorcycle in 1907, Curtiss was now officially the fastest man in the air as well.

The news that Wilbur had filed suit in New York reached Reims at the very moment of Curtiss's triumph. It was no surprise. The Wrights had given ample warning, and had discussed the situation with Courtlandt Field Bishop at some length when he visited with them just before their return from Europe that spring. Bishop, now the major stockholder in the Herring-Curtiss firm, took their comments very seriously.

The Wrights made a persuasive case for patent infringement, pointing to Herring's presence at Kitty Hawk in 1902, their repeated contacts with Curtiss and the members of the AEA since 1906, and the broad and complete nature of their patent coverage. "They . . . put things in a very bad light, both on moral and legal grounds," Bishop remarked to Monroe Wheeler, the Hammondsport judge who was serving as president of the Herring-Curtiss Company.[18]

Curtiss and Herring allayed Bishop's concerns. Together at Reims, Curtiss and his principal backer assured reporters that the mid-wing ailerons of the *Golden Flier* and the Reims machine were not covered in the Wright patent. The matter was now in the hands of Judge John R. Hazel, of the Federal Circuit Court in Buffalo. Until such time as Judge Hazel either ruled in their favor or issued a restraining order against them, the Herring-Curtiss Company would remain in operation and Glenn Curtiss would continue to fly.[19]

Orville and Katharine were in Berlin preparing for a series of demonstration flights to satisfy the requirements of two additional contracts when the news of the patent suit broke. "I have just read in the papers of the filing of suits against Curtiss & Co.," Orville wrote to his brother on August 24. "I think it would be a good plan to give out an interview in which the announcement is made of suing all who have any connection with infringing machines."[20] Wilbur thought the matter over and filed an additional suit against Ralph Saulnier, a Blériot importer, in the Federal Circuit Court in New York on October 20.

The first of the agreements that had brought Orville and Katharine to Germany was with Herr Scherl, publisher of the Berlin newspaper *Lokal-Anzieger.* Scherl's representative, Captain Alfred Hildebrandt, a German officer and aeronautical writer, had called on Wilbur not long after he arrived at Pau in January 1909, offering a substantial sum in exchange for a series of flights to be staged in Berlin later that year. The Wrights, anxious to pursue the contacts that they had made in Germany in 1907, accepted.[21]

Some weeks later, Captain Richard von Kehler visited the Wrights at Centocelle. Kehler, whom Wilbur had met in 1907, was the managing director of the Studien Gesselschaft, the Society for Airship Studies which had sponsored the development of the Parseval dirigible.[22]

The wealthy members of the Gesselschaft were interested in forming a German company to produce Wright aircraft under an arrangement similar to that concluded with Lazare Weiller and the CGNA. In exchange for the German patent rights, a sales monopoly in Germany, Turkey, Denmark, Sweden, Norway, and Luxembourg, and the usual course of demonstration flights and pilot training, the new firm—to be known as Flugmaschine Wright Gesellschaft—would provide the Wrights with a cash payment of 200,000 marks, stock in the new firm, and a 10 percent royalty on every machine sold. It was precisely the sort of agreement that the Wrights had hoped to conclude in Germany. They accepted immediately.

The Germans, well aware that they did not have a single pilot or airplane capable of competing at Reims, welcomed Orville and Katharine with great fanfare. The meet shaping up in France was very much on Orville's mind as well—he came within a hairsbreadth of postponing the German flights and rushing to France as a last-minute entry. It required an urgent cable from Will to keep him in place. Orv wrote back to reassure his brother that he would not go to Reims, but added: "if I had gone . . . I think we would have taken everything."[23]

Orville took every opportunity to prove this during the course of the nineteen flights that he made from military parade grounds at Berlin and Potsdam between August 30 and October 4. He moved the family name back into the record books, recapturing the world marks for altitude, flight duration, and duration with a passenger.[24]

The Germans had waited a long time to see an airplane in flight. Crowds of up to 200,000 people, as large as any that had gathered at Reims, came to see Orv fly. At times the crush was frightening. On September 17, following a flight witnessed by members of the royal family, Orville joined Katharine and Mr. and Mrs. Charles Flint, who were touring Germany. After several minutes during which the crowd threatened to overwhelm them, Orville left his sister and guests in order to draw the well-wishers away.[25]

The Kaiser and his family were taken with the Wrights. As part of the official response to the French spectacular at Reims, the Emperor had arranged for Count von Zeppelin to fly the great airship LZ 6 from Friedrichshafen to Berlin. The Kaiser insisted that Orville join him in greeting the count upon his arrival in Berlin on August 29, and hosted both heroes of the air at a dinner that evening. Two weeks later, on September 15, Orville flew from Frankfurt to Mannheim aboard the LZ 6.[26]

Crown Prince Friedrich Wilhelm was an enthusiastic supporter of the Wrights. Orville took the young man up for a fifteen-minute flight on October 2. As a memento of the occasion, the first member of any royal family to fly removed a stickpin from his tie and presented it to Orville. The diamond-encrusted "W," he explained, could as easily stand for Wright as for Wilhelm.[27]

By the time Orville completed his duties in Germany, Wilbur was also back in the air, and in the news. While he was in New York filing the patent suits in August, representatives of the Hudson-Fulton Celebration Aeronautics Committee had offered Wilbur a $15,000 contract for a flight of at least ten miles in length or one hour in duration plus any other flights he would be willing to make during the two weeks following September 25. The flights would be the highlight of a great celebration in honor of the centennial of the first voyage of Robert Fulton's North River Steamboat and the three hundredth anniversary of Henry Hudson's entry into New York Harbor. To add spice to the proceedings, the committee also offered Glenn Curtiss a

$5,000 contract for a flight from Governors Island to Grant's Tomb and back.[28]

Wilbur accepted his offer and was back in New York on September 20 with a crated airplane and Charlie Taylor to assist in its assembly. A day later Glenn Curtiss stepped off the ship from France. On the morning of September 22 he visited Wilbur at Governors Island, where hangars had been provided for both of them. The meeting was outwardly pleasant. Wilbur plied the man against whom he had already filed an infringement suit with questions about Reims.[29]

Curtiss traveled to Hammondsport for a welcoming ceremony, returning to New York with a new airplane on September 29. The Reims Racer was no longer available—Herring had accepted $5,000 from Rodman Wanamaker to exhibit the craft in his department store, provided that it could appear immediately after the return from France.[30]

Curtiss, his one-week contract about to expire, made one short hop early the next morning. Convinced that the underpowered substitute airplane was unequal to the task of flying on a windy day, he rolled it back into the hangar and left.

Wilbur saw a golden opportunity to show Curtiss up. He took off for the first time at nine o'clock that morning and flew a two-mile circuit of Governors Island. The standard Wright Flyer looked a bit different this time. Never having flown over water for any distance, Wilbur purchased a bright red canoe from a New York store, sealed it with a canvas cover, and strapped it between the skids on the underside as a flotation device. The short test flight was to determine what impact the canoe would have on the handling quality of the airplane.

Satisfied that all was in order, Will announced that he would make his first public flight before noon. He took off and, to everyone's delight, headed straight toward the Statue of Liberty on Bedloe's Island. The airplane dipped into a sharp bank around the statue's waist as the hundreds of ships gathered in the harbor for the celebration tooted and honked. The Wrights might eschew competition, but they had some showmanship in them.[31]

High winds kept Wilbur and Curtiss on the ground the next two days. Curtiss made a second attempt to fly to Grant's Tomb late on the evening of Saturday, October 2, but as before he was scarcely off the ground when he realized that flying was simply too dangerous in the prevailing high winds. Faced with another contract obligation in

St. Louis in only four days, he withdrew from his agreement with the Aeronautic Committee.

Wilbur turned up on Governors Island early on the morning of Monday, October 4, and announced that he was not only prepared to make the long flight as he had promised, but would combine it with the flight which Curtiss had contracted to make. He was off the ground at 9:53 that morning, the canoe still tied between the skids and two small American flags fluttering from the elevator struts. He flew ten miles up the Hudson, passing over the enormous fleet of U.S. and foreign ships assembled for the Hudson-Fulton Celebration. One million New Yorkers witnessed some portion of the flight.

Wilbur flew the twenty-mile round trip to Grant's Tomb in 33 minutes, 33 seconds, averaging 36 miles per hour. "It was an interesting trip," he wrote to Milton, "and at times rather exciting." New Yorkers certainly thought so. For a time, Wilbur had recaptured the excitement of the year before.[32]

Wilbur canceled a second flight planned for that afternoon when the engine blew a cylinder head straight through the top of the wing. He packed his gear and boarded a train for Washington the next morning. There was still one task to complete under the terms of the Army contract—pilot training for a select group of officers.

The parade ground at Fort Myer had been only marginally acceptable as an area for the demonstration flights. A larger and more open spot would be required for the daily in-flight instruction. Frank Lahm found just such a place during the course of a balloon flight, a large pasture near the Maryland Agricultural College at College Park, a Washington suburb.

When Wilbur reached College Park on October 6, the U.S. Army's only flying machine, the aircraft flown at Fort Myer that spring, was waiting in the hangar at the new flying field. Wilbur made fifty-five flights between October 8 and November 2. Most of his time was devoted to teaching two students, Lieutenants Frank Lahm and Frederick E. Humphreys, to fly. Benny Foulois, also desperate to go through the training course, had been ordered to represent the government at an aeronautical congress in France. He left early and reached College Park on October 19, in time to receive his first three lessons.

Wilbur set his final record at College Park: 46 miles per hour over a measured 500-meter course. He also took a friend of Katharine's, Mrs. Ralph Van Deman, aloft—the first American woman to fly from

American soil. Wilbur's final flight was a two-minute hop with Frank Lahm as a passenger on November 2. It was the last time he would ever fly in public, and one of his last flights as a pilot.[33]

But if one era was ending, another had begun. While in New York for the Hudson-Fulton Celebration, Wilbur had met Clinton R. Peterkin. Peterkin was only twenty-four years old, and looked younger, but his appearance and age belied his experience. He had gone to work as an office boy at the investment banking firm of J. P. Morgan at fifteen. Since that time, he had kept his eyes and ears open and had repeatedly demonstrated uncanny business judgment.[34]

Recently recovered from an illness and anxious to make his mark in the world, Peterkin called on Wilbur at the Park Hotel, offering to spearhead the establishment of an American company to manufacture and sell Wright machines. Wilbur liked the brash young man. He listened to his proposition, then cautioned that he and his brother would only consider an arrangement in which important men of affairs, "men whose names would carry weight," were involved.[35]

Peterkin took the matter straight to J. P. Morgan. Morgan, who had met the Wrights in Europe the year before, was interested, and promised to attract his acquaintance, Elbert Gary, the head of U.S. Steel, into the venture. Peterkin next drew DeLancy Nicoll, a Wall Street lawyer, into the new firm. Nicoll, in turn, opened other doors. Within a matter of weeks Peterkin's list of investors included Cornelius Vanderbilt; August Belmont; Morton Plant, chairman of the board for the Southern Express Company and vice-president of the Chicago, Indianapolis and Louisville; Thomas F. Ryan, director of Bethlehem Steel; and Theodore P. Shonts, president of the New York Interborough subway.[36]

Aware that things were moving more rapidly than he expected, Wilbur made a quick trip back to New York from College Park on October 29. Suitably impressed with the preliminary list of investors, he asked Peterkin to contact Russell and Fred Alger, of the Packard Motor Car Company, with whom the Wrights had earlier discussed forming a company. In addition, Robert Collier, of *Collier's Weekly*, should be included. Many details remained. Peterkin discovered to his surprise that many of the largest investors objected to Morgan and Gary, convinced that they would dominate the board of directors. The two men voluntarily withdrew.[37]

Wilbur was on the dock to meet Orville and Katharine when they disembarked from Europe on November 4. They traveled straight home to Dayton, where the family was reunited for the first time in many months. The first order of business was a financial stocktaking. Lorin, a bookkeeper by profession, had become the family accountant. Since the receipt of the original 25,000 franc forfeiture payment from the Letellier syndicate in 1906, he had deposited a quarter of a million dollars in local banks and building and loan associations.

The money included the first payments from the French syndicate; the prize money and various cash awards earned or accepted in Europe in 1908; the fees paid by Pirelli and his Italian friends for the flights and flight training at Centocelle; and the payments from Short Brothers for the use of the Wright patents and the sale of several aircraft. Over the past six months alone they had received $30,000 from the Army contract, $48,000 from the two German contracts, and $12,500 of the agreed-upon $15,000 from the Hudson-Fulton Celebration committee. "It is doubtful whether I ever get any more," Will remarked to his father on the subject of the Hudson-Fulton money. "The treasury is about empty."[38]

Now there was Peterkin's proposal for an American Wright Company. If they agreed to the terms, they would receive $100,000 in cash for their patent rights and expertise. In addition, they would be given one third of the total shares, plus a 10 percent royalty on every machine built and sold. As the owner of the Wright patents, the new firm would take charge of prosecuting infringers, relieving the Wrights of all legal expenses, pursuing additional suits, and establishing a mechanism for licensing of patent rights.[39]

The arrangement was ideal—the terms were excellent, and the investors men with impeccable credentials in the world of business and finance. The brothers signed.

The Wright Company was incorporated under the laws of the State of New York on November 22, 1909, with a capital stock issue of $1 million. Wilbur would serve as president. Orville and Andrew Freedman, a New York financier, were elected vice-presidents. The board of directors included August Belmont, Robert J. Collier, Cornelius Vanderbilt, and Russell Alger.

The future, as Wilbur told Chanute, seemed very bright indeed. "All of us are in very good health. Father, though in his eighty-second year, is still quite active. My own health owing to the outdoor life of the past year is better than in former years. I trust that you will retain well your strength and enjoyment of life."[40]

chapter 30

OF POLITICS AND PATENTS

January 1910

The Wrights both hoped that the formation of the new company would remove the burden of business affairs from their shoulders, freeing them to return to research. As Wilbur explained to Chanute: "The general supervision of the business will be in our hands though a general manager will be secured to directly have charge. We will devote most of our time to experimental work."[1]

The new board of directors established corporate headquarters for the Wright Company in the Night and Day Bank Building at 527 Fifth Avenue, New York, but the factory would be in Dayton. Frank Russell, a cousin of Russell and Frank Alger, was hired as factory manager. He reported to the Wright Company in January 1910. Wilbur and Orville, cramped for space and loath to set up the manager of a major corporation in a bicycle repair shop, helped Russell find temporary quarters behind a plumbing store a block or so away.

So far as they were concerned, that was the end of their involvement in the day-to-day operations of the front office. To underscore their disinterest in paperwork, Wilbur called on Russell a few days later carrying a container stuffed with letters addressed to the new company. "I don't know what you want to do with this," he remarked. "Maybe they should be opened. But of course if you open a letter, there's always the danger that you may decide to answer it, and then you're apt to find yourself involved in a long correspondence."[2]

While the brothers would no longer have to concern themselves with the sale of flying machines, only they could run the production side of the business.

Ground was broken for a Wright Company factory at 2701 Home Road in Dayton in January 1910. Until that building was ready for operation in November, the Wrights rented factory space in a corner of the Speedwell Motor Car Company plant at 1420 Wisconsin Boulevard.[3] The old pattern airplanes, what the brothers would always call their 1907 machines, were a thing of the past. The Wrights built two new prototype designs in the temporary quarters at Speedwell.

They called the first of these new types the "Model B." Clearly, while they had never applied the term "Model A" to the machines constructed since 1905, they thought of them as such. The Model B was a radical departure from its predecessors, with the elevator in the rear and wheels mounted on the skids. The development of a four-cylinder, 40-horsepower engine to propel the Model B enabled them to dispense with catapult launching. The Model R, a smaller, single-seat machine developed for speed and altitude competitions, was the second aircraft designed and built at Speedwell.

So long as they were directly in charge, the Wrights paid meticulous attention to the details of the machines on which they would risk their lives. Grover Loening, who went to work as Orville's assistant in 1913, recalled that his boss "directed all of the design work in the shop, even to small metal fittings, and many a time I had designed some detail and made a fine drawing of it, only to find that meanwhile Orville had gone into the shop and, with one of his old trusted mechanics, such as Charlie Taylor or Jim Jacobs, he would not only have designed the part, but had it made right there."[4]

But the Wrights' primary goal was to establish their priority as the inventors of the airplane and to defend themselves against those who would profit at their expense. They chose the patent courts of America and Europe as their arena.

On January 3, 1910, Judge Hazel of the Federal Circuit Court in Buffalo issued an injunction restraining the Herring-Curtiss Company from the manufacture, sale, or exhibition of airplanes. The decision surprised everyone but Wilbur and Orville. Patent complaints are adjudicated through a legal process as involved as any murder trial, and just as time-consuming. A difficult infringement suit may require many months, even years, to run its course, particularly if an appeal is involved.[5]

In the case of *Wright* v. *Herring-Curtiss*, the opposing attorneys took hundreds of pages of sworn testimony. They collected reams of technical material, quizzed expert witnesses to buttress their arguments, and tied all of it together with complex legal briefs.

The judge could not begin to weigh the evidence until he had command of the technical issues involved. His next step was to ensure that the examiner issuing the patent had correctly applied the confusing welter of regulations governing the patent process. Only then could he determine whether, and to what extent, the defendant had infringed on a protected feature of the invention.

Fully aware of the length of time required, the Wrights sought to prevent Glenn Curtiss from profiting while the case was in progress. When Wilbur filed his suit in Buffalo on August 18, 1909, therefore, he also asked Judge Hazel to issue a preliminary injunction forbidding the Herring-Curtiss Company from using the technology in question until the court reached a decision.

In view of the complexity of most patent suits and the ruinous consequences of such a restraint on the defendant, injunctions of this sort were uncommon. Knowledgeable individuals following *Wright* v. *Herring-Curtiss* assumed that the general rule would apply here as well. They were wrong. Judge Hazel, ruling that the evidence on hand was sufficient to indicate that the final judgment would support the Wrights, issued the injunction.

Stunned, Curtiss posted a $10,000 bond with the court and filed an appeal. He could legally continue flying until the appelate court issued a ruling, but he took a terrible risk in doing so. If Judge Hazel's decision was upheld, Curtiss would have to negotiate a settlement with the Wrights covering all of the monies earned during the time the injunction was in effect. It would spell financial ruin.

Having dealt with Glenn Curtiss, the Wrights next took action to put foreign aviators out of business as well. On January 4, 1910, the day after the injunction was issued in Buffalo, the Wright Company filed for a second injunction restraining the French aviator Louis Paulhan from giving exhibition flights inside the United States with machines that infringed the Wright patent.

Paulhan had won a Voisin machine in a model airplane competition in 1908, and emerged as one of the most popular and successful competitors at Reims. Invited to compete in an airshow to be held at Dominguez Field in Los Angeles, he arrived in New York in January 1910 with four machines—two Farmans and two Blériots. Taking the recent action of Judge Hazel into consideration, Judge Learned Hand, of the United States Circuit Court for the Southern District of New York, issued a restraint on February 17. Like Curtiss, Paulhan would have to post a bond ($25,000, later reduced to $6,000) if he wished to continue his exhibition flights prior to the adjudication of his case.

Having already earned some $20,000 at Los Angeles and other points on his U.S. tour, Paulhan returned to France.[6]

Only one of the Wright suits against an individual pilot actually came to trial. The English aviator Claude Grahame-White earned a grand total of $100,000 during a U.S. tour in 1911. The Wright Company sued him for half of that amount. The decision, handed down on January 24, 1912, was in favor of the plaintiffs, in the amount of $1,700. The sum was much smaller than requested, but enough to demonstrate that the American climate would not be congenial to aviators until the patent situation was finally resolved.[7]

Individuals like Curtiss, Paulhan, and Grahame-White could choose to post bond and take their chances in court, but corporate investors were unwilling to take that risk. The original injunction of January 3, 1910, doomed the already shaky Herring-Curtiss Company. The problems began in October 1909, when the board of directors met at Hammondsport to develop a strategy for fighting the Wright patent suit. Herring was asked to turn over the patent documents that he had pledged to the firm. Surely these materials, predating the Wright patent, would settle the issue. Rather than complying, as his backers had every right to expect, Herring equivocated.

The board, meeting again in a special session that December, threatened Herring with a court order if he did not produce the documents at once. As the discussion grew more heated, Herring and his lawyer withdrew from the boardroom for a private talk. When they did not return, the board members went looking, and discovered that the two men had left the building. Herring returned to New York and went into hiding to avoid being served with the court order for the patent documents. He could not comply. There were no patents—only a yellowing application based on a motorized version of the Chanute-Herring triplane that had been rejected by the Patent Office in 1896, and bits and pieces of correspondence with the Patent Office since that time.[8]

Judge Hazel's injunction, arriving on the heels of Herring's precipitous departure from the firm, finished the company. Unable to sell airplanes or to send an exhibition team into the field, income ceased to flow. Creditors, sensing trouble, quickly drained the treasury. The company filed for bankruptcy on April 10, 1910.

The Herring-Curtiss firm did not die a clean death. Courtlandt Field Bishop sided with Herring in a new lawsuit, claiming that the bankruptcy petition was nothing more than a ruse to get rid of Herring.

The suit was rejected and a decree of bankruptcy issued in December 1910.

In fact, Herring and Bishop were correct. On June 14, 1910, the United States Circuit Court of Appeals withdrew the injunction issued against Curtiss by Judge Hazel. The legal tradition against granting injunctions in cases of this sort prevailed. Curtiss was now free to do business until a decision was handed down in the suit.

The success of the appeal was a stroke of double good fortune for Curtiss. Not only was he free to produce flying machines again, but the original company, and the burden of an unwanted partner, were removed. Anxious to set up entirely on his own, he purchased his old plant back from the Herring-Curtiss trustees at auction, and by December 1911 was back in business as the Curtiss Aeroplane and Motor Company.[9]

The story was far from over. Seven years later, when Curtiss was flush with money as a result of lucrative war contracts with the U.S. and British governments, Herring returned for another round. Still holding two thousand shares of stock in the old company, he pointed out that while Herring-Curtiss had gone bankrupt, the company had not been legally dissolved. He brought suit on the old charges, claiming once again that the whole episode was trumped up to remove him from the business. The suit was dismissed in 1923. Herring appealed the decision and eventually won a reversal in the New York Supreme Court, which established a panel of arbitrators to work out the financial arrangements.

Herring died in 1926. Curtiss lived until 1930, fighting the suit, which was carried on by Herring's family with all the resources at their command. His widow, Lena Curtiss, was unwilling to continue the effort, however, and settled out of court for a sum that may have been as high as half a million dollars, although most of the money went for legal fees. Augustus Herring did not live to see it, but he had finally succeeded in making a fortune in the flying-machine business.[10]

The preliminary injunctions issued by Judges Hazel and Hand gave the Wright brothers an effective monopoly in the flying-machine business in America for the first six months of 1910. Even when the restraints were removed in June of that year, the Wright patent suits continued to threaten American pilots and aircraft builders. Having forced the Herring-Curtiss Company out of business and placed Glenn Curtiss and other competing aviators in legal jeopardy, the Wrights, through their foreign licensees, launched a direct attack on their European competitors.

Late in 1910, the Compagnie Générale de Navigation Aérienne brought suit against six rival aircraft manufacturers (Blériot, Farman, Esnault-Pelterie, Clément-Bayard, Antoinette, and Santos-Dumont) for infringement on the Wrights' French patents. The case was tried before the Third Civil Tribunal, composed of three judges and a substitute, a state's attorney boasting special technical qualifications.[11]

The substitute, who was charged with advising the court on technical matters, issued a statement in March 1911 suggesting that, while the Wrights deserved all recognition and credit for the invention of the airplane, their patent application was invalidated by prior disclosure. Chanute's lecture to the Aéro-Club in the spring of 1903, coupled with the publication of Wilbur's first speech to the Western Society of Engineers, had revealed the essential features of the Wright technology prior to the grant of any patent.[12]

Wilbur, who had journeyed to France to testify at the trial, was much alarmed. The substitute, he complained, "gave us bushels of brightly colored husks, but the kernels went to the infringers."[13]

He need not have worried. The Tribunal handed down its decision a month later, on April 29. The judges did not fully agree with the substitute, ruling in favor of the CGNA in every case except that against Santos-Dumont, the only defendant who had not profited by his use of the protected technology. The court did offer the aviators a small loophole, however. Before passing final judgment, a panel of three aeronautical authorities was established to determine whether the key elements of the Wright patent had been anticipated by other aeronautical pioneers.

Discouraged, Blériot announced his willingness to reach an immediate agreement with the Wrights. The others restrained him, insisting on waiting for the final decision of the court, and following it with an appeal if necessary.

Led by Robert Esnault-Pelterie, the most original of the French experimenters, the defendants in the French suit spent the next five years keeping their cause alive before a series of courts and panels. In large measure, the real blame for the protracted legal problems in France lay with the CGNA. The firm, plagued by weak leadership, gave up most of its business and nearly all of the profit to the Astra company, one of its original contract builders. At the same time, CGNA's pursuit of infringers was halfhearted at best. The questions of infringement and compensation were still not fully resolved when the Wrights' French patents expired in 1917.[14]

In Germany, the Patent Office itself sat in judgment on infringement cases, which reached the court system only on appeal. Late in 1911 a consortium of five rival aircraft builders brought suit against Captain von Kehler and the incorporators of the German Wright Company. The Patent Office declared the Wright patent invalid on the grounds of prior disclosure, again citing the Chanute speech and Wilbur's lecture to the Western Society of Engineers. The Wrights and their German licensees appealed to the Imperial Supreme Court at Leipzig, which upheld the decision.[15]

The patent suits absolutely consumed Wilbur and Orville's time and energy during the period 1910–12. They were also responsible for significantly altering the way in which the world viewed the brothers. Prior to 1910, most Europeans regarded the Wrights as a pair of grand eccentrics. They were geniuses, of course, but of an extraordinarily naive and otherworldly sort. The French were genuinely puzzled by these two men who did not smoke, drink, gamble, or pursue women. Even François Peyrey, a great admirer, described Wilbur as "This ascetic, who is ignorant of practically everything in life."[16]

Their own countrymen, on the other hand, cast them in the mythic role of prototypical Americans. These were good American boys, who, as President Taft remarked, kept their noses to the grindstone and put business before pleasure. The brothers were proof that the old virtues of family solidarity and commitment, hard work and perseverance, retained their validity in the new century.

The Wrights were never without their defenders. Outside the aeronautical community, pro-Wright feeling predominated. The airplane was a product of their hard work and genius; they deserved compensation for their efforts. The brothers had every right to stand up and fight for what was theirs.

Even within aviation circles there were always those who believed that the patent suits were perfectly justified. Charles Hayward, for example, the author of *Practical Aerodynamics*, the most useful guidebook available to first-generation aircraft builders, argued that the "perfect flood of criticism—even abuse and vilification" directed against the Wrights as a result of the patent suits was "misguided, to say the least." The situation was simple:

> There is . . . presented on the one hand a patentee who, after years of labor and expenditure of a considerable sum of money, has succeeded in

inventing a device of an absolutely revolutionary nature; on the other hand, an enormous number of investigators in the same field who wish to avail themselves of his hard earned success without in any way contributing to the reward which should be his.[17]

The aeronautical clubs and organizations that sponsored flying meets and contests fell into step behind the Wrights. The Aero Club of America led the way, signing an agreement with the Wright Company on April 8, 1910. The club agreed to sanction only those meets approved by the Wright Company; the company, in turn, agreed to license only those local promoters whom the club had approved.[18]

It was an ingenious arrangement that served the needs of both parties. The Wrights used the agreement as a public relations device. Who could accuse them of attempting to create a monopoly, or of stifling progress, when they were allowing their competitors to fly infringing machines at specifically sanctioned meets without any fear of legal consequences? The club, on the other hand, could continue to sponsor the meets that were its lifeblood while remaining within the law.

The aviators saw things a bit differently. The patent suits threatened their economic survival. Henry Toulmin had earned his fee: the Wright patents were broad and free of loopholes. If the courts decided in their favor, the brothers would enjoy an absolute monopoly in the flying-machine trade and could demand license fees that would break the backs of their competitors. There were only two choices available to those who would fly: negotiate with the Wrights for the use of the patents, or accept the challenge of a battle in court. For the most part, they were not the sort of men to turn their backs on a fight.

The patents wars were joined, not only before the bar of justice, but also in the court of public opinion. The men whom the Wrights regarded as infringers were anxious to demonstrate that they too stood on moral ground. Louis Blériot led the way in portraying the Wrights as avaricious monopolists threatening to retard the development of aeronautics:

I merely wish to say that it was regrettable to see at the dawn of a science (to encourage which all should have united in their efforts), inventors make the unjustifiable claim of monopolizing an idea, and, instead of bringing their help to their collaborators, prevent them, for no reason, from profiting by some ideas which they should have been happy to see generalized.[19]

The Wrights expected that sort of response from men whom they were about to haul into court, but they were surprised when Octave Chanute agreed with the critics. Chanute put his thoughts on record as early as August 1909, telling the editor of *Aeronautics* that he thought "the Wrights have made a blunder by bringing suit at this time." They would antagonize those who should be their colleagues and slow the natural development of aircraft technology. They might even damage their cause by forcing the defendants to search for prior patents, "which will invalidate their more important claims."[20]

"Personally," Chanute told a reporter for the *New York World*, "I do not think that the courts will hold that the principle underlying the warping tips can be patented." Pointing to Mouillard's experiments with the patented trailing edge tabs, he explained that "there is no question that the fundamental principle was well known before the Wrights incorporated it in their machines."[21]

Warping was something that many inventors had worked to develop, "from the time of Leonardo da Vinci." Chanute himself had introduced the Wrights to the work of their predecessors. "When the Wrights wanted to start, they wrote to me that they had read my book on gliding and asked if I would permit them to use the plans of my biplane. . . . I turned over all my data which included a copy of the Mouillard patent and information given to me by Dr. Langley and his young engineers Manly, Herring and Huffaker, and made them free of it."[22]

Wilbur, who had always been closest to Chanute, wrote on January 20, 1910, requesting an explanation. Chanute's recent remarks in the press represented an opinion "quite different from that which you expressed in 1901 when you became acquainted with our methods." Judges in the United States and Europe had considered and rejected any possibility that the Mouillard patent might have anticipated theirs. Nor could they find any references in *Progress in Flying Machines* to early experiments that might predate their own work with wing warping. Wilbur restated their case in the clearest possible terms: "It is our view that morally the world owes its almost universal use of our system of lateral control entirely to us. It is also our opinion that legally it owes us."[23]

Chanute's reply was distinctly unfriendly. While the means by which the Wrights achieved lateral control (the use of lines and cables linked to a control with which to warp the wings) was original to them, "it does not follow that it covers the general principle of warping or twisting the wings, the proposals for doing this being ancient."

Chanute doubted that the courts would uphold the Wright patents. "Therefore it was that I told you in New York that you were making a mistake by abstaining from prize-winning contests while public curiosity is yet so keen, and by bringing suits to prevent others from doing so. This is still my opinion and I am afraid, my friend, that your usually sound judgment has been warped by the desire for great wealth."[24] Furthermore, Wilbur in his recent remarks had given the impression that Chanute had "thrust" himself upon the Wrights in 1901. He asked that the brothers be careful, in future, to mention the fact that they had initially solicited his advice.

Both brothers found the revelations contained in Chanute's letter to be nothing short of "incredible."

> We never had the slightest ground for suspecting that when you repeatedly spoke to us in 1901 of the originality of our methods, you referred only to our methods of driving tacks, fastening wires, etc., and not to the novelty of our general systems. Neither in 1901, nor in the five years following, did you in any way intimate to us that our general system of lateral control had long been a part of the art. . . . Therefore it came to us with somewhat of a shock when you calmly announced that this system was already a feature of the art well known, and that you meant only the mechanical details when you referred to its novelty. If the idea was really old in the art, it is somewhat remarkable that a system so important that individual ownership of it is considered to threaten strangulation of the art was not considered worth mentioning then, nor embodied in any machine built prior to ours.[25]

Will brushed aside Chanute's accusation of greed, and his complaint that the Wrights were misrepresenting their relationship with him. Just how honest had Chanute been about their relationship?

> . . . we have also had grievances extending back as far as 1902, and on one occasion several years ago we complained to you that the impression was being spread broadcast by newspapers that we were mere pupils and dependants of yours. You indignantly denied that you were responsible for it. When I went to France I found everywhere an impression that we had taken up aeronautical studies at your special instigation; that we obtained our first experience on one of your machines; that we were pupils of yours and put into material form a knowledge furnished by you; that you provided the funds; in short, that you furnished the science and money while we contributed a little mechanical skill, and that when success had been achieved you magnanimously stepped aside and permitted us to enjoy the rewards.[26]

Wilbur closed on a warmer note. The problems that were driving them apart were of long standing and would not be resolved easily. But with a bit of effort on both of their parts, they ought to be able to forge a joint statement outlining the role that Chanute had played in their work.

Unwilling to draw back or compromise, Chanute did not respond. Instead, he wrote to Spratt, describing Wilbur's "violent letter." "I will answer him in a few days," Chanute commented, "but the prospects are that we will have a row. I am reluctant to engage in this, but think I am entitled to some consideration for such aid as I may have furnished."[27]

When a response had still not arrived by the end of April, Wilbur wrote again—in a very different tone. He explained that his frank remarks were occasioned by a fear that serious misunderstandings were undermining a friendship that meant a great deal to him.

> My brother and I do not form many intimate friendships, and do not lightly give them up. I believed that unless we could understand exactly how you felt, and you could understand how we felt, our friendship would tend to grow weaker instead of stronger. Through ignorance or thoughtlessness, each would be touching the other's sore spots and causing unnecessary pain. We prize too highly the friendship which meant so much to us in the years of our early struggles to see it worn away by uncorrected misunderstandings, which might be corrected by a frank discussion.[28]

Chanute finally responded on May 14. He refused to apologize, but did try to clarify his earlier remarks. His health was bad and he planned to travel to Europe for a rest. "I hope, upon my return . . . that we will be able to resume our former relations."

He did not make the trip, nor was there any further contact between them. Octave Chanute died at home on November 23, 1910. The family wired the news to Wilbur, who immediately boarded a train for the funeral in Chicago.[29]

Other old friends were slipping away. George Spratt, for example, was firmly convinced that the success of the Wright brothers had grown from his suggestion of measuring the characteristics of an airfoil by directly balancing lift against drag on a test rig. He believed that he deserved some credit for that, and wrote to tell the Wrights so.[30]

Wilbur responded on October 16, 1909, admitting that Spratt's idea had sparked their own imaginations. They had acknowledged that debt, and attempted to repay it by making all of the wind-tunnel data available to him. "I cannot help feeling that in so doing we returned the loan with interest, and that the interest many times outweighed in value the loan itself."[31] Spratt did not agree, and another friendship was ended.

Even Albert Francis Zahm, whose behavior toward Orville during his stay in Washington in 1908 had been nothing short of unctuous, demonstrated that his friendship had a price. When Wilbur visited him in Washington in November 1909 to obtain a single affidavit for use in the preliminary hearings, there did not seem to be a problem.

The first indication of trouble came in a letter from Zahm dated January 27, 1910. "You will probably regard me as a renegade friend," Zahm noted, "if the defense in the approaching litigation succeed in securing my professional service against you, but I hope you will remember that I have never declined, or hesitated, to serve you when the opportunity arose."[32] The message was clear: Zahm's services as a witness were for sale to the highest bidder.

The Wrights had no intention of paying any man to tell the truth. Wilbur replied swiftly, expressing his regret that Zahm might decide to testify for Curtiss, but assuring him that "such service carried out in a spirit of fairness" need not interrupt "the friendship that has always existed between us."[33]

Zahm disagreed. On February 7 he wrote back: "Apparently you are not very much concerned about my position in the patent litigation, seeing that you made no effort to secure my professional services."[34] Unable to accept that the Wrights did not regard his support as worthy of purchase, Zahm immediately signed up with the Curtiss defense team.

Zahm, convinced that the Wrights had rejected him, spent the rest of a very long career (he died in 1954) working to discredit them in turn. In his testimony, and in his *Aerial Navigation*, published in 1911, Zahm argued that the invention of the airplane was the result of a slow accretion of information rather than a flash of brilliance in the minds of Wilbur and Orville Wright. He claimed to have suggested the need for three-axis control himself in a paper presented at the 1893 Chicago conference, noting that "the combination of the torsional wings and a double rudder, either fixed or movable, has been public property since that date."[35]

The judges considered his testimony and rejected it, a fact that only stiffened his resolve to attack the Wrights. Wilbur and Orville had found a bitter and tenacious opponent, whom they would hear from again.

At the very moment that friends were deserting them, the Wrights were themselves sued for infringing on a patent. Both cases bordered on the ridiculous. Still, they had to expend time and energy in dealing with them.

The first of the two suits began in January 1910, when Charles H. Lamson, who had constructed one of the machines that Herring had attempted to fly at Kitty Hawk in 1902, began making outrageous statements in the newspapers. Lamson, now a Los Angeles jeweler, claimed that he was the true inventor of the "airship feature" in dispute in the Wright-Curtiss trial. He stated that, at Chanute's behest, he had constructed a glider for the Wrights and shipped it to their camp at Kitty Hawk in 1902. As the whole world knew, the Wrights flew their powered machine the following year.

Wilbur sent Chanute a copy of the Lamson article, citing it as an example of the sort of "misrepresentation" with which Chanute's name had been connected and noting that "the story ought to be corrected." In point of fact Chanute was very much at fault, though there was no malice involved. He had told Lamson that he was commissioning the glider as a gift to the Wrights. The Wrights simply refused to accept it as such. That original misunderstanding provided a firm foundation for the rest of Lamson's fantasy.

Lamson took it all very seriously. In January 1901 he had obtained a patent on a special kite design, including the rocking-wing principle embodied in his 1902 glider. Convinced that the Wrights would never have flown without uncovering the "secrets" hidden in his patent, he brought suit for infringement. His lawyer, Israel Ludlow, was an aeronautical pioneer of some repute, having flown a series of man-lifting kites of his own design. It was the very definition of a nuisance suit, but it dragged on until 1912, when the Federal Circuit Court for the Southern Division of Ohio, Western Division, handed down a final ruling in favor of the Wrights.[36]

The second suit brought against the Wrights was even less firmly based in reality. Inventor Erastus E. Winkley had developed and patented an automatic control device for sewing machines. Obsessed with the notion that the Wrights had stolen his invention as the basis for their own control system, he filed for an interference hearing with the Patent Office in May 1912. The Commissioner of Patents ruled in favor of the Wrights that August.[37]

chapter 31

"THE MONTEBANK GAME"

January 1910-April 1912

A ny hope of returning to a life of research vanished before 1910 was many months old. Wilbur took on much of the legal burden. Orville was involved as well, giving testimony and making periodic court appearances, but he devoted most of his time to getting the production side of the operation running.

The small crew of carpenters, mechanics, and machinists set to work in rented quarters at the Speedwell plant built several prototype Model B aircraft and two versions of a special racing design, the Model R, or Roadster. The serious business of producing aircraft for sale began after the move into the new factory on Home Road in November 1910. Once established there they could build two airplanes a month, complete with engines.

The problem was what to do with the airplanes once they were built. The sale of a single airplane to the Army had, for the moment, satisfied the demand for land-based military flying machines in the United States. It was never a large market—before 1915, when Orville left the company, the Wrights sold a total of fourteen airplanes to the U.S. Army.[1]

As Chanute had prophesied, the exhibition business was booming. The first American air show, held in Los Angeles in the spring of 1910, drew enormous crowds. During the weeks that followed, the aviators who had flown at Dominguez Field spread out across the nation, introducing thousands of spectators to the miracle of flight.

Curtiss never doubted that there was a fortune to be made in exhibition flying. Undaunted by his failure to fulfill the Hudson-Fulton contract, he traveled to St. Louis to perform with the dirigible balloon crowd—Tom Baldwin, Roy Knabenshue, and a newcomer named Lincoln Beachey. He did well at Dominguez Field, leaving $6,500 richer than when he arrived.

He captured an even more impressive prize on May 29, 1910. At the time of the Hudson-Fulton Celebration, the *New York World* had offered $10,000 for a flight from Albany to New York City. Curtiss flew the 151 miles in 2 hours and 51 minutes, averaging 52 miles per hour. In addition to the major prize, the Aero Club of America awarded him the Scientific American Trophy for the Albany to Pough-keepsie leg of the journey. A three-time winner, he now took perma-nent possession.

More important, the Hudson River flight electrified the public. The *New York Times* devoted over four pages to the story, which was front-page news in every other paper in town. The owners and editors of big city dailies immediately recognized the value of sponsoring flights of their own. The Philadelphia *Public Ledger* and the *New York Times* put up $10,000 for the first round trip flight between the two cities. The *Times* offered an additional $25,000 for the first flight from New York to Chicago. Not to be outdone, William Randolph Hearst established the ultimate distance prize—$50,000 for a flight from coast to coast in thirty days or less.[2]

Charles K. Hamilton grabbed the New York to Philadelphia prize in short order. Taking off from Governors Island early on the morning of June 13, 1910, he flew to Philadelphia and back in eleven hours, with two stops along the way.

Hamilton was a legend among the devil-may-care fraternity of the air. A small man with an uncontrollable shock of red hair, he seems to have gone through life with a cigarette perpetually dangling from his lips and "an aura of alcohol generally surrounding him."[3]

Hamilton began his aeronautical career as a parachute daredevil, venturing aloft beneath a hot-air balloon, cutting loose several thou-sand feet in the air, and returning to earth by opening and discarding one parachute after another. The crowds loved it.

He mastered the airship, accompanying Roy Knabenshue on the county fair circuit for several years, then traveled to Hammondsport in the early fall of 1909 determined to fly an airplane. When Curtiss refused to accept him as a student, Hamilton waited until no one was looking, walked out onto the flying field, and soloed without instruc-tion.

It was typical. Hamilton was a fatalist, a man without fear. Suffering from tuberculosis, he did not expect to live long, and flew accordingly. During his short career he ran up an incredible string of crashes, breaking both legs and one ankle, smashing his collarbone, fracturing at least two ribs, dislocating an arm, and getting badly burned by steam escaping from a smashed radiator. "There is little left of the original Hamilton," his colleague Lincoln Beachey once joked. Yet Charles Hamilton died in bed on January 22, 1914, not yet thirty years old.[4]

Wilbur and Orville were aghast at such behavior. At the same time, they recognized that they would have to find a Hamilton of their own if they wished to make money building and flying airplanes. Against their better judgment, they decided to enter the exhibition business.

They put themselves in experienced hands. On January 17, 1910, Wilbur cabled A. Roy Knabenshue, asking him to come to Dayton to discuss the organization of a flying team. Knabenshue agreed to an arrangement with the Wright Company and was on board by mid-March.[5]

Knabenshue would handle bookings, logistics, the pilots and their problems. Orville accepted responsibility for selecting the team members and teaching them to fly. In addition, he would handle the lucrative contract flight-training program for Army and Navy officers and teach the handful of wealthy civilian enthusiasts who could afford the price of an airplane and instruction.

The flying would be done at Simms Station, the old Huffman Prairie. They would send out a working party to prepare the field and construct a new and larger hangar when the weather eased in the spring. In the meantime, Orville began operations at a winter flying field in Montgomery, Alabama. He and Charlie Taylor arrived with a new airplane and five student pilots on March 24.[6]

Walter Brookins, "Brookie," was the first of the new Wright-Fliers. Twenty-one years old, he was a West Side kid whom the Wrights had known since he was four. He had been a student of Katharine's at Central High, and had spent every free moment of the last few years hanging around the bicycle shop. Orville took Brookins up for the first time on March 28. Like all the Model A and B machines, the craft flown at Montgomery featured an elevator lever at the far right of one seat and the far left of the other. A single wing-warping control was mounted between the seats, so that it could be shared by both pilot and student. As Orville was right-handed, Brookins automatically became a left-handed pilot.[7]

The Wright exhibition team in training at Montgomery, Alabama, in 1910.

The training went smoothly. By April 30, Brookins was flying with Orville as a passenger. The young man soloed on May 5. The other students were a varied lot. Arch Hoxsey, a twenty-six-year-old automobile racer whom Knabenshue had hired to tune his dirigible engine in Pasadena, was, like Brookins, a natural. A. L. Welsh, a young Washingtonian who had seen the Wrights fly at Fort Myer, also showed promise. Spencer Crane, a Dayton automobile enthusiast, did less well and dropped out of the program. J. W. Davis, of Colorado Springs, failed to qualify as a pilot but remained with the exhibition team as a mechanic.[8]

Orville and Welsh left for Dayton on May 7 to begin operations at Huffman Prairie. Brookins, suddenly promoted to the rank of instructor, remained behind in Montgomery until May 25 to give Hoxsey additional time in the air.

Orville began flying at Huffman Prairie on May 10. He completed Welsh's training in short order and started instructing a fresh batch of pilots for the Wright exhibition team. Duval La Chapelle, an American living in France who had worked as Wilbur's mechanic in 1908–09, was the first. La Chapelle, who failed to mention his poor eyesight, nearly destroyed a hangar at the conclusion of his first solo.

Frank Coffyn, a wealthy young New Yorker, had pulled a few strings for a chance to become a member of the team. After seeing Louis Paulhan fly in New York in the spring of 1908, Coffyn persuaded his father, a vice-president of the Phoenix National Bank, to arrange an introduction to Wilbur. "Well, Frank, you come out to Dayton in about a month," Wilbur told him, "and we'll see how we like one another."[9]

Ralph Johnstone, a Kansas City man, was another Knabenshue candidate. A pure daredevil, he had made his living as a trick bicycle rider since the age of fifteen. Mid-air flips from a springboard were his specialty. Phil O. Parmalee, J. Clifford Turpin, Howard Gill, and Leonard Bonney rounded out the Wright team.

Teaching all these men to fly kept Orville busy. He made nearly 250 flights from Huffman Prairie in 1910, over 100 of them during the last three weeks in May. Change was in the air. Orv test-flew the first Model B early in July, and conducted the first experiments with wheeled machines on July 21.[10]

Wilbur flew only once, on May 21. It was the last time that he would ever fly as a pilot in the United States. Four days later, Orville took his brother up as a passenger, the only time they flew together. That was also the day on which Milton made his only flight.[11]

The Wright team flew its first exhibition at the Indianapolis Motor Speedway on June 13–18. It was especially exciting for Frank Coffyn, who soloed while the meet was in progress. Walter Brookins had his share of excitement, too—he was descending from a record altitude of over 6,000 feet when a valve broke, forcing him to glide in for his first dead stick landing.[12]

The Wright crew was very green indeed, and most of the flying at Indianapolis consisted of straightforward laps around the track. The promoters were disappointed. "The age is one of speed and competition," remarked one speedway official, "and I want to see a flock of airships fighting for first place under the wire."[13]

Things grew more exciting as the aviators gained experience. Ralph Johnstone set a new Canadian altitude record at Montreal early in July. Moving on to Atlantic City, Brookins won $5,000 for exceeding his own world altitude mark. Curtiss was there as well, earning $5,000 for a series of flights over the ocean. He was training his own exhibition team at Hammondsport, and intended to take on the Wright Fliers at every opportunity.

The Curtiss crowd was free-form, operating under the loose control of Jerome Fanciulli, the publicist who managed the exhibition operation. The pilots were well paid, receiving 50 percent of the revenues resulting from an appearance. "We were taught by the Wrights that the Curtiss crowd was just no good at all," Frank Coffyn recalled. "We turned our noses up at them. But we found out later on, by flying at the same meets, that they were a pretty nice bunch of fellows."[14]

Pilots in the Wright camp were subject to much stricter supervision. All the standard family rules were in effect. There was no drinking, gambling, or flying on Sundays. The pay was much less—a set fee of $20 per week and $50 for every day a man flew. For the Wright Company, it was an ideal arrangement. The brothers demanded $1,000 for for each day that they flew at a meet. The company received $6,000 per man for a standard one-week meet, plus any prize money earned; the pilot received $320. Small wonder that the year 1910 was a good one for the Wright Company, with profits approaching $100,-000. Half of that amount went to the Wright brothers.[15]

The crowds flocked in increasing numbers to see the members of the two teams perform at makeshift flying fields—and their reaction fascinated the pilots. "They thought you were a fake, you see." That was the way pioneer Curtiss aviator Beckwith ("Becky") Havens remembered it. "There wasn't anybody there who believed an airplane would really fly. In fact, they'd give odds. But when you flew, oh my, they would carry you off the field."[16]

"Flight was generally looked upon as an impossibility," Orville recalled, "and scarcely anyone believed in it until he had actually seen it with his own eyes." People reacted in unexpected ways to their first sight of an airplane in the sky. Wilbur noticed an "intensity of enjoyment" and a sense of exhilaration among the spectators. He recalled one man who wandered away from the 1909 trials at Fort Myer muttering, over and over again, "My God! My God!"[17]

A Chicago clergyman attending his first air meet thought that he had never seen "such a look of wonder on the faces of the multitude. From the grey-haired man to the child, everyone seemed to feel that it was a new day in their lives."[18] A reporter noticed the same look on the faces of those attending the meet at Dominguez Field: "Thirty-thousand eyes are on those rubber-tired wheels, waiting for the miraculous moment—historical for him who has not witnessed it. Suddenly, something happens to those whirling wheels—they slacken their speed, yet the vehicle advances more rapidly. It is the moment of miracle."[19]

As the president of the Indianapolis Speedway suggested, spectators were also drawn by less exalted motives. The excitement of simply watching a man fly quickly gave way to a hunger for speed and aerial thrills. The sense of competition helped to keep the crowds coming. Everyone knew that the Wrights and Curtiss were locked in a courtroom struggle. To many, the flying field seemed the most appropriate place to settle the dispute.

Soon, star performers on each team were vying for the crowd. Arch Hoxsey and Ralph Johnstone took one another on at meet after meet, each struggling to top the other's performance. It was all part of the show—as was the danger.

The first major accident involving a member of the Wright team occurred at Asbury Park, New Jersey, on August 10. Fifty thousand people came to see Walter Brookins make the first flight of a ten-day meet. Three times Brookins aborted his takeoff run when press photographers crowded in front of the oncoming machine.

Finally in the air, Brookins circled the field for twenty minutes, then cut his engine and came in for a landing, only to see the photographers standing precisely where he intended to touch down. He nosed his aircraft straight into the ground to avoid crashing into them. "Well, all they had to do was raise the flap of the hospital tent and drag me in," he recalled. "I had a broken nose, a broken ankle and several teeth knocked out. And the ship was a complete wreck."[20]

A few days later it was Ralph Johnstone's turn. Orville originally planned for all of the team to fly a single Model A. When Brookins destroyed that machine in the crash, Orv ordered Taylor and the mechanics to assemble one of the new Model B aircraft on the spot. Unaccustomed to the long landing roll resulting from the use of wheels, Johnstone miscalculated and smashed into a line of parked automobiles. "We all laughed at him," recalled Frank Coffyn.[21]

Brookins was back in the air in time to win the distance and endurance prizes at the Squantum Meadows Meet, near Boston, on September 3–13. At the same time, Hoxsey suffered his first serious accident flying at the Wisconsin State Fair in Milwaukee. Losing control during a low-level pass in front of the grandstand, his machine dropped precipitously to the ground, injuring a number of spectators.

Both brothers were concerned about the risks their pilots were taking. Three days after the accident in Milwaukee, Hoxsey and Johnstone, who were preparing for yet another exhibition in Detroit, received a letter from Wilbur:

I am very much in earnest when I say that I want no stunts and spectacular frills put on the flights there. If each of you can make a plain flight of ten to fifteen minutes each day keeping always within the inner fence wall away from the grandstand and never more than three hundred feet high it will be just what we want. Under no circumstances make more than one flight each day apiece. Anything beyond plain flying will be chalked up as a fault and not as a credit.[22]

Hoxsey and Johnstone had not won fame as the "Stardust Twins" for their caution and knew that the crowds did not come to watch them fly in sedate circles. The Dive of Death, a nose-down plunge from 1,000 feet with a pullout at the last possible minute, was what packed them in.

The stunts continued, along with the accidents. Johnstone crashed at Kinloch Park, St. Louis, early in October. He lost control of his aircraft in a turn and landed so hard that his motor broke loose from its mount and came smashing forward, missing the pilot by inches. Undaunted, ex-President Theodore Roosevelt made a short flight with Arch Hoxsey the next day.[23]

On October 22–30, the entire team reported for duty at Belmont Park, New York. The size of the field gathered for the competition at the Long Island racetrack indicated the enormous growth in American aviation over the past year. The Wright and Curtiss teams entered four aviators each. In addition, there were seven independent American competitors: Clifford Burke Harmon with his newly acquired Farman machine; French-trained Earl Ovington, flying a Blériot type constructed by the New York–based Queen Monoplane Company; John Moisant, who had recently flown the Channel in his Blériot; and millionaire Harry Harkness, proud owner of the first American Antoinette.

It was the first international meet held in America. Nine French pilots brought a collection of Farman and Blériot aircraft. England was represented by Claude Grahame-White, James Radley, and William McArdle, also flying Farman and Blériot machines. Grahame-White was the best known of the group. Just the week before he had landed and taken off from West Executive Avenue, between the White House and the War Department Building. Alec Ogilvie, the final English entry, flew a Wright Model R. A friend of the Wrights, he had traveled to Dayton in September to take possession of the machine, a modified Model B with a four-cylinder, 35-horsepower engine.

The aviators were drawn to Belmont by the promise of $72,300

This special Model R, "Baby Grand," designed to capture the Gordon Bennett trophy at Belmont Park in 1910, was destroyed in a crash before the race.

worth of prizes. The meet would be capped by the second running of the James Gordon Bennett speed classic, which Curtiss had won at Reims the year before. In addition, there would be a $10,000 race around the Statue of Liberty and a host of speed, altitude, and duration contests.

The Wright team came to Belmont Park with a special Model R, determined not to let Curtiss win the Gordon Bennett Cup a second time. Dubbed the Baby Grand, it had a wingspan of only 21 feet and an eight-cylinder engine that developed 50–60 horsepower. Orville was clocked at 70 mph during test flights on October 25.

The Wright pilots entered a variety of contests. Ralph Johnstone caused a flurry of excitement when he set a new world altitude record of over 9,200 feet on October 25. Brookins took an early lead flying the Baby Grand in an endurance contest that day. He was forced to land after only twelve laps of the course, but the smart money was betting that he would win the Gordon Bennett competition—the only one that really mattered to the Wrights.

Their hopes were dashed during a trial flight before Brookins's first official speed run on October 29. The tiny airplane smashed to earth when the engine stopped cold in a turn. Brookins was rushed to a nearby hospital with minor injuries. Grahame-White, whom the Wrights sued for infringement, won the 1910 Gordon Bennett. Victory in the Statue of Liberty race went to John Moisant.[24]

The Wrights did not leave Belmont with empty pockets. Ralph Johnstone set another altitude record on the last day of the meet. It raised their total prize earnings to $15,000, plus an additional $20,000 for sanctioning the meet.[25] But it was clear that they had lost their technological edge. After Belmont, the inventors of the airplane resigned themselves to a position back in the middle of the pack.

Hoxsey flew at Baltimore on November 2, then, accompanied by Johnstone and Walter Brookins, now recovered, he moved on to a Denver air meet that opened on November 16. Johnstone took off first on the afternoon of November 17, climbing aloft and winging over into a spiraling dive. He did not pull out.

Hoxsey, also in the air, watched in horror as the crowd broke through the police cordon and streamed toward the tangle of wreckage. By the time he landed and made his way to the scene, Johnstone's body, smashed beyond recognition, had been stripped of gloves and other items of clothing. He was the first American pilot to die in a crash.[26]

Orville was on board ship at the time of Johnstone's death. He and Katharine had watched Phil Parmalee take off from Simms Station on November 7 with two bolts of dress silk strapped into the passenger seat of a Model B. An hour and six minutes later he landed at a field outside Columbus, sixty-five miles away, and turned the material, the world's first air-freight shipment, over to an agent of the Morehouse-Martens Department Store.[27]

Orville sailed from New York aboard the *Kronprinzessin Cecile* on November 15. He learned of both the Denver accident and Chanute's death when he landed at Bremen on November 23. This was a business trip with no flying involved. His friend Count de Lambert met him at the dock with the latest news from France, none of it good. Weiller's syndicate, founded only two years before, was virtually out of business. The Astra company, which had constructed most of the French machines for CGNA under contract, was taking over. The legal complications of the changeover might take years to untangle. In the meantime, profits plummeted.[28]

The situation in Germany was no more promising. Flugmaschine Wright Gesellschaft had an impressive factory, with a main building large enough to accommodate the construction of five machines at once. The materials and workmanship Orv thought "first class." The flying field, and the German pilots operating the license-built Wright machines, were also impressive.[29]

The business side of the operation was another matter. Orville regarded Herr Klose, the manager of the operation, as "incompetent to handle the business." He took no interest in the infringement suits pending in the German Patent Office, and paid scant attention to the company books.[30]

Royalty payments to the Wrights were handled in the most cavalier fashion. Pilots came into the factory and constructed their own Wright machines, which were exempt from royalty. The company was also selling machines on the installment plan, with the royalty to the Wrights coming from the fianl check—if there was a final check. Nor were royalties paid on company-owned training machines.

Orville spent a few days discussing the design of a new machine for the German military. It was a pointless exercise. The procurement officers demanded that the craft feature "the latest inventions of the Wright brothers in control," so long as all of the steering was done with the feet.[31]

Wilbur kept his brother abreast of the latest news from home. Johnny Moisant, the young aviator who had done so well at Belmont, was touring the country with a "flying circus." The operation netted only $600 for a three-day appearance in Chattanooga, and $200 for a single day in Memphis. Knabenshue, on the other hand, booked Brookins, Hoxsey, and Parmalee into San Francisco for $22,500. Parmalee would fly the rebuilt Baby Grand at the event.[32]

Wilbur did not succeed in cheering his brother. "I have about made up my mind to let the European business go," Orville wrote. "I don't propose to be bothered with it all my life and I see no prospect of its ever amounting to anything unless we send a representative here to stay to watch our interests."[33]

Orville returned to Dayton on December 29 thoroughly discouraged. He had been gone less than a month and a half. Two days later Johnny Moisant was killed while flying near New Orleans. That same afternoon, Hoxsey and Brookins took off from Dominguez Field, Los Angeles. Hoxsey climbed to 7,000 feet in search of yet another altitude record, gave up, and nosed over into a spiraling dive. Like his friend Johnstone, he did not recover.

Only a week earlier, Frank Russell had announced that the Wright Company would pay a monthly annuity to Johnstone's widow. Now he told reporters that they would pick up Hoxsey's funeral expenses and contribute to the support of his mother.

Ralph Johnstone and Arch Hoxsey were the first members of the Wright Fliers to die in aircraft accidents. Others would follow. Six of the nine men who served on the team (Johnstone, Hoxsey, Parmalee,

Welsh, Gill, and Bonney) died in crashes. All but Bonney—who died in a machine of his own design in 1928—were killed in Wright aircraft before the year 1912 was half over.

The situation was as bad for other Wright pilots. Almost one quarter of the thirty-five men killed in aircraft crashes by the end of 1910 died in Wright or Wright-type machines constructed by licensed builders. Eugène Lefebvre, the first man after Selfridge to die in an airplane, was a Wright pilot. So was C. S. Rolls, who purchased one of the first machines from Short Brothers.[34]

Some aviators began to regard the Wright machines as fatally flawed. That was not the case. The Dayton-built Wright aircraft were the sturdiest machines in the air. If they were less stable than some other types, they repaid the pilot by giving him absolute control. These were airplanes that would do precisely what the pilot asked of them.

The same could not be said of many of the license-built machines. The aircraft in which C. S. Rolls died, for example, had been hastily modified. The collapse of that modified structure caused the crash. The same was true of the German- and Italian-built machines in which European aviators died.

The only safety problem with the Wright machines could have been remedied with a few pennies worth of belting. No aircraft of the period had seat belts. Brookins believed that Johnstone fell out of his seat during the dive. Wilbur accepted that judgment, and suggested that the same thing might have happened to Hoxsey.

The Wrights remained in the exhibition business for eleven months after Hoxsey's crash, but profits were falling and the brothers were rapidly losing interest in "the montebank game." They dissolved the team in November 1911.

That did not mean there would be less activity at Huffman Prairie. Orville made hundreds of flights from the old field between 1911 and 1915, testing nine of the thirteen distinct aircraft types developed by the Wright Company. Huffman remained a world center of aeronautical achievement.

It was also a teaching center. Late in his life Orville compiled a list of 115 individuals who had learned to fly there. It included the pioneers of U.S. military aviation. Lieutenants Frank Lahm and Charles DeForest Chandler, who began their instruction at College Park, completed their training in Dayton. The first naval aviators, Lieutenants Kenneth Whiting and John Rodgers, soloed at the Prairie. One junior officer, Lieutenant Henry H. "Hap" Arnold, rose to the rank of five-star general, commanded the U.S. Army Air Forces in World War II, and served as the first Chief of Staff of the newly created U.S. Air Force.[35]

Calbraith Perry Rodgers, the first man to complete a coast-to-coast flight across America, soloed at Huffman Prairie. So did Canadian Roy Brown, who would one day be credited with the death of Captain Manfred von Richthofen, Germany's ace in World War I. Eddie Stinson, the founder of Stinson Aircraft, was also on the list.

The average student pilot of the period received nothing more than encouragement before being turned loose to conquer the air on his own. Those whom Orville Wright taught to fly were more fortunate. The world's first pilot had given a great deal of thought to the business of flight instruction.

The experiences of "Hap" Arnold and Thomas DeWitt Milling, who arrived in Dayton for flight training in April 1911, were typical. "Our primary training took place in the factory," Arnold recalled, "for in addition to learning to fly we found we would have to master the construction and maintenance features of the Wright machine. . . ." With orientation out of the way, Cliff Turpin and Al Welsh introduced the novice aviators to the business of flying.[36]

As Arnold noted: "No two types of controls were the same in those days, and from the student's point of view the Wright system was the most difficult." Since 1900, the controls had grown ever more cumbersome. By 1910 the pilot negotiating a turn had to move one lever to the front or rear to initiate a bank, while bending his wrist to the right or left to operate the rudder. Nor could he neglect the elevator, operated with the other hand.

Contrast this to the Curtiss system in which a control wheel was pushed forward or pulled back to control the elevator, and turned to the right or left as a steering wheel to operate the rudder. A shoulder yoke controlled the ailerons. Every movement—pushing and pulling, turning the wheel and leaning—was natural and instinctive.

A new pilot had to *think* about flying a Wright machine, and that was a dangerous thing. To provide his students with some practice before risking life and limb, Orville developed the world's first flight simulator—an old airplane balanced on sawhorses set up in the rear of the factory.

"It was probably taken out of commission due to its age and need of general overhauling," recalled Grover Cleveland Bergdoll, who learned to fly at Huffman Prairie in 1912. "The motor was taken out, but the propellers were still in place. It was mounted on a kind of wooden trestle which permitted it to tip over from side to side, and would not remain in a horizontal position if left to itself."[37] "Hap" Arnold described how it worked:

> The lateral controls were connected with small clutches at the wingtips, and grabbed a moving belt running over a pulley. A forward motion, and the clutch would snatch the belt, and down would go the left wing. A backward pull and the reverse would happen. The jolts and teetering were so violent that the student was kept busy just moving the lever back and forth to keep on an even keel. That was primary training, and it lasted for a few days.[38]

"It was an improvised affair," Bergdoll noted, "but did its work well for years." One of his fellow students, Fred Southard, of Youngstown, Ohio, "used to sit in this trainer for days and days at a time and practiced so long that he could read a newspaper and keep the wings balanced without any thought of the same." Southard was unable to transfer his expertise to the air, however. Every time he went up with instructor Al Welsh, he would push or pull the warping lever in the wrong direction. Welsh gave him up as a hopeless case, and Orville refused to let him take possession of the machine he had already purchased. Southard decided to take matters into his own hands.[39]

Arriving at the field early on the morning of May 21, 1912, he smashed the lock on the hangar where his airplane was stored and took off. "He got no more than fifty feet up," recalled Bergdoll, "when the plane rolled over on one side and skidded to the ground a total wreck and Southard killed. Evidently he had pulled the warping lever in the wrong direction for the last time."[40]

"Hap" Arnold took his first lesson on May 3, and soloed ten days later, a veteran of twenty-eight flights—3 hours, 48 minutes of flying time. Al Welsh, his instructor, told him it was about average.[41]

Most of the civilian graduates of the Wright school set up as exhibition pilots, traveling the county fair circuit, and vying for the rich distance prizes established by American newspapers. Harry Atwood, Cal Rodgers, and Bob Fowler were among the best of the bunch.

Harry Atwood left Huffman Prairie determined to win the $50,000 Hearst Prize for the first flight from coast-to-coast. There was no time to waste. According to the rules established by the Hearst papers, the prize would lapse unless the flight was completed by October 1, 1911.

Money was Atwood's big problem. Given the primitive nature of aeronautical technology, this would be as much an expedition as a flight. The aviator would have to equip himself with at least two airplanes, one to fly and the other for spare parts. He would also need several spare engines, a crew of mechanics, and a means of moving the ground crew and equipment across the nation in his wake.

Unable to raise that kind of money, Atwood decided on a shorter but still very impressive flight from St. Louis to New York via Chicago, where he would compete in a scheduled air meet. The publicity, he hoped, would attract funding for the longer flight. He left St. Louis in a Model B on August 16 and landed at Governors Island nine days later. The flight was front-page news, but no sponsors came forward.[42]

Cal Rodgers, a complete unknown, emerged as the big money winner at Chicago, earning $11,285 for the longest flight of the meet. At thirty-two, he was older than most of the pilots. He was bigger as well, six feet four inches tall and weighing almost two hundred pounds. Rodgers's family had deep roots in America. One ancestor, Oliver Hazard Perry, defeated the British in the Battle of Lake Erie in 1813; another, Matthew Calbraith Perry, opened Japan in 1854. His grandfather was a rear admiral in the Union Navy, and his father a career cavalry officer, who died just before Cal was born.[43]

Cal Rodgers came to Huffman Prairie in June 1911 to visit his cousin, Navy Lieutenant John Rodgers, a Wright student. Intrigued, Cal enrolled in the school himself. Confident after his victory at the Chicago meet, he convinced officials of the Armour Meat-Packing Company to sponsor his try for the Hearst transcontinental prize. Recognizing an opportunity to publicize a new grape beverage, "Vin Fizz," the company agreed to pay for Rodgers's airplane, to lease a train that would shadow him across the nation, and to pay 5 cents for every mile that he flew. Rodgers would pay for gas, oil, crew, and spare parts.

Rodgers traveled to Dayton to confer with Orville and purchase a new Model EX, a small, high-powered version of the Model B. He also offered Charlie Taylor $10 a day plus expenses to serve as his chief mechanic, twice what Charlie was getting at the Wright Factory. Charlie was not getting along with manager Frank Russell and jumped at the chance. Informed of the arrangement, Orville advised his old friend to think of the project as a leave of absence.[44]

Rodgers took off from a racetrack near Sheepshead Bay, Long Island, on September 17, headed west. His entourage—wife Mabel, Charlie Taylor, and the other members of the support team—followed in a special three-car train steaming out of New York on the Erie Railroad tracks.

Rodgers suffered his first crash while taking off from Middletown, New York, the next morning. Brushing across the top of a willow tree, he lost control and fell into a chicken coop. He was fine but the EX required major repairs.

By September 23, he had progressed to Elmira, New York. That afternoon, he destroyed the left side of his machine in a crash.

Cal Rodgers finally rolled his wheels into the surf at Long Beach, California, on December 10, eighty-four days after leaving Sheepshead Bay. He had suffered five disastrous crashes, each requiring major repairs to the *Vin Fizz*—not to mention innumerable hard landings, aborted takeoffs, broken fuel lines, blown valves, and engine failures.

He ended the flight with a pair of crutches strapped to the wing of the airplane. He had broken his ankle landing at Pasadena on November 12 and spent a month in bed before attempting the short final leg of his journey to the Pacific shore. Only the honor of the thing sustained him—he was not even close to the one-month time limit for the Hearst Prize.

Bob Fowler, another recent graduate of Huffman Prairie, had taken off from San Francisco on September 11, heading his Model B east toward the Rockies. An ex-automobile racer, he planned to dash across the continent in twenty days. The first attempt ended the next day with a crash near Alta, California. Fowler was not injured, but his machine had to be completely rebuilt. He set off again on September 23, but turned back at the Donner Pass, still unable to make his way over the Rockies. Finally, he selected a Southern route that avoided the mountains. He landed at Jacksonville, Florida, on February 8, 1912, 112 days after his takeoff from Los Angeles.[45]

Two months later, on April 3, Calbraith Perry Rodgers crashed into the surf near Long Beach. Spectators reported that he lost control after swerving to avoid a flock of seagulls. He died instantly of a broken neck.

chapter 32

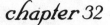

"A SHORT LIFE. . ."

March 1911-March 1912

W ilbur Wright was forty-five in the spring of 1912—and very tired. "During the past three months most of my time has been taken up with lawsuits," he told a friend. "I have been away from home most of the time."[1] It had been his turn to journey to Europe in 1911, responding to a summons from Henry Peartree, who handled legal matters for Flint & Company in France. Wilbur left for Paris on March 12, and did not return home until August. Orville's trip to Germany in 1910 had been short and relatively relaxing. Typically, Will stayed longer and was on the go the entire time.

He began with a visit to the licensees, where things had not improved since Orv's visit in 1910. Lazare Weiller's syndicate was virtually defunct. The Société Astra, which built the airplanes that CGNA sold, had taken over the entire operation. The changeover did not improve sales. "I have spent the best part of four or five days on the accounts," Wilbur wrote his brother, "and can very readily see where the trouble with our business came from. It was partly incompetence, partly a poor system of bookkeeping which prevented them from ever knowing where they were at, and *principally* bum motors. There have been three or four different times that we have gained the lead so far as the army [purchasing office] is concerned, and each time have lost it again because the motors were no good."[2] In fact, Wilbur believed that Astra could never make a success of the business. Its machines were not up to Wright standards and its business practices were hopeless.

The Wrights would not grow rich on the profits from the sale of license-built machines in France, but they might expect some healthy royalty payments if the French patent court ruled in their favor. Wilbur worked hard, offering lengthy testimony and doing his best to assist Peartree. The court ruled in favor of the Wrights, but there were any number of legal loopholes.

Robert Esnault-Pelterie and the others attempted to use one of those loopholes, arguing that the wing-warping technique had been anticipated by French pioneers. The appeal to French pride led to the formation of the Ligue Aérienne, a nationalist organization whose members "made it their purpose to convince themselves and the world that France was the birthplace of human flight."[3]

Initially, the defense argued that Alberto Santos-Dumont had been the first to fly. The court rejected that argument out of hand. Santos-Dumont was not only heavily influenced by what he knew of the Wrights, but he had not flown until 1906. The chauvinists then reached further back into history to propose Clément Ader.

The court paid an official visit to the Conservatoire des Arts et Métiers, where the batlike Ader machine was on exhibit, complete with a label claiming that the craft had flown 300 meters in 1897. Wilbur knew that it was not true. Commandant Henri Bonel, who had been there, assured the Wrights that the machine had not left the ground.

Borrowing a ladder, Wilbur climbed up to take a closer look—the control system was impossible and the wings had so few ribs that they would never hold their shape in flight. "The whole machine is ridiculous," he told Orv. Disgusted and only half joking, Will suggested that they offer a prize to call the French bluff. "I am intending to offer in our names a prize of 450,000 frs., to be known as the 'Prix de Satory' [the 1897 trials were conducted at Satory, France], to commemorate the experiment of 9 October, 1897, the prize to be given to the person who makes the longest flight *exceeding one hundred* meters with a machine having its wings, screws, and actuating arrangements exact duplicates of those of the *Avion*. . . ."[4]

The aging Clément Ader testified that his plan to turn the machine by running the propeller on one side more rapidly than that on the other corresponded to the Wright system of wing warping. Not even the defense attorneys could swallow that. Undaunted, the leaders of the Ligue Aérienne finally cited Louis Mouillard. Here, they claimed, was the true father of wing warping. Chanute had transmitted Mouillard's notion of lateral control to the Wrights, who had taken it as their own.

Wilbur explained to the court, as he had to Chanute, that Mouillard's plan called for slowing the speed of one wing relative to the other, inducing a flat turn. The notion of a banking turn involving the simultaneous action of both wings with the rudder was entirely absent. Moreover, Mouillard had never flown the glider.

The court listened, and seemed to agree with Wilbur, but it was clear that the judicial process would not be speedy. There was no sense in his remaining in Paris.[5]

Things were no better in Germany or England. He found the German company just as shaky as Orville had reported. During his stay in Berlin Wilbur made at least one flight, probably with Captain Paul Engelhard.[6]

There were fewer problems in England, but Wilbur was displeased with the way in which individual pilots modified their "Wright machines." He told Katharine about one fellow who had "added porches, attics and sheds" to his craft, "till it looks like an old farm house which has been in the family for three or four generations." The man was able to lunge several hundred feet through the air with the thing, but his technique left much to be desired. "When he jams a wing into the ground and whirls around suddenly, he says he has found by experience that he can turn quicker that way than any other."[7]

It was all very discouraging. As he wrote to Orville from Berlin in June:

If I could get free from business with the money we already have in hand I would rather do it than continue in business at a considerable profit. Only two things lead me to put up with responsibilities and annoyances for a moment. First, the obligations to people who put money into our business, and second, the reluctance a man normally feels to allow a lot of scoundrels and thieves to steal his patents, subject him to all kinds of troubles or even try to cheat him out of his patents entirely. So far as Europe is concerned I do not feel that we are in debt to either the French or German companies. We have not had a square deal from either of them. All the money we ever got from either of these companies will be fully paid for by future work and worries. But I hate to see the French infringers wreck our business and abuse us and then go unscathed. . . . For the good of the public and the protection of others we ought to do our share to discourage such people a little.[8]

Orville met him at the dock in New York on August 9, and they returned to Dayton together. After a few days rest, Wilbur was ready to resume the fight. He brought suit against the sponsors of an unauthorized Chicago air meet, then traveled back to New York to offer still more testimony in the Curtiss case.

Orville was just as anxious to see Glenn Curtiss brought to justice, but there were other priorities. He was off to Kitty Hawk for the first time in four years on October 7, accompanied by Lorin, Lorin's ten-year-old Horace (known as Buster, or Bus), and Alexander Ogilvie, their English pilot friend. The trip was proof that the press of business and the patent suits had not completely halted aeronautical research at the Wright Company, at least so far as Orville was concerned.

Having achieved controlled flight, the brothers had turned to consider automatic stability as early as 1905–06. They recognized that absolute control carried with it the penalty of instability, but were willing to pay that price to obtain complete command of their machine. Next, they were anxious to take a step back and see if it might not be possible to keep an airplane flying straight and level without the intervention of the pilot.[9]

They applied for a patent on such a device on February 8, 1908. Well into development by 1911, the automatic stabilizing system was based on a feedback mechanism—a pendulum (roll-yaw) and a vane (pitch) which sensed changes in attitude and activated the wing-warping and elevator controls through compressed-air cylinders to restore equilibrium.

Orville designed a new aircraft to test the prototype system. The 1911 glider bore a general resemblance to the standard Model B, but was smaller and weighed only a third as much.

Orville and his party arrived at the old camp on October 10. It was a shambles. Parts of the 1905–08 machine were poking out of the sand. Orville had considered bringing them home with him, but rejected the notion. The parts were "too badly damaged by the weather and the field mice that made an abode in them."[10]

The work went quickly. Most of the first week was devoted to flying kites on the beach with Bus and exploring the Sound side of the Banks in a rented motorboat. The crates containing the glider arrived at the Kitty Hawk dock on October 13. Four newsmen were waiting for Orville when he nosed his boat into the old dock to pick up the machine: D. Bruce Salley, the Norfolk reporter who had ferreted out their story in 1903; John Mitchell of the Associated Press; Van Ness Harwood of the *New York Herald;* and a representative of the *New*

York World. Two more, Arnold Krockman and a Mr. Berges, both representing the *New York American,* strolled into camp on October 20.[11]

Orville made them welcome, but decided that there would be no tests of the automatic stability system so long as reporters were present. It was just as well. The business of test-flying the new glider proved to be challenge enough. In the air for the first time on October 16, he discovered that both the rudder and elevator were too small; he added an additional vertical stabilizer in front and a larger elevator at the rear, both scavenged from the parts scattered around the camp site. By the end of the afternoon he had completed a glide of 1,223 feet.

Orville and Alec Ogilvie both did some gliding the next day. Orv, still tinkering with the craft, added a sliding arrangement enabling him to move the front vertical surface two feet fore and aft. The last flight of the day was a near disaster: Orville flew the machine straight into the side of the sandhill. He was not injured, but the entire left side of the machine was smashed.

There was another accident on October 23. Ogilvie and Lorin had just released the machine into the air when it reared up and flipped over on its back. Once again, Orville walked away from a crash that severely damaged his machine.

Tuesday, October 24, dawned cool and sunny. The wind was blowing across the top of the big hill at 40 miles per hour. Orville made twenty glides that day, several of them quite spectacular. On one flight he rose to an altitude of 50 feet and remained in the air for 5 minutes, 29 seconds. On two other occasions he stayed up for 7 minutes, 15 seconds. The best flight of the day—9 minutes, 45 seconds— was almost unbelievable. Orville seemed to hang suspended in the air, moving back and forth over one spot for almost ten full minutes. The crew measured his path across the ground when it was all over and discovered that he had moved a total distance of only 40 yards.

Once again, Kitty Hawk had rewarded the Wrights with perfect conditions. The weather, combined with the aerodynamic improvements built into the machines since the last time they had gone gliding in 1903, resulted in the first example of true soaring. The long flight of October 24 would stand as a world's record for unpowered, heavier-than-air flight for ten years. It was Orville's longest standing record.

The good flying weather held for a few more days. Orville made thirty-one flights on October 25 and twenty-four on October 26, his

last day on the dunes. None of them approached the record performances of October 24, but they proved that Orville's initial demonstration of soaring was a genuine breakthrough, not the result of a
meteorological fluke.

Three thousand miles to the west of Kitty Hawk, John Joseph
Montgomery was also back in the air. Any doubts he might have felt
as a result of the death of Dan Maloney aboard the flimsy Santa Clara
glider in 1905 had apparently vanished. With the assistance of a new
financial backer, James Plew, and a publicist, Victor Lougheed, he
was testing a high-wing monoplane glider on the rolling hills near
Evergreen, California.[12]

The Wrights had finally met Montgomery at the Belmont Meet the
year before. The picture of enthusiasm, he claimed that his new machine was so successful his pilots were looping the loop with it. Things
had gotten so dangerous he was forced to limit the extent to which
the controls could be operated, just to keep the "boys" flying safe. "Of
course there was no doubt in our minds as to whether his statement
should be believed," Orv remarked to Tom Baldwin, "but it was hard
to tell whether his statement was a result of an illusion, or whether
it was simply a plain falsehood."[13]

When news of Orville's soaring flights appeared in the newspapers,
Victor Lougheed told the press that it would be "utterly impossible
to remain aloft five minutes without the use of artificial power."
Lougheed traveled to Kitty Hawk determined to expose the "hoax"
once and for all. "When he learned at first hand from half a dozen
persons who had been eyewitnesses that the reports were really true,
he skipped out without even seeing the machine!" Orv reported to
Tom Baldwin.[14]

John Montgomery made his last flight on October 31 while Orville
was packing up camp at Kitty Hawk. Witnesses reported that he lost
control when his machine was struck by a gust. Montgomery's wife
and his mechanic ran to the glider and found the pilot unconscious, his
skull penetrated by a long stove bolt. Montgomery, whose one short
glide from Otay Mesa in 1885 had earned him the distinction of being
the first American glider pilot, died before the doctor arrived.[15]

Increasingly, the Wrights found themselves focusing on the past.
On October 26, the day on which Orville made his last glides from the
big Kill Devil Hill, the machine that he had flown for the Army at Fort
Myer in 1909 was enshrined in the National Museum of the Smithsonian Institution.

Lieutenant Foulois had been ordered to transport the aircraft to Fort Sam Houston, Texas, before his own training at College Park was completed. Foulois, who would rise to command the U.S. Army Air Corps during the years prior to World War II, liked to describe himself as the world's first correspondence-school pilot. Arriving at his assigned post without having soloed, he taught himself to fly, writing to Orville for advice when he ran into problems.[16]

Army brass took little interest in their only active pilot and airplane—during the first year, Foulois and his enlisted mechanics paid for some repairs to the machine out of their own pockets. After two years of service, Foulois received permission to ship the dilapidated Flyer back to the factory in Dayton for a complete refitting. Orville took one look and advised against it. The War Department relented, purchasing a new machine and offering the Wrights a contract to restore the world's first military airplane for presentation to the Smithsonian.

Wilbur's writing was taking a historical turn as well. Anxious to correct the false claims put forward by members of the Ligue Aérienne, he published articles assessing the contributions of Ader and Mouillard. Having demonstrated that neither deserved as much credit as was claimed for them, it seemed only fair to identify the more substantial contributors. When the brothers discovered that Otto Lilienthal's widow and children were in financial distress, they sent the family a check for $1,000 in recognition of the extent to which the pioneer had influenced their own early work.[17]

All too often, potential buyers regarded the Wrights as historic figures rather than suppliers of up-to-date machines. By the end of 1911 even the U.S. War Department was convinced that the inventors of the airplane could no longer compete with European manufacturers. Orville fought that notion. "If the American government will make purchases equal to those of the French government," he wrote to Captain Charles DeForest Chandler, "American manufacturers can easily meet all of the conditions required of foreign machines."[18]

In Europe, government subsidies to aircraft builders had fueled a rapid advance since 1906: "You are, no doubt, aware that in France whenever a manufacturer turns out a new type of machine which is not a flat failure, the government takes over the machine and, if it is specially good, orders several additional ones." The French Ministry of War had spent over $1,250,000 to purchase 250 French-built machines during the past two years. Orville argued that while government subsidies had enabled the French to close the technological gap quickly, American machines remained competitive.

> We believe that at the present time the foreign machines excel the American only in one particular—that of speed. Contests . . . have clearly demonstrated the superior development of the American machines in ability to fly in high winds and in strength and safety of construction. . . . In the matter of weight-carrying, we would call your attention to the flights made at Detroit with the Alger brothers' Wright machine in which three men, weighing nearly 500 pounds, in addition to hydroplane pontoons, were carried with a four cylinder motor of 30 horsepower. . . . We do not think that any foreign machine has ever approached this performance.[19]

It was a weak sales pitch. By the winter of 1911 all interested observers could see that the cutting edge of flight technology had overtaken and passed the Wright Company. The reasons were clear enough, as Wilbur explained to his French friend, M. Hévésy:

> We had hoped in 1906 to sell our invention to governments for enough money to satisfy our needs and devote our time to science, but the jealousy of certain persons blocked this plan, and compelled us to rely on our patents and commercial exploitation. We wished to be free from business cares so that we could give all our own time to advancing the science and art of aviation, but we have been compelled to spend our time on business matters instead during the past five years. When we think what we might have accomplished if we had been able to devote this time to experiments, we feel very sad, but it is always easier to deal with things than with men, and no one can direct his life entirely as he would choose.[20]

The patent suits remained the biggest drain on their time, particularly Wilbur's. He was constantly on the move from mid-December 1911 through the early spring of 1912, shuttling back and forth between New York and Dayton in an attempt to deal with the Grahame-White, Lamson, Winkley, and Herring-Curtiss suits, all of which seemed to be coming to a head.[21]

The constant travel and the pressure of court appearances took its toll. Orville recalled that his brother would "come home white" following a visit with the lawyers. In late April, Wilbur fell seriously ill while on a trip to Boston. Newspapers speculated that the original indisposition was a result of eating contaminated shellfish. He felt better by the time he arrived home on May 2, but it was obvious that he was not himself.[22]

That afternoon the four of them—Milton, Wilbur, Orville, and Katharine—packed a picnic lunch and drove across town to Hawthorn Hill. Wilbur and Orville had purchased seventeen acres near the corner of Park Drive and Harmon Avenue in the affluent suburb of Oakwood in February, and the local architectural firm of Schenck & Williams was already at work on plans for the house that they would build there.[23]

When they got home, Wilbur complained of a temperature. Milton summoned Dr. D. B. Conklin, who diagnosed malarial fever. The patient's temperature was noticeably higher the next morning, although he did not feel particularly ill.

The lingering fever did not keep him from work. He made a trip to Huffman Prairie on May 4, then sat down to write an angry letter to Frederick Fish, a Wright Company attorney, who had suggested postponing hearings in the Herring-Curtiss case until the fall. Wilbur had asked Toulmin to insist on a speedy disposition. Convinced that he had not made the point sufficiently clear, Wilbur wrote in terms Fish could not possibly misunderstand:

> Unnecessary delays by stipulation of counsel have already destroyed fully three fourths of the value of our patent. The opportunities of the last two years will never return again. At the present moment almost innumerable competitors are entering the field, and for the first time are producing machines which will really fly. These machines are being put on the market at one half less than the price which we have been selling our machines for.
>
> The real season for flying as far as money-making is concerned extends from September to the middle of November. If the case goes over to fall, it will be practically the same thing as delaying a whole year. The bare fact that the case is before the Court during the summer would have great value, even though the decision is not rendered until September.[24]

It was Wilbur's last letter. By the afternoon of May 8 he was noticeably weaker. Dr. Conklin, back for a second look, was no longer certain that this was malaria. "There seems to be a sort of typhoidal fever prevailing," Milton wrote in his diary. For the members of this family, there could have been nothing worse. All of them remembered Orville's bout with typhoid in 1896. It was particularly ironic that Wilbur, always so careful to avoid contaminated food and water, should be stricken.

Wilbur knew that he was failing. On May 10 he sent for Ezra

Kuhns, a lawyer who had gone to high school with Orv. With Kuhns as a witness, he dictated his will to Mabel Beck, his own secretary.

The other members of the family could only wait and hope. Assured by the doctors that his brother was in no immediate danger, Orville left for Washington to deliver a new airplane on May 16. Wilbur lapsed into unconsciousness two days later. Orville caught the first train back to Dayton and was at his brother's bedside once again on May 20.

Dr. Conklin and old Dr. Spitler, the physician who had pulled Orv through his bout with the disease twelve years before, prescribed opiates. When there was no apparent improvement by May 22, the two local men called in Dr. Bushiemer, a Cincinnati specialist. Reuchlin arrived from Kansas on May 24.

Conklin and Spitler came at 7:00 A.M. on May 27 and stayed for most of the day. Wilbur's bladder was failing and he seemed to be having difficulty with digestion. The bishop, certain that his son was near death, slept that night with his clothes on.[25]

Wilbur lingered for two more days, dying "without a struggle," as his father reported, at 3:15 on the morning of May 30. With his usual meticulous care, Milton noted that his son was forty-five years, one month, and fourteen days old. The loving father reserved his deeper feelings for the privacy of his diary:

> A short life, full of consequences. An unfailing intellect, imperturbable temper, great self-reliance and as great modesty, seeing the right clearly, pursuing it steadfastly, he lived and died.[26]

Milton estimated that the family had received a thousand telegrams of condolence by the afternoon of May 30. They came from the President, the heads of Europe, men of industry like Lord Northcliffe ("Deepest sympathy dear Katharine and Orville Wright. Very great grief in England at World's loss"), and from hundreds of ordinary citizens, including Glenn Hammond Curtiss. "Flowers come from individuals and societies," Milton noted, "most beautiful. . . ."[27] One newspaper reported that by the time of the funeral there were enough flowers to fill a boxcar.

Wilbur was front-page news for the last time. Newspapers across the nation and around the globe offered glowing tributes, calling him the "Inventor of the Airplane," the "Father of Flight," "Conqueror of the Air," and "the man who made flying possible."[28]

The family would have preferred a quiet funeral, but public pressure was too great to ignore. Wilbur's body was transported to the First Presbyterian Church on Saturday morning, June 1. Twenty-five thousand people had filed past the coffin by the time the funeral began at three o'clock. The service lasted only twenty minutes, and was conducted without music.

The Reverend Dr. Maurice Wilson, pastor of the church, quoted from the Bible, and read an account of Wilbur's career prepared by Reuchlin. Then a United Brethren preacher from Huntington, Indiana, who had remained a family friend through all the church crises, read the words of Martin Luther's hymn, "A Mighty Fortress Is Our God."

The graveside services were limited to family members and the eight pallbearers. At 3:30 P.M. all activity in the city stopped: church bells tolled, automobiles pulled to the curb, streetcars halted in their tracks, and the switchboards refused to accept calls as Wilbur Wright was laid to rest next to his mother in Woodland Cemetery.[29]

Ezra Kuhns came to the house to read the will on June 3. Wilbur had left an estate that was eventually valued by the probate court at $279,298.40. Milton, the first beneficiary, received his son's "earnest thanks for his example of a courageous, upright life and for his earnest sympathy with everything tending to my true welfare," and the sum of $1,000, to be used for such "little unusual expenditures as might add to his comfort and pleasure."[30]

The great bulk of the estate—$150,000 in cash—was to be divided equally between Reuch, Lorin, and Katharine. The remainder, including all of the patents and jointly held shares in the various Wright companies, went to Orville, "who I am sure will use the property in very much the same manner as we would use it together in case we would both survive to old age."[31]

As executor, Orville was determined to treat his brother's will as sacrosanct. Reuch presented the only real problem. Having distanced himself from the other members of the family years before, he felt guilty about accepting a share of the estate equal to Lorin and Katharine's. After some struggle with his conscience, he returned $1,000 to the bishop. But Milton sent back the money with the comment that he and Orville were determined to carry out every provision of the will in exact detail.[32]

"Probably Orville and Katharine felt the loss most," Milton suggested in his diary. "They say little."[33] Both of them found it difficult to conceive of life without Wilbur. Orville would later say that there were times when he suddenly awoke to the fact that Wilbur had not simply stepped into the next room for a few minutes.

Brother and sister were drawn closer together by shared grief and a touch of bitterness. They did not regard Will's death as pure providence—other factors had been at work. He had been worn out by the patent fight, his energy drained and his resistance lowered. The men who had forced them into court time after time bore a share of the responsibility. Together, they rededicated themselves to carrying on the fight their brother had begun.[34]

Less than two weeks after Wilbur's death, Orville and Katharine left for Washington to attend the funerals of Art Welsh and Lieutenant Leighton Hazelhurst, killed while flying a new Wright Model C-1 at College Park, Maryland, on June 11. Welsh, anxious to complete the Army acceptance tests required for the purchase of the machine, had nosed down into a shallow dive, then pulled sharply up as he prepared to climb to the altitude stipulated by the contract. Nosing up too steeply, he stalled and crashed.

Orv and Katharine left for the annual pilgrimage to Europe on February 12, 1913. In London on February 21 they presided, at long last, over the formation of a British Wright Company. Orville, who was now president of the American Wright Company, became chairman of the board of the new English firm.

The arrangement with Short Brothers had already enabled the Wrights to make what money they could from the sale of their machines in England. The new company would not produce many airplanes, but it did play an important role in persuading the English government to make a lump-sum payment of £15,000 for all unauthorized use of the Wright patent in England.[35]

They arrived in Leipzig on February 26, just in time to hear the German Supreme Court render a verdict in the long-standing German patent suit. With "great regret," the court upheld the ruling of the Patent Office. Although the Wrights were indeed the inventors of wing warping, they had forfeited all rights through prior disclosure, but were still entitled to patent control over the combined use of wing warping and the rudder. Orville once remarked to an early biographer that the German verdict was something akin to excusing a pickpocket because the victim had indicated the location of his purse.[36]

They went on to Paris in time to assist Flint Company attorneys with the final presentation to the French high court. The ruling seemed to be completely in favor of the Wrights. Even the use of the rudder disconnected from the wing-warping system was allowed. Once again, however, the judges accepted a defense motion for yet another panel of experts to study prior art. Peartree and the Flint lawyers advised Orville that the infringers would be able to keep the proceedings alive until the patent expired in 1917. Accepting the inevitable, they decided to leave for home.

They sailed for America on March 9. For once, there was good news waiting in New York. On February 27, Judge Hazel handed down his final decision in the case of *Wright* v. *Curtiss*, upholding the Wright position. Curtiss was enjoined from the continued manufacture, sale, or exhibition of aircraft.[37]

Curtiss immediately appealed and was allowed to continue operations until the Federal Appeals Court handed down its ruling, but his situation did not look hopeful. It seemed to Orville that they were very close to the legal vindication he and Will had sought so long.

They arrived back home on March 19—just in time for the greatest natural disaster in the city's history. A hard rain began to fall on Easter Sunday, March 23. Dayton, at the confluence of the Miami, Stillwater, and Mad rivers with Wolf Creek, had always been prone to flooding. Six times in its history rampaging waters had swept through the streets of the city.

This time it was far worse. Torrential rains poured down all over the area drained by the rivers and creeks that met in the center of Dayton. By Monday afternoon, the Miami River was rising at the rate of six inches per hour. Flooding was inevitable.

The real disaster began with the collapse of an earthen dam containing the Loramie Reservoir in Shelby County, Ohio, at seven o'clock the next morning. The water poured down the valley of the Miami past Sidney, Piqua, and Troy to reach Dayton that afternoon. The levee along Stratford Avenue was breached at about four o'clock; within an hour water was pouring though additional breaks on East Second and Fifth streets. West Dayton, built on low-lying land bounded by the Miami and Wolf Creek, got the worst of it.[38]

Orville and Katharine overslept on the morning of March 25, and rushed out of the house for an appointment in another part of town. High water made it impossible for them to return to Hawthorn Street late that afternoon. They spent the night at the home of E. L. Lorenz, a friend who lived on higher ground a few blocks away on Summit Street.

Like thousands of other Daytonians, Orville had a sleepless night.

His concern for Milton's safety was paramount. The telephones were completely out of service; before nightfall Orv and Katharine posted notices asking anyone with information as to the bishop's whereabouts to contact them at Summit Street. The next day a passer-by informed them that he was safe.

Milton and his next-door neighbor, Mrs. Wagner, had been rescued by a good Samaritan with a canoe and taken to William Hartzell's house on Williams Street just before nightfall. Milton estimated that Hawthorn Street lay under eight feet of water by nine o'clock that evening.[39]

Orville had other worries that first night. The priceless photographic negatives of the flying-machine experiments of 1900–05 were in the old shed at the rear of the house. Letters, diaries, and other records of the invention of the airplane were stored in his second-floor office at the bicycle shop on Third Street, where the water was said to be over twelve feet deep. Fires fed by escaping gas broke out all over the city that night. From his vantage point on high ground Orville could see the glow created by a major blaze in the neighborhood of the bike shop. The entire West Side business district was in danger of going up in flames.

The floodwaters receded by March 30, enabling the citizens of Dayton to assess the damage: 371 lives had been lost and property damage was estimated at $100 million. Determined that nothing of the sort would ever happen again, local leaders banded together to form the Miami Conservancy District, an intergovernmental agency that would oversee the construction and operation of a system of local flood-control dams. The effort was a success—the dams were built and the conservancy program became the model for similar programs undertaken across the nation.

The Wrights had escaped with their lives and property losses of less than $5,000. Like everyone else they now faced a daunting clean-up effort. One reporter left a graphic description of the scene on the West Side:

> The streets are seas of yellow ooze. Garden fences and hedges are twisted or torn away. Reeking heaps of indescribable refuse lie moldering where there were smooth lawns and bright flower beds. The houses that stand are all smeared with dirt that shows the height of the flood. But inside the houses, that is the dreadful thing. The rooms that the water filled are like damp caves. Mud lies thick on the floors, the walls are streaked with slime, and the paper hangs down in dismal festoons.

Some pictures may remain hanging, but they are all twisted and tarnished. The furniture is a jumbled mass of confusion and filth. But the worst is the reek of death about the place.[40]

The things that had remained downstairs at 7 Hawthorn Street and in the bicycle shop were a total loss. Fortunately, the materials relating to the invention of the airplane survived with little damage. Rummaging through the shed, Orville found that some of the emulsion had begun to peel from a few of the glass plate negatives, but none was a total loss. The most important photo—the plate that John Daniels exposed just after the machine lifted off the rail for the first time on December 17, 1903—had lost only a small bit of emulsion in one corner. The image was undamaged.

The records of their experiments were safe as well. The water had not reached the second-floor office, and the fire that swept through other buildings on West Third left the bicycle shop untouched. Even the remnants of the 1903 airplane, stored in the low shed at the back, survived unharmed. The precious bits of wood and fabric, submerged beneath twelve feet of water, were protected from damage by a thick layer of mud.

Of all the surviving reminders of their early work, the world's first airplane was probably least important to Orville. He and his brother had never given much thought to their old machines. Each of the three gliders had been discarded in turn at Kitty Hawk, as had the 1905 airplane when its career was concluded in 1908. They stored the 1904 machine over a single winter in the shed at Huffman Prairie; the following spring the wings and frame were hauled out and burned to make room for the new machine.

The 1903 airplane was the only one they had saved, stowing the shipping crates away behind the bike shop without unpacking them. Now it had survived the great flood. Orville cleaned the mud off the top of the crates as best he could, and put them back in the shed. Soon he would be very glad that those shattered bits of wood and torn fabric had been preserved one more time.

chapter 33

THE END OF AN ERA

April 1913-October 1915

T he Wright factory escaped the flood. Orville called the men back
to work on April 10, but only five of them made it to the plant.
"There is some prospect that the street railway service will be
resumed in the early part of next week," he told a friend, "in which
case I think we will have a fairly full force."[1]

As master of those workmen and president of the company, Orville
was badly out of his depth. Wilbur had not been especially fond of
management, but he had worked hard at it, driven by an ambition that
would not permit failure. At the deepest level, he had undertaken the
search for a practical airplane as a means of distinguishing himself
from the common herd. The opportunity to stand in the spotlight on
his own terms and to be accepted as an equal by the industrialists who
had invested in the Wright Company was proof that he had achieved
his goal. For Wilbur, the stresses of the company presidency were
offset by very real psychic rewards.

Orville had almost none of his brother's restless ambition nor the
energy and drive to succeed that came with it. Alone with his friends
he was a delightful conversationalist; among strangers he grew silent
and withdrawn. He had few illusions about his capacity for leadership.
The thought of attending a board meeting, let alone presiding at one,
was abhorrent to him. Moreover, with the single exception of Robert
Collier, he felt little other than contempt for the rich New Yorkers
whom Wilbur had regarded as friends and associates.[2]

Orville accepted the presidency of the Wright Company because he

455

had no choice. The position enabled him to maintain control over his own financial destiny while at the same time drawing on corporate resources to carry out litigation at company expense.

He would use the power of his office, but he had no intention of reshaping himself into the image of a corporate executive. From the members of the board of directors to the men on the shop floor in Dayton, they would have to take him as he was.

Nor did he make any secret of his distaste for management. Orville physically distanced himself from the factory, maintaining his old office above the bicycle shop. In addition, he insisted on conducting business through intermediaries like Mabel Beck, his forceful and protective secretary, who became a legend in the company.[3]

Yet there was no doubt who was in charge. Wilbur had never been especially fond of Frank Russell. Orville, who liked him even less, fired Russell less than a year after taking over the reins. He hired a replacement, Grover Loening, during a business trip to New York in July 1913.

Loening, a recent graduate of Columbia, had met Wilbur in New York in 1909. The young man subsequently worked as chief engineer of the tiny Queen Aeroplane Company in New York, and constructed a flying boat of his own design.

Loening's earlier acquaintance with Wilbur was relevant. Throughout their relationship, Orville would treat him as a younger brother—a young Wilbur, in fact. He enjoyed his company, and tried to lure him into the sort of arguments he and Wilbur had found so productive. For his part, Loening was extraordinarily fond of his employer but not blind to his weaknesses. "Factory organization was pretty rough," he recalled many years later. "Orville . . . would delay making an important decision and drive us all nuts trying not to disobey his orders on the one hand and yet not knowing what to do."[4]

Loening admired the fact that no one ever put anything over on Orville, but he was puzzled by his apparent lack of vision, saying: "He certainly did not have any 'big business' ideas or any great ambition to expand. He seemed to be lacking in push." Part of the problem, Loening thought, was that Orville missed his brother. In addition, he was battling recurrent back pain resulting from the crash at Fort Myer in 1908.[5]

The patent suit was the most serious problem, however. Loening described the ongoing court battle with Glenn Curtiss as "the one great hate and obsession" preying on "the minds and characters" of both Orville and Katharine. He saw the patent fight as a two-edged sword. While it might ultimately put the competition out of business, it also monopolized Orville's attention and discouraged any attempt to incorporate the latest technical advances into the design of Wright aircraft.[6]

The standard Wright production of 1913, the Model C, was an obsolete machine. Compared to contemporary European aircraft, it was slow, tail-heavy, and unstable. Other flying-machine builders, notably Esnault-Pelterie and Blériot, pioneered a natural control arrangement combining the use of a stick and rudder pedals. Orville retained the cumbersome and confusing system of twin levers developed in 1908.

In part, Orville's technical conservatism was based on a reluctance to move too far from the classic Wright pattern developed at the start of the century. Until the patent suit was settled, there was a danger that a radical design change might be seen as an admission that the original required improvement. Moreover, Orville was reluctant to adopt innovations pioneered by men whom he had accused of infringing on his ideas.

Take the case of the flying boat. Since the day in 1910 when the French aviator Henri Fabre lifted off the water for the first time, hydroaeroplanes—flying boats—had enjoyed enormous popularity. Recognizing the extent to which the Wrights would dominate the U.S. Army market, Glenn Curtiss made a concerted effort to sell his machines to the U.S. Navy. He offered the Navy a cut-rate flight training program, staged the first takeoff and landing from U.S. naval vessels, and paid close attention as the Navy formulated its requirements.

His most important achievement, however, was the development of the flying boat. Curtiss began his experiments in the fall of 1908 with the rebuilt version of the *June Bug* called the *Loon.* He continued to develop his ideas with a variety of machines during 1909–11, finally introducing the Model E, his first genuinely practical flying boat, in 1912.

The Model E and subsequent variants were so successful that Curtiss not only dominated the U.S. Navy market but received the first great batch of orders from European purchasers. In 1913 he completed work on the *America,* a giant flying boat designed to cross the Atlantic. With the advent of war, the Curtiss Aeroplane and Motor Company would become the major supplier of large flying boat patrol aircraft to both the British and American governments.[7]

Orville could trace his interest in flying boats to 1907, when he and

Will had dreamed of a surprise appearance over the fleet during the Jamestown celebration. His first successful water takeoff and landing were made with a Model CH on a secluded stretch of the Miami River in 1913. Essentially a Model C fitted with a 240-pound pontoon, the clumsy machine was a far cry from the sleek Curtiss Model E with its rakish boat hull.

Grover Loening designed the first Wright flying boat, the Model G of 1913–14. Orville did not make it easy for him, insisting that the craft should in no way resemble the Curtiss boats. The result was much inferior and fell short of U.S. Navy requirements.[8]

The Wright Company floundered through the years 1912–15. New machines developed during this period failed to keep pace with the competition; more important, the standard Model C fell into ill repute with the U.S. Army. Art Welsh and Lieutenant Leighton Hazelhurst were the first men killed in a Model C, dying in the crash at College Park on June 11, 1912. The next fatalities at College Park came on the afternoon of September 28, when Lieutenant Lewis Rockwell drove his Model B straight into the ground at 50 miles per hour, killing himself and his passenger, Corporal Frank Scott.

The death toll continued to mount. Lieutenant Loren H. Call died in a Model B crash at Fort Sam Houston on July 8, 1913. Lieutenant Moss Love was killed in a Model C at the Army's new North Island, California, facility on September 4. Lieutenant Perry C. Rich died when his Model C nosed into Manila Bay on November 14. Ten days later Lieutenant Hugh Kelly and flight instructor Eric Ellington died in a second Model C crash at North Island.[9]

Ellington's death convinced Grover Loening that there was a major defect in the design of the Model C. "He was one of the leading Wright pilots in the Army and was constantly corresponding with us on details of his machine and his troubles," the engineer recalled. "Finally, one morning I read of his death in the papers and arrived in the office, only to find a long letter from him, predicting that something would happen, as he was feeling sure the Wright Model C was too tail heavy and didn't answer the controls properly."[10]

Orville rejected the notion of a fundamental design problem, maintaining it was a matter of pilot error. The Model C was equipped with a new six-cylinder engine developing 60 horsepower—the aviators simply were not accustomed to so much power.[11]

Most of the crashes, he was convinced, were caused by stalls. The pilots misjudged the angle of attack, diving and climbing at too steep an angle. He developed an angle-of-incidence indicator—a simple pointer that sensed small changes in the angle of attack and warned the pilot when his climb or dive became too steep.

Orville thought that the automatic pilot on which he had been at work since 1905 would also help to solve the problem. The device, complete and ready for testing by the fall of 1913, was designed to keep an airplane flying straight and level without the intervention of the pilot. It included a pendulum to control the wing warping and a horizontal vane to operate the elevator, both working through ser-vomotors powered by a wind-driven generator.[12]

He received a patent on the automatic pilot in October 1913, by which time he had installed a prototype system on a special single-seat Model E. He had tested the thing in secret and knew that it worked. The first public demonstration would be a particularly sweet moment, for he had found a way to use the invention to triumph over Glenn Curtiss.

In 1911, Orville's friend Robert Collier established what was to become the most prestigious award in American aviation. The Collier Trophy was to be presented annually for the most significant contri-bution to aeronautics made during the year. Curtiss had won the trophy two years running for his flying boats. Orville was determined to snatch the award from him in 1913.

Remembering Wilbur's stratagem for winning the Coupe Michelin at the last minute, Orville scheduled his first public demonstration of the automatic pilot for December 31. He made a total of seventeen flights before the Aero Club of America observers gathered at Huff-man Prairie that day. The most spectacular performance included a takeoff followed by seven full circles of the field with his hands held high in the air.[13]

Orville was awarded the Collier Trophy on February 5, 1914, but it proved to be a hollow triumph. In the spring of 1913, just as he was putting the finishing touches on his automatic stabilizer, a twenty-year-old engineer named Lawrence Sperry reported to the Curtiss flight school at Hammondsport for pilot training. The son of Elmer Sperry, who had developed a gyroscopic stabilizing system for ships, Lawrence was determined to perfect a similar device for aircraft.

Sperry earned his wings and traveled with the Curtiss crowd to winter quarters at North Island, California, a five-mile-long sandbar separating San Diego Bay from the Pacific, where the work on the gyroscopic stabilizer continued. Like Orville, young Sperry developed a mechanism that would sense deviations from straight and normal flight and apply corrective action.

Rather than using mechanical vanes and pendulums, however, he established a stable platform for two gyroscopes in the cockpit of a Curtiss flying boat. One gyro sensed deviations in the yaw axis and operated the rudder. The other functioned for the roll and pitch axes and controlled the ailerons and elevator.

Sperry unveiled his invention on June 18, 1914, as part of a great safety competition sponsored by the Aéro-Club de France and the French War Department. He took a Curtiss C-2 off the Seine, climbed to altitude, and flew back down the river. At the appropriate moment, his mechanic, Emile Cachin, crawled seven feet out onto one wing as Sperry lifted his hands from the controls and stood up in the cockpit. The airplane flashed past the judges as the crowd went wild.[14]

Orville's automatic stabilizer worked, but Sperry had broken entirely new ground. His brilliant solution to the problem rivaled what the Wrights themselves had achieved in the invention of the airplane. Not only did it form the basis for all subsequent automatic stability systems, it opened an entire range of new possibilities. The enormously complex inertial navigation system that guided the first men to the Moon in 1969 was directly rooted in Sperry's automatic pilot of 1914.

In the summer of 1913, with attention focused on the bottom line of corporate account books and general operations in Dayton, the board of directors of the Wright Company dispatched the company treasurer, Alpheus Barnes, to keep a close eye on the situation. Orville, working through Loening, remained in charge of production. Barnes took over bookkeeping, advertising, and contract negotiation.

Loening remembered Barnes as "a hearty, well-built, and genial character, smoking cigars continually and full of good stories," who regarded Orville's Dayton friends as provincial hicks. From Orville's point of view, the company treasurer was the worst of the New York crowd. That, Loening commented, "did not bother Barnes much." In addition to his other duties, Loening served as a mediator between the two men.[15]

Orville and Barnes could not even agree on a response to good news. On January 13, 1914, the United States Circuit Court of Appeals upheld the original decision in the case of *Wright* v. *Curtiss*. The Wright patent was valid and Glenn Hammond Curtiss had infringed upon it. This time it seemed that Curtiss had run out of space in which to maneuver. His only possible resort was to the Supreme Court of the United States, and there were no apparent legal grounds on which to base such an appeal.

Alpheus Barnes and his New York colleagues were overjoyed. Grover Loening listened for hours as the treasurer spun bright visions of what such a decision would mean to the company—opening the way for a legal monopoly as all-inclusive and remunerative as that granted to the Bell Telephone Company.[16]

It might have worked. Loening spent considerable time in later years speculating on what might have occurred if Barnes and the other members of the board of directors had been given a free hand to expand production and exploit a monopoly.

> There were untold millions of dollars ready in New York to be invested in such a trust. In no time Curtiss and what other companies there were could have been closed down or bought up, and we would have seen a totally different development of flying starting here and spreading to Europe exactly as the telephone monopoly did. When we look back on it, it might have been a better thing for aviation. Many destructive rivalries would have been stopped, and with the World War just getting ready to start, one hesitates to think what a difference a great rich legal trust might have made.[17]

"At any rate," Loening concluded, "it did not happen because of one man—Orville Wright. With the winning of the suit, his revenge on Curtiss seemed satisfied, and all he wanted was tribute—royalties from everyone."[18] Badgered by the New York board to take immediate action that would drive Curtiss and the others out of business, Orville refused, announcing that everyone, with the possible exception of Curtiss, would be free to continue doing business so long as they paid the Wright Company a 20 percent royalty on every machine produced.

W. Starling Burgess, a wealthy yacht designer turned aircraft builder, was among those who jumped at Orville's offer. Glenn L. Martin of California was another. But those men ran very small operations compared to the Curtiss Aeroplane Company.

By the early spring of 1914, Curtiss was the largest and most successful producer of aircraft in the United States, the only firm that could compete with leading European manufacturers. Glenn Curtiss was a man of few illusions. He knew that the offer made to other manufacturers would not be available to him. The Wright Company would take legal action to shut him down. Not long before, Henry Ford had been caught in just such a situation.

When Ford entered the automobile business before the turn of the century, the Selden patent had dominated that industry. Unlike the Wright brothers, George Selden was not an inventor in any important sense, but he had taken note of the rapid development of lightweight steam and internal-combustion engines during the years after 1870 and had drawn some conclusions. The day of the "road engine," the self-propelled vehicle, was not far distant. He filed for a patent in 1879, describing his "invention" in such broad terms that it would be virtually impossible to build a "road engine" without infringing upon it. His plan was to wait until someone else built such a machine, then launch a patent infringement suit that would make his fortune.

Selden kept his patent application pending until 1895, by which time there were, at long last, a handful of auto builders to sue. When the preliminary decisions were handed down in his favor, most of the manufacturers caved in and agreed to pay a royalty for use of the patent. Henry Ford was the only major auto builder to fight to the end, emerging victorious just months before the Selden patent would have lapsed.

There was an enormous difference between the Selden case and that of Wilbur and Orville Wright. The Wright patent covered a brilliant achievement that deserved protection under the law. Selden had simply found a legal loophole to exploit the system. Henry Ford, however, was unable to distinguish between the two situations. Convinced that this was a repetition of his own experience, Ford offered Curtiss the services of W. Benton Crisp, the lawyer who had finally broken the Selden patent.[19]

With Crisp's assistance, Curtiss devised a new strategy. Accepting the fact that the combined use of wing warping and rudder was fully covered in the Wright patent, and that his ailerons were analagous to wing warping, he announced that henceforth he would construct machines designed to use only one aileron at a time. That is, he would disconnect the ailerons on the right and left wings so that simultaneous action would no longer be possible. While that might make his machines more difficult to fly, it would also place them outside the bounds of the Wright patent.

In fact, a comparable situation was covered in Claim 1 of the Wright patent. Unfortunately, Claim 1 had not been cited or included in the earlier suit and had yet to be adjudicated. Curtiss had found his loophole. The Wright Company would have to bring suit all over again.

Orville was outraged but strangely indecisive. He recognized that the whole business was nothing more than a ploy to buy time, yet he refused to take action.

The board of directors were as angry at Orville as they were at Curtiss. Quick legal action on the basis of the original ruling might force Curtiss out of business, preserving the dream of monopoly. By dragging his feet, Orville allowed his rival to catch his breath and devise a fresh legal gambit.

The Wright-Curtiss feud had become a public relations disaster. While the Wright Company had its defenders, it was increasingly portrayed as a cutthroat organization, determined to smash honest competitors by fair means or foul. The fact that Curtiss continued to prosper throughout the period of the patent suits was generally overlooked. Moreover, there was a growing assumption that the patent suits had retarded the development of American aeronautics, enabling European competitors to forge ahead.

It is impossible to gauge the impact of the patent wars on the growth of aviation in America. Clearly other factors, including government subsidies, prize competitions, and international rivalry, provide a full explanation for the rapidity of European advance during 1906–14. At the most basic level, the situation was proof of the old adage that it is sometimes better to be a fast second. The French, having lost the race for the invention of the airplane, had swept past the Wrights and everyone else by sheer momentum.

At the same time, the Wright-Curtiss feud did create serious divisions within the American aeronautical community. As Grover Loening noted, these divisions extended into the tiny band of U.S. Army aviators:

> The army at this time had Curtiss pusher planes that, if anything, were more dangerous than the Wrights'. And to make matters worse, the vicious Curtiss vs. Wright rivalry that existed in the commercial flying game had, like an insidious disease, fastened itself on the army flyers. What was at first good-natured kidding (such as sending messages from one hangar to another not to fly their planes over the former, please, because so many things fell off them in the air as to endanger the people on the ground) grew into deadly serious jealousy and spite, affecting everyone, even down to the mechanics.[20]

But the rivalry was the least of their problems. On February 9, 1914, Lieutenant Harry Post was killed while flying a Wright Model C at North Island. The Army had originally purchased six Model C aircraft; five of those machines had now killed six men. One half of all the Army pilots who had died in air crashes to date had met their end in Model C aircraft. Selfridge, Rockwell, Scott, and Call had been killed flying earlier Wright machines. So far as Major Samuel Reber, the officer in charge of Army aviation, was concerned, that was enough.

Reber called for a board of investigation, which determined that the design of the Model C, not pilot error, was primarily responsible for the accidents. The officers suggested that the rear elevator was too small and weak to enable a pilot to recover from a rapid descent.[21]

Orville disagreed with their conclusions but did his best to cooperate. After a series of conferences with Reber, Thomas Milling, and others in Dayton, Oscar Brindley, the leading instructor at Huffman Prairie, was dispatched to North Island to study the training situation. His initial report noted that aircraft maintenance was a major problem. Reber responded by advertising for a civilian engineer to oversee the airworthiness of machines in the Army inventory and organizing a small research and development unit.

Loening, who "did not see much of an immediate future with the Wright Company the way things were going," applied for the job and was hired. For years thereafter he was convinced that Orville regarded him as disloyal and ungrateful. Loening's first step after arriving at North Island was to declare all the Wright and Curtiss pushers unsafe to fly. "The pusher planes were not only easily stallable," he explained, "but in a crash the engine generally fell on and crushed the pilot."[22]

Loening and the group of pilots and mechanics who were assisting him went a step further, rebuilding one of the antiquated Burgess tractor machines into an adequate training aircraft that reflected the latest European developments. The engineers at the Curtiss Company scarcely needed that lesson, being already involved in the development of a modern tractor machine of their own. The Curtiss Model J, unveiled later in 1914, was the first step toward the immortal JN-4D "Jenny" of World War I.[23]

Curtiss now had an entire staff of engineers and designers. Orville had no taste for that sort of corporate expansion and no desire for personal power. Even more surprising, he had little interest in managing a research and development program that would keep him at the forefront of aeronautical advance. Uncomfortable with the pressures of the job, he was fully aware that the company fortunes had dived under his leadership.

He knew precisely what had to be done. In the early spring of 1914 he began to buy up the company shares held by members of the board of directors. The project was risky—most of his own capital was tied up in the company. For the first time in his life, Orville was forced to borrow very large sums of money.[24]

The attempt to gain full control of the company helps to explain Orville's behavior during these months. His refusal to file a new suit against Curtiss was almost certainly part of a carefully considered plan to discourage and alienate his own board. The New Yorkers were dumbstruck when he vetoed their request to hire a new lawyer with close connections to the Wilson administration, a man who could bring high-level influence to bear against Curtiss. It was a clear signal that Orville would stop at nothing in his efforts to frustrate the company board and encourage them to sell out.

The strategy worked. Orville bought up the stock held by every member of the board with the exception of his friend Robert Collier. But the takeover was expensive. In order to close the deal, he had to guarantee a 100 percent profit on each man's investment, exclusive of dividends. The problem now was to make good on his enormous investment.

In full control at last, Orville's indecision vanished. His first step was to fire Alpheus Barnes. With personal business out of the way, he brought suit against the Curtiss Aeroplane and Motor Company on November 16, 1914. Over the next few months he spent long hours with the company lawyers preparing depositions to be used against Curtiss when the new case came to trial. In addition, he filed for a new patent incorporating changes and improvements developed since 1906.[25]

Orville was now ready to reveal the final step in his plan: putting the Wright Company up for sale. In spite of the reverses suffered in 1913–14, it remained a going concern. In addition to the factory in Dayton, the Wright name was still worth a great deal to anyone interested in manufacturing airplanes. Moreover, by renewing his pursuit of Curtiss in the courts, Orville underscored the continuing value and importance of his patents.

In the end, Orville proved to be a very successful businessman. His handling of the negotiations for the sale was masterful. The final agreement with a group of New York financiers was signed on October 15, 1915. Although the full amount of the purchase price was not disclosed, the *New York Times* reported that Orville received roughly

$1.5 million, plus an additional $25,000 for his services as chief consulting engineer during the first year of the new company's operation.[26]

The reorganized Wright Company made a valiant effort to keep
pace with advances in aeronautical technology. The first models developed under the new management, the Wright K and L, were tractor
biplanes that bore little resemblance to the old Wright pattern. Ultimately, however, the effort was unsuccessful. The Wright Company
continued to lose money until 1916, when it merged with the Glenn L.
Martin Company and the Simplex Automobile Company of New
Brunswick, New Jersey, to create the Wright-Martin Company. The
new organization transferred operations to the Simplex manufacturing plant and obtained a major contract from the French government
for the production of 450 Hispano-Suiza aircraft engines.[27]

Wright-Martin prospered as an engine, rather than airframe, producer. Dissatisfied with that orientation, Glenn Martin left the firm to
reestablish his own Glenn L. Martin Company in 1917. The Wright-
Martin Company was reorganized once again in 1919 as the Wright
Aeronautical Company; it would emerge as the most innovative and
successful aeronautical engine company in the nation during the
1920s.

With the sale of the company in 1915, Orville walked away from the
entire business. He did not have much serious involvement in developing the last of the Wright Company machines, nor did the new management feel that he had done much to earn his contract salary. The
arrangement was not renewed and Orville broke his final connection
with the firm that he and his brother had founded only five years
before.

The patent suit was no longer his problem. Orville accepted the
appellate court decision of January 1914 as his final vindication. The
Wright Company continued to pursue the matter in court, but there
would never be a firm legal resolution of the remaining issues. The
situation was further complicated by the fact that Curtiss, which now
held a number of significant patents of its own, began to threaten
other companies with infringement suits.

With American entry into World War I in April 1917, the government took steps to resolve the entire patent mess. Representatives of
the concerned companies formed a Manufacturers Aircraft Association. As part of a plan developed by W. Benton Crisp, who was still
working as a Curtiss retainer, the members of the new organization

entered into cross-licensing agreements permitting a member firm use of the patented technology after payment of a blanket fee. In exchange for that agreement, the principal patent holders, Wright-Martin and Curtiss, resolved their differences and received $2 million each. Seven years after Wilbur brought the original suit against Curtiss, the patent wars died.[28]

The extent to which the old animosities were left behind was evident in 1929, when Clement M. Keys merged Wright Aeronautical and Curtiss Aeroplane and Motor to form a giant new combine, Curtiss-Wright, the second-largest manufacturer of aircraft and engines in the nation. Scarcely anyone noticed the irony.

chapter 34

CARRYING ON ALONE

November 1915

O rville Wright was forty-three when he sold the Wright Company
in the fall of 1915. The arrangement freed him from burdensome duties and left him a very wealthy man. He paid off the
loans that had financed the company takeover and spread the profits
through a program of investments that gradually increased his fortune and enabled the family to live well for the rest of their lives.

Orville broke one more tie with the past soon after disposing of the
company. In June 1916, he began work on a one-story laboratory at
15 North Broadway, just down the block and around the corner from
the bicycle shop.[1]

He and Will had long dreamed of a specialized workshop where they
could recapture the thrill of discovery. The brothers had purchased
the lot in 1909, when they were too involved with business problems
to plan the laboratory. Now it would be Orville's building alone. He
moved in that November, finally giving up the lease on the old shop
at 1127 West Third that held so many memories.

Orville was not certain what sort of research he would pursue, but
he did have several ideas he was anxious to explore and a group of
friends willing to invest in him. Those friends—Edward A. Deeds,
Charles F. Kettering, and the Harold Talbotts, a father and son
team—were long-time associates and business partners.

Deeds and Kettering earned their reputations while working under
John H. Patterson at the National Cash Register Company. They
founded a company of their own in 1914, the Dayton Engineering

Laboratories (DELCO), to produce an automobile self-starter developed by Kettering in Deeds's barn. The profits of that venture were plowed into a second firm, the Dayton Metal Products Company, which they founded with the Talbotts, local building contractors.[2]

The Dayton Airplane Company was their next joint project. The new firm was organized immediately after the Wright-Martin Company shifted production from Dayton to New Jersey in March 1917. The original Wright Company factory buildings had been leased to another firm, but some of the department heads and many trained workmen were reluctant to move. Orville believed that the availability of this pool of skilled labor inspired Edward Deeds "to start a small company to carry out some experiments in connection with some ideas of mine which he wished to see brought out."[3]

Whatever Orville's ideas were, the new company did not pursue them. War had raged in Europe for over three years and, in spite of President Wilson's assurances, America was being drawn into the conflict. Deeds and his associates knew nothing about airplanes but they were convinced that their experience in solving production problems could be helpful when there was a fortune to be made in military contracts.

Moreover, they had several major advantages over potential competitors, including their friendship with Orville Wright, who not only loaned his name to the enterprise but signed on as consulting engineer. Other friends were even more useful. Howard Coffin, president of the Hudson Motor Car Company and an old friend of Deeds and Kettering, was the new head of the Aircraft Production Board, an agency charged with mobilizing American industry to produce enough airplanes to darken the skies over the battlefields of Europe.

With American entry into the war, Deeds was commissioned a colonel and placed in command of aircraft procurement for the Aircraft Production Board. He divested himself of his financial interest in the firm, which had been reorganized as the Dayton-Wright Company in April, then awarded his old associates two contracts for the production of 4,400 aircraft, 4,000 warplanes, and 400 trainers. Dayton-Wright operated out of a series of buildings constructed at South Field, near Dayton, on land owned by Edward Deeds.[4]

Orville was commissioned a major in the Aviation Section of the Signal Officers Reserve Corps, but he did not wear a uniform or refer to his rank in correspondence. He told his English friend Griffith Brewer that there was some talk of calling him to Washington for the duration. Instead, he was ordered to remain at home, working with the engineers at Dayton-Wright.

Air Service officials decided that the time lost in designing and testing new American aircraft could be saved by contracting with U.S. manufacturers for the production of proven European models. A sample De Havilland 4, a British-built two-seat observation and bombing aircraft, was delivered to Dayton-Wright in April 1917. The company had a contract to produce four thousand of those machines, and four hundred J-1 trainers designed by an American firm, Standard Aircraft.

The task of building the DH-4s was more difficult than Dayton-Wright officials had supposed. The first problem was to prepare a complete set of new drawings, including the basic design changes required to accommodate an American-built Liberty engine power plant rather than the Rolls-Royce original.

Orville was heavily involved in these preparations that spring, summer, and fall, but he was far more interested in another project—the Kettering Bug. Designed to be sent against targets far behind German lines, the Bug was an unmanned flying bomb powered by a four-cylinder engine. Orville went to work on the project in the fall of 1917 and remained with it for the next year. The Bug showed promise, but was still in development when the Armistice was signed.[5]

The officials of Dayton-Wright took full advantage of Orville's public relations value. He piloted an airplane for the last time on May 13, 1918, flying one of his 1911 machines in formation with the first Dayton-built DH-4 while the newsmen snapped away. After landing, he climbed into the DH-4 and went up again for a second ride, this time as a passenger.

Dayton-Wright needed all the favorable publicity it could get. The record of the company, and of the U.S. airframe and engine industry as a whole, was mixed. There were some bright spots, notably the development of the beautifully engineered Liberty engine and the production of such American-designed and built aircraft as the Curtiss JN-4D "Jenny" trainer. The disappointments, however, were overwhelming.

The promised aerial armada failed to materialize. A trickle of U.S.-built aircraft arrived in France, but in numbers much lower than predicted. The quality of the American product was questioned as well. The legend of the "flaming coffin" would be applied to the Dayton-built DH-4s before war's end.

Grover Loening was among the small manufacturers who complained that their bids for government contracts had been rejected in favor of large firms that substituted influence in Washington for experience in aircraft construction. Dayton-Wright was their favorite target.

It was Gutzon Borglum, a sculptor with an ego to match the size of the faces that he would one day carve from the rock of Mount Rushmore, who first raised the cry of scandal. Borglum, a self-styled aviation expert, wrote to President Wilson in the fall of 1917 complaining that the Aircraft Production Board had ignored a design he submitted. Newspapers echoed the charges of collusion and conspiracy. A Senate investigating committee substantiated a great many of the allegations, including the fact that Deeds had shown favoritism to his friends. President Wilson appointed Charles Evans Hughes, ex-presidential candidate and future Chief Justice of the Supreme Court, to head a special commission to study the aircraft procurement program.

The Hughes Commission did not bring charges against Deeds, but it documented examples of mismanagement and favoritism and suggested that the Army court-martial him. The Army finally decided against such drastic action. Orville himself testified before the Hughes Committee, but he was neither a stockholder nor a decision maker in the Dayton-Wright Company, and avoided being tarnished.

Dayton-Wright survived the scandal. After the war, the firm produced a series of interesting aircraft, including the R.B. Racer, and the XPS-1, the first airplane in the U.S. Army inventory to feature retractable landing gear. General Motors bought the company in 1919, and kept it going until June 1, 1923, when the automotive giant pulled out of the airplane business.

Orville retained a tenuous connection with the company until GM closed the doors, serving as a consulting engineer on special projects, including the R.B. Racer. He remained in his West Side laboratory most of the time, as he had during the war, making occasional trips out to the plant to consult with old friends like James H. Jacobs, one of the men who went back to the old days of the original Wright Company.

Together, the two of them developed and patented the split flap, a trailing edge device designed to increase lift and enable a pilot to reduce the speed of his machine in a steep dive. Even here there was disappointment. A Navy Bureau of Aeronautics Report issued in January 1922 dismissed the split flap as being of no value. Twenty years later, a new generation of naval aviators operating Douglas SBD Dauntless dive bombers in the Pacific would return a very different verdict.[6]

The split flap was Orville's last important technical contribution to aeronautics. With the demise of Dayton-Wright, he retired from active flight research and severed his final ties with American industry.

Yet during the mid-1920s, Orville emerged as one of the most revered men of his generation. There was a mythic quality to his fame. As the sole survivor of the team that had given flight to the world, he was seen as the living embodiment of an American tradition of heroic invention that stretched back to the early years of the Republic. He was, quite literally, a legend in his own time—an exemplar and an inspiration for future generations of Americans.

For all his fame, Orville remained something of a puzzle. Those who met him were frequently startled by the disparity between their expectations and reality. A *New Yorker* reporter who visited Dayton to do a profile of Orville in 1930 expected to meet a legend. Instead, he found a "gray man . . . dressed in gray clothes." "Not only have his hair and his mustache taken on that tone, but [also] his curiously flat face . . . a timid man whose misery at meeting you is so keen that, in common decency, you leave as soon as you can."[7]

Orville could never mask his painful shyness. He was uncomfortable even when accepting the plaudits of an admiring crowd. At the same time, he knew that he could not escape that role. The result was an unsatisfactory compromise between his desire for privacy and the need to represent Wilbur and the other members of the family with dignity. Orville was the honored guest at scores of banquets over the years, but he absolutely refused to speak from the podium. He would not so much as offer an after-dinner thank you into a microphone, although he did, on occasion, write comments to be read by others. Requests for radio interviews were dismissed out of hand, and there are no known recordings of his voice.

There were those who sought to trap him into making a short speech. On the occasion of the fortieth anniversary of powered flight in 1943, he was honored by cabinet members, congressional leaders, and high-ranking military officers at a black-tie dinner in Washington. As usual, he agreed to attend only with the understanding that he would not be invited to speak.

The chairman had no intention of honoring that agreement. Without warning, Orville was asked to step forward and present the Collier Trophy to his one-time student, General "Hap" Arnold. Stony-faced, he walked to the podium, handed the trophy to the embarrassed Arnold, and returned to his chair without uttering a word.[8]

The tension between desire and duty was also apparent in the record of Orville's long-time service on various aeronautical boards and commissions. His most important and longstanding relationship with a government agency began in 1920, when President Wilson appointed him a member of the National Advisory Committee for Aeronautics (NACA).

Founded in 1915, the NACA was charged with aiding the fledgling American aircraft industry by conducting research and development. The agency was not in the business of building airplanes; its job was to identify key research problems whose solution would open the way to further progress. The first and most important of the NACA facilities, the Langley Research Center, opened at Hampton Roads, Virginia, in 1917. The discoveries emerging from wind tunnels and laboratories at Langley over the next twenty years help to explain the rise of the U.S. aircraft industry from a position of weakness in 1918 to world leadership by 1940.

The work of the NACA was directed by the committee whose name it bore. And the members had supervisory authority over the heart of the organization—the research program.

Orville remained a member of the NACA longer than anyone else in the history of the committee. His record of attendance at the annual and semiannual meetings over a period of twenty-eight years was exemplary, yet his personal contributions had no special impact on the NACA program. He concentrated on those issues of greatest interest to him, such as championing the cause of the small inventors who wrote in search of advice or assistance. He participated in discussions but rarely exercised leadership.[9]

His service on the board overseeing the operation of the Daniel and Florence Guggenheim Fund for the Promotion of Aeronautics followed a similar pattern. The single most important privately funded effort to improve the quality of American aeronautical enterprise during the interwar years, the Guggenheim Fund began operation in 1926 and went out of business in 1930. The Guggenheims did not intend the fund to be self-perpetuating; rather, they were convinced that a sudden infusion of cash aimed at particular areas of research over a short period might lead to major breakthroughs in aeronautics. They were right.

An elder statesman of aeronautics, Orville spent much of his time attending conferences during the 1920s and 1930s. Here he sits with fellow members of the board of
the Daniel and Florence Guggenheim Fund for the Promotion of Aeronautics at Port
Washington, Long Island, December 13, 1928. (Standing, from the right: Nobel laureate Robert Millikan, Harry Guggenheim, Charles Lindbergh. Seated, from the right:
William F. Durand, Orville Wright, Daniel Guggenheim.)

The fund underwrote the establishment of aeronautical engineering programs at major universities from coast to coast. Perhaps the
most visible result of this program was the creation of the Guggenheim Aeronautical Laboratory at the California Institute of Technology (GALCIT). Under the leadership of the redoubtable Hungarian
scientist/engineer Theodore von Karman, GALCIT quickly became a
major center for research into the esoteric realm of high-speed flight
and rocket-engine technology.

The members of the Guggenheim board funded pioneering research
leading to the development of early "blind-flying" instruments and
sponsored the most important of all U.S. aircraft safety competitions.
The fund was short-lived but had an extraordinary impact. Through
his faithful attendance at meetings and his participation in the deliber-
ations of the board, Orville helped to shape a program of lasting
importance. His name was a distinct asset to the work of the fund. As
in the case of the NACA, however, he rarely exercised leadership on
the Guggenheim board.[10]

Like his grandfather and father before him, he responded to pressure by establishing a buffer between himself and the outside world. That was Mabel Beck's role. She was the gatekeeper who screened those who wished to contact Orville Wright. After Katharine and the nieces, she was the most important woman in his life.

Roy Knabenshue brought Miss Beck into the Wright Company as his secretary in 1910. Following the dissolution of the exhibition team, she went to work in the president's office as Wilbur's secretary. Orville liked her and kept her on. Within a matter of months she had become indispensable to him.

Her job was her life. No one came to Orville Wright except through her and, as an old friend of Orville's once remarked, "she was not one to be smarty with."

Acerbic and abrasive, Miss Beck was never a favorite with those closest to Orville. Even the men whom he regarded as his best friends—aeronautical journalist Earl Findley, the English writer Griffith Brewer, and Wright biographer Fred Kelly, for example—approached her with caution. They may not have liked Miss Beck, but they could not afford to offend her.

Orville was never a prompt or reliable correspondent. Mabel Beck was the channel though which most of his friends communicated with him. That presented special problems for men like Findley and Kelly, whose friendship with Orville had economic and professional value.

Both were journalists who built their early reputations at least in part on the success of interviews with Orville. In later life, Findley earned his living as the editor of *U.S. Air Services*, a leading aeronautical trade journal. Quotes, articles, and opinions from Orville became a hallmark of the magazine.

Kelly, a free-lance columnist and writer, based some of his most successful pieces on the career of his friend. He was the authorized biographer of the Wright brothers, and the editor of the first volume of their published papers.

For both Kelly and Findley, access to the historic letters, diaries, journals, and photos stored in the laboratory on North Broadway was through Miss Beck. She knew the story, and the materials, as well as Orville did. She was the one who answered their questions, or urged Orville to do so. And when Orville was displeased, Miss Beck delivered the bad news.

Findley could cite bitter experience. In 1915, at the very beginning of their friendship, Orville agreed to allow Findley and a young friend, John R. McMahon, to prepare a biography of the Wright brothers.

They visited Dayton, interviewed Orville, Milton, and Katharine at length, and were given limited access to the papers.

They worked for six months on a first draft, which Findley mailed to Orville. Confined to bed with back pain, Orville thought the manuscript entirely too personal and chatty. Rather than explaining his feelings directly, he asked Mabel Beck to reject it, commenting: "I would rather have the sciatica." She did so, using precisely those words.[11]

The family regarded Miss Beck with undisguised disdain. "After some twenty years," Lorin's daughter Ivonette recalled,

> she became more and more possessive. She knew that with her knowledge of the Wright story in all its aspects, she had a job for life. Knowing Orville, she was sure he'd never make a change. She felt the power of her position and seemed to want to alienate everyone from Orville in order to have his full attention for herself. She tried to alienate my father, Lorin, but was not successful. She tried to push her way into Orville's household, but she ran into spunky little Carrie [Kayler Grumbach, the Wright housekeeper for half a century], who was a match for her. Carrie told "Mr. Orv" if "that woman" ever came in the front door of the house, she would leave by the back door.[12]

Orville chided friends and family members for their inability to get along with Miss Beck, almost as though she was one of the practical jokes he took such delight in playing. Where Mabel Beck was concerned, not even Katharine could move her brother. It was clear that Orville approved of his secretary's manner and placed enormous value on her services.

Miss Beck was his first line of defense, but Orville developed other far more subtle means of insulating himself from the world. Consider, for example, the design for living embodied in his home, Hawthorn Hill, and in his summer retreat on Georgian Bay.

The decision to leave 7 Hawthorn Street, where the family had lived for forty-two years, did not come easily, but the old neighborhood was changing for the worse. Wilbur and Orville originally selected a small lot on the corner of Salem Avenue and Harvard Boulevard, but Katharine thought it too near the center of the city. She wanted a wooded lot on high ground. Wilbur and Orville grumbled, then acquiesced.

Hawthorn Hill, named for the lovely old hawthorn trees that dominated the crest of a rise overlooking Dayton, was the ideal compromise. The brothers bought the seventeen-acre site near the corner of Park Drive and Harmon Avenue in the affluent suburb of Oakwood in February 1912.[13] The new house began as Katharine's dream, but Orville took it over. Katharine believed that his original rough plans for the colonial mansion were inspired by the stately homes he had seen in Virginia in 1908 and 1909.

Wilbur took little interest in the project. Orville sent the preliminary floor plans to him during his stay in Europe in 1911. "You are wasting entirely too much space on halls," Wilbur replied.[14] For his part he wanted nothing more than a bedroom and a bath of his own. He died before construction began.

Orville turned his preliminary drawings over to the local architectural firm of Schenck & Williams, but followed every detail of the planning and construction. The interior and furnishings received the same close attention. Everything about the house had to be perfect. Painters unable to match the precise shade of red stain for the doors and woodwork were taken off the job. He did the work himself.

"When the carpeting first arrived," his niece recalled, "the design around the border wasn't exactly in line with the fireplace in the living room. Orville drew a detailed sketch of how the carpet should fit around the fireplace and sent it off to the rugmakers in Ireland. He got it changed to suit him."[15]

The house was Orville's machine for living. He designed the basic plumbing, heating, and electrical systems himself. "Knowing that rain water was mineral free," one family member explained, "he used it for all hot and cold bath water. He had it piped from the roof into a first cistern. To remove the sediment, color, and odor, he designed . . . a special filter through which he pumped this water into the second cistern. To clean this filter there was a system for pumping a backflow of the purified water through the filter, periodically."[16]

Water was dispensed in Orville's enormous second-floor bathroom through a series of circular shower pipes surrounding the bather from shoulder to knees. Special shields beneath the floor prevented any staining of the first-floor ceilings.

It was the same with the heating system. Standard controls were not acceptable. Orville regulated the temperature with a wire running from the furnace in the basement through the living room and on up to his bedroom. He was especially proud of an industrial vacuum system built into the walls so that Carrie had simply to plug her hose into an outlet in a room and throw the switch.[17]

Orville took great pleasure in maintaining all this. He devoted forty years of effort to fiddling with furnaces, plumbing, and wiring. With-

Orville, Katharine, and the bishop moved into their new home, Hawthorn Hill, in 1913.

out his constant attention they would have ceased to function. Carrie never did use the built-in vacuum—it seldom worked and created nothing but problems. When the National Cash Register Company purchased Hawthorn Hill as a guest house following Orville's death, its first move was to install a rational plumbing and heating system.

The house was filled with examples of domestic ingenuity.[18] Orville drilled a vertical hole in each arm of his favorite overstuffed easy chair to accommodate a homemade bookholder that could be shifted from side to side. The reading glasses on the stand next to the chair had only one temple; Orville removed the other so he could whip them on and off with ease. The walls of the surrounding rooms were covered in expensive damask that had to be stripped, washed, and rehung each year. Orville designed and built a special tool to do the job.

The summer home was as much a part of his life as Hawthorn Hill, and he shaped it in precisely the same way. Recovering from a severe bout of sciatica in the spring of 1916, he treated his father and sister to a three-month family vacation, the first they had ever taken.

Canadian citizens, in a gesture of support for the war effort, were renting out summer homes to vacationing Americans and investing the proceeds in war bonds. Orville chose a cottage on Waubeck Island, in Lake Huron's Georgian Bay. He fell in love with neighboring Lambert Island while exploring the Bay that summer. Before they returned to Dayton, Orville was the proud owner of the entire island, twenty acres of rocky Canadian real estate, complete with seven buildings: a main house; three smaller cottages; a pumphouse; an icehouse; and a tool shed. Thereafter he would return every summer until World War II.[19]

Orville had designed Hawthorn Hill himself. At Lambert Island he rearranged the existing buildings to suit his taste. "For exercise he was continually remodeling or moving the cabins," his grandnephew George Russell explained. "We cut up one cabin into several small sections and moved it several hundred feet and remodeled it to fit with the island."[20] He ripped out the old docks as well, replacing them with new models designed to survive the harsh winters.

As in Dayton, the plumbing system was a matter of special concern. Water was pumped out of the lake and into a 300-gallon water tower with an old gasoline motor that only Orville could start. From there it was piped into the kitchen of the main cabin, where a special line ran into the back of the icebox. Cold water was always on tap.

"Orville's Railway" was a special project that required several years to complete. Initially, it was nothing more than a small cart used to haul ice and baggage up a steep path of crushed gravel to the cottages on the crest of the hill. Within a few years Orville replaced that primitive system with a new cart running on a set of wooden rails. A cable and drum system driven by an outboard motor drew the cart up the incline. As with the pump, Orville was the only one who could operate the railway with any assurance.[21]

Outboard motors were the prime movers on Lambert Island. The automatic clothes washer consisted of a large metal tub set on a rod mounted at a 45-degree angle. Clothes were soaked, then placed in the tub. A Johnson motor down on the lake pumped a stream of water through a hose aimed at the tub. The clothes were thoroughly washed and spun in a single operation.[22]

Orville practiced the cooking skills developed at Kitty Hawk in the kitchen of the main house, which was filled with examples of his ingenuity. Fond of toast, he developed two special implements to guarantee a perfect product every time: a gauge to ensure that each slice of bread was cut to a precise thickness, and a toaster, con-structed of two sheets of metal, to compress each slice as it was toasting.

The domestic spaces that Orville fashioned with such care, and the bits and pieces of homespun technology with which he furnished them, were his psychological shield. Wrapped in an environment of his own design and construction, he created a private world that he could control.

Orville did his best to draw every member of the family into that private world. On April 3, 1917, Bishop Milton Wright, eighty-eight years old, died. The services, held two days later at Hawthorn Hill,

Orville (right), Katharine (second right), Horace (fourth left), Lorin (second left), and other family members enjoy a picnic.

were followed by burial next to Susan in the family plot at Woodland Cemetery.

Orville was head of the Wright clan now. Like his father, he was devoted to the notion of family. He shared Milton's passion for genealogy, picking up the search for lost and obscure Wright ancestors. He hired lawyers and researchers to locate the homestead near Hillsboro, Virginia, where his mother had been born. When they returned with a suggested birthplace that did not match descriptions offered by his aunt and cousins, he sent them back to work. As always, he wanted only precise knowledge.[23]

But the family was changing. Reuch died in 1920 and Lorin in 1939. Their children were growing older, going off to college, and starting families of their own. Orville was careful not to let the youngsters slip away, and he worked hard to draw their husbands, wives, and children into the circle. His strategy for accomplishing that was pure Orville.

Lorin's daughters, Ivonette and Leontine, were both married at Hawthorn Hill. "Uncle Orv" lost little time in teasing the new spouses and playing gentle practical jokes on them. Ivonette's new husband, Harold S. ("Scribze") Miller, was initiated at the annual Hawthorn

Hill Christmas dinner in 1919. Every person found his or her place at the table marked by a plain envelope containing a twenty-dollar bill—except for Miller, who found a small box of candy. "He thanked Uncle Orv for it," Ivonette recalled,

> and nothing more was said for awhile. Then someone spoke up and said to Scribze, "I'll bet there's a bill in yours somewhere, why don't you look and see?" Scribze said he was satisfied but because we all insisted, he opened the box of candy and went all through it—no money. He was becoming more and more embarrassed by the minute. Uncle Orv was chuckling all through the procedure, but said nothing. Finally, someone said, "Why don't you take the box apart? I'm sure it's in there somewhere." That he did, and slipped in under the cover of the box was his twenty dollar bill. Uncle Orv had carefully taken the cover off and pasted it back together again.[24]

Leontine's husband, John Jameson, was welcomed in similar fashion. They were married on a hot day in June 1923. Orville rigged a special cooling device, a fan blowing over a tub of cracked ice, in the hall where the groom was waiting for the ceremony to begin. "The blessedly cool air that was wafted over me was a lifesaver, I can tell you," Jameson recalled many years later. "Uncle Orv's eyes danced as they always did when his ingenuity triumphed over a difficulty—or when he successfully pulled off a practical joke. Thereafter he always delighted in reminding me how he 'put John on ice.' "[25]

Orville loved a good argument, and tried to goad those closest to him into impassioned debate. That had always been his way with Wilbur, and he saw no reason to change. He needled John Jameson, an advertising executive, about his profession. "What did I think about the economic wastefulness of advertising and how it exploited the people? He would mischievously try to goad me into an argument, which he loved and I usually avoided, because he could be pretty merciless at that game."[26]

Harold Miller, who operated a savings and loan company, faced a similar grilling on the ethics of moneylending. Orville went so far as to argue the case for Soviet communism in an effort to spark an argument with him:

> We never saw any of this hurtful aspect, and we did enjoy his playful teasing. We could always see the "tease" coming on, for it was always telegraphed ahead. His lips worked in a hidden smile in preparation, causing a "twitch" to his mustache in that familiar way when he was getting ready with something. We enjoyed his teasing way as much as he did, for we learned that he only teased those he cared for.[27]

The teasing and joking was Orville's way of drawing newcomers into the family circle, making them feel a part of things, and letting them know that he cared about them. It worked. Harold Miller and John Jameson grew extraordinarily fond of him, and he of them.

Over the years he invited even distant relatives to spend time with him at Hawthorn Hill or Lambert Island. He offered career advice and assistance to the youngsters, and helped to put several of them through college.

This concern for family members was genuine, but it was not purely altruistic. Like his father and grandfather, the family was to be his shelter from life.

No incident more clearly underscores the importance of family unity and trust in Orville's mind than his break with Katharine in 1926. The two had grown extraordinarily close over the years. Katharine was her brother's staunchest defender, his strongest supporter, his best friend. He was closer to her than to anyone else in life, including Wilbur.

Orville believed that he and his sister were bound by a firm understanding—they were the sole survivors. Through it all, from Milton's early church difficulties to the patent wars, they had avoided any entangling personal relationships outside the family circle. Their sole allegiance was to one another.

In this family, such informal agreements had the force of law. They loved, trusted, and depended upon one another to an extraordinary degree, but each expected the other to stick to a bargain.

In later life, Orville assumed that the old bargain of mutual and exclusive support was still in effect between Katharine and himself. He was satisfied and had no intention of violating the pact. No one would ever have a more important place in his life than his sister.

Katharine was less comfortable with the arrangement. In the summer of 1926 she announced her engagement to Henry J. Haskell, an old college friend and fellow Oberlin trustee. They had been courting for over a year before they even told Orville of the relationship.

Orville was dumbfounded. He turned his back on his sister, who married Haskell on November 20, 1926—at Oberlin rather than in her own home. The Haskells moved to Kansas City, where Henry became the editor and part owner of the Kansas City *Star*. Katharine was desperate for a reconciliation with her brother; Orville remained unyielding.

Two years after the wedding, Katharine contracted pneumonia. It

In 1915 Katharine told a visitor that, while they loved Hawthorn Hill, "we were always happy on Hawthorn Street."

was obvious that she would not survive, yet Orville refused to go to her. He finally traveled to Kansas City at Lorin's insistence, arriving in time to be with her when she died on March 3, 1929. With Haskell's approval, he brought Katharine's body back to Dayton and laid her to rest next to their father, mother, and older brother.

Some members of the family blamed the estrangement on the jealous influence of Mabel Beck, with whom Katharine had never gotten along. It is not necessary to look for any outside influence. From Orville's point of view, it was brutally simple: Katharine violated a sacred pact. In admitting another man into her life, she had rejected her brother. Katharine, of all people, had shaken his faith in the inviolablity of the family ties that provided his emotional security.[28]

chapter 35

THE SMITHSONIAN FEUD

January 1914-January 1940

From the year 1869, when the great debate over secret societies erupted within the Church of the United Brethren in Christ, until Orville's death in 1948, there was scarcely a time when the members of the Wright family were not deeply involved in one controversy or another. They had survived them all: the Radical-Liberal fight; the schism; the Old Constitution–New Constitution legal suits; the Keiter affair; and the long string of disputes involving the invention of the airplane, culminating in the patent suits of 1910–15.

With the sale of the company, Orville hoped to retire from the battle. Instead, he was drawn into the longest and most publicized controversy of his career—a feud with officials of the Smithsonian Institution that would last for almost thirty years.

It began with the Curtiss patent suit. The U.S. Circuit Court of Appeals handed down its final decision in favor of the Wright Company on January 13, 1914, but that was not the end of the matter. Curtiss and patent specialist W. Benton Crisp had found that it might be possible to fly an airplane in which each aileron was operated separately without violating any of the provisions already upheld. Curtiss announced that he would do just that, forcing Orville and his company to bring an entirely new suit.

At best, the strategy was little more than a stopgap measure. Orville filed the new complaint on November 16, 1914. There was every indication that he would be upheld once again, but it would take time. Curtiss used that time to mount a fresh attack on the basic validity of the patent.

The fact that the Wrights had been the first to fly was essential to the broad interpretation of their patent. Curtiss could not prove that anyone else had flown before the Wrights. He might, however, be able to demonstrate that some experimenter had been *capable* of flight before December 17, 1903, but had not actually flown for reasons beyond his control. It would not be a strong legal argument, but Curtiss had few alternatives.

Looking for a suitable candidate, Curtiss began to consider the work of Samuel Pierpont Langley, who had died in 1906. Charles D. Walcott, now secretary of the Smithsonian, had played an important role in funding the 1903 Aerodrome and was anxious to redeem the reputation of his old friend.

Walcott had set a Langley Memorial Tablet into the wall of the Smithsonian Castle, established a Langley Medal for contributions to aeronautics, and created a Langley Laboratory that he hoped would become a national facility for aeronautical research. May 6, the day on which the first of the steam-powered Aerodrome models had been flown in 1896, was proclaimed an official holiday at the Institution— Langley Day.

On January 21, 1914, eight days after the U.S. Circuit Court handed down its decision in favor of the Wrights, Lincoln Beachey, the best-known American stunt pilot of the day, wired the Smithsonian requesting to borrow the surviving parts of the 1903 Aerodrome so that he could rebuild and fly the craft. Beachey was scarcely a disinterested party—he had learned to fly at the Curtiss school, had been the star aerial performer on the Curtiss exhibition team, and remained a Curtiss stockholder.

Smithsonian administrator Richard Rathbun passed the telegram on to Walcott with a recommendation: "I do not think you will want to grant Mr. Beachey's request." Alexander Graham Bell, a Smithsonian regent, and a friend of both Langley and Walcott, agreed. Bell felt that the Langley machine was too valuable an artifact to be tampered with or risked in flight, although he did suggest that an exact replica might be constructed.[1]

Walcott refused Beachey, but the idea took hold. The ultimate step in redeeming Langley's reputation would be to fly the Aerodrome, proving that, had conditions been only slightly different, the honors heaped on Wilbur and Orville Wright might have gone to Samuel Pierpont Langley.

When Glenn Curtiss brought one of his float planes to Washington to participate in the 1914 Langley Day celebration, he remarked to

Walcott that he "would like to put the Langley aeroplane itself in the air."[2] This time Walcott jumped at the chance. Without informing Bell or any of the Smithsonian regents, he authorized A. F. Zahm, a Curtiss witness in the patent trial who was now in charge of the Langley Laboratory, to turn over the fuselage, engine, propellers, various bits of tubing, and "a few wing ribs" of the old machine to Curtiss. In addition, Walcott provided $2,000 to underwrite rebuilding and testing.

"The main objects of these renewed trials," Zahm explained, "were first to show whether the original Langley machine was capable of sustained free flight with a pilot, and secondly, to determine more fully the advantages of the tandem wing type of aeroplane."[3] There were better ways to test tandem-wing airplanes than by rebuilding the shattered remnants of an eleven-year-old machine that had refused to fly in the first place. Clearly, the only real purpose of the tests was to demonstrate that the Langley machine had been "capable" of flight in 1903.

Curtiss, the Smithsonian, and Zahm all stood to benefit if the craft proved airworthy. Curtiss could return to court arguing that the pioneer status granted the Wright patent was unwarranted. Walcott would demonstrate to the world that his old friend Langley had not really failed after all. And Zahm would gain revenge on Orville for the supposed slights offered to him at the outset of the patent suit in 1910.

Curtiss and Zahm announced that they would return the Aerodrome to its condition at the time of the 1903 tests. If that was their goal, they failed to achieve it. The wings constructed in the Curtiss plant differed from the originals in chord, camber, and aspect ratio.[4] The trussing system that linked the wings to the fuselage also bore little resemblance to the 1903 original. The kingposts had been relocated, and the wires were trussed to different spars at different points. This was particularly important, for most knowledgeable authorities believed that the failure of the wing structure, not a catapult defect, had been responsible for the disaster of 1903.

There were the other changes. Curtiss fitted the craft with his own yoke and wheel control system. After the first trial, the original rudder under the midpoint of the craft was tied off, and the large cruciform tail altered to serve as both rudder and elevator. Finally, Curtiss rejected the old catapult launch system, mounting the machine on floats. This last change can be excused in the name of self-preservation, though it does not seem to have occurred to anyone at the time that Curtiss had finally come up with a way to land the machine safely, something impossible with the original craft.

On the morning of May 28, 1914, the rebuilt Aerodrome, with Curtiss at the controls, lifted off the surface of Lake Keuka and flew 150 feet. After a few additional short hops, it was taken back into the shop, where the 1903 Langley engine was replaced with a modern Curtiss power plant and additional changes were made to the structure. Further flights followed with the altered craft that fall.

Walcott and Zahm were overjoyed. In an account of the tests published in the 1914 Smithsonian *Annual Report,* Zahm claimed the Aerodrome had demonstrated that, "with its original structure and power, it is capable of flying with a pilot and several hundred pounds of useful load. It is the first airplane in history of which this can truthfully be said." Far from providing a list of the alterations that had transformed failure into success, Zahm reported that the old Aerodrome had flown "without modification." "With a thrust of 450 pounds," he concluded, "the Langley aeroplane, without floats, restored to its original condition and provided with stronger bearings, should be able to carry a man and sufficient supplies for a voyage lasting practically the whole day."[5]

That was only the beginning. The 1915 *Report* repeated the claim that "The tests thus far made have shown that former Secretary Langley had succeeded in building the first aeroplane capable of sustained free flight with a man."[6] Similar statements were repeated in later Smithsonian publications.

Then there was the matter of labeling. When the Aerodrome was shipped back from Hammondsport, Walcott ordered it returned to its original 1903 condition. It was then exhibited in the Arts and Industries Building with a label explaining that it was "the first man-carrying aeroplane in the history of the world capable of sustained free flight."

Orville Wright was justifiably outraged. At the very outset of their careers, he and his brother had written to the Smithsonian for advice as to useful readings in the field of aeronautics. They were always careful to mention that the involvement of the world-renowned Samuel Langley in aeronautics had given them initial confidence. At the same time, they owed no technical debt to Langley, nor had they ever believed that his machine was capable of flight.

The Wright brothers' relationship with the Smithsonian began to sour after Langley's death. Walcott, at Bell's suggestion, presented the first Langley Medal to the Wrights. In preparing the text of their remarks for publication, however, the secretary used a section of an earlier Wright letter which "helped to create a false impression over the world that the Wrights had acknowledged indebtedness to Langley's scientific work."[7]

The brothers also became suspicious when, in 1910, Walcott all but refused their offer to donate the 1903 Wright airplane to the Smithsonian. Walcott had written in March 1910 requesting "one of your machines, or a model thereof, for exhibition purposes." The Wrights responded by offering to have a model of any of their craft constructed for the museum; or they could "reconstruct the 1903 machine with which the first flights were made at Kitty Hawk. Most of the parts are still in existence."

Walcott replied that the Smithsonian would really prefer the 1908 (actually 1909) military Flyer. In addition, he requested several scale models of Wright aircraft and some full-scale engines to display in conjunction with specimens from the Langley collection, "making the exhibit illustrate two very important steps in the history of the aeronautical art."[8]

The Smithsonian planned to exhibit the 12–16-horsepower Wright engine of 1903 next to the 52-horsepower Langley engine; a 1909 Wright aircraft with parts of the 1903 Langley machine; and small-scale models of manned Wright aircraft beside the larger unmanned Langley steam models of 1896. Small wonder that suspicions were aroused.

Now the Smithsonian was sponsoring the reconstruction and testing of the Langley machine by a man with whom the Wrights were locked in a bitter patent fight, and the work was to be overseen by A. F. Zahm, scarcely disinterested. Orville was worried, and anxious to obtain accurate information about the goings-on at Hammondsport.

Griffith Brewer traveled to Hammondsport on Orville's behalf in June 1914, just after the bits and pieces of the Aerodrome arrived from Washington. Orville's staunchest ally throughout the Smithsonian controversy, Brewer first met the brothers in 1908. A short hop with Wilbur at Le Mans gave him the distinction of being the first Englishman to fly. He helped to arrange the production of the first English Wright machines by Short Brothers, and after Wilbur's death, Orville entrusted him with the task of organizing the English Wright Company.

Brewer came to Dayton in 1914 to spend three months with Orville and Katharine. He planned to work on a book on the history of the airplane and to complete the requirements for a pilot's license. It was the first of thirty visits that he would make to Hawthorn Hill and Lambert Island by 1941.

Orville asked his friend for a favor. As a distinguished representative of the British aeronautical community, Brewer was in a perfect position to request a tour of the facility at Hammondsport, during which he could nose about for information on the Aerodrome project. Brewer agreed, and returned to Dayton with a series of photographs and other information suggesting that Curtiss workmen were making serious alterations to the old Langley machine.[9]

A year later, with the reconstruction of the Aerodrome complete and testing under way, Orville dispatched Lorin to the scene, putting him on a train for upstate New York on June 3, 1915. Arriving in Hammondsport the following day, Lorin looked around the Curtiss hangars on Lake Keuka shore and snapped a few photos of the Aerodrome. Up and about early the next morning, he watched through a pair of field glasses as Curtiss pilot Walter Johnson attempted a takeoff with the rebuilt craft. Johnson raced along the surface of the lake for perhaps 330 yards when the rear wings folded up.

Lorin reached the hangars just as the bedraggled machine was being towed ashore. He immediately began snapping pictures, attracting the attention of a group of workmen in the process. When Johnson confronted him and demanded the exposed film, Lorin had no choice but to comply. Fortunately, many of the changes made in the Aerodrome had already been documented by Brewer, or were visible in the photographs released by the Smithsonian.[10]

Orville was not certain how to respond. After the sale of the Wright Company he had no further legal interest in the patent suit and no immediate need to take action over the Langley trials. He was busy with his war work at Dayton-Wright, and concerned about the extent to which anything he said might be misunderstood. "A denial of these [Smithsonian] statements by me might have been looked upon by the public as a jealous attack upon the work of a man [Langley] who was dead," as he later told Chief Justice William Howard Taft, chairman of the Smithsonian's Board of Regents.[11]

Curtiss would undoubtedly have raised the issue had the patent suit been pressed to a conclusion. In 1916–17 he took one more step in that direction, building and flying an aircraft designed by the French experimenter Alexandre Goupil in 1883. As in the case of the Aerodrome, he took considerable liberties in transforming the original design into a flyable airplane.

The Curtiss lawyers were prepared to argue that the 1914 Aerodrome trials and the tests of the Goupil machine in 1916–17 demonstrated that other experimenters were capable of flight before the Wrights. We will never know how a court might have reacted to that argument. The suit collapsed in 1917 with the creation of a patent pool covering the entire industry, complete with a system of payments to the holders of both the Wright and Curtiss patents.

The legal issues were resolved by 1921, but Orville was growing more concerned. At the Smithsonian, Walcott and Zahm were busy rewriting the history of the airplane on the basis of the 1914 Hammondsport trials. Their message was clear: The Wrights may have been the first to fly, but Langley had been capable of doing it before them.

It was apparent that people, from the man on the street to trained engineers who should have known better, were listening. The *Literary Digest* proclaimed Dr. Langley "Discoverer of the Air," while *L'Aérophile,* the single most important aeronautical trade journal, praised the Smithsonian for doing "posthumous justice to a great pioneer." If Orville did not take action soon, the Smithsonian version would make its way into the history books.

"It was not until 1921 that I became convinced that the officials of the Smithsonian, at least Dr. Walcott, were fully acquainted with the character of the tests at Hammondsport," Orville explained. "I had thought up to that time that they might have been ignorant of the fundamental changes which had been incorporated in the machine before these tests were made, and that when these changes were pointed out to them, they would hasten to correct their erroneous reports. They did not do this, but have continued to repeat their earlier statements."[12]

It would not be easy to counter the Smithsonian effort, and Orville was reluctant to involve himself. Fortunately, Griffith Brewer was more than willing to help. On October 20, 1921, he gave a lecture entitled "Aviation's Greatest Controversy" on the subject of the 1914 Langley tests to the Royal Society of the Arts. Stripping away the propaganda issued by the Smithsonian over the previous eight years, he catalogued the changes made to the 1903 Aerodrome during the first and second episodes of rebuilding at Hammondsport. To most unbiased observers the evidence seemed overwhelming—the 1914 tests had not demonstrated that the 1903 Langley Aerodrome was capable of flight.[13]

The Brewer report sparked an immediate reaction. A new crop of articles with such titles as "On a Matter of Fraud" and "The Scandal of the First Man-Carrying Aeroplane" appeared in the press. Aviation leaders who had accepted the Smithsonian assertions at face value were stunned. The English aeronautical engineer Leonard Bairstow spoke for many when he commented that "the Hammondsport trials were not part of the work of Langley, and in the opinion of many of us were ill-advised."[14]

Although public opinion was swinging in his favor, Orville felt like David battling Goliath. He hoped that Smithsonian officials would retract their false claims for the 1903 Aerodrome and offer a public apology. Instead, Walcott and his staff ignored what was happening. Orville's attempts to go over Walcott's head by writing to Chief Justice Taft were no help. The members of the Smithsonian establishment were content to sit quietly until the storm of controversy passed.

In the end, Orville proved to be a better strategist than either his father or his brother in their legal battles. In the spring of 1925, he announced that he would send the 1903 Wright airplane to the Science Museum of London. The decision created a furor. In response to those who asked him to reconsider, Orville replied:

> I believe that my course in sending our Kitty Hawk machine to a foreign museum is the only way of correcting the history of the flying machine, which by false and misleading statements has been perverted by the Smithsonian Institution. In its campaign to discredit others in the flying art, the Smithsonian has issued scores of these false and misleading statements. They can be proved to be false and misleading from documents. But the people of today do not take the trouble to examine the evidence.
>
> With this machine in any American museum the national pride would be satisfied; nothing further would be done and the Smithsonian would continue its propaganda. In a foreign museum this machine will be a constant reminder of the reasons for its being there, and after the people and petty jealousies of this day are gone, the historians of the future may examine the evidence impartially and make history accord with it. Your regret that this old machine must leave the country can hardly be so great as my own.[15]

Most Americans were not aware that the 1903 Wright airplane was still in existence. Orville himself had scarcely given it any thought until 1916, when Massachusetts Institute of Technology officials asked to exhibit the historic craft as part of the ceremonies marking the opening of two new Institute buildings. He and Jim Jacobs of the Dayton-Wright Company pulled the parts out of the crate and began the job of reconstruction, adding new material only where absolutely necessary to repair the damage that had occurred in 1903.

The world's first airplane was displayed at MIT on June 11–13, 1916. Walcott requested the loan of the machine that December, but Orville would no longer consider such an arrangement with the organization that had sponsored the Hammondsport tests. It was shown again at the Pan-American Aeronautical Exhibition at the Grand Central Palace in New York on February 8–15, 1917, and twice more in Dayton during the years 1918–25.

Sending the 1903 machine to a foreign museum was a stroke of political genius. Orville's announcement galvanized public attention and put the Smithsonian on the defensive. The world's first airplane was a national treasure. Ultimately, the National Museum could not allow the craft to remain abroad where it would serve as a perpetual reminder of the controversy. Now Orville could afford to sit and wait.

Lester Gardner, founder of *Aviation,* became a spokesman for the Wright cause:

> For many years it has been no secret that the original Wright airplane would not be entrusted to the Smithsonian so long as the influences that had conducted the Langley propaganda in this country were in charge. . . . But now that Orville Wright has decided to send it to the English Museum the public may awake to some of the damage done by the zeal of Langley's friends.[16]

Secretary Walcott, on the defensive for the first time, attempted to buttress his position. Recognizing that he could no longer base his claim that the Langley Aerodrome had been "capable" of flight solely on the Hammondsport tests, he invited Joseph S. Ames and David Wilson Taylor, both recognized aviation authorities and distinguished members of the National Advisory Committee for Aeronautics, to offer a judgment.

Ames and Taylor were apparently not provided with a complete list of the changes made to the Aerodrome in 1914. While they admitted that the 1914 machine had been much stronger than that of 1903, they concluded that "structurally the original Langley machine was capable of level and controlled flight." They argued that, although the Wrights "were the first to navigate the air," Langley, "after years of effort, following a different road, was in sight of the same goal."[17]

Orville Wright disagreed, as did most of the rest of the American aeronautical community and the qualified engineers who have examined the craft since that time. But Walcott, resting his case on the report, refused to budge.

Charles D. Walcott died in 1927. His successor, Charles Greeley Abbot, reduced the label on the Aerodrome to read: "Langley Aerodrome—The Original Langley Flying Machine of 1903, Restored." Moreover, in 1928 the Smithsonian Board of Regents passed a resolution declaring that "to the Wrights belongs the credit of making the first successful flight with a power-propelled, heavier-than-air machine carrying a man." The resolution was meaningless. No one, not even Walcott, had questioned the Wrights priority in having *made* the first flight. The controversy involved the capability of the Langley machine to fly.

Charles Abbot and Orville met and corresponded, seeking a solution that would satisfy Orville without unduly embarrassing the Smithsonian. Speaking in Washington on December 17, 1933, Abbot suggested the creation of a committee to mediate the differences between them, and proposed that Charles Lindbergh should head the group. Orville accepted, spelling out his understanding of the arrangement.

He suggested that the work of the committee should be limited to a study of the specific problem, that is, the Smithsonian claim that the 1914 Hammondsport tests had demonstrated the capability of the 1903 Aerodrome for flight. If the committee judged that the machine was so capable, Orville would bring the 1903 Wright airplane home. If Wright was vindicated, however, he would expect the Smithsonian to "rectify the offenses committed by it in the past in its own publications by printing full corrections in these same publications. These corrections shall be unequivocal, and shall be given a prominence and circulation equal to that given to the former statements of which they are a correction, so that in the future the matters involved can not be misunderstood."[18]

Lindbergh, anxious to help, met with Abbot and Wright independently in January 1934. He told both men that he believed the first step should be to establish the basic facts in the case. He asked Orville Wright to begin the process by preparing a statement of the important differences between the 1903 Aerodrome and the machine flown at Hammondsport in 1914.

Lindbergh met with Abbot again in late January. In a letter describing that meeting to Orville Wright, Abbot said that Lindbergh feared he would not be able to devote enough time to the problems involved, and suggested that the Secretaries of War, Navy, and Commerce each be asked to name an individual to serve on a committee to weigh the evidence. Abbot then proposed that this committee be asked to address five specific questions:

1. In what ways was the 1914 machine similar to the 1903 Aerodrome?
2. In what ways was it different?
3. What bearing did the 1914 tests have on a determination of the capacity of the 1903 machine to fly?
4. What bearing did the flights of Langley's models in 1896 and 1903 have on the determination of the capacity of the full-scale 1903 Aerodrome to fly?
5. What other facts, if any, would assist in determining the capacity of the 1903 Aerodrome to fly?

Orville was not willing to accept such a committee. Each of the Secretaries, he noted, already had some official connection with the Smithsonian. He left unspoken the obvious fact that he should have an opportunity to participate in the selection process. Moreover, he believed that Abbot's proposed charge to the group was much too broad. Orville was really interested in only two things: a published list of the differences between the 1903 Aerodrome and the 1914 Hammondsport machine, and an admission by the Smithsonian that the craft was heavily modified.[19]

Orville then proceeded as if the committee proposal had never been made. He sent Lindbergh a list based on Griffith Brewer's 1921 paper, with the specific dimensions of the 1903 Langley Aerodrome on one side of the page and those of the 1914 machine on the other, so that any reader could see the differences at a glance.

Lindbergh passed this list on to Abbot who, finding no substantial errors, proposed that it be published as part of a long article which would include:

1. An account of Langley's work up to 1903.
2. A history of the Aerodrome from 1903 to 1914.
3. Republication of Zahm's original article of 1914.
4. Orville's comparison of the 1903 and 1914 machines.
5. Zahm's notes on Orville's list of changes.
6. The facts relating to the subsequent exhibition of the 1903 machine since 1914.

Once again, Orville demurred. Abbot was suggesting that his simple comparison of the 1903 and 1914 machines be buried in a mass of extraneous material, including a republication of the offending article that launched the controversy in the first place. On March 15, 1935, he wrote to Abbot outlining in clear and precise terms the sort of article that might lead to the return of the 1903 Wright Flyer.[20]

> Instead of a paper such as you have proposed may I offer the following suggestion: That the Smithsonian publish a paper presenting a list of specifications in parallel columns of those features of the Langley machine of 1903 and the Hammondsport machine of 1914, in which there were differences, with an introduction stating that the Smithsonian now finds that it was misled by the Zahm report of 1914; that through the Zahm paper the Institution was led to believe that the aeroplane tested at Hammondsport was "as nearly as possible in its original condition"; that as a result of this misinformation the Smithsonian had published erroneous statements from time to time alleging that the original Langley machine, without modification, or with only such modifications as were necessary for the addition of floats, had been successfully flown at Hammondsport in 1914; that it ask its readers to disregard all of its former statements and expressions of opinion regarding the flights at Hammondsport in 1914, because these were based on misinformation as the list to follow will show. The list and specifications are to be agreed upon by the Smithsonian, Colonel Lindbergh and myself.[21]

It was Orville Wright's last word on the subject. He would not require the Smithsonian to admit that the 1903 Aerodrome was incapable of flight. A simple admission that the Smithsonian statements relating to the 1914 tests were untrue would do. Abbot did not respond to the proposal.

Lindbergh, both fascinated and puzzled by the controversy, offered a thoughtful assessment in a 1939 diary entry. The fault, he believed, lay "primarily with the Smithsonian people. But Orville Wright is not an easy man to deal with in the matter. I don't blame him much, though, when I think of the way he was treated for a period of years. He has encountered the narrow-mindedness of science and the dishonesty of commerce."[22]

The tide of public opinion was clearly running in Orville's favor. During the next eight years Abbot was bombarded with scores of petitions, most of them the result of a drive sponsored by the aviation magazine *Contact*, asking that the Smithsonian take the requisite steps to get back the 1903 Flyer. Bills were introduced into Congress calling for an investigation and the creation of a committee to resolve the dispute. A new organization, Men With Wings, was established to support the return of the airplane from England. Private citizens and aviation leaders offered to mediate a solution.

Liberty, Collier's, and other national magazines took up the cry with articles entitled "Bring Home the Wright Plane," "The Road to Justice," and "Bring Back Our Winged Exile." With the exception of the acerbic English editor C. G. Grey, the aviation trade press was almost exclusively pro-Wright. Some of these journals, notably Earl Findley's *U.S. Air Services,* the oldest-surviving American aviation magazine, waged editorial campaigns against the Smithsonian.

It was an extraordinarily difficult time for Abbot. By the mid-1930s, the feud threatened to do irreparable damage to the reputation of the Institution. Orville was portrayed as the oppressed citizen beset by a powerful government bureaucracy blind to justice.[23]

By 1940 both men had given up hope of reaching an agreement. In response to a letter from the president of the National Cash Register Corporation asking that he make one more attempt to negotiate a solution, Abbot replied: "I regret that the Institution's experience on this subject during the past ten years, when it has made many efforts to compose these differences, has been so unpleasant and discouraging that without trustworthy assurances of success, the Institution would now hesitate to move at all . . . lest it should only arouse renewed misrepresentation."[24]

From the time of his entry into the controversy, Charles Abbot had labored under a delusion. He expected to negotiate a solution. It was a misunderstanding that everyone else at the Smithsonian shared, including Paul E. Garber, the Institution's resident aeronautical expert, who found it hard to understand why his boss and Orville Wright could not "put their legs under the same table" and talk the situation out.[25]

Orville had no interest in reaching a compromise. The Smithsonian had lied about the 1914 tests of the Aerodrome, and would have to make amends or face the consequences. In preparing his will in 1937, he stipulated that the 1903 airplane should remain in London after his death unless the will was amended by a subsequent letter from him indicating a change of heart.

The controversy with the Smithsonian represented the most publicized challenge to the priority of the Wrights, but it was by no means the only attempt to obtain some measure of posthumous credit for a flying-machine pioneer at Wilbur and Orville's expense. The specter of John Montgomery, for example, refused to be laid to rest.

In 1917 Montgomery's widow Regina, together with his mother, brothers, and sister, brought suit against the Wright-Martin Company, holders of the original Wright patents, and the U.S. government, which had arranged the joint license agreement that ended the Wright-Curtiss patent suit. The plaintiffs argued that the Wrights had infringed on an essential provision of the patent granted to Montgomery in 1906 for the glider design that killed Dan Maloney. The Wright patent referred to the wings of the airplane as "normally flat." The Montgomery patent, however, described wings with a parabolic curve, as in the arc of a circle. As a Montgomery attorney noted, everyone knew that practical airplanes have curved wings.[26]

Henry Toulmin's use of the phrase "normally flat" had nothing to do with camber. He was referring to the fact that in normal flight the wings were flat across the span. When warped to turn or bank, they had a helical twist. Toulmin did not refer to camber, reasoning that the increased efficiency of arched wings was so well known that it was not patentable. A precise description of the Wright wing camber had no value in the patent, although it would reveal important proprietary information on the wind-tunnel studies.

Orville offered depositions on behalf of Wright-Martin in 1920 and 1921. He also assembled the 1903 airplane in January 1921 for a complete set of photographs to be used in the trial. The Montgomery heirs dropped the Wright-Martin suit as a hopeless cause that year. Many years later, Orville's friend Fred C. Kelly edited his 1920–21 depositions into a short book, *How We Invented the Airplane,* which remains the best first-person account of the Wright story.[27]

The Montgomery suit against the federal government continued until 1928, when the court handed down a final decision in favor of the defendants. The judges in the case noted: "It seems to us idle to contend that Montgomery was a pioneer in this particular field." Yet the Montgomery legend continued to grow. Family members and enthusiastic Californians refused to let his story die.

Publicist Victor Lougheed led the way, making totally unfounded claims for his one-time business associate. James Montgomery did his part, telling and retelling the story of his brother's early work, extending the number and length of his flights in the process.

The process of enshrinement was complete by the mid-twentieth century when Hollywood took up the cause of this "forgotten" California pioneer. Glenn Ford portrayed Montgomery in the film *Gallant Journey,* while Walt Disney opened his cartoon history of flight with a comic version of the story. Monument builders and the anonymous bureaucrats responsible for naming schools, highways, and airfields followed, enthusiastically endorsing Montgomery as the man who "opened the skies for all mankind."

The strange case of Gustav Weisskopf, or Whitehead, first came to public attention through an article published in *Scientific American* on June 8, 1901. Written by Stanley Yale Beach, son of the editor of the magazine, the story provided a detailed description of a mono-plane "built after the model of a bird or bat," by a Bavarian immigrant named Whitehead living in Bridgeport, Connecticut. Ten days later the *New York Herald* followed up with a well-illustrated piece enti-tled "Connecticut Night Watchman Thinks He Has Found Out How to Fly." The article included Whitehead's offhand remark that he had already flown his machine for a distance of a half mile.[28]

On August 18, 1901, the Bridgeport *Sunday Herald* carried what purported to be an eyewitness account of yet another half-mile flight. In another article published in the *American Inventor* for April 1902, Whitehead claimed to have made flights of two and seven miles over Long Island Sound in January of that year.[29]

The stories created a brief flurry of excitement, but interest quickly died when no corroboration followed and no further flights were an-nounced. Langley dispatched a Smithsonian employee to Atlantic City when the Whitehead machine was exhibited at Young's Pier. He re-turned with the comment that the craft did not appear to be air-worthy.[30]

Whitehead remained on the scene for a number of years. In 1904 he built and flew gliders vaguely reminiscent of the Chanute craft of 1896. By 1911 he was working on an unsuccessful helicopter design featuring sixty rotors. He also constructed an unsuccessful flying machine for Stanley Beach, who remained a major supporter.

Whitehead exhibited photos of his machines, including a fuzzy image reputed to be the 1901 or 1902 machine in the air, at the two New York Aero Shows of 1906, and later in a Bridgeport store win-dow. He also displayed his line of aeronautical engines at exhibitions in New York and St. Louis. The engines apparently worked better than the flying machines; at least one of them powered a pioneer aircraft built by a New Yorker.

Never part of the mainstream, Whitehead became a laughingstock when he announced plans to fly the Atlantic in an outlandish machine after World War I. He died a pauper in 1927.

The first serious retelling of the Whitehead story came in an article published by Stella Randolph, an aspiring writer, and Harvey Phillips, an aero history buff, in the June 1935 issue of *Popular Aviation*. Two years later, Ms. Randolph offered a more complete account in her first book, *The Lost Flights of Gustave Whitehead*.

Ms. Randolph told the compelling story of a poor inventor who had achieved great things only to have his work forgotten. "If this tale is true," the Los Angeles *Times* noted, "the little be-moustached Bavarian . . . sped farther, faster and better than the Wrights." The Washington *Herald* added that "the history of aviation may move back a page from the Wright brothers flight at Kitty Hawk, N.C. to the experimental flights of Gustav Whitehead at Bridgeport, Conn."[31]

It did not take long for the first holes to appear in the Whitehead yarn. In 1935, John Crane, a young Harvard Ph.D., inspired by the Randolph and Phillips article, traveled to Bridgeport to investigate the story. He began with the original news article of August 18, 1901. Three alleged witnesses were named in the account. One, Richard Howell, the editor who had written the piece, was dead. Another, Andrew Cellic, could not be located. No one remembered a local resident by that name, nor did he appear in any of the turn-of-the-century Bridgeport directories.

Crane did find the third man—and James Dickie offered unequivocal testimony. He remembered Whitehead, but denied ever having seen him fly. He had not been present on the morning in question, and regarded the entire story as a hoax concocted by Howell on the basis of planned flights that Whitehead had described during an interview.

Crane also talked to some of the reputed witnesses whom Stella Randolph had interviewed. One man gave her a particularly detailed account after having been promised a financial interest in her book. Most of the other testimony fell apart in similar fashion. Even the members of Whitehead's family could not recall his having specifically mentioned the long flights of 1901–02 at the time.[32]

The evidence continued to accumulate. Financial supporters, especially Stanley Beach, who had originally convinced his father to underwrite Whitehead's work, rejected the claim. "I do not believe that any of his machines ever left the ground," Beach commented, "in spite of the assertions of many people who think they saw them fly. I think I was in a better position during the nine years that I was giving Whitehead money to develop his ideas, to know what his machines could do, than persons who were employed by him for a short period of time, or those who have remained silent for thirty-five years about what would have been an historic achievement in aviation."[33]

Orville believed that Crane's evidence, and the evidence of common sense, would prevail. If Whitehead had really flown one half mile in 1901 or seven miles in 1902, why did he abandon that machine in favor of gliders designed by other men almost a decade before? If he had flown in 1901, why could he not do so thereafter?

In October 1937, Orville remarked to writer Fred Black that he suspected Stella Randolph's book had "originated in the mind of A. F. Zahm, of whom you already know. He has been quite active in this matter, as I have learned from several sources." This was not a case of paranoia on Orville's part. In May 1935, a month before Ms. Randolph's first article appeared and two years before her book was published, Zahm wrote to Emerson Newell, a leading member of the Curtiss defense team at the time of the Wright-Curtiss suit, requesting any information collected on Whitehead for use in court.[34]

Zahm, who was now employed as an aeronautical expert by the Library of Congress, continued his search for material that would support the Whitehead claim, offering a reward to anyone who could provide proof of the story. Such proof was never forthcoming, but Zahm seldom missed an opportunity to argue that the tale was true. In his own self-serving history of early aeronautics, *Early Power-plane Fathers* (1951), he commented that Stella Randolph's book "evinces notable research," and concluded that Whitehead "must either be credited with a real flight or denounced as a charlatan. The latter course would be ungracious, indeed repugnant to the code of honor prevailing among reputable men. . . ."[35]

Like the Montgomery story, the tale of Gustav Whitehead refused to die. It resurfaced again in 1945 when a radio announcer introduced Charles Whitehead as the son of the man who had invented the airplane. *Liberty* Magazine included the story in an article on the broadcaster, which was reprinted in the July 1945 issue of *Reader's Digest*.

"The Gustav Whitehead story is too incredible and ridiculous to require serious refutation," Orville commented to Alexander McSurley of *Aviation News* in 1945. Nevertheless, he responded to the new round of publicity with an article of his own, "The Mythical Whitehead Flights," published in the August 1945 issue of *U.S. Air Services*. It did not lay the Whitehead issue to rest.

The Whitehead supporters are still with us—livelier than ever. A more militant generation took up the cause in the early 1960s, determined to obtain what they regard as a fair hearing for their case. They found and interviewed the last group of Bridgeport residents who claimed to have seen Whitehead fly six decades before, and scoured local newspapers for additional information. In spite of their effort, the story has not been materially strengthened since 1937. The tale was not true then and it is not true today. The voices have simply grown louder and more strident.

In recent years, partisans have built and flown a "replica" of the Whitehead machine. The fact that the original drawings and engineering data required for an accurate reproduction no longer exist does not seem to have deterred them. Ironically, the Smithsonian Institution is charged with being so pro-Wright as to refuse to consider the possibility that there might be a kernel of truth in the Whitehead story. That would have tickled Orville.[36]

By the end of his life, Orville realized that he would never be able to lay the rival first-flight claims to rest. The problem involved psychology rather than historical truth. However persuasively he might argue, whatever the courts might rule, there would always be someone anxious to defend the cause of yet another candidate for the honor of having been first to fly. The fact that none of those claims has ever been proved does not seem to matter. A. F. Zahm would have been tickled at that.

He would be less pleased by the fact that no one has ever come close to stripping Wilbur and Orville Wright of their title as the inventors of the airplane. The various claimants have had almost no lasting impact on public opinion. The great mass of Americans have never doubted the priority of the Wrights. Nor should they.

chapter 36

OF MEN AND MONUMENTS

1920-1940

T he twenty-five years during which Orville faced challenges from the Smithsonian, Zahm, Montgomery, and Whitehead also saw him permanently enshrined as one of the great heroes of American history. Medals and awards—among them the American Distinguished Flying Cross and the French Legion of Honor—flowed in from every direction. Between 1915 and 1947 he received a grand total of eleven honorary degrees from colleges and universities in Europe and America, including Harvard, Yale, the University of Michigan, the University of Cincinnati, Earlham, and the University of Munich.[1]

Distinguished visitors to Dayton were obliged to call at Hawthorn Hill. The celebrities ranged from Carl Akeley, the big-game hunter and showman, Nobel Laureate Dr. Robert Millikan, poet Carl Sandburg, and physicist Michael Pupin, to such aviation personalities as General William Mitchell, Admiral Richard Byrd, and the great scientist/engineer Theodore von Karman.

The two most memorable visitors were Charles Lindbergh and Franklin Roosevelt. Lindbergh came to Dayton at Orville's invitation on June 22, 1927, less than a month after he had flown the Atlantic. The stopover was a signal honor. Lindbergh, on his way back to St. Louis for the first time since his triumphant return to New York, had promised his financial backers he would make no further public appearances before returning home.

He landed the *Spirit of St. Louis* at Wright Field, the new Army

Air Corps research and development facility just outside the city limits, where Orville and General William Gilmore were waiting with a car to take them along a parade route through downtown Dayton. When Lindbergh explained his promise, Orville ordered the car driven straight to Hawthorn Hill.

Thousands of Daytonians waiting to catch a glimpse of their hero streamed out to Oakwood. "Dinner was about to be served," Ivonette Wright Miller recalled,

> when from nowhere people began to appear on the front lawn. Soon the front lawn was crowded, then the side lawns and the hillside at the back. It was not a crowd but a mob, pushing and shoving, trampling the flower beds and bushes, climbing trees, all clamoring for a look at Lindbergh. When people came up on the porch, the occupants of the house took refuge on the second floor. But the mob persisted, demanding at least a glimpse of their hero. Finally, Orville Wright, more to save his house from ruin than to gratify the crowds, appealed to Lindbergh, and he made a brief appearance on a little balcony of the front portico, tall and boyish, with Orville Wright at his side. The crowd seemed satisfied and dispersed.[2]

The following day, Orville drove Lindbergh down to the laboratory on North Broadway. Harold Miller, who was a member of the small party accompanying them, remembers a moment that typified Orville's enthusiasm. As they were walking into the building Orville saw a crowd of old friends watching from the street. With an enormous smile on his face, Orville looked at Miller and pointed to Lindbergh with his hand behind his back, scarcely able to control his glee at being seen with the young hero.[3]

President Franklin Roosevelt's visit to Dayton on October 16, 1940, had a very different tone. Orville's politics are difficult to categorize. He had some faintly socialist notions about production and finance. An admirer of Roosevelt's, he was deeply honored by an invitation to join the President and James Cox, ex-governor of Ohio and 1920 Democratic candidate for President (with FDR as his running mate), for a parade and tour of Dayton. When the trip was complete, the presidential car drove back to Hawthorn Hill and was about to turn up the long, winding drive. Orville tapped the chauffeur on the shoulder and asked to be let out on the street, preferring not to take the President out of his way.[4]

The banquets, medals, awards, honorary degrees, and visits from distinguished guests were only the beginning. The Wright brothers were the most memorialized Americans of the twentieth century. Of all their countrymen, only Washington, Jefferson, and Lincoln have inspired commemorative zeal to match.

The mythic stature attained by the brothers reflected the nature of their achievement. The airplane was not simply a bit of new technology; it was something akin to a miracle. Flight symbolized the most basic human yearnings. To fly was to achieve freedom, control, power, and an escape from restraint.

And the invention came from such an unexpected quarter. The Wrights had no special training in science or engineering. While both were well educated, neither had completed the formal coursework required for his high school diploma. Before the summer of 1899, they seemed the most ordinary of men.

That was part of their fascination. They were the quintessential Americans, whose success seemed compounded of hard work, perseverance, and common sense, with a liberal dollop of Yankee ingenuity—raised to the level of genius. It was Horatio Alger writ large. They were proof that the values of an older America retained their validity in a new, complex, and somewhat frightening world.

The first monument planned to honor the Wrights was to have been built at Huffman Prairie. At the time of Wilbur's death in 1912, forty prominent Daytonians formed a Wright Memorial Committee to commemorate the events that had occurred there. They proposed to erect two Greek columns, "if possible obtained from the ruins near Athens," in the middle of the Prairie. The simple columns would be "thoroughly in keeping with the unassuming modesty of Wilbur and Orville Wright, and fittingly mark this historic spot which will be known to posterity as the cradle of aviation." In spite of Torrence Huffman's enthusiasm and some interest on the part of the Greek government, the project languished.[5]

Early the next year, the sculptor Gutzon Borglum offered his own design. He suggested that the committee commission "a heroic figure, part human, part divine, or rather of a human being transformed into an angelic spirit with wings, typifying man's mastery of the air."[6] Nothing came of this proposal either.

The earliest memorial actually built and dedicated to the Wrights stands on the open field of Camp d'Auvours, near Le Mans, where Wilbur flew in 1908. Dedicated in 1912, the great black granite boulder was badly scarred as Allied troops fought their way through this area in 1944, but the simple inscription remains intact:

WILBUR ET ORVILLE WRIGHT
KITTY HAWK, 1903

The American ambassador to France unveiled Paul Landowski's sculptural tribute to the Wrights, a figure with arms stretched up toward the heavens, in Le Mans in 1920. The French Armée de l'Air dedicated yet another monument on the site of the old Wright flying school at Pau in 1935.[7]

The first American monument to the Wrights, a five-foot marble shaft, still stands in the front yard of what was once the Methodist parsonage in Kitty Hawk. In 1927, when the federal government announced plans for a great Wright Brothers National Memorial to be constructed four miles to the south at Kill Devil Hills, the citizens of Kitty Hawk, led by Captain William Tate, raised $210 to mark this spot where the first Wright machine, the 1900 glider, had been assembled and flown. This, they argued, was "the bona fide cradle of aviation."[8]

The little obelisk is seldom seen by the tourists who throng to modern Kill Devil Hills and Nags Head each summer. Kitty Hawk, the tiny fishing village that Wilbur and Orville Wright knew, is a collection of widely spaced houses clustered around a school, post office, and convenience store set a mile back from the main beach road. Ask a local citizen for directions to the Wright brothers' monument and they will send you to Kill Devil Hills, where the grandest of all memorials to the brothers was finally dedicated in 1932.

It is a lovely thing, a great pylon of Mount Airy granite with wings sculpted into the sides and an aeronautical beacon on top that can be seen for miles around at night. The memorial was conceived in 1926 by Congressman Lindsay Warren as a means of attracting tourist dollars to boost the Outer Banks into the twentieth century.

At the time, the thin chain of sand islands paralleling the North Carolina coast remained, as Orville Wright once remarked, "like the Sahara." The sole access to the mainland was by ferry, and the only roads on the Banks were wooden "corduroy" affairs that could be moved in response to the shifting sands.

North Carolina legislators and the local members of the Kill Devil Hills Memorial Association agreed that Warren's proposal was a fine idea. Dayton citizens were not so sure. Fred Marshall, editor of the Dayton-based aviation magazine *Slipstream,* took the lead in the fight against Kill Devil Hills as the site, pointing out that the Outer

Banks remained as remote and inaccessible as they had been in 1903. "Who will ever visit this monument if it is built in the wind swept dunes at Kitty Hawk?"[9]

Marshall offered an alternative—"a practical and inspiring" museum to house the 1903 Wright airplane, still on loan to the Science Museum of London. The best spot for such a museum, he suggested, was on a high bluff behind the newly established Wright Field, with a clear view of Huffman Prairie.

Marshall was ignored. A $50,000 appropriation bill introduced by Warren's ally, Senator Hiram Bingham of Connecticut, breezed through committee, passed both houses, and was signed into law by President Coolidge on March 2, 1927. Architects Robert Perry Rogers and Alfred Eastman Poor won the $5,000 prize for the monument design. Warren, Bingham, Orville Wright, and Amelia Earhart dedicated the cornerstone on December 17, 1928, in the presence of two hundred "pilgrims" who had braved a series of difficult bus, automobile, and boat rides to reach the site.[10]

The Army Quartermaster Corps now had to build the memorial. The first problem facing Captain John A. Gilman, who had recently completed work on the Tomb of the Unknown Soldier at Arlington Cemetery, and his assistant, Captain W. H. Kindervater, was Kill Devil Hill itself. It was not a hill at all, but a ninety-foot sand dune that was moving across the narrow Outer Banks at a speed of twenty feet a year. During the quarter of a century since 1903, it had traveled some 600 feet toward an eventual resting place in the waters of Currituck Sound. If the dune was to serve as the foundation for a monument, it would have to be permanently stabilized.

Beginning early in 1929, Gilman spent $27,500 to accomplish that task. The area was fenced to keep the hogs and cattle out, then covered with a two-inch layer of straw, leaf, and wood mold extending 300 feet up the slope. Tough, hardy imported grasses—bitter tannic, hairy vetch, and marram—were planted in the artificial topsoil. Once this band of vegetation took root, Gilman extended the planting up to the summit on the northeast side where the prevailing wind struck the dune, then over the rest of the slope.

By the summer of 1930, the majestic moving dune was transformed into a stable hill, carpeted with green weeds and shrubs. A few watermelon vines even found a foothold near the top. Gilman and his crew started work on the monument itself in February 1931. Finished the following spring, the granite shaft measured sixty feet from the five-pointed star at the base to the tip of the beacon. The hill raises the total height of the structure to 151 feet above sea level.[11]

On November 19, 1932, another party of distinguished guests made their way over the new Wright Memorial Bridge and down a concrete highway to attend the dedication of the finished monument. Warren's plan to use the monument to lure tourists to the Outer Banks was an enormous success—development followed on a scale beyond his wildest dreams. Wilbur and Orville Wright would no longer recognize the string of neon-bedecked motels, restaurants, gift shops, condominiums, and elegant beach houses that lines the route to their old camp.

During the twenties and thirties memorials to the Wrights sprang up virtually everywhere the brothers had worked and flown, including College Park, Maryland; Fort Myer, Virginia; and Montgomery, Alabama. Wilbur's birthplace, a farmhouse near New Castle, Indiana, became a state historic park. Local historical groups in Iowa, Indiana, Ohio, and Virginia marked the sites of the various Wright homesteads. But Henry Ford's purchase of the house at 7 Hawthorn and the bicycle shop at 1127 West Third marked the beginning of the most important preservation project involving the Wright brothers.

Henry Ford, who had made his fortune on the shop floors of urban Detroit, was convinced that his success was based on unyielding adherence to the precepts of an older America. A confirmed social engineer, he saw the historic village and museum as a means of passing on the strength of simple rural virtue to a new generation.

Ford began his recreation of the past by restoring the old Ford farm and homestead to its condition in 1876, the year in which his mother died. That project was followed in 1923 by the purchase and restoration of the Wayside Inn in Sudbury, Massachusetts.

The Wayside Inn project has been celebrated as a major step in the historic preservation movement. It was an important step in Ford's thinking as well, demonstrating the educational value of a restored complex, including a famous building, a working farm, an old-time school, and quaint shops.

But the history of colonial and early nineteenth-century America was of little interest to Ford. He was convinced that his own past—the lives of ordinary, hardworking Americans of the post-Civil War era—represented the nation's Golden Age. Greenfield Village was designed to capture Ford's roseate memories of those years.

It took shape in an empty field near the Ford engineering laboratory, a mile or so from the huge River Rouge plant. There were two components: a vast museum filled with the objects of American industry and everyday life; and a village made up of historic structures gathered from across the nation. The entire complex would illustrate the way in which the men and women of Ford's generation had applied rural values in building a new industrial America.[12]

Ford was a firm believer in the "Great Man" theory of history, and he thought there was no greater man than Thomas Alva Edison. He named his historic complex the Edison Institute, and moved both the laboratory in which Edison had worked for forty years at Fort Myers, Florida, and the buildings at Menlo Park, New Jersey, where the great man and his team had developed the electric light, onto the site.

By 1936, Greenfield Village—the outdoor-museum portion of the Institute—was taking shape. It included a few traditional American buildings, such as the Stephen Foster, William Holmes McGuffey, and Noah Webster houses, but concentrated chiefly on fledgling business and industry—a pottery, sawmill, blacksmith and tinsmith shops, a Cape Cod windmill, cooper shop, mine-pumping engine, and machine shop.

In choosing his American heroes, Ford avoided the traditional emphasis on political leaders and military men, although he did acquire an Illinois courthouse associated with Abraham Lincoln. Luther Burbank's birthplace and laboratory and Charles Steinmetz's camp seemed more appropriate to him.

Buildings representing Wilbur and Orville Wright fit perfectly into the scheme of Greenfield Village, but the acquisition of the Wright home and bicycle shop owed far more to Detroit newsman William E. Scripps than it did to Henry Ford. Scripps, an aviation enthusiast who served as president of the Early Birds, a national club for pioneer aviators, had long dreamed of a facility where the papers and memorabilia of fliers could be preserved. That project never materialized, but his early discussions with Ford did achieve results.[13]

The first sign that something was afoot came with Orville's initial visit to Greenfield Village on June 27, 1936. Then, on July 2, Charles Webbert, the Wrights' old landlord, sold the building at 1127 West Third to Ford for $13,000. The Dayton *Daily News* broke the story four days later.

Reaction in Dayton was mixed. Some congratulated Ford on acquiring a historic structure that would probably not have been preserved if left in the hands of local citizens. Others were less pleased. "It is an outrage to let a thing like this happen," argued Judge James

Douglas of the Court of Common Pleas. "First England takes the first airplane and now Henry Ford takes the original workshop. . . ."[14]

Henry Ford and his son Edsel paid their first visit to Dayton with Fred Black, the man in charge of Greenfield Village, on October 27. They saw the old bike shop while it was still in place, and discussed plans for its removal and restoration with Orville. The Fords also discovered that the house at 7 Hawthorn might be available. Orville could not understand the Fords' interest in so undistinguished a building, but promised to see what he could do.

Milton had willed the house to Katharine, who sold it to Lottie Jones, the washerwoman who had worked for them on Hawthorn Street. Within a month Orville had arranged the sale for $4,100.[15]

Edward Cutler, Ford's preservation specialist, arrived in Dayton to make drawings and photos of both buildings in October. Ford workmen had marked, disassembled, moved, and reassembled them on new foundations in Greenfield Village by February 1937.

Furnishing the interior of the house and shop proved more difficult than expected. Orville provided a few pieces and a great many of the books from the house on Hawthorn Street. Lottie Jones had preserved some additional items in the house itself. She and her sons milked the Ford establishment for all it was worth, sending several shipments of "newly discovered" material to Detroit on consignment. Fred Black finally returned to Dayton to request a complete list of everything available, so that he could make his selection and reach a financial agreement with the family.[16]

The Ford organization located Charlie Taylor, working in the toolroom at North American Aviation in Los Angeles, and hired him to participate in restoring the bicycle shop. He helped Orville and Mabel Beck to locate surviving machine tools used in the shop at the turn of the century, then signed on as a guide once the buildings were opened to the public.[17]

The house and bicycle shop were dedicated with appropriate ceremony on April 16, 1938—Wilbur's birthday. Charles Kettering, now head of the General Motors Laboratory, served as toastmaster. Frank Lahm, Griffith Brewer, and Walter Brookins also spoke briefly. That Sunday evening, the Ford Hour radio program ran a special tribute to the Wrights.

The buildings are still in Greenfield Village. You can stand in the room where Orville was born in 1871, and the one in which Wilbur died in 1912, or peek into the workshop where a kite, three gliders, and three powered flying machines took shape between 1900 and 1905. The furnishings, particularly those in the typically overstuffed turn-of-the-century Sunday parlor, offer a sense of middle-class life and the taste of the times.

There are personal touches as well. Orville's mandolin leans against a wall of the sitting room, as though he has just walked out the door. "Orv began lessons on the mandolin," Katharine wrote their father not long before Wilbur left for Kitty Hawk in 1900. "We are getting even with the neighborhood at last for the noise they have made on pianos. He sits around and picks that thing until I can hardly stay in the house."[18]

The interiors of the two buildings have been meticulously restored. It is only when you walk outside that you realize how completely Henry Ford succeeded in transplanting the two structures into an environment of his own imagining. Set on a generous plot of neatly manicured grass, framed by shrubs and trees, the Wright home and the world's most famous bicycle shop have become central features of Ford's idealized vision of small-town America. The reality of West Dayton—the sense of bustle and activity, change, opportunity, and excitement that marked the streetcar suburb in which the Wrights lived and worked—is entirely absent.

Dayton had lost its two most historic buildings, but it did eventually get its great monument. It stands just where Fred Marshall thought it should, on the high bluff overlooking Huffman Prairie, two miles to the east. Dedicated on August 19, 1940, Orville Wright's sixty-ninth birthday, the memorial is a multifaceted thirty-foot shaft of pink North Carolina marble. General "Hap" Arnold flew in for the occasion and told his audience that the monument would "stand as a shrine to aviation as the Plymouth Rock is to America."[19]

You can stand at the stone rail behind the monument and see Huffman Prairie off in the distance. It is one of the few places of importance in the story of Wilbur and Orville Wright that has not changed much since their time. Torrence Huffman leased the Prairie, and 2,075 additional acres which included both the Beard and Stauffer farms, back to the original owners, the people of the United States, on May 22, 1917. All of this land was incorporated into Wilbur Wright Field, a base where the first generation of American combat airmen received their basic training. By the end of 1917, eleven squadrons were operating eighty-five Curtiss JN-4 "Jennies," and thirty-two Standard S-1 training aircraft in the neighborhood of the last Wright hangar, which remained standing into the mid-1920s.

Together with Fairfield Air Depot and the Air Service Engineering Division headquarters at McCook Field in Dayton, Wilbur Wright became a center of American flight research during the years following World War I. Air Service test pilots flew the giant six-engine NBL-1, the Barling Bomber, here when the runways at McCook Field proved too short. The talented cadre of engineers and technicians at Wilbur Wright prepared the Douglas DWC World Cruisers for the first circumnavigation of the globe, and the Fokker "Bird of Paradise" for the first flight from the mainland to Hawaii.

Of course, there was a price to be paid. Lieutenants Frank Stuart Patterson and Leroy Swann were killed in a DH-4 crash on June 19, 1918. Lieutenant Alexander Bliss II died while practicing for the 1924 Pulitzer Race. The wooden propeller of Captain Burt Skeel's Curtiss racer shattered as he dived toward the starting line a few days later. Horrified spectators saw the machine burst apart in the air and fall to earth just outside the boundary of what had once been Huffman Prairie.

Most of the test flying was transferred to nearby Wright Field when that facility replaced old McCook in 1927. In an effort to avoid confusion, Wilbur Wright was renamed Patterson Field in 1931. The two bases were finally merged to form Wright-Patterson Air Force Base in January 1948.[20]

Like the previous owners, the U.S. Air Force has been hardpressed to find a use for the old Prairie. For many years it served as a safety zone beyond the officers' club skeet range. Occasional proposals to turn the area into a bomb dump or an emergency pull-off ramp for aircraft that run into trouble out on the main runway have not been pursued.

They used to mow the Prairie regularly each summer. Local ecologists have convinced base officials to put a stop to that, and the area has gradually resumed its former appearance. There are plans to burn the field periodically, a process that will drive out intruding plant species and encourage the growth of indigenous native flora.

In the end, Huffman Prairie is the most appropriate of all monuments to the memory of Wilbur and Orville Wright—the spot where they first flew, preserved inviolate and surrounded by a giant research complex dedicated to the advancement of flight technology. A visit to the imposing granite shaft up on Wright Hill seems uninspiring compared with the opportunity to retrace their footsteps down here in the tall grass where it all began.

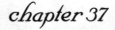

chapter 37

THE FINAL CHAPTER

1940-1948

For thirty years Orville Wright's place of business was the plain brick building he had constructed on North Broadway. Visiting reporters found it quite ordinary. There was a reception area for Miss Beck; an inner office with Orville's desk, files, and drawing table; and a large work area that ran across the back of the building. Orville referred to this room as his laboratory. In fact, with the exception of a large wind tunnel capable of testing models at speeds of up to 50 miles per hour, there was little to distinguish it from any other well-equipped machine shop.

Still, it was difficult to believe that the inventor of the airplane was not at work in his lab on some project that would eventually yield wonders for a grateful humanity. Orville summed it up in a story he told to his friend, Dayton clergyman Charles Seasholes. One morning while puttering around the shop he noticed two small boys peeking through an open window. One boy asked his companion what in the world Orville was doing. The other replied, with a note of derision in his voice: "Why, he's inventing!"[1]

Orville had a great deal in common with those two boys. He did not pursue technology to make a fortune, improve the world, or earn immortal fame, although the airplane had accomplished all those things for him. The psychological complexity of Wilbur's motives or the meticulous care with which Edison analyzed the market for a new device before launching into the development process were entirely foreign to him.

His interest in technological problem solving was that of a small boy blessed with insatiable curiosity and a childlike enthusiasm for all things mechanical. How did it work? What could be learned by taking it apart and putting it back together? How could it be improved? His choice of mechanical problems was inspired by that curiosity, and had little to do with social utility or corporate balance sheets.

Free of the necessity of earning a living or pleasing anyone but himself, Orville spent most of his time in the laboratory doing exactly what he wanted—tinkering. His forays with screwdriver and pliers occasionally led him astray. Having purchased a brand-new IBM electric typewriter for Miss Beck, nothing would do but to take it apart and see what made it tick. When Miss Beck looked in, she found him surrounded by a bewildering array of parts. An IBM serviceman summoned to the scene commented that he was paid to fix the machines, not to build them. He scooped up the parts and told Orville a new machine would be delivered from the factory.[2]

Ivonette Miller recalled another occasion on which he disassembled the regulator of a brand-new gas stove—"After that, it never did work right." But for every failure there were a great many successes. Orville took particular pride in having repaired a complicated ship's clock, a present from Griffith Brewer, after several leading Dayton jewelers told him the job was impossible.[3]

His reputation as a driver was not the best. "It was said that the police of Oakwood closed their eyes and held their breath until O.W. and another prominent Daytonian passed through on their way to their offices," one relative noted. "The police didn't feel they could arrest either one because of their prominence, so they kept their fingers crossed."[4]

He customized his cars as carefully as he did his homes. Because of the old back injury, the bounce and jolt of travel caused him excruciating pain, so he had his automobiles fitted with a special system of heavy-duty shock absorbers. Grandnephew George Russell recalled the long drives from Dayton to Lambert Island in the comfort of Orville's 1929 Pierce Arrow. "With everything loaded in the car, including Wilbur [sic-Orville] and myself, the car was steady as a rock. We never felt a bump."[5]

Orville put in his share of time under the hood. Convinced that the carburetor of that same Pierce Arrow was malfunctioning, he drilled a series of holes. Then, discovering that he had only made the problem worse, he carefully filled each of the holes with a wooden plug.[6]

Orville Wright—the cobbler at his last—c. 1947.

He worked on a number of small-scale inventions, some of which, like an automatic transmission system, were intended to help the motorist. But for the most part there seems to have been little rhyme or reason to his inventive projects. He worked on whatever interested him at the moment.

For a time, he focused on the development of an automatic record changer. As one relative recalled:

> He didn't like the radio, but he wanted his phonograph to change records automatically. He'd pile up a lot of records and, consulting the chart with the names of the selections, he'd press a button to select one and eject another. I don't remember whether he ever got it working right, but I do remember he came to our house asking us if we had any old records— he was breaking so many he was running out of supplies![7]

The failure of the record changer provided members of the family with an opportunity to pay Orville back for some of the teasing they had endured over the years. Lorin's nephew, Alfred "Peek" Andrews, remembers that "The whole family was having fun teasing him about the records he was breaking in attempting to perfect the apparatus. He enjoyed so much teasing all of us we were happy to have a chance to reciprocate."[8]

The youngsters growing up in the house recalled that Wilbur and Orville had always been fascinated by toys. In telling the story of the invention of the airplane, Orville seldom failed to mention the toy helicopter that had sparked their curiosity in the first place.

When the nieces and nephews, now grown and with families of their own, gathered for Christmas at Hawthorn Hill in 1923, Orville had a new gadget to show them—a toy he remembered from his own childhood and thought a new generation of Wrights would enjoy.

"It was a contraption with a narrow base board about eighteen inches long," Ivonette recalled.

On one end it had a spring board that could be put under tension and then be released by a trigger. It had a launching seat on it and a little wooden clown with wire hooks for arms. On the other end of the base was a revolving double trapeze with a counter balancing clown holding to the bottom side. When a similar clown was released from the spring board, it flew through the air and caught the top side of the trapeze to revolve.[9]

Adult members of the family were also intrigued by the Flips and Flops, as Orville called his clowns. Ivonette's husband, Harold Miller, saw them as a business opportunity. The president of a local savings and loan institution, Miller had recently invested in the Miami Wood Specialty Company, a small firm manufacturing novelty items. He asked Orville if he would consider allowing the company to manufacture the toy clowns.

That was all the encouragement Orville needed. He launched into a series of tests to determine the best angle for the seat, the ideal spring tension, and other details. He presented the results to Harold Miller and applied for a patent, the last he would ever be granted.

Miami Wood Specialties prospered. Lorin Wright eventually bought into the firm, making it something of a family venture. When the sales of Flips and Flops began to decline, the partners turned to advertising specialties, including small wooden gliders with the name of the client printed on them. Orville not only designed and built the small printing press used to apply the advertising, but produced the specialized equipment that cut the parts out of thin sheets of wood.

Such attention to small-scale projects might be considered an enormous step down for the man who had been a full partner in the

invention of the airplane. But Orville was simply giving free rein to
his unbounded mechanical curiosity. The carburetor, record changer,
and Flips and Flops all help to clarify the working relationship that
had existed between the two brothers.

Wilbur had been interested in systems, in the big picture. Orville
was the one who could make it work. He thought in terms of particular mechanisms—the bits and pieces that went together to form the
big picture. He was the one who had developed the printing press that
surprised professional printers. The self-oiling bike hub had been his
pride and joy. More significant, he had played a leading role in developing the wind tunnel and designing the all-important balances. He
was a born inventor, whose fingers itched for a screwdriver and pliers.

There were those who thought that Orville should channel his efforts in more useful directions. Charles Lindbergh urged him to write
an autobiography. Lindbergh, like others before him, found it
"strange to look at this quiet, mild, gray-headed man and to realize
that he is the one who flew the plane at Kitty Hawk on the December
day. . . ."[10] The two men, who much admired one another, were
frequently thrown together at NACA meetings. Lindbergh seldom
lost an opportunity to encourage Orville to go to work on a book.

"He has talked of doing this for years," he noted in his diary after
a meeting with Orville in Washington in October 1939,

> . . . but he has never started, as far as anyone knows, and he shows no
> indication of starting now. It is a tragedy, for Wright is getting well on
> in years, and no one else is able to tell the story as he can. It seems that
> Wright does not trust anyone else to tell it properly. The words and
> phrases people use in telling of the achievements of Orville Wright and
> his brother are never quite satisfactory and never of sufficiently compre-
> hensive accuracy. Wright tells me that "no one else quite understands
> the spirit and conditions of those times." What people say about them
> in articles is never "quite accurate."[11]

Orville told Lindbergh that he might write such a book himself
someday, but added that

> he does not like to write and that he has not the ability to do it well. There
> are many writers who would be glad to do a book in co-operation with
> him, but the writers do not understand aviation well enough to suit him;
> he prefers a technical person. But when Ed Warner [a well-known aero-
> nautical engineer and writer] once offered to take six months off from
> his work, to do a book with Wright, the offer was never accepted. And
> I am afraid the book will never be written, although I intend to talk to
> Wright about it again.[12]

At an NACA conference in Dayton only a month later, in November 1939, Lindbergh sat between Orville and Edward Warner at dinner. His attempts to raise the subject met "with no more success than before."

Lindbergh tried to enlist others, including Vannevar Bush of MIT. Aware that Earl Findley was one of Orville's oldest and closest friends, Lindbergh visited him in September 1940. Findley surprised Lindbergh by admitting that once, a quarter of a century before, he had written a biography of the Wright brothers. He fetched the manuscript out, explaining that Orville had rejected it as being too personal.

> He had spent six months in the writing at a time when his finances were in a condition which made it very difficult to put the manuscript aside without publication. I could see that he had been badly hurt by the whole affair—so badly hurt that it was still somewhat painful to discuss the matter, even after the lapse of a quarter century. I think he was hurt even more by Wright's feeling that the manuscript was unsatisfactory than by the loss of six months' work.[13]

Lindbergh asked Findley if he would mind his raising the issue with Orville once more. Findley, with some reluctance, agreed.

Neither Lindbergh nor Findley was aware just how much Orville had disliked the manuscript when it was first submitted to him in 1915. It had been the occasion of his comment to Mabel Beck: "I would rather have the sciatica."

Nor had Findley told Lindbergh the entire story. In preparing the manuscript, he had taken on a young partner, John R. McMahon. The two of them had traveled to Dayton, spent considerable time with the family, and been given limited access to the Wright papers. McMahon, who had more interest in publishing than in preserving a friendly relationship with Orville, stewed over the rebuff for fourteen years. Finally, in 1929, he submitted a rewritten version as a series of articles, "The Real Fathers of Flight," to *Popular Science Monthly*. The following year he brought out a slightly altered version as a book, *The Wright Brothers: Fathers of Flight.*

Orville was outraged by what he regarded as McMahon's treachery. Only a year before those articles appeared in *Popular Science*, Mitchell Charnley had published *The Boys' Life of the Wright Brothers*, first as a series in the magazine *American Boy*, then as a book. Charnley had not contacted Orville, basing his account on the published writings of the brothers and news and magazine stories that had appeared over the years.

Both Charnley and McMahon steered away from any serious discussion of the technology, concentrating instead on the personalities
of the brothers and their family life. Orville saw this as an unwarranted intrusion into his private life. In addition, he was appalled by
what he regarded as an extraordinary number of errors in both books.
Ever the technician, he insisted that a proper book on the work of the
Wright brothers should focus only on the technology, and be absolutely free of error.

Following the appearance of McMahon's articles, Orville pressured
Findley to halt publication of the book. Findley, badly bruised by the
rejection of the original manuscript, did his best to stop his one-time
partner, but to no avail. Orville then contacted the publisher, Little,
Brown and Company, and negotiated some changes. The most significant involved the relative importance of Wilbur's hockey accident.

In *Popular Science,* McMahon had written:

. . . his athletic activity led to an accident without which the world would
have no airplane today.

Orville's negotiations resulted in an alteration that read:

. . . his athletic activity led to an accident that was not less than fateful,
at least this is a statement of high probability.[14]

One subsequent biographer, John Evangelist Walsh, has argued
that Orville feared the original passage would reveal that the invention of the airplane was rooted in Wilbur's state of mind, thus reducing his own role. It is far more likely that Orville simply refused to
probe the psychological forces that had driven his brother. What they
had accomplished was important. Why they had done it was beyond
knowing.

In spite of the changes, Orville's disgust with the book was deep
and unrelenting. Soon after publication he received a copy from a
distant relative asking him to autograph it as a souvenir for her
daughter. He refused, keeping the book and sending an autographed
photo of the first flight instead, along with an impassioned letter on
the evils of John McMahon and his book.

Lindbergh eventually gave up on Orville and the autobiography. He
encouraged Findley to give his manuscript to a library where it could
remain sealed until the principals were dead.

Fred C. Kelly was not so easily discouraged. Like Findley, he had
first met Orville as a young reporter a quarter of a century before.

Kelly had actually been working as a newsman in Xenia at the time of the flights at Huffman Prairie in 1904–05, although he did not then know the Wrights. A free-lance writer and columnist, he published his first interview with Orville, "Flying Machines and the War," in the July 5, 1915, issue of *Collier's*.

Kelly's sense of humor and way with words impressed Orville, and the two became fast friends. Over the years, Kelly would publish one article after another, many of them humorous, based on interviews and comments from the inventor of the airplane.

The idea of writing a biography of the Wrights emerged slowly. By 1939, Kelly was determined to move ahead, aware that handling Orville would be a difficult and delicate task. He first convinced his friend to cooperate in preparing a long article, "How the Wright Brothers Began," for a 1939 issue of *Harper's*.

As Kelly had feared, Orville was demanding, and never fully satisfied with the finished product. As with Findley's manuscript, he found it too personal and not sufficiently technical. Kelly persevered, arguing that while he might not be able to describe the technical details of invention, he could give the world an accurate depiction of the life and times of the brothers.

Using the *Harper's* piece as a jumping-off point, Kelly continued to write, sending Orville long sections of manuscript for comment. Almost without realizing it, Orville agreed to let Kelly produce a book with the understanding that he would have an opportunity to go over every word.

As one family member commented, "writing a book with Orville Wright looking over your shoulder would not be an easy task." Kelly had to prod and beg for Orville's response to each new section. At one point, with the manuscript half finished, Orville asked Kelly to call a halt, offering to pay him for the time spent so far. The author was silent for a moment, then asked Orville if he would have been willing to give up on the morning of December 17, 1903. Orville chuckled, and returned to work on the manuscript.[15]

Determined to avoid Findley's experience, Kelly sought to guarantee Orville's continued cooperation and eventual permission to publish the book as an authorized biography. The answer was to put Orville in his debt. There was an obvious way to accomplish that. Kelly wrote to Charles Abbot, suggesting that he would be willing to assist in resolving the long-standing dispute with the Smithsonian by negotiating a statement that would satisfy Orville Wright.[16]

Kelly knew precisely what would work—the publication of the differences between the 1903 Aerodrome and the 1914 machine flown at Hammondsport, plus a disavowal of the 1914 Zahm report. With considerable finesse, he moved Abbot toward just such a statement. It finally appeared, as Orville had demanded, in a volume of the *Smithsonian Miscellaneous Collections* on October 24, 1942, preceded by a note:

> This paper has been submitted to Dr. Orville Wright, and under date of October 8, 1942, he states that the paper as now prepared will be acceptable to him if given adequate publication.[17]

The long feud was over, although Orville did not say so to Abbot. Officially, he did not respond to the publication. Unofficially, however, he took the immediate steps required to ensure the eventual presentation of the 1903 machine to the Smithsonian.

Officials of the Science Museum in London, frightened by the threat of war during the Munich crisis, had removed the airplane from exhibition for safekeeping in September 1938. It was returned to display in October once the crisis had passed, but went back into storage for good with the onset of the Blitz in July 1940.[18]

On December 8, 1943, Orville wrote to inform the director of the Science Museum that he would be asking for the return of the machine once the war was over and it could be safely transported back across the Atlantic. He planned to announce his decision in the presence of President Roosevelt at the 1943 Collier Trophy dinner, to be held in Washington in honor of the fortieth anniversary of powered flight. When Roosevelt was unable to attend, Orville remained silent—and the Smithsonian was left guessing.

The letter to the Science Museum was not made public. It did, however, fulfill the condition of Orville's 1937 will for the return of the aircraft. To make doubly sure there would be no misunderstanding, Orville spelled out his wishes in a new will, never signed, that he was developing with the assistance of a lawyer at the time of his death:

> I give and bequeath to the U.S. National Museum of Washington, D.C., for exhibition in the National Capital only, the Wright aeroplane (now in the Science Museum, London, England) which flew at Kitty Hawk, North Carolina, on the 17th of December, 1903.[19]

Fred Kelly had triumphed. Perhaps because of his assistance in settling the Smithsonian dispute, perhaps simply out of friendship,

Orville finally approved the manuscript for publication. It was not what he had hoped for, but it did tell the story in relatively straightforward fashion. Released by Harcourt, Brace on May 13, 1943, *The Wright Brothers: A Biography Authorized by Orville Wright* has remained in print for over forty years.

Aging, but satisfied that the Smithsonian controversy was behind him at last, Orville remained active and visible throughout World War II. The round of banquets, honors, awards, and dedications peaked as the fortieth anniversary of powered flight approached in 1943. He pursued a private bit of war work in the laboratory, laboring to develop a code machine for the armed forces. At the end of the war, President Truman honored him with the Award of Merit for distinguished service to the NACA throughout the conflict.

With an air war being waged around the globe, reporters came in increasing numbers to ask if Orville had any regrets about the invention of the airplane. When they had put that question in 1918, he had assured them that he did not; he and his brother had always assumed that the possibility of death from the skies would deter war. He stil, didn't have any regrets, but he had grown more cynical over the years. In answer to his friend Lester Gardner's letter of congratulations on the occasion of his seventy-fourth birthday in August 1945, he wrote: "I once thought the aeroplane would end wars. Now I wonder if the aeroplane and the atomic bomb can do it."[20]

With the coming of peace, his old friend Edward Deeds involved him in a major restoration project. In 1946, Deeds, now chairman of the board of the National Cash Register Company, decided to build a park to commemorate the role the Miami Valley had played in the history of transportation. A special building devoted to the achievements of Wilbur and Orville Wright would be the centerpiece.

He approached Orville early in 1947, outlining his plans and requesting assistance in choosing a Flyer to be included in the display. Orville first suggested that Deeds obtain a replica of the 1903 machine. The original craft had been removed from storage in England, but, at the request of the Science Museum, Orville had agreed not to demand its return officially until a new set of drawings and an accurate replica had been completed. Perhaps the English would be willing to build a second replica for the city of Dayton.

After thinking it over for a few days, Orville contacted Deeds a second time, suggesting that an original airplane of much greater significance to Dayton—the 1905 machine flown at Huffman Prairie—might be available. Deeds was enthusiastic, and ordered Carl Beust, head of his patent department, to place the company facilities at Orville's disposal.

The story of the preservation and restoration of the historic 1905 Flyer begins in 1911. The old craft was abandoned in camp when the brothers left Kitty Hawk in 1908. Orville had considered bringing the pieces back with him when he returned to the camp with the new glider in 1911, but decided against it when he saw how much damage time, the elements, and souvenir hunters had done.

Pieces of the 1905 airplane had been pulled from crates and scattered across the sand. Wild animals and vacationers had rooted through the pile and made a discouraging mess of things. When they broke camp at the end of that short season, yet another historic machine, the 1911 glider, was left behind with the tattered remnants of its 1905 predecessor.

Soon after Orville's return from the Outer Banks that year, the Wrights received a letter from Zenas Crane, a wealthy Massachusetts paper manufacturer, requesting that they donate one of their old machines to the Berkshire Museum, established by him in Pittsfield, Massachusetts. Orville replied that nothing of the sort was available. But he added that if Crane was interested, he might be able to hire members of the Kill Devil Hills lifesaving crew to gather up the various scattered parts and ship them to Pittsfield.

Crane followed Orville's advice. For a $25 shipping fee, he became the proud possessor of the entire 1911 glider, and the wings, rudder, elevator, and various bits of wood and wire of the world's first practical airplane.

Crane had only the slightest notion which two machines he had salvaged and he knew almost nothing about Wright airplanes. Fortunately, the lifesavers who had done the packing had separated the parts of the two aircraft. Just as fortunately, Crane set his carpenters to work "reassembling" the 1911 parts first. If one machine had to be sacrificed, the world's first soaring machine was marginally more expendable than the world's first genuine airplane.

Working from photographs, Crane's workmen cut, bent, and twisted the 1911 glider parts into a rough facsimile of the 1902 glider. Orville could make no sense of the photographs of the reconstruction that Crane provided—only when he visited the Berkshire Museum did the awful truth dawn on him. He absolutely refused to give Crane permission to exhibit the craft, which was eventually scrapped. The historic 1911 glider was gone forever.

With a clear notion of just how valuable the remaining bits and pieces of the 1905 machine were, Crane, his relatives, and friends spent the next thirty years pleading for Orville's assistance in mounting a restoration effort. Orville had the engine of the 1905 craft in his Dayton laboratory, along with an assortment of other parts that could be used in refurbishing the machine. And he had received a number of letters over the years from individuals requesting that he identify the parts they had found in the old Wright camp while vacationing on the Outer Banks during the period 1908–11. Those parts would be a valuable addition to a restoration effort.

Orville held back, refusing to become involved and discouraging Crane from proceeding on his own. He was convinced that the Pittsfield workmen who had unintentionally butchered the 1911 craft should not be allowed to attempt the same thing with the 1905 machine.

He had not forgotten the parts stored in the basement of the museum, however. Deeds's offer provided him with an opportunity to see that the job was finally done the right way. The first step would have to be handled with tact. After years of discouraging Zenas Crane, Orville would now have to approach the Berkshire Museum requesting that it turn the parts over to him.

Stuart C. Henry, the new director, proved cooperative. Crane was dead, and his museum had evolved into a gallery specializing in American art, with a small natural history collection and no serious interest in airplanes. By mid-December 1947, the remains of the 1905 airplane were back in Dayton.

Orville had already reassembled most of the parts of the 1905 engine, with the exception of the crankshaft and flywheel, which had been employed in the 1926 restoration of the 1903 airplane. Serious work on the airplane itself began early in 1947. Harvey Geyer, an experienced mechanic who had worked for the Wright Company from 1910 to 1912, volunteered to undertake the job under Orville's supervision.

As Deeds noted: "Mr. Wright, in characteristic fashion, spared no pains to insure authenticity in every detail." That was an understatement—Orville leaped into the task.[21]

The 1905 airplane was unveiled at Deeds Carillon Park with considerable fanfare in June 1950. Orville did not live to see that day. He suffered his first heart attack on October 10, 1947, while running up the front steps of the main NCR building to keep an appointment. Hospitalized for four days, he spent his time teasing the nurse and working out a means to improve the efficiency and comfort of the

The restoration of the 1905 Wright airplane for Deeds Park in Dayton was the last great project of Orville's life.

oxygen tents. He was released on October 14, after being cautioned to slow down.[22]

He spent the morning of January 27, 1948, fixing the doorbell at Hawthorn Hill. His second heart attack came after he had arrived at the laboratory. Miss Beck immediately summoned a physician from across the street and called Carrie Grumbach at the house. Carrie reached the laboratory before the ambulance pulled away. Orville Wright died in his bed at Miami Valley Hospital three days later, at 10:30 P.M. on January 30. He was seventy-seven years old.

Edward Deeds took charge of the funeral arrangements. The choice of a minister to conduct the services for a national figure who had not been to church or shown the slightest interest in religion for over half a century was a problem. Orville had once remarked that there were only two clergymen in Dayton whom he admired—a black preacher from the West Side and the Reverend Charles Lyon Seasholes, pastor of the First Baptist Church. Seasholes it would be.

Distinguished Americans flocked to Dayton for the funeral at the First Baptist Church on February 2. The leaders of the official delegation included General Carl Spaatz, Chief of Staff of the newly created U.S. Air Force; John Victory, long-time secretary of the NACA; Dr. Francis W. Reichelderfer, chief of the U.S. Weather Bureau; and Alexander Wetmore, the new secretary of the Smithsonian Institution.

Reverend Seasholes's eulogy summed up what most Americans had always thought about Orville Wright. A genius, he was also "a man who was just one of folks like us—middle class, mid-Western American, with simple, devout parents, and simple and modest way of life."[23]

Four jet fighters circled over Dayton as the funeral cortege drove toward Woodland Cemetery that afternoon. Flags flew at half mast from coast to coast; local schools were dismissed at noon. As they laid him to rest, the four jets swooped low over the cemetery in formation, dipped their wings, and flew off. All of them—Susan, Milton, Wilbur, Katharine, and now Orville—were together again.[24]

Reporters hounded the family over the next week. What was to become of the 1903 airplane? For the moment, there was no answer to that question. Officials of the Science Museum had not made Orville's 1943 letter public, and he had not announced his intentions.

Family and friends assumed that Orville had named Mabel Beck as his executor, and waited patiently for the secretary to produce a will. When nothing happened, Harold Miller proceeded to Orville's bank to check on its whereabouts. Bank officials then contacted Orville's lawyer, Charles Funkhouser, who produced the will. To everyone's surprise, Orville had named Miller and Harold Steeper, both nephews by marriage, as his executors.

He left an estate slightly in excess of $1 million. For the most part, the executors' duties were simple enough. There was a large $300,000 bequest to Oberlin, Katharine's alma mater; the remainder of the estate was broken up into bequests for members of the family, old friends, and employees.

The treatment of the historic materials that were part of the estate presented far greater problems. What was to become of the vast collection of letters, notebooks, scrapbooks, and photographs chronicling the invention of the airplane? The will charged the executors with the disposition of those materials.

So long as Albert Zahm had served on the staff of the Library of Congress, that repository of the papers of great Americans had been out of the question. Soon after Zahm's retirement in 1945, however, Orville had opened discussions with Archibald McLeish, the distinguished poet who was serving as Librarian of Congress.[25]

Immediately after the funeral, Miller and Steeper received word from the Library that the papers ought to be regarded as a national treasure. The Library of Congress it would be—with one stipulation. Some means would have to be found to publish sections of the papers.

Marvin W. McFarland, a young scholar fresh from wartime service with the Army Air Forces, was placed in charge of the program. The original plan called for the publication of pamphlets containing items from the collection on special topics—a booklet on propeller research, another on the wind-tunnel tests, and so on. What finally evolved was far more useful—an edited set of the most important materials from the collection that would enable the brothers to tell the complete story of the invention of the airplane in their own words. Initially planned as a three-volume set, later reduced to two, *The Papers of Wilbur and Orville Wright* were published by McGraw-Hill in 1953. They remain today as one of the finest sets of published American historical papers—a monument to the scholarship of McFarland and his colleagues.

The Library of Congress had decided to take only those materials relating to the history of flight. As a result, a wealth of purely family items—letters, papers, photos, and documents tracing the history of the Wrights back to their roots in seventeenth-century New England—remained in Ivonette and Harold Miller's basement in Dayton for another quarter of a century. On May 2, 1974, the Millers and the other surviving heirs of the Orville Wright estate donated this second major collection to a local facility named, appropriately enough, The Wright State University.

Determining the most appropriate home for the world's first airplane was more complex. When Miller and Steeper studied the 1937 will, they discovered the passage deeding the machine to the Science Museum, unless Orville had revoked that clause with a letter indicating a new disposition. Judge Love of the Montgomery County Probate Court ordered Harold Miller to look for such a document. He began in the most obvious place—with Mabel Beck.

Miss Beck admitted that such a letter existed, but refused to produce it. Miller left the office at once and called Earl Findley in Washington, who, in turn, called Miss Beck, reminding her of her obligation to respect Orville's wishes. She turned the letter over to Miller at a meeting in Edward Deeds's office the following day. The news that Orville Wright had relented and asked that the world's first airplane be sent to the Smithsonian was announced the same afternoon.[26]

There was jubilation at the Smithsonian. When the new secretary, Alexander Wetmore, had first been informed of the stipulation regarding the airplane in the 1937 will, he had remarked to General "Hap" Arnold that, "So far as I know, no such instrument [a letter calling the machine back to the U.S.] was ever issued."[27] Believing that the airplane would stay in England, Wetmore planned to have a full-scale replica of the 1903 Wright Flyer constructed for the museum.

Once the executors announced the existence of the letter, Wetmore immediately opened discussions with the heirs, and with the British government, to arrange the return as expeditiously as possible. Problems still remained to be solved. The executors and the lawyer for the estate insisted on steps to ensure that the Wright heirs would not be liable for an enormous inheritance tax on the priceless relic.

The final arrangement, approved by the Internal Revenue Service, called for the executors to sue the heirs for possession of the machine. This clarification of ownership was required to ensure that no heir would be able to return to the executors with a claim that he or she had been cheated out of a share of money that might have been made from the sale of the airplane to the highest bidder, or through exhibition fees. The executors stated in open court that, as the aircraft was beyond price, it would be sold to the United States National Museum for the sum of one dollar, thus freeing the estate of any potential tax obligation for the artifact. The people of the United States were the ultimate beneficiaries.[28]

The contract for the sale of the world's first airplane to the museum would include other provisions as well, safeguards against a reopening of the feud. The airplane, for example, was never to be exhibited outside the Washington area. A specified label, approved by a committee of Orville Wright's old friends, was always to appear with the machine on exhibition. Finally, if the Smithsonian recognized any other aircraft as having been capable of powered, sustained, and controlled flight with a man on board before December 17, 1903, the executors of the estate would have the right to take possession of the machine once again. The Smithsonian signed.

The long feud came to an end on the morning of December 17, 1948. Eight hundred and fifty people attended the ceremony in the North Hall of the Smithsonian's Arts and Industries Building. They sat in chairs ranged along the east wall, facing a temporary speakers' platform—and the great, tattered flag that Francis Scott Key had seen still flying over Fort McHenry in the dawn's early light of September 14, 1814.

The Star Spangled Banner was but one of the American icons crowded into this building. George Washington's uniform, Thomas Jefferson's writing desk, Benjamin Franklin's stove, the oldest American locomotive, gowns worn by each First Lady since Martha Washington—precious physical reminders of two hundred years of American life were stuffed into every corner of the National Museum.

Visitors entered this cluttered treasure house through the North Hall, which housed the most popular single object in the museum, the *Spirit of St. Louis.* The silver Ryan monoplane had held the place of honor, suspended high above the central entrance doors, since its arrival at the Smithsonian in 1928. A month before the ceremony, workmen carefully moved the *Spirit* toward the rear of the hall to make room for a new centerpiece. Charles Lindbergh did not complain. When curator Paul Garber informed him of the impending move, Lindbergh remarked that he was honored to know that his machine would be sharing the hall with the world's first airplane, the 1903 Wright Flyer.

The ceremony began promptly at 10:00 A.M., for timing was of some importance. Precisely fifty-five years before, just after ten o'clock on the morning of December 17, 1903, the Wright Flyer had rolled down a sixty-foot takeoff rail laid out on the sand flats some four miles south of the fishing village of Kitty Hawk, North Carolina, and climbed into the air.

Alexander Wetmore opened the proceedings with a short welcoming speech, then he introduced the Honorable Fred Vinson, Chief Justice of the United States and chancellor of the Smithsonian Institution. Vinson in turn welcomed the guests and called Major General Luther D. Miller, Chief of Chaplains of the U.S. Air Force, to the podium to offer the invocation. Colonel Robert Landry, President Truman's Air Force aide, read a greeting from the President, after which Sir Oliver Franks, British ambassador to the United States, made a few appropriate remarks.

Milton Wright, a nephew of the Wright brothers, then came forward to present the world's first airplane to the National Museum. Vice-President Alben W. Barkeley accepted on behalf of the people of the United States with a speech which one of those present remembered as "poor, and poorly read." The U.S. Air Force band concluded with "The Star-Spangled Banner." The Wright Flyer had come home.[29]

Many of the guests who filed out of the historic North Hall after the ceremony planned to attend a black-tie dinner that evening at which the prestigious Collier Trophy would be awarded to Captain Charles Yeager, John Stack, Lawrence Bell, and other members of the

NACA/Air Force/industry team which had conducted the first supersonic flight research program.

A few of the guests, it is to be hoped, paused to read the label on the world's first airplane, hanging at long last where it had always belonged. It may have led them to wonder at the progress wrought in the forty-four short years separating Kitty Hawk from the sound barrier.

THE ORIGINAL WRIGHT BROTHERS AEROPLANE
THE WORLD'S FIRST POWER-DRIVEN,
HEAVIER-THAN-AIR MACHINE IN WHICH MAN
MADE FREE, CONTROLLED, AND SUSTAINED FLIGHT
INVENTED AND BUILT BY WILBUR AND ORVILLE WRIGHT
FLOWN BY THEM AT KITTY HAWK, NORTH CAROLINA
DECEMBER 17, 1903
BY ORIGINAL SCIENTIFIC RESEARCH THE WRIGHT BROTHERS
DISCOVERED THE PRINCIPLES OF HUMAN FLIGHT
AS INVENTORS, BUILDERS, AND FLYERS THEY
FURTHER DEVELOPED THE AEROPLANE,
TAUGHT MAN TO FLY, AND OPENED
THE ERA OF AVIATION

NOTES

PROLOGUE

1. Details of what occurred on May 25, 1910, are to be found in Milton Wright's diary entry for that day, box 10, file 4, The Wright Brothers Collection, Wright State University Archives, Dayton, Ohio.

2. George Burba, "Orville Wright—A Sketch," Dayton *Daily News*, January 4, 1909.

3. Ivonette Wright Miller, ed., *Wright Reminiscences* (Dayton, Ohio: Privately printed, 1978), p. 64.

4. Fred C. Kelly, ed., *Miracle at Kitty Hawk: The Letters of Wilbur and Orville Wright* (New York: Farrar, Straus & Young, 1951), p. 47.

5. Katharine Wright to Milton Wright, September 25, 1901, in ibid., p. 46.

6. *New York Times*, June 1, 1909.

7. Harry Harper, *My Fifty Years in Flying* (London: Associated Newspapers, 1956), p. 110.

8. Quoted in *New York Times*, June 1, 1909.

9. Milton Wright to the Editor of *Who's Who*, October 4, 1908, in Miller, ed., *Wright Reminiscences*, p. 168.

10. Jess Gilbert, "A Tribute," in ibid., p. 184.

11. Miller, ed., *Wright Reminiscences*, p. 62; see also John R. McMahon, *The Wright Brothers: Fathers of Flight* (New York: Little, Brown, 1930), p. 11.

12. Wilbur Wright to Octave Chanute, October 28, 1906, in Marvin W. McFarland, ed., *The Papers of Wilbur and Orville Wright* (New York: McGraw-Hill, 1953), vol. 2, pp. 731–732.

CHAPTER 1

1. Milton Wright, undated manuscript, "Facts and Dates," box 8, file 8, The Wright Brothers Collection, Wright State University Archives (cited hereafter as Wright Collection, WSU).

2. Milton Wright to Mrs. Cornelius Vanderbilt, November 29, 1899, box 14, file 7, WSU.

3. Milton Wright, undated manuscript (probably 1912), "Ancestors," box 8, file 8, WSU.

4. Ibid.

5. Ibid.; Milton Wright, undated manuscript, "My Father's Life," box 8, file 8; and Milton Wright, manuscript dated February 1912, "My Grand Parents and Parents," box 8, file 8, WSU; H. A. Thompson, *Our Bishops* (Dayton, Ohio: United Brethren Publishing House, 1903), pp. 525–549; Paul Rodes Koontz and Walter Edwin Roush, *The Bishops: Church of the United Brethren in Christ* (Dayton, Ohio: Otterbein Press, 1950), vol. 2, pp. 60–75.

6. "Ancestors."

7. Porter Wright to Dan Wright, assorted letters, box 11, file 6, WSU.

8. Asahel Wright to Dan Wright, January 3, 1827, box 11, file 6, WSU.

9. Asahel Wright to Dan Wright, Dec. 26, 1828, and February 20, 1829; copies in box 11, file 5, WSU. Originals in Dayton Collection, Montgomery County Public Library.

10. Sanford C. Cox, *Recollections of the Early Settlement of the Wabash Valley* (Freeport, N.Y.: Books for Libraries Press, 1970), pp. 16, 25.

11. *Indiana: A Guide to the Hoosier State* (New York: Oxford University Press, 1941), p. 107.

12. "Ancestors."

13. "My Grand Parents and Parents," p. 6.

14. Ibid., p. 7; "My Father's Life"; see other descriptions in manuscript and printed sources cited in note 5.

15. "My Grand Parents and Parents," p. 7; see also Thompson, *Our Bishops*, p. 527; Koontz and Roush, *The Bishops*.

16. "My Grand Parents and Parents."

17. Thompson, *Our Bishops*, p. 532.

18. "Ancestors."

19. Ibid.

20. Ibid.; see also Thompson, *Our Bishops;* Koontz and Roush, *The Bishops*.

21. "Ancestors."

22. Ibid.

23. Ibid.

24. Ibid.

25. Ibid.

26. On the history of the Church of the United Brethren in Christ, see Daniel Berger, *History of the Church of the United Brethren in Christ* (Dayton, Ohio: United Brethren Publishing House, 1906); A. W. Drury, *History of the Church of the United Brethren in Christ* (Dayton, Ohio: United Brethren Publishing House, 1924); Paul H. Fetters, *Trials and Triumphs* (Huntington, Ind.: Department of Church Services, 1984); Frank S. Mead, *Handbook of Denomination in the U.S.* (New York: Abingdon-Cokesbury, 1950); Robert T. Handy, *A History of the Churches in the United States and Canada* (New York: Oxford University Press, 1977); various issues of *The United Brethren Yearbook* also contain useful historical information. For Milton Wright's White River Conference, see Augustus Cleland Wilmore, *History of the White River Conference of the Church of the United Brethren in Christ* (Dayton, Ohio: United Brethren Publishing House, 1925).

27. Milton Wright Teaching Certificates, box 8, file 8, WSU.

28. Milton Wright manuscript letter, January 7, 1916, box 8, file 8, WSU.

29. Ibid.

30. Milton Wright to William Wright, December 24, 1855, and March 17, 1853; box 8, file 9, WSU.

31. Milton Wright manuscript letter, January 16, 1916, box 8, file 8, WSU.

CHAPTER 2

1. The details of the Koerner-Fry (or Fryer) families fascinated Orville Wright, who shared his father's enthusiasm for genealogy. His correspondence with W. E. Martin, a Leesburg, Va., lawyer, about his mother's background and birthplace provide the basis for this section; box 12, file 11. See also Koerner Letters, box 12, files 8–10, Wright State University Archives (cited hereafter as WSU).

2. Orville Wright quoted in Fred C. Kelly, *The Wright Brothers: A Biography Authorized by Orville Wright* (New York: Harcourt, Brace, 1943), p. 10.

3. H. A. Thompson, *Our Bishops* (Dayton, Ohio: United Brethren Publishing House, 1903), p. 529.

4. Jess B. Gilbert, "A Tribute," in Ivonette Wright Miller, ed., *Wright Reminiscences* (Dayton, Ohio: Privately printed, 1978), pp. 183–184.

5. Milton Wright Diary, May 28, 1857, box 8, file 11, WSU (cited hereafter as Diary). The author has made use of a complete typed transcript of Milton Wright's diary prepared for the Wright family by the Wright State University Archives.

6. Diary, June 19, 1857.

7. Milton Wright to William Wright, July 4, 1857, box 8, file 9, WSU; see also Diary, July 4, 1857.

8. Milton Wright to William Wright, July 4, 1857, box 8, file 9, WSU.

9. Diary, July 6–18, 1857; Milton Wright to Dan and Catherine Wright, August 11, 1857, box 8, file 9, WSU.

10. Diary, July 20, 1857.

11. Diary, August 2, 1857.

12. Ibid.

13. Diary, November 1859.

14. Diary, November 14, 1859.

15. Milton Wright to Wilbur Wright, July 4, 1908, box 6, The Papers of Wilbur and Orville Wright, Manuscript Division, Library of Congress (cited hereafter as Wright Papers, LC).

16. Milton Wright to Wilbur Wright, October 11, 1907, box 5, Wright Papers, LC.

17. Milton Wright, untitled notes inserted in Diary for 1859, WSU.

18. Ibid.

19. Milton Wright to William Wright, November 27, 1862, box 5, WSU.

20. Ibid.; Milton Wright, untitled notes inserted in Diary for 1859, WSU; Milton Wright to William Wright, October 22, 1863, box 5, WSU.

21. Assorted deeds and titles, box 97, Wright Papers, LC; Milton Wright, untitled notes inserted in Diary for 1859, WSU.

22. Ibid.

23. Thompson, *Our Bishops*, p. 532; Diary, special notes on 1861, added later to 1858 Diary.

24. Interview with Milton Wright entitled "Wilbur Wright Born in Henry County," undated newspaper clipping, Wright Scrapbooks, 1909, Wright Papers, LC.

25. *The Reform Leaflet* (October 1881), vol. 1, no. 1, 2; see also April 1882; July 1882, WSU.

26. Thompson, *Our Bishops*, p. 549.

CHAPTER 3

1. A. W. Drury, *History of the City of Dayton and Montgomery County, Ohio* (Dayton, Ohio: S. J. Clarke Co., 1909), vol. 1, p. 574; Sam Bass Warner, *Streetcar Suburbs: The Process of Growth in Boston, 1870–1900* (New York: Atheneum, 1970), and John W. Repps, *The Making of Urban America: A History of City Planning in the United States* (Princeton, N.J.: Princeton University Press, 1968), are the best studies of the development of streetcar suburbs like West Dayton. Other details rest in part on the work of Allan Fletcher, *The Wright Brothers' Home and Cycle Shop in Greenfield Village*, a thesis in the University of Michigan Program in Museum Practice, June 30, 1972, and on discussions with curators of Greenfield Village, Dearborn, Mich.

2. Montgomery County Recorder's Office, Deed Record J-4; Fletcher, *Wright Brothers' Home.*

3. U.S. Census, 1890 and 1900, Ward 5, Enumeration District 54, National Archives.

4. The figures are the author's estimates based on loose notes in M. Wright Diaries and assorted biographical materials, deeds, and legal documents; Wright Papers, boxes 96–98, LC.

5. For games and childhood life in West Dayton, see "Fox and Townball Were Early Sports," Dayton *Journal* (June 16, 1909), and John R. McMahon, *The Wright Brothers: Fathers of Flight* (Boston: Little, Brown, 1930), p. 22.

6. Milton Wright to Reuchlin Wright, November 9, 1899, box 5, Wright Papers, LC.

7. Ibid.; McMahon, *Wright Brothers*, p. 24.

8. McMahon, *Wright Brothers*, p. 32.

9. Ivonette Wright Miller, "Ivonette Wright Miller's Reminiscences," in Miller, ed., *Wright Reminiscences* (Dayton, Ohio: Privately printed, 1978), pp. 3–4.

10. Wilbur Wright, Last Will and Testament, May 10, 1912, in Alfred Stokes Andrews, *The Andrews, Clapp, Stokes, Wright, Van Cleve Genealogies* (Fort Lauderdale, Fla.: Privately printed, 1984), p. 502.

11. Wilbur Wright, April 3, 1912, in Marvin W. McFarland, ed., *The Papers of Wilbur and Orville Wright* (New York: McGraw-Hill, 1953), vol. 1, p. v.

12. McMahon, *Wright Brothers*, p. 21.

13. H. A. Thompson, *Our Bishops* (Dayton, Ohio: United Brethren Publishing House, 1903), p. 543.

14. Ibid.

15. Ibid., pp. 545–546.

16. Ibid., pp. 542–543; see also Paul Rodes Koontz and Walter Edwin Roush, *The Bishops: Church of the United Brethren in Christ* (Dayton, Ohio: Otterbein Press, 1950), and Paul R. Fetters, *Trials and Triumphs: A History of the Church of the United Brethren in Christ* (Huntington, Ind.: Church of the United Brethren in Christ, Department of Church Services, 1984), pp. 237–238.

17. Fetters, *Trials and Triumphs*, pp. 237–238.

18. Information on the houses in Cedar Rapids and Adair is from Milton Wright's Diary, passim, Wright State University Archives.

19. McMahon, *Wright Brothers*, p. 28.

20. Interview with Milton Wright, "Wilbur Wright Born in Henry County," undated newspaper clipping, Wright Scrapbooks, 1909, Wright Papers, LC.

21. Fred C. Kelly, ed., *Miracle at Kitty Hawk* (New York: Farrar, Straus & Young, 1951), p. 3. Original in Wright Papers, LC.

CHAPTER 4

1. Milton Wright to Susan Wright, June 2, 1888, box 5, Wright Papers, Library of Congress.

2. Milton Wright to Katharine Wright, May 3, 1888, box 5, Wright Papers, LC.

3. Milton Wright to Katharine Wright, October 15, 1887, box 5, Wright Papers, LC.

4. Milton Wright to Susan Wright, September 11, 1888, box 5, Wright Papers, LC.

5. Fred C. Kelly, *The Wright Brothers* (New York: Harcourt, Brace, 1943), p. 15.

6. Octave Chanute, *Progress in Flying Machines* (New York: The American Engineer and Railroad Journal, 1894), pp. 55–56. See also "Remarks by Milton Wright," Smithsonian Institution Press Release, December 17, 1948, 28; Ivonette Wright Miller, ed., *Wright Reminiscences* (Dayton, Ohio: Privately printed, 1978), p. 4; Milton Wright to Reuchlin Wright, November 9, 1899, box 5, Wright Papers, LC; and C. H. Gibbs-Smith, *Aviation: An Historical Survey* (London: HMSO, 1970), pp. 46–47.

7. Orville Wright, Deposition, January 13, 1920, in Marvin W. McFarland, ed., *The Papers of Wilbur and Orville Wright* (New York: McGraw-Hill, 1953), vol. 1, p. 3.

8. Grace Boston, "Wright Boys Interested in Aviation When They Were School Boys in This City," Cedar Rapids *Evening Gazette* (Sept. 19, 1928); "Remembering When Orville and Wilbur Wright Were Iowa Schoolboys," undated article, Wright Scrapbooks, 1928, Wright Papers, LC.

9. "Remarks by Milton Wright."

10. "Teacher Tells of Boys; They Caused No Trouble," Dayton *Herald,* June 16, 1909.

11. Kelly, *Wright Brothers,* p. 1.

12. Ibid., p. 5.

13. Boston, "Wright Boys."

14. "Teacher Tells of Boys."

15. Milton Wright, Diaries, 1878, WSU.

16. Milton Wright to Wilbur Wright, October 3, 1907, box 6, Wright Papers, LC. Dr. Adrian J. Kinnane offers a similar interpretation of Reuchlin's rebellion in "The Crucible of Flight."

17. H. A. Thompson, *Our Bishops* (Dayton, Ohio: United Brethren Publishing House, 1903), p. 546. For an example of the bishop's attitude toward politicians, see Milton Wright to Wilbur Wright, August 27, 1908, box 6, Wright Papers, LC.

18. Ibid.

19. *Reform Leaflet,* vol. 1, no. 1, box 8, file 4, WSU.

20. Thompson, *Our Bishops,* p. 544.

21. Lorin Wright to Susan Wright, October 31, 1882, box 5, Wright Papers, LC.

22. Ibid.; see also other letters, box 5.

23. Philomatheon Program, box 3, file 4, WSU.

24. Assorted report cards, box 3, file 3, WSU.

25. Interview with Milton Wright entitled "Wilbur Wright Born in Henry County," undated newspaper clipping, Wright Scrapbooks, Wright Papers, LC.

26. Susan Wright to Milton Wright, June 20, 1884, box 8, file 10, WSU.

CHAPTER 5

1. A. W. Drury, *History of the Church of the United Brethren in Christ* (Dayton, Ohio: United Brethren Publishing House, 1924), p. 475.

2. Paul Fetters, *Trials and Triumphs* (Huntington, Ind.: Department of Church Services, 1984), pp. 234–270, provides the clearest description of the crisis.

3. Ibid.

4. Dayton *Daily Journal*, May 25, 1885.

5. *Lutheran Standard* quoted in the *Christian Conservator*, July 15, 1885.

6. Dayton *Daily Journal*, May 27, 1885.

7. Susan Wright to Milton Wright, September 20, 1888, July 23, 1888, and September 20, 1888; all in file 10, box 8, Wright Collection, WSU.

8. Milton sent his son detailed advice on farming during these years. See, for example, Milton Wright to Reuchlin Wright, December 1901, box 5, Wright Papers, LC.

9. Katharine Wright to Milton Wright, September 25, 1902, box 5, Wright Papers, LC.

10. Reuchlin Wright to Milton Wright, September 17, 1901, box 6, Wright Papers, LC.

11. Wilbur Wright to Reuchlin Wright, May 20, 1902, box 7, Wright Papers, LC.

12. Reuchlin Wright to Milton Wright, April 2, 1911, box 6, Wright Papers, LC.

13. Reuchlin Wright to Milton Wright, October 6, 1912, box 6, Wright Papers, LC.

14. Lorin's letters to Katharine offer a classic picture of life on the Kansas frontier in the roaring eighties. See, for example, Lorin Wright to Katharine Wright, November 29, 1887, box 5, Wright Papers, LC.

15. Lorin Wright to Katharine Wright, August 4, 1888, August 15, 1888, November 12, 1888, and May 30, 1888; all in box 5, Wright Papers, LC.

16. Lorin Wright to Katharine Wright, November 12, 1888, box 5, Wright Papers, LC.

17. Dayton *Daily News*, December 18, 1927, "Ed Ellis Tells of the Boys' Characteristics," undated article, Wright Scrapbooks, 1909, Wright Papers, LC; Wilbur Wright grade cards, Wright Collection, file 3, box 3, WSU.

18. Milton Wright, "Notes for Who's Who," October 26, 1907, in Ivonette Wright Miller, ed., *Wright Reminiscences* (Dayton, Ohio: Privately printed, 1978), p. 170.

19. Wilbur Wright to Milton Wright, September 12, 1894, box 7, Wright Papers, LC; also in Fred C. Kelly, ed., *Miracle at Kitty Hawk* (New York: Farrar, Straus & Young, 1951), pp. 8–10.

20. Wilbur Wright to George Spratt, January 23, 1902, in Marvin W. McFarland, ed., *The Papers of Wilbur and Orville Wright* (New York: McGraw-Hill, 1953), vol. 1, p. 205.

21. Wilbur Wright to George Spratt, December 2, 1903, in ibid., vol. 1, p. 390.

22. Interview with Milton Wright, "Wilbur Wright Born in Henry County," undated newspaper clipping in Wright Scrapbooks, 1909, Wright Papers, LC.

23. Wilbur Wright, *Scenes in the Church Commission During the Last Day of Its Session* (Dayton, Ohio: Wright Brothers, Job Printers, 1888).

24. Ibid.

25. See Paul Fetters, *Trials and Triumphs* (Huntington, Ind.: Church of the United Brethren in Christ, 1984), pp. 267–270, for details of the crisis.

26. Wilbur Wright to Milton Wright, August 13, 1888, box 6, Wright Papers, LC.

27. Wilbur Wright to the Rev. Mr. McGee, April 13, 1888, box 41, Wright Papers, LC.

28. Wilbur Wright to Milton Wright, August 23, 1888, box 6, Wright Papers, LC.

29. Fetters, *Trials and Triumphs*, pp. 273–274.

30. Ibid., p. 275.

31. Walter E. Musgrave, *The Church of the United Brethren in Christ: Its Teachings and Progress* (Huntington, Ind.: Church of the United Brethren in Christ, 1945), p. 76; Drury, *History*, p. 475.

32. Milton Wright, Diary, July 4, 1889, file 4, box 9, Wright Collection, WSU.

CHAPTER 6

1. Walter E. Musgrave, *The Church of the United Brethren in Christ: Its Teachings and Progress* (Huntington, Ind.: Church of the United Brethren in Christ, 1945), p. 77; Paul R. Fetters, *Trials and Triumphs: A History of the Church of the United Brethren in Christ* (Huntington, Ind.: Church of the United Brethren in Christ, 1984), p. 306.

2. *Proceedings of the Twenty-Third General Conference of the United Brethren in Christ* (Huntington, Ind.: United Brethren Publishing Enterprise, 1901), p. 196.

3. Fetters, *Trials and Triumphs*, p. 314.

4. Musgrave, *The Church of the United Brethren in Christ*, pp. 75–76.

5. Ibid., p. 76.

6. Milton Wright to Katharine Wright, October 15, 1887, and May 30, 1889; both in box 5, Wright Papers, LC.

7. Milton Wright to Katharine Wright, August 9, 1889, box 5, Wright Papers, LC.

8. Milton Wright, Diary, September 18, 1893, box 9, file 5, WSU.

9. Milton Wright to Wilbur Wright, October 11, 1907, box 5, Wright Papers, LC.

10. Milton Wright to Katharine Wright, September 12, 1892, box 5, Wright Papers, LC.

11. Ibid.

12. For more on Milton's complex attitude toward women in the professions, see Milton Wright, "Women as Physicians," *The Religious Telescope* (January

1870), in H. A. Thompson, *Our Bishops* (Dayton, Ohio: United Brethren Publishing House, 1903), p. 543.

13. Lorin Wright to Milton Wright, July 12, 1889, box 5, Wright Papers, LC.

14. For information on the Reuchlin and Lorin Wright families, see A. S. Andrews, *The Andrews, Clapp, Stokes, Wright and Van Cleve Genealogies* (Fort Lauderdale, Fla.: Privately printed, 1984), pp. 447–483.

15. Milton Wright to Wilbur Wright, September 9 and 14, 1908, box 6, Wright Papers, LC.

16. Milton Wright to Wilbur Wright, June 28, 1908, box 6, Wright Papers, LC.

17. Milton Wright to Wilbur Wright, August 11, 1907, box 6, Wright Papers, LC.

18. Milton Wright to Wilbur Wright, September 19, 1907, box 6, Wright Papers, LC.

19. Milton Wright to Wilbur Wright, August 27, 1908, box 6, Wright Papers, LC.

20. Milton Wright to Wilbur Wright, August 4, 1907, box 6, Wright Papers, LC.

21. Milton Wright to Wilbur Wright, July 23, 1908, box 6, Wright Papers, LC.

22. Wilbur Wright to Milton Wright, December 1, 1898, box 6, Wright Papers, LC.

CHAPTER 7

1. Fred C. Kelly, *The Wright Brothers* (New York: Harcourt, Brace, 1943), p. 13.

2. Orville Wright grade cards, file 3, box 3, Wright Collection, WSU.

3. William Werthner, "Personal Recollections of the Wrights," *Aero Club of America Bulletin* (July 1912), 13.

4. Kelly, *Wright Brothers*, p. 17.

5. Miscellaneous items printed by the Wright brothers, file 17, box 3, Wright Collection, WSU.

6. Orville Wright to Milton Wright, July 20, 1888, box 4, Wright Papers, LC.

7. Charles J. Bauer, "Ed Sines: Pal of the Wrights," *Popular Aviation* (June 1938), 40.

8. All quotations from *The West Side News* and *The Evening Item* are drawn from the complete file of original issues in the Dayton Collection of the Dayton and Montgomery County Public Library. Microfilm copies of the entire run of both newspapers are available at the Library of Congress, the Ohio Historical Society, and the Wright State University.

9. Orville Wright to Milton Wright, October 16, 1891, in Fred C. Kelly, ed., *Miracle at Kitty Hawk* (New York: Farrar, Straus & Young, 1951), pp. 6–7.

10. *Thanksgiving Tid-Bits* (1891), box 3, file 10, WSU.

11. The bit of doggerel is quoted in Marvin W. McFarland, ed., *The Papers of Wilbur and Orville Wright* (New York: McGraw-Hill, 1953), vol. 1, p. 696, note 1. All three original issues of *The Tattler* are in the collection of the Dayton and Montgomery County Public Libarary.

12. "Circuit Court of 7 Hawthorn St.," box 3, file 6, WSU.

13. Ivonette Wright Miller, "Character Study," in Miller, ed., *Wright Reminiscences* (Dayton, Ohio: Privately printed, 1978), p. 61.

CHAPTER 8

1. Wilbur Wright to Katharine Wright, September 18, 1892, box 5, Wright Papers, LC.

2. Ibid.

3. Ibid.

4. Detroit *Tribune* (May 1, 1896); W J McGee, "Fifty Years of American Science," in A. Hunter Dupree, ed., *Science and the Emergence of Modern America* (Chicago: University of Chicago Press, 1953), p. 325; other quotes from Robert Smith, *A Social History of the Bicycle* (New York: American Heritage, 1972), passim.

5. *Eleventh Census of the United States, 1900* vol. X, pt. 1, p. 325.

6. David Hounshell, *From the American System to Mass Production* (Baltimore: Johns Hopkins University Press, 1984).

7. Mitchell R. Charnley, *The Boys' Life of the Wright Brothers* (New York: Harper & Brothers, 1928), pp. 40–41.

8. Wilbur Wright, "The Rights of Cyclists," *Snap-Shots of Current Events* (Oct. 29, 1894), vol. 1, no. 1.

9. *Williams' Dayton Directory* (Philadelphia: Williams & Co., 1895), p. 931.

10. Wilbur Wright to Milton Wright, September 12, 1894, box 6, Wright Papers, LC.

11. Wilbur Wright to Milton Wright, October 2, 1894, box 6, Wright Papers, LC.

12. Wilbur Wright to Milton Wright, September 1894, box 6, Wright Papers, LC.

13. The only complete collection of *Snap-Shots* is in the Dayton Room, Dayton and Montgomery County Public Library.

14. Orville Wright to Milton Wright, October 8, 1895, box 6, Wright Papers, LC.

15. Charles J. Bauer, "Ed Sines: Pal of the Wrights," *Popular Aviation* (June 1938), 78.

16. Milton Wright to Reuchlin Wright, March 17, 1896, box 6, Wright Papers, LC.

17. *Snap-Shots* (April 17, 1896), vol. 2, no. 6, 1.

18. "Wright Cycle Co., Makers, 1127 West Third Street, Dayton, Ohio," reprinted in *Wheelman* (November 1980), no. 17, 14.

18. Binghamton *Republican* (June 4, 1896). Clipping in S. P. Langley Scrapbooks, Ramsey Rare Book Room, National Air and Space Museum, Washington, D.C.

19. Rev. E. S. Upford and Rev. John Scudder, both quoted in *New York Herald* (June 17, 1895).

20. Minneapolis *Tribune* (Sept. 14, 1895).

21. James Means, "Wheeling and Flying," *The Aeronautical Annual* (Boston, 1896), p. 25.

22. Ibid.

CHAPTER 9

1. "Ed Ellis Tells of the Boys' Characteristics," Dayton *Herald* (June 16, 1909).

2. Katharine Wright, quoted in Ivonette Wright Miller, "Ivonette Miller's Reminiscences," in Ivonette Wright Miller, ed., *Wright Reminiscences* (Dayton, Ohio: Privately printed, 1978), p. 4.

3. Ibid.

4. Charles E. Taylor, "My Story of the Wright Brothers," *Collier's Magazine* (Dec. 25, 1948).

5. "Wilbur Wright Is Named in Divorce Suit by Frenchman—Plot Suspected," Dayton *Herald* (June 8, 1908).

6. "He's Too Clean Says Life Chum," Dayton *Herald* (June 8, 1908).

7. "What He Thinks of Newspaper Scandals," Dayton *Herald* (June 8, 1908).

8. Jess Gilbert, "A Tribute," in Miller, ed., *Wright Reminiscences*, p. 183.

9. The discussion of Agnes Osborn is based on conversations with Mrs. Elizabeth Rehling, Mrs. Osborn's daughter, and with members of the Wright family.

10. Katharine Wright to Orville and Wilbur Wright, June 22, 1900, box 4, Wright Papers, LC.

11. Ibid.

12. Katharine Wright to Orville and Wilbur Wright, September 4, 1900, box 4, Wright Papers, LC.

13. Katharine Wright to Orville Wright, October 5, 1902, box 4, Wright Papers, LC.

14. Katharine Wright to Milton Wright, October 25, 1903, box 4, Wright Papers, LC.

15. Marvin W. McFarland, *The Papers of Wilbur and Orville Wright* (New York: McGraw-Hill, 1953), vol. 1, p. 57, note 8.

16. Katharine Wright to Milton Wright, September 11, 1901, box 4, Wright Papers, LC.

17. Katharine Wright to Milton Wright, September 21, 1901, box 4, Wright Papers, LC.

18. Orville Wright to Katharine Wright, September 11, 1902, box 6, Wright Papers, LC.

19. Katharine Wright to Milton Wright, September 12, 1900, box 4, Wright Papers, LC.

20. Katharine Wright to Milton Wright, April 17, 1901, box 4, Wright Papers, LC.

21. Katharine Wright to Milton Wright, September 5, 1900, box 4, Wright Papers, LC.

22. Katharine Wright to Milton Wright, September 28, 1903, box 4, Wright Papers, LC.

23. Katharine Wright to Milton Wright, November 1, 1903, box 4, Wright Papers, LC. Katharine's letters to Milton of 1900–03 are filled with repeated health complaints and expressions of loneliness.

24. Katharine Wright to Wilbur and Orville Wright, July 10, 1905, box 4, Wright Papers, LC.

25. Katharine Wright to Wilbur and Orville Wright, July 13, 1905, box 4, Wright Papers, LC.

26. Katharine Wright to Wilbur and Orville Wright, July 17, 1905, box 4, Wright Papers, LC.

27. Katharine Wright to Wilbur and Orville Wright, July 19, 1905, box 4, Wright Papers, LC.

28. Katharine Wright to Milton Wright, July 27, 1905, box 4, Wright Papers, LC.

29. Katharine Wright to Milton Wright, August 1, 1905, box 4, Wright Papers, LC.

30. Milton Wright to Katharine Wright, September 26, 1908, box 5, Wright Papers, LC.

31. Milton Wright to Katharine Wright, February 22, 1909, box 6, Wright Papers, LC.

32. Leontine Wright Jameson, "Reminiscences," in Miller, ed., *Wright Reminiscences*, p. 113.

33. Miller, ed., *Wright Reminiscences*, p. 2. For another view of the candy-making operation, see Horace Wright, "Recollections," in ibid., p. 153.

34. Horace Wright, "Recollections," p. 158.

35. Miller, ed., *Wright Reminiscences*, p. 3.

36. Milton Wright, "Remarks on Behalf of the Estate of Orville Wright, in Presenting the Kitty Hawk Aeroplane to the United States of America," Smithsonian Institution Press Release, December 17, 1948, Smithsonian Institution Archives.

37. Horace Wright, "Recollections," in Miller, ed., *Wright Reminiscences*, p. 156.

38. Ivonette Wright Miller, Untitled Reminiscences, author's collection, p. 22.

39. Miller, ed., *Wright Reminiscences*, p. 4.

40. Ibid.

41. Milton Wright, "Remarks."

42. Miller, ed., *Wright Reminiscences*, pp. 3–4.

43. Ibid.

44. Wilbur Wright to Lulu Billheimer Wright, June 18, 1901, box 7, Wright Papers, LC. Dr. Adrian Kinnane calls attention to the important insights represented in this letter in his "The Crucible of Flight."

45. Ibid.

46. Ibid.

47. Ibid.

CHAPTER 10

1. Paul H. Boller, Jr., *Presidential Campaigns* (New York: Oxford University Press, 1984), p. 72.

2. Details of spring and summer 1896 are drawn from the following sources:

3. John Trowbridge, "Darius Green and His Flying Machine," in Hazel Felaman, ed., *Poems That Live Forever* (New York: Macmillan, 1965), pp. 204–207.

4. Simon Newcomb, "Is the Airship Coming?" *McClure's* (September 1901), 562–565; George Melville, "The Engineer and the Problem of Aerial Navigation," *North American Review* (December 1901), 820–821; John Le Conte, "The Problem of the Flying Machine," *Popular Science Monthly* (November 1888), 69.

5. The treatment of aeronautical cranks is based on a series of unidentified clippings found in a Samuel Pierpont Langley scrapbook dated 1896, Ramsey Rare Book Room, National Air and Space Museum, and the historical scrapbooks of the Institute of Aeronautical Sciences, AIAA History Collection, Manuscript Division, LC.

6. The description of Langley's arrival at Widewater with Bell, and the details of the appearance of the town, are based on an undated Washington *Star* clipping found in the Samuel Pierpont Langley scrapbook for 1896.

7. Samuel Pierpont Langley, *Experiments in Aerodynamics* (Washington, D.C.: Smithsonian Institution Press, 1891).

8. Samuel Pierpont Langley, notebook entitled "Aerodromics 10," pp. 120–126, Ramsey Rare Book Room, National Air and Space Museum. For detailed treatments of the Aerodrome experiments, see Samuel Pierpont Langley, "Experiments with the Langley Aerodromes," *Report of the Board of Regents of the Smithsonian Institution for 1904* (Washington, D.C.: Smithsonian Institution Press, 1905), pp. 113–125; Samuel Pierpont Langley, "The Flying Machine," *McClure's* (June 1897), 646–660; and Samuel Pierpont Langley, *Researches and Experiments in Aerial Navigation*, (Washington, D.C.: Smithsonian Institution Press, 1908).

9. Description of the events of August 2, 1896, is based on R. W. Wood, "Lilienthal's Last Flights," Boston *Transcript* (Aug. 16, 1896). For additional reading on Lilienthal, see "The Flying Man," *McClure's* (September 1894), 1–10; "The Flying Man," *Aeronautics* (April 1894), 85–87; "Lilienthal's Experiments in Flying," *Nature* (Dec. 20, 1894), 177–179; and "Our Teachers in Soaring Flight," *Aeronautical Annual* (Boston, 1897), 84–91. The best available biography is Werner Schwipps, *Lilienthal* (Berlin: Arami-Verlag GmbH, 1979).

10. The only English translation is Otto Lilienthal, *Birdflight as the Basis of Aviation: A Contribution Toward a System of Aviation* (London, 1911).

11. Wood, "Lilienthal's Last Flights."

12. Ibid.

13. Ibid.

14. Ibid.

CHAPTER 11

1. Alice Chanute Boyd, "Some Memories of My Father," unpublished manuscript, box 45, Octave Chanute Collection, Manuscript Division, Library of Congress. A copy is also contained in the Chanute biographical file, National Air and Space Museum. The extracts and details of Chanute's life that follow are all drawn from the same source.

2. Leavenworth *Daily Tribune* (March 6, 1873); *Parsons Sun* (March 15, 1873); Quincy *Daily Evening Call* (March 10, 1873).

3. "Early Presidents of the Society," *Civil Engineering* (December 1937), 871.

4. Milton Wright describes his trip to the fair in his Diaries for the period, Wright State University Library.

5. A. F. Zahm, "Diary of the Aeronautical Congress of 1893, By Professor A.F. Zahm, General Secretary," October 19, 1892, unpublished manuscript in A. F. Zahm Collection, Notre Dame Archives, Notre Dame University, South Bend, Ind.

6. Pittsburgh *Dispatch* (Jan. 23, 1894).

7. Octave Chanute, *Progress in Flying Machines* (New York: Forney, 1894).

8. For biographical details, see "Augustus Herring," *Dictionary of American Biography;* J. V. Martin, "The Aircraft Conspiracy," *The Libertarian* (March 1924), 120–127; and A. M. Herring biographical file, Archives, National Air and Space Museum.

9. A. F. Zahm quoted in Carl Dienstbach, "Invention of the Chanute Glider," *American Aeronaut* (June 1908), 163; See also A. M. Herring, "Dynamic Flight," *Aeronautical Annual* (Boston, 1896), pp. 89–101.

10. For a detailed treatment of the 1896 trials, see Octave Chanute, "Recent Experiments in Gliding Flight," *The Aeronautical Annual* (Boston, 1897), 30–53; Octave Chanute, "Evolution of the Two-Surface Flying Machine," *Aeronautics* (October 1908), 9–10; and Octave Chanute, "Experiments in Flying," *McClure's* (June 1900).

CHAPTER 12

1. Milton Wright to Katharine Wright, August 31, 1896, box 4, Wright Papers, LC.

2. Wilbur Wright, "Some Aeronautical Experiments," in Marvin W. McFarland, ed., *The Papers of Wilbur and Orville Wright* (New York: McGraw-Hill, 1953, cited hereafter as *Papers*), vol. 1, p. 103.

3. Milton Wright, Diary, October 21, 1896, box 9, file 6, Wright Brothers Collection, WSU.

4. Orville Wright, Deposition, in McFarland, ed., *Papers*, vol. 1, p. 3.

5. Wilbur Wright, "Brief and Digest of the Evidence for Complainant on Final Hearing," The Wright Co. vs. Herring-Curtiss Co. and Glenn H. Curtiss in Equity No. 400, pp. 4–25; copy in Wright State University Archives.

6. Wilbur Wright to the Smithsonian Institution, May 30, 1899, in McFarland, ed., *Papers*, vol. 1, pp. 4–5.

7. Wilbur Wright to Milton Wright, September 23, 1900, in Fred C. Kelly, ed., *Miracle at Kitty Hawk: The Letters of Wilbur and Orville Wright* (New York: Farrar, Straus & Young, 1951), pp. 30–31; Katharine Wright to Milton Wright, September 26, 1900, in ibid., pp. 31–32.

8. Milton Wright to the Editor of *Who's Who*, October 4, 1908, quoted in Ivonette Wright Miller, ed., *Wright Reminiscences* (Dayton, Ohio: Privately printed, 1978), pp. 68–69.

9. Milton Wright to Wilbur Wright, August 2, 1908, box 6, Wright Papers, LC.

10. Milton Wright to Katharine Wright, March 22, 1909, box 6, Wright Papers, LC.

11. Milton Wright, Diary, May 30, 1912, WSU.

12. Milton Wright to the Editor of *Who's Who*, October 4, 1908, in Miller, ed., *Wright Reminiscences*, p. 69.

13. Wilbur Wright, "Brief and Digest . . ."

14. Wilbur Wright, "Some Aeronautical Experiments," p. 5.

15. James Means, "Wheeling and Flying," *The Aeronautical Annual*, 2 (Boston, 1896), p. 25.

16. Fred C. Kelly, *The Wright Brothers* (New York: Ballantine Books, 1975), p. 183.

CHAPTER 13

1. Orville Wright, Deposition, in Marvin W. McFarland, ed., *The Papers of Wilbur and Orville Wright*, (New York: McGraw-Hill, 1953, cited hereafter as *Papers*), vol. 1, p. 7.

2. Wilbur Wright, "Some Aeronautical Experiments," in ibid., vol. 1, p. 103; see also Wilbur Wright, "Brief and Digest of the Evidence for Complainant on Final Hearing," The Wright Co. vs. Herring-Curtiss Co. and Glenn H. Curtiss in Equity No. 400, pp. 4–25; copy in Wright State University Archives.

3. Wilbur Wright to Octave Chanute, May 13, 1900, in *Papers*, vol. 1, pp. 16–17.

4. Wilbur Wright, "Brief and Digest . . ."

5. Ibid.

6. Orville Wright, Deposition, in *Papers*, vol. 1, pp. 8–9.

7. Author's conversation with Mrs. Elizabeth Rehling, daughter of Agnes Osborn, May 20, 1986. My thanks go to Mrs. Rehling for her many kindnesses, and to Harold and Ivonette Miller for introducing me to her.

8. Orville Wright, Deposition, in *Papers*, vol. 1, p. 11.

9. Wilbur Wright to Octave Chanute, May 13, 1900, in *Papers*, vol. 1, pp. 16–17.

10. Orville Wright, Deposition, in *Papers*, vol. 1, p. 12.

11. I have not provided detailed footnotes for the lengthy discussion that follows of the calculations required in designing the 1901 Wright glider. For background, readers should consult McFarland, ed., *Papers*, vol. 1, pp. 575–577.

Harry Coombs with Martin Caidin, *Kill Devil Hill: Discovering the Secret of the Wright Brothers* (Boston: Houghton Mifflin, 1979), pp. 361–375, provides a good account of the mathematics of airplane design. I am enormously indebted to Dr. Howard Wolko of the Aeronautics Department, National Air and Space Museum, for his own understanding of the process—and much else besides.

CHAPTER 14

1. Wilbur Wright to Octave Chanute, May 13, 1900, in Marvin W. McFarland, ed., *The Papers of Wilbur and Orville Wright* (New York: McGraw-Hill, 1953, cited hereafter as *Papers*), vol. 1, pp. 15–19.

2. Octave Chanute to Wilbur Wright, May 17, 1900, in ibid., pp. 19–21.

3. Wilbur Wright to Instrument Division, U.S. Weather Bureau, November 21, 1899; Wilbur Wright to Chief, U.S. Weather Bureau, December 9, 1899, in ibid., p. 2.

4. *Monthly Weather Review* (September 1899), 440–441.

5. Joseph J. Dosher to Wilbur Wright, August 18, 1900, in Fred C. Kelly, ed., *Miracle at Kitty Hawk: The Letters of Wilbur and Orville Wright* (New York: Farrar, Straus & Young, 1951), p. 25.

6. William Tate to Wilbur Wright, August 18, 1900, in ibid.

7. Wilbur Wright to Octave Chanute, August 10, 1900, in *Papers*, vol. 1, p. 22.

8. Wilbur Wright to Milton Wright, September 3, 1900, in Kelly, ed., *Miracle*, pp. 25–26.

9. Katharine Wright to Milton Wright, September 5, 1900, in Kelly, ed., *Miracle*, p. 27.

10. Wilbur Wright, Fragmentary Memo, Notebook A [1900–01], in *Papers*, vol. 1, pp. 23–25.

11. Ibid.

12. Ibid.

13. Wilbur Wright to Milton Wright, September 23, 1900, in ibid., pp. 25–27.

14. U.S. Department of Agriculture, Weather Bureau Daily Journal—Kitty Hawk, N.C., 1900, Record Group 27, National Archives. Determination of the day of first flight was worked out by comparing Dosher's record book with Orville's letters cited above.

15. John R. McMahon, *The Wright Brothers: Fathers of Flight* (Boston: Little, Brown, 1930). The reconstruction of the first manned flight draws heavily on the author's experience in flying a replica 1902 Wright glider constructed by Mr. Rick Young, of Petersburg, Va. The author's debt to Rick Young and his wife Sue is the sort that can never be repaid.

16. Orville Wright to Katharine Wright, October 14, 1900, in *Papers*, vol. 1, p. 28.

17. Ibid., p. 28.

18. Ibid., p. 29.

19. Ibid., p. 30.

20. Ibid.

21. Orville Wright to Katharine Wright, October 18, 1900, in ibid., p. 37.

22. Wilbur Wright to Milton Wright, November 23, 1903, in ibid., p. 383, note 6.

23. Orville Wright to Katharine Wright, July 28, 1901, in ibid., p. 73.

24. Orville Wright to Katharine Wright, October 14, 1900, in ibid., p. 32.

25. Wilbur Wright to Milton Wright, September 23, 1900, in ibid., p. 25.

26. Orville Wright to Katharine Wright, October 14, 1900, in ibid., p. 32.

27. Ibid.

28. Ibid.

29. Robert Frost, "A Trip to Currituck, Elizabeth City, and Kitty Hawk (1894)," *North Carolina Folklore* (May 1968), vol. 16, no. 1, 3–9.

30. Orville Wright to Katharine Wright, October 14, 1900, in *Papers*, vol. 1, p. 32.

31. Ibid., p. 33.

32. Ibid., p. 33.

33. William Tate, "I Was Host to the Wright Brothers at Kitty Hawk," *U.S. Air Services* (December 1943), 29–30.

34. Wilbur Wright, Notebook A [1900–01], in *Papers*, vol. 1, pp. 23–25.

35. Orville Wright to Katharine Wright, October 18, 1900, in ibid., pp. 34–37.

36. Ibid., p. 38.

CHAPTER 15

1. Octave Chanute to Wilbur Wright, November 29, 1900, in Marvin W. McFarland, ed., *The Papers of Wilbur and Orville Wright* (New York: McGraw-Hill, 1953 cited hereafter as *Papers*), vol. 1, p. 47.

2. Octave Chanute to Paul Renard, November 22, 1908, in ibid., vol. 2, p. 940. See also Wilbur Wright to Octave Chanute, January 20, 1910, and Octave Chanute to Wilbur Wright, January 23, 1910, ibid., pp. 979–980. The Wrights came to regard Chanute as being too imprecise for their taste, and guilty of "guessing." See, for example, Milton Wright, manuscript notes, January 7, 1916, box 8, file 8, Wright Papers, WSU; John R. McMahon, *The Wright Brothers: Fathers of Flight* (Boston: Little, Brown, 1930), p. 10; Wilbur Wright to Octave Chanute, December 1, 1900, in *Papers*, vol. 1, pp. 46–47; Octave Chanute to Wilbur Wright, December 2, 1900, in ibid., p. 49; and Wilbur Wright to Octave Chanute, December 3, 1900, in ibid., p. 49.

3. Octave Chanute to Wilbur Wright, November 23, 1900, in ibid., p. 44.

4. Wilbur Wright to Octave Chanute, November 26, 1900, in ibid., p. 45.

5. Wilbur Wright to Octave Chanute, May 12, 1901, in ibid., p. 54.

6. Orville Wright, Deposition of January 13, 1920, in *Montgomery* v. *U.S.*, in *Papers*, vol. 2, p. 547.

7. Wilbur Wright to Octave Chanute, June 19, 1901, in ibid., vol. 1, p. 55.

8. Charles Taylor, "My Story of the Wright Brothers," *Collier's* (Dec. 25, 1948), vol. 122, no. 26, 27, 68, and 70.

9. For biographical information on Edward Chalmers Huffaker, see Tom D. Crouch, *A Dream of Wings: Americans and the Airplane, 1875–1905* (New York: W. W. Norton, 1981), passim.

10. For biographical information on George Spratt, see William Trimble, *High Frontier: A History of Aeronautics in Pennsylvania* (Pittsburgh: University of Pittsburgh Press, 1982).

11. Octave Chanute to Wilbur Wright, June 29, 1901, in *Papers*, vol. 1, p. 56.

12. Ibid.

13. Wilbur Wright to Octave Chanute, July 1, 1901, in ibid., p. 64.

14. Octave Chanute to Wilbur Wright, July 3, 1901, in ibid.

15. Wilbur Wright to Octave Chanute, July 4, 1901, in ibid.

16. Wilbur Wright to Octave Chanute, July 26, 1901, in ibid., p. 70.

17. Orville Wright to Katharine Wright, July 28, 1901, in ibid., p. 72.

18. Ibid., p. 73.

19. Ibid.

20. Ibid., p. 74.

21. Wilbur Wright to Octave Chanute, July 26, 1901, in ibid., p. 70.

22. Wilbur Wright, "Some Aeronautical Experiments," in ibid., p. 109.

23. Orville Wright to Katharine Wright, July 28, 1901, in ibid., pp. 71–74.

24. Wilbur Wright Diary A, 1900–1901, pp. 22–23, in ibid., p. 77.

25. Wilbur Wright to Milton Wright, July 18, 1901, in ibid., pp. 68–69.

26. Wilbur Wright, "Some Aeronautical Experiments," in ibid., p. 111.

27. Wilbur Wright, "Brief and Digest of the Evidence for the Complainant on Final Hearing," The Wright Co. vs. Herring-Curtiss Co. and Glenn H. Curtiss in Equity No. 400, pp. 4–25. Original transcript, National Archives.

28. Chanute-Huffaker Diary, July 23, 1901, pp. 165–166, in *Papers*, vol. 1, p. 81.

29. Wilbur Wright to George Spratt, September 21, 1901, in ibid., p. 118.

30. Wilbur Wright, "Brief and Digest. . . ."

31. Fred C. Kelly, *The Wright Brothers: A Biography Authorized by Orville Wright* (New York: Ballantine Books, 1956), p. 167.

CHAPTER 16

1. Katharine Wright to Milton Wright, August 26, 1901, in Marvin W. McFarland, ed., *The Papers of Wilbur and Orville Wright* (New York: McGraw-Hill, 1953 cited hereafter as *Papers*), vol. 1, p. 84.

2. Wilbur Wright to Octave Chanute, August 29, 1901, in ibid., p. 85.

3. Wilbur Wright, "Brief and Digest of the Evidence for the Complainant on Final Hearing," The Wright Company vs. Herring-Curtiss, Co., and Glenn H. Curtiss in Equity No. 400, pp. 4–25; copy in Wright State University Archives.

4. The material on the Keiter affair is based primarily on assorted news clippings in boxes 96–98, Wright Papers, LC, and on Keiter Affair Documents, in file 6–7, box 8, Wright Brothers Collection, WSU. All quotes are drawn from "Church in Turmoil," [Chicago] *Sunday Chronicle* (Aug. 24, 1902).

5. Katharine Wright to Milton Wright, September 3, 1901, in *Papers*, vol. 1, p. 91.

6. Wilbur Wright to Octave Chanute, September 5, 1901, in ibid., p. 93.

7. Katharine Wright to Milton Wright, September 25, 1901, in ibid., p. 99.

8. Wilbur Wright, "Some Aeronautical Experiments," *Journal of the Western Society of Engineers* (December 1901), in ibid., p. 100.

9. Wilbur Wright to George Spratt, September 21, 1901, in ibid., p. 118.

10. Octave Chanute to Wilbur Wright, September 13, 1901, in ibid., p. 98.

11. Wilbur and Orville Wright, "The Wright Brothers Aeroplane," *The Century* (September 1908).

12. Wilbur Wright to Octave Chanute, September 26, 1901, in *Papers*, vol. 1, p. 121.

13. Wilbur Wright to Octave Chanute, November 2, 1901, in ibid., p. 145.

14. Wilbur Wright to Octave Chanute, October 6, 1901, in ibid., p. 124.

15. A few examples of the paper records survive in the collection of the Franklin Institute.

16. The description of the difficulties in reassembling the balances is based on the author's experience.

17. Octave Chanute to Wilbur Wright, November 18, 1901, in *Papers*, vol. 1, p. 156. The most complete and accurate treatment of the range of Wright wind-tunnel tests is to be found in Appendix II, ibid., pp. 547–593.

18. Ivonette Wright Miller, "Character Study," in Miller, ed., *Wright Reminiscences* (Dayton, Ohio: Privately printed, 1978), p. 60.

CHAPTER 17

1. Octave Chanute to Wilbur Wright, December 19, 1901, in Marvin W. McFarland, ed., *The Papers of Wilbur and Orville Wright* (New York: McGraw-Hill, 1953, cited hereafter as *Papers.*), vol. 1, p. 183.

2. Wilbur Wright to Octave Chanute, December 23, 1901, in ibid., p. 184.

3. Wilbur Wright to Octave Chanute, January 19, 1902, in ibid.

4. Octave Chanute to Wilbur Wright, May 5, 1902, in ibid., p. 232.

5. Wilbur Wright to Octave Chanute, February 11, 1902, in ibid., p. 215.

6. Wilbur Wright to Octave Chanute, February 7, 1902, in ibid., p. 213.

7. Wilbur Wright to Octave Chanute, May 5, 1902, in ibid., p. 232.

8. Wilbur Wright to Octave Chanute, February 7, 1902, in ibid., p. 213.

9. Octave Chanute to Wilbur Wright, February 13, 1902, in ibid., p. 215.

10. Ferdinand Ferber, "Que valent les Brevets Wright?" *L'Aérophile* (July 1, 1908).

11. Octave Chanute to Wilbur Wright, March 4, 1902, in *Papers*, vol. 1, p. 223.

12. Octave Chanute to James Means, May 31, 1897, box 24, book 34, p. 366, Octave Chanute Papers, Manuscript Division, Library of Congress.

13. A.M. Herring to Octave Chanute, March 17, 1901, and January 5, 1902, in ibid., box 2.

14. Wilbur Wright to Octave Chanute, May 29, 1902, in *Papers*, vol. 1, p. 234.

15. Wilbur Wright to Octave Chanute, June 2, 1902, in ibid., p. 235.

16. Wilbur Wright to Octave Chanute, July 9, 1902, in ibid., p. 238.

17. Katharine Wright to Milton Wright, August 20, 1902, in ibid., p. 244.

18. Octave Chanute to Wilbur Wright, August 26, 1902, in ibid., p. 244.

19. Wilbur Wright to Octave Chanute, September 5, 1902, in ibid., p. 247.

20. Wilbur Wright to Octave Chanute, September 2, 1902, in ibid., p. 246.

21. Wilbur Wright to Octave Chanute, September 21, 1902, in ibid., p. 257.

22. Orville Wright, Diary B, 1902, pp. 22–31, in ibid., p. 260.

23. *Papers*, p. 269, note 3.

24. Orville Wright, Notebook C, October 11, 1902, in ibid., p. 273.

25. S. P. Langley to Octave Chanute, October 17 and October 23, 1902, in ibid., p. 282.

26. Orville Wright to Katharine Wright, October 23, 1902, in ibid., pp. 279–280.

CHAPTER 18

1. See, for example, Wright Cycle Co. to Daimler Manufacturing Co., December 3, 1902, in Marvin W. McFarland, ed., *The Papers of Wilbur and Orville Wright* (New York: McGraw-Hill, 1953, cited hereafter as *Papers*), vol. 1, p. 287.

2. Orville and Wilbur Wright, "The Wright Brothers Aeroplane," *The Century* (September 1908).

3. Orville Wright, "How We Made the First Flight," *Flying* (December 1913).

4. Ibid.

5. Charles E. Taylor, "My Story of the Wright Brothers," *Collier's* (Dec. 25, 1948), p. 68.

6. Leonard S. Hobbs, *The Wright Brothers Engines and Their Design* (Washington, D.C.: Smithsonian Institution Press, 1971), is the best source in print on Wright power plant technology.

7. Taylor, "My Story," p. 68.

8. Ibid.

9. Octave Chanute to Wilbur Wright, December 9, 1902, in *Papers*, vol. 1, p. 290.

10. Wilbur Wright to Octave Chanute, December 11, 1902, in ibid.

11. Rodney K. Worrell, "The Wright Brothers Pioneer Patent," *American Bar Association Journal* (October 1979), 1514.

12. Ibid.

13. On the career of Baden-Powell, see Alfred Gollin, *No Longer an Island: Britain and the Wright Brothers, 1902–1909* (Stanford, Calif.: Stanford University Press, 1984), pp. 20–24.

14. Baden-Powell to Octave Chanute, September 22, 1902, Octave Chanute Papers, Manuscript Division, Library of Congress.

15. Octave Chanute to Baden-Powell, October 21, 1902, Chanute Papers, LC.

16. J. Lawrence Pritchard, "The Wright Brothers and the Royal Aeronautical Society: A Survey and a Tribute," *Royal Aeronautical Society Journal* (December 1953), 766.

17. On Patrick Y. Alexander's career, see Major C. C. Turner, *Old Flying Days* (New York: Arno Press, 1971), p. 11; see also Gollin, *No Longer an Island*, pp. 22–33.

18. "Memorandum by Wilbur Wright Esq," February 8, 1907, in Gollin, *No Longer an Island*, p. 29.

19. Octave Chanute to Wilbur Wright, March 7, 1903, in *Papers*, vol. 1, p. 299.

20. Octave Chanute to Wilbur Wright, March 13, 1903, in ibid., p. 301.

21. Octave Chanute to Wilbur Wright, April 4, 1903, in ibid.

22. On the career of Alberto Santos-Dumont, see Peter Wykeham, *Santos-Dumont: A Study in Obsession* (New York: Harcourt, Brace and World, 1962).

23. Quoted in Douglas Botting, *The Giant Airships* (Alexandria, Va.: Time-Life Books, 1980), p. 29.

24. de Rue [Ferdinand Ferber], "Expériences d'Aviation," *L'Aérophile* (February 1903).

25. See Ernest Archdeacon, "M. Chanute en Paris," *La Locomotion* (April 11, 1903), 225–227.

26. *L'Aérophile* (April 1903).

27. Archdeacon, "M. Chanute en Paris," 226.

28. Comte de la Vaulx, *La Triomphe de la Navigation Aérienne* (Paris, 1911), p. 274.

29. Archdeacon, "M. Chanute en Paris," 226.

30. de La Vaulx, *La Triomphe*, p. 274.

31. Ferber to Archdeacon, April 1903, in Archdeacon, "M. Chanute en Paris," 226.

CHAPTER 19

1. Orville Wright to George Spratt, June 7, 1903, in Marvin W. McFarland, ed., *The Papers of Wilbur and Orville Wright* (New York: McGraw-Hill, 1953, cited hereafter as *Papers*), vol. 1, p. 313.

2. Octave Chanute to Wilbur Wright, June 30, 1903, in ibid., p. 335.

3. Wilbur Wright to Octave Chanute, July 14, 1903, in ibid., p. 341.

4. Wilbur Wright to Octave Chanute, July 22, 1903, in ibid., p. 345.

5. Octave Chanute to Wilbur Wright, July 23, 1903, in ibid., p. 346.

6. Wilbur Wright to Octave Chanute, July 24, 1903, in ibid.

7. Octave Chanute to Wilbur Wright, July 27, 1903, in ibid., p. 348.

8. Wilbur Wright to Octave Chanute, August 23, 1903, in ibid., p. 350.

9. Wilbur Wright to Octave Chanute, September 19, 1903, in ibid., pp. 354–355.

10. Ibid., vol. 2, Appendix 5, "Aeroplanes and Motors," p. 1187.

11. S. P. Langley to Octave Chanute, June 1897, Chanute Papers, LC.

12. Wilbur Wright to Octave Chanute, October 13, 1903, in *Papers* vol. 1, p. 364.

13. Orville Wright to Katharine Wright, November 1, 1903, in ibid., p. 375, note 2.

14. Ibid., p. 374.

15. Ibid.

16. Ibid., p. 337, note 1.

17. Orville Wright to Katharine and Milton Wright, November 15, 1903, in ibid., p. 381.

18. Orville Wright, Diary D, November 15, 1903, in ibid., p. 380.

19. For a more complete treatment of the Langley Aerodrome program, see Tom D. Crouch, *A Dream of Wings: Americans and the Airplane, 1875–1905* (New York: W. W. Norton, 1981).

20. Orville Wright to Milton Wright, December 15, 1903, in *Papers*, vol. 1, p. 393.

21. Wilbur Wright to Milton Wright and Katharine Wright, December 14, 1903, in ibid., pp. 392–393.

22. Wilbur Wright to Milton Wright and Katharine Wright, November 23, 1903, in ibid., p. 383.

23. William O. Saunders, "Then We Quit Laughing," *Collier's* (Sept. 17, 1927), 24.

24. William Tate, "With the Wrights at Kitty Hawk," *The Aeronautical Review* (December 1928), 128–132.

25. Orville Wright to Samuel Acheson, January 22, 1937, in *Papers*, vol. 1, p. 397.

26. Milton Wright, Diary, December 14, 1903, box 8, WSU.

27. *Papers*, plate 71.

28. Ivonette Wright Miller, Unpublished reminiscences, author's collection.

29. Octave Chanute to Katharine Wright, December 17, 1903, in *Papers*, vol. 1, p. 397.

30. Ivonette Wright Miller, Unpublished reminiscences.

31. Wright Scrapbooks, 1903, Wright Papers, LC.

32. Orville Wright to Katharine Wright, December 23, 1903, in *Papers*, vol. 1, p. 400.

CHAPTER 20

1. Fred C. Kelly, ed., *Miracle at Kitty Hawk: The Letters of Wilbur and Orville Wright* (New York: Farrar, Straus & Young, 1951), p. 120.

2. John R. McMahon, *The Wright Brothers: Fathers of Flight* (Boston: Little, Brown, 1930), p. 149.

3. Wilbur Wright to Albert Francis Zahm, December 22, 1905, in Marvin W. McFarland, ed., *The Papers of Wilbur and Orville Wright* (New York: McGraw-Hill, 1953, cited hereafter as *Papers*), vol. 1, p. 537.

4. F. Ferber to Octave Chanute, January 27, 1904, Chanute Papers, Manuscript Division, Library of Congress (cited hereafter as Chanute Papers, LC).

5. F. Ferber to E. Archdeacon, n.d. [1904], in vol. 1, *Papers*, p. 424, note 1.

6. Victor Tatin, "L'Analyse des Expériences d'Aviation," *L'Aérophile* (February 1904). The quotations that follow are from the same source.

7. Augustus Moore Herring to the Wright brothers, December 26, 1903, in *Papers*, vol. 1, p. 413, note 2.

8. Octave Chanute to Wilbur Wright, December 27, 1903, in ibid., p. 401; Octave Chanute to Patrick Alexander, January 18, 1904, Chanute Papers, LC.

9. Octave Chanute to Wilbur Wright, January 20, 1903, Chanute Papers, LC.

10. Wilbur Wright to Octave Chanute, January 18, 1904, Chanute Papers, LC.

11. Octave Chanute to Wilbur Wright, January 23, 1910, *Papers*, vol. 1, pp. 980–981.

12. Wilbur Wright to Octave Chanute, June 21, 1904, in Kelly, ed., *Miracle*, p. 130.

13. William Werthner, "Personal Recollections of the Wrights," *Aero Club of America Bulletin* (July 1912), vol. 1, 13. See also Orville Wright botany notebook, and William Werthner, *Plant Descriptions and Field Notes, Season of '87*, both in Wright Collection, series 2, file 3, box 3, WSU.

14. The comment from Huffman appears in an undated Dayton news article (c. 1908), Wright Scrapbooks, 1908, Wright Papers, LC.

15. The comment from Waddell appears in ibid.

16. Wilbur Wright to Octave Chanute, May 27, 1904, in *Papers*, vol. 1, p. 437.

17. Fred C. Kelly, *The Wright Brothers: A Biography Authorized by Orville Wright* (New York: Ballantine Books, 1956), p. 84.

18. Arthur Renstrom, *Wilbur and Orville Wright: A Chronology Commemorating the One Hundredth Anniversary of the Birth of Orville Wright* (Washington, D.C.: U.S. Government Printing Office, 1975). Renstrom provides a complete checklist of all Wright flights, 1900–14.

19. Wilbur Wright to Octave Chanute, August 8, 1904, in *Papers*, vol. I, pp. 448–449.

20. Kelly, *Wright Brothers*, p. 76.

21. A. I. Root, "Our Homes," *Gleanings in Bee Culture*, (Jan. 1, 1905), vol. 33, no. 1, 38.

22. Wilbur Wright, Diary E, November 9, 1904, in *Papers*, vol. 1, p. 463.

CHAPTER 21

1. Alfred Gollin, *No Longer an Island: Britain and the Wright Brothers, 1902–1909* (Stanford, Calif.: Stanford University Press, 1984), pp. 64–65.

2. Halford Mackinder, "The Geographic Pivot of History," *The Geographical Journal* (April 1904), 441; see Gollin, *No Longer an Island*, for a more complete treatment.

3. L. S. Amery, *My Political Life* (London, 1953), vol. 1, p. 229. See also Gollin, *No Longer an Island*.

4. Percy B. Walker, *Early Aviation at Farnborough, Vol. 2, The First Aeroplanes* (London: Macdonald, 1974), p. 12.

5. Ibid., p. 18.

6. "Wright Brothers' English Negotiations," February 8, 1907, in Gollin, *No Longer an Island*, p. 69.

7. Wilbur Wright to Octave Chanute, June 1, 1905, in Fred C. Kelly, ed., *Miracle at Kitty Hawk: The Letters of Wilbur and Orville Wright* (New York: Farrar, Straus & Young, 1951), p. 42.

8. Wilbur and Orville Wright to J. E. Capper, January 10, 1905, quoted in Walker, *Early Aviation*, pp. 24–25.

9. Wilbur and Orville Wright to R. M. Nevin, January 18, 1905, in Kelly, ed., *Miracle*, p. 135.

10. G. L. Gillispie to R. M. Nevin, in ibid., p. 137.

11. Wilbur Wright to Octave Chanute, June 1, 1905, in Marvin W. McFarland, ed., *The Papers of Wilbur and Orville Wright* (New York: McGraw-Hill, 1953, cited hereafter as *Papers*), vol. 1, p. 494.

12. "Fads, Frauds and Follies Cripple Nation's Finances," *Brooklyn Eagle*, March 11, 1904; Tom D. Crouch, *A Dream of Wings: Americans and the Airplane, 1875–1905* (New York: W. W. Norton, 1981), offers a more complete discussion of the congressional reaction to the failure of the Langley program.

13. J. E. Capper to G.O.C. Royal Engineers, Aldershot Command, in Walker, *Early Aviation*, p. 26.

14. Ibid.

15. Ibid., p. 30.

16. Wilbur and Orville Wright to H. N. Dumbleton, March 1, 1905, in ibid.

17. R. H. Brade to Wilbur and Orville Wright, May 13, 1905, in ibid., p. 34.

18. Wilbur Wright, Diary F, 1905, *Papers*, vol. 1, p. 501.

19. For a more complete treatment of Montgomery, see Arthur Dunning Spearman, *John Joseph Montgomery: Father of Basic Flying* (Santa Clara, Calif.: University of Santa Clara, 1967).

20. Wilbur Wright to Octave Chanute, August 6, 1905, in *Papers*, vol. 1, p. 504.

21. For the best technical treatment of the 1905 Flyer, see Frederick J. Hooven, "Longitudinal Dynamics of the Wright Brothers Early Flyers: A Study in

Computer Simulation of Flight," in Howard Wolko, ed., *The Wright Flyer: An Engineering Perspective* (Washington, D.C.: Smithsonian Institution Press, 1987).

22. Hildebrandt, "The Wright Brothers' Flying Machine," *The American Magazine of Aeronautics* (January 1908), 13–16.

23. Ibid., p. 14.

24. Ibid., p. 15.

25. Quoted in Fred C. Kelly, *The Wright Brothers* (New York: Harcourt, Brace, 1943), pp. 108–109.

26. Kelly, *Wright Brothers*, remains a useful treatment of the Wrights' relationship with the press.

CHAPTER 22

1. Orville Wright to George Spratt, June 7, 1903, in Marvin W. McFarland, ed., *The Papers of Wilbur and Orville Wright* (New York: McGraw-Hill, 1953, cited hereafter as *Papers*), vol. 1, p. 313.

2. Octave Chanute to Wilbur Wright, January 23, 1910, in ibid., vol. 2, p. 981.

3. Percy B. Walker, *Early Aviation at Farnborough: Vol. 2 The First Aeroplanes* (London: Macdonald, 1974), p. xv.

4. Wilbur Wright to Octave Chanute, January 29, 1910, in *Papers*, vol. 2, p. 983.

5. Wright Brothers to W. H. Taft, October 9, 1905, in Fred C. Kelly, ed., *Miracle at Kitty Hawk: The Letters of Wilbur and Orville Wright* (New York: Farrar, Straus & Young, 1951), p. 149.

6. J. C. Bates to Wright Brothers, October 16, 1905, in ibid., p. 149.

7. J. C. Bates to Wright Brothers, October 24, 1905, in ibid., p. 151.

8. Walker, *Early Aviation*, pp. 35–43.

9. H. Foster to Wright Brothers, [?] December 8, 1905, in ibid., p. 42.

10. R. M. Ruck to Brig. Gen. Wolfe Murray, January 18, 1906, in ibid., p. 46.

11. F. Ferber to Wilbur Wright, October 21, 1905, in *Papers*, vol. 1, p. 524.

12. Wilbur Wright to F. Ferber, November 4, 1905, in ibid.

13. Carl Dienstbach, "Dus Zwiete Lebansjahr der Praktische Flugmaschine," *Illustriete Aeronautische Mitteilungen* (February 1906), 50–54.

14. "The Wright Aeroplane and Its Fabled Performances," *Scientific American* (Jan. 13, 1906), 40.

15. Wilbur Wright to Octave Chanute, December 4, 1905, in *Papers*, vol. 2, p. 529.

16. Charles Harvard Gibbs-Smith, *The Rebirth of European Aviation, 1902–1908* (London: HMSO, 1974), p. 192.

17. Wilbur Wright to Octave Chanute, April 28, 1906, in Kelly, ed., *Miracle*, p. 175.

18. Wilbur Wright to Lt. Col. A.E.W. Gleichen, July 31, 1906, in Walker, *Early Aviation*, p. 55.

19. J. E. Capper to Director, Fortifications and Works, September 6, 1906, in ibid., p. 59.

20. For full details of the work of J. W. Dunne, see Walker, *Early Aviation*, pp. 163–263.

21. "The Wright Aeroplane and Its Performances," *Scientific American* (April 7, 1906), 291–292.

22. On the personality and appearance of G. H. Curtiss, see C. R. Roseberry, *Glenn Curtiss: Pioneer of Flight* (Garden City, N.Y.: Doubleday, 1972).

23. Roseberry, *Curtiss*, pp. 49–53; Kelly, ed., *Miracle*, p. 435.

24. "Fliers or Liars," *New York Herald* (Paris Edition), February 10, 1906.

CHAPTER 23

1. Octave Chanute to Wilbur Wright, October 15, 1906, in Marvin W. McFarland, ed., *The Papers of Wilbur and Orville Wright* (New York: McGraw-Hill, 1953, cited hereafter as *Papers*), vol. 2, pp. 730–731.

2. Wilbur Wright to Octave Chanute, October 10, 1906, in ibid., p. 729.

3. Ibid., p. 730.

4. Octave Chanute to Wilbur Wright, October 15, 1906, in ibid., pp. 730–731.

5. Octave Chanute to Wilbur Wright, November 1, 1906, in ibid., p. 733.

6. Wilbur Wright to Octave Chanute, November 2, 1906, in ibid., p. 734.

7. "L'Aéroplane Archdeacon et les expériences de Merlimont," *L'Aérophile* (June 1905). Charles Harvard Gibbs-Smith, *The Rebirth of European Aviation, 1902–1908: A Study of the Wright Brothers' Influence* (London: HMSO, 1974), has served as a general guide to early European aeronautics.

8. Robert Esnault-Pelterie, "Expériences d'Aviation exécutées en 1904, en vérification de celles des frères Wright," *L'Aérophile* (June 1905).

9. Ibid.

10. "L'Aéroplane Archdeacon . . . " *L'Aérophile* (June 1905).

11. Gabriel Voisin, *Men, Women and 10,000 Kites* (London: Putnam, 1963).

12. Ibid.

13. Ibid.

14. Ibid.

15. Ibid.

16. Biographical material on Blériot and information on his early aircraft can be found in Simone Rubel Blériot, "Souvenirs d'Enfance," *Icare* (1979), 97; Michael L'Hospice, *Match Pour La Manche* (Paris, 1964); Charles Fontaine, *Comment Blériot a Traversé La Manche* (Paris, 1909). Tom D. Crouch, *Blériot XI: The Story of a Classic Aircraft* (Washington, D.C.: Smithsonian Institution Press, 1982), is virtually the only full treatment of the subject in English.

17. *New York Herald* (Paris Edition), November 13, 1906 (?). Undated copy of article found in Bell Scrapbooks, Archives, National Air and Space Museum.

18. Ernest Archdeacon, in Gibbs-Smith, *Rebirth*, p. 223.

19. Undated and unidentified article in Bell Scrapbooks, NASM.

20. *New York Herald* (?), undated article, 1906, Bell Scrapbooks, NASM.

21. Ibid.

CHAPTER 24

1. Milton Wright, Diary, November 30, 1906, box 10, file 2, WSU.

2. Charles Ranlett Flint, *Memories of an Active Life: Men and Ships and Sealing Wax* (New York: Putnam, 1923).

3. Fred C. Kelly, *The Wright Brothers* (New York: Harcourt, Brace, 1943), pp. 118–119.

4. "The Genesis of the First Successful Aeroplane," *Scientific American* (Dec. 15, 1906), 402.

5. Kelly provides the best discussion of the evolving proposals moving back and forth between the Wrights and Flint representatives.

6. Wilbur Wright to Octave Chanute, December 20, 1906, in Marvin W. McFarland, ed., *The Papers of Wilbur and Orville Wright* (New York: McGraw-Hill, 1953, cited hereafter as *Papers*), vol. 2, p. 743.

7. Wilbur Wright to Octave Chanute, January 28, 1907, in ibid., p. 749.

8. Kelly, *Wright Brothers*, pp. 97–98.

9. Dayton *Herald*, May 21, 1907; Orville Wright to H. C. Richardson, February 17, 1926, in *Papers*, vol. 2, pp. 1137–1138.

10. Wilbur Wright to Milton Wright, July 20, 1907, in ibid., 803–804.

11. Orville Wright to Board of Ordnanace and Fortification, May 17, 1907, in ibid., p. 761.

12. Orville Wright to Board of Ordnanace and Fortification, May 31, 1907, in ibid., p. 766.

13. H. O. Berg to Flint and Co., May 26, 1907, in Fred C. Kelly, ed., *Miracle at Kitty Hawk: The Letters of Wilbur and Orville Wright* (New York: Farrar, Straus & Young, 1951), p. 205.

14. Alfred Gollin, *No Longer an Island: Britain and the Wright Brothers, 1902–1909* (Stanford, Calif.: Stanford University Press, 1984), pp. 213–221.

15. Wilbur Wright to Orville Wright, June 11, 1907, in *Papers*, vol. 2, p. 773.

16. Ibid.

17. Wilbur Wright to Katharine Wright, June 8, 1907, in Kelly, ed., *Miracle*, p. 212.

18. Wilbur Wright to Orville Wright, May 30, 1907; Wilbur Wright to Katharine Wright, July 24, 1907; and Wilbur Wright to Katharine Wright, June 18, 1907; all in ibid., pp. 209, 227, and 217.

19. Wilbur Wright, Diary, July 17, 1907, in *Papers*, vol. 2, p. 798. See also Wilbur Wright, "Flying as a Sport—Its Possibilities," *Scientific American* (Feb. 29, 1908), p. 135.

20. Wilbur Wright, Diary, July 8, 1907, in ibid., p. 790.

21. F. Ferber to Georges Besançon, *L'Aérophile* (June 1907), 107–108.

22. Wilbur Wright, Diary, July 24, 1907, in *Papers*, vol. 2, pp. 807–808.

23. Orville Wright to Wilbur Wright, July 11, 1907, in ibid., p. 793.

24. Orville Wright to Wilbur Wright, July 1, 1907, in ibid., p. 783.

25. Wilbur Wright to Milton Wright, July 2, 1907, in ibid., pp. 803–804.

26. Ibid., p. 803.

27. Ibid.

28. Wilbur Wright to Octave Chanute, September 2, 1907, in ibid., p. 819.

29. Wilbur Wright, Diary, August 17–September 11, 1907, in ibid., p. 839.

30. Wilbur Wright to Octave Chanute, September 2, 1907, in ibid., p. 819.

31. Wilbur Wright to Octave Chanute, December 9, 1907, in ibid., p. 839.

32. Ibid.

33. Stephen F. Tillman, *Man Unafraid: The Miracle of Military Aviation* (Washington D.C.: Army Times Publishing Co., 1958), pp. 14–15.

34. Ibid., p. 15.

35. All material on the Grand Prix is drawn from appropriate issues of *L'Aérophile;* C. H. Gibbs-Smith, *The Rebirth of European Aviation, 1902–1908* (London: HMSO, 1974); and C. H. Gibbs-Smith, *The Invention of the Aeroplane, 1799–1909* (London: Faber & Faber, 1965).

36. Orville Wright to Milton Wright, November 19, 1907, in Kelly, ed., *Miracle*, pp. 240–241.

37. Ibid.

38. Gibbs-Smith, *Rebirth*, p. 245.

CHAPTER 25

1. Wilbur Wright to Milton Wright, November 22, 1907, in Fred C. Kelly, ed., *Miracle at Kitty Hawk: The Letters of Wilbur and Orville Wright* (New York: Farrar, Straus & Young, 1951), p. 241.

2. Stephen Tillman, *Man Unafraid: The Miracle of Military Aviation* (Washington, D.C.: Army Times Publishing Co., 1954), p. 15.

3. Wilbur Wright to Octave Chanute, December 3, 1907, in Marvin W. McFarland, ed., *The Papers of Wilbur and Orville Wright* (New York: McGraw-Hill, 1953 cited hereafter as *Papers*), vol. 2, pp. 835–836.

4. Tillman, *Man Unafraid*, pp. 13–17.

5. Ibid., p. 16.

6. Ibid., p. 17; and James Means to Octave Chanute, January 10, 1908, Octave Chanute Papers, Manuscript Division, Library of Congress.

7. Wilbur Wright to Octave Chanute, January 16, 1908, in *Papers*, vol. 2, p. 849.

8. Tillman, *Man Unafraid*, pp. 17–19.

9. Wilbur Wright to Octave Chanute, April 8, 1908, in *Papers*, vol. 2, p. 861.

10. The discussion of Bell and the AEA is based on a variety of sources, including Louis Casey, *Curtiss: The Hammondsport Era, 1907–1915* (New York: Crown, 1981); J. W. Parkin, *Bell and Baldwin: Their Development of Aerodromes and Hydrodromes at Baddeck, Nova Scotia* (Toronto: University of Toronto, 1964); and C. H. Roseberry, *Glenn Curtiss: Pioneer of Flight* (Garden City, N.Y.: Doubleday, 1972).

11. Parkin, *Bell and Baldwin,* p. 215.

12. Ibid.

13. Thomas E. Selfridge to Orville Wright, January 15, 1908, in Kelly, ed., *Miracle,* p. 248.

14. Casey, *Curtiss,* p. 15.

15. Ibid., pp. 6–34.

16. Unless otherwise noted, the treatment of the 1908 Kitty Hawk trials is based on Wilbur Wright, Diary T, in *Papers,* vol. 2, pp. 862–880.

17. See Fred Kelly, notes on the Wrights and the newsmen in 1903 and 1908. Final correspondence folder, Fred C. Kelly, Papers of Wilbur and Orville Wright, Manuscript Division, Library of Congress. See also Fred C. Kelly, *The Wright Brothers* (New York: Harcourt, Brace, 1943).

18. Byron Newton, "Watching the Wright Brothers Fly," *Aeronautics* (June 1908), 8; see also Arthur Ruhl, "History at Kill Devil Hill," *Collier's* (May 30, 1908), 18–19; Carl Dienstbach, "The Recent Flights of the Wright Brothers in North Carolina," *American Aeronautics* (June 1908), 209–211; "American Aeronautics Disclosure of the Wright Brothers' Secret," *American Aeronautics* (June 1908), 6–10; and Mark Sullivan, *Our Times* (New York: Scribner's, 1927), vol. 2, pp. 607–613.

19. Newton, "Watching the Wright Brothers Fly."

20. Ibid.

21. Ibid.

22. See assorted news articles, Wright Scrapbooks, 1908, Wright Papers, LC.

23. *Papers,* May 15, 1908, vol. 2, p. 879.

24. Wilbur Wright to Katharine Wright, May 19, 1908, in ibid., p. 881.

CHAPTER 26

1. Wilbur Wright to Katharine Wright, May 19, 1908, in Marvin W. McFarland, ed., *The Papers of Wilbur and Orville Wright* (New York: McGraw-Hill, 1953, cited hereafter as *Papers*), vol. 2, p. 881.

2. Wilbur Wright to Orville Wright, May 29, 1908, in ibid., p. 888.

3. Ibid.

4. Orville Wright to Wilbur Wright, May 23, 1908, in ibid.

5. Wilbur Wright to Orville Wright, June 28, 1908, in ibid., p. 903.

6. Wilbur Wright to Orville Wright, June 3, 1908, in ibid., p. 886.

7. Orville Wright to Glenn Curtiss, July 20, 1908, in ibid., p. 907.

8. Wilbur Wright, Diary T, June 9, 1908, in ibid., p. 895.

9. Wilbur Wright to Orville Wright, June 3, 1908, in ibid., p. 886.

10. Wilbur Wright to Orville Wright, June 17, 1908, in ibid., p. 900.

11. Ibid.

12. Wilbur Wright to Orville Wright, June 20, 1908, in Fred C. Kelly, ed., *Miracle at Kitty Hawk* (New York: Farrar, Straus, & Young, 1951), p. 275.

13. Wilbur Wright to Orville Wright, July 9, 1908, in ibid., p. 289.

14. Wilbur Wright to Katharine Wright, August 2, 1908, in ibid.

15. Wilbur Wright to Orville Wright, August 9, 1908, in ibid., p. 291.

16. *Daily Mirror* (London), August 13, 1908.

17. *The Times* (London), August 14, 1908.

18. *Le Figaro*, August 11, 1908.

19. *L'Aérophile*, August 11, 1908.

20. *L'Auto*, August 9, 1908.

21. C. H. Gibbs-Smith, *The Rebirth of European Aviation, 1902–1908* (London: HMSO, 1974), p. 287.

22. *Le Matin*, September 5, 1908.

23. Wilbur Wright to Orville Wright, August 15, 1908, in *Papers*, vol. 2, p. 913.

CHAPTER 27

1. Orville Wright to Katharine Wright, August 31, 1908, in Fred C. Kelly, ed., *Miracle at Kitty Hawk: The Letters of Wilbur and Orville Wright* (New York: Farrar, Straus & Young, 1951, cited hereafter as *Miracle*), p. 301.

2. Wilbur Wright to Milton Wright, September 13, 1908, in ibid., p. 309.

3. Orville Wright to Katharine Wright, August 27, 1908, in *ibid.*, p. 298.

4. Orville Wright to Wilbur Wright, August 23, 1908, in *Papers*, vol. 2, p. 915.

5. Ibid.

6. Benjamin D. Foulois with Martin Caiden, *From the Wright Brothers to the Astronauts* (New York: McGraw-Hill, 1968), p. 54.

7. Stephen Tillman, *Man Unafraid: The Miracle of Military Aviation* (Washington, D.C.: Army Times Publishing Co., 1958), pp. 26–27; Foulois, *From the Wright Brothers*, pp. 48–49.

8. Foulois, *From the Wright Brothers*, p. 54.

9. Ibid., p. 54.

10. Signal Corps, "Log of the Wright Airplane," August 25, 1908, in *Papers*, vol. 2, p. 916.

11. Complete details of the flights at Fort Myer can be found in Arthur G. Renstrom, *Wilbur and Orville Wright: A Chronology* (Washington, D.C.: Library of Congress, 1975), pp. 165–166.

12. Orville Wright to Wilbur Wright, September 6, 1908, in Kelly, ed., *Miracle*, p. 303.

13. Some details of the account of September 17 are based on articles of that date and the next in the *New York Times* and the Washington *Evening Star*.

14. Orville Wright to Wilbur Wright, November 14, 1908, in *Papers*, vol. 2, pp. 936–937.

15. Octave Chanute to Katharine Wright, September 29, 1908, in ibid., p. 929.

16. Milton Wright, Diary, September 17, 1908, in ibid., p. 925.

17. John R. McMahon, *The Wright Brothers: Fathers of Flight* (New York: Little, Brown, 1930), p. 208.

18. François Peyrey, *Les Oiseaux Artificiels* (Paris: H. Dunod et E. Pinat, 1909), pp. 194–196; Wilbur Wright to Katharine Wright, September 20, 1908, in Kelly, ed., *Miracle*, p. 315; Wilbur Wright to Katharine Wright, September 29, 1908, in *Papers*, vol. 2, p. 925.

19. Wilbur Wright to Katharine Wright, September 20, 1908, in Kelly, ed., *Miracle*, p. 315.

20. Ibid.

21. Quoted in Foulois, *From the Wright Brothers*, p. 57.

22. Ibid.

CHAPTER 28

1. Katharine Wright to Agnes Osborn, September 22, 1908, author's collection. Thanks to Mrs. E. Rehling.

2. Ibid.

3. Octave Chanute to Katharine Wright, September 29, 1908, in Marvin W. McFarland, ed., *The Papers of Wilbur and Orville Wright* (New York: McGraw-Hill, 1953, cited hereafter as *Papers*), vol. 2, p. 929.

4. Washington *Evening Star*, September 22, 1908.

5. Ibid.; see also C. H. Roseberry, *Glenn Curtiss: Pioneer of Flight* (Garden City, N.Y.: Doubleday, 1972), pp. 130–131.

6. Wilbur Wright to Katharine Wright, September 20, 1908, in *Papers*, vol. 2, p. 927.

7. Orville Wright to Wilbur Wright, November 14, 1908, in ibid., p. 936.

8. Arthur G. Renstrom, *Wilbur and Orville Wright: A Chronology* (Washington, D.C.: Library of Congress, 1975, cited hereafter as *Chronology*), provides the most complete and detailed list of all Wright flights.

9. B. Baden-Powell, "A Trip with Wilbur Wright," *Aeronautics* (December 1908).

10. Wilbur Wright to Orville Wright, October 9, 1908, in Fred C. Kelly, ed., *Miracle at Kitty Hawk* (New York: Farrar, Straus & Young, 1951), p. 323.

11. Ross Browne Interview, Columbia University Oral History Collection, p. 17.

12. C. H. Gibbs-Smith, *The Invention of the Aeroplane, 1799–1909* (London: Faber & Faber, 1965), pp. 122–165.

13. Renstrom, *Chronology*, p. 164.

14. Wilbur Wright to Orville Wright, April 9, 1909, in *Papers*, vol. 2, p. 949.

15. John McMahon, *The Wright Brothers: Fathers of Flight* (Boston: Little, Brown, 1930), p. 217.

16. Fred C. Kelly, *The Wright Brothers* (New York: Harcourt, Brace, 1943), p. 155.

17. Ibid.

18. Wilbur Wright to Orville Wright, April 4, 1909, in *Papers*, vol. 2, p. 949.

19. Milton Wright, Diary, April 19, 1909, box 10, file 3, WSU.

20. Wilbur Wright to Orville Wright, April 4, 1909, in *Papers*, vol. 2, p. 950.

21. Renstrom, *Chronology*, p. 32.

22. "Wrights Hear of Their Fame," *New York Globe* (May 12, 1908). All description of the reception in New York is based on material in Wright scrapbooks at the Library of Congress and the Dayton Public Library.

23. Ibid.

24. Wilbur Wright to Octave Chanute, June 6, 1909, in *Papers*, vol. 2, p. 953.

25. Renstrom, *Chronology*, p. 41.

26. Octave Chanute to Wilbur Wright, June 16, 1909, in *Papers*, vol. 2, p. 955.

27. Ibid.

CHAPTER 29

1. Wilbur Wright to Octave Chanute, June 6, 1909, in Marvin W. McFarland, ed., *The Papers of Wilbur and Orville Wright* (New York: McGraw-Hill, 1953, cited hereafter as *Papers*), vol. 2, p. 954.

2. *New York Times*, June 29, 1909.

3. Carl Dienstbach, "The Revelations at Fort Myer," *American Aeronaut* (September 1909), vol. 1, no. 2, 81.

4. Benjamin D. Foulois, *From the Wright Brothers to the Astronauts* (New York: McGraw-Hill, 1968), p. 62.

5. *New York Times*, July 3, 1909.

6. *New York Times*, August 11, 1908.

7. Foulois, *From the Wright Brothers*, p. 64.

8. Ibid.

9. C. H. Gibbs-Smith, "The Man Who Came By Air," *Shell Aviation News*, June 19, 1959, 2.

10. The most complete treatment of the AEA is in J. H. Parkin, *Bell and Baldwin* (Toronto: University of Toronto Press, 1964); see also Louis S. Casey, *Curtiss: The Hammondsport Era, 1907–1915* (New York: Crown, 1981).

11. The best account of the history of the Herring-Curtiss firm is in C. R. Roseberry, *Glenn H. Curtiss: Pioneer of Flight* (Garden City, N.Y.: Doubleday, 1972), pp. 159–162.

12. Ibid., p. 154.

13. Casey, *Curtiss*, pp. 55, 61; Roseberry, *Glenn H. Curtiss*, pp. 167–168, 173.

14. Charles Harvard Gibbs-Smith, *The Invention of the Aeroplane, 1799–1909* (London: Faber & Faber, 1965), pp. 213–220.

15. Casey, *Curtiss*, p. 46.

16. Heinrich Adams, *Fluq von Heinrich Adams Unser Flieger von Wilbur und Orville Wright* (Leipzig: C. F. Amelaags Verlag, 1909), p. 104.

17. Gibbs-Smith, *Invention of the Aeroplane*, pp. 213–220.

18. Roseberry, *Glenn H. Curtiss*, pp. 170–171.

19. Ibid.

20. Orville Wright to Wilbur Wright, August 24, 1909, in Fred C. Kelly, ed., *Miracle at Kitty Hawk* (New York: Farrar, Straus & Young, 1951), p. 343.

21. Arthur G. Renstrom, *Wilbur and Orville Wright: A Chronology* (Washington, D.C.: Library of Congress, 1975, cited hereafter as *Chronology*), pp. 40–47.

22. Ibid., p. 47.

23. Orville Wright to Wilbur Wright, September 28, 1909, in Kelly, ed., *Miracle*, p. 348.

24. Ibid.

25. Ibid.

26. Renstrom, *Chronology*, pp. 179–180.

27. Fred C. Kelly, *The Wright Brothers* (New York: Harcourt, Brace, 1943), p. 264; author's interview with Ivonette Wright Miller.

28. Renstrom, *Chronology*, p. 181.

29. Grover Loening, *Our Wings Grow Faster* (New York: Doubleday, Doran, 1935), pp. 9–13.

30. Clara Studer, *Sky-Storming Yankee: The Life of Glenn Curtiss* (New York: Stackpole, 1937), p. 195; Roseberry, *Glenn H. Curtiss*, p. 220.

31. Renstrom, *Chronology*, pp. 44–45.

32. Ibid., p. 45.

34. Kelly, *Wright Brothers*, pp. 164–165.

35. Ibid.

36. Ibid.; Milton Wright, Diary, November 25, 1909, box 10, file 4, WSU.

37. Kelly, *Wright Brothers*, pp. 164–165.

38. The figures are drawn from a close study of the Wright letters, papers, and diaries for the period. The final estimate is my own. For quote, see Wilbur Wright to Milton Wright, October 31, 1909, in Kelly, ed., *Miracle*, p. 352.

39. Kelly, *Wright Brothers*, p. 166.

40. Wilbur Wright to Octave Chanute, December 6, 1909, in *Papers*, vol. 2, p. 971.

CHAPTER 30

1. Wilbur Wright to Octave Chanute, December 6, 1909, in Marvin W. McFarland, ed., *The Papers of Wilbur and Orville Wright* (New York: McGraw-Hill, 1953, cited hereafter as *Papers*), vol. 2, p. 971.

2. Fred C. Kelly, *The Wright Brothers* (New York: Harcourt, Brace, 1943), p. 166.

3. For a complete account of the Wright factory locations, see Mary Ann Johnson, *A Field Guide to Flight: On the Aviation Trail in Dayton, Ohio* (Dayton, Ohio: Landfall Press, 1986).

4. Grover Loening, *Our Wings Grow Faster* (New York: Doubleday, Doran, 1935), p. 33.

5. C. W. Hayward, *Practical Aeronautics* (Chicago: American Technical Society, 1917), part 2, pp. 55–85, remains by far the most useful introduction to the aeronautical patent suits. See also Arthur G. Renstrom, *Wilbur and Orville Wright: A Bibliography* (Washington, D.C.: Library of Congress, 1968), pp. 100–122, for a listing of all patents and suits, as well as the most complete bibliography available on the subject.

6. Hayward, *Practical Aeronautics*, part 2, p. 66.

7. Ibid., p. 80.

8. C. R. Roseberry, *Glenn Curtiss: Pioneer of Flight* (Garden City, N.Y.: Doubleday, 1972), pp. 430–435; James V. Martin, "When Will Merit Count in Aviation?" *The Libertarian* (October 1924), 589–608.

9. Roseberry, *Glenn Curtiss*, pp. 430–435.

10. Ibid., pp. 453–455, 479.

11. Hayward, *Practical Aeronautics*, part 2, pp. 55–85; Kelly, *Wright Brothers*, pp. 176–183.

12. Hayward, *Practical Aeronautics*, part 2, pp. 71–73.

13. Wilbur Wright to Octave Chanute, March 31, 1911, in *Papers*, vol. 2, p. 1022.

14. Hayward, *Practical Aeronautics*, part 2, pp. 55–85.

15. Ibid., p. 70.

16. François Peyrey, *Les Oiseaux Artificiels* (Paris: H. Dunod et E. Pinat, 1909), p. 202.

17. Hayward, *Practical Aeronautics*, part 2, p. 505.

18. *Aeronautics* (April 10, 1910); Arthur G. Renstrom, *Wilbur and Orville Wright: A Chronology* (Washington, D.C.: Library of Congress, 1975, cited hereafter as *Chronology*), p. 50.

19. Quoted in Hayward, *Practical Aeronautics*, part 2, p. 521.

20. Octave Chanute to Ernest Jones, August 20, 1909, in *Papers*, vol. 2, p. 962.

21. *New York World*, June 17, 1910.

22. Chicago *Daily News*, undated clipping, Chanute Scrapbook, Octave Chanute Papers, Manuscript Division, Library of Congress.

23. Wilbur Wright to Octave Chanute, January 20, 1910, in *Papers*, vol. 2, p. 979.

24. Octave Chanute to Wilbur Wright, January 23, 1910, in ibid., p. 980.

25. Wilbur Wright to Octave Chanute, January 29, 1910, in ibid., p. 982.

26. Ibid.

27. Octave Chanute to George Spratt, February 2, 1910, in ibid., p. 978.

28. Wilbur Wright to Octave Chanute, April 28, 1910, in ibid., p. 991.

29. Renstrom, *Chronology*, p. 53.

30. Wilbur Wright to George Spratt, October 16, 1909, in *Papers*, vol. 2, p. 978.

31. Ibid.

32. A. F. Zahm to Wilbur Wright, January 27, 1910, in ibid., p. 1094.

33. Wilbur Wright to A. F. Zahm, January 29, 1910, in ibid.

34. A. F. Zahm to Wilbur Wright, February 7, 1910, in ibid., p. 1094.

35. Ibid., p. 1095.

36. *Aeronautics* (July 1910), 21–22; Israel Ludlow, "Criticism of the Court's Decision. . . ." *Aircraft* (April 1910), 75; Israel Ludlow, "The Wright Company Is a Menace. . . ." *Aircraft* (May 1910), 94–95; and Hayward, *Practical Aeronautics*, part 2, pp. 505–524.

37. Hayward, *Practical Aeronautics*, part 2, p. 62.

CHAPTER 31

1. James C. Fahey, *U.S. Army Aircraft, 1908–1946* (New York: Ships and Aircraft, 1946), p. 6.

2. Sherwood Harris, *First to Fly: Aviation's Pioneer Days* (New York: Simon & Schuster, 1970), p. 117.

3. Ibid., p. 178.

4. Ibid.

5. Fred C. Kelly, *The Wright Brothers* (New York: Harcourt, Brace, 1943), pp. 166–167, 171.

6. Arthur G. Renstrom, *Wilbur and Orville Wright: A Chronology* (Washington D.C.: Library of Congress, 1975, cited hereafter as *Chronology*), pp. 187–190.

7. Kelly, *Wright Brothers*, pp. 168, 171.

8. Ibid., p. 169.

9. Frank Coffyn, "Flying with the Wrights," *The World's Work* (December 1929), 80–86; Frank Coffyn, "Flying As It Was," *Sportsman Pilot* (May 19, 1939), 30–32; Frank Coffyn, Interview in the files of the Columbia Oral History Project.

10. Renstrom, *Chronology*, p. 51.

11. Marvin W. McFarland, ed., *The Papers of Wilbur and Orville Wright* (New York: McGraw-Hill, 1953, cited hereafter as *Papers*), vol. 2, p. 996.

12. Houston Peterson, *See Them Flying: Houston Peterson's Air-Age Scrapbook, 1909–1910* (New York: R. W. Baron, 1969), pp. 192–195.

13. Harris, *First to Fly*, p. 166.

14. Coffyn, interview.

15. Ibid.

16. Beckwith Haven Interview in Columbia University Oral History Collection quoted in Roger E. Bilstein, *Flight in America, 1900–1983* (Baltimore: The Johns Hopkins University Press, 1984), p. 18.

17. Fred C. Kelly, "They Wouldn't Believe the Wrights Had Flown," *Harpers*, vol. 81 (August 1940), p. 300. Orville Wright quoted in Mark Sullivan, *Our Times: The United States, 1900–1925* (New York: Scribner's, 1931), vol. 2, p. 599.

18. J. A. Adams, "The Man Higher Up," *The Advance*, LX (Oct. 6, 1910), 12.

19. Charles K. Field, "On the Wings of Today," *Sunset*, 24 (March 1910), 249.

20. Peterson, *See Them Flying*, pp. 212–213.

21. Coffyn, interview.

22. Wilbur Wright to Arch Hoxsey, September 19, 1910, in *Papers*, vol. 2, p. 998.

23. Renstrom, *Chronology*, p. 42.

24. Henry Serrano Villard, *Contact! The Story of the Early Birds* (New York: Bonanza Books, 1953), pp. 106–112.

25. Wilbur Wright to Orville Wright, December 3, 1910, in *Papers*, vol., 2, p. 1006.

26. Harris, *First to Fly*, pp. 215–216.

27. Renstrom, *Chronology*, p. 53.

28. Orville Wright to Wilbur Wright, November 24, 1910, in *Papers*, vol. 2, p. 1001.

29. Orville Wright to Wilbur Wright, November 27, 1910, in ibid., p. 1002.

30. Ibid.

31. Ibid.

32. Wilbur Wright to Orville Wright, December 9, 1910, in ibid., p. 1006.

33. Orville Wright to Wilbur Wright, November 27, 1910, in ibid., p. 1004.

34. Villard, *Contact!*, pp. 242–243.

35. A complete list of the pilots trained at Huffman Prairie appears on the monument on Wright Hill overlooking the field.

36. H. H. Arnold, *Global Mission* (New York: Harper, 1949), pp. 16–17.

37. Harris, *First to Fly*, pp. 160–162.

38. Arnold, *Global Mission*, pp. 18–19.

39. Harris, *First to Fly*, pp. 160–162.

40. Ibid., p. 161–162.

41. Arnold, *Global Mission*, pp. 19–20.

42. Harris, *First to Fly*, p. 258.

43. Calbraith Perry Rodgers biographical file, Library, National Air and Space Museum.

44. Charles Taylor, "My Story of the Wright Brothers," *Collier's* (Dec. 25, 1948).

45. *New York Times*, April 4, 1912.

CHAPTER 32

1. Wilbur Wright to Henry Peartree, March 7, 1911, in Marvin W. McFarland, ed., *The Papers of Wilbur and Orville Wright* (New York: McGraw-Hill, 1953, cited hereafter as *Papers*), vol. 2, p. 1018; Arthur Renstrom, *Wilbur and Orville Wright: A Chronology* (Washington, D.C.: Library of Congress, 1975, cited hereafter as *Chronology*) pp. 54–57.

2. Wilbur Wright to Orville Wright, March 31, 1911, in *Papers*, vol. 2, p. 1020.

3. Wilbur Wright, "What Ader Did," *Aero Club of America Bulletin* (April 1912).

4. Wilbur Wright to Orville Wright, March 31, 1911, in *Papers*, vol. 2, p. 1020.

5. Ibid; Wilbur Wright, "What Ader Did."

6. Renstrom, *Chronology*, p. 66.

7. Wilbur Wright to Katharine Wright, June 28, 1911, in Fred C. Kelly, ed., *Miracle at Kitty Hawk* (New York: Farrar, Straus & Young, 1951), p. 384.

8. Wilbur Wright to Orville Wright, June 30, 1911, in ibid., pp. 384–385.

9. See, for example, Wilbur Wright, June 9, 1907, in *Papers*, vol. 2, pp. 771–772.

10. Tom D. Crouch, "A Machine of Practical Utility: The 1905 Wright Flyer," *Timelines* (August–September 1905), 24–37.

11. For a complete treatment of the 1911 glider trials, see *Papers*, vol. 2, pp. 1024–1029; Renstrom, *Chronology*, pp. 57, and 199–202.

12. On J. J. Montgomery, see Arthur Dunning Spearman, *John Joseph Montgomery, 1858–1911: The Father of Basic Flying* (Santa Clara, Calif.: University of Santa Clara Press, 1967).

13. Orville Wright to T. S. Baldwin, November 18, 1911, in *Papers*, vol. 2, p. 1029.

14. Ibid.

15. Spearman, *John Joseph Montgomery.*

16. Benjamin D. Foulois, *From the Wright Brothers to the Astronauts* (New York: McGraw-Hill, 1968), pp. 79–95.

17. Renstrom, *Chronology*, p. 57.

18. Orville Wright to C. DeF. Chandler, December 29, 1911, in *Papers*, vol. 2, p. 1031.

19. Ibid.

20. Wilbur Wright to M. Hévésy, January 25, 1912, in ibid., p. 1035.

21. Renstrom, *Chronology*, pp. 57–59.

22. John McMahon, *The Wright Brothers: Fathers of Flight* (Boston: Little, Brown, 1930), p. 266.

23. Renstrom, *Chronology*, p. 58.

24. Wilbur Wright to Frederick Fish, May 4, 1912, in *Papers*, vol. 2, p. 1042.

25. Milton Wright, Diary, May 27, 1912, box 10, file 5, WSU.

26. Ibid., May 30, 1912.

27. Ibid., May 31, 1912.

28. Wright Scrapbooks, 1912, Wright Papers, LC.

29. Ibid.

30. Last Will and Testament of Wilbur Wright, in Alfred Andrews, *The Andrews, Clapp, Stokes, Wright, Van Cleve Genealogies* (Fort Lauderdale, Fla.: Privately printed, 1984), p. 502.

31. Ibid.

32. Milton Wright to Reuchlin Wright, August 16, 1912, in *Papers*, vol. 2, p. 1048.

33. Milton Wright, Diary, June 3, 1912, box 10, file 5, WSU.

34. Ivonette Wright Miller, ed., *Wright Reminiscences* (Dayton, Ohio: Privately printed, 1978), pp. 14–15.

35. Renstrom, *Chronology*, p. 65.

36. McMahon, *Wright Brothers*, pp. 275–276.

37. Renstrom, *Chronology*, p. 61.

38. Logan Marshall, *The True Story of Our National Calamity of Flood, Fire and Tornado* (no place: I. T. Myers, 1913).

39. Milton Wright, Diary, March 25, 1913, box 10, file 5, WSU.

40. Quoted in Marshall, *True Story*, p. 16.

CHAPTER 33

1. Orville Wright to Andrew Freeman, April 11, 1913, in Marvin W. McFarland, ed., *The Papers of Wilbur and Orville Wright* (New York: McGraw-Hill, 1953, cited hereafter as *Papers*), vol. 2, p. 1066.

2. Grover Loening, *Our Wings Grow Faster* (Garden City, N.Y.: Doubleday, Doran, 1935), p. 44; Grover Loening, *Takeoff into Greatness: How American Aviation Grew So Big So Fast* (New York: Putnam, 1968), pp. 54–61.

3. Ivonette Wright Miller, ed., *Wright Reminiscences* (Dayton, Ohio: Privately printed, 1978), p. 118.

4. Loening, *Our Wings*, p. 44.

5. Ibid.

6. Ibid., p. 45.

7. Louis Casey, *Curtiss: The Hammondsport Era, 1907–1915* (New York: Crown, 1981), pp. 84–137.

8. Loening, *Takeoff*, pp. 54–61.

9. Stephen F. Tillman, *Man Unafraid* (Washington, D.C.: The Army Times, 1958), pp. 154–185.

10. Loening, *Our Wings*, p. 47.

11. Orville Wright to Lt. William C. Sherman, September 6, 1913, in *Papers*, vol. 2, p. 1063; Orville Wright to Sherman, October 15, 1913, in ibid., p. 1066; Orville Wright to Lt. Col. Samuel Reber, December 5, 1913, in ibid., p. 1068.

12. John McMahon, *The Wright Brothers: Fathers of Flight* (Boston: Little, Brown, 1930), p. 291; Orville Wright, "Automatic Stability," *Smithsonian*

Annual Report (Washington, D.C.: Smithsonian Institution Press, 1914), pp. 201–216; U.S. Patent No. 1,122, 348.

13. *New York Times* (Jan. 6, 1914); Arthur G. Renstrom, *The Wright Brothers: A Chronology* (Washington, D.C.: Library of Congress, 1975, cited hereafter as *Chronology*), p. 206.

14. William Wyatt Davenport, *Gyro! The Life and Times of Lawrence Sperry* (New York: Scribner's, 1978), pp. 90–113.

15. Loening, *Our Wings*, p. 44.

16. Ibid., pp. 44–46.

17. Ibid., p. 46.

18. Ibid.

19. Robert Scharff and Walter Taylor, *Over Land and Sea: A Biography of Glenn Hammond Curtiss* (New York: McKay, 1968), p. 218; C. R. Roseberry, *Glenn Curtiss: Pioneer of Flight* (Garden City, N.Y.: Doubleday, 1972), p. 357.

20. Loening, *Our Wings*, p. 49.

21. Tillman, *Man Unafraid*, p. 155.

22. Loening, *Our Wings*, p. 50.

23. Casey, *Curtiss*, pp. 176–196.

24. See Loening, *Takeoff*, 62–63; Fred C. Kelly, ed., *Miracle at Kitty Hawk* (New York: Farrar, Straus & Young, 1951), p. 403; and Fred C. Kelly, *The Wright Brothers* (New York: Harcourt, Brace, 1943), p. 285.

25. Renstrom, *Chronology*, p. 65.

26. *New York Times*, October 16, 1915. Orville refused to reveal an exact figure, simply referring to "a very large sum."

27. John B. Rae, *Climb to Greatness: The American Aircraft Industry, 1920–1960* (Cambridge: MIT Press, 1968), p. 5.

28. Ibid.

CHAPTER 34

1. Arthur G. Renstrom, *Wilbur and Orville Wright: A Chronology* (Washington, D.C.: Library of Congress, 1975, cited hereafter as *Chronology*), p. 67.

2. See Stuart Leslie, *Boss Kettering* (New York: Columbia University Press, 1983); Isaac Marcosson, *Colonel Deeds: Industrial Builder* (New York: Dodd, Mead, 1948); and Howard Mingos, "The Birth of an Industry," in G. E. Simonsons, ed., *The History of the American Aircraft Industry: An Anthology* (Cambridge: MIT Press, 1968), pp. 10–95.

3. "Interrogation of Orville Wright by Judge Charles Evans Hughes," *Hughes Aircraft Investigation, Testimony of Witnesses, May to October, 1918, United States Department of Justice*, vol. 23, pp. 175–193. Copy in National Archives.

4. Leslie, *Boss Kettering*, pp. 219–229; Mingos, "Birth of an Industry," p. 21.

5. See National Air and Space Museum and USAF Museum technical files, Kettering Bug. See also Henry H. Arnold, *Global Mission* (New York: Harper, 1949), pp. 74–76.

6. Marvin W. McFarland, ed., *The Papers of Wilbur and Orville Wright* (New York: McGraw-Hill, 1953, cited hereafter as *Papers*), vol. 2, p. 1149; Fred C. Kelly, ed., *Miracle at Kitty Hawk* (New York: Farrar, Straus & Young, 1951), p. 462; Renstrom, *Chronology*, p. 100.

7. Eric Hodgins, "Heavier-Than-Air," *The New Yorker* (Dec. 13, 1930), 29–32.

8. *Papers*, vol. 2, pp. 1175–1177; *New York Times* (Dec. 18, 1940); Ivonette Wright Miller, ed., *Wright Reminiscences* (Dayton, Ohio: Privately printed, 1978), pp. 34–35.

9. Alex Roland, *Model Research: The National Advisory Committee for Aeronautics, 1915–1958* (Washington, D.C.: Government Printing Office, 1985), p. 52.

10. Richard P. Hallion, *Legacy of Flight: The Guggenheim Contribution to American Aviation* (Seattle: University of Washington Press, 1977).

11. John Evangelist Walsh, *One Day at Kitty Hawk: The Untold Story of the Wright Brothers and the Airplane* (New York: Crowell, 1975), pp. 4, 5, 250; Marvin W. McFarland, "Orville Wright and Friend," *U.S. Air Services* (August 1956), 5–7. McFarland believed that it was Katharine who delivered the bad news. If he is correct, the particular story is of course ruined; the extent to which Findley and Kelly handled Mabel Beck with kid gloves remains clear, however. See the correspondence of both men with Orville, Wright Papers, LC.

12. Ivonette Wright Miller, Unpublished reminiscences, author's collection.

13. Graham Justice, "Hawthorn Hill Has a Special Place in World History," *NCR World* (June 1965).

14. Wilbur Wright to Orville Wright, May 26, 1911, Kelly, ed., *Miracle*, p. 382.

15. Justice, "Hawthorn Hill," 4.

16. Jay Peartree, "Summers," in Miller, ed., *Reminiscences*, p. 133.

17. Ibid.; Justice, "Hawthorn Hill," 4.

18. Thanks to the kindness of Ivonette and Harold Miller and the staff of the National Cash Register Co., the author was privileged to spend a night in Orville's bedroom at Hawthorn Hill. These observations were made at that time.

19. Robert Hadeler, "My Summers with Orville Wright," in Miller, ed., *Reminiscences*, p. 145.

20. George Russell in ibid.

21. Ibid., p. 144.

22. Peartree in ibid., p. 138.

23. Orville's notes on his mother's birthplace are in file 11, box 12, Wright Papers, WSU.

24. Miller, ed., *Reminiscences*, pp. 21–22.

25. John Hulbert Jameson Autobiography, in Alfred Stokes Andrews, *The Andrews, Clapp, Stokes, Wright, Van Cleve Genealogies* (Fort Lauderdale, Fla.: Privately printed, 1984), pp. 470–471.

26. Ibid., p. 471.

27. Peartree, "Summers," p. 141.

28. See Grace Goulder, *Ohio Scenes and Citizens* (Cleveland: World, 1964), pp. 117–123; John R. McMahon, *The Wright Brothers: Fathers of Flight* (Boston: Little, Brown, 1930), pp. 298–299. Orville's estrangement from his sister is obviously a sensitive topic within the family; nevertheless, the substance of the account here is drawn from the observations of family and friends. Two friends in particular, Marvin W. McFarland and C. H. Gibbs-Smith, both now dead, first called my attention to the psychological implications of the situation. Those discussions sparked my own first thoughts on the importance of family to the Wrights. In a sense, they were the real origin of this book. C. H. Gibbs-Smith had actually seen Katharine's letters to C. S. Rolls and described them to me.

CHAPTER 35

1. Lincoln Beachey to Smithsonian, January 21, 1914; Richard Rathbun to Charles Walcott, January 21, 1914, RG 46, Smithsonian Institution Archives.

2. A. F. Zahm, "The First Man-Carrying Aeroplane. . . ." Smithsonian *Annual Report* (Washington D.C., 1914), p. 218.

3. Ibid.

4. Griffith Brewer, "Aviation's Greatest Controversy," *Aeronautical Journal* (December 1921), vol. 25, 620–664, offers the best summary of the differences between the two machines.

5. Zahm, "The First Man-Carrying Aeroplane," 222.

6. Smithsonian *Annual Report* (Washington D.C., 1915), p. 122.

7. Fred C. Kelly, *The Wright Brothers* (New York: Harcourt, Brace, 1943), p. 185.

8. Charles Walcott to Wilbur Wright, March 7, 1910; Wilbur Wright to Charles Walcott, March 26, 1910; and April 11, 1910; all in Wright Papers, LC.

9. Griffith Brewer, *Fifty Years of Flying* (London: Air League of the British Empire, 1946), p. 111.

10. Memorandum by Lorin Wright, July 5, 1915, in Marvin McFarland, ed., *The Papers of Wilbur and Orville Wright* (New York: McGraw-Hill, 1953), vol. 2, p. 1090.

11. Orville Wright to William Howard Taft, May 14, 1925, in Wright Papers, "Smithsonian Controversy," Library of Congress.

12. Ibid.

13. Brewer, *Fifty Years*, p. 111.

14. Leonard Bairstow, "The Work of Samuel Pierpont Langley," manuscript in Samuel Langley Papers, Smithsonian Institution Archives.

15. Kelly, *Wright Brothers*, p. 194.

16. Lester Gardner, *Aviation* (May 18, 1925), in "Who Made the First Flying Machine?" *The Aeroplane* (June 3, 1925), 530.

17. Joseph Ames and David Wilson Taylor, "A Report on the Langley Machine," June 3, 1925, box 111, folder 3, Smithsonian Institution Archives.

18. Orville Wright, Mimeographed press statement, July 1937, Wright Papers, LC.

19. Kelly, *Wright Brothers*, p. 198.

20. Lindbergh, Wright, Abbot correspondence, Wright Papers, LC, and Wright-Smithsonian Controversy files, Smithsonian Institution Archives.

21. Orville Wright to Charles Abbot, March 15, 1935, in Wright Papers, LC.

22. Charles A. Lindbergh, *The Wartime Diaries of Charles Lindbergh* (New York: Harcourt Brace Jovanovich, 1970), p. 188.

23. Letters and memoranda on Macmillan and Goldstrum, box 107, Smithsonian Institution Archives.

24. Charles Abbot to John Ahlers, August 20, 1940, Wright Papers, LC.

25. Paul Edward Garber, personal conversation with the author.

26. Understanding of the various Montgomery-Wright suits rests on a reading of a file on the Montgomery case in the papers of C. D. Walcott, Smithsonian Institution Archives; U.S. Court of Claims, Case No. 33852, R. M. Montgomery et al. vs. the United States, Complainant's Affidavits, Wright Papers, box 73, LC. Arthur Dunning Spearman, *John Joseph Montgomery: The Father of Basic Flying* (Santa Clara Calif.: University of Santa Clara Press, 1967), is not particularly satisfactory, but it is the only biography of Montgomery and does cover the court proceedings, after a fashion and from a biased point of view.

27. Orville Wright, *How We Invented the Airplane*, edited and with commentary by Fred C. Kelly (New York: McKay, 1952).

28. "Connecticut Night Watchman . . ." *New York Herald* (June 16, 1901); Stanley Y. Beach, "A New Flying Machine," *Scientific American* (June 8, 1901), 19.

29. "Flying," Bridgeport *Sunday Herald* (Aug. 18, 1901); [G. Whitehead], "The Whitehead Flying Machine," *American Inventor* (April 1, 1901), 1–2.

30. C. Manly to F. Hodge, September 20, 1901, *Aerodromics 10*, 29, 441, Ramsey Rare Book Room, National Air and Space Museum.

31. Quotes appearing on the original dust jacket of Stella Randolph's *The Lost Flights of Gustave Whitehead* (Washington D.C.: Places, Inc., 1937.)

32. John Crane, "Did Whitehead Actually Fly?" *National Aeronautic Association Magazine* (December 1936).

33. Quoted in C. H. Gibbs-Smith's unpublished manuscript on flight claims, a copy of which was presented to me. I am forever indebted to CHGS for his early guidance and support.

34. *Papers*, vol. 2, pp. 1165–1167, note 8.

35. Albert Francis Zahm, *Early Powerplane Fathers* (South Bend, Ind.: Notre Dame University Press, 1951).

36. The most blatant attack on the Smithsonian is contained in William O'Dwyer and Stella Randolph, *History by Contract* (West Germany: Fritz Major & Sohn, 1978).

CHAPTER 36

1. Arthur G. Renstrom, *Wilbur and Orville Wright: A Chronology* (Washington, D.C.: Library of Congress, 1975), passim. Renstrom provides a complete list of honors and awards.

2. Ivonette Wright Miller, ed., *Wright Reminiscences* (Dayton, Ohio: Privately printed, 1978), pp. 25–26.

3. John Jameson Autobiography in Alfred Andrews, *The Andrews, Clapp, Stokes, Wright, Van Cleve Genealogies* (Fort Lauderdale, Fla.: Privately printed, 1984), pp. 470–471; personal conversations with Harold and Ivonette Miller.

4. Miller, ed., *Reminiscences,* p. 31.

5. "The Proposed Wright Brothers Memorial," *Aero Club of America Bulletin* (July 1912), vol. 1, no. 6, 5.

6. "Wilbur Wright Memorial Designed Here," Dayton *Daily News* (Jan. 22, 1913).

7. "France and the Wright Brothers," *Légion d'Honneur* (April 1933), vol. 1, 206–215; "The Wilbur Wright and Hubert Latham Monuments," *The Aero* (London, December 1912), vol. 6, 352; Wright Brothers Memorials, Library, National Air and Space Museum (cited hereafter as NASM files).

8. Undated news clipping and assorted materials, NASM files.

9. [Fred Marshall], "In Honor of the Wrights," *Slipstream* (November 1927), vol. 8, no. 11, 9–10; "Wright Memorial Site Criticized," *Slipstream* (January 1928), vol. 9, no. 1, 7–8.

10. The treatment of the monument at Kill Devil Hills is based on a thorough reading of the sources cited in Arthur G. Renstrom, *Wilbur and Orville Wright: A Bibliography* (Washington, D.C.: Library of Congress, 1968), pp. 138–146.

11. For Wright Hill Memorial, see "Wright Hill Dedicated at Dayton," *U.S. Air Services* (September 1940) vol. 25, no. 9, 10–11; "Have You Ever Visited Wright Hill?" *NCR Factory News* (August–September 1940), 1–6; and "Dedication of the Wright Brothers Monument," *Air Corps News Letter* (Sept. 1, 1940), vol. 23, no. 17, 7.

12. The best discussions of Henry Ford and Greenfield Village are to be found in Allan Nevins and Frank Ernest Hill, *Ford: Expansion and Challenge, 1915–1935* (New York: Scribner's, 1957); William Greenleaf, *From These Beginnings: The Early Philanthropies of Henry and Edsel Ford, 1911–1936* (Detroit: Wayne State University Press, 1964); and Roger Butterfield, "Henry Ford, the Wayside Inn and the Problem of History Is Bunk," *Pro-*

ceedings of the Massachusetts Historical Society (January–December 1965), vol. 78, 60. For a contemporary view by a Ford publicist, see William Adams Simmonds, *Henry Ford and Greenfield Village* (New York: Frederick Stokes, 1938).

13. The information on the acquisition of the home and bicycle shop is drawn from Allan Fletcher, *The Wright Brothers' Home and Cycle Shop in Greenfield Village*, a thesis in the University of Michigan Program in Museum Practice, June 30, 1972.

14. Dayton *Journal Herald*, July 5, 1936.

15. Fletcher, *The Wright Brothers' Home*, p. 44.

16. Personal conversation of the author with Ivonette and Harold Miller.

17. Undated clippings, Hawthorn Hill scrapbook.

18. Katharine Wright to Milton Wright, quoted in Ivonette Wright Miller, unpublished reminiscences, author's collection.

19. See references quoted in note 11.

20. The best treatment of the history of Wright-Patterson Air Force Base and its predecessors is Louise Walker and Shirley E. Wickham, *From Huffman Prairie to the Moon: The History of Wright-Patterson Air Force Base* (Dayton, Ohio: Office of History, 27501 Air Base Wing, 1986).

CHAPTER 37

1. Charles Lyon Seasholes, "A Letter to Mr. and Mrs. Harold S. Miller," in Ivonette Wright Miller, ed., *Wright Reminiscences* (Dayton, Ohio: Privately printed, 1978), p. 195.

2. James McConnaughey, "Powered Plane Was Only One of Orville Wright's Gadgets," Kettering-Oakwood *Times* (Nov. 9, 1969).

3. Ibid.

4. Ivonette Wright Miller, in Miller, ed., *Reminiscences*, p. 16.

5. George Russell, "Reminiscences," in ibid., p. 143.

6. Wilkinson Wright, personal conversation with the author.

7. Ivonette Wright Miller, in McConnaughey, "Powered Plane."

8. Alfred S. Andrews, in Miller, ed., *Reminiscences*, p. 89.

9. Miller, ed., *Reminiscences*, pp. 23–24.

10. Charles A. Lindbergh, *The Wartime Journals of Charles Lindbergh* (New York: Harcourt Brace Jovanovich, 1970), p. 277.

11. Ibid.

12. Ibid.

13. Ibid., p. 383.

14. John Evangelist Walsh, *One Day at Kitty Hawk: The Untold Story of the Wright Brothers and the Airplane* (New York: Crowell, 1975), p. 253.

15. Miller, ed., *Reminiscences*, p. 32.

16. Ibid.

17. Charles Greeley Abbot, "The 1914 Test of the Langley Aerodrome," *Smithsonian Miscellaneous Collections* (Washington D.C., Oct. 24, 1942), vol. 103, no. 8.

18. Arthur G. Renstrom, *Wilbur and Orville Wright: A Chronology* (Washington, D.C.: Library of Congress, 1975), pp. 100–103.

19. Notes, Wright-Langley Controversy files, Smithsonian Institution Archives; and typed copy of Orville Wright Will and Probate Petition, Probate Court of Montgomery County, Ohio, August 6, 1948, in RG 46, box 107, folder 6, Smithsonian Institution Archives.

20. Orville Wright to Lester Gardner, August 28, 1945, in Marvin W. McFarland, ed., *The Papers of Wilbur and Orville Wright* (New York: McGraw-Hill, 1953, cited hereafter as *Papers*), vol. 2, p. 1176.

21. Undated clipping, Wright Scrapbooks, 1947, Wright Papers, LC.

22. Miller, ed., *Reminiscences*, p. 39.

23. Undated news clipping, Wright Scrapbooks, 1948, LC.

24. Ibid.; Miller, ed., *Reminiscences*, p. 40.

25. *Papers*, vol. 1, pp. vii–xx.

26. Miller, ed., *Reminiscences*, pp. 41–42.

27. Alexander Wetmore to Henry H. Arnold, February 6, 1948, RG 46, box 108, Smithsonian Institution Archives.

28. Author's conversations with Harold S. Miller, executor, Orville Wright estate; Probate petition.

29. Description of the ceremony is based on primary materials including programs, invitations, and correspondence in RG 46, box 107, Smithsonian Institution Archives. The quotation, "poor, and poorly read," is from Miller, ed., *Reminiscences*, p. 46.

BIBLIOGRAPHY

Much ink has been spilled in attempts to portray Wilbur and Orville Wright and their achievements. What follows is intended to introduce the reader to the major sources consulted during the preparation of *The Bishop's Boys*, and to offer suggestions for those interested in further reading.

GENERAL:

Arthur G. Renstrom, *Wilbur and Orville Wright: A Bibliography* (Washington, D.C.: Library of Congress, 1968), serves as a starting point for any discussion of the Wright literature. The 2,055 items catalogued represent the vast bulk of what was said about Wilbur and Orville prior to 1968. The bibliography prepared by Dominick Pisano of the National Air and Space Museum for Richard P. Hallion, ed., *The Wright Brothers: Heirs of Prometheus* (Washington, D.C.: Smithsonian Institution Press, 1978), is a useful guide to materials published since Renstrom.

MANUSCRIPTS:

The majority of materials relating to Wilbur and Orville Wright are held by two repositories: the Manuscript Division of the Library of Congress, and the Wright State University Archives, Dayton, Ohio. For the most part, letters, diaries, the great bulk of the brothers' correspondence, and other material relating to the invention of the airplane will be found in the Library of Congress. The fine collection at Wright State consists of what was once, incorrectly, regarded as the less important family and legal material. Patrick A. Nolan and John Zamonski, *The Wright Brothers Collection: A Guide to the Technical, Business and Legal, Genealogical, Photographic, and Other Archives at Wright State University* (New York: Garland Publishing, 1977), is a very useful guide to that collection. A much shorter aid is available for Wright materials at the Library of Congress. An additional smaller collection of original Wright material can be found at the Franklin Institute.

The Dayton Room of the Dayton and Montgomery County Public Library main-
tains the only complete collection of newspapers published by the brothers, as well
as several fine unduplicated scrapbooks, and scattered materials relating to the
family and to Milton's church career. Other major scrapbook collections include
those in the Wright Collection at the Library of Congress, and the Bell and
Langley scrapbooks in the National Air and Space Museum Library. One interesting single scrapbook is in Orville's library at Hawthorn Hill.

PHOTOGRAPHS:

The original glass plate negatives taken by Orville Wright as a record of the
invention of the airplane are in the Library of Congress, which also holds one of
the finest general photo collections relating to the brothers. A set of microfilm
cards, including all the original glass plate images, is available for sale through
the Library. The National Air and Space Museum Archive has another fine photo
collection, all of which are included on a single laser-read video disc sold by the
museum. The Wright State University is the third major repository of Wright
images, many of them family snapshots not available elsewhere. Arthur G. Renstrom, *Wilbur and Orville Wright: Pictorial Materials, a Documentary Guide*
(Washington, D.C.: Library of Congress, 1982), lists virtually all known photographs of the brothers except for those covered in Nolan and Zamonski, *The
Wright Brothers Collection.*

Film of the Wrights and their machines is available in a number of repositories.
The best collections are at the National Archive Motion Picture Branch; the USAF
Central Audio-Visual Depository, Norton Air Force Base, and the National Air
and Space Museum, Washington, D.C.

PRINTED PAPERS:

Marvin W. McFarland, ed., *The Papers of Wilbur and Orville Wright: Including
the Chanute-Wright Letters and Other Papers of Octave Chanute* (New York:
McGraw-Hill, 1953), 2 vols., and Fred C. Kelly, ed., *Miracle at Kitty Hawk: The
Letters of Wilbur and Orville Wright* (New York: Farrar, Straus & Young, 1951),
reproduce the bulk of the useful manuscript material on the invention of the
airplane. The *Papers,* in particular, represent one of the finest jobs of historical
editing in this century.

BIOGRAPHIES:

There are seven noteworthy biographies of Wilbur and Orville Wright:

John R. McMahon, *The Wright Brothers: Fathers of Flight* (Boston: Little,
Brown, 1930).

Fred C. Kelly, *The Wright Brothers: A Biography Authorized by Orville Wright*
(New York: Harcourt, Brace, 1943).

Elsbeth E. Freudenthal, *Flight into History: The Wright Brothers and the Air
Age* (Norman, Okla.: University of Oklahoma Press, 1949).

John Evangelist Walsh, *One Day at Kitty Hawk: The Untold Story of the Wright
Brothers and the Airplane* (New York: Crowell, 1975).

Rosamond Young and Catharine Fitzgerald, *Twelve Seconds to the Moon: A Story of the Wright Brothers* (Dayton, Ohio: The Journal Herald, 1978).

Harry Coombs with Martin Caidin, *Kill Devil Hill: Discovering the Secret of the Wright Brothers* (Boston: Houghton Mifflin, 1979).

Fred Howard, *Wilbur and Orville: A Biography of the Wright Brothers* (New York: Alfred A. Knopf, 1987).

Fred Kelly had the enormous advantage of working directly with Orville Wright—his book has a flavor all the others lack. But he faced a disadvantage as well. The fact that Orville was looking over his shoulder limited the judgments he could make on the brothers and their work. His book is still marginally the best. Fred Howard offers a wealth of detail. Coombs, an engineer and aircraft company executive, provides fresh insight of real value into the Wright technology. Walsh is critical of Orville. Freudenthal too was generally critical, tending to favor Chanute's point of view over that of the Wrights.

Two books on which I have relied heavily are Ivonette Wright Miller's *Wright Reminiscences* (Dayton, Ohio: Privately printed, 1978) and Arthur G. Renstrom's *Wilbur and Orville Wright: A Chronology Commemorating the One Hundredth Anniversary of the Birth of Orville Wright* (Washington, D.C.: Library of Congress, 1975). Mrs. Miller's book, filled with the reminiscences of family and friends, is a priceless source of information on life at 7 Hawthorn Street. The day-by-day account offered by Renstrom, complete with the list of flights made by the brothers, is extraordinarily valuable to any scholar.

Special note should be taken of the work of Dr. Adrian Kinnane, a clinical psychologist at the Meyer Treatment Center of the George Washington University. His unpublished study, "The Crucible of Flight," offers considerable insight into the dynamics of the Wright family and the importance of family values in the story of Wilbur and Orville Wright.

The following have proved especially useful in preparing this book:

Abbot, C. G., "The 1914 Test of the Langley Aerodrome," *Smithsonian Institution Miscellaneous Collections* (Washington, D.C.: Smithsonian Institution Press, Oct. 24, 1942).

———, *The Relations Between the Smithsonian Institution and the Wright Brothers* (Washington, D.C.: Smithsonian Institution Press, 1928).

Adams, Heinrich, *Flug von Heinrich Adams Unser Flieger von Wilbur und Orville Wright* (Leipzig: C. F. Amelaags Verlag, 1909).

Adler, Cyrus, *I Have Considered the Days* (Philadelphia: Jewish Publication Society of America, 1941).

Aero Club of America, *Navigating the Air* (New York: Doubleday, 1907).

"L'Aéroplane Archdeacon et les expériences de Merlimont," *L'Aérophile* (June 1905).

Albertson, Catharine, *Wings Over Kill Devil Hill and Legends of the Dunes* (Elizabeth City, N.C.: Privately printed, 1928).

Amery, L. S., *My Political Life* 2 vols. (London, 1953).

Andrews, A. S., *The Andrews, Clapp, Stokes, Wright, Van Cleve Genealogies* (Fort Lauderdale, Fla.: Privately printed, 1984).

Archdeacon, Ernest, "M. Chanute en Paris," *La Locomotion* (April 11, 1903), 225–227.

Arnold, Henry H., *Global Mission* (New York: Harper & Brothers, 1949).

Baden-Powell, B.F.S. "A Trip with Wilbur Wright," *Aeronautics* (December 1908).

Bauer, Charles J., "Ed Sines: Pal of the Wrights," *Popular Aviation* (June 1938), 40.

Beck, Mabel, "The First Airplane After 1903," *U.S. Air Services* (December 1954), 9–10.

Berger, Daniel, *History of the Church of the United Brethren in Christ* (Dayton, Ohio: United Brethren Publishing House, 1906).

Botting, Douglas, *The Giant Airships* (Arlington, Va.: Time-Life Books, 1980).

Brewer, Griffith, *Fifty Years of Flying* (London: Air League of the British Empire, 1946).

———, "Aviation's Greatest Controversy," *Aeronautical Journal* (December 1921), 620–664.

Butterfield, Roger, "Henry Ford, the Wayside Inn and the Problem of History Is Bunk," *Proceedings of the Massachusetts Historical Society* (January–December 1965), 60.

Casey, Louis, *Curtiss: The Hammondsport Era, 1907–1915* (New York: Crown, 1981).

Chandler, Capt. C. DeF., and Frank P. Lahm, *How Our Army Grew Wings: Airmen and Aircraft Before 1914* (New York: Ronald, 1943).

Chanute, Octave, *Progress in Flying Machines* (New York: M. N. Forney, 1894).

———, "Gliding Experiments," *Journal of the Western Society of Engineers* (November 1897), 593–628.

———, "Experiments in Flying," *McClure's Magazine* (June 1900), 127–133.

Charnley, Mitchell V., *The Boys' Life of the Wright Brothers* (New York: Harper & Brothers, 1928).

Coffyn, Frank, "Flying with the Wrights," *World's Work* (December 1929), 80–86.

———, "Flying As It Was—Early Days in the Wrights' School," *Sportsman Pilot* (May 15, 1939), 14–15.

Coles, Thomas R., "The 'Wright Boys' as a Schoolmate Knew Them," *Out West* (January 1910), 36–38.

Conover, Charlotte Reeve, *Dayton: An Intimate History* (New York: Lewis Historical Publishers, 1932).

Cox, Sanford C., *Recollections of the Early Settlement of the Wabash Valley* (Freeport, N.Y.: Books for Libraries Press, 1970).

Crane, John B., "Did Whitehead Actually Fly?" *National Aeronautic Association Magazine* (December 1936).

Crouch, Tom D., *Blériot XI: The Story of a Classic Airplane* (Washington, D.C.: Smithsonian Institution Press, 1982).

———, *A Dream of Wings: Americans and the Airplane, 1875–1905* (New York: W. W. Norton, 1981).

Davenport, William Wyatt, *Gyro! The Life and Times of Lawrence Sperry* (New York: Scribner's, 1978).

"Dedication of the Wright Brothers Monument," *Air Corps Newsletter* (September 1940), 7.

Dienstbach, Carl, "Dus Zwiete Lebansjahr der Praktische Flugsmacshine," *Illustriete Aeronautische Mitteilungen* (February 1906), 50–54.

———, "The Recent Flights of the Wright Brothers in North Carolina," *American Aeronautics* (June 1908), 209–211.

———, "The Revelations at Fort Myer," *American Aeronaut* (September 1909), 81.

Drury, A. W., *History of the City of Dayton and Montgomery County, Ohio* (Dayton, Ohio: S. J. Clarke Co., 1909).

———, *History of the Church of the United Brethren in Christ* (Dayton, Ohio: United Brethren Publishing House, 1924).

Dupree, Hunter, *Science and the Emergence of Modern America* (Chicago: University of Chicago Press, 1953).

Esnault-Pelterie, Robert, "Expériences d'Aviation exécutées en 1904, en vérification de celles des frères Wright," *L'Aérophile* (June 1905).

Fahey, James C., *U.S. Army Aircraft, 1908–1946* (New York: Ships and Aircraft, 1946).

Ferber, Ferdinand [de Rue], "Expériences d'Aviation," *L'Aérophile* (February 1903).

———, "Wilbur Wright à Paris," *L'Aérophile* (June 1907), 167–168.

Fetters, Paul H., *Trials and Triumphs: A History of the Church of the United Brethren in Christ* (Huntington, Ind.: Church of the United Brethren in Christ, Department of Church Services, 1984).

Fisk, Fred C. "The Wright Brothers' Bicycles," *The Wheelmen* (November 1980), 2–15.

Fletcher, Allan, *The Wright Brothers' Home and Cycle Shop in Greenfield Village* (Unpublished thesis, University of Michigan Program in Museum Practice, June 30, 1972). Copy in Greenfield Village Archives.

Flint, Charles, *Memories of an Active Life: Men and Ships and Sealing Wax* (New York: Putnam, 1923).

Foulois, Benjamin D., *From the Wright Brothers to the Astronauts* (New York: McGraw-Hill, 1968).

Frost, Robert, "A Trip to Currituck, Elizabeth City, and Kitty Hawk (1894)," *North Carolina Folklore* (May 1968), vol. 16, 3–9.

"Genesis of the First Successful Aeroplane," *Scientific American* (Dec. 15, 1906), 402.

Gibbs-Smith, Charles H., *The Aeroplane: An Historical Survey* (London: HMSO, 1960).

———, *The Wright Brothers: A Brief Account of Their Work* (London: HMSO, 1963).

——, *The Invention of the Aeroplane, 1799–1909* (London: Faber & Faber, 1965).

——, *Aviation: An Historical Survey from Its Origins to the End of World War II* (London: HMSO, 1970).

——, *The Rebirth of European Aviation, 1902–1908: A Study of the Wright Brothers' Influence* (London: HMSO, 1974).

Gollin, Alfred, *No Longer an Island: Britain and the Wright Brothers, 1902–1909* (Stanford, Calif.: Stanford University Press, 1984).

Goulder, Grace, *Ohio Scenes and Citizens* (Cleveland: World, 1964).

Greenleaf, William, *From These Beginnings: The Early Philanthropies of Henry and Edsel Ford, 1911–1936* (Detroit: Wayne State University Press, 1964).

Harper, Harry, *My Fifty Years in Flying* (London: Associated Newspapers, 1956).

Harris, Sherwood, *The First to Fly: Aviation's Pioneer Days* (New York: Simon & Schuster, 1970).

Hatch, Alden, *Glenn Curtiss: Pioneer of Naval Aviation* (New York: Messner, 1942).

"Have You Ever Visited Wright Hill?" *NCR Factory News* (August–September 1940).

Hayward, Charles B., *Practical Aeronautics: An Understandable Presentation of Interesting and Essential Facts in Aeronautics*, Parts 1 and 2 (Chicago: American Technical Society, 1917).

Hildebrandt, Capt. Alfred, "The Wright Brothers' Flying Machine," *The American Magazine of Aeronautics* (January 1908), 13–16.

The History of Montgomery County, Ohio (Chicago: W. H. Beers, 1882).

Hobbs, Leonard S., *The Wright Brothers' Engines and Their Design* (Washington, D.C.: Smithsonian Institution Press, 1971).

Hodgins, Eric, "Heavier-Than-Air," *The New Yorker* (Dec. 13, 1930), 29–32.

Hounshell, David, *From the American System to Mass Production* (Baltimore: Johns Hopkins University Press, 1984).

Indiana: A Guide to the Hoosier State (New York: Oxford University Press, 1941).

Johnson, Mary Ann, *A Field Guide to Flight: On the Aviation Trial in Dayton, Ohio* (Dayton, Ohio: Landfall Press, 1986).

Justice, Graham, "Hawthorn Hill Has a Special Place in World History," *NCR Factory News* (June 1965).

Kinnane, Adrian, "The Crucible of Flight," unpublished manuscript.

——, "A House United: Morality and Invention in the Wright Brothers Home," *The Psychohistory Review* (Spring 1988), 367–397.

Koontz, Paul R., and Walter Edwin Roush, *The Bishops: Church of the United Brethren in Christ*. 2 Vols. (Dayton, Ohio: Otterbein Press, 1950).

Langley, Samuel Pierpont, *Experiments in Aerodynamics* (Washington, D.C.: Smithsonian Institution Press, 1891).

———, *Memoir on Mechanical Flight* (Washington, D.C.: Smithsonian Institution Press, 1911).

Leslie, Stuart, *Boss Kettering* (New York: Columbia University Press, 1983).

Lindbergh, Charles A., *The Wartime Journals of Charles Lindbergh* (New York: Harcourt Brace Jovanovich, 1970).

Loening, Grover C., *Our Wings Grow Faster* (New York: Doubleday, Doran, 1935).

———, *Takeoff into Greatness: How American Aviation Grew So Big So Fast* (New York: Putnam, 1968).

Lougheed, Victor, *Vehicles of the Air: A Popular Exposition of Modern Aeronautics* (Chicago: Reilly & Britton, 1909).

Ludlow, Israel, "Criticism of the Court's Decision. . . ." *Aircraft* (April 1910), 75.

———, "The Wright Company Is a Menace," *Aircraft* (May 1910), 94–95.

Mackinder, Halford, "The Geographical Pivot of History," *The Geographical Journal* (April 1904), 441.

Marcosson, Isaac F., *Colonel Deeds: Industrial Builder* (New York: Dodd, Mead, 1948).

Marshall, Fred, "In Honor of the Wrights," *Slipstream* (November 1927), 9–10.

———, "Wright Memorial Site Criticized," *Slipstream* (January 1928), 7–8.

Marshall, Logan, *The True Story of Our National Calamity of Flood, Fire and Tornado* (no place: L. T. Myers, 1913).

Martin, James V., "When Will Merit Count in Aviation? The Life Story of Augustus M. Herring, Inventor of the Aeroplane," *The Libertarian* (Greenville, S.C. October 1924), 589–608.

McFarland, Marvin W., "Orville Wright and Friend," *U.S. Air Services* (August 1956), 5–7.

Means, James Howard, ed., *The Aeronautical Annual* (Boston, 1895, 1896, 1897).

Mingos, Howard, "The Birth of an Industry," in G. E. Simonson, ed., *The History of the American Aircraft Industry: An Anthology* (Cambridge: MIT Press, 1968), pp. 10–95.

Musgrave, Walter E., *The Church of the United Brethren in Christ: Its Teachings and Progress* (Huntington, Ind.: Church of the United Brethren in Christ, 1945).

Nevins, Allen, and Frank Hill, *Ford: Expansion and Challenge, 1915–1935* (New York: Scribner's, 1957).

Newton, Byron, "Watching the Wright Brothers Fly," *Aeronautics* (June 1908), 8.

O'Dwyer, William, and Stella Randolph, *History by Contract* (West Germany: Fritz Major & Sohn, 1978).

Outlaw, Edward R., Jr. *Old Nag's Head: Some Personal Recollections* (Norfolk, Va.: Liskey Lithography, 1956).

Parkin, J. H., *Bell and Baldwin: Their Development of Aerodromes and Hydrodromes at Baddeck, Nova Scotia* (Toronto: University of Toronto Press, 1964).

Peterson, Houston, *See Them Flying: Houston Peterson's Air-Age Scrapbook, 1909–1910* (New York: R. W. Baron, 1969).

Peyrey, François, *Les Oiseaux Artificiels* (Paris: H. Dunod et E. Pinat, 1909).

———, *Les Premiers Hommes-oiseaux: Wilbur et Orville Wright* (Paris: Guiton, 1909).

Pritchard, J. Lawrence, "The Wright Brothers and the Aeronautical Society: A Survey and a Tribute," *Royal Aeronautical Society Journal* (December 1953).

"The Proposed Wright Brothers Memorial," *Aero Club of America Bulletin* (July 1912), 5.

Rae, John B., *Climb to Greatness: The American Aircraft Industry, 1920–1960* (Cambridge: MIT Press, 1968).

Randolph, Stella, *The Lost Flights of Gustave Whitehead* (Washington, D.C.: Places, Inc., 1937).

Root, Amos I., "Our Homes," *Gleanings in Bee Culture* (January 1905), 38.

Roseberry, C. R., *Glenn Curtiss: Pioneer of Flight* (Garden City, N.Y.: Doubleday, 1972).

Ruhl, Arthur, "History at Kill Devil Hill," *Collier's Weekly* (May 30, 1908), 18–19.

Scharff, Robert, and Walter S. Taylor, *Over Land and Sea: A Biography of Glenn Hammond Curtiss* (New York: McKay, 1968).

Smith, Robert, *A Social History of the Bicycle* (New York: American Heritage, 1972).

Spearman, Arthur Dunning, *John Joseph Montgomery, 1858–1911: Father of Basic Flying* (Santa Clara, Calif.: University of Santa Clara Press, 1967).

Stuckey, Ronald, and Karen Reese, eds., *The Prairie Peninsula: In the Shadow of Transeau* (Columbus, Ohio: Ohio State University, 1981).

Studer, Clara, *Sky-Storming Yankee: The Life of Glenn Curtiss* (New York: Stackpole, 1937).

Sullivan, Mark, *Our Times: The United States, 1900–1925.* 5 vols. (New York: Scribner's, 1927).

Tate, William, "With the Wrights at Kitty Hawk," *Aeronautic Review* (December 1928), 188–192.

———, "I Was Host to the Wright Brothers at Kitty Hawk," *U.S. Air Services* (December 1943), 29–30.

Tatin, Victor, "L'Analyse des Expériences d'Aviation," *L'Aérophile* (February 1904).

Taylor, Charles, "My Story of the Wright Brothers, As Told to Robert S. Ball," *Collier's Weekly* (Dec. 25, 1948), vol. 122, no. 26, 26–27, 68, 70.

Thompson, H. A., *Our Bishops* (Dayton, Ohio: United Brethren Publishing House, 1903).

Tillman, Stephen F., *Man Unafraid: The Miracle of Military Aviation* (Washington, D.C.: The Army Times, 1954).

Trimble, William F., *A History of Aeronautics in Pennsylvania* (Pittsburgh: University of Pittsburgh Press, 1982).

Turner, Major C. C., *Old Flying Days* (New York: Arno Press, 1971).

Vaulx, Comte de la, *La Triomphe de la Navigation Aérienne* (Paris, 1911).

Villard, Henry Serrano, *Contact! The Story of the Early Birds* (New York: Bonanza Books, 1953).

Voisin, Gabriel, *Men, Women and 10,000 Kites* (London: Putnam, 1963).

Walker, Percy B., *Early Aviation at Farnborough*. Vol. 2: *The First Airplanes* (London: Macdonald, 1974).

Weaver, Henry M., "Letter Read by Mr. Frank Lahm Before the Aviation Committee of the Aéro-Club de France, December 29, 1905," *Aeronautical Journal* (July–September 1916), 97–99.

Werthner, William, "Personal Recollections of the Wrights," *Aero Club of America Bulletin* (July 1912), 13.

"The Wilbur Wright and Hubert Latham Memorials," *The Aero* (December 1912), 352.

Wilmore, Augustus Cleland, *History of the White River Conference of the Church of the United Brethren in Christ* (Dayton, Ohio: United Brethren Publishing House, 1925).

Wolko, Howard, ed., *The Wright Flyer: An Engineering Perspective* (Washington, D.C.: Smithsonian Institution Press, 1987).

Worrel, Rodney K., "The Wright Brothers' Pioneer Patent," *American Bar Association Journal* (October 1979), 1512–1518.

"The Wright Aeroplane and Its Fabled Performances," *Scientific American* (Jan. 13, 1906), 40; (April 7, 1906), 291–292.

"Wright Hill Dedicated in Dayton," *U.S. Air Services* (September 1940), 10–11.

Wright, Orville, "The Wright Brothers' Aeroplane," *Century Magazine* (September 1908), 641–650.

———, "How We Made the First Flight," *Flying* (December 1913), 10–12.

———, "Automatic Stability," *Smithsonian Annual Report* (Washington, D.C.: Smithsonian Institution Press, 1914), 201–216.

———, "Why the 1903 Airplane Is Sent to the British Museum," *U.S. Air Services* (March 1928), 30–31.

———, "The Mythical Whitehead Flights," *U.S. Air Services* (August 1945), 9.

———, edited and with commentary by Fred C. Kelly, *How We Invented the Airplane* (New York: McKay, 1953).

Wright, Wilbur, *Scenes in the Church Commission During the Last Day of Its Session* (Dayton, Ohio: Wright Brothers, 1888).

———, "Angle of Incidence," *The Aeronautical Journal* (July 1901), 47–49.

———, "Die Wagerechte Lage Während des Gleitfluges," *Illustriete Aeronautische Mitteilungen* (July 1901), 108–109.

———, "Some Aeronautical Experiments," *Journal of the Western Society of Engineers* (December 1901), 489–510.

———, "Experiments and Observations in Soaring Flight," *Journal of the Western Society of Engineers* (August 1903), 400–417.

——, "Octave Chanute's Work in Aviation," *Aeronautics* (January 1911), 4.

——, "What Mouillard Did," *Aero Club of America Bulletin* (April 1912), 2–4.

——, "What Clément Ader Did," *Aero Club of America Bulletin* (May 1912), 17–19.

Wykeham, Peter, *Santos-Dumont: A Study in Obsession* (London: Putnam, 1962).

Zahm, Albert Francis, *Aerial Navigation* (New York: Appleton, 1911).

——, "The First Man-Carrying Aeroplane. . . ." *Smithsonian Annual Report* (Washington, D.C.: Smithsonian Institution Press, 1914), 218.

——, *Early Powerplane Fathers* (South Bend, Ind.: Notre Dame University Press, 1951).

INDEX